1961	1962	1963	1964	1965	1966	1967	1968	1969	1970	1971	1972	1973	1974	1975
145.5	158.7	168.1	179.6	199.1	217.0	221.3	233.6	244.3	233.2	236.6	261.7	284.7	280.4	252.3
126.7	130.3	135.4	140.9	146.2	154.0	156.9	162.9	169.5	173.8	169.5	172.9	174.6	173.6	169.8
245.5	263.4	282.1	306.2	324.8	349.7	367.6	397.2	432.4	458.6	480.7	511.7	531.7	524.8	530.3
377.3	437.0	471.4	456.3	505.0	593.3	677.3	678.2	645.4	547.1	491.6	477.3	466.4	459.7	451.3
120.6	124.7	132.1	137.5	143.8	152.9	158.2	165.4	173.9	182.5	184.0	191.1	192.4	187.4	183.3
93.4	97.3	106.0	120.6	132.3	136.3	125.9	130.0	141.6	131.8	120.6	134.1	152.6	147.8	118.8
92.4	112.4	124.5	127.6	163.2	160.3	141.1	168.9	169.7	136.6	171.1	186.8	217.6	187.9	159.2
119.0	125.4	131.3	141.1	146.6	152.1	150.6	155.0	154.7	153.9	157.8	180.8	181.5	164.7	153.4
118.5	126.6	131.3	141.8	154.3	163.7	163.7	182.8	192.2	188.0	198.4	217.5	226.4	206.0	196.3
145.9	151.4	159.1	168.9	179.8	193.4	203.9	207.4	217.5	211.3	213.2	227.6	233.5	230.0	215.2
224.8	249.5	273.3	299.0	333.7	363.4	380.2	427.7	462.4	481.2	511.9	576.2	629.7	652.5	595.0
139.8	144.1	149.4	156.2	159.9	165.8	173.3	178.0	183.9	186.6	192.5	202.8	206.8	209.6	208.4
38.6	38.7	38.8	38.7	38.8	38.6	38	37.8	37.7	37.1	36.9	37	36.9	36.5	36.1
672	650	635	634	632	627	613	606	619	623	609	628	642	697	752
2,859	2,948	3,010	3,097	3,232	3,317	3,248	3,350	3,575	3,588	3,704	3,889	4,097	4,020	3,525
16,326	16,853	16,995	17,274	18,062	19,214	19,447	19,781	20,167	19,367	18,623	19,151	20,154	20,077	18,323
11,747	11,153	11,109	11,022	10,325	8,994	8,569	8,023	7,518	7,798	8,156	8,478	8,274	8,529	8,901
34,142	35,098	36,013	37,278	38,837	40,743	42,495	44,160	46,023	47,302	48,276	50,007	51,897	53,471	54,345
1.0	1.0	0.9	0.9	0.9	0.9	0.8	0.8	0.8	0.8	0.8	0.8	0.8	0.8	0.9
4.3	4.4	4.4	4.5	4.5	4.6	4.4	4.4	4.6	4.6	4.7	4.7	4.8	4.6	4.1
24.8	25.3	25.1	24.9	25.4	26.4	26.1	26.1	25.9	24.6	23.5	23.3	23.7	23.1	21.3
17.9	16.7	16.4	15.9	14.5	12.3	11.5	10.6	9.7	9.9	10.3	10.3	9.7	9.8	10.4
51.9	52.6	53.1	53.8	54.6	55.9	57.1	58.2	59.1	60.1	60.8	60.9	61.0	61.6	63.3
2.14	2.22	2.28	2.36	2.46	2.56	2.68	2.85	3.04	3.23	3.45	3.7	3.94	4.24	4.53
9.47	9.69	9.83	10.01	10.22	10.35	10.5	10.73	10.93	11.03	11.19	11.5	11.58	11.48	11.22
692	640	715	834	911	874	879	906	877	753	885	951	924	759	802
3,059	2,794	3,083	3,539	3,787	3,533	3,448	3,412	3,154	2,571	2,871	2,955	2,717	2,055	1,987
4.4	4.3	4.3	4.4	4.5	5.1	5.5	6.2	7.0	8.0	7.4	7.2	7.4	8.6	8.8
135.8	147.0	157.9	162.1	175.4	197.8	212.1	245.3	276.3	279.6	295.9	338.1	380.3	419.6	430.5
129.1	139.4	147.0	154.9	165.7	187.3	213.4	239.2	258.7	286.9	316.3	345.0	375.8	424.2	497.4
6.7	7.6	10.9	7.2	9.7	10.5	−1.3	6.1	17.6	−7.3	−20.4	−6.9	4.5	−4.6	−66.9
238.4	248.0	254.0	256.8	260.8	263.7	266.6	289.5	278.1	283.2	303.0	322.4	340.9	343.7	394.7

FOUNDATIONS *of* MICROECONOMICS

The challenge and thrill of learning a new subject is like climbing a mountain. When we set out at the mountain's base, we are unsure of the way up. Along the way, we sometimes feel lost. But as we progress upward, we see ever more clearly the path we've followed, even the parts where we felt lost, and we see how our path fits into a bigger and broader picture.

Students, like mountaineers, benefit enormously from the experience of those who have scaled the peaks before them and from the maps that these earlier climbers have made. They also benefit from practicing on smaller peaks. And they gain perspective by pausing on the climb and looking back at where they've been on their ascent.

Our aims in *Foundations of Microeconomics* are to travel with you on a journey of discovery, to support you every step of the way so that you are never disoriented or lost, and to help you understand and appreciate the economic landscape that surrounds you.

The cover of this text symbolizes our aims. The mountain range is the terrain of economics that we're going to scale, understand, and appreciate. The rising sun and *Foundations* icon are our light sources—the clearest and most sharply focused explanations and illustrations of economic principles and ideas. The icon also emphasizes the idea of building blocks that fit one on top of another but that stand on a firm foundation. Each block is a small and easily handled object that can be understood on its own and then more keenly appreciated as part of a larger picture.

FOUNDATIONS *of* MICROECONOMICS

Robin Bade

University of Western Ontario

Michael Parkin

University of Western Ontario

Boston San Francisco New York
London Toronto Sydney Tokyo Singapore Madrid
Mexico City Munich Paris Cape Town Hong Kong Montreal

Editor-in-Chief	Denise Clinton
Acquisitions Editor	Victoria Warneck
Associate Editor	Roxanne Hoch
Executive Development Manager	Sylvia Mallory
Senior Project Manager	Mary Clare McEwing
Supplements Editor	Meredith Gertz
Senior Administrative Assistant	Dottie Dennis
Senior Media Producer	Melissa Honig
Marketing Manager	Adrienne D'Ambrosio
Online Marketing Specialist	Jennifer Berkley
Managing Editor	James Rigney
Senior Production Supervisor	Nancy Fenton
Senior Design Manager	Regina Hagen
Technical Illustrator	Richard Parkin
Electronic Publisher	Sally Simpson
Senior Manufacturing Buyer	Hugh Crawford
Copy Editor	Barbara Willette
Indexer	Robin Bade
Development, Design, and Project Management	Elm Street Publishing Services, Inc.

Library of Congress Cataloging-in-Publication Data

Bade, Robin.
Foundations of microeconomics ; Robin Bade, Michael Parkin.
p. cm.
Includes index.
ISBN 0-201-47383-6 (alk. paper)
1. Microeconomics. I. Parkin, Michael, 1939– II. Title
HB172 .B233 2002
338.5—dc21 2001022087

Printed in the United States of America.

1 2 3 4 5 6 7 8 9 10—WCT—05 04 03 02 01

To Erin, Tessa, Jack,

and Abby

About the Authors

Robin Bade was an undergraduate at the University of Queensland, Australia, where she earned degrees in mathematics and economics. After a spell teaching high school math and physics, she enrolled in the Ph.D. program at the Australian National University, from which she graduated in 1970. She has held faculty appointments at the University of Edinburgh in Scotland, at Bond University in Australia, and at the Universities of Manitoba, Toronto, and Western Ontario in Canada. Her research on international capital flows appears in the *International Economic Review* and the *Economic Record.*

Robin first taught the principles of economics course in 1970 and has taught it (alongside intermediate macroeconomics and international trade and finance) most years since then. She developed many of the ideas found in this text while conducting tutorials with her students at the University of Western Ontario.

Michael Parkin studied economics in England and began his university teaching career immediately after graduating with a B.A. from the University of Leicester. He learned the subject on the job at the University of Essex, England's most exciting new university of the 1960s, and at the age of 30 became one of the youngest full professors. He is a past president of the Canadian Economics Association and has served on the editorial boards of the *American Economic Review* and the *Journal of Monetary Economics.* His research on macroeconomics, monetary economics, and international economics has resulted in more than 160 publications in journals and edited volumes, including the *American Economic Review*, the *Journal of Political Economy*, the *Review of Economic Studies*, the *Journal of Monetary Economics*, and the *Journal of Money, Credit, and Banking*. He is author of the best-selling textbook, *Economics* (Addison-Wesley), now entering its Sixth Edition.

Robin and Michael are a wife-and-husband duo. Their most notable joint research created the Bade-Parkin Index of central bank independence and spawned a vast amount of research on that topic. They don't claim credit for the independence of the new European Central Bank, but its constitution and the movement toward greater independence of central banks around the world were aided by their pioneering work. Their joint textbooks include *Macroeconomics* (Prentice-Hall), *Modern Macroeconomics* (Pearson Education Canada), and *Economics: Canada in the Global Environment*, the Canadian adaptation of Parkin, *Economics* (Addison-Wesley). They are dedicated to the challenge of explaining economics ever more clearly to an ever-growing body of students.

Music, the theater, art, and walking on the beach provide their relaxation and fun. They don't have a dog, and if they did, they wouldn't call it Keynes.

Microeconomics

Brief Contents

Contents

PART 5 PRICES, PROFITS, AND INDUSTRY PERFORMANCE 283

Preface

Why?

With Parkin's *Economics* (now entering its sixth edition) an established, best-selling principles of economics textbook, why have we written *Foundations of Microeconomics* and its companion Foundations of Macroeconomics? Is this rational behavior?

We think so. We have been driven to write Foundations by what our own students and several hundred of our fellow economists in colleges and universities across the United States have repeatedly told us. Economics is a core competency for the responsible citizen and is a foundation tool for every type of career. But the challenges of learning and teaching economics are formidable. Our students have diverse backgrounds and learning styles. We must fit an entire course in microeconomics into too few weeks. And we must meet the challenge of using new technologies in our classrooms.

As we contemplated these challenges, it became clear to us that to meet them, we needed to rethink the way we teach our subject and to create a new learning system for our students.

LOWERING THE BARRIERS TO ENTRY

Most economics professors want to teach a serious, analytical course that explains the core principles of our subject and helps students apply these principles in their lives and jobs. We are not content to teach "dumbed-down" economics. But most students drown rather than learn to swim when thrown into the deep end of the pool. In this book and its accompanying learning tools, we make painstaking efforts to lower the barriers to learning and to reach out to the beginning student.

We focus on core concepts. We steer a steady path between an overload of detail that swamps the students and a minimalist approach that leaves the student dangling with too much unsaid. We explain tough concepts with the simplest, most straightforward language possible, and we reinforce them with clear, fully explained graphs. And we offer students a rich array of active learning tools that provide alternative ways of accessing and mastering the material.

Focus on Core Concepts

Each chapter of *Foundations* concentrates on a manageable number of main ideas (most commonly three or four) and reinforces each idea several times throughout the chapter. This patient, confidence-building approach guides students through unfamiliar terrain and helps them to focus their efforts on the most important tools and concepts of our discipline.

Diagrams That Tell the Whole Story

We developed the style of our diagrams with extensive feedback from faculty focus group participants and student reviewers. All figures make consistent use of color to show the direction of shifts and contain detailed, numbered captions designed to direct students' attention step by step through the action. Because beginning students of economics are often apprehensive about working with graphs, we have made a special effort to present material in as many as three ways—with graphs, words, and tables—in the same figure. And in an innovation that seems necessary but is to our knowledge unmatched, nearly all of the information supporting a figure appears on the same page as the figure itself. No more flipping pages back and forth!

Many Learning Tools for Many Learning Styles

Our text and its integrated print and electronic learning package recognize that our students have a variety of learning styles. Some learn easily by reading the textbook; others benefit from audio and visual reinforcement. All students can profit from an active learning approach. Your students' textbooks come with access to a suite of innovative learning tools, including tutorial software, an eText featuring animated graphs with audio voiceovers, interactive quizzing, and more.

PRACTICE MAKES PERFECT

Everyone agrees that the only way to learn economics is to do it! Reading and remembering doesn't work. Active involvement, working problems, repeated self-testing: These are the ingredients to success in this subject. We have structured this text and its accompanying electronic and print tools to encourage learning by doing. The central device that accomplishes this goal is a tightly knit learning system based on our innovative *Checklist-Checkpoints* structure.

Checklists

Each chapter opens with a *Chapter Checklist*—a list of (usually) three or four tasks the student will be able to perform after completing the chapter. Each item in the Checklist corresponds to a major section of the chapter that engages the student with a conversational writing style, well-chosen examples, and rich and carefully designed illustrations.

Checkpoints

A full-page *Checkpoint*—containing a Practice Problem with solution and a parallel Exercise—immediately follows each chapter section. The Checkpoints serve as stopping points and encourage students to review the concept and to practice using it before moving on to new ideas. Diagrams and tables bring added clarity to the Checkpoint problems and solutions.

Each Checkpoint also contains an exact page reference to corresponding material in the Study Guide as well as a reference to the corresponding section of eFoundations, our online learning environment. We describe these learning tools more fully below.

Chapter Checkpoints

At the end of each chapter, a *Chapter Checkpoint* summarizes what the student has just learned with a set of key points, a list of key terms, and a set of exercises, many of which send the student to our Web site for further information or data.

Conveying the Excitement

Students learn best when they can see the point of what they are studying. We show the point in a series of *Eye On ...* features and in *Economics in the News*. Current and recent events appear in *Eye on the U.S. Economy* boxes. We place our present experience in global and historical perspectives with *Eye on the Global Economy* and *Eye on the Past* boxes. *All of our Eye On ...* boxes connect theory with reality.

Economics in the News, which appears once each chapter, is a brief news item with questions for discussion or assignment. A Web link provides access to a more complete version of the news item, together with links to other relevant information. The Instructor's Manual contains answers to the questions, and a set of PowerPoint presentations enables the news story to be discussed and illustrated in the classroom.

ORGANIZATION

Our text focuses on core topics with maximum flexibility. We cover all the standard topics of the principles of microeconomics curriculum. And we do so in the order that is increasingly finding favor in the principles course. We believe that a powerful case can be made for teaching the subject in the order in which we present it here. We introduce and explain the core ideas about efficiency and fairness early and then cover major policy issues in a series of chapters that use only the tools of demand and supply and the ideas of marginal benefit, marginal cost, and consumer and producer surplus. Topics such as consumer choice and cost curves, which are more technical, are covered later.

Extensive reviewing suggests that most teachers agree with us. But we recognize that there is a range of opinion about sequencing, and we have structured our text so that it works equally well if other sequences are preferred.

Deciding the order in which to teach the components of microeconomics involves a tradeoff between building all the foundations and getting to policy issues early in the course. There is little disagreement that the place to begin is with production possibilities and demand and supply. We provide a carefully paced and thoroughly modern treatment of these topics.

Following the order of this text, the course quickly gets to interesting policy issues. Two further chapters lay the foundation: elasticity in Chapter 5 and a discussion of the efficiency and fairness of markets in Chapter 6. Introducing students to both efficiency and fairness (equity) issues early in the course enables a more complete and engaging discussion of topics such as taxes, price floors and ceilings, externalities, public goods, and the tax system, all of which we cover in Chapters 7 through 9. Teaching this material early in the course maintains student interest, directly serves the role of the principles course as a foundation for citizenship, and provides an immediate payoff from learning the demand-supply and related tools. Only when these policy issues have been covered do we dig more deeply behind the consumption and production decisions.

Teachers who prefer to cover policy issues later in the course can skip Chapter 6 and the chapters of Part 3 and move straight from elasticity to consumer choice (Chapter 10) and then on to the economics of the firm. The policy-related chapters can be covered at any chosen later point in the course. The special chapter on farms and cities (Chapter 20) can be covered at any time after Chapters 5 and 8. This chapter provides an opportunity to apply the concepts of elasticity of demand and supply, price floors, and externalities and helps the student to appreciate the power of economics as an aid to understanding everyday situations and problems.

A RICH ARRAY OF SUPPORT MATERIALS FOR THE STUDENT

Foundations of Microeconomics is accompanied by the most comprehensive set of learning tools ever assembled. All the components of our package are organized by Checkpoint topic so that the student may move easily between the textbook, the Study Guide, eText, interactive tutorial, and online quiz, while mastering a single core concept.

The variety of tools that we provide enables students to select the path through the material that best suits their individual learning styles. The package is technology enabled, not technology dependent. Active learners will make extensive use of the *Foundations Interactive* software tutorial and the animated graphics of eText, our online version of the textbook. Reflective learners may follow a print-only path if they prefer.

Study Guide

Tom Meyer (Patrick Henry Community College) and Mark Rush (University of Florida) have prepared a Study Guide that is available in both print and electronic formats. The Study Guide provides an expanded Chapter Checklist that enables the student to break the learning tasks down into smaller, bite-sized pieces; self-test materials; expanded explanations of the solutions to the practice problems in the text; and additional practice problems. To ensure consistency across the entire package, the authors who wrote the questions for the Test Bank also wrote the self-test questions for the Study Guide.

Foundations Interactive

A Java and JavaScript tutorial software program that runs in a Web browser, *Foundations Interactive* contains electronic interactive versions of most of the textbook figures. The student manipulates the figures by changing the conditions that lie behind them and observes how the economy responds to events. Quizzes that use five question types (fill-in-the-blank, true-or-false, multiple-choice, numeric, and complete-the-graph) can be worked with, or optionally without, detailed feedback. *Foundations Interactive* is available through the Web site and on CD-ROM.

eFoundations

The *e*Foundations icons found throughout the textbook refer students to the Foundations Web site, a powerful online learning environment and self-assessment tool. On the Web site, students will find:

- The textbook—the *entire textbook in HTML* with hyperlinks and animated figures, more than 100 of which are accompanied by audio explanations prepared by Morris Knapp (Miami Dade Community College)
- *Foundations Interactive*—tutorials, quizzes, and graph tools that with a click of the mouse make curves shift and graphs come to life
- The Study Guide—the entire study guide, free, online—with online quizzes
- Economics in the News updated daily during the school year
- Online "Office Hours"—ask your question via email and one of us will answer you within 24 hours!
- Economic links—links to sites that keep you up to date with what's going on in the economy and that enable you to work end-of-chapter Web-based exercises

The power of *e*Foundations lies not just in the breadth and depth of learning tools available, but also in the way that we have linked the tools together. For example, suppose that a student logs on to eFoundations to take a multiple-choice quiz from the *e*Study Guide. When the quiz is submitted for a grade, the student receives a scorecard with an explanation of why answers are correct or incorrect, *and a hyperlink to the part of the eText that the student should read to better understand the concept*. The student is thus able to navigate easily through the site and to maximize the payoff from her or his study efforts.

The Econ Tutor Center

Staffed by qualified, experienced college economics instructors, the Econ Tutor Center is open five days a week, seven hours a day. Tutors can be reached by phone, fax, and email. The Econ Tutor Center hours are designed to meet your students' study schedules, with evening hours Sunday through Thursday. Students receive one-on-one tutoring on examples, related exercises, and problems. Please contact your Addison-Wesley representative for information on how to make this service available to your students.

Economist.com Edition

The premier online source of economic news analysis, Economist.com provides your students with insight and opinion on current economic events. Through an agreement between Addison-Wesley and *The Economist*, your students can receive a low-cost subscription to this premium Web site for 3 months, including the complete text of the current issue of *The Economist* and access to *The Economist's* searchable archives. Other features include web-only weekly articles, news feeds with current world and business news, and stock market and currency data. Professors who adopt this special edition will receive a complimentary one-year subscription to *The Economist* and Economist.com.

The Wall Street Journal Edition

Addison-Wesley is also pleased to provide your students with access to *The Wall Street Journal*, the most respected and trusted daily source for information on business and economics. For a small additional charge, Addison-Wesley offers your students a 10-week subscription to *The Wall Street Journal* print edition and *The Wall Street Journal Interactive Edition*. Adopting professors will receive a complimentary one-year subscription of both the print and interactive versions.

Financial Times Edition

Featuring international news and analysis from FT journalists in more than 50 countries, the *Financial Times* will provide your students with insights and perspectives on economic developments around the world. The *Financial Times Edition* provides your students with a 15-week subscription to one of the world's leading business publications. Adopting professors will receive a complimentary one-year subscription to the *Financial Times* as well as access to the Online Edition at FT.com.

A QUALITY ASSURED SUPPORT SYSTEM FOR THE INSTRUCTOR

Our instructor resource tools are the most comprehensive, carefully developed, and accurate materials ever made available. We recognize and respect the desire of every instructor to use a text and package that contain no nasty surprisesæthat are safe. This text and package are safe! *Foundations Interactive*, the Study Guide, the Web site, *and the Test Banks* all key off the Checkpoints in the textbook. The entire package has a tight integrity. We are the authors of *Foundations Interactive* and the Web site and we've played a key role in reviewing and revising the Study Guide, Instructor's Manual, and Test Banks to ensure that every element of the package achieves the level of coherence that students and teachers need.

Instructor's Manual

Prepared by Carol Dole (State University of West Georgia) and Mark Rush, the Instructor's Manual contains chapter outlines and road maps, answers to in-text exercises and Economics in the News questions, additional exercises with solutions, and a virtual encyclopedia of suggestions on how to enrich class presentation and use class time efficiently.

Three Test Banks

Three separate Test Banks, with more than 11,000 questions, provide multiple-choice, true-false, numerical, fill-in-the-blank, short-answer, and essay questions. Mark Rush reviewed and edited questions from six dedicated principles instructors to form one of the most comprehensive testing systems on the market. Our questions authors are Seemi Ahmad (Dutchess Community College), Sue Bartlett (University of South Florida), Jack Chambless (Valencia Community College), Paul Harris (Camden County Community College), William Mosher (Assumption College), and Terry Sutton (Southeast Missouri State University). These same questions authors also wrote questions for the Study Guide and Web site to ensure consistency across the entire package.

PowerPoint Resources

Working closely with Charles Pflanz (Scottsdale Community College), we have played a large role in creating the PowerPoint tools. Every figure and table—every single one, even those used in Checkpoint questions and solutions—is included in the PowerPoint lecture notes, many of them animated so that you can build them gradually in the classroom. We have created these figures and determined the optimal build sequence for those that are animated. They are all produced with the same degree of clarity and precision as the figures in the text.

For instructors who prefer to make up their own PowerPoint notes and who want larger versions of the figures, we've also provided a set of full-screen figures that can be used alone or can be cut and pasted into the instructor's own PowerPoint presentations. We've also provided special PowerPoint shows on the Economics in the News feature of each chapter. These materials might be used to motivate when starting a new topic, or used as a wrap-up and summary.

eFoundations

The instructor side of eFoundations includes all of the same resources as for students, but with the addition of PowerPoint lecture notes, classroom experiments resources, and an online "Consult the Authors" feature—ask your questions and make your suggestions via e-mail, and one of us will answer you within 24 hours!

Overhead Transparencies

Full-color overhead transparencies of *all* figures from the text will improve the clarity of your lectures. They are available to qualified adopters of the text (contact your Addison-Wesley sales representative).

Instructor's Resource Disk with Computerized Test Banks

This CD-ROM contains Computerized Test Bank files, Test Bank and Instructor's Manual files in Microsoft Word, and PowerPoint files. All three Test

Banks are available in Test Generator Software (TestGen-EQ with QuizMaster-EQ). Fully networkable, it is available for Windows and Macintosh. TestGen-EQ's graphical interface enables instructors to view, edit, and add questions; transfer questions to tests; and print different forms of tests. Tests can be formatted by varying fonts and styles, margins, and headers and footers, as in any word-processing document. Search and sort features let the instructor quickly locate questions and arrange them in a preferred order. QuizMaster-EQ, working with your school's computer network, automatically grades the exams, stores the results on disk, and allows the instructor to view and print a variety of reports.

FastFax Testing

FastFax Testing is designed for instructors who do not have access to a computer or an assistant who can help prepare tests for students. Simply choose from a large pool of questions in the print testbank and include custom headers, if you like. Fill out the test information sheet that lists instructor-selected questions and test preferences that describe how the test should be generated. You may even request multiple forms of a test and receive answer keys for each one.

Turnaround time is usually 48 hours or less and test pages can be mailed or faxed back to you by the date the test is needed. FastFax Testing is fast, reliable, and free to qualified adopters of this text.

CourseCompass

A dynamic, interactive online course management tool powered by BlackBoard, CourseCompass provides flexible tools and rich content resources that enable instructors to easily and effectively customize online course materials to suit their needs. Now instructors can track and analyze student performance on an array of Internet activities. Please contact your Addison-Wesley representative for more details.

ACKNOWLEDGMENTS

Working on a project such as this generates many debts that can never be repaid. But they can be acknowledged, and it is a special pleasure to be able to do so here and to express our heartfelt thanks to each and every one of the following long list, without whose contributions we would have had a lesser product.

Mark Rush is our Study Guide, Instructor's Manual, and Test Bank coordinator and manager. He assembled, polished, wrote, and rewrote these materials to ensure their close consistency with the text. He and we were in constant contact as all the elements of our text and package came together. Mark also made many valuable suggestions for improving the text and the Checkpoints. His contribution went well beyond that of a reviewer. And his effervescent sense of humor kept us all in good spirits along the way. Working closely with Mark, Tom Meyer wrote content for the Study Guide and Carol Dole wrote content for the Instructor's Manual and questions for *Foundations Interactive*. Seemi Ahmad, Sue Bartlett, Jack Chambless, Paul Harris, William Mosher, and Terry Sutton provided questions for the Study Guide and Test Banks. Charles Pflanz created the PowerPoint presentations and Morris Knapp provided the audio for the animated figures on our Web site.

The ideas that ultimately became Foundations began to form over dinner at the Andover Inn in Andover, Massachusetts, with Denise Clinton and Sylvia Mallory. We gratefully acknowledge Sylvia's role not only at the birth of this project but also in managing the entire development team. Denise has been our ongoing inspiration for almost ten years. She is the most knowledgeable economics editor in the business, and we are privileged to have the benefit of her enormous experience.

The arrival at Addison-Wesley of Victoria Warneck has blessed us with the talents of an outstanding sponsoring editor. We are in awe of Victoria's extraordinary editorial craft. It has been, and we hope will for many future editions remain, a joy to work with her.

Mary Clare McEwing has been our indomitable development editor. She, with help from Dottie Dennis, has rounded up the best group of reviewers we've ever worked with. And she has steered the project along through three full redrafts and polishes. Mary Clare also began the design process with focus groups that told us what teachers and students look for in the design of a textbook. And Gina Hagen converted the raw ideas into this outstandingly designed text. Meredith Nightingale provided the detailed figure designs.

Meredith Gertz did an incredible job as editor of our print supplements and coordinated the work of our large team of coauthors. Andrea Basso helped Meredith by managing the reviews of all our print supplements.

Melissa Honig, our technology guru, built our Web site and worked tirelessly to help develop *Foundations Interactive*. She has been a constant source of high energy, good sense, level headed advice, and quickly found creative solutions to all our technology problems. And Roxanne Hoch provided cheerful editorial assistance and managed the creation of the PowerPoint resources.

Nancy Fenton, our unflappable production supervisor, ensured that all the elements eventually came together to bring our text out on schedule. Sally Simpson, our electronic production administrator, performed her magic to make our pages look beautiful. Jim Rigney managed the supplements production process and ensured that all the print supplements stayed on schedule. And Hugh Crawford oversaw the manufacturing process, and worked with the printers and binders to produce beautiful, on-time books.

Our marketing manager, Adrienne D'Ambrosio, has added enormous value, not only by being acutely intelligent and having a sensitive understanding of the market, but also by sharpening our vision of our text and package. Jenny Jefferson stayed late many nights fielding requests from the sales force and Jennifer Berkley managed our online marketing efforts.

Karen Hill and Ingrid Mount of Elm Street Publishing Services provided development, photo research, and production coordination. Our copy editor, Barbara Willette and supplements copy editor Sheryl Nelson gave our work a thorough review and helpful polish.

Richard Parkin, our technical illustrator, created the figures in the text, the dynamic figures in the online version of the text, the illustrations in *Foundations Interactive*, and the animated versions of the figures in the PowerPoint presentations and contributed many ideas to improve the clarity of our illustrations. Laurel Davies created and edited the Foundations Interactive database and acted as its accuracy checker and reviewer.

Jeannie Gillmore, our personal assistant, worked closely with us in creating *Foundations Interactive* and served as a meticulous accuracy checker. Kevin Young Beckwith of Clark University also provided a careful accuracy review. Jane McAndrew, economics librarian at the University of Western Ontario, went the extra mile on many occasions to help us track down the data and references we needed. Ann Parkin came to our rescue in the closing weeks of this project and helped with a final accuracy check of the pages, table of contents, glossary, and index.

Finally, our reviewers, whose names appear on the following pages, have made an enormous contribution to this text. In the many texts that we've now written, we've never seen reviewing of the quality that we enjoyed on this project. It has been a pleasure (if at times a challenge) to respond constructively to their many excellent suggestions.

Robin Bade
Michael Parkin
London, Ontario, Canada
robin@econ100.com
michael.parkin@uwo.ca

Reviewers

Seemi Ahmad, Dutchess Community College
William Aldridge, Shelton State Community College
Ali Ataiifar, Delaware County Community College
John Baffoe-Bonnie, Pennsylvania State University Delaware County Campus
Sue Bartlett, University of South Florida
John Bethune, Barton College
David Bivin, Indiana University–Purdue University at Indianapolis
Geoffrey Black, Boise State University
Barbara Brogan, Northern Virginia Community College
Christopher Brown, Arkansas State University
Nancy Burnett, University of Wisconsin at Oshkosh
Robert Carlsson, University of South Carolina
Jack Chambless, Valencia Community College
Robert Cherry, Brooklyn College
Quentin Ciolfi, Brevard Community College
Jim Cobbe, Florida State University
John Cochran, Metropolitan State College
Carol Conrad, Cerro Coso Community College
Kevin Cotter, Wayne State University
Elizabeth Crowell, University of Michigan at Dearborn
Susan Dadres, Southern Methodist University
Jeffrey Davis, ITT Technical Institute (Utah)
Dennis Debrecht, Carroll College
Al DeCooke, Broward Community College
Vince DiMartino, University of Texas at San Antonio
Carol Dole, State University of West Georgia
John Dorsey, University of Maryland College Park
Marie Duggan, Keene State College
Carl Enomoto, New Mexico State University
Rudy Fichtenbaum, Wright State University
Kaya Ford, Northern Virginia Community College
Robert Francis, Shoreline Community College
Arthur Friedberg, Mohawk Valley Community College
Julie Gallaway, Southwest Missouri State University
Neil Garston, California State University at Los Angeles
Kirk Gifford, Ricks College
Mark Gius, Quinnipiac College
Randall Glover, Brevard Community College
Stephan Gohmann, University of Louisville
Richard Gosselin, Houston Community College
Warren Graham, Tulsa Community College
Dennis Hammett, University of Texas at El Paso
Leo Hardwick, Macomb Community College
Paul Harris, Camden County Community College
Gus Herring, Brookhaven College
Steven Hickerson, Mankato State University
Andy Howard, Rio Hondo College

Yu Hsing, Southeastern Louisiana University
Matthew Hyle, Winona State University
Harvey James, University of Hartford
Russell Janis, University of Massachusetts at Amherst
Arthur Kartman, San Diego State University
Diane Keenan, Cerritos College
John Keith, Utah State University
Douglas Kinnear, Colorado State University
Morris Knapp, Miami-Dade Community College
Steven Koch, Georgia Southern University
Joyce Lapping, University of Southern Maine
Tom Larson, California State University, Los Angeles
Robert Lemke, Florida International University
Tony Lima, California State University at Hayward
Kenneth Long, New River Community College
Michael Magura, University of Toledo
Mark Maier, Glendale College
Paula Manns, Atlantic Cape Community College
Kathryn Marshall, Ohio State University
Drew E. Mattson, Anoka-Ramsey Community College
Diego Mendez-Carbajo, Illinois Wesleyan University
Thomas Meyer, Patrick Henry Community College
Meghan Millea, Mississippi State University
Michael Milligan, Front Range Community College
Jenny Minier, University of Miami
William Mosher, Assumption College
Melinda Nish, Salt Lake Community College
Lee Nordgren, Indiana University at Bloomington
William C. O'Connor, Western Montana College–University of Montana
Charles Okeke, College of Southern Nevada
Tim Petry, North Dakota State University
Charles Pflanz, Scottsdale Community College
Barbara Ross-Pfeiffer, Kapiolani Community College
Jeffrey Rous, University of North Texas
Udayan Roy, Long Island University
Mark Rush, University of Florida
Joseph Santos, South Dakota State University
Ted Scheinman, Mount Hood Community College
Jerry Schwartz, Broward Community College
Terry Sutton, Southeast Missouri State University
James Thorson, Southern Connecticut State University
Marc Tomljanovich, Colgate University
Cynthia Royal Tori, Valdosta State University
Ngoc-Bich Tran, San Jacinto College South
Nora Underwood, University of California, Davis
Jack Wegman, Santa Rosa Junior College
Jason White, Northwest Missouri State University
Barbara Wiens-Tuers, Pennsylvania State University Altoona
Joachim Zietz, Middle Tennessee State University
Armand Zottola, Central Connecticut State University

Part 1

Introduction

Chapter 1

Getting Started

CHAPTER CHECKLIST

When you have completed your study of this chapter, you will be able to:

1. **Define economics, distinguish between microeconomics and macroeconomics, and explain the questions of microeconomics.**
2. **Describe the work of economists as social scientists.**
3. **Explain five core ideas that define the economic way of thinking.**
4. **Explain why economics is worth studying.**

You are studying microeconomics at a time of enormous change. New businesses such as Amazon.com are bringing e-commerce into our homes and transforming the way we shop. MP3 music and DVD movies are transforming the way we play. But inequality is increasing: The less educated are falling behind. And despite the burst of economic expansion enjoyed by Americans, much of the world remains untouched by the new economy. Of the world's 6 billion people, more than a billion survive on $1 a day or less. Disturbed by the combination of increasing wealth and persistent poverty, some people are pointing to globalization as the source of growing inequality.

You've just glimpsed at some of the economic issues in today's world. Your course in microeconomics will help you to understand the powerful forces that are shaping our economic world and help you to navigate it. Our goal throughout this text and its accompanying study guide, CD, and Web site is to help you to learn microeconomics and to apply its lessons in your everyday life and work.

1.1 DEFINITIONS AND QUESTIONS

All economic questions and problems arise because human wants exceed the resources available to satisfy them. We want good health and long lives. We want good schools, colleges, and universities. We want well-run day-care facilities. We want a peaceful and secure world. We want spacious and comfortable homes. We want a huge range of sports and recreational equipment from running shoes to jet skis. We want the time to enjoy our favorite sports, video games, novels, music, movies, travel to exotic places, and just hanging out with friends.

In the everyday world of politics and the media, it is easy to get carried away with the idea that we can have it all. A random sample of news headlines might include these:

Everyone must get the best health care.

There must be a computer in every classroom.

We cannot afford to stop exploring space.

We must stop polluting our lakes and rivers.

Most people would agree that each headline expresses a desirable goal. But we might not be able to achieve them all. The ability of each of us to satisfy our wants is limited by time and by the incomes we earn and the prices we pay for the things we buy. These limits mean that everyone ends up with some unsatisfied wants. Our ability as a society to satisfy our wants is limited by the productive resources that exist. These resources include the gifts of nature, our own labor and ingenuity, and tools and equipment that we have produced.

Scarcity
The condition that arises because the available resources are insufficient to satisfy wants.

Our inability to satisfy all our wants is called **scarcity**. The poor and the rich alike face scarcity. A child wants a $1.00 can of soda and two 50¢ packs of gum but has only $1.00 in his pocket. He faces scarcity. A millionaire wants to spend the weekend playing golf *and* spend the same weekend at the office attending a business strategy meeting. She faces scarcity. A society wants to provide vastly improved health care, install a computer in every classroom, explore space, clean polluted lakes and rivers, and so on. Society also faces scarcity.

Not only do I want a cracker—we all want a cracker!

Faced with scarcity, we must make choices. We must *choose* among the available alternatives. The child must *choose* the soda *or* the gum. The millionaire must *choose* the golf game *or* the meeting. As a society, we must *choose* among health care, computers, space exploration, the environment, and so on.

Economics is the social science that studies the choices that individuals, businesses, government, and entire societies make as they cope with scarcity. The subject divides into two main parts:

Economics
The social science that studies the choices that individuals, businesses, governments, and entire societies make as they cope with scarcity.

- Microeconomics
- Macroeconomics

Microeconomics

Microeconomics is the study of the choices that individuals and businesses make, the way these choices interact, and the influence that governments exert on these choices. Some examples of microeconomic questions are: Why are more people buying SUVs and fewer people buying minivans? Why, when Sony Corporation launched its new PlayStation 2, did it ship too small a quantity to the United States? How would a tax on e-commerce affect the growth of the Internet?

Microeconomics
The study of the choices of individuals and businesses, the interaction of these choices, and the influence that governments exert on these choices.

Macroeconomics

Macroeconomics is the study of the aggregate (or total) effects on the national economy and the global economy of the choices that individuals, businesses, and governments make. Some examples of macroeconomic questions are: Why did production and jobs expand so rapidly in the United States during the 1990s? Why has Japan been in a long period of economic stagnation? Why does the Federal Reserve sometimes raise interest rates and sometimes lower them?

Macroeconomics
The study of the aggregate (or total) effects on the national economy and the global economy of the choices that individuals, businesses, and governments make.

The distinction between microeconomics and macroeconomics is similar to the distinction between two views of a display of national flags in an Olympic stadium. The micro view is of a single participant and the actions he or she is taking. The macro view is the patterns formed by the joint actions of all the people participating in the entire display.

Microeconomic Questions

The economic choices that individuals, businesses, and governments make and the interactions of those choices answer the three major questions:

- What?
- How?
- For whom?

What?

Goods and services
The objects that people value and produce to satisfy human wants. Goods are physical objects and services are work done for people.

What goods and services get produced and in what quantities? **Goods and services** are the objects that people value and produce to satisfy human wants. Goods are physical objects such as golf balls. Services are tasks performed for people such as haircuts. The nation's farms, factories, construction sites, shops, and offices produce a dazzling array of goods and services that range from necessities such as food, houses, and apartments to leisure items such ocean cruises, SUVs, and DVD players.

What determines the quantities of corn we grow, homes we build, and DVD players we produce? How do these quantities change over time? And how are they affected by the ongoing changes in technology that make an ever-wider array of goods and services available to us?

How?

How are goods and services produced? In a vineyard in France, basket-carrying workers pick the annual grape crop by hand. In a vineyard in California, a huge machine and a few workers do the same job that a hundred French grape pickers do. Look around you and you will see many examples of this phenomenon—the same job being done in different ways. In some supermarkets, checkout clerks key in prices. In others, they use a laser scanner. One farmer keeps track of his livestock feeding schedules and inventories by using paper-and-pencil records, while another uses a personal computer. GM hires workers to weld auto bodies in some of its plants and uses robots to do the job in others.

Why do we use machines in some cases and people in others? Do mechanization and technological change destroy more jobs than they create? Do they make us better off or worse off?

For Whom?

For whom are the various goods and services produced? The answer to this question depends on the incomes that people earn and the prices they pay for the goods and services they buy. At given prices, a person who has a high income is able to buy more goods and services than a person who has a low income. Doctors earn much higher incomes than do nurses and medical assistants. So doctors get more of the goods and services produced than nurses and medical assistants get.

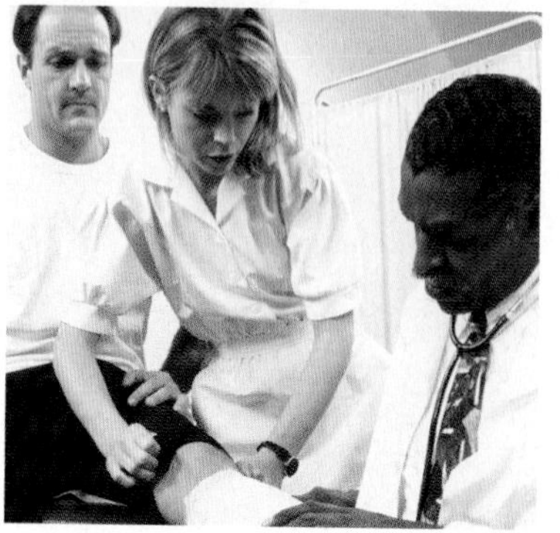

You probably know about many other persistent differences in incomes. Men, on the average, earn more than women. Whites, on the average, earn more than minorities. College graduates, on the average, earn more than high school graduates. Americans, on the average, earn more than Europeans, who in turn earn more, on the average, than Asians and Africans earn. But there are some significant exceptions. The people of Japan and Hong Kong now earn an average income similar to that of Americans. And there is a lot of income inequality throughout the world.

What determines the incomes we earn? Why do doctors earn larger incomes than nurses? Why do white male college graduates earn more than minority female high school graduates? Why do Americans earn more, on the average, than Africans?

Microeconomics will help you to answer the questions we've just reviewed. It will show you how the economic choices that individuals, businesses, and governments make and the interactions of those choices end up determining *what*, *how*, and *for whom* goods and services get produced.

CHECKPOINT 1.1

1 **Define economics, distinguish between microeconomics and macroeconomics, and explain the questions of microeconomics.**

Study Guide pp. 2–5 

*e*Foundations 1.1 

Practice Problems 1.1

1. Economics studies choices that arise from one fact. What is that fact?
2. Sort the following issues into microeconomic and macroeconomic issues:
   a. People must install catalytic converters in their cars.
   b. U.S. unemployment should be much lower.
   c. Your local county opens a neighborhood gym for teenagers.
3. Match the following headlines with the What, How, and For whom questions:
   a. With more research, we will cure cancer.
   b. A good education is the right of every child.
   c. What will the government do with its surplus?

Exercises 1.1

1. Every day, we make many choices. Can't we avoid having to make choices?
2. Check your local media for headlines that concern three microeconomic issues and three macroeconomic issues.
3. Check your local media for headlines that ask two of each of the What, How, and For whom questions.

Solutions to Practice Problems 1.1

1. The fact is scarcity—human wants exceed the resources available.

2a. Microeconomic issue because it deals with the choices made by individual people.
2b. Macroeconomic issue because it refers to the national economy.
2c. Microeconomic issue because the government's decision interacts with teenagers' decisions.

3a. More research is a How question, and a cure for cancer is a What question.
3b. Good education is a What question, and every child is a For whom question.
3c. Who will get the surplus is a For whom question.

1.2 ECONOMICS: A SOCIAL SCIENCE

We've defined economics as the *social science* that studies the choices that individuals and societies make as they cope with scarcity. We're now going to look at the way economists go about their work as social scientists and at some of the problems they encounter.

The major goal of economists is to discover how the economic world works. In pursuit of this goal, economists (like all scientists) distinguish between two types of statements:

- What *is*
- What *ought to be*

Statements about what *is* are called *positive* statements. They say what is currently understood about the way the world operates. A positive statement might be right or wrong. And we can test a positive statement by checking it against the data. When a chemist does an experiment in her laboratory, she is attempting to check a positive statement against the facts.

Statements about what *ought to be* are called *normative* statements. These statements depend on values and cannot be tested. When Congress debates a motion, it is ultimately trying to decide what ought to be. It is making a normative statement.

To see the distinction between positive and normative statements, consider the controversy about global warming. Some scientists believe that 200 years of industrial activity and the large quantities of coal and oil that we burn are increasing the carbon dioxide content of the earth's atmosphere with devastating consequences for life on this planet. Other scientists disagree. The statement "Our planet is warming because of an increased carbon dioxide buildup in the atmosphere" is a positive statement. It can (in principle and with sufficient data) be tested. The statement "We should cut back on our use of carbon-based fuels such as coal and oil" is a normative statement. You may agree with or disagree with this statement, but you can't test it. It is based on values. Health-care reform provides another economic example of the distinction. "Universal health care will cut the amount of work time lost to illness" is a positive statement. "Every American should have equal access to health care" is a normative statement.

The task of economic science is to discover and catalog positive statements that are consistent with what we observe in the world and that enable us to understand how the economic world works. This task is a large one that can be broken into three steps:

- Observing and measuring
- Model building
- Testing

Observing and Measuring

The first step toward understanding how the economic world works is to observe and measure it. Economists keep track of huge amounts of economic data. Some examples are the amounts and locations of natural and human resources, wages and work hours, the prices and quantities of the different goods and services produced, taxes and government spending; and the volume of international trade.

Model Building

The second step is to build models. An **economic model** is a description of some aspect of the economic world that includes only those features of the world that are needed for the purpose at hand. A model is simpler than the reality it describes. What a model includes and what it leaves out result from *assumptions* about what is essential and what are inessential details.

Economic model
A description of some aspect of the economic world that includes only those features of the world that are needed for the purpose at hand.

You can see how ignoring details is useful—even essential—to our understanding by thinking about a model that you see every day, the TV weather map. The weather map is a model that helps to predict the temperature, wind speed and direction, and precipitation over a future period. The weather map shows lines called isobars—lines of equal barometric pressure. It doesn't show the interstate highways. The reason is that we think the location of the highways has no influence on the weather but the air pressure patterns do have an influence.

An economic model is similar to a weather map. It tells us how a number of variables are determined by a number of other variables. For example, an economic model of the 1994 Los Angeles earthquake might tell us the effects of the earthquake and the government's relief efforts on the number of houses and apartments, rents and prices, jobs, and commuting times.

Economists use a variety of methods to describe their economic models. Most commonly, the method is mathematical. And if you plan on a career in economics, you will study a good deal of math. But the basic ideas of all economic models can be described using words and pictures or diagrams. That is how economic models are described in this text.

A rare exception is a model called the Phillips Economic Hydraulic Computer shown here. Bill Phillips, a New Zealand-born engineer-turned-economist created this model using plastic tubes and plexiglass tanks at the London School of Economics in 1949. The model still works today in a London museum.

Testing

The third step is testing models. A model's predictions might correspond to or conflict with the data. If there is a conflict, the model needs to be modified or rejected. A model that has repeatedly passed the test of corresponding well with real-world data is the basis of an economic theory. An **economic theory** is a generalization that summarizes what we understand about the economic choices that people make and the economic performance of industries and nations.

Economic theory
A generalization that summarizes what we understand about the economic choices that people make and the economic performance of industries and nations based on models that have repeatedly passed the test of corresponding well with real-world data.

The process of building and testing models creates theories. For example, meteorologists have a theory that if the isobars form a particular pattern at a particular time of the year (a model), then it will snow (reality). They have developed this theory by repeated observation and by carefully recording the weather that follows specific patterns of isobars.

Economics is a young science. Although philosophers have written about economic issues since the time of the ancient Greeks, it is generally agreed that as a modern social science, economics was born in 1776 with the publication of Adam Smith's *The Wealth of Nations*. Over the years since then, economists have discovered many useful theories. But in many areas, economists are still looking for answers. The gradual accumulation of economic knowledge gives most economists some faith that their methods will eventually provide usable answers.

But progress in economics comes slowly. A major reason is that it is difficult in economics to unscramble cause and effect.

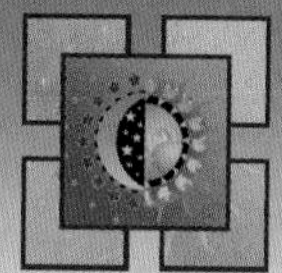

Eye On The PAST

Adam Smith and the Birth of Economics as a Modern Social Science

Many people had written about economics before Adam Smith, but he made economics a social science.

Born in 1723 in Kirkcaldy, a small fishing town near Edinburgh, Scotland, Smith was the only child of the town's customs officer. Lured from his professorship (he was a full professor at 28) by a wealthy Scottish duke who gave him a pension of £300 a year—ten times the average income at that time—he devoted ten years to writing his masterpiece, *An Inquiry into the Nature and Causes of the Wealth of Nations*, published in 1776.

Why, Adam Smith asked in that book, are some nations wealthy while others are poor? He was pondering these questions at the height of the Industrial Revolution. During these years, new technologies were applied to the manufacture of textiles, iron, transportation, and agriculture.

Adam Smith answered his questions by emphasizing the role of the division of labor and free markets. To illustrate his argument, he used the example of a pin factory. He guessed that one person, using the hand tools available in the 1770s, might make 20 pins a day. Yet, he observed, by using those same hand tools but breaking the process into a number of individually small operations in which people specialize—by the division of labor—ten people could make a staggering 48,000 pins a day. One draws out the wire, another straightens it, a third cuts it, a fourth points it, a fifth grinds it. Three specialists make the head, and a fourth attaches it. Finally, the pin is polished and packaged.

But a large market is needed to support the division of labor: One factory employing ten workers would need to sell more than 15 million pins a year to stay in business!

Unscrambling Cause and Effect

Are computers getting cheaper because people are buying them in greater quantities? Or are people buying computers in greater quantities because they are getting cheaper? Or is some third factor causing both the price of a computer to fall and the quantity of computers to increase? Economists want to answer questions like these, but doing so is often difficult. The central idea that economists (and all scientists) use to unscramble cause and effect is *ceteris paribus*.

Ceteris Paribus

Ceteris paribus
Other things remaining the same (often abbreviated as ***cet. par.***)

Ceteris paribus is a Latin term (often abbreviated as *cet. par.*) that means "other things being equal" or "if all other relevant things remain the same." Ensuring that other things are equal is crucial in many activities and all successful attempts to make scientific progress use this device. By changing one factor at a time and holding all the other relevant factors constant, we isolate the factor of interest and are able to investigate its effects in the clearest possible way.

Economic models, like the models in all other sciences, enable the influence of one factor at a time to be isolated in the imaginary world of the model. When we use a model, we are able to imagine what would happen if only one factor changed. But *ceteris paribus* can be a problem in economics when we try to test a model.

Laboratory scientists, such as chemists and physicists, perform controlled experiments by holding all the relevant factors constant except for the one under investigation. In economics, we observe the outcomes of the *simultaneous* operation of many factors. Consequently, it is hard to sort out the effects of each individual factor and to compare the effects with what a model predicts. To cope with this problem, economists take three complementary approaches:

- Natural experiments
- Statistical investigations
- Economic experiments

Natural Experiments

A natural experiment is a situation that arises in the ordinary course of economic life in which the one factor of interest is different and other things are equal (or similar). For example, Canada has higher unemployment benefits than the United States, but the people in the two nations are similar. So to study the effects of unemployment benefits on the unemployment rate, economists might compare the United States with Canada.

Statistical Investigations

Statistical investigations look for correlations. **Correlation** is the tendency for the values of two variables to move in a predictable and related way. For example, there is a correlation between the amount of cigarette smoking and the incidence of lung cancer. There is also a correlation between the size of a city's police force and the city's crime rate. Two economic examples are correlation between household income and spending and correlation between the price of a telephone call and the number of calls made. We must be careful to interpret a correlation correctly. Sometimes a correlation shows the strength of a *causal* influence of one variable on the other. For example, smoking causes lung cancer, and higher incomes cause higher spending. Sometimes the direction of causation is hard to determine. For example, does a larger police force *detect* more crimes or does a higher crime rate cause a larger police force to be hired? And sometimes a third factor causes both correlated variables. For example, advances in communication technology have caused both a fall in the price of phone calls and an increase in the quantity of calls. So the correlation between the price and quantity of phone calls has a deeper cause.

Correlation
The tendency for the values of two variables to move in a predictable and related way.

Sometimes, the direction of cause and effect can be determined by looking at the timing of events. But this method must be handled with care because of a problem known as the *post hoc* fallacy.

Post Hoc *Fallacy* Another Latin phrase—*post hoc ergo propter hoc*—means "after this, therefore because of this." The ***post hoc* fallacy** is the error of reasoning that a first event *causes* a second event because the first occurred before the second. Suppose you are a visitor from a far-off world. You observe lots of people shopping in early December, and then you see them opening gifts and celebrating on Christmas Day. Does the shopping cause Christmas, you wonder? After a deeper study, you discover that Christmas causes the shopping. A later event causes an earlier event.

***Post hoc* fallacy**
The error of reasoning that a first event *causes* a second event because the first occurred before the second.

Just looking at the timing of events often doesn't help to unravel cause and effect in economics. For example, the stock market booms, and some months later the economy expands—jobs and incomes grow. Did the stock market boom cause the economy to expand? Possibly, but perhaps businesses started to plan the expansion of production because a new technology that lowered costs had become available. As knowledge of the plans spread, the stock market reacted to *anticipate* the economic expansion.

To disentangle cause and effect, economists use economic models to interpret correlations. And when they can do so, economists perform experiments.

Economic Experiments

Economic experiments put real subjects in a decision-making situation and vary the influence of interest to discover how the subjects respond to one factor at a time. Most economic experiments are done using students as the subjects. But some use the actual people whose behavior economists want to understand and predict. An example of an economic experiment on actual subjects is one designed to discover the effects of changing the way welfare benefits are paid in New Jersey. Another experiment was conducted to discover how telecommunications companies would bid in different types of auctions for the airwave frequencies they use to transmit cellular telephone messages. Governments have made billions of dollars using the results of this experiment.

CHECKPOINT 1.2

Study Guide pp. 5–6

*e*Foundations 1.2

2 Describe the work of economists as social scientists.

Practice Problems 1.2

1. Classify each of the following statements as positive or normative:
   - **a.** There is too much poverty in the United States.
   - **b.** An increase in the gas tax will cut pollution.
   - **c.** Cuts to social security in the United States have been too deep.
2. Provide two examples of the *post hoc* fallacy.

Exercises 1.2

1. Classify each of the following statements as positive or normative:
   - **a.** More scholarships to students from poor families will reduce U.S. poverty.
   - **b.** Free trade will harm developing countries.
   - **c.** Cuts to public education in the United States have been too high.
2. How might an economist test one of the positive statements in Exercise 1?

Solutions to Practice Problems 1.2

1a. A normative statement. It cannot be tested.
1b. A positive statement. An experiment will test it.
1c. A normative statement. It cannot be tested.

2. Examples are: New Year celebrations cause January sales. A booming stock market causes a Republican president to be elected.

1.3 THE ECONOMIC WAY OF THINKING

You've seen that to understand what, how, and for whom goods and services are produced, economists build and test models of peoples' choices and the interactions of those choices. Five core ideas summarize the economic way of thinking about people's choices, and these ideas form the basis of all microeconomic models. The ideas are:

- People make rational choices by comparing costs and benefits.
- Cost is what you *must give up* to get something.
- Benefit is what you gain when you get something and is measured by what you are *willing to give up* to get it.
- A rational choice is made on the margin.
- People respond to incentives.

Rational Choice

The most basic idea of economics is that in making choices, people act rationally. A **rational choice** is one that uses the available resources to most effectively satisfy the wants of the person making the choice.

Rational choice
A choice that uses the available resources to most effectively satisfy the wants of the person making the choice.

Only the wants and preferences of the person making a choice are relevant to determine its rationality. For example, you might like chocolate ice cream more than vanilla ice cream, but your friend prefers vanilla. So it is rational for you to choose chocolate and for your friend to choose vanilla.

A rational choice might turn out to have been not the best choice after the event. A farmer might decide to plant wheat rather than soybeans. Then, when the crop comes to market, the price of soybeans might be much higher than the price of wheat. The farmer's choice was rational when it was made, but subsequent events made it less profitable than a different choice.

The idea of rational choice provides an answer to the first question: What goods and services will get produced and in what quantities? The answer is: Those that people rationally choose to produce!

But how do people choose rationally? Why have we chosen to build an interstate highway system and not an interstate high-speed railroad system? Why have most people chosen to use Microsoft's Windows operating system rather than another? Why do more people today choose to drink bottled water and sports energy drinks than in the past?

We make rational choices by comparing *costs* and *benefits*. But economists think about costs and benefits in a special and revealing way. Let's look at the economic concepts of cost and benefit.

Cost: What You *Must Give Up*

Whatever you choose to do, you could have done something else instead. You could have done lots of things other than what you actually did. But one of these other things is the *best* alternative given up. This alternative that you must give up to get something is the **opportunity cost** of the thing that you get. The thing that you could have chosen—the highest-valued alternative forgone—is the cost of the thing that you did choose.

Opportunity cost
The opportunity cost of something is the best thing you must give up to get it.

"There's no such thing as a free lunch" is not a clever but empty saying. It expresses the central idea of economics: that every choice involves a cost.

We use the term *opportunity cost* to emphasize that when we make a choice in the face of scarcity, we give up an opportunity to do something else. You can quit school right now, or you can remain in school. Suppose that if you quit school, the best job you can get is at McDonald's, where you can earn $10,000 during the year. The opportunity cost of remaining in school includes the things that you could have bought with this $10,000. The opportunity cost also includes the value of the leisure time that you must forgo to study.

Opportunity cost is *only* the alternative forgone. It does not include all the expenditures that you make. For example, when you contemplate whether to remain in school, your expenditure on tuition is part of the opportunity cost of remaining in school. But the cost of your school meal voucher is *not* part of the opportunity cost of remaining in school. You must buy food whether you remain in school or not.

Sunk cost
A previously incurred and irreversible cost.

Also, past expenditures that cannot be reversed are not part of opportunity cost. Suppose you've paid your term's tuition and it is nonrefundable. If you now contemplate quitting school, the paid tuition is irrelevant. It is called a sunk cost. A **sunk cost** is a previously incurred and irreversible cost. Whether you remain in school or quit school, having paid the tuition, the tuition is not part of the opportunity cost of remaining in school.

Benefit: Gain Measured by What You Are *Willing to Give Up*

Benefit
The benefit of something is the gain or pleasure that it brings.

The **benefit** of something is the gain or pleasure that it brings. Benefit is how a person *feels* about something. You might be extremely anxious to get the latest version of a video game. It will bring you a large benefit. And you might have almost no interest in the latest Yo Yo Ma cello concerto. It will bring you a small benefit.

Economists measure the benefit of something by what a person is *willing to give up* to get it. You can buy CDs, sodas, or magazines. The sodas or magazines that you are *willing to give up* to get a CD measure the benefit you get from a CD.

On the Margin

A choice on the **margin** is a choice that is made by comparing *all* the relevant alternatives systematically and incrementally. For example, you must choose how to divide the next hour between studying and e-mailing your friends. To make this choice, you must evaluate the costs and benefits of the alternative possible allocations of your next hour. You choose on the margin by considering whether you will be better off or worse off if you spend an extra few minutes studying or an extra few minutes e-mailing.

The margin might involve a small change, as it does when you're deciding how to divide an hour between studying and e-mailing friends. Or it might involve a large change, as it does, for example, when you're deciding whether to remain in school for another year. Attending school for part of the year is no better (and might be worse) than not attending at all—it is not a *relevant* alternative. So you likely will want to commit the entire year to school or to something else. But you still choose on the margin. It is just that the marginal change is now a change for one year rather than a change for a few minutes.

Margin
A choice on the margin is a choice that is made by comparing *all* the relevant alternatives systematically and incrementally.

Marginal Cost

The cost of a one-unit increase in an activity is called **marginal cost**. Marginal cost is what you *must* give up to get one more unit of something. Think about your marginal cost of going to the movies for a third time in a week. Your marginal cost is what you must give up to see that one additional movie. It is *not* what you give up to see all three movies. The reason is that you've already given up something for two movies, so you don't count this cost as resulting from the decision to see the third movie.

The marginal cost of any activity increases as you do more of it. You know that going to the movies decreases your study time and lowers your grade. Suppose that seeing a second movie in a week lowers your grade by five percentage points. Seeing a third movie will lower your grade by more than five additional percentage points. Your marginal cost of movie going is increasing.

Marginal cost
The cost that arises from a one-unit increase in an activity. The marginal cost of something is what you *must* give up to get one more unit of it.

Marginal Benefit

The benefit of a one-unit increase in an activity is called marginal benefit. **Marginal benefit** is what you gain when you get *one more* unit of something. Think about your marginal benefit from the movies. You've been to the movies twice this week, and you're contemplating going for a third time. Your marginal benefit is the benefit you will get from the one additional movie. It is *not* the benefit you get from all three movies. The reason is that you already have had the benefit from two movies, so you don't count this benefit as resulting from the third movie.

Marginal benefit is *measured by* the most you are *willing to give up* to get *one more* unit of something. And a fundamental feature of marginal benefit is that it usually diminishes. The benefit from seeing the first movie in the week is greater than the benefit from seeing the second movie in the week. Because the marginal benefit decreases as you see more movies in the week, *you are willing to give up less* to see one more movie. You know that going to the movies decreases your study time and lowers your grade. Suppose that you were willing to give up ten percentage points to see your second movie. You won't be willing to take such a big hit on your grades to see the third movie in a week. Your marginal benefit of movie going is decreasing.

Marginal benefit
The benefit that arises from a one-unit increase in an activity. The marginal benefit of something is *measured* by what you are *willing to* give up to get one more unit of it.

Making a Rational Choice

So will you go to the movies for that third time in a week? If the marginal cost is less than the marginal benefit, your rational choice will be to see the third movie. If the marginal cost exceeds the marginal benefit, your rational choice will be to spend the evening studying. We make a rational choice and use our scarce resources in the way that makes us as well off as possible when we take those actions for which marginal benefit exceeds or equals marginal cost.

Responding to Incentives

Incentive
An inducement to take a particular action.

In making our choices, we respond to incentives. An **incentive** is an inducement to take a particular action. An incentive can be a "carrot"—a reward that comes from an increase in benefit or a decrease in cost. And an incentive can be a "stick"—a punishment that comes from a decrease in benefit or an increase in cost. A change in marginal benefit or a change in marginal cost brings a change in the incentives that we face and leads us to change our actions.

For example, for most students, the marginal benefit of studying in the days just before a test is greater (or at least is perceived to be greater) than the marginal benefit of studying a month before a test. Because the marginal benefit of studying increases as a test date approaches, we observe an increase in study time and a decrease in leisure pursuits during the last few days before a test. And the more important the test, the greater is this effect.

A change in marginal cost also changes incentives. For example, suppose that last week, you found your course work easy. You scored 100 percent on all your practice quizzes. The marginal cost of taking off an evening to enjoy a movie was low. Your grade on this week's test will not suffer. So you have a movie feast. But this week, suddenly, the going has gotten tough. You are just not getting it. Your practice test scores are low and you know that if you take off even one evening, your grade on next week's test will suffer. The marginal cost of seeing a movie is higher this week than last week. So you decide to give the movies a miss next week.

The central idea of economics is that we can measure changes in incentives, and these measurements enable us to predict the choices that people make as their circumstances change.

CHECKPOINT 1.3

3 **Explain five core ideas that define the economic way of thinking.**

Study Guide pp. 6–8 

***e*Foundations 1.3** 

Practice Problem 1.3

Kate usually plays tennis for two hours a week, and her grade on each math test is usually 70 percent. Last week, after playing two hours of tennis, Kate thought long and hard about playing for another hour. She decided to play another hour of tennis and cut her study time by one additional hour. But the grade on last week's math test was 60 percent.

a. What was Kate's opportunity cost of the third hour of tennis?

b. Given that Kate made the decision to play the third hour of tennis, what can you conclude about the comparison of her marginal benefit and marginal cost of the second hour of tennis?

c. Was Kate's decision to play the third hour of tennis rational?

d. Did Kate make her decision at the margin?

Exercises 1.3

1. Bill Gates gives away a lot of money: $200 million to put computers in libraries that can't afford them and $135 million to universities, cancer research, a children's hospital, and the Seattle Symphony. Doesn't Bill Gates experience scarcity? Are his donations rational? In making these donations, might Bill Gates have responded to any incentive?

2. Steve Fossett spent a lot of money trying to be the first person to circumnavigate the world in a hot-air balloon. Anheuser-Busch offered a prize of $1 million for the first balloonist to do so in 15 days nonstop. What was the opportunity cost of Steve Fossett's adventure? But Steve Fossett was not the first person to circumnavigate the world in a balloon, so did he get any benefits? Why did Anheuser-Busch offer the prize?

3. Tony is an engineering student, and he is considering taking an extra course in history. List the things that might be part of his costs and benefits of the history course. Think of an incentive that might encourage him to take the course.

Solution to Practice Problem 1.3

a. Kate's opportunity cost of the third hour of tennis was the ten percentage point drop in her grade. If Kate had not played tennis for the third hour, she would have studied and her grade would not have dropped. The best alternative forgone is her opportunity cost of the third hour of tennis.

b. The marginal benefit from the second hour of tennis must have exceeded the marginal cost of the second hour because Kate chose to play tennis for the third hour. If the marginal benefit did not exceed the marginal cost, she would have chosen to study and not play tennis for the third hour.

c. If for Kate, marginal benefit exceeded marginal cost, her decision was rational.

d. Kate made her decision at the margin because she considered the benefit and cost of *one additional hour*.

1.4 WHY ECONOMICS IS WORTH STUDYING

In 1961, Mick Jagger, then the 19-year-old lead singer with a group that would become the Rolling Stones, enrolled in an economics degree program at the London School of Economics. During the day, he was learning about opportunity cost, and each night, his rock group was earning today's equivalent of $120. Mick soon realized that his opportunity cost of remaining in school was too high, and so he dropped out. (A faculty advisor is reputed to have told Mick that he wouldn't make much money in a rock band. But within a few months, the Rolling Stones, along with the Beatles, shot to international stardom and multimillion-dollar recording contracts!)

Mick Jagger used one of the big ideas of economics to make his own rational decision. And you can do the same. Let's look at the benefits and costs of studying economics and check that the benefits outweigh the costs.

Two main benefits from studying economics are:

- Understanding
- Expanded career opportunities

Understanding

George Bernard Shaw, the great Irish dramatist and thinker, wrote, "Economy is the art of making the most of life." Life is certainly full of economic problems, some global or national in scope and some personal.

Every day, on television, on the Internet, and in newspapers and magazines, we hear and read about global or national economic issues: Should Nike pay higher wages to its workers in Asia? Is there too much economic inequality in the world today? How can we improve health care, welfare, and education? Are taxes too high or too low? Will the Federal Reserve increase interest rates next week?

And every day in your own life, you're confronted with personal economic choices: Will you buy pizza or pasta? Will you skip class today? Will you put your summer earnings in the bank or the stock market?

Studying economics equips you with tools and insights that help you to understand the world's problems and to participate in the political debate that surrounds them and to understand and solve your personal economic problems.

John Maynard Keynes, a famous British economist of the twentieth century, wrote, "The ideas of economists . . . , both when they are right and when they are wrong, are more powerful than is commonly understood. Indeed the world is ruled by little else. Practical men [and women, he would have written today], who believe themselves to be quite exempt from any intellectual influences, are usually the slaves of some defunct economist."

Keynes was correct. You can't ignore economic ideas. They are all around you. You use them every day in your personal life and in your work. You use them when you vote and when you argue with your friends. But you don't need to be the slave of some defunct economist. By studying economics, you will learn how to develop your own ideas and to test them against the ideas of others. As you progress with your study of economics, you will start to listen to the news and read your newspaper with a deeper understanding of what's going on. You will also find yourself increasingly using the economics that you are learning as you make your own economic choices.

Expanded Career Opportunities

Robert Reich, a former U.S. Secretary of Labor, predicts that the three big jobs of the twenty-first century will be what he calls *problem identifying*, *problem solving*, and *strategic brokering*. The people who are good at these tasks command soaring incomes. And there is no better way to train yourself in these skills than to study economics. You can think of economics as a workout regimen for your brain. Almost everything that you study in economics is practice at thinking abstractly and rigorously about concrete things. You will constantly be asking, "What if?" Although students of economics learn many useful economic concepts, it is the training and practice in abstract thinking that really pay off.

Most students of economics don't go on to major in the subject. And even those who do major in economics don't usually go on to become economists. Rather, they work in fields such as banking, business, management, finance, insurance, real estate, marketing, law, government, journalism, health care, and the arts. A course in economics is a very good choice for a pre-med, pre-law, or pre-MBA student.

Economics graduates are not the highest-paid professionals. But they are close to the top, as you can see in Figure 1.1. Engineers and computer scientists, for example, earn up to 20 percent more than economics graduates. Economics graduates earn more than most others, and significantly, they earn more than business graduates.

FIGURE 1.1
Average Incomes

*e*Foundations 1.4 

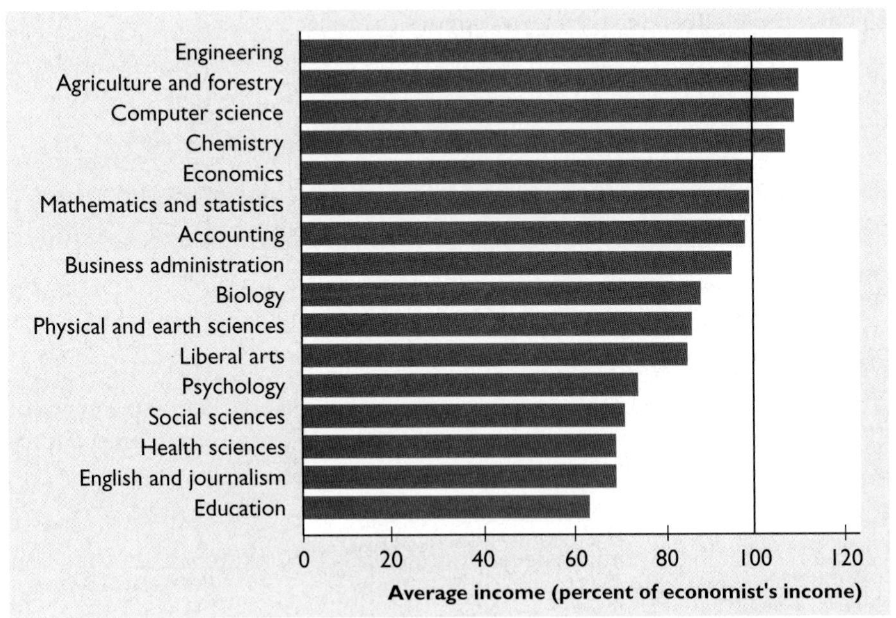

Graduates in disciplines that teach *problem identifying*, *problem solving*, and *strategic brokering* (engineering, computer science, and economics) are at the top of the earnings distribution.

SOURCES: U.S. Department of Commerce, Bureau of the Census, *Current Population Reports*, Series P-70, No. 32, "Educational Background and Economic Status: Spring 1990," and *Statistical Abstract of the United States*, 1994, Table 246, and authors' calculations.

The Costs of Studying Economics

Regardless of what you study, you must buy textbooks and supplies and pay tuition. So these expenses are *not* part of the opportunity cost of studying economics.

One cost of studying economics is forgone knowledge of some other subject. If you work hard at studying economics, you must forgo learning some other subject. You can't study everything.

Another cost, and the main cost of studying economics, is forgone leisure time. Economics is a demanding subject, and it takes time to master. Most students say that they find it difficult. They often complain that they understand the subject when they read the textbook or listen to their instructor but then, when they take an exam, they just can't figure out the correct answers.

The trick is practice, or learning-by-doing. Economics is not a subject that you learn by memorizing things. You must memorize definitions and technical terms. But beyond that, memory is not your main mental tool. Working problems and learning how to analyze and solve problems are the key. And this activity is time consuming.

Benefits Versus Costs

So which is larger: the benefit or the cost? Economics says that only you can decide. You are the judge of value or benefit to yourself. So you must weigh the benefits and the costs that we've identified (and consider any others that are important to *you*).

If you're clear that the benefits outweigh the costs, you're well on your way to having a good time in your economics course. If the costs outweigh the benefits, don't waste your time. Life is too short.

If you're on the fence, try to get more information. But if you remain on the fence, complete this one course in economics and then decide.

CHECKPOINT 1.4

Study Guide pp. 9–10 

*e*Foundations 1.4

4 Explain why economics is worth studying.

Practice Problem 1.4

A student is choosing between an economics course and a popular music course. List two opportunity costs and two benefits from taking a course in economics.

Exercise 1.4

Why did Mick Jagger quit his economics course? What are some of the benefits that Mick Jagger might have given up?

Solution to Practice Problem 1.4

Opportunity costs include the leisure forgone and forgone appreciation of popular music. Benefits include expanded career opportunities, better understanding of the world, and better problem-solving skills.

CHAPTER CHECKPOINT

Key Points

1 Define economics, distinguish between microeconomics and macroeconomics, and explain the questions of microeconomics.

- Economics is the social science that studies the choices that individuals, businesses, governments, and entire societies make as they cope with scarcity.
- Microeconomics is the study of the choices that individuals and businesses make, the way these choices interact, and the influence that governments exert on these choices.
- Macroeconomics is the study of the aggregate effects on the national economy and the global economy of the choices that individuals, businesses, and governments make.
- Choices that individuals, businesses, and governments make and the interactions of those choices end up determining *what* goods and services get produced, *how* they get produced, and *for whom* they get produced.

2 Describe the work of economists as social scientists.

- Positive statements are about what is, and they can be tested. Normative statements are about what ought to be, and they cannot be tested.
- To explain the economic world, economists build and test economic models.
- Economists use the *ceteris paribus* assumption to try to disentangle cause and effect, and they use natural experiments, statistical methods, and economic experiments.

3 Explain five core ideas that define the economic way of thinking.

- People make rational choices by comparing *costs* and *benefits*.
- Cost is what you *must give up* to get something.
- Benefit is what you gain when you get something and is measured by what you are *willing to give up* to get it.
- A rational choice is made on the margin.
- People respond to incentives.

4 Explain why economics is worth studying.

- The benefits of studying economics are understanding of the economic world and expanded career opportunities.
- The costs of studying economics are forgone knowledge of some other subject and leisure time.

Key Terms

Benefit, 14
Ceteris paribus, 10
Correlation, 11
Economic model, 9
Economic theory, 9
Economics, 5
Goods and services, 6
Incentive, 16
Macroeconomics, 5
Margin, 15
Marginal benefit, 15
Marginal cost, 15
Microeconomics, 5
Opportunity cost, 13
Post hoc fallacy, 11
Rational choice, 13
Scarcity, 4
Sunk cost, 14

Exercises

1. Label each of the following news items as involving a microeconomic or macroeconomic issue:
   a. An increase in the tax on cigarettes will decrease teenage smoking.
   b. It would be better if the United States spent more on cleaning up the environment and less on space exploration.
   c. A government scheme called "work-for-the-dole" will reduce the number of people who are unemployed.
   d. An increase in the number of police on inner-city streets will reduce the crime rate.

2. Label each of the following news items as involving a What, How, or For whom question:
   a. Today most stores use computers to keep their inventory records, whereas 20 years ago most stores used paper records.
   b. It would be better if the United States spent more on cleaning up the environment and less on space exploration.
   c. A doubling of the gas tax might lead to a better public transit system.

3. Label each of the following news items as a positive or a normative statement:
   a. The poor pay too much for housing.
   b. The number of farms in the United States has decreased over the last 50 years.
   c. The population in rural areas in the United States has remained constant over the past decade.

4. Explain how economists try to unscramble cause and effect. Explain why economists use the *ceteris paribus* assumption.

5. What is correlation? What approaches do economists use to try to sort out the cause and effect relationship that correlation might indicate? Describe each of these approaches.

6. What is the *post hoc* fallacy? Provide two examples of the *post hoc* fallacy.

7. Pam, Pru, and Pat are deciding how they will celebrate the New Year. Pam prefers to go on a cruise, is happy to go to Hawaii, but does not want to go skiing. Pru prefers to go skiing, is happy to go to Hawaii, but does not want to go on a cruise. Pat prefers to go to Hawaii or to take a cruise but does not want to go skiing. Their decision is to go to Hawaii. Is this decision rational? What is the opportunity cost of the trip to Hawaii for each of them? What is the benefit each person gets?

8. Your school has decided to increase the intake of new students next year. What economic concepts would your school consider in reaching its decision? Would the school make its decision at the margin?

9. In California, most vineyards use machines and a few workers to pick grapes, while some vineyards use no machines and many workers.
   a. Which vineyards have made a rational choice? Explain your answer.
   b. In choosing how to pick grapes, do vineyards make their choice at the margin? Do incentives play a role?

APPENDIX: MAKING AND USING GRAPHS

When you have completed your study of this appendix, you will be able to:

1 **Interpret a scatter diagram, a time-series graph, and a cross-section graph.**

2 **Interpret the graphs used in economic models.**

3 **Define and calculate slope.**

4 **Graph relationships among more than two variables.**

Basic Idea

A graph represents a quantity as a distance and enables us to visualize the relationship between two variables. To make a graph, we set two lines called *axes* perpendicular to each other, like those in Figure A1.1. The vertical line is called the y-axis, and the horizontal line is called the x-axis. The common zero point is called the *origin*. In Figure A1.1, the x-axis measures temperature in degrees Fahrenheit. A movement to the right shows an increase in temperature, and a movement to the left shows a decrease in temperature. The y-axis represents ice cream consumption, measured in gallons per day. To make a graph, we need a value of the variable on the x-axis and a corresponding value of the variable on the y-axis. For example, if the temperature is 40°F, ice cream consumption is 5 gallons a day at point A in the graph. If the temperature is 80°F, ice cream consumption is 20 gallons a day at point B in the graph. Graphs like that in Figure A1.1 can be used to show any type of quantitative data on two variables.

FIGURE A1.1
Making a Graph

e/**Foundations A1.1** 

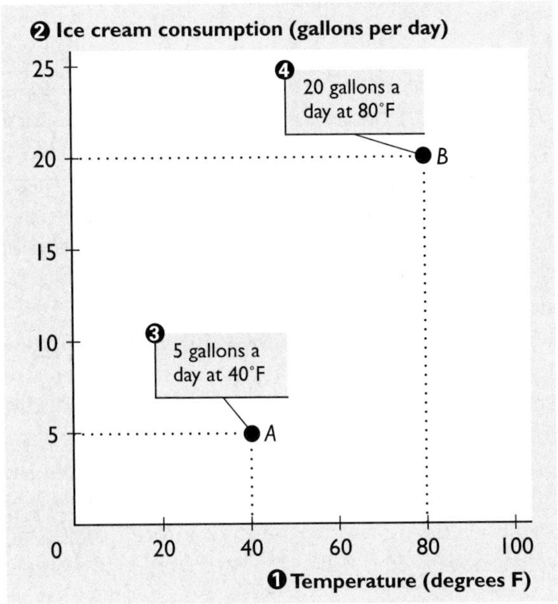

All graphs have axes that measure quantities as distances.

❶ The horizontal axis (x-axis) measures temperature in degrees Fahrenheit. A movement to the right shows an increase in temperature.

❷ The vertical axis (y-axis) measures ice cream consumption in gallons per day. A movement upward shows an increase in ice cream consumption.

❸ Point A shows that 5 gallons of ice cream are consumed on a day when the temperature is 40°F.

❹ Point B shows that 20 gallons of ice cream are consumed on a day when the temperature is 80°F.

Interpreting Data Graphs

Scatter diagram
A graph of the value of one variable against the value of another variable.

A **scatter diagram** is a graph of the value of one variable against the value of another variable. It is used to reveal whether a relationship exists between two variables and to describe the relationship. Figure A1.2 shows two examples.

Figure A1.2(a) shows the relationship between consumption and income. Each point shows consumption per person and income per person in the United States in a given year from 1990 to 1999. The points are "scattered" within the graph. The label on each point shows its year. The point marked 96 shows that in 1996, income per person was $21,400 and consumption per person was $19,700. This scatter diagram reveals that as income increases, consumption also increases.

Figure A1.2(b) shows the relationship between the number of minutes of international phone calls made from the United States and the average price per minute. This scatter diagram reveals that as the price per minute falls, the number of minutes called increases.

Time-series graph
A graph that measures time on the *x*-axis and the variable or variables in which we are interested on the *y*-axis.

A **time-series graph** measures time (for example, months or years) on the *x*-axis and the variable or variables in which we are interested on the *y*-axis. Figure A1.2(c) shows an example. In this graph, time (on the *x*-axis) is measured in years, which run from 1970 to 2000. The variable that we are interested in is the price of coffee, and it is measured on the *y*-axis.

A time-series graph conveys an enormous amount of information quickly and easily, as this example illustrates. It shows when the value is:

1. High or low. When the line is a long way from the x-axis, the price is high. When the line is close to the x-axis, the price is low.
2. Rising or falling. When the line slopes upward, as in 1976, the price is rising. When the line slopes downward, as in 1978, the price is falling.
3. Rising or falling quickly and slowly. If the line is steep, then the price is rising or falling quickly. If the line is not steep, the price is rising or falling slowly. For example, the price rose quickly in 1976 and 1977 and slowly in 1993. The price fell quickly in 1978 and slowly during the early 1980s.

Trend
A general tendency for the value of a variable to rise or fall.

A time-series graph also reveals whether the variable has a trend. A **trend** is a general tendency for the value of a variable to rise or fall. You can see that the price of coffee had a general tendency to fall from the mid-1970s to the early 1990s. That is, although the price rose and fell, it had a general tendency to fall.

With a time-series graph, we can compare different periods quickly. Figure A1.2(c) shows that the 1980s were different from the 1970s. The price of coffee fluctuated more violently in the 1970s than it did in the 1980s. This graph conveys a wealth of information, and it does so in much less space than we have used to describe only some of its features.

Cross-section graph
A graph that shows the values of an economic variable for different groups in a population at a point in time.

A **cross-section graph** shows the values of an economic variable for different groups in a population at a point in time. Figure A1.2(d) is an example of a cross-section graph. It shows average income per person in the ten largest metropolitan areas in the United States in 1995. This graph uses bars rather than dots and lines, and the length of each bar indicates average income per person. Figure A1.2(d) enables you to compare the average incomes per person in these ten metropolitan areas. And you can do so much more quickly and clearly than by looking at a list of numbers.

FIGURE A1.2
Data Graphs

*e*Foundations **A1.1**

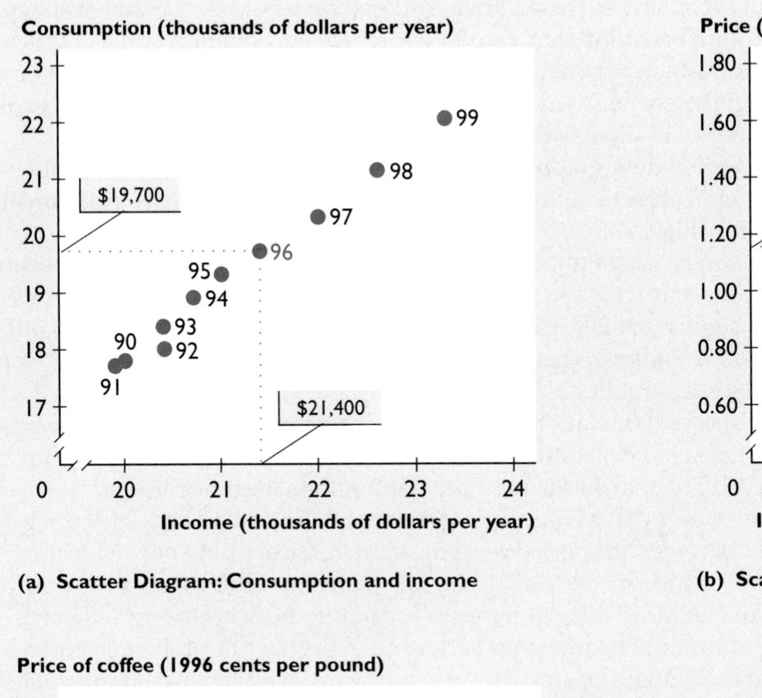

(a) Scatter Diagram: Consumption and income

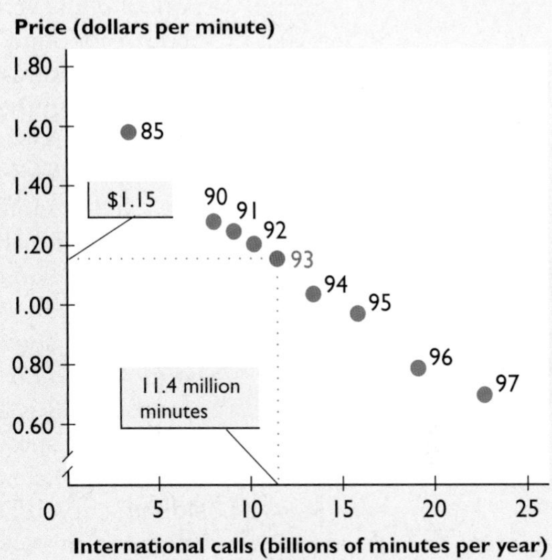

(b) Scatter Diagram: Price and quantity of calls

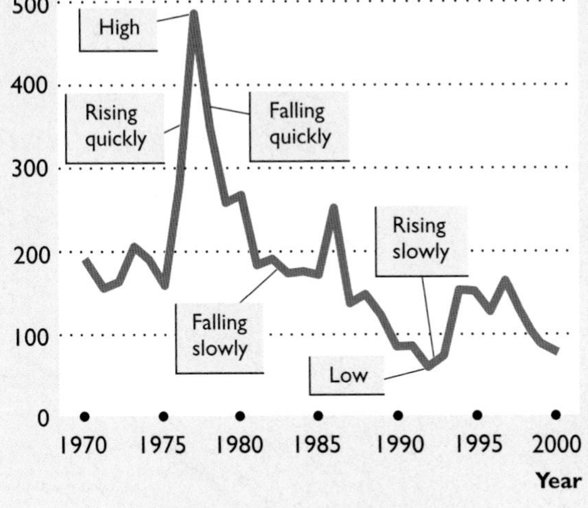

(c) Time Series: The price of coffee

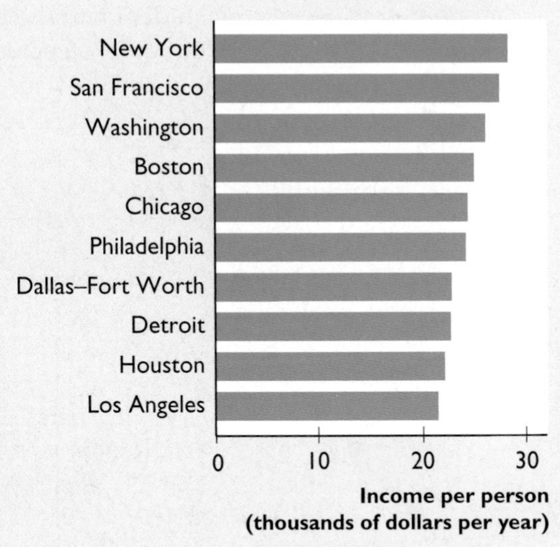

(d) Cross Section: Income per person

A scatter diagram reveals the relationship between two variables. In part (a), as income increases, consumption increases. In part (b), as the price per minute falls, the number of minutes called increases.

A time-series graph plots the value of a variable on the *y*-axis against time on the *x*-axis. Part (c) plots the price of coffee each year from 1970 to 2000. The graph shows when the price of coffee was high and low, when it increased and decreased, and when it changed quickly and slowly.

A cross-section graph shows the value of a variable across the members of a population. Part (d) shows the average income per person in each of ten large U.S. metropolitan areas in 1995.

Interpreting Graphs Used in Economic Models

We use graphs to show the relationships among the variables in an economic model. An *economic model* is a simplified description of the economy or of a component of the economy such as a business or a household. It consists of statements about economic behavior that can be expressed as equations or as curves in a graph. Economists use models to explore the effects of different policies or other influences on the economy in ways similar to those used to test model airplanes in wind tunnels and models of the climate.

Positive relationship or direct relationship
A relationship between two variables that move in the same direction.

Linear relationship
A relationship that graphs as a straight line.

Figure A1.3 shows graphs of the relationships between two variables that move in the same direction. Such a relationship is called a **positive relationship** or **direct relationship**.

Part (a) shows a straight-line relationship, which is called a **linear relationship**. The distance traveled in 5 hours increases as the speed increases. For example, point *A* shows that 200 miles are traveled in 5 hours at a speed of 40 miles an hour. And point *B* shows that the distance traveled increases to 300 miles if the speed increases to 60 miles an hour.

Part (b) shows the relationship between distance sprinted and recovery time (the time it takes the heart rate to return to its normal resting rate). An upward-sloping curved line that starts out quite flat but then becomes steeper as we move along the curve away from the origin describes this relationship. The curve slopes upward and becomes steeper because the extra recovery time needed from sprinting another 100 yards increases. It takes less than 5 minutes to recover from sprinting 100 yards but more than 10 minutes to recover from sprinting 200 yards.

Part (c) shows the relationship between the number of problems worked by a student and the amount of study time. An upward-sloping curved line that starts out quite steep and becomes flatter as we move away from the origin shows this

FIGURE A1.3
Positive (Direct) Relationships

*e*Foundations **A1.1** 

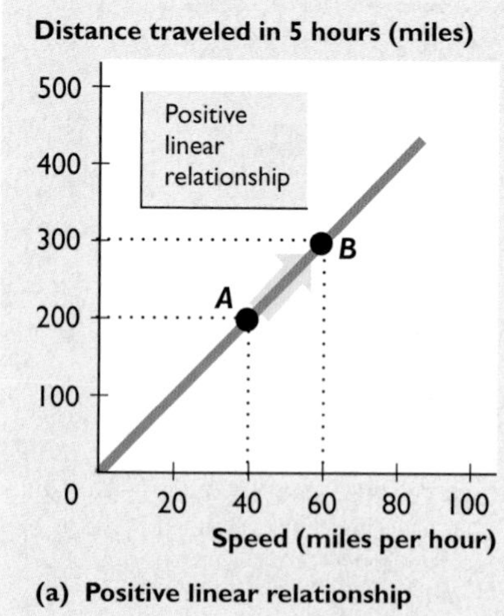

(a) **Positive linear relationship**

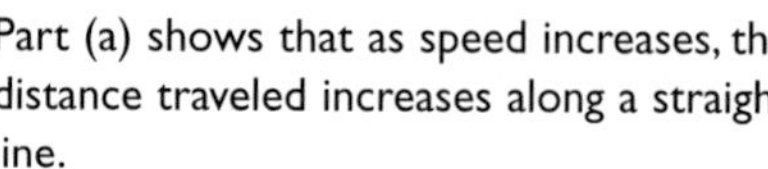
Part (a) shows that as speed increases, the distance traveled increases along a straight line.

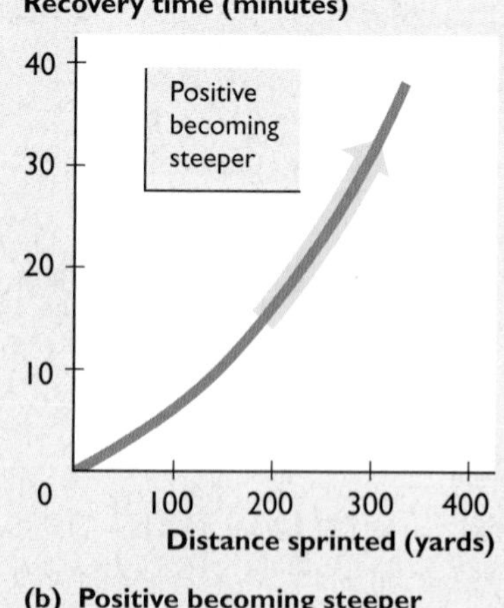

(b) **Positive becoming steeper**

Part (b) shows that as the distance sprinted increases, recovery time increases along a curve that becomes steeper.

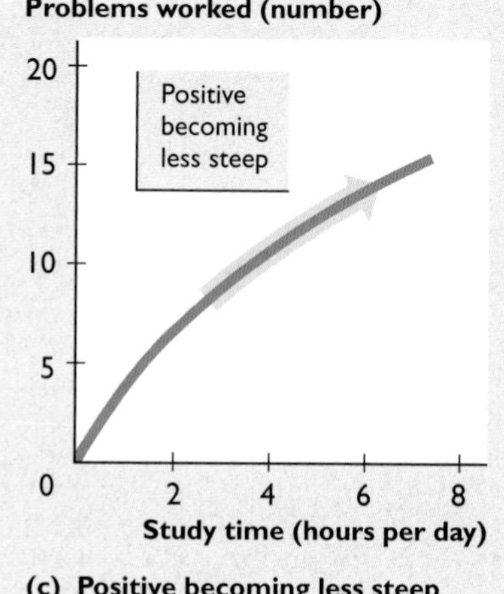

(c) **Positive becoming less steep**

Part (c) shows that as study time increases, the number of problems worked increases along a curve that becomes less steep.

relationship. Study time becomes less effective as you increase the hours worked and become more tired.

Figure A1.4 shows relationships between two variables that move in opposite directions. Such a relationship is called a **negative relationship** or **inverse relationship**.

Negative relationship or inverse relationship
A relationship between two variables that move in opposite directions.

Part (a) shows the relationship between the number of hours for playing squash and the number of hours for playing tennis when the total hours available is five. One extra hour spent playing tennis means one hour less playing squash and vice versa. This relationship is negative and linear.

Part (b) shows the relationship between the cost per mile traveled and the length of a journey. The longer the journey, the lower is the cost per mile. But as the journey length increases, the cost per mile decreases, and the fall in the cost is smaller, the longer the journey. This feature of the relationship is shown by the fact that the curve slopes downward, starting out steep at a short journey length and then becoming flatter as the journey length increases. This relationship arises because some of the costs are fixed, such as auto insurance, and the fixed costs are spread over a longer journey.

Part (c) shows the relationship between the amount of leisure time and the number of problems worked by a student. Increasing leisure time produces an increasingly large reduction in the number of problems worked. This relationship is a negative one that starts out with a gentle slope at a small number of leisure hours and becomes steeper as the number of leisure hours increases. This relationship is a different view of the idea shown in Figure A1.3(c).

Many relationships in economic models have a maximum or a minimum. For example, firms try to make the largest possible profit and to produce at the lowest possible cost. Figure A1.5 shows relationships that have a maximum or a minimum.

FIGURE A1.4
Negative (Inverse) Relationships

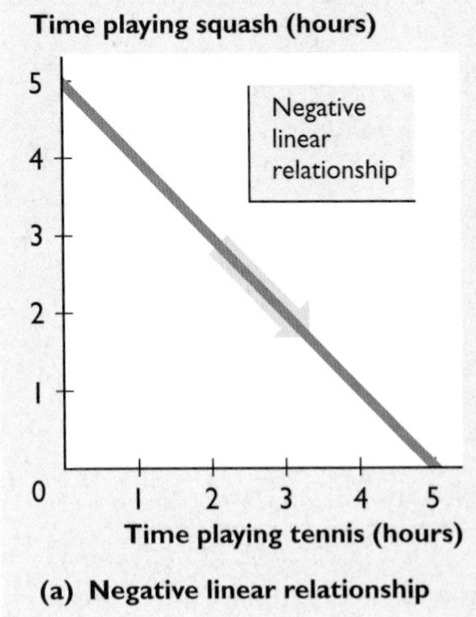

(a) Negative linear relationship

Part (a) shows that as the time playing tennis increases, the time playing squash decreases along a straight line.

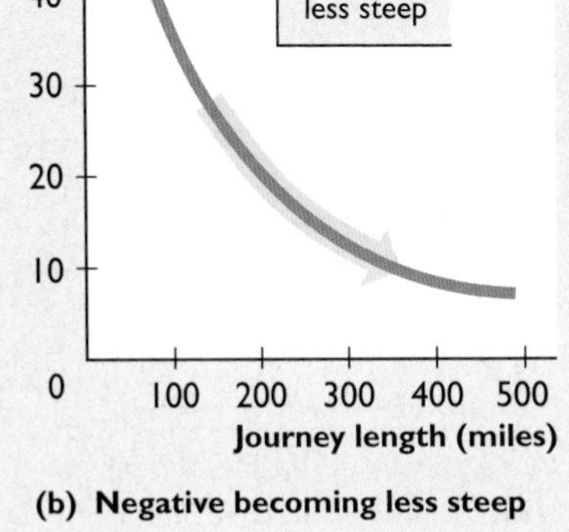

(b) Negative becoming less steep

Part (b) shows that as the journey length increases, the cost of the trip falls along a curve that becomes less steep.

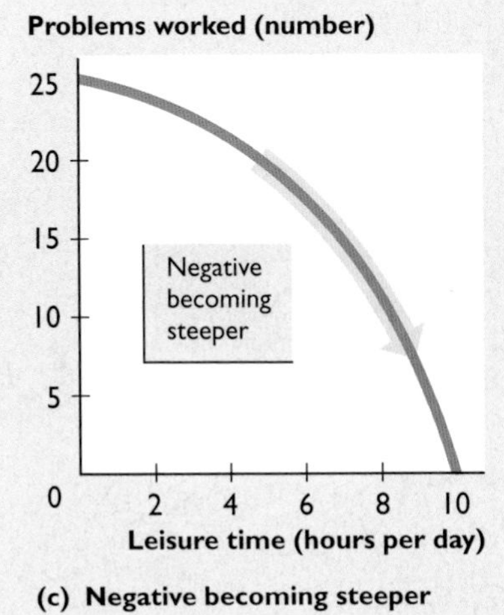

(c) Negative becoming steeper

Part (c) shows that as leisure time increases, the number of problems worked decreases along a curve that becomes steeper.

FIGURE A1.5

Maximum and Minimum Points

*e*Foundations **A1.1** 

In part (a), as the rainfall increases, the curve ❶ slopes upward as the yield per acre rises, ❷ is flat at point *A*, the maximum yield, and then ❸ slopes downward as the yield per acre falls.

In part (b), as the speed increases, the curve ❶ slopes downward as the cost per mile falls, ❷ is flat at the minimum point *B*, and then ❸ slopes upward as the cost per mile rises.

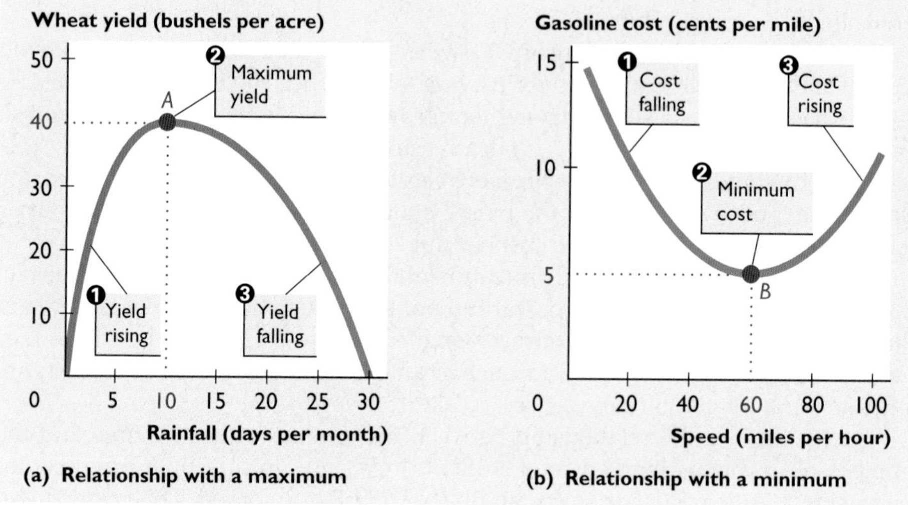

(a) Relationship with a maximum

(b) Relationship with a minimum

Part (a) shows the relationship that starts out sloping upward, reaches a maximum, and then slopes downward. Part (b) shows a relationship that begins sloping downward, falls to a minimum, and then slopes upward.

Finally, there are many situations in which, no matter what happens to the value of one variable, the other variable remains constant. Sometimes we want to show the independence between two variables in a graph. Figure A1.6 shows two graphs in which the variables are independent.

FIGURE A1.6

Variables That Are Unrelated

*e*Foundations **A1.1** 

In part (a), as the price of bananas increases, the student's grade in economics remains at 75 percent. These variables are unrelated, and the curve is horizontal.

In part (b), the vineyards of France produce 3 billion gallons of wine no matter what the rainfall in California is. These variables are unrelated, and the curve is vertical.

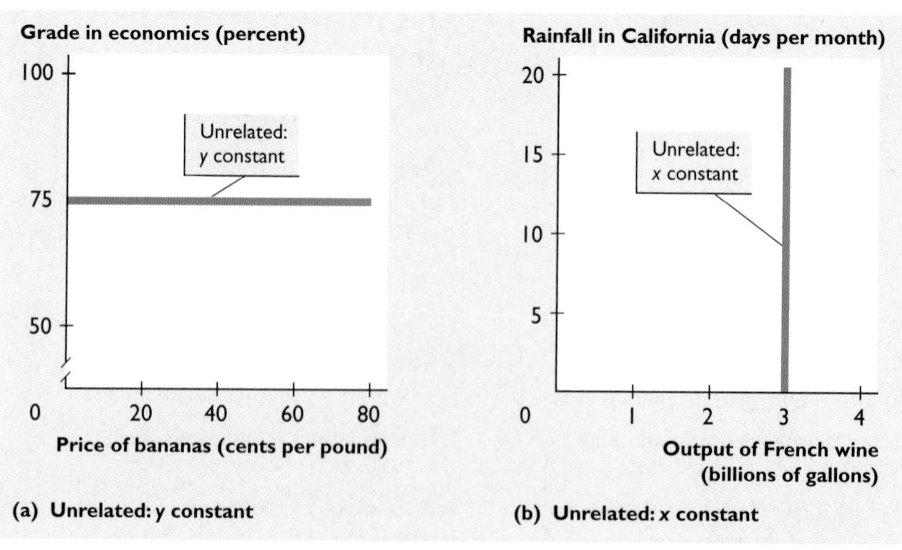

(a) Unrelated: *y* constant

(b) Unrelated: *x* constant

The Slope of a Relationship

We can measure the influence of one variable on another by the slope of the relationship. The **slope** of a relationship is the change in the value of the variable measured on the y-axis divided by the change in the value of the variable measured on the x-axis. We use the Greek letter Δ (delta) to represent "change in." So Δy means the change in the value of y, and Δx means the change in the value of x, and the slope of the relationship is

$$\Delta y \div \Delta x.$$

Slope
The change in the value of the variable measured on the *y*-axis divided by the change the value of the variable measured on the *x*-axis.

If a large change in y is associated with a small change in x, the slope is large and the curve is steep. If a small change in y is associated with a large change in x, the slope is small and the curve is flat.

Figure A1.7 shows you how to calculate slope. The slope of a straight line is the same regardless of where on the line you calculate it—the slope is constant. In part (a), when x increases from 2 to 6, y increases from 3 to 6. The change in x is +4—that is, Δx is 4. The change in y is +3—that is, Δy is 3. The slope of that line is 3/4. In part (b), when x increases from 2 to 6, *y decreases* from 6 to 3. The change in y is *minus* 3—that is, Δy is –3. The change in x is plus 4—that is, Δx is 4. The slope of the curve is –3/4. In part (c), we calculate the slope at a point on a curve. To do so, place a ruler on the graph so that it touches point A and no other point on the curve, then draw a straight line along the edge of the ruler. The slope of this straight line is the slope of the curve at point A. This slope is 3/4.

FIGURE A1.7
Calculating Slope

*e*Foundations A1.1 

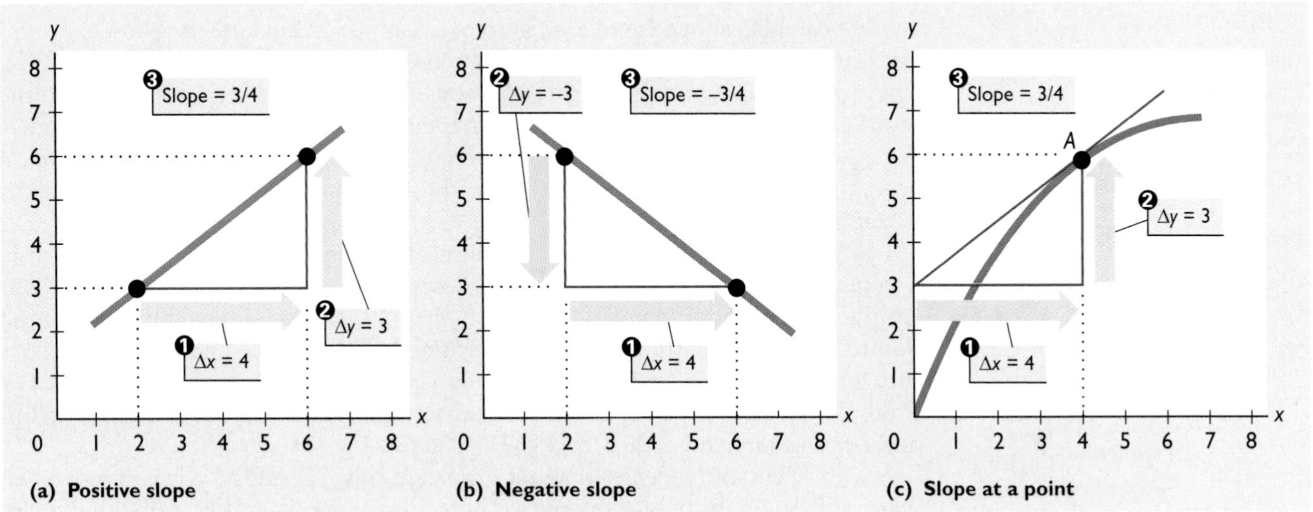

In part (a), ❶ when Δx is 4, ❷ Δy is 3, so ❸ the slope (Δy/Δx) is 3/4.

In part (b), ❶ when Δx is 4, ❷ Δy is –3, so ❸ the slope (Δy/Δx) is –3/4.

In part (c), the slope of the curve at point *A* equals the slope of the red line. ❶ When Δx is 4, ❷ Δy is 3, so ❸ the slope (Δy/Δx) is 3/4.

Relationships Among More Than Two Variables

We have seen that we can graph the relationship between two variables as a point formed by the x and y values. But most of the relationships in economics involve relationships among many variables, not just two. For example, the amount of ice cream consumed depends on the price of ice cream and the temperature. If ice cream is expensive and the temperature is low, people eat much less ice cream than when ice cream is inexpensive and the temperature is high. For any given price of ice cream, the quantity consumed varies with the temperature; and for any given temperature, the quantity of ice cream consumed varies with its price.

Figure A1.8 shows a relationship among three variables. The table shows the number of gallons of ice cream consumed each day at various temperatures and ice cream prices. How can we graph these numbers?

To graph a relationship that involves more than two variables, we use the *ceteris paribus* assumption.

Ceteris Paribus

The Latin phrase *ceteris paribus* means "other things remaining the same." Every laboratory experiment is an attempt to create *ceteris paribus* and isolate the relationship of interest. We use the same method to make a graph.

Figure A1.8(a) shows an example. This graph shows what happens to the quantity of ice cream consumed when the price of ice cream varies while the temperature remains the same. The curve labeled 70°F shows the relationship between ice cream consumption and the price of ice cream if the temperature is 70°F. The numbers used to plot that curve are those in the first and fourth columns of the table in Figure A1.8. For example, if the temperature is 70°F, 10 gallons are consumed when the price is 60¢ a scoop and 18 gallons are consumed when the price is 30¢ a scoop. The curve labeled 90°F shows consumption as the price varies if the temperature is 90°F.

We can also show the relationship between ice cream consumption and temperature while the price of ice cream remains constant, as shown in Figure A1.8(b). The curve labeled 60¢ shows how the consumption of ice cream varies with the temperature when the price of ice cream is 60¢ a scoop, and a second curve shows the relationship when the price of ice cream is 15¢ a scoop. For example, at 60¢ a scoop, 10 gallons are consumed when the temperature is 70°F and 20 gallons when the temperature is 90°F.

Figure A1.8(c) shows the combinations of temperature and price that result in a constant consumption of ice cream. One curve shows the combination that results in 10 gallons a day being consumed, and the other shows the combination that results in 7 gallons a day being consumed. A high price and a high temperature lead to the same consumption as a lower price and a lower temperature. For example, 10 gallons of ice cream are consumed at 90°F and 90¢ a scoop, at 70°F and 60¢ a scoop, and at 50°F and 45¢ a scoop.

With what you've learned about graphs in this Appendix, you can move forward with your study of economics. There are no graphs in this textbook that are more complicated than the ones you've studied here.

FIGURE A1.8
Graphing a Relationship Among Three Variables

*e*Foundations **A1.1** 

Price (cents per scoop)	Ice cream consumption (gallons per day)			
	30°F	50°F	70°F	90°F
15	12	18	25	50
30	10	12	18	37
45	7	10	13	27
60	5	7	10	20
75	3	5	7	14
90	2	3	5	10
105	1	2	3	6

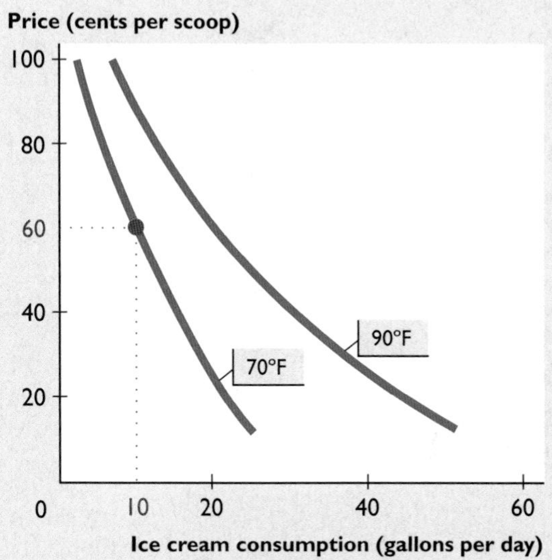

(a) Price and consumption at a given temperature

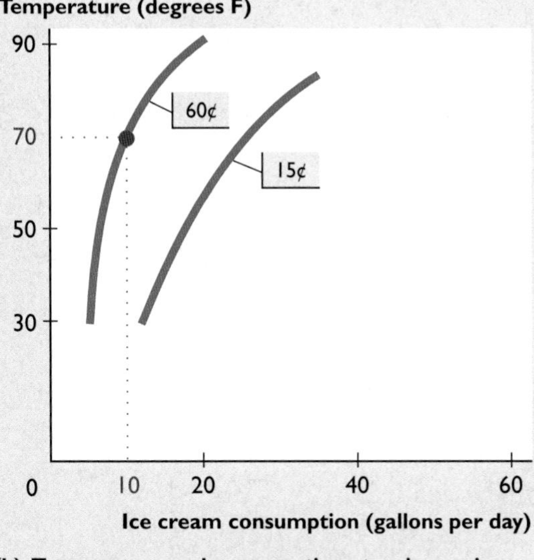

(b) Temperature and consumption at a given price

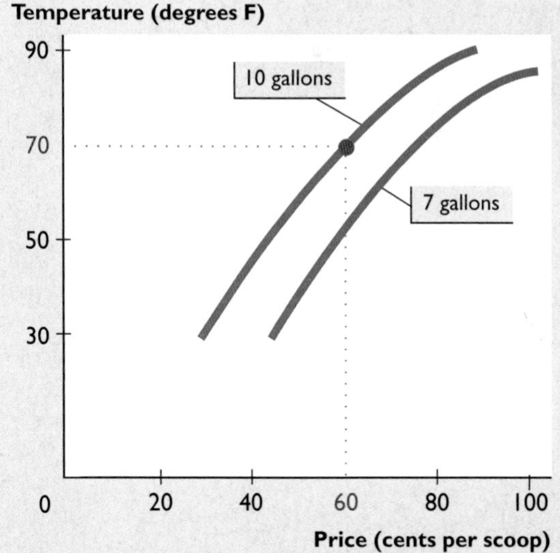

(c) Temperature and price at a given consumption

The table tells us how many gallons of ice cream are consumed each day at different prices and different temperatures. For example, if the price is 60¢ a scoop and the temperature is 70°F, 10 gallons of ice cream are consumed. This set of values is highlighted in the table and each part of the figure.

Part (a) shows the relationship between price and consumption when temperature is held constant. One curve holds temperature at 90°F, and the other at 70°F.

Part (b) shows the relationship between temperature and consumption when price is held constant. One curve holds the price at 60¢ a scoop, and the other at 15¢ a scoop.

Part (c) shows the relationship between temperature and price when consumption is held constant. One curve holds consumption at 10 gallons, and the other at 7 gallons.

APPENDIX CHECKPOINT

Study Guide pp. 14–19

*e*Foundations A1.1

Exercises

The spreadsheet provides data on the U.S. economy: Column A is the year, the other columns are actual and projected expenditures per person on recorded music (column B), Internet services (column C), and movies in theaters (column D). Use this spreadsheet to answer exercises 1, 2, 3, 4, and 5.

	A	B	C	D
1	1992	43	4	23
2	1993	47	5	24
3	1994	56	6	25
4	1995	57	11	25
5	1996	57	17	27
6	1997	55	26	29
7	1998	56	32	30
8	1999	58	37	31
9	2000	62	43	32
10	2001	66	48	33
11	2002	69	53	34

1. Draw a scatter diagram to show the relationship between expenditure on recorded music and expenditure on Internet services. Describe the relationship.

2. Draw a scatter diagram to show the relationship between expenditure on Internet services and expenditure on movies in theaters. Describe the relationship.

3. Draw a scatter diagram to show the relationship between expenditure on recorded music and expenditure on movies in theaters. Describe the relationship.

4. Draw a time-series graph of expenditure on Internet services. Say in which year(s) (a) expenditure was highest, (b) expenditure was lowest, (c) expenditure increased the most, and (d) expenditure increased the least. Also, say whether the data show a trend and describe its direction.

5. Draw a time-series graph of expenditure on recorded music. Say in which year(s) (a) expenditure was highest, (b) expenditure was lowest, (c) expenditure increased the most, and (d) expenditure increased the least. Also, say whether the data show a trend and describe its direction.

6. Draw a graph to show the relationship between the two variables x and y:

x	0	1	2	3	4	5	6	7	8
y	0	1	4	9	16	25	36	49	64

   a. Is the relationship positive or negative?
   b. Calculate the slope of the relationship between x and y when x equals 2 and when x equals 4.
   c. How does the slope of the relationship change as the value of x increases?
   d. Think of some economic relationships that might be similar to this one.

7. Draw a graph to show the relationship between the two variables x and y:

x	0	1	2	3	4	5	6	7	8
y	60	49	39	30	22	15	9	4	0

   a. Is the relationship positive or negative?
   b. Calculate the slope of the relationship between x and y when x equals 2 and when x equals 4.
   c. How does the slope of the relationship change as the value of x increases?
   d. Think of some economic relationships that might be similar to this one.

Price (dollars per ride)	Balloon rides (number per day)		
	50°F	70°F	90°F
5	32	50	40
10	27	40	32
15	18	32	27
20	10	27	18

8. The table provides data on the price of a balloon ride, the temperature, and the number of rides a day. Draw graphs to show the relationship between:
   a. The price and the number of rides, holding the temperature constant.
   b. The number of rides and the temperature, holding the price constant.
   c. The temperature and the price, holding the number of rides constant.

Chapter 2

The U.S. Economy

CHAPTER CHECKLIST

When you have completed your study of this chapter, you will be able to:

1. Describe the patterns and changes in *what* goods and services are produced in the United States.
2. Describe the patterns and changes in *how* goods and services are produced in the United States.
3. Describe *for whom* goods and services are produced in the United States.
4. Use the circular flow model to provide a picture of how households, firms, and government interact to determine what, how, and for whom goods and services are produced.

Economic activity arises from scarcity—the available resources are insufficient to meet all our wants. Microeconomics studies the choices that individuals, businesses, and governments make as they cope with scarcity. These choices and the interactions among them determine *what* goods and services get produced, *how* they are produced, and *for whom* they are produced.

Most of your microeconomics course is about the theories that *explain,* and in some cases enable economists to make *predictions* about, these choices and their consequences. But in this chapter, we are going to *describe* the main features of the U.S. economy. You will learn about the resources available and how they are used. You will learn what, how, and for whom goods and services are produced. And you will learn about the division of economic activity between individuals and businesses and governments.

2.1 WHAT GOODS AND SERVICES ARE PRODUCED?

Walk around a shopping mall and pay close attention to the range of goods and services that are being offered for sale. Go inside some of the shops and look at the labels to see where various items are manufactured. The next time you travel on an interstate highway, look at the large trucks and pay attention to the names and products printed on their sides and the places in which the trucks are registered. Open the Yellow Pages and flip through a few sections. Notice the huge range of goods and services that businesses are offering.

You've just done a sampling of *what* goods and services are produced and consumed in the United States today.

What We Consume

Because people buy millions of different goods and services, we can describe what they buy only if we classify them in large groups. Even then, we would need several pages of small print to list the types and quantities of goods and services that people buy.

Rather than trying to describe *everything* that people buy, we focus on a few major items, and that is what Figure 2.1(a) does. It shows the expenditures on the five largest items on which we spend our incomes. Medical care—all the goods and services that maintain good health—is now the largest single category of expenditure and is 17 percent of household expenditure. Housing is 15 percent of household expenditure. Transportation comes next at 12 percent and food is 11 percent of total expenditure, only a little more than recreation at 8 percent.

FIGURE 2.1
What We Consume

*e*Foundations 2.1 

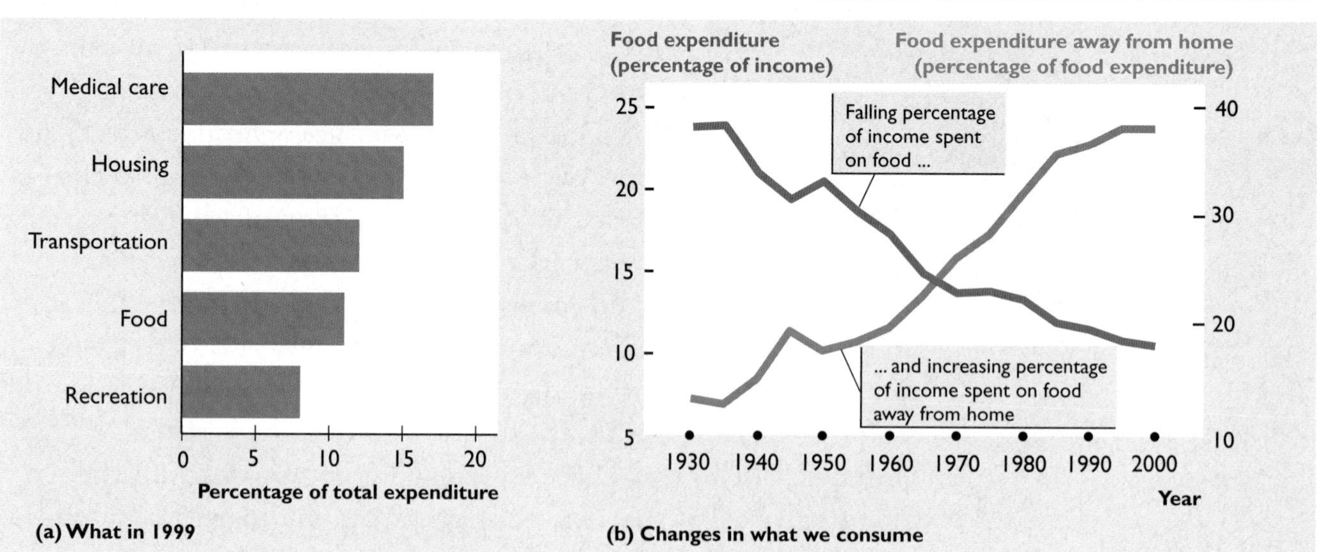

SOURCE: U.S. Census Bureau, *Statistical Abstract of the United States*, 1999.

Medical care, housing, transportation, food, and recreation are the items on which Americans spend the largest share of their income.

Americans spend a falling share of their total expenditure on food and other necessities and an increasing share on services, such as meals away from home.

The data in Figure 2.1(a) show the situation in the United States at the end of the 1990s. How have spending patterns changed over time? The main answer is that over time, incomes have increased, and as they have done so, expenditure on the necessities of life has taken a smaller percentage of income and expenditure on services has taken a larger percentage of income. Figure 2.1(b) illustrates one aspect of this change by looking at our expenditures on food. Total expenditure on food has fallen from 24 percent of income in 1930 to 11 percent in 1999. But the amount that we spend on food away from home has increased from 13 percent of total food expenditure in 1930 to almost 40 percent of food expenditure in 1999.

What We Produce

Businesses located in the United States produce most of the goods and services that people in the United States buy. Businesses in the rest of the world produce goods and services that the United States imports.

By far the largest part of what we produce today is services, not goods. Figure 2.2 shows the largest five items in each category. Real estate services are the largest item and represent 11 percent of the value of total production. These services are those of realtors and others who help individuals and businesses to buy and sell real estate. Retail and wholesale trade are the next two largest categories. Health services and education complete the largest five services. (Medical-care expenditures in Figure 2.1 are larger than health services in Figure 2.2 because expenditures cover services and *goods* such as drugs and medical equipment.)

The largest categories of goods—construction, electronic equipment such as computers, food, industrial equipment, and chemicals—each account for less than 4 percent of the value of total production.

FIGURE 2.2
What We Produce

*e*Foundations 2.1 

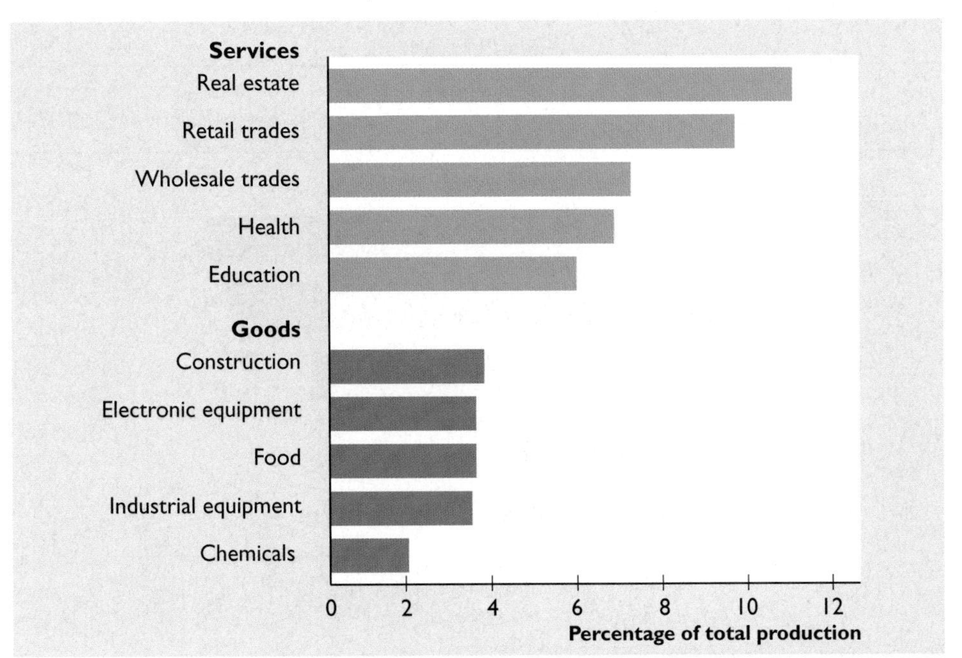

SOURCE: Bureau of Economic Analysis.

Real estate services, retail and wholesale trades, health, and education are the largest five service items produced.

Construction, electronic equipment, food, industrial equipment, and chemicals are the largest five goods produced.

Services production exceeds goods production and is growing faster.

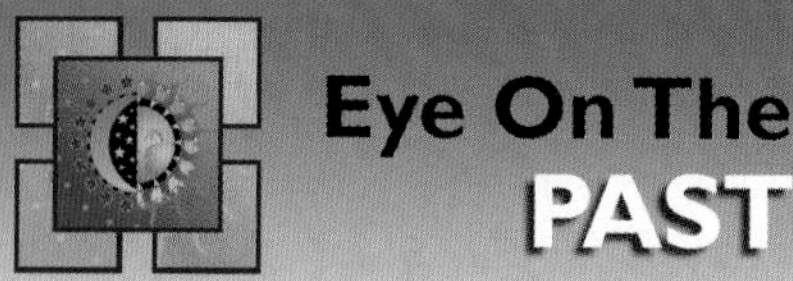

Changes in What We Produce

Sixty years ago, one American in four worked on a farm. That number has shrunk to one in thirty-five. The number of people who produce goods—in mining, construction, and manufacturing—has also shrunk from one person in three to one in five. In contrast, the number of people who produce services has expanded from one in two to almost four out of five. These changes in employment reflect changes in what we produce—services.

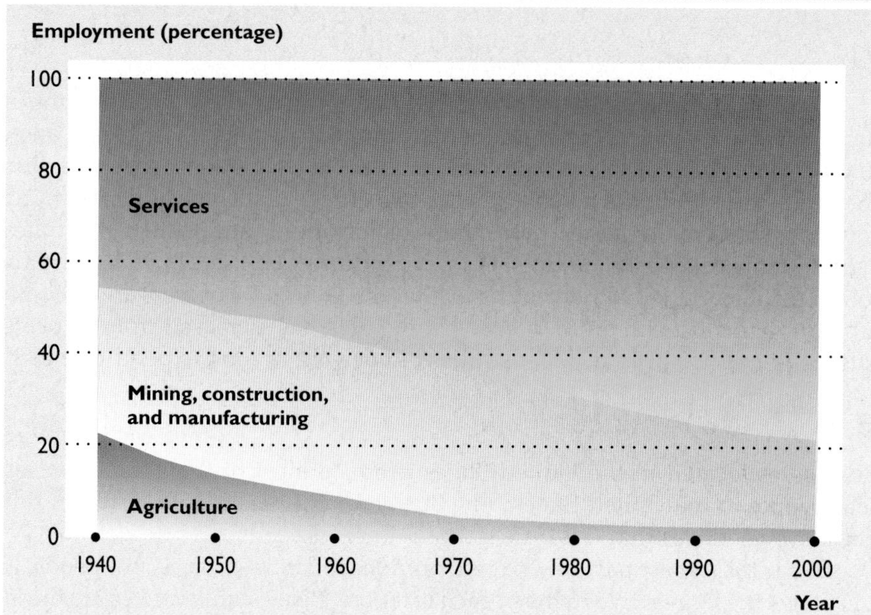

SOURCE: U.S. Census Bureau, *Statistical Abstract of the United States*, 2000.

What We Buy from the Rest of the World

Some of what is produced in the United States is sold to the rest of the world. And we buy some of what we consume from the rest of the world. Figure 2.3 shows the major items that we buy from other countries. We use a large amount of oil for transportation, generating electricity, and heating; and we buy some of this oil from the Middle East, Canada, and Mexico. Most of our clothing, office equipment, televisions, VCRs, and toys and sporting goods are produced in Asia.

FIGURE 2.3
What We Buy from the Rest of the World

*e*Foundations 2.1 

Oil, clothing, office equipment, televisions and VCRs, and toys and sporting goods are the biggest items that we import from other countries.

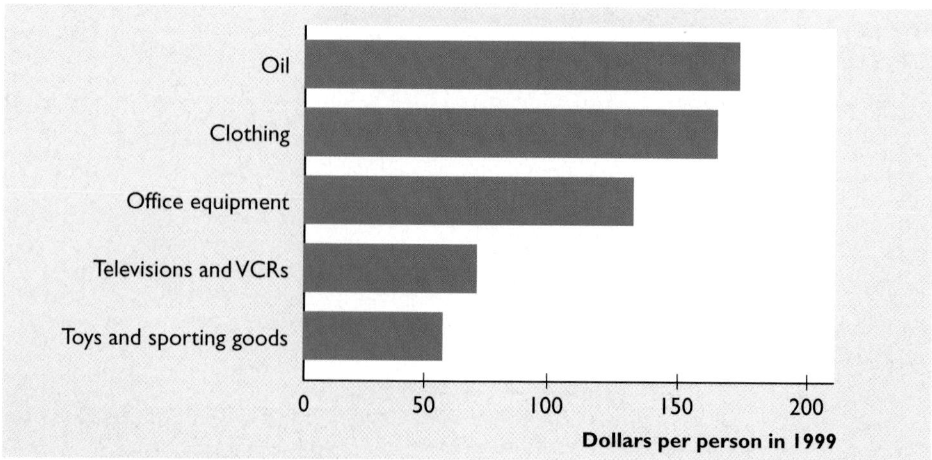

SOURCE: Bureau of Economic Analysis.

CHECKPOINT 2.1

1 **Describe the patterns and changes in *what* goods and services are produced in the United States.**

Study Guide pp. 25–26

eFoundations 2.1

Practice Problems 2.1

1. On which goods and services do Americans spend most of their incomes?
2. How have the goods and services on which Americans spend most of their incomes changed since the 1930s?

Exercises 2.1

1. Which goods and services do businesses in the United States produce and which do they import from the rest of the world?
2. How have the goods and services produced by businesses in the United States and imported from the rest of the world changed since the 1930s?

Solutions to Practice Problems 2.1

1. Americans spend 17 percent of their incomes on health, 15 percent on housing, 12 percent on transportation, 11 percent on food, and 8 percent on recreation.
2. In the 1930s, Americans spent 24 percent of their income on food and today, they spend 11 percent on food. In the 1930s, Americans spent 13 percent of their food expenditure on meals outside the home. Today, Americans spend 40 percent of their food expenditure on meals outside the home.

2.2 HOW ARE GOODS AND SERVICES PRODUCED?

Factors of production
The productive resources used to produce goods and services—land, labor, capital, and entrepreneurship.

Goods and services are produced by using productive resources. Economists call the productive resources **factors of production**. Factors of production are grouped into four categories:

- Land
- Labor
- Capital
- Entrepreneurship

Land

Land
The "gifts of nature," or *natural resources,* that we use to produce goods and services.

In economics, **land** includes all the "gifts of nature" that we use to produce goods and services. Land is what, in everyday language, we call *natural resources.* It includes land (in the everyday sense); minerals, energy, water, and air; and wild plants, animals, birds, and fish.

Some of these resources are renewable, and some are nonrenewable. The U.S. Geological Survey maintains a national inventory of the quantity and quality of natural resources and monitors changes to that inventory. The most recent inventory is for 1997.

Figure 2.4(a) shows how the surface area of the United States is used and how that use is *very slowly* changing. The United States covers 1,944 million acres. In

FIGURE 2.4
Land Use in the United States

*e*Foundations 2.2 

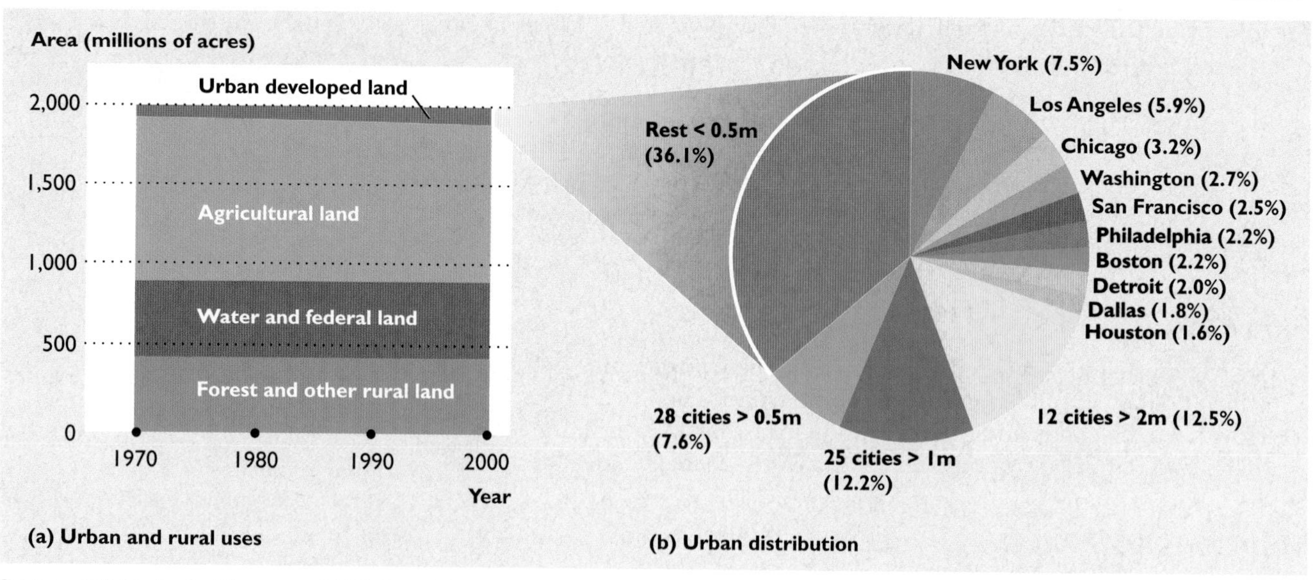

SOURCE: U.S. Geological Survey and U.S. Census Bureau.

Part (a) shows how the 1,944 million acres covered by the United States are used. Agriculture, water and federal lands, and forests cover 94 percent of the land area. Built-up urban areas use only 105 million acres, up from 70 million acres in 1982.

Part (b) shows the dense urban distribution of land use. A quarter of the population lives in the six largest cities (or metropolitan areas), almost a third lives in the ten largest cities, and more than half lives in cities that exceed 1 million.

1997, 930 million of these acres were in agricultural use (either as cropland, pastureland, or rangeland). Agricultural land has decreased from 970 million acres in 1982. The 35 million acres that have gone from agricultural use have been converted to built-up urban land. Urban land use has increased from 70 million acres in 1982 to 105 million acres in 1997. Water and federal land (lakes and rivers, national parks, and other federal lands) cover a roughly constant 450 million acres. Forests and other rural land cover another roughly constant 450 million acres.

People live on a very small proportion of the nation's land area and for the most part in a few very large cities (or metropolitan areas). Figure 2.4(b) shows where Americans live. You can see that one quarter of the population lives in the six largest cities. Almost one third lives in the ten largest cities. More than one half of the population lives in cities that exceed 1 million people.

Our land surface and water resources are renewable. Some of our mineral resources can be recycled, but many mineral resources, and all those that we use to create energy, can be used only once. They are nonrenewable resources. Figure 2.5 shows the current reserves of the three major energy resources: coal, oil, and natural gas. Because nations can buy and sell these resources, the relevant quantities are the world totals, not the resources of a single nation. Figure 2.5 shows the known quantities in both the United States and the rest of the world.

The world has a huge known reserve of coal, and a large part of that coal reserve is in the United States. At current rates of use and if the rates of use continue to grow at the same pace as in the past, the U.S. known coal reserves will last for 77 years and the rest of the world's known coal reserves will last about 79 years. The rest of the world has large reserves of gas—sufficient to last for 40 years—and oil—sufficient to last for 27 years. But the United States has only small known reserves of oil and gas—sufficient to last for about 7 years.

The known or proven quantities of natural resources grow over time as more sources are discovered. Also, over time more fuel-efficient technologies get developed. So the time until energy resources run out will be longer, perhaps much longer, than the numbers in the previous paragraph.

FIGURE 2.5
U.S. and Global Nonrenewable Energy Resources

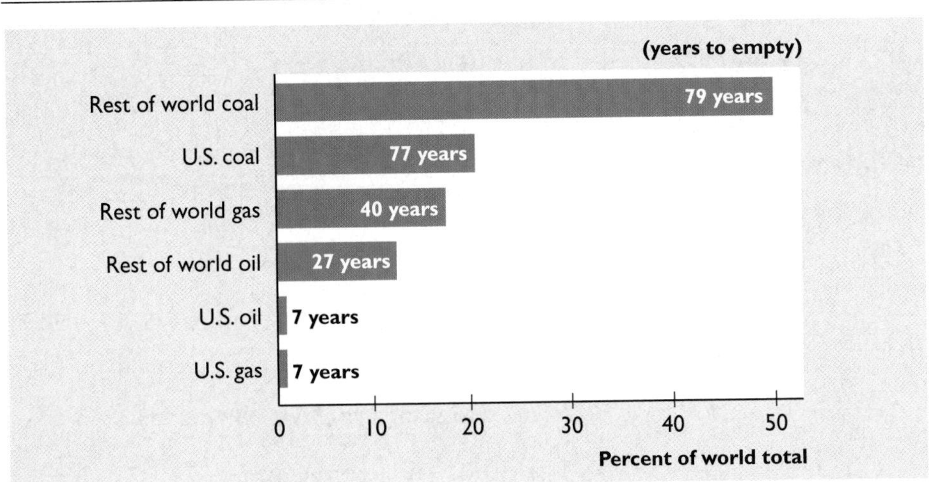

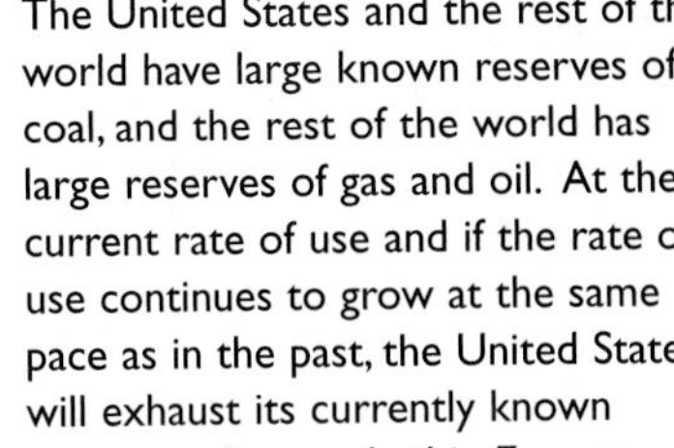
The United States and the rest of the world have large known reserves of coal, and the rest of the world has large reserves of gas and oil. At the current rate of use and if the rate of use continues to grow at the same pace as in the past, the United States will exhaust its currently known reserves of gas and oil in 7 years.

SOURCE: U.S. Department of Energy.

Labor

Labor
The work time and work effort that people devote to producing goods and services.

Labor is the work time and work effort that people devote to producing goods and services. It includes the physical and the mental efforts of all the people who work on farms and construction sites and in factories, shops, and offices. The Census Bureau and Bureau of Labor Statistics measure the nation's labor force every month.

In the United States today, 141 million people have jobs or are available for work and they provide about 25 billion hours of labor a year. In the world as a whole, 3 billion people work some 6 trillion hours a year.

The quantity of labor increases as the adult population increases. The quantity of labor also increases if a larger percentage of the population takes jobs. During the past 50 years, a larger proportion of women have taken paid work and this trend has increased the quantity of labor available.

Figure 2.6 shows the changes in the number of men and women and their total in the U.S. labor force since 1980. In 1980, a labor force of 106 million consisted of 61 million men and 45 million women. In 2000, a labor force of 141 million consisted of 75 million men and 66 million women.

Human capital
The knowledge and skill that people obtain from education, on-the-job training, and work experience.

The quality of labor depends on how skilled people are. Economists use a special name for human skill: human capital. **Human capital** is the knowledge and skill that people obtain from education, on-the-job training, and work experience. You are building your own human capital right now as you work on your economics course and other subjects. And your human capital will continue to grow when you get a full-time job and become better at it. Human capital improves the *quality* of labor. Today, more than 80 percent of the population of the United States

FIGURE 2.6
Labor in the United States

*e*Foundations 2.2 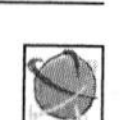

In 2000, 75 million men and 66 million women worked in the United States. The growth of the female work force has been more rapid than the growth in the male labor force because an increasing percentage of women have sought paid work.

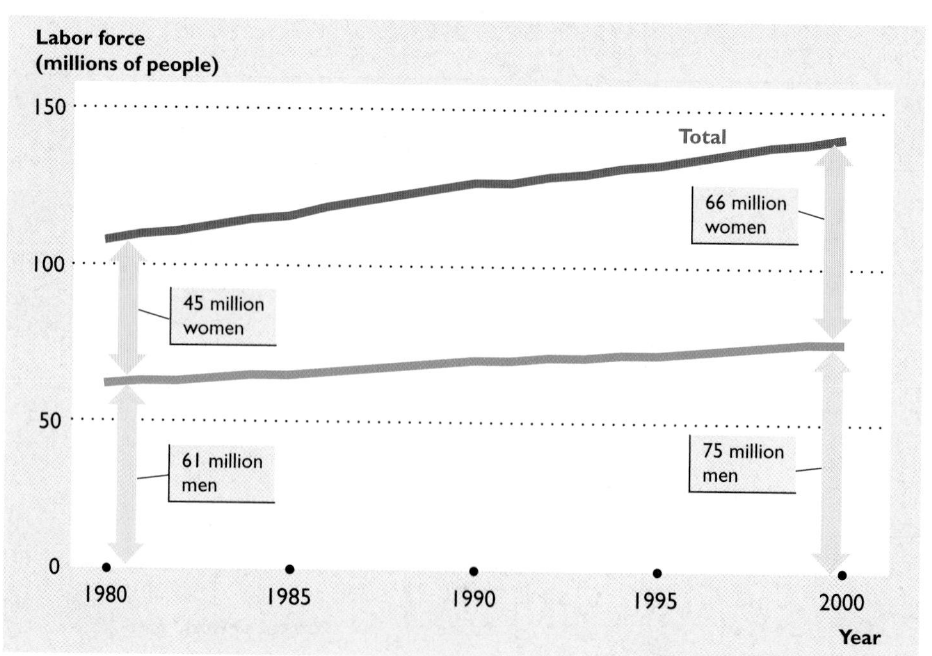

SOURCE: Bureau of Labor Statistics.

have completed high school and 25 percent have a college or university degree. Figure 2.7 shows a measure of the growth of human capital in the United States over the past century. In 1910, some 25 percent of the population had less than five years of elementary school and fewer than 3 percent had a college or university degree. You can see how the number of high school and college graduates has increased steadily over the past 90 years.

Capital

In addition to human capital, economists distinguish between two meanings of capital—*financial* capital and *physical* capital. In everyday language, we talk about money, stocks, and bonds as being capital. For example, we talk about firms raising capital by issuing stock or bonds. These items are *financial capital*, and they are not productive resources. They play an important role in enabling people to lend to businesses, and they provide businesses with financial resources, but they are *not* used to produce goods and services. They are not capital.

Capital consists of the tools, instruments, machines, buildings, and other constructions that have been produced in the past and that businesses now use to produce goods and services. Capital includes hammers and screwdrivers, computers, auto assembly lines, office towers and warehouses, interstate highways, dams and power plants, airports and airplanes, shirt factories, and cookie shops. The Bureau of Economic Analysis in the U.S. Department of Commerce keeps track of the total value of capital, which grows over time. In the United States today, the value of capital is around $20 trillion. In the world as a whole, the value of capital exceeds $130 trillion.

Capital
The tools, instruments, machines, buildings, and other constructions that have been produced in the past and that businesses now use to produce goods and services.

FIGURE 2.7
Measures of Human Capital

*e*Foundations 2.2 

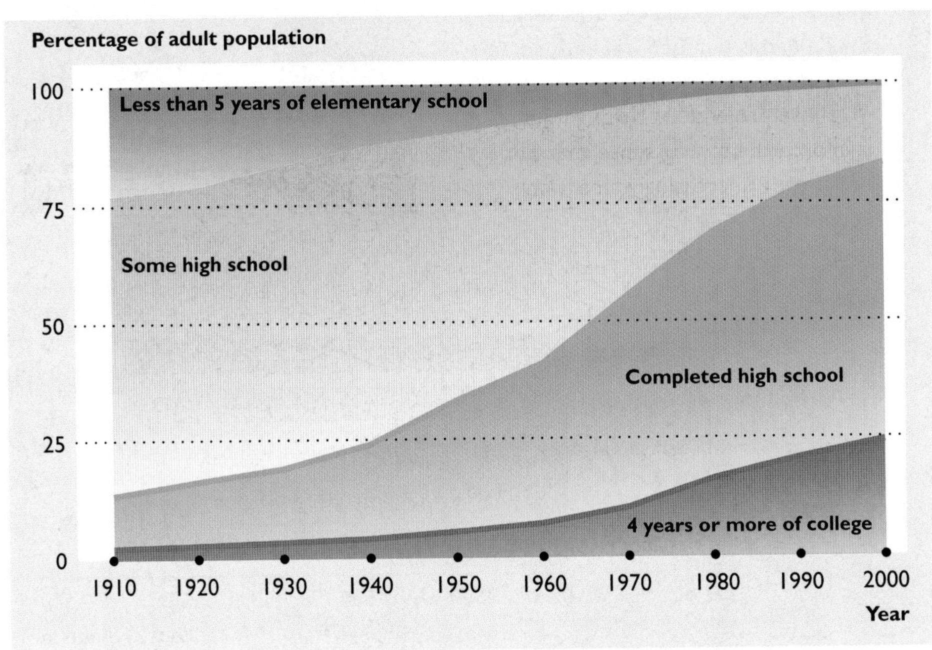

SOURCE: U.S. Census Bureau, *Statistical Abstract of the United States*, 1999.

In 2000, 25 percent of the population had 4 years or more of college, up from fewer than 3 percent in 1910. A further 58 percent had completed high school, up from 11 percent in 1910.

Entrepreneurship

Entrepreneurship
The human resource that organizes labor, land, and capital.

Entrepreneurship is the human resource that organizes labor, land, and capital. Entrepreneurs come up with new ideas about what and how to produce, make business decisions, and bear the risks that arise from these decisions.

The quantity of entrepreneurship is hard to describe or measure. At some periods, there appears to be a great deal of imaginative entrepreneurship around. People such as Steven Jobs and Steven Wozniak, who created the Apple computer; Bill Gates, who founded the Microsoft empire; and Michael Dell, who established Dell Computers, are examples of extraordinary entrepreneurial talent. But these highly visible entrepreneurs are just the tip of an iceberg that consists of hundreds of thousands of people who run businesses, large and small.

How We Produce in the New Economy

The new economy consists of the jobs and businesses that produce Internet services, e-commerce, database and other information services, and other computer-driven services. The new economy also consists of the biotechnology industries.

These new economy sectors are indeed growing rapidly. But they are not really the heart of tomorrow's economy.

Tomorrow's economy, like today's economy, will be an increasingly service-oriented economy.

In 1996, some 15 million people worked in general clerical and sales jobs. By 2006, their number will be swelled by another 2 million workers, an increase of 14 percent since 1996. Clerical work and retail selling are the core of tomorrow's economy.

Health care and personal care make up a second large and fast-growing area. The nearly 6 million workers in these jobs will grow to 8 million by 2006.

Food preparation and serving will grow by 1 million workers to more than 7 million by 2006. This increase continues the trend toward people buying an ever-increasing proportion of their meals away from home.

The education sector will also expand quickly with close to a million more teachers by 2006, an increase of 33 percent since 1996.

The computer-driven economy will expand rapidly too. In fact, it will grow more quickly than any of the areas we've just reviewed. In 1996, about 1 million people worked in this sector. By 2006, this number will have somewhat more than doubled.

These projections through 2006 reinforce the strong sense that our economy is increasingly a service economy.

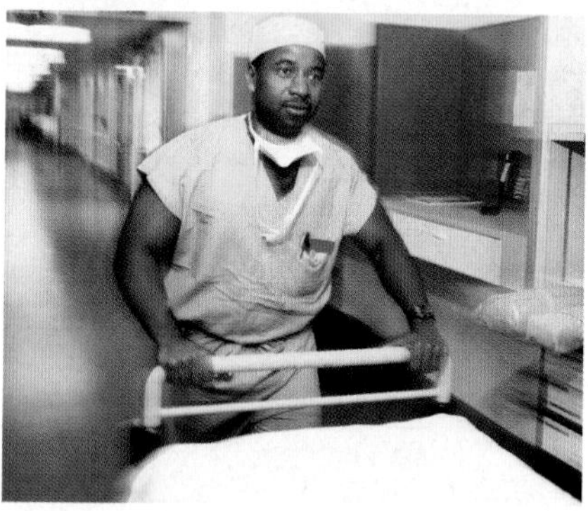

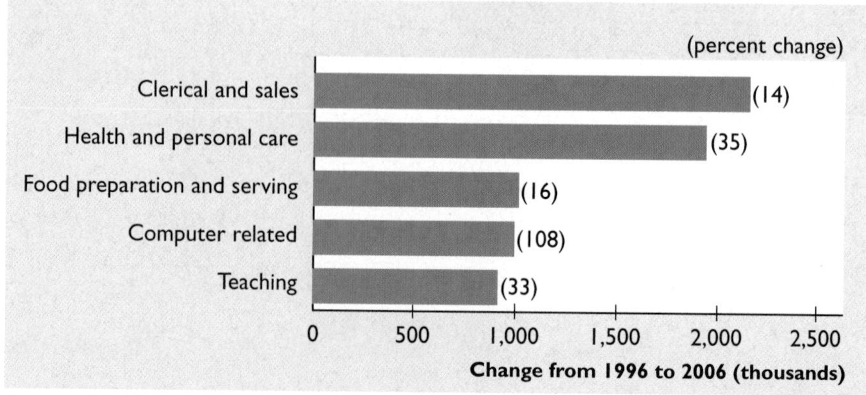

SOURCE: U.S. Census Bureau, *Statistical Abstract of the United States*, 2000.

CHECKPOINT 2.2

2 **Describe the patterns and changes in *how* goods and services are produced in the United States.**

Study Guide pp. 26–28 

eFoundations 2.2

Practice Problems 2.2

1. Describe how land is used in the United States and comment on the view that urban sprawl is destroying our environment.
2. Which energy resources will run out first? What will the United States use to produce electricity when its oil and natural gas are all gone?
3. Classify each of the following as one of the four factors of production:
   a. The Mississippi River
   b. School teachers
   c. A car-park attendant
   d. Robot owned by General Motors
   e. A cruise ship

Exercises 2.2

1. Describe the changes that have occurred in the labor force and the human capital of the United States during the last few decades.
2. How much longer will the world's nonrenewable energy sources last and what do you think will happen when they are used up?
3. Divide the following items into those that are factors of production and those that are not, and for each factor of production, classify it as land, labor, capital, or entrepreneurship.
   a. The arch in St. Louis
   b. Niagara Falls
   c. U.S. senators
   d. NASA rocket launcher
   e. A U.S. government bond
   f. A ski run at Aspen

Solutions to Practice Problems 2.2

1. The United States covers 1,944 million acres. Forests, parks, water, and other federal land covers 450 million acres, agriculture uses 930 million acres, and other forest and rural land covers about 450 million acres. Urban land covers 105 million acres. It is true that urban sprawl is using former farmland. But over the past 20 years, only 35 million acres, or 1.8 percent of land, has been transferred from agricultural to urban use. Forests and parks have not decreased.
2. Oil and natural gas will run out first. Coal reserves are very large, and known reserves will last for almost 80 years at the current rate of use and if the rate of use continues to grow as it has in the past. So most likely, the United States will continue to use coal to generate electricity after the oil and gas are gone.
3. Economists classify **a.** the Mississippi River as land; **b.** school teachers as labor; **c.** a car-park attendant as labor; **d.** a robot owned by General Motors as capital; **e.** a cruise ship as capital.

2.3 FOR WHOM ARE GOODS PRODUCED?

Who gets the goods and services that are produced depends on the incomes that people earn and the goods and services that they choose to buy. A large income enables a person to buy large quantities of goods and services. A small income leaves a person with few options and small quantities of goods and services.

You know of lots of people who earn very large incomes. Tiger Woods *won* $9.2 million in 2000 and earned substantially more than this amount in endorsements. The average major league baseball player's salary in 1999 was $1.7 million, and some stars, such as the Atlanta Braves' Chipper Jones, the New York Mets' Mike Piazza, the Rangers' Alex Rodriguez, and the L.A. Dodgers' Kevin Brown, signed multiyear contracts worth more than $15 million a year. News anchors Tom Brokaw, Peter Jennings, and Dan Rather; morning show host Katie Couric; and interviewer Barbara Walters all earn several million dollars a year.

You know of even more people who earn very small incomes. Servers at McDonald's average around $6.35 an hour. Checkout clerks, gas station attendants, and textile and leather workers earn less than $10 an hour.

Rent
Income paid for the use of land.

Wages
Income paid for the services of labor.

Interest
Income paid for the use of capital.

Profit (or loss)
Income earned by an entrepreneur for running a business.

Functional distribution of income
The percentage distribution of income among the factors of production.

Personal distribution of income
The percentage distribution of income among individual persons.

People earn their incomes by selling the services of the factors of production they own. **Rent** is paid for the use of land, **wages** are paid for the services of labor, **interest** is paid for the use of capital, and entrepreneurs receive a **profit** (or incur a **loss**) from running their businesses.

Which factor of production in the United States earns more income: labor or capital? And how is income distributed among individuals? Figure 2.8 provides some answers. Part (a) shows the **functional distribution of income**, which is the percentage distribution of income among the factors of production. Labor earns most of the income—71 percent of total income in 1999. Capital income—corporate income and net interest income—was 18 percent in 1999. The proprietors of businesses, whose earnings are a mixture of labor and capital income, earned 9 percent of total income in 1999. Rental income of persons was 2 percent in 1999. These percentages remain remarkably constant over time.

Figure 2.8(b) shows the **personal distribution of income**, which is the percentage distribution of income among individual persons. The incomes are shown for five groups, each of which represents 20 percent of the population. If incomes were equal, each 20 percent group would earn 20 percent of total income. You know that incomes are unequal, and the figure provides a measure of just how unequal they are.

The 20 percent of individuals with the lowest incomes earn only 4 percent of total income. The highest income of this group in 1999 was about $22,000. The second lowest 20 percent earn about 9 percent of total income. The highest income of this group in 1999 was about $40,000. The next 20 percent—the middle 20 percent—earn 15 percent of total income. The highest income of this group in 1999 was about $60,000. All three of these groups—the lowest 60 percent of individuals—earn only 28 percent of total income.

The second highest 20 percent earn 23 percent of total income. The highest income in this group in 1999 was about $90,000. So 80 percent of individuals earn less than $90,000 a year.

The richest 20 percent of individuals earn 49 percent of total income. We don't know the highest income in this group, but some of the famous names that we started out with are examples of high earners. So the richest 20 percent get half the goods and services produced, and the other 80 percent get the other half.

FIGURE 2.8
For Whom?

*e*Foundations 2.3 

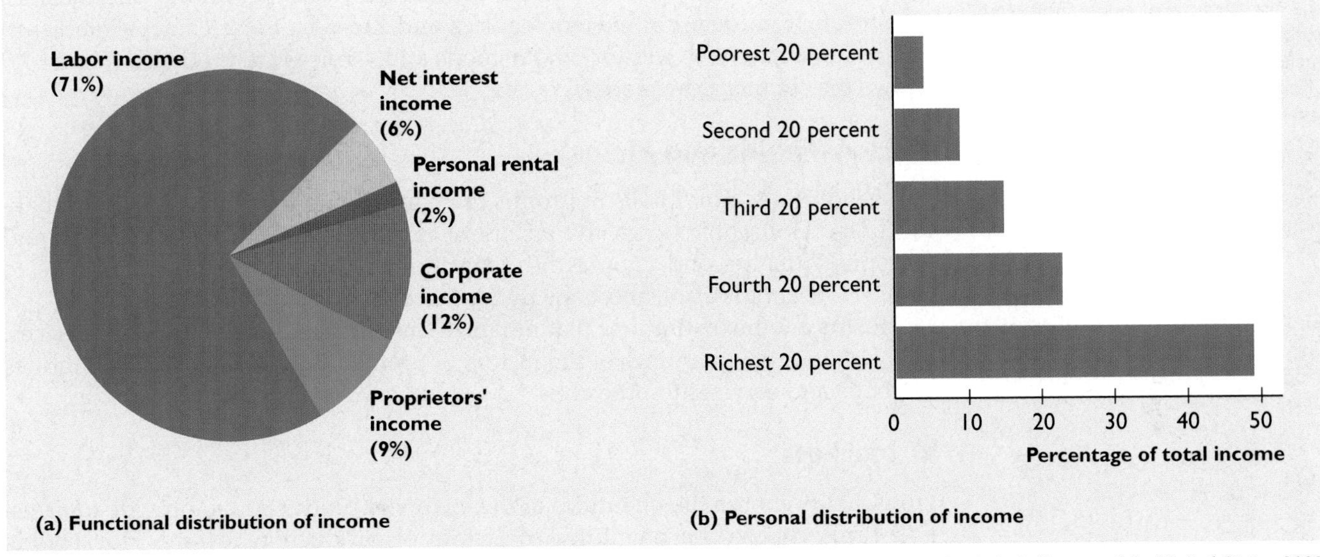

SOURCE: U.S. Census Bureau, *Statistical Abstract of the United States*, 2000.

CHECKPOINT 2.3

3 **Describe *for whom* goods and services are produced in the United States.**

Study Guide pp. 28–30

*e*Foundations 2.3 

Practice Problems 2.3

1. Distinguish between the functional distribution of income and the personal distribution of income.
2. How can wages account for 70 percent of all incomes when the 20 percent of the population with the highest incomes earn 49 percent of total income?

Exercise 2.3

1. If everyone were to consume an equal quantity of goods and services, what percentage of total income would the richest 20 percent of individuals have to transfer to lower income groups? What percentage would the second richest 20 percent have to transfer?

Solutions to Practice Problems 2.3

1. The functional distribution of income is the percentage of total income received by each factor of production. The personal distribution of income is the percentage of total income received by individual persons.
2. Many individuals own large amounts of capital and earn the largest incomes. In addition, many of these individuals earn high salaries.

2.4 CIRCULAR FLOWS

Circular flow model
A model of the economy that shows the circular flow of expenditure and incomes that result from decision makers' choices and the way those choices interact to determine what, how, and for whom goods and services are produced.

We can organize the data you've just studied using the **circular flow model**—a model of the economy that shows the circular flow of expenditures and incomes that result from decision makers' choices and the way those choices interact to determine what, how, and for whom goods and services are produced. Figure 2.9 shows the circular flow model.

Households and Firms

Households
Individuals or groups of people living together as decision-making units.

Firms
The institutions that organize the production of goods and services.

Households are individuals or groups of people living together as decision-making units. Households own the factors of production—land, labor, capital, and entrepreneurship—and choose the quantities of these resources to provide to firms. Households also choose the quantities of goods and services to buy.

Firms are the institutions that organize the production of goods and services. Firms choose the quantities of the factors of production to hire and the quantities of goods and services to produce.

Markets

Households choose the quantities of the factors of production to provide to firms, and firms choose the quantities of factors of production to hire. Households choose the quantities of goods and services to buy, and firms choose the quantities of goods and services to produce. How are these choices coordinated and made compatible? The answer is: by markets.

Market
Any arrangement that brings buyers and sellers together and enables them to get information and do business with each other.

A **market** is any arrangement that brings buyers and sellers together and enables them to get information and do business with each other. An example is the market in which oil is bought and sold—the world oil market. The world oil market is not a place. It is the network of oil producers, oil users, wholesalers, and brokers who buy and sell oil. In the world oil market, decision makers do not meet physically. They make deals by telephone, fax, and the Internet.

Goods markets
Markets in which goods and services are bought and sold.

Factor markets
Markets in which factors of production are bought and sold.

Figure 2.9 identifies two types of markets: goods markets and factor markets. **Goods markets** are markets in which goods and services are bought and sold. **Factor markets** are markets in which factors of production are bought and sold.

Real Flows and Money Flows

When households choose the quantities of land, labor, capital, and entrepreneurship to offer in factor markets, they respond to the incomes they receive—rent for land, wages for labor, interest for capital, and profit for entrepreneurship. When firms choose the quantities of factors to hire, they respond to the rent, wages, interest, and profits they must pay to households.

Similarly, when firms choose the quantities of goods and services to produce and offer for sale in goods markets, they respond to the dollar amounts that they receive from the expenditures that households make. When households choose the quantities of goods and services to buy, they respond to the dollar amounts they must pay to firms.

Figure 2.9 shows the flows that result from these decisions made by households and firms. The real flows are shown in orange. These are the flows of the factors of production that go from households through factor markets to firms and the goods and services that go from firms through goods markets to households. The money flows go in the opposite direction. These flows are the payments made in exchange for factors of production (blue flow) and expenditures on goods and services (red flow).

Lying behind these real flows and money flows are millions of individual decisions about what to consume, what to produce, and how to produce. These decisions result in buying plans by households and selling plans by firms in goods markets. And the decisions result in selling plans by households and buying plans by firms in factor markets. When these buying plans and selling plans are carried out, they determine the prices that people pay and the incomes they earn and so determine for whom goods and services are produced. You'll learn in Chapter 4 how markets coordinate the buying plans and selling plans of households and firms and make them compatible.

Firms produce most of the goods and services that we consume. But governments provide some of the services that we enjoy. And governments play a big role in modifying for whom goods and services are produced by changing the distribution of income. So now we're going to look at the government sector of the U.S. economy. We'll also add government to the circular flow model.

FIGURE 2.9
The Circular Flow Model

*e*Foundations **2.4** 

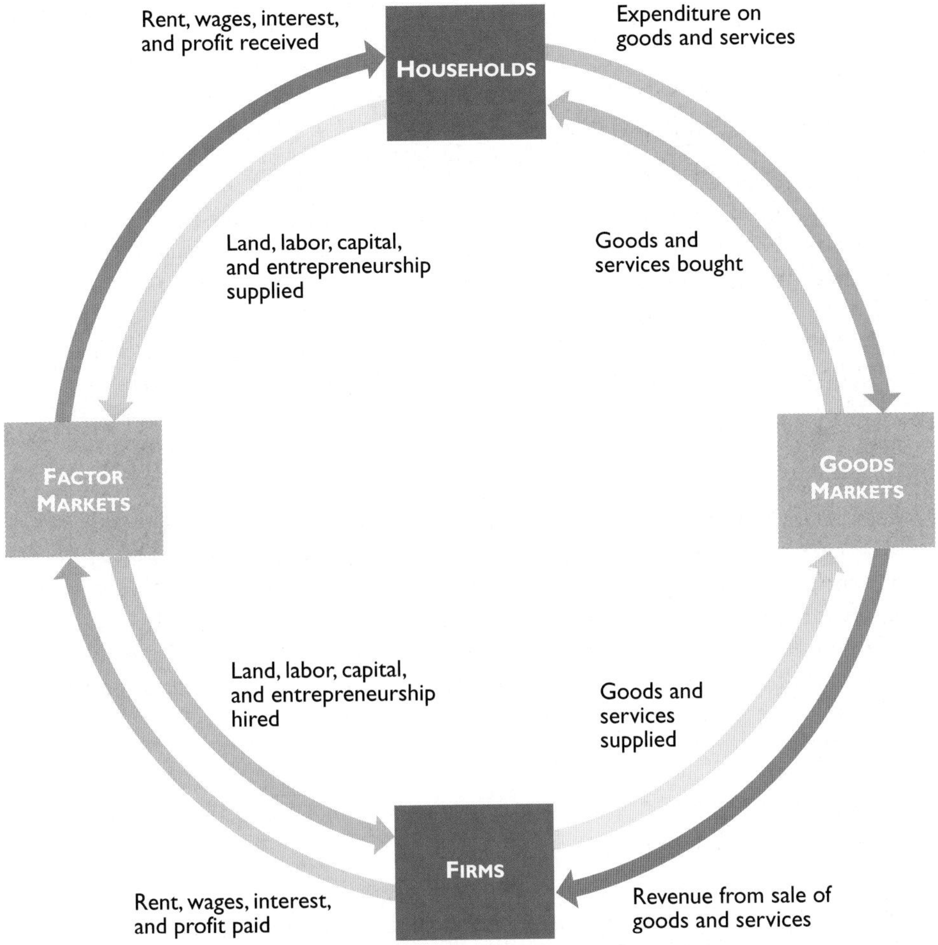

Rent, wages, interest, and profit received

HOUSEHOLDS

Expenditure on goods and services

Land, labor, capital, and entrepreneurship supplied

Goods and services bought

FACTOR MARKETS

GOODS MARKETS

Land, labor, capital, and entrepreneurship hired

Goods and services supplied

FIRMS

Rent, wages, interest, and profit paid

Revenue from sale of goods and services

The orange flows are the factors of production that go from households through factor markets to firms and the goods and services that go from firms through goods markets to households.

The flows in the opposite direction are the payments made in exchange for the factors of production (the blue arrows) and the goods and services (the red arrows).

The choices that generate these flows determine what, how, and for whom goods and services are produced.

The Government Sector

The government sector of the U.S. economy consists of more than 86,000 separate organizations, some tiny like the Yuma, Arizona, school district and some enormous like the U.S. federal government. We divide the government sector into:

- Federal government
- State and local government

Federal Government

The federal government's major expenditures are to provide:

1. Goods and services
2. Social security and welfare benefits
3. Transfers to state and local governments

The goods and services provided by the federal government include the legal system, which defines property rights and enforces contracts, and national defense. Social security and welfare benefits, which include income for retired seniors and programs such as Medicare and Medicaid, are transfers from the federal government to households. Transfers to state and local governments are designed to provide more equality across the states and regions.

The federal government finances its expenditures by collecting a variety of taxes. The main taxes paid to the federal government are:

1. Personal income taxes
2. Corporate (business) income taxes
3. Social security taxes

In 2000, the federal government spent and raised in taxes more than $2 trillion—about 20 percent of the total value of all the goods and services produced in the United States in that year.

State and Local Government

The state and local governments' major expenditures are to provide:

1. Local goods and services
2. Welfare benefits

Goods and services provided by state and local governments include the state courts and law enforcement, schools, roads, garbage collection and disposal, water supplies, and sewage management. Welfare benefits provided by state governments include unemployment benefits and aid to low-income families.

State and local governments finance these expenditures by collecting taxes and receiving transfers from the federal government. The main taxes paid to the state and local governments are:

1. Sales taxes
2. Property taxes
3. State income taxes

In 2000, the state and local governments spent more than $1.2 trillion—about 12 percent of the total value of all the goods and services produced in the United States in that year.

Government in the Circular Flow

Figure 2.10 adds the government sector to the circular flow model. As you study this figure, first notice that the outer circle is the same as Figure 2.9. In addition to these private sector flows, the government sector purchases goods and services from firms. The red arrows that run from the government through the goods markets to firms show this flow.

Households and firms pay taxes to the government. The green arrows running directly from households and firms to government show these flows. Also, the government makes cash payments to households and firms. The green arrows running directly from government to households and firms show these flows. Taxes and transfers are direct transactions with government and do not go through the good markets and factor markets.

Not part of the circular flow and not visible in Figure 2.10, governments provide the legal framework within which all transactions occur. For example, they operate the courts and legal system that enable contracts to be written and enforced.

FIGURE 2.10
Government in the Circular Flow

*e*Foundations **2.4** 

Households
Rent, wages, interest, and profit
Expenditures on goods and services
Transfers
Taxes
Government purchases of goods and services
Factor Markets
Government
Goods Markets
Transfers
Taxes
Government purchases of goods and services
Rent, wages, interest, and profit
Firms
Expenditures on goods and services

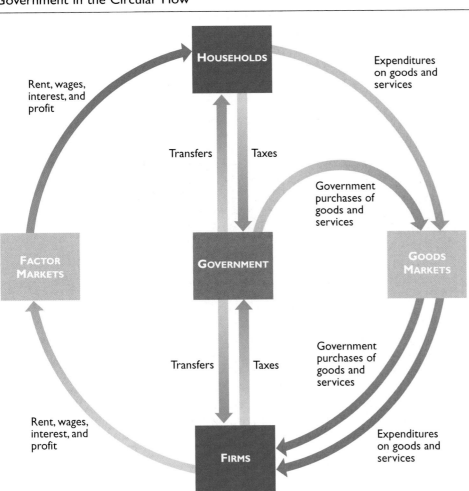

The government purchases goods and services from firms in goods markets (the red arrows). Households and firms pay taxes to and receive transfers from governments (the green arrows).

Federal Government Expenditures and Revenue

What are the main items of expenditures by the federal government on goods and services and transfers? And what are its main sources of tax revenue? Figure 2.11 answers these questions.

You can see that by far the largest part of what the federal government spends is the social security payments and other benefits paid to individuals. National defense also takes a big slice of the federal government's expenditures. The interest payment on the national debt is another large item. The **national debt** is the total amount that the government has borrowed to make expenditures that exceed tax revenue—to run a government budget deficit. The national debt is a bit like a large credit card balance. And paying the interest on the national debt is like paying the minimum required monthly payment.

National debt
The total amount that the government has borrowed to make expenditures that exceed tax revenue—to run a government budget deficit.

Transfers to other levels of government also use up a large part of the federal government's expenditures. Purchases of goods and services (other than national defense) are relatively small, and subsidies and aid to other countries take a tiny slice of expenditures.

Most of the tax revenue of the federal government—almost a half of it—comes from personal income taxes. And two thirds of the rest comes from social security taxes. Corporate income taxes are a small part of the federal government's revenue.

FIGURE 2.11
Federal Government Expenditures and Revenue

*e*Foundations 2.4 

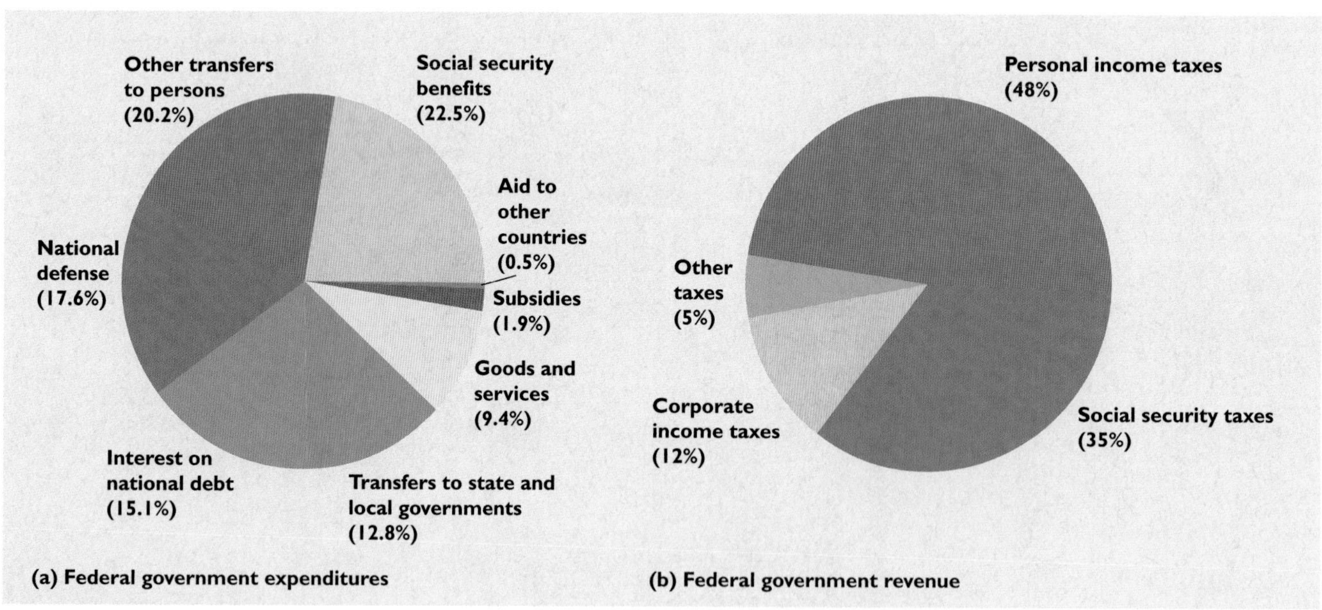

SOURCE: Bureau of Economic Analysis.

Social security benefits and other transfers to persons take the largest slice of federal government expenditures. National defense, interest on the national debt, and grants to state and local governments also take a large share.

Most of the federal government's revenue comes from personal income taxes and social security taxes. Corporate income taxes are only a small part of total revenue.

State and Local Government Expenditures and Revenue

What are the main items of expenditures by the state and local governments on goods and services and transfers? And what are their main sources of revenue? Figure 2.12 answers these questions.

You can see that education is by far the largest part of the expenditures made by state and local governments. This item covers the cost of public schools, colleges, and universities. It absorbs 40 percent of total expenditures—approximately $400 billion, or $1,500 per person.

Welfare benefits are the second largest item, and it takes 20 percent of total expenditures. Highways are the next largest item, and it accounts for 8 percent of total expenditures. The remaining 32 percent is spent on other local public goods and services such as police services, garbage collection and disposal, sewage management, and water supplies.

Sales taxes and transfers from the federal government bring in similar amounts—about 25 percent of total revenue. Property taxes account for 21 percent of total revenue. Individual incomes taxes account for 15 percent, and corporate income taxes account for 3 percent. The remaining 13 percent comes from other taxes such as estate taxes.

FIGURE 2.12
State and Local Government Expenditures and Revenue

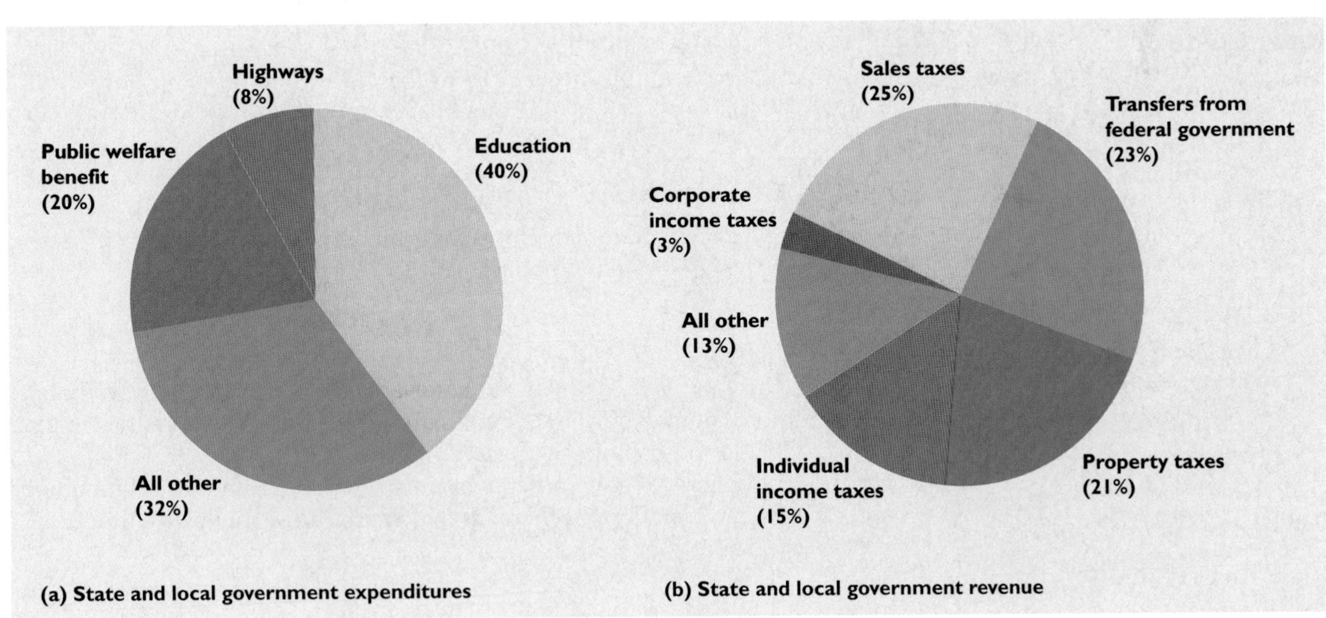

SOURCE: Bureau of Economic Analysis.

Education, highways, and public welfare benefits take the largest slice of state and local government expenditures.

Most of the state and local government revenue comes from sales taxes, property taxes, and transfers from the federal government.

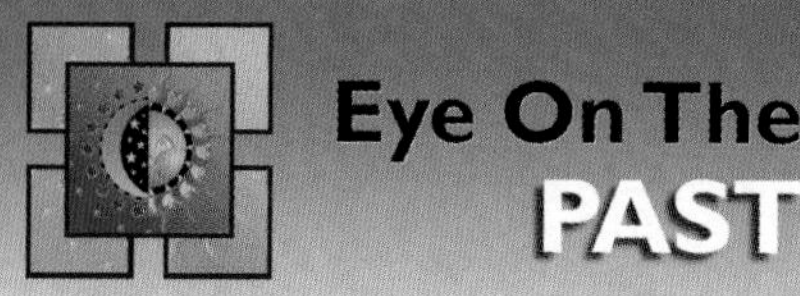

The Changing Size of the Federal Government

The federal government's expenditure took 44 percent of total expenditure during World War II. Fluctuations in defense spending are driven by the state of war and peace. Nondefense spending increased steadily through the 1960s and 1970s, stabilized during the 1980s, and decreased slightly during the 1990s.

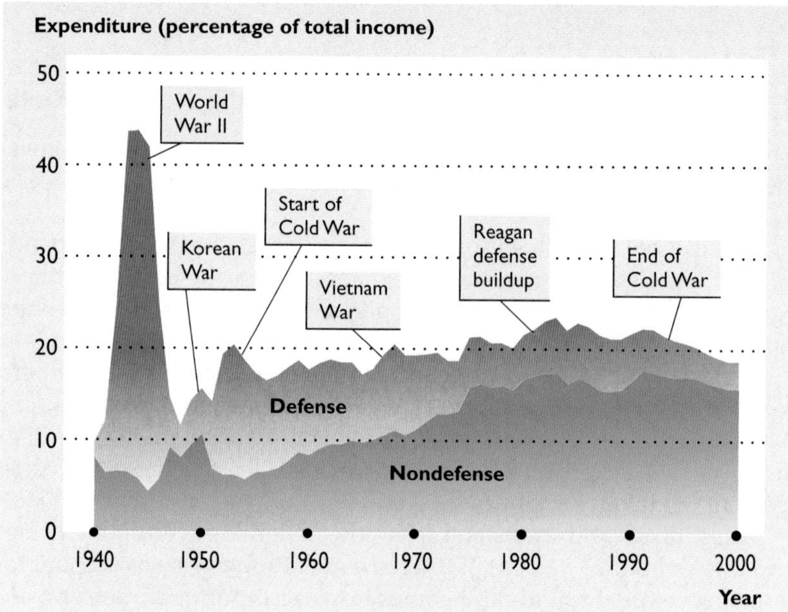

SOURCE: *Economic Report of the President*, 2000.

CHECKPOINT 2.4

Study Guide pp. 30–32

***e*Foundations 2.4**

4 **Use the circular flow model to provide a picture of how households, firms, and government interact to determine what, how, and for whom goods and services are produced.**

Practice Problem 2.4

What are the real flows and money flows that run between households, firms, and government in the circular flow model?

Exercises 2.4

1. What are the choices made by households and firms that determine what, how, and for whom goods and services are produced? Where, in the circular flow model, do those choices appear?
2. How do the actions of governments modify what, how, and for whom goods and services are produced? Where, in the circular flow model, do those choices appear?

Solution to Practice Problem 2.4

The real flows are the services of factors of production from households to firms and the goods and services from firms to households and from firms to government. The money flows are factor incomes, household expenditures, taxes, and transfers.

CHAPTER CHECKPOINT

Key Points

1 Describe the patterns and changes in *what* goods and services are produced in the United States.

- Medical care, housing, transportation, food, and recreation are the largest expenditure items. Real estate services, retail and wholesale trades, health services, and education are the largest production items.
- Food is a decreasing component, and services are an increasing component of total production.

2 Describe the patterns and changes in *how* goods and services are produced in the United States.

- A small and slowly increasing proportion of land is being built up.
- Increased employment of women and a better-educated population have increased the quantity and quality of labor.
- The quantity of capital increases over time.
- Some highly visible entrepreneurs and thousands of small entrepreneurs organize the other factors of production and create the new ideas that keep changing what and how goods and services are produced.

3 Describe *for whom* goods and services are produced in the United States.

- People earn incomes for the factors of production they own: rent for land, wages for labor, interest for capital, and profit for entrepreneurship.
- More than 70 percent of total income comes from labor.
- The richest 20 percent of the population consumes half of the goods and services produced, and the other 80 percent share the remaining half.

4 Use the circular flow model to provide a picture of how households, firms, and government interact to determine what, how, and for whom goods and services are produced.

- The circular flow model shows the real flows of factors and goods and the corresponding money flows of incomes and expenditures.
- Government in the circular flow receives taxes, makes transfers, and buys goods and services.

Key Terms

Capital, 41
Circular flow model, 46
Entrepreneurship, 42
Factor markets, 46
Factors of production, 38
Firms, 46
Functional distribution of income, 44
Goods markets, 46
Households, 46
Human capital, 40
Interest, 44
Labor, 40
Land, 38
Market, 46
National debt, 50
Personal distribution of income, 44
Profit (or loss), 44
Rent, 44
Wages, 44

Exercises

1. Which of the following items are not factors of production and why?
   a. Vans used by a baker to deliver bread
   b. 1,000 shares of Amazon.com
   c. Undiscovered oil
   d. A garbage truck
   e. A pack of bubble gum
   f. The President of the United States
   g. Disneyland

2. Thinking about the trends in what and how goods and services are produced:
   a. Which jobs will grow fastest during the next decade? Explain your answer.
   b. What types of jobs will most people most likely be doing 50 years from now? Explain your answer.
   c. What do you think will happen to the quantity of human capital over the next decade? Explain your answer.
   d. Do you think that at some future time, there will be no jobs? Why or why not?

3. If the trends in land use in the United States that we saw from 1982 to 1997 continue into the future:
   a. How long would it take for all the land currently used by agriculture to become built up urban land?
   b. Do you think it likely that the trend of the 1980s and 1990s will continue indefinitely? Explain why or why not.

4. Looking at the world's currently known reserves of nonrenewable energy resources:
   a. Which resources will most likely be used up first?
   b. If the United States runs out before other countries do, how will the United States cope with the scarcity of nonrenewable energy sources?

5. You've seen that the distribution of income is unequal. Why do you think it is unequal and do you think it matters?

6. You've seen that the government grew larger through the mid-1980s and shrank slightly after that time. Do you think the government is too big or too small? Provide your reasons.

7. Why do you think all levels of government get such a small part of their revenue from taxing businesses? Wouldn't it be better if businesses paid more tax and individuals paid less? Explain your answer.

8. On a circular flow diagram, show the flows in which the following items occur:
   a. Capital owned by households and used by firms
   b. Computers sold by firms to governments and households
   c. Labor hired by firms
   d. Land rented to businesses
   e. Taxes paid by households and firms
   f. Unemployment benefits
   g. Wages paid by firms
   h. Dividends paid by businesses
   i. Profit paid to entrepreneurs

Chapter 3

The Economic Problem

CHAPTER CHECKLIST

When you have completed your study of this chapter, you will be able to:

1. **Use the production possibilities frontier to illustrate the economic problem.**
2. **Calculate opportunity cost.**
3. **Define efficiency and describe an efficient use of resources.**
4. **Explain how specialization and trade expand production possibilities.**

You learned in Chapter 1 that all economic problems arise from scarcity, that scarcity forces us to make choices, and that in making choices, we try to get the most value out of our scarce resources by comparing marginal costs and marginal benefits. You learned in Chapter 2 what, how, and for whom goods and services are produced in the U.S. economy. And you used your first economic model, the circular flow model, to illustrate the choices and interactions that determine what, how, and for whom goods and services are produced.

In this chapter, you will study another economic model: one that illustrates scarcity, choice, and cost and that helps us to understand the choices that people and societies actually make. You will also learn about the central idea of economics— *efficiency*. And you will discover how we can expand production by specializing and trading with each other.

3.1 PRODUCTION POSSIBILITIES

Every working day in the mines, factories, shops, and offices and on the farms and construction sites across the United States, we produce a vast array of goods and services. In the United States in 2000, 230 billion hours of labor equipped with $20 trillion worth of capital produced $9 trillion worth of goods and services. Globally, 6 trillion hours of labor and $100 trillion of capital produced $45 trillion worth of goods and services.

Although our production capability is enormous, it is limited by our available resources and by technology. At any given time, we have fixed quantities of the factors of production and a fixed state of technology. Because our wants exceed our resources, we must make choices. We must rank our wants and decide which wants to satisfy and which to leave unsatisfied. In using our scarce resources, we make rational choices.

To make a rational choice, we must determine the costs and benefits of the alternatives. In the rest of this chapter, we're going to study an economic model that makes the ideas of scarcity, costs and benefits, and rational choice more concrete. We're also going to learn about the economic concept of efficiency.

To illustrate the limits to production, we focus our attention on two goods only and hold the quantities produced of all the other goods and services constant. That is, we use the *ceteris paribus* assumption. We look at a *model* of the economy in which everything remains the same except for the production of the two goods we are currently considering.

Production Possibilities Frontier

Production possibilities frontier
The boundary between the combinations of goods and services that can be produced and the combinations that cannot be produced, given the available factors of production and the state of technology.

The **production possibilities frontier** is the boundary between the combinations of goods and services that can be produced and the combinations that cannot be produced, given the available factors of production—land, labor, capital, and entrepreneurship—and the state of technology. Let's look at the production possibilities frontier for bottled water and CDs.

Land can be used for either water-bottling plants or CD factories. Labor can be trained to work as water bottlers or as CD makers. Capital can be devoted to tapping springs and making water filtration plants or to the computers and lasers that make CDs. And entrepreneurs can devote their creative talents to managing water resources and bottling factories or to running electronics businesses that make CDs. In every case, the more resources that get used to produce bottled water, the fewer are left for producing CDs.

We can illustrate the production possibilities frontier by using either a table or a graph. The table in Figure 3.1 describes six production possibilities for bottled water and CDs—alternative combinations of quantities of these two goods that we can produce.

One possibility, in column *A*, is to devote no factors of production to making bottled water, so bottled water production is zero. In this case, we can devote all the factors of production to making CDs and produce 15 million a year. Another possibility, in column *B*, is to devote resources to bottled water production that are sufficient to produce 1 million bottles a year. But the resources that are being used in water-bottling plants must be taken from CD factories. So we can now produce only 14 million CDs a year. Columns *C*, *D*, *E*, and *F* show other possible combinations of the quantities of these two goods that we can produce. In column *F*, we use all our resources to produce 5 million bottles of water a year and have no resources to devote to producing CDs.

The graph in Figure 3.1 illustrates the production possibilities frontier, *PPF*, for bottled water and CDs. It is a graph of the production possibilities in the table. The x-axis shows the production of bottled water, and the y-axis shows the production of CDs. Each point on the graph labeled *A* through *F* represents the corresponding column in the table. For example, point *B* represents the production of 1 million bottles of water and 14 million CDs. These quantities also appear in column *B* of the table.

The *PPF* is a valuable tool for illustrating the effects of scarcity and its consequences. It puts three features of production possibilities in sharp focus. They are the distinctions between:

- Attainable and unattainable combinations
- Full employment and unemployment
- Tradeoffs and free lunches

FIGURE 3.1

The Production Possibilities Frontier

*e*Foundations 3.1 

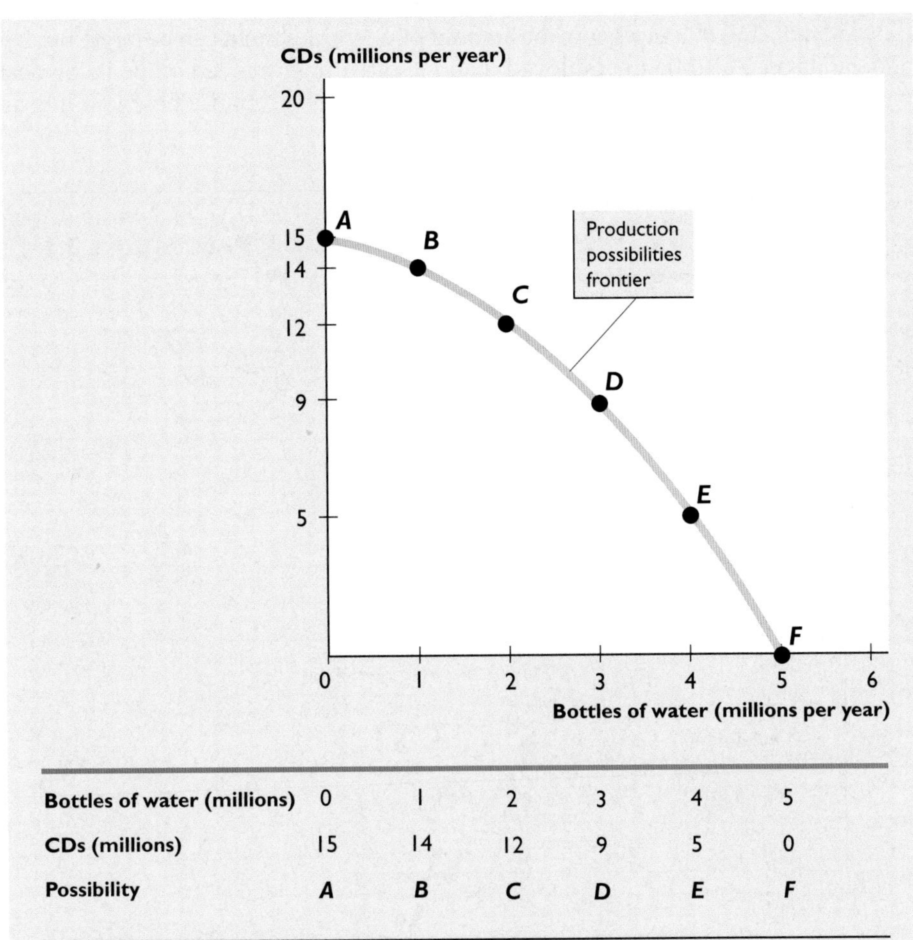

Bottles of water (millions)	0	1	2	3	4	5
CDs (millions)	15	14	12	9	5	0
Possibility	*A*	*B*	*C*	*D*	*E*	*F*

The table and the figure show the production possibilities frontier for bottled water and CDs. Point *A* tells us that if we produce no bottled water, the maximum quantity of CDs we can produce is 15 million a year. Points *A*, *B*, *C*, *D*, *E*, and *F* in the figure represent the columns of the table. The line passing through these points is the production possibilities frontier.

Attainable and Unattainable Combinations

Because the *PPF* shows the *limits* to production, it separates attainable combinations from unattainable ones. We can produce combinations of bottled water and CDs that are smaller than those on the *PPF*, and we can produce any of the combinations *on* the *PPF*. These combinations of bottled water and CDs are attainable. But we cannot produce combinations that are larger than those on the *PPF*. These combinations are unattainable.

Figure 3.2 emphasizes the attainable and unattainable combinations. Only the points on the *PPF* and inside it (in the orange area) are attainable. The combinations of bottled water and CDs beyond the *PPF* (in the white area), such as the combination at point *G*, are unattainable. These points illustrate combinations that cannot be produced with our current resources and technology. The *PPF* tells us that we can produce 4 million bottles of water and 5 million CDs at point *E* or 2 million bottles of water and 12 million CDs at point *C*. But we cannot produce 4 million bottles of water and 12 million CDs at point *G*.

Full Employment and Unemployment

Full employment occurs when all the available factors of production are being used. Unemployment occurs when some factors of production are not used.

The most noticed unemployment affects labor. There is always some unemployed labor, and in a recession, the amount of unemployment can be large. But land and capital can also be unemployed. Land is often unemployed while its owner is trying to work out the land's most valuable use. Look around where you live and

FIGURE 3.2

Attainable and Unattainable Combinations

*e*Foundations 3.1 

The production possibilities frontier, *PPF*, separates attainable combinations from unattainable ones. We can produce at any point inside the *PPF* (the orange area) or *on* the frontier. Points outside the production possibilities frontier such as point *G* are unattainable.

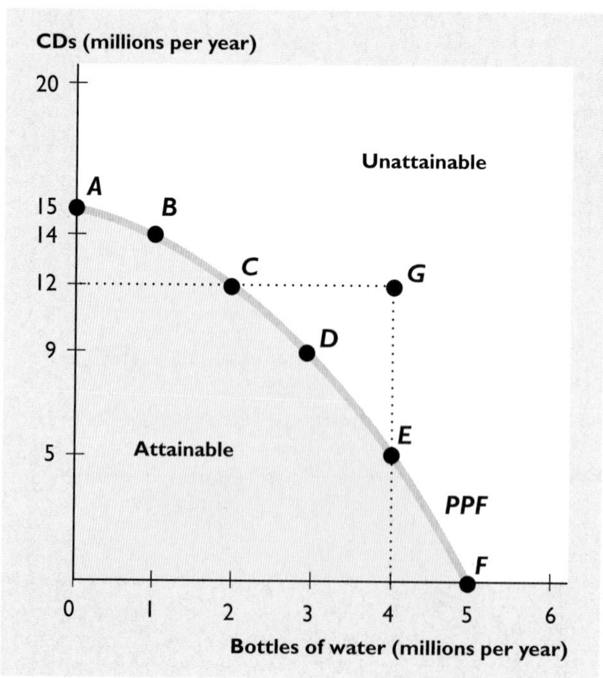

you'll probably be able to find at least one or two city blocks that are currently unemployed. Capital often lies idle. For example, thousands of automobiles are unemployed in parking lots; and restaurant tables and kitchens are often unemployed.

Figure 3.3 illustrates the effects of unemployment. With unemployed resources, the economy might produce at point *H*. Here, with some resources *employed*, it is possible to produce 3 million bottles of water and 5 million CDs. But with full employment, it is possible to move to points such as *D* or *E*. At point *D*, there are more CDs and the same quantity of bottled water as at point *H*. And at point *E*, there are more bottles of water and the same quantity of CDs as at point *H*.

Tradeoffs and Free Lunches

A **tradeoff** is a constraint or limit to what is possible that forces an exchange or a substitution of one thing for something else. If the federal government devotes more resources to finding a cure for AIDS and cuts its transfers to state and local governments, a move that forces state and local governments to increase class sizes and cut back on school libraries and computer facilities, we face a tradeoff between health care and education. If the federal government devotes more resources to national defense and fewer resources to NASA's space exploration program, we face a tradeoff between defense and the space program.

Tradeoff
A constraint or limit to what is possible that forces an exchange or a substitution of one thing for something else.

If lumber producers cut down fewer trees to conserve spotted owls, we face a tradeoff between paper products and wildlife. If Ford Motor Company decreases the production of trucks to produce more SUVs, we face a tradeoff between two types of vehicle. If a student decides to take an extra course and cut back on her weekend job, she faces a tradeoff between course credits and income.

FIGURE 3.3
Full Employment and Unemployment

*e*Foundations 3.1 

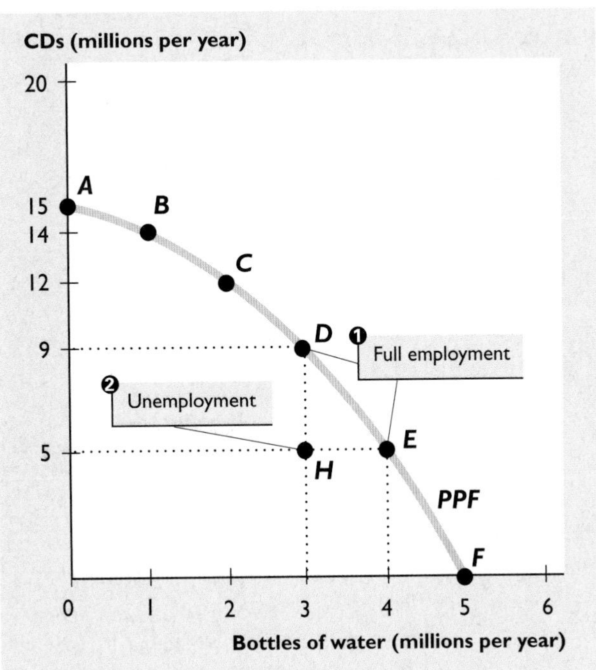

1. When resources are fully employed, production occurs at points on the *PPF* such as *D* and *E*.
2. When resources are unemployed, production occurs at a point inside the frontier such as point *H*.

The *PPF* in Figure 3.4 illustrates the idea of a tradeoff. If we produce at point *E* and would like to produce more CDs, we must forgo some bottled water. For example, we might move from point *E* to point *D*. We exchange some bottles of water for some CDs.

Economists often express the central idea of economics—that every choice involves an opportunity cost—with the saying "There is no such thing as a free lunch." (See Chapter 1, p. 11.) But suppose some resources are not being used or are not being used in their most productive way. Isn't it then possible to avoid opportunity cost and get a free lunch?

The answer is yes. You can see this answer in Figure 3.4. If production is taking place *inside* the *PPF* at point *H*, then it is possible to move to point *D* and increase the production of CDs by using currently unused resources or by using resources in their most productive way. There is a free lunch.

So when production takes place at a point on the *PPF*, we face a tradeoff. But we don't face a tradeoff if we produce inside the *PPF*. More of some goods and services can be produced without producing less of some others.

Because of scarcity and the attempt to get the most out of our scarce resources, we do not leave factors of production idle or use them unproductively if we can avoid it. And if such a situation arises, people seek ways of putting their resources to productive employment. It is for these reasons that economists emphasize the tradeoff idea and deny the existence of free lunches. We might *occasionally* get a free lunch, but we *persistently* face tradeoffs.

FIGURE 3.4

Tradeoffs and Free Lunches

*e*Foundations 3.1 

❶ When production is *on* the *PPF*, we face a tradeoff. If we are producing 5 million CDs a year at point *E*, to produce 9 million CDs at point *D*, we must trade some bottled water for CDs and move along the *PPF*.

❷ When production is *inside* the *PPF*, there is a free lunch. If we are producing 5 million CDs a year at point *H*, to produce 9 million CDs at point *D*, we move to the *PPF* and get a free lunch.

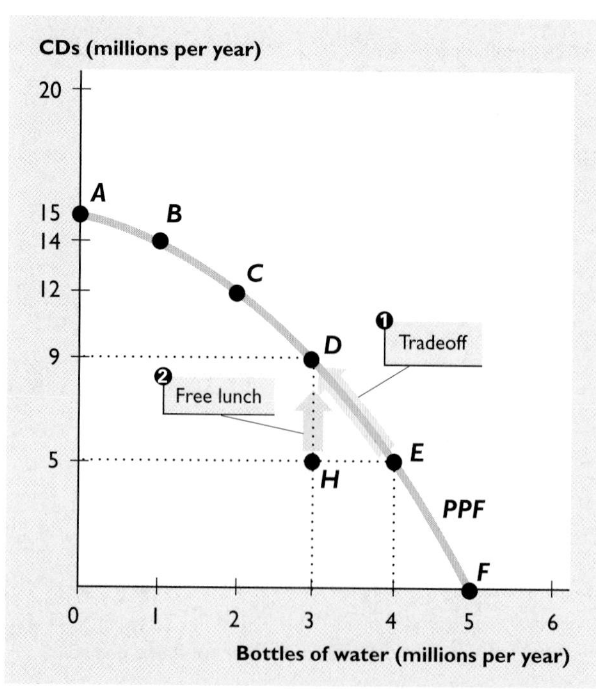

CHECKPOINT 3.1

1 **Use the production possibilities frontier to illustrate the economic problem.**

Study Guide pp. 38–41 

*e*Foundations 3.1

Practice Problems 3.1

1. Robinson Crusoe, the pioneer of the television program *Survivor*, lived alone on a deserted island. He spent his day fishing and picking fruit. He varied the time spent on these two activities and kept a record of his production. Table 1 shows the numbers that Crusoe wrote in the sand. Use these numbers to make Crusoe's *PPF* if he can work only 8 hours a day.
2. Which combinations (pounds of each) are attainable and which are unattainable: (i) 10 fish and 30 fruit, (ii) 13 fish and 26 fruit, (iii) 20 fish and 21 fruit?
3. Which combinations (pounds of each) use all of Crusoe's available 8 hours a day: (i) 15 fish and 21 fruit, (ii) 7 fish and 30 fruit, (iii) 18 fish and 0 fruit?
4. Which combinations (pounds of each) provide Crusoe with a free lunch and which confront him with a tradeoff when he increases fruit by 1 pound: (i) 0 fish and 36 fruit, (ii) 15 fish and 15 fruit, (iii) 13 fish and 26 fruit?

TABLE 1

Hours	Fish (pounds)		Fruit (pounds)
0	0		0
1	4.0	or	8
2	7.5	or	15
3	10.5	or	21
4	13.0	or	26
5	15.0	or	30
6	16.5	or	33
7	17.5	or	35
8	18.0	or	36

Exercises 3.1

1. In the winter, both fish and fruit are harder to find and Robinson Crusoe can work only 5 hours a day. Table 2 shows the quantities that Crusoe can produce in winter. Use these numbers to make Crusoe's *PPF* in winter.
2. Which combinations (pounds of each) are attainable and which are unattainable: (i) 9 fish and 13 fruit, (ii) 10 fish and 13 fruit, (iii) 7 fish and 18 fruit?
3. Which combinations (pounds of each) use all of Crusoe's available 5 hours a day: (i) 11 fish and 0 fruit, (ii) 10 fish and 6 fruit, (iii) 4 fish and 20 fruit?
4. Which combinations provide Crusoe with a free lunch and which confront him with a tradeoff when he increases fish by 1 pound: (i) 10 fish and 7 fruit, (ii) 4 fish and 20 fruit?

TABLE 2

Hours	Fish (pounds)		Fruit (pounds)
0	0		0
1	4	or	7
2	7	or	13
3	9	or	19
4	10	or	24
5	11	or	28

Solutions to Practice Problems 3.1

1. Table 3 sets out Crusoe's *PPF*. He has 8 hours a day for fishing and fruit picking. He can produce the combinations of fish and fruit that lie on his *PPF* if he uses a total of 8 hours a day. If he picks fruit for 8 hours, he picks 36 pounds and catches no fish—row *A*. If he picks fruit for 7 hours, he picks 35 pounds and has 1 hour for fishing in which he catches 4 pounds—row *B*. Check that you can construct the other rows of Table 3.
2. (i) 10 fish and 30 fruit is attainable because on row *D*, Crusoe can produce 10.5 fish and 30 fruit. (ii) 13 fish and 26 fruit is attainable—row *E*. (iii) 20 fish and 21 fruit is unattainable because when Crusoe picks 21 pounds of fruit, he can catch only 15 pounds of fish (row *F*).
3. (i) 15 fish and 21 fruit uses all 8 hours—it is on his *PPF* (row *F*). (ii) 7 fish and 30 fruit does not use all 8 hours—it is inside his *PPF* (row C). (iii) 18 fish and 0 fruit uses all 8 hours—it is on his *PPF* (row *I*).
4. (i) 0 fish and 36 fruit involves a tradeoff because it is on his *PPF*. (ii) 15 fish and 15 fruit provides a free lunch because it is inside his *PPF*. (iii) 13 fish and 26 fruit involves a tradeoff because it is on his *PPF*.

TABLE 3

Possibility	Fish (pounds)		Fruit (pounds)
A	0	and	36
B	4.0	and	35
C	7.5	and	33
D	10.5	and	30
E	13.0	and	26
F	15.0	and	21
G	16.5	and	15
H	17.5	and	8
I	18.0	and	0

3.2 OPPORTUNITY COST

You've just seen that along the *PPF*, all choices involve a tradeoff. But what are the terms of the tradeoff? How much of one item must be forgone to obtain an additional unit of another item—a large amount or a small amount? The answer is given by opportunity cost—what you must give up to get something (see p. 13). The production possibilities frontier enables us to calculate opportunity cost.

The Opportunity Cost of a Bottle of Water

The opportunity cost of a bottle of water is the decrease in the quantity of CDs divided by the increase in the number of bottles of water as we move down along the *PPF* in Figure 3.5.

At point *A*, we produce no bottles of water and 15 million CDs. At point *B*, we produce 1 million bottles of water and 14 million CDs. If we move from point *A* to point *B*, the quantity of water increases by 1 million bottles and the quantity of CDs decreases by 1 million. So the opportunity cost of 1 bottle of water is 1 CD.

At point *C*, we produce 2 million bottles of water and 12 million CDs. If we move from point *B* to point *C*, the quantity of water increases by 1 million bottles and the quantity of CDs decreases by 2 million. So the opportunity cost of 1 bottle of water is now 2 CDs.

Repeat these calculations, moving from *C* to *D*, from *D* to *E*, and from *E* to *F*, and check that you can obtain the opportunity costs shown in the table and graph.

FIGURE 3.5

Calculating the Opportunity Cost of a Bottle of Water

*e*Foundations 3.2 

Movement along *PPF*	Decrease in quantity of CDs	Increase in quantity of bottled water	Decrease in CDs divided by increase in bottled water
A to *B*	1 million	1 million	1 CD per bottle
B to *C*	2 million	1 million	2 CDs per bottle
C to *D*	3 million	1 million	3 CDs per bottle
D to *E*	4 million	1 million	4 CDs per bottle
E to *F*	5 million	1 million	5 CDs per bottle

Moving down the *PPF* from *A* to *F*, the opportunity cost of bottled water increases as the quantity of bottled water produced increases.

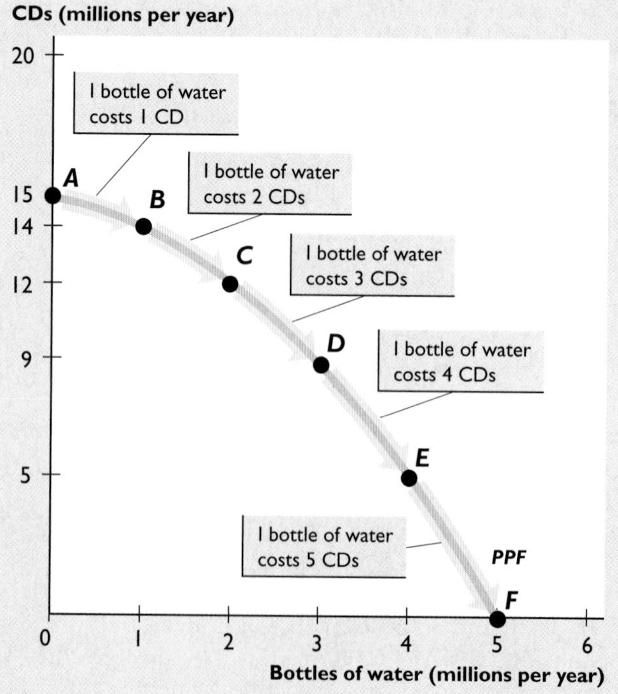

The Opportunity Cost of a CD

The opportunity cost of a CD is the decrease in the quantity of water divided by the increase in the quantity of CDs as we move up along the *PPF* in Figure 3.6.

At point *F*, we produce no CDs and 5 million bottles of water. At point *E*, we produce 5 million CDs and 4 million bottles of water. If we move from point *F* to point *E*, the quantity of CDs increases by 5 million and the quantity of water decreases by 1 million bottles. So the opportunity cost of 1 CD is ⅕ of a bottle of water.

At point *D*, we can produce 9 million CDs and 3 million bottles of water. If we move from point *E* to point *D*, the quantity of CDs increases by 4 million and the quantity of water decreases by 1 million bottles. So the opportunity cost of a CD is now ¼ of a bottle of water.

At point *C*, we can produce 12 million CDs and 2 million bottles of water. If we move from point *D* to point *C*, the quantity of CDs increases by 3 million and the quantity of water decreases by 1 million bottles. So the opportunity cost of a CD is now ⅓ of a bottle of water.

Again, repeat these calculations, moving from *C* to *B* and from *B* to *A*, and check that you can obtain the opportunity costs shown in the figure.

Opportunity Cost Is a Ratio

You've seen that to calculate the opportunity cost of a bottle of water, we divide the quantity of CDs forgone by the increase in the quantity of water. And to calculate the opportunity cost of a CD, we divide the quantity of bottled water

FIGURE 3.6
Calculating the Opportunity Cost of a CD

*e*Foundations **3.2** 

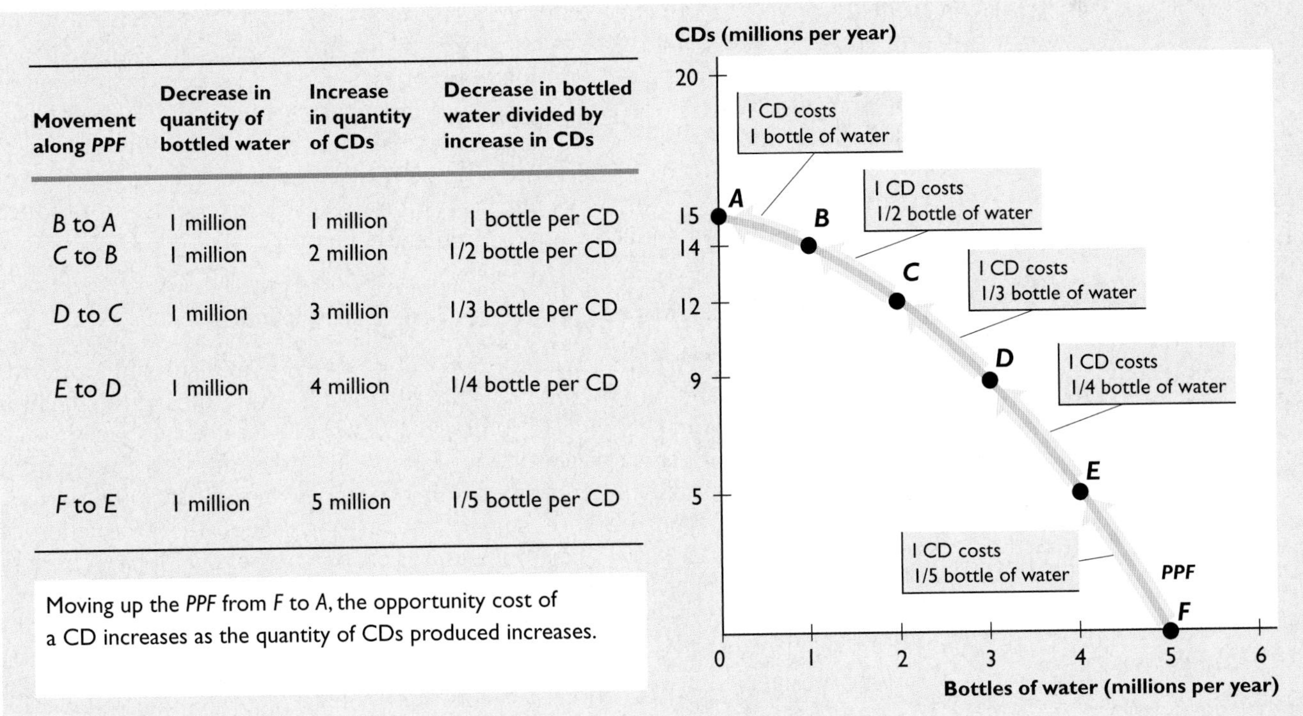

Movement along *PPF*	Decrease in quantity of bottled water	Increase in quantity of CDs	Decrease in bottled water divided by increase in CDs
B to A	1 million	1 million	1 bottle per CD
C to B	1 million	2 million	1/2 bottle per CD
D to C	1 million	3 million	1/3 bottle per CD
E to D	1 million	4 million	1/4 bottle per CD
F to E	1 million	5 million	1/5 bottle per CD

Moving up the *PPF* from F to A, the opportunity cost of a CD increases as the quantity of CDs produced increases.

forgone by the increase in the quantity of CDs. So opportunity cost is a ratio—the change in the quantity of one good divided by the change in the quantity of the other good. The opportunity cost of producing water is equal to the inverse of the opportunity cost of producing CDs. Check this proposition by returning to the calculations we've just worked through. When we move along the *PPF* from point *C* to point *D*, the opportunity cost of a bottle of water is 3 CDs. The inverse of 3 is ⅓, so if we increase the production of CDs and decrease the production of water by moving from *D* to *C*, the opportunity cost of a CD must be ⅓ of a bottle of water. This number is correct—it is the number we've just calculated.

Increasing Opportunity Cost

The opportunity cost of a bottle of water increases as the quantity of bottled water produced increases. The opportunity cost of a CD increases as the quantity of CDs produced increases. The phenomenon of increasing opportunity cost is reflected in the shape of the *PPF*. It is bowed outward. When a large quantity of CDs and a small quantity of water are produced—between points *A* and *B* in Figure 3.5—the frontier has a gentle slope. A given increase in the quantity of bottled water costs a small decrease in the quantity of CDs, so the opportunity cost of a bottle of water is a small quantity of CDs.

When a large quantity of bottled water and a small quantity of CDs are produced—between points *E* and *F* in Figure 3.5—the frontier is steep. A given increase in the quantity of bottled water costs a large decrease in the quantity of CDs, so the opportunity cost of a bottle of water is a large quantity of CDs.

The production possibilities frontier is bowed outward because resources are not equally productive in all activities. Production workers with many years of experience working for Aqua Springs are very good at bottling water but not very good at making CDs. So if we move some of these people from Aqua Springs to Sony, we get a small increase in the quantity of CDs but a large decrease in the quantity of bottled water.

Similarly, engineers and production workers who work at Sony are good at making CDs but not very good at bottling water. So if we move some of these people from Sony to Aqua Springs, we get a small increase in the quantity of bottled water but a large decrease in the quantity of CDs. The more we try to produce of either good, the less productive are the additional resources we use to produce that good and the larger is the opportunity cost of a unit of that good.

Increasing Opportunity Costs Are Everywhere

Just about every activity that you can think of is one with an increasing opportunity cost. We allocate the most skillful farmers and the most fertile land to the production of food. And we allocate the best doctors and least fertile land to the production of health-care services. If we shift fertile land and tractors away from farming to hospitals and ambulances and ask farmers to become hospital porters, the production of food drops drastically and the increase in the production of health-care services is small. The opportunity cost of a unit of health-care services rises. Similarly, if we shift our resources away from health care toward farming, we must use more doctors and nurses as farmers and more hospitals as hydroponic tomato factories. The decrease in the production of health-care services is large, but the increase in food production is small. The opportunity cost of a unit of food rises.

CHECKPOINT 3.2

2 **Calculate opportunity cost.**

Study Guide pp. 41–43

*e*Foundations 3.2 

Practice Problems 3.2

1. Use Robinson Crusoe's production possibilities shown in Table 1 to calculate his opportunity cost of a pound of fish. Make a table that shows Crusoe's opportunity cost of a pound of fish as he increases the time he spends fishing and decreases the time that he spends picking fruit.
2. If Crusoe increases his production of fruit from 21 pounds to 26 pounds and decreases his production of fish from 15 pounds to 13 pounds, what is his opportunity cost of a pound of fruit? Explain your answer.
3. If Crusoe is producing 10 pounds of fish and 20 pounds of fruit, what is his opportunity cost of a pound of fruit and a pound of fish? Explain your answer.

TABLE 1

Possibility	Fish (pounds)	Fruit (pounds)
A	0	36
B	4.0	35
C	7.5	33
D	10.5	30
E	13.0	26
F	15.0	21
G	16.5	15
H	17.5	8
I	18.0	0

Exercises 3.2

1. Use Robinson Crusoe's production possibilities in winter shown in Table 2 to calculate his opportunity cost of a pound of fruit. Make a table that shows Crusoe's opportunity cost of a pound of fruit as he increases the time he spends picking fruit and decreases the time he fishes.
2. If Crusoe currently catches 7 pounds of fish and picks 13 pounds of fruit a day, calculate his opportunity cost of a pound of fruit and of a pound of fish. Explain your answer.
3. If Crusoe increases the fish caught from 7 to 9 pounds and decreases the fruit picked from 19 to 13 pounds, what is his opportunity cost of a pound of fish? Explain your answer.
4. Does Crusoe's opportunity cost of a pound of fruit increase as he spends more time picking fruit? Explain why or why not.

TABLE 2

Possibility	Fish (pounds)	Fruit (pounds)
A	0	28
B	4	24
C	7	19
D	9	13
E	10	7
F	11	0

Solutions to Practice Problems 3.2

1. Crusoe's opportunity cost of a pound of fish is the decrease in fruit divided by the increase in fish as he moves along his *PPF*, increasing the time he spends fishing and decreasing the time he spends picking fruit. For example, when Crusoe spends no time fishing, he produces the quantities in row *A* in Table 1. When he spends more time fishing and moves to row *B* in Table 1, the increase in fish is 4 pounds and the decrease in fruit picked is 1 pound. So the opportunity cost of a pound of fish is ¼ pound of fruit. Check that you can derive the other rows of Table 3.
2. The opportunity cost of a pound of fruit is ⅖ pound of fish. When fruit increases by 5 pounds, fish decreases by 2 pounds. The opportunity cost of a pound of fruit is 2 pounds of fish divided by 5 pounds of fruit. This opportunity cost is the inverse of the opportunity cost of fish (Table 3, move from *E* to *F*).
3. If Crusoe is producing 10 pounds of fish and 20 pounds of fruit, his opportunity cost of fruit and of fish is zero because he can increase the production of both without decreasing the production of either. He is producing a combination inside his *PPF*.

TABLE 3

Move from	Increase in fish (pounds)	Decrease in fruit (pounds)	Opportunity cost of fish (pounds of fruit)
A to *B*	4.0	1	0.25
B to *C*	3.5	2	0.57
C to *D*	3.0	3	1.00
D to *E*	2.5	4	1.60
E to *F*	2.0	5	2.50
F to *G*	1.5	6	4.00
G to *H*	1.0	7	7.00
H to *I*	0.5	8	16.00

3.3 USING RESOURCES EFFICIENTLY

Ralph Nader says that we should expand the use of clean solar technologies and burn less oil and coal. He also says that we should create clean mass transit systems and decrease our reliance on the automobile. Political leaders of all parties say that we should hire more teachers to reduce class size and improve education. They also want to spend more on prescription drug plans for seniors and improve health care for the uninsured. Some political leaders want to enter into a new phase of defense spending and create an effective antimissile defense system. All of these policy proposals and the political debates that surround them are about efficiency.

Efficiency
A situation in which the quantities of goods and services produced are those that people value most highly—in which we cannot produce more of a good or service without giving up some of another good or service that people value more highly.

Economists use the idea of efficiency in a broad way that cuts to the heart of these debates. In economics, **efficiency** occurs when we produce the quantities of goods and services that people value most highly. To put it another way, resource use is *efficient* when we cannot produce more of a good or service without giving up some of another good or service that people value more highly.

If people value a pollution-free environment more highly than they value cheap electric power, it is efficient to use high-cost clean technologies to produce electricity. In this case, Ralph Nader's proposal to limit the use of coal and oil and expand the use of solar energy sources could be efficient. If people value the flexibility of being able to choose when and where to travel more highly than they value low-cost, low-pollution, safe transportation, it is efficient to use high-cost, polluting, accident-prone automobiles.

So just what is the efficient energy policy: one that favors clean energy technologies or one that burns oil and coal? What is the efficient method of urban transportation: one that uses a clean mass transit system or a system of freeways and private automobiles? And what are the efficient quantities of education, health care, and national defense?

These are questions that have enormous consequences for human welfare, and they are difficult questions. But you can see the essence of the answers by thinking about the simpler question: What is the efficient quantity of bottled water to produce? The answer to this question provides the principles that underlie the answers to all questions about how to use our scarce resources.

Two Conditions for Efficiency

Efficiency is achieved when two conditions are met:

- Production efficiency
- Allocative efficiency

Production Efficiency

Production efficiency
A situation in which we cannot produce more of one good or service without producing less of some other good or service—production is at a point *on* the *PPF*.

We achieve **production efficiency** if we cannot produce more of one good or service without producing less of some other good or service. When production is efficient, we are at a point *on* the *PPF*. If we are at a point *inside* the *PPF*, production is *inefficient* because we have some *unemployed* resources or resources are not being used most productively. Bringing those resources into their most productive use enables more of both goods to be produced.

You've seen that when resources are unemployed, It is possible to produce more of a good without incurring a cost. So production is not efficient. Only when all resources are fully employed and the economy is operating on the *PPF* is it impossible to produce more of one good or service without producing less of another good or service.

Allocative Efficiency

Allocative efficiency
The most highly valued combination of goods and services on the *PPF*.

We achieve **allocative efficiency** when we produce the combination of goods and services on the *PPF* that we value most highly. All the combinations of goods and services on the *PPF* achieve production efficiency. Each of these combinations is such that, to produce more of one good or service, we must produce less of the other. But only one of these combinations achieves allocative efficiency. That is, only one combination is the most highly valued. To find this combination, we need some additional information that is not contained in the *PPF*. We need to know the value of each available combination. We express value in terms of the marginal benefit people receive.

Marginal Benefit

You learned in Chapter 1 (pp. 14–15) that the *benefit* of something is the gain or pleasure that it brings. Benefit is how a person *feels* about something. We defined *marginal benefit* as the benefit that a person receives from consuming one more unit of a good or service.

You also learned in Chapter 1 that economists measure the benefit of something by what a person is *willing to* give up to get it. So a person's *marginal* benefit of a good or service is what that person is *willing to give up* to get *one more* unit of it.

It is a general principle that the more we have of any good or service, the smaller is our marginal benefit from it—the principle of decreasing marginal benefit. To understand the principle of decreasing marginal benefit, think about your own marginal benefit from bottled water. If bottled water is very hard to come by and you can buy only one or two bottles a year, you will be very pleased to get one more bottle. The marginal benefit of that bottle of water is high. In this situation, you are willing to give up quite a lot of some other good or service to get one more bottle of water. But if there is plenty of bottled water around and you have as much as you can drink, you will get almost no benefit from one more bottle. So you are willing to give up almost nothing for that bottle of water.

The principle of diminishing marginal benefit applies to all goods and services. You get a lot of pleasure from one slice of pizza. A second slice is fine, too, but not quite as satisfying as the first one. But eat three, four, five, six, and more slices, and each additional slice is less enjoyable than the previous one. You get diminishing marginal benefit from pizza. So the more pizza you have, the less of some other good or service you would be willing to give up to get one more slice.

Although marginal benefit expresses a person's *feeling* toward a good or service, it is nonetheless a real, objective phenomenon. It is as real as the physical limits to production that we express in the *PPF*. The *PPF* shows what is *feasible*. Marginal benefit is an expression of what is *desirable*. And we need a way of describing marginal benefit that is as concrete as the *PPF*.

Let's see how economists describe marginal benefit.

Marginal Benefit Schedule and Curve

We describe marginal benefit by using either a marginal benefit schedule or a marginal benefit curve. Figure 3.7 illustrates these concepts, and we continue to use the same two goods as before: bottled water and CDs. The marginal benefit from a bottle of water can be expressed as the number of CDs that a person is willing to forgo to get one more bottle. This amount decreases as the quantity of bottled water available increases.

Begin by looking at the table below the graph. In column *A*, 1 million bottles of water are available, and at that quantity, people are willing to give up 4.5 CDs for a bottle of water. As the quantity of bottled water available increases, the amount that people are willing to give up for an additional bottle falls—3.5 CDs per bottle when 2 million bottles are available in column *B*, 2.5 CDs per bottle when 3 million bottles are available in column *C*, and 1.5 CDs per bottle when 4 million bottles are available in column *D*.

The marginal benefit curve is a graph of the marginal benefit schedule. The points *A*, *B*, *C*, and *D* on the marginal benefit or *MB* curve correspond to the columns *A*, *B*, *C*, and *D* of the marginal benefit schedule.

The marginal benefit from a bottle of water and the opportunity cost of a bottle of water that you studied on p. 62 are both measured in CDs per bottle. But they are *not* the same concept. The opportunity cost of a bottle of water is the quantity of CDs that people *must forgo* to get another bottle. The marginal benefit from a bottle of water is the quantity of CDs that people are *willing to forgo* to get another bottle.

FIGURE 3.7
Marginal Benefit of a Bottle of Water

*e*Foundations 3.3 

The table and the figure show the marginal benefit of bottled water. Point *A* tells us that if we produce 1 million bottles of water a year, the maximum quantity of CDs that people are willing to give up for an additional bottle of water is 4.5 CDs. Points *A*, *B*, *C*, and *D* in the figure represent the columns of the table. The line passing through these points is the marginal benefit curve. The marginal benefit of bottled water decreases as the quantity of bottled water produced increases.

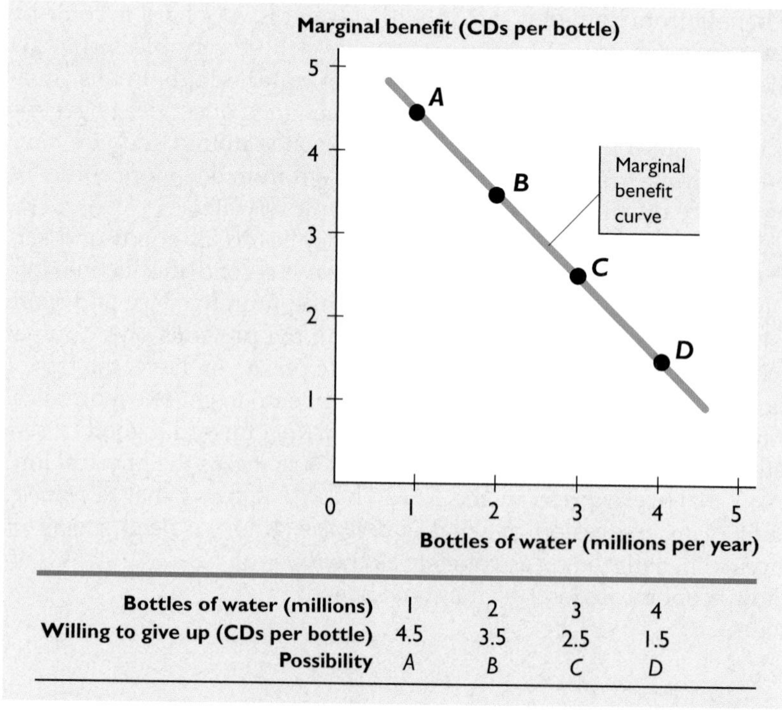

Bottles of water (millions)	1	2	3	4
Willing to give up (CDs per bottle)	4.5	3.5	2.5	1.5
Possibility	*A*	*B*	*C*	*D*

Marginal Cost

To achieve allocative efficiency, we must compare the marginal benefit of a bottle of water with its marginal cost. We defined *marginal cost* in Chapter 1 (p. 15) as the opportunity cost of producing one more unit of a good or service. You've seen how we can calculate opportunity cost as we move along the production possibilities frontier. We can calculate marginal cost in a similar way. The marginal cost of a bottle of water is the opportunity cost of one additional bottle—the quantity of CDs that must be given up to get one more bottle of water—as we move along the *PPF*.

Figure 3.8 illustrates the marginal cost of a bottle of water. It is based on the opportunity cost numbers that you've already calculated. Recall that the opportunity cost of the first 1 million bottles of water is 1 million CDs. So on the average, 1 bottle of water costs 1 CD. We graph this cost midway between zero and 1 million on the graph. The opportunity cost of the second 1 million bottles of water is 2 million CDs. So on the average, 1 bottle of water costs 2 CDs over this range. We graph this cost midway between 1 million and 2 million on the graph.

Figure 3.8 shows that the marginal cost curve of bottled water slopes upward. That is, as the quantity of bottled water produced increases, the marginal cost of bottled water increases. This increasing marginal cost occurs for the same reason the opportunity cost increases.

Let's use the concepts of marginal benefit and marginal cost to discover the efficient quantity of bottled water to produce.

FIGURE 3.8

Marginal Cost of a Bottle of Water

e **Foundations 3.3** 

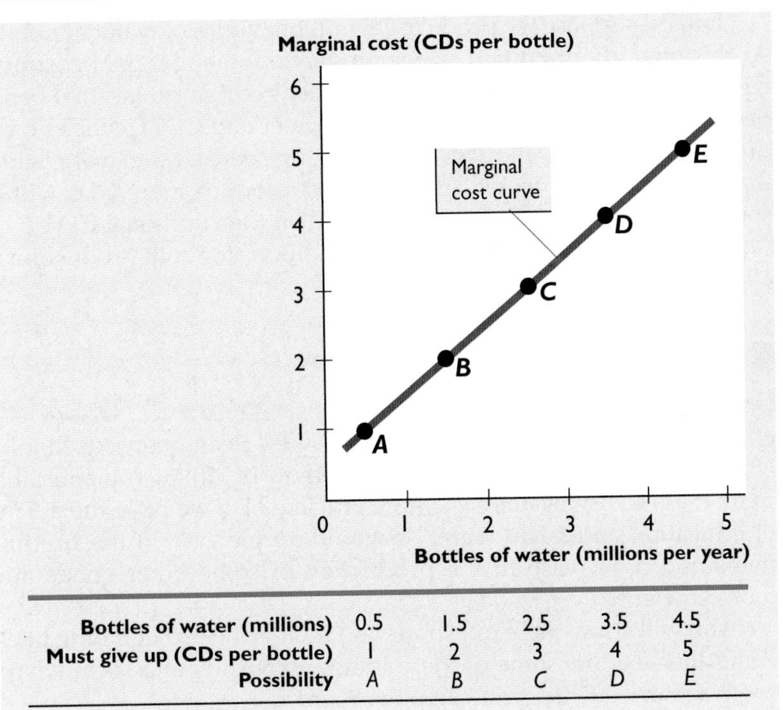

Bottles of water (millions)	0.5	1.5	2.5	3.5	4.5
Must give up (CDs per bottle)	1	2	3	4	5
Possibility	*A*	*B*	*C*	*D*	*E*

The table and the figure show the marginal cost of bottled water. Marginal cost is the opportunity cost of producing one more unit and is derived from the *PPF*. Points *A*, *B*, *C*, *D*, and *E* in the figure represent the columns of the table. The marginal cost curve shows that the marginal cost of a bottle of water increases as the quantity of bottled water produced increases.

Efficient Use of Resources

Resource use is efficient when we produce the goods and services that we value the most highly. That is, when we are using our resources efficiently, we cannot produce more of any good without producing less of something else that we value even more highly.

We can illustrate an efficient use of resources by continuing to use the example of bottled water and CDs. Figure 3.9(a) shows the production possibilities frontier (the same as in Figure 3.1 on p. 57). And Figure 3.9(b) shows the marginal cost (*MC*) and marginal benefit (*MB*) of bottled water.

Suppose we produce 1.5 million bottles of water a year at point *A* on the *PPF* in Figure 3.9(a). This combination of water and CDs meets the conditions for production efficiency because it is on the *PPF*. But does it meet the conditions for allocative efficiency? To answer this question, we need to compare marginal benefit and marginal cost in Figure 3.9(b). The marginal benefit from bottled water is 4 CDs per bottle, but the marginal cost of bottled water is only 2 CDs per bottle. Because people value an additional bottle of water more highly than it costs to produce, we are producing too many CDs and not enough bottled water. We can get more value from our resources by moving some of them out of CD production and into bottled water production.

Now suppose that we produce 3.5 million bottles of water a year at point *C* on the *PPF*. Again, this point meets the conditions for production efficiency because it is on the *PPF*. To check whether it meets the conditions for allocative efficiency, we again need to compare marginal benefit and marginal cost. The marginal benefit from bottled water is now 2 CDs per bottle, but the marginal cost of bottled water is 4 CDs per bottle. People now value an additional bottle of water less highly than it costs to produce. So we are producing too much bottled water and too few CDs. We can get more value from our resources by moving some of them out of bottled water production and into CD production.

Finally, suppose we produce 2.5 million bottles of water at point *B* on the *PPF*. At this quantity of bottled water production, the marginal cost of bottled water equals the marginal benefit. Both marginal cost and marginal benefit are 3 CDs per bottle. This combination of bottled water and CDs is efficient. We cannot produce more bottled water without giving up some CDs that we value more highly than the additional water. And we can't produce more CDs without giving up some water that we value more highly than the additional CDs.

So point *B* on the *PPF* meets the conditions for both production efficiency and allocative efficiency.

ECONOMICS *in the* NEWS

July 18, 2000

Pre-sliced Apples Going to Market

Two Washington apple packing and marketing companies are offering bagged apple slices.

Questions

Do you think the opportunity cost of producing sliced apples is large and do you think it increases much as the quantity of sliced apples produced increases?

Draw a PPF for sliced apples and whole apples that incorporates your answer to the previous question.

What are the benefits of sliced apples compared to whole apples?

What determines the efficient quantities of sliced apples and whole apples?

 **eFoundations 3.3**

Efficiency in the U.S. Economy

Does our economy achieve an efficient use of resources? Do we have an efficient energy policy, or would a policy that favors clean-energy technologies be more efficient? Do we have an efficient method of urban transportation, or would more mass transit systems be more efficient? Do we have the efficient quantities of education and health care, or would an increase in the production of these items and a decrease in the production of some other goods and services be more efficient?

You will study these questions and their answers beginning in Chapters 6 and 7 and then explore some of these issues more fully and learn what we can do to try to achieve efficiency in Chapters 8 and 9.

FIGURE 3.9
The Efficient Quantity of Bottled Water

*e*Foundations 3.3 

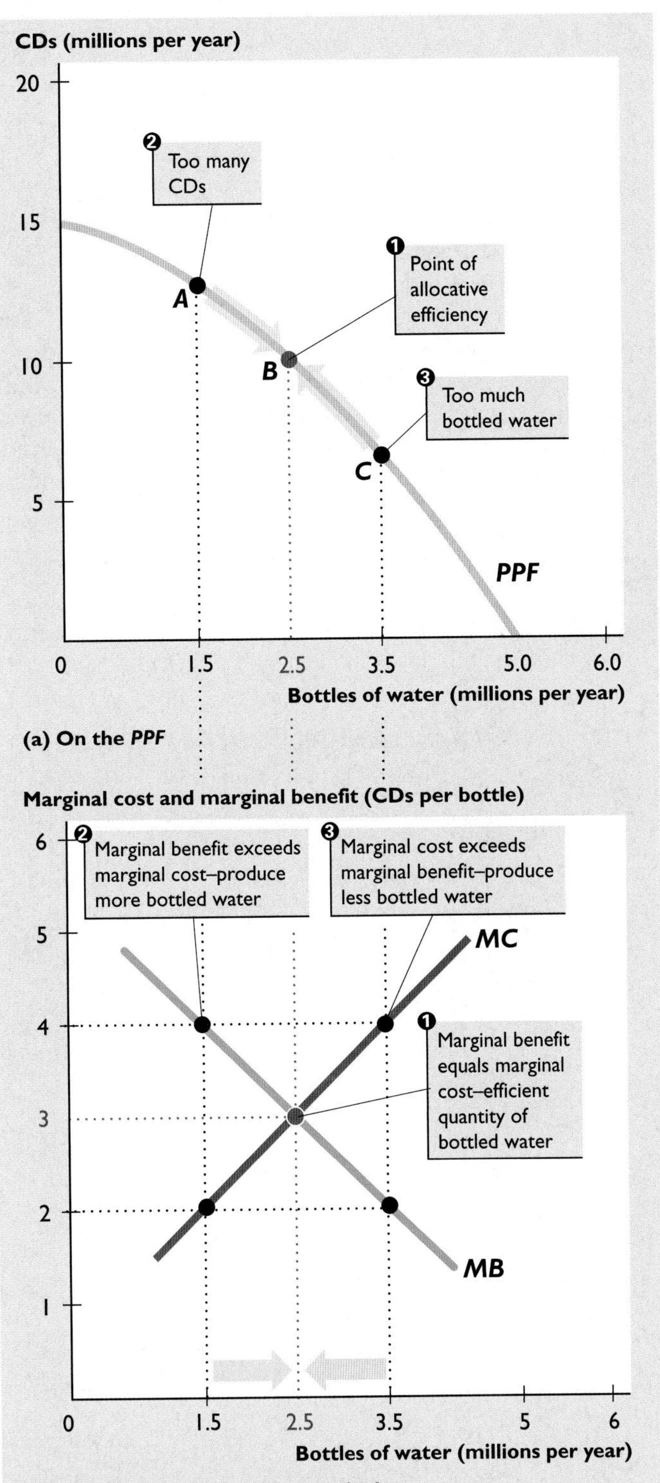

❶ Production efficiency occurs at all points on the *PPF* in part (a). But only point *B* meets the condition for allocative efficiency, which occurs where the marginal benefit of bottled water (*MB*) equals the marginal cost of bottled water (*MC*) in part (b).

❷ At point *A*, too many CDs are being produced and too little bottled water is being produced. The marginal benefit of bottled water exceeds the marginal cost.

❸ At point *C*, too much bottled water is being produced and too few CDs are being produced. The marginal cost of bottled water exceeds the marginal benefit.

CHECKPOINT 3.3

Study Guide pp. 43–46

*e*Foundations 3.3

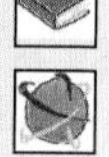

3 **Define efficiency and describe an efficient use of resources.**

TABLE 1

Possibility	Bananas (bunches)	Coffee (pounds)
A	70	40
B	50	100
C	30	140
D	10	160

Practice Problems 3.3

1. Table 1 shows a nation's production possibilities of bananas and coffee. Use the table to calculate the nation's marginal cost of a bunch of bananas. Draw the marginal cost curve.
2. Use the following data to draw the nation's marginal benefit curve for a bunch of bananas:
   i. When 20 bunches of bananas are available, people are willing to give up 3 pounds of coffee to get an additional bunch of bananas.
   ii. When 40 bunches of bananas are available, people are willing to give up 2 pounds of coffee to get an additional bunch of bananas.
   iii. When 60 bunches of bananas are available, people are willing to give up 1 pound of coffee to get an additional bunch of bananas.
3. Use the data in Practice Problems 1 and 2 to calculate the efficient use of the nation's resources.

Exercise 3.3

Use the *PPF* shown in Figure 1(a) and the marginal benefit curve shown in Figure 1(b) to find the efficient quantities of yogurt and ice cream.

FIGURE 1

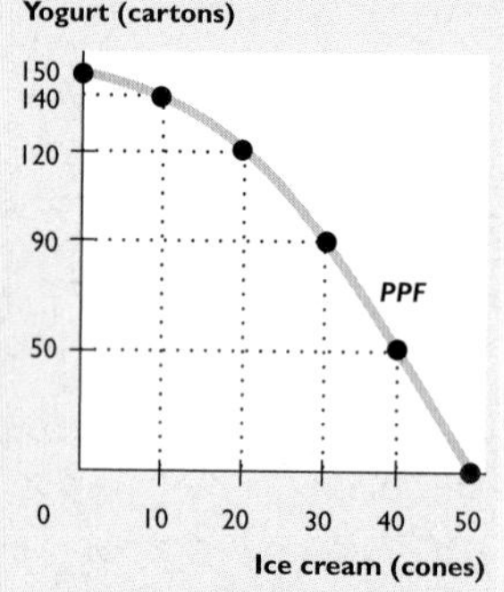

(a) *PPF*

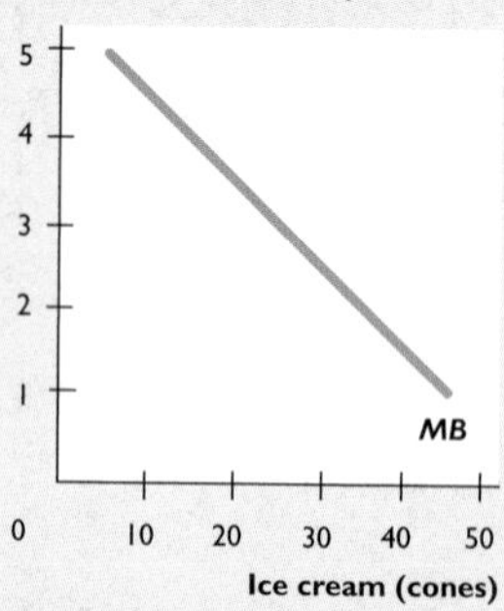

(b) Marginal benefit

Solutions to Practice Problems 3.3

1. Figure 2 shows the marginal cost curve. When the quantity of bananas increases from 10 to 30 pounds, the quantity of coffee decreases from 160 to 140 pounds. Bananas increase by 20 pounds and coffee decreases by 20 pounds. So the opportunity cost of 1 bunch of bananas is 1 pound of coffee. In the figure, marginal cost is 1 pound of coffee at the midpoint between 10 and 30 pounds, which is 20 bunches of bananas. When the quantity of bananas increases from 30 to 50 pounds, coffee decreases from 140 to 100 pounds. Bananas increase by 20 pounds, and coffee decreases by 40 pounds. So the opportunity cost of 2 bunches of bananas is 1 pound of coffee. In the figure, marginal cost is 2 pounds of coffee at the midpoint between 30 and 50 pounds, which is 40 bunches of bananas.
2. Figure 2 shows the marginal benefit curve, which plots the data given. The marginal benefit curve slopes downward because as more bananas are available, the marginal benefit from an additional bunch of bananas decreases.
3. The nation uses its resources efficiently when it produces 40 bunches of bananas and (approximately) 120 pounds of coffee. When the nation produces 40 bunches of bananas and 120 pounds of coffee, it produces on the *PPF* (production efficiency), and it is the highest-valued combination because marginal benefit equals marginal cost (allocative efficiency).

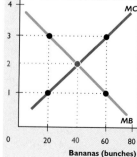

FIGURE 2

Coffee (pounds per bunch)

4, 3, 2, 1, 0; *MC*; *MB*; 20, 40, 60, 80; Bananas (bunches)

3.4 SPECIALIZATION AND EXCHANGE

People can produce several goods, or they can concentrate on producing one good and then exchange some of their own good for those produced by others. Concentrating on the production of only one good is called *specialization*. We are going to discover how people gain by specializing in the production of the good in which they have a *comparative advantage*.

Comparative Advantage

A person has a **comparative advantage** in an activity if that person can perform the activity at a lower opportunity cost than someone else. Let's explore the idea of comparative advantage by looking at two water-bottling plants, one operated by Tom and the other operated by Nancy.

Comparative advantage
The ability of a person to perform an activity or produce a good or service at a lower opportunity cost than someone else.

Tom produces both water and bottles, and Figure 3.10 shows his production possibilities frontier. If Tom uses all his resources to produce water, he can produce 1,333 gallons an hour, and if he uses all his resources to make bottles, he can produce 4,000 bottles an hour. For each additional 1,000 gallons of water produced, Tom must decrease his production of bottles by 3,000.

Tom's opportunity cost of producing 1 gallon of water is 3 bottles.

Similarly, if Tom wants to increase his production of bottles, he must decrease his production of water. For each 1,000 bottles produced, he must decrease his production of water by 333 gallons. So

Tom's opportunity cost of producing 1 bottle is 0.333 gallon of water.

FIGURE 3.10
Production Possibilities at Tom's Water-Bottling Plant

Bottles (thousands per hour)
5
4
3
2
1
0
Tom's opportunity costs:
1 gallon of water costs 3 bottles
1 bottle costs 1/3 of a gallon of water
4,000 bottles
Tom's *PPF*
Tom's production point
1,333 gallons
1 2 3 4 5
Water (thousands of gallons per hour)

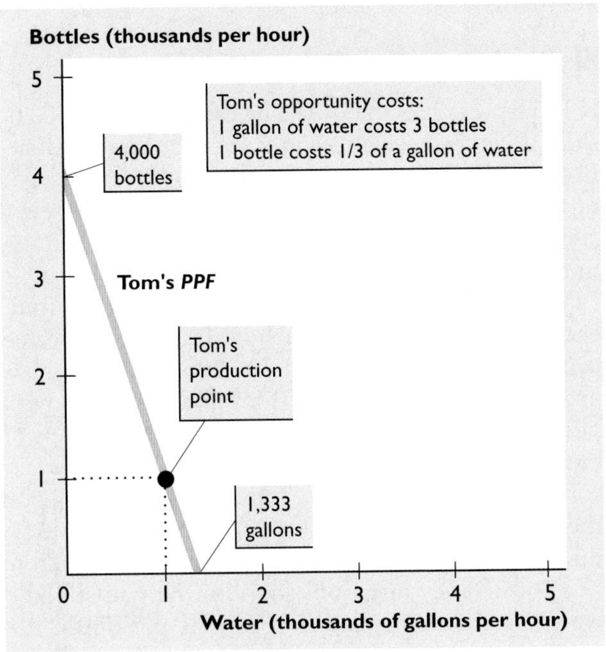

Tom can produce bottles and water along the production possibility frontier *PPF*. For Tom, the opportunity cost of 1 gallon of water is 3 bottles and the opportunity cost of 1 bottle is ⅓ of a gallon of water. If Tom produces at point *A*, he can produce 1,000 gallons of water and 1,000 bottles an hour.

Tom's *PPF* is linear because his workers have similar skills so if he reallocates them from one activity to another, he faces a constant opportunity cost.

Nancy also produces water and bottles. But Nancy owns a much better spring than Tom. At the same time, her bottle-making equipment is less productive than is Tom's. These differences between the two plants mean that Nancy's production possibilities frontier—shown along with Tom's *PPF* in Figure 3.11—is different from Tom's. If Nancy uses all her resources to produce water, she can produce 4,000 gallons an hour. If she uses all her resources to make bottles, she can produce 1,333 an hour. Nancy's *PPF* is linear, like Tom's, so she faces a constant opportunity cost. For each 1,000 additional bottles produced, she must decrease her production of water by 3,000 gallons.

Nancy's opportunity cost of producing 1 bottle is 3 gallons of water.

Similarly, if Nancy wants to increase her production of water, she must decrease her production of bottles. For each additional 1,000 gallons of water produced, she must decrease her production of bottles by 333. So

Nancy's opportunity cost of producing 1 gallon of water is 0.333 bottle.

Suppose that Tom and Nancy produce both bottles and water and that each produces 1,000 bottles and 1,000 gallons of water—1,000 gallons of bottled water—an hour. That is, each produces at point *A* on their production possibilities frontiers. Total production is 2,000 gallons of bottled water an hour.

In which of the two activities does Nancy have a comparative advantage? Recall that comparative advantage is a situation in which one person's opportunity cost of producing a good is lower than another person's opportunity cost of producing that same good. Nancy has a comparative advantage in producing water. Nancy's opportunity cost of a gallon of water is 0.333 bottle, whereas Tom's opportunity cost of a gallon of water is 3 bottles.

Because Nancy has a comparative advantage in water and Tom has a comparative advantage in bottles, they can both gain from specialization and exchange.

Achieving the Gains from Trade

If Tom specializes in bottles, he can produce 4,000 bottles an hour—point *B* on his *PPF*. If Nancy specializes in water, she can produce 4,000 gallons an hour—point *B'* on her *PPF*. By specializing, Tom and Nancy together can produce 4,000 gallons of water and 4,000 bottles an hour—double their total production without specialization. By specialization and exchange, Tom and Nancy can get *outside* their individual production possibilities frontiers.

To achieve the gains from specialization, Tom and Nancy must trade with each other. Suppose that each hour, Nancy produces 4,000 gallons of water, Tom produces 4,000 bottles, and Nancy supplies Tom with 2,000 gallons of water in exchange for 2,000 bottles. Tom and Nancy move along the red "Trade line" to point *C*. At this point, each produces 2,000 gallons of bottled water an hour—double their previous production rate.

By specializing and trading with each other, both Tom and Nancy can double their production from 1,000 to 2,000 bottles of water an hour. The increases in production that each of them achieves are the gains from specialization and exchange.

Both Nancy and Tom share in the gains. Nancy gets bottles for 1 gallon of water per bottle instead of 3 gallons per bottle. Tom gets water for 1 bottle per

FIGURE 3.11
The Gains from Specialization

*e*Foundations 3.4

❶ Tom and Nancy each produce at point *A* on their respective *PPF*s. Tom has a comparative advantage in bottles and Nancy has a comparative advantage in water.

❷ If Tom specializes in bottles, he produces at point *B* on his *PPF*.

❸ If Nancy specializes in water, she produces at point *B*' on her *PPF*.

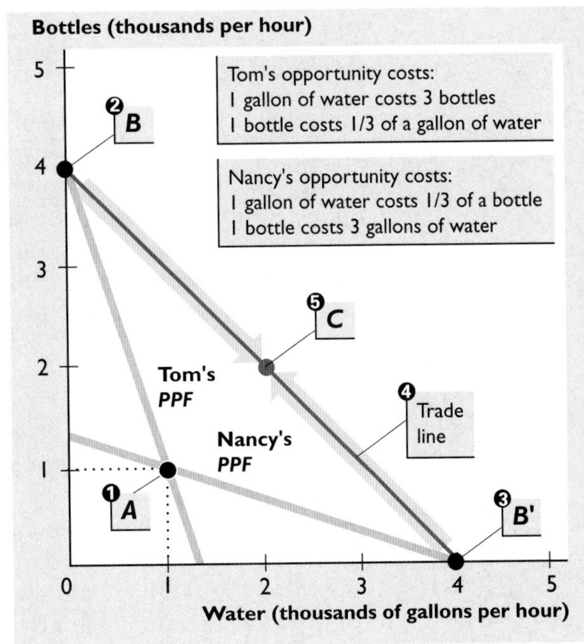

❹ They exchange water for bottles along the red "Trade line." Nancy buys bottles from Tom for less than her opportunity cost of producing them, and Tom buys water from Nancy for less than his opportunity cost of producing it.

❺ Each goes to point *C*—a point outside his or her individual *PPF*—where each has 2,000 bottles of water an hour. Tom and Nancy increase production with no change in resources.

gallon instead of 3 bottles per gallon. Nancy gets her bottles more cheaply and Tom gets his water more cheaply than when they produced both water and bottles.

Absolute Advantage

Suppose that Nancy invents a production process that makes her four times as productive as she was before in the production of both water and bottles. With her new technology, Nancy now has an **absolute advantage**—she is more productive than Tom in both activities.

Absolute advantage
When one person is more productive than another person in several or even all activities.

But Nancy does not have a *comparative* advantage in both goods. She can produce four times as much of *both* goods as before, but her *opportunity cost* of 1 bottle is still 3 gallons of water. Her opportunity cost is higher than Tom's. So Nancy can still get bottles at a lower cost by trading water for bottles with Tom.

The key point to recognize is that it is *not* possible for *anyone* to have a comparative advantage in everything, even though they might have an absolute advantage in everything. So gains for specialization and trade are always available when opportunity costs diverge.

The principle of comparative advantage and the gains from specialization and exchange explain why each individual specializes in a small range of economic activities. It is also the driving force behind international trade. Mexico and the United States, like Tom and Nancy, can *both* gain by specializing in the activities in which they have a comparative advantage and trading with each other. The absolute advantage of the United States is no obstacle to reaping mutual gains from trade.

CHECKPOINT 3.4

Study Guide pp. 46–48 

*e*Foundations 3.4 

4 **Explain how specialization and trade expand production possibilities.**

Practice Problem 3.4

Tony and Patty produce scooters and snowboards. Figure 1 shows their production possibilities per day.

a. Calculate Tony's opportunity cost of a snowboard.
b. Calculate Patty's opportunity cost of a snowboard.
c. Who has a comparative advantage in producing snowboards?
d. Who has a comparative advantage in producing scooters?
e. If they specialize and trade, how many snowboards and scooters will they produce?

FIGURE 1

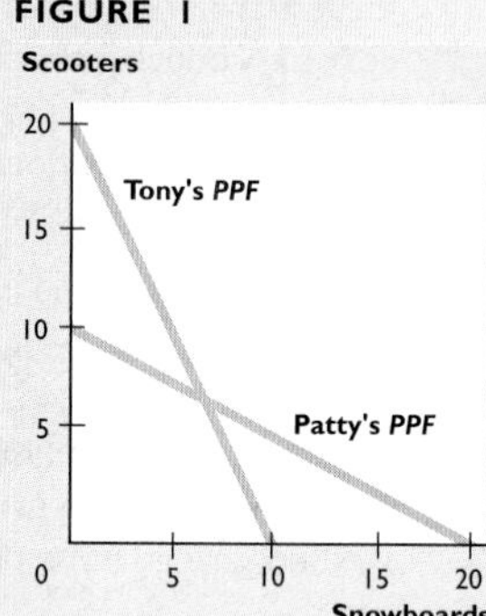

FIGURE 2

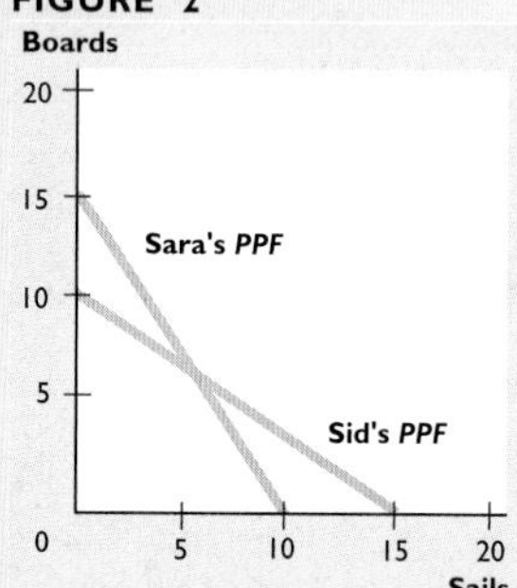

Exercises 3.4

1. Sara and Sid produce boards and sails for windsurfing. Figure 2 shows their production possibilities per day.
   a. Calculate Sara's opportunity cost of a board.
   b. Calculate Sid's opportunity cost of a board.
   c. Who has a comparative advantage in producing boards?
   d. Who has a comparative advantage in producing sails?
   e. If they specialize and trade, how many boards and sails will they produce?
2. Sid in Exercise 1 installs a new machine that doubles his production possibilities.
   a. Who now has a comparative advantage in producing boards?
   b. Are there any gains for Sara and Sid if they specialize and trade? Explain why or why not.

Solution to Practice Problem 3.4

a. Tony's opportunity cost of a snowboard is 2 scooters. If Tony uses all his resources to make scooters, he can make 20 a day. If he uses all his resources to make snowboards, he can make 10 a day. For each snowboard made, Tony forgoes making 2 scooters.

b. Patty's opportunity cost of a snowboard is ½ of a scooter. If Patty uses all her resources to make scooters, she can make 10 a day. If she uses all her resources to make snowboards, she can make 20 a day. For each snowboard made, Patty forgoes making ½ of a scooter.

c. Patty has a comparative advantage in producing snowboards because her opportunity cost of a snowboard is less than Tony's.

d. Tony has a comparative advantage in producing scooters. For each scooter made, Tony forgoes making ½ of a snowboard. His opportunity cost of a scooter is ½ of a snowboard. For each scooter made, Patty forgoes making 2 snowboards. Her opportunity cost of a scooter is 2 snowboards. Tony's opportunity cost is lower than Patty's.

e. Patty specializes in snowboards, and Tony specializes in scooters. Together, they produce 20 snowboards and 20 scooters.

CHAPTER CHECKPOINT

Key Points

1 Use the production possibilities frontier to illustrate the economic problem.

- The production possibilities frontier, *PPF*, describes the limits to what we can produce by fully and efficiently using all our available resources.
- Points inside and on the *PPF* are attainable. Points outside the *PPF* are unattainable.

2 Calculate opportunity cost.

- Along the *PPF*, the opportunity cost of X (the item in the x-axis) is the decrease in Y (the item on the y-axis) divided by the increase in X.
- The opportunity cost of Y is the inverse of the opportunity cost of X.
- The opportunity cost of producing a good increases as the quantity of the good produced increases.
- Opportunity cost increases because resources are not equally productive in all activities.

3 Define efficiency and describe an efficient use of resources.

- Production efficiency and allocative efficiency deliver an efficient use of resources.
- Production efficiency occurs at *all* points *on* the *PPF*. Points *inside* the *PPF* are inefficient.
- The point on the *PPF* that achieves allocative efficiency is the one at which marginal cost equals marginal benefit.

4 Explain how specialization and trade expand production possibilities.

- People differ in their production abilities.
- A person has a comparative advantage in an activity if he or she can perform that activity at a lower opportunity cost than someone else.
- We gain by specializing in the activity in which we have a comparative advantage and trading.

Key Terms

Exercises

1. People can now obtain music from Web sites such as Napster and MP3.
   a. How has the *PPF* for recorded music and other goods and services changed?
   b. Is there still a tradeoff between recorded music and other goods and services, or is the opportunity cost of recorded music now zero?

2. AIDS has become an acute problem in Africa.
   a. How has the spread of AIDS influenced the *PPF* of the economies of Africa?
   b. Has the spread of AIDS increased the opportunity cost of some goods and services? Has it decreased the opportunity cost of anything?

TABLE 1

Entertainment (units)		Good food (units)
100	and	0
80	and	30
60	and	50
40	and	60
20	and	65
0	and	67

3. On Survivor Island, the only resources are 5 units of capital and 10 hours of labor a day. Table 1 shows the maximum quantities of entertainment and good food that Survivor Island can produce.
   a. Draw Survivor Island's production possibilities frontier.
   b. If Survivor Island produces 50 units of entertainment and 50 units of good food, is its production attainable? Are all its resources fully employed? What is the opportunity cost of a unit of entertainment?
   c. If Survivor Island produces 40 units of entertainment and 60 units of good food, is its production attainable? Is there a tradeoff? What is the opportunity cost of a unit of entertainment?
   d. What can you say about the opportunity cost of a unit of good food as Survivor Island allocates more resources to producing good food?
   e. What is the marginal cost of a unit of entertainment when Survivor Island produces 60 units of entertainment and 50 units of good food?
   f. If the efficient quantity of entertainment is 40 units, what is the marginal benefit from entertainment?

TABLE 2

Robot services (units)		Other goods and services (units)
0	and	2,000
1	and	1,900
2	and	1,700
3	and	1,400
4	and	1,000
5	and	500

4. Table 2 shows the quantities of robots and other goods and services that the country Alpha can produce along its production possibilities frontier.
   a. If Alpha increases its production of robots from 0 to 1 a year, what is the opportunity cost of the robot? Explain.
   b. If Alpha increases its production of robots from 0 a year to 2 a year, what is the opportunity cost of producing the 2 robots? Explain.

5. In 8 hours, Willy can produce either 50 sundaes or 20 pizzas. In 8 hours, Wendy can produce either 20 sundaes or 50 pizzas.
   a. Calculate Willy's opportunity cost of a sundae.
   b. Calculate Wendy's opportunity cost of a sundae.
   c. Who has a comparative advantage in producing pizzas?
   d. If Willy and Wendy specialize, how many sundaes and how many pizzas will they produce?

6. Tom can produce either 5 kites and 3 jigsaw puzzles an hour or 3 kites and 4 jigsaw puzzles an hour. Tessa can produce either 6 kites and 2 jigsaw puzzles an hour or 2 kites and 5 jigsaw puzzles an hour.
   a. Who has a comparative advantage in producing kites?
   b. Tom and Tessa specialize in producing the good in which they have a comparative advantage. Who produces kites and who produces jigsaw puzzles?
   c. Would Tom and Tessa get any gains from specializing production and trading with each other?

Chapter 4

Demand and Supply

CHAPTER CHECKLIST

When you have completed your study of this chapter, you will be able to:

1 **Distinguish between quantity demanded and demand and explain what determines demand.**

2 **Distinguish between quantity supplied and supply and explain what determines supply.**

3 **Explain how demand and supply determine price and quantity in a market and explain the effects of changes in demand and supply.**

Because we face scarcity, we must make choices. One of these choices is to specialize in the activity in which we have a comparative advantage. Because we specialize, we sell the services of our factors of production in factor markets and we buy the goods and services that we consume in goods markets.

In this chapter, you study the tools of demand and supply that explain how markets work. You will learn how the choices people make about what to buy and sell determine the quantities and prices of the goods and services produced and consumed and the quantities of the factors of production employed.

Throughout your course in microeconomics, you will use these demand and supply tools to understand the forces that allocate scarce resources. Soon, you will find yourself using the tools of demand and supply in your everyday life whenever you need to think about a price or a quantity.

COMPETITIVE MARKETS

When you need a new pair of running shoes, want a bagel and a latte, plan to upgrade your stereo system, or need to fly home for Thanksgiving, you must find a place where people sell those items or offer those services. The place in which you find them is a *market*. You learned in Chapter 3 that a market is any arrangement that brings buyers and sellers together. A market has two sides: buyers (demanders) and sellers (suppliers). There are markets for *goods* such as apples and hiking boots, for *services* such as haircuts and tennis lessons, for *resources* such as computer programmers and earthmovers, and for other manufactured *inputs* such as memory chips and auto parts. There are also markets for money such as Japanese yen and for financial securities such as Yahoo! stock. Only imagination limits what can be traded in markets.

Some markets are physical places where the buyers and sellers meet and where an auctioneer or a broker helps to determine the prices. Examples of this type of market are the New York Stock Exchange and wholesale fish, meat, and produce markets.

Some markets are groups of people spread around the world who never meet and know little about each other but are connected through the Internet or by telephone. Examples of this type of market are the e-commerce markets and currency markets.

But most markets are unorganized collections of buyers and sellers. You do most of your trading in this type of market. An example is the market for basketball shoes. The buyers in this $3 billion-a-year market are the 45 million Americans who play basketball (or those who want to make a fashion statement) and are looking for a new pair of shoes. The sellers are the tens of thousands of retail sports equipment and footwear stores. Each buyer can visit several different stores, and each seller knows that the buyer has a choice of stores.

Markets vary in the intensity of competition that buyers and sellers face. In this chapter, we're going to study a *competitive market* that has so many buyers and so many sellers that no one can influence the price.

4.1 DEMAND

First, we'll study the behavior of buyers in a competitive market. The **quantity demanded** of any good, service, or resource is the amount that people are willing and able to buy during a specified period and at a specified price. For example, when spring water costs $1 a bottle, you decide to buy 2 bottles a day. The 2 bottles a day is your quantity demanded of spring water.

Quantity demanded
The amount of any good, service, or resource that people are willing and able to buy during a specified period at a specified price.

The quantity demanded is measured as an amount *per unit of time*. For example, your quantity demanded of water is 2 bottles *per day*. We could express this quantity as 14 bottles per week or some other number per month or per year. But without a time dimension, a particular number of bottles has no meaning.

Many things influence buying plans, and one of them is price. We look first at the relationship between quantity demanded and price. To study this relationship, we keep all other influences on buying plans the same and we ask: How, other things remaining the same, does the quantity demanded of a good change as its price varies? The law of demand provides the answer.

The Law of Demand

The **law of demand** states:

> **Other things remaining the same, if the price of a good rises, the quantity demanded of that good decreases; and if the price of a good falls, the quantity demanded of that good increases.**

So the law of demand states that when all else remains the same, if the price of a Palm Pilot falls, people will buy more Palm Pilots; or if the price of a baseball ticket rises, people will buy fewer tickets.

Why does the quantity demanded increase if the price falls, all other things remaining the same?

The answer is that, faced with a limited budget, people always have an incentive to find the best deals they can. If the price of one item falls and the prices of all other items remain the same, the item with the lower price is a better deal than it was before. So people buy more of this item. Suppose, for example, that the price of bottled water fell from $1 a bottle to 25 cents a bottle while the price of Gatorade remained at $1 a bottle. Wouldn't some people switch from Gatorade to water? By doing so, they save 75 cents a bottle, which they can spend on other things they previously couldn't afford.

Think about the things that you buy and ask yourself: Which of these items does *not* obey the law of demand? If the price of a new textbook were lower, other things remaining the same (including the price of a used textbook), would you buy more new textbooks? Then think about all the things that you do not now buy but would if you could afford them. How cheap would a PC have to be for you to buy *both* a desktop and a laptop? There is a price that is low enough to entice you!

Demand Schedule and Demand Curve

Demand is the relationship between the *quantity demanded* and the *price* of a good when all other influences on buying plans remain the same. The quantity demanded is *one* quantity at *one* price. *Demand* is a *list of quantities at different prices* illustrated by a demand schedule and a demand curve.

Demand
The relationship between the quantity demanded and the price of a good when all other influences on buying plans remain the same.

Demand schedule
A list of the quantities demanded at each different price when all other influences on buying plans remain the same.

Demand curve
A graph of the relationship between the quantity demanded of a good and its price when all other influences on buying plans remain the same.

A **demand schedule** is a list of the quantities demanded at each different price when all the other influences on buying plans remain the same. The table in Figure 4.1 is one person's (Tina's) demand schedule for bottled water. It tells us that if the price of water is $2 a bottle, Tina buys no water. Her quantity demanded is 0 bottles a day. If the price of water is $1.50 a bottle, her quantity demanded is 1 bottle a day. Tina's quantity demanded increases to 2 bottles a day at a price of $1.00 a bottle and to 3 bottles a day at a price of 50 cents a bottle.

A **demand curve** is a graph of the relationship between the quantity demanded of a good and its price when all the other influences on buying plans remain the same. The points on the demand curve labeled *A* through *D* represent the rows *A* through *D* of the demand schedule. For example, point *B* on the graph represents row *B* of the demand schedule and shows that the quantity demanded is 1 bottle a day when the price is $1.50 a bottle. Point C on the demand curve represents row C of the demand schedule and shows that the quantity demanded is 2 bottles a day when the price is $1.00 a bottle.

The downward slope of the demand curve illustrates the law of demand. Along the demand curve, when the price of the good *falls*, the quantity demanded *increases*. For example, in Figure 4.1, when the price of a bottle of water falls from $1.00 to 50 cents, the quantity demanded increases from 2 bottles a day to 3 bottles a day. And when the price *rises*, the quantity demanded *decreases*. For example, when the price rises from $1.00 to $1.50 a bottle, the quantity demanded decreases from 2 bottles a day to 1 bottle a day.

FIGURE 4.1
Demand Schedule and Demand Curve

*e*Foundations 4.1 

The table shows a demand schedule, which lists the quantity of water demanded at each price if all other influences on buying plans remain the same. At a price of $1.50 a bottle, the quantity demanded is 1 bottle a day.

The demand curve shows the relationship between quantity demanded and price, everything else remaining the same. The downward-sloping demand curve illustrates the law of demand. When the price falls, the quantity demanded increases; and when the price rises, the quantity demanded decreases.

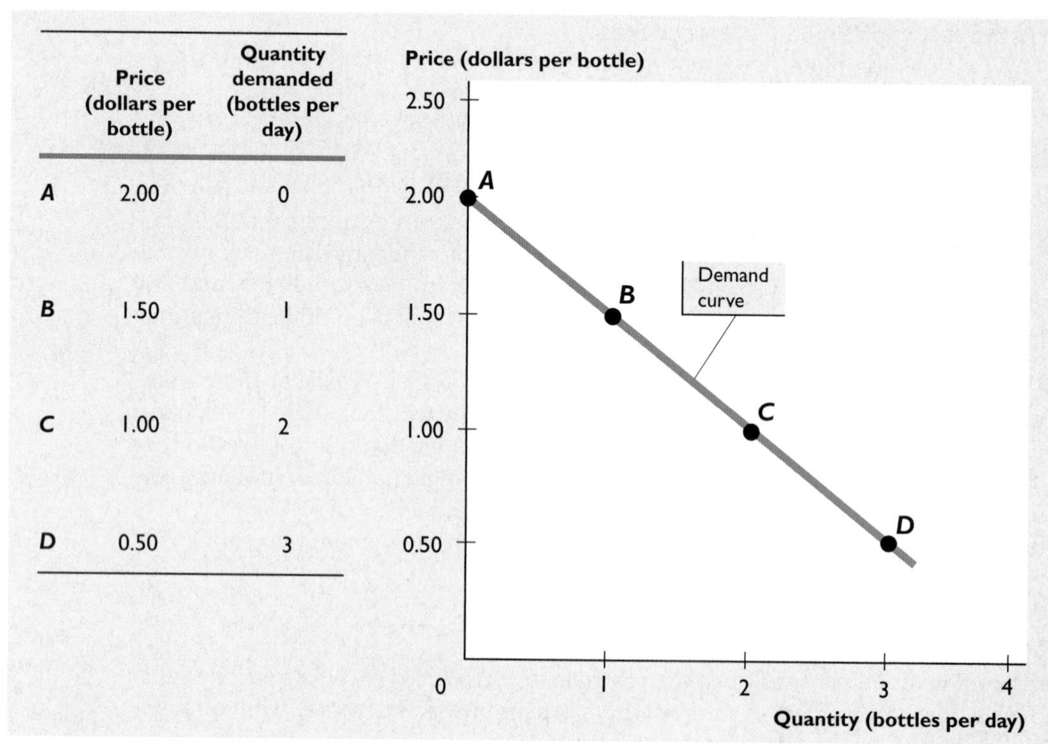

	Price (dollars per bottle)	Quantity demanded (bottles per day)
A	2.00	0
B	1.50	1
C	1.00	2
D	0.50	3

Individual Demand and Market Demand

The demand schedule and the demand curve that you've just studied are for one person. To study a market, we must determine the market demand.

Market demand is the sum of the demands of all the buyers in a market. To find the market demand, imagine a market in which there are only two buyers: Tina and Tim. The table in Figure 4.2 shows three demand schedules: Tina's, Tim's, and the market demand schedule. Tina's demand schedule is the same as before. It shows the quantity of water demanded by Tina at each different price. Tim's demand schedule tells us the quantity of water demanded by Tim at each price. To find the quantity of water demanded in the market, we sum the quantities demanded by Tina and Tim. For example, at a price of $1.00 a bottle, the quantity demanded by Tina is 2 bottles a day, the quantity demanded by Tim is 1 bottle a day, and so the quantity demanded in the market is 3 bottles a day.

Tina's demand curve in part (a) and Tim's demand curve in part (b) are graphs of the two individual demand schedules. The market demand curve in part (c) is a graph of the market demand schedule. At a given price, the quantity demanded on the market demand curve equals the sum of the quantities demanded on the individual demand curves.

Market demand
The sum of the demands of all the buyers in a market.

FIGURE 4.2
Individual Demand and Market Demand

*e*Foundations 4.1 

Price (dollars per bottle)	Quantity demanded (bottles per day)				
	Tina		Tim		Market
2.00	0		0		0
1.50	1		0		1
1.00	2	+	1	=	3
0.50	3		2		5

The market demand schedule is the sum of the individual demand schedules, and the market demand curve is the horizontal sum of the individual demand curves.

At a price of $1 a bottle, the quantity demanded by Tina is 2 bottles a day and the quantity demanded by Tim is 1 bottle a day, so the total quantity demanded in the market is 3 bottles a day.

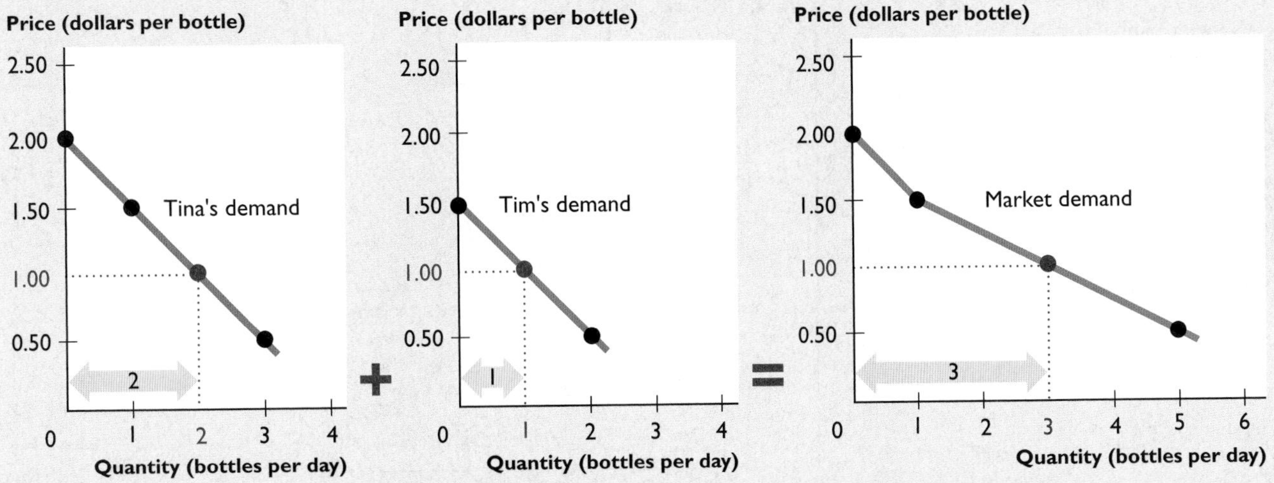

(a) Tina's demand

(b) Tim's demand

(c) Market demand

Changes in Demand

Change in the quantity demanded
A change in the quantity of a good that people plan to buy that results from a change in the price of the good.

Change in demand
A change in the quantity that people plan to buy when any influence on buying plans other than the price of the good changes.

The demand curve shows how the quantity demanded changes when the price changes but *all other influences on buying plans remain the same.* When the price changes, we call the resulting change in buying plans a **change in the quantity demanded**, and we illustrate this change by a movement along the demand curve.

When any influence on buying plans other than the price of the good changes, there is a **change in demand**. When demand changes, *the demand curve shifts.* Figure 4.3 illustrates two changes in demand. Initially, the demand curve is D_0. When the demand for bottled water decreases, the demand curve shifts leftward to D_1. On demand curve D_1, the quantity demanded is smaller at each price. And when the demand for bottled water increases, the demand curve shifts rightward to D_2. On demand curve D_2, the quantity demanded is greater at each price.

The main influences on buying plans that change demand are:

- Prices of related goods
- Income
- Expectations
- Number of buyers
- Preferences

Prices of Related Goods

Substitute
A good that can be consumed in place of another good.

A change in the price of one good can bring a change in the demand for a related good. Related goods are either substitutes or complements. A **substitute** for a good is another good that can be consumed in its place. Chocolate cake is a substitute for cheesecake, a taxi ride is a substitute for a subway ride, and bottled water is a substitute for Gatorade.

FIGURE 4.3
Changes in Demand

*e*Foundations 4.1 

A change in any influence on buyers' plans, other than a change in the price of the good itself, changes demand and shifts the demand curve.

❶ When demand decreases, the demand curve shifts leftward from D_0 to D_1.

❷ When demand increases, the demand curve shifts rightward from D_0 to D_2.

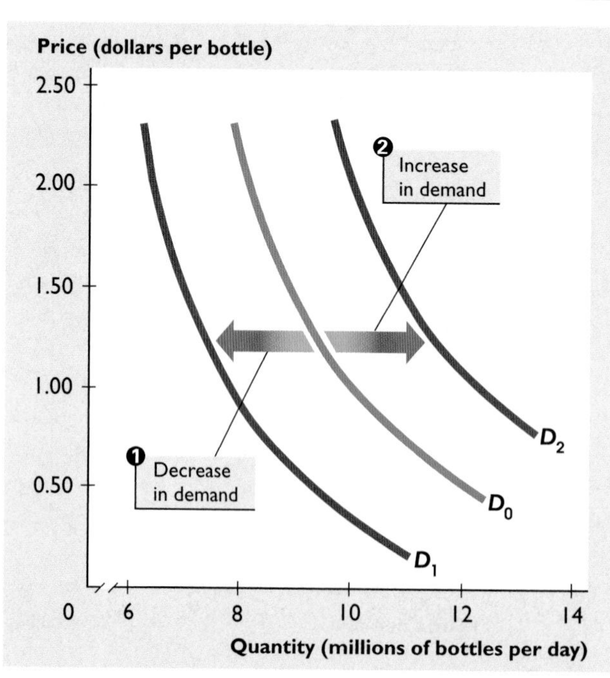

A **complement** of a good is another good that is consumed with it. Salsa is a complement of tortilla chips, wrist guards are a complement of in-line skates, and bottled water is a complement of fitness center services.

Complement
A good that is consumed with another good.

A Change in the Price of a Substitute The demand for a good *increases* if the price of one of its substitutes *rises*; and the demand for a good *decreases* if the price of one of its substitutes *falls*. That is, the demand for a good and the price of one of its substitutes move in the *same direction*. For example, cheesecake and chocolate cake are substitutes, so the demand for cheesecake increases when the price of chocolate cake rises.

A Change in the Price of a Complement The demand for a good *decreases* if the price of one of its complements *rises*; and the demand for a good *increases* if the price of one of its complements *falls*. That is, the demand for a good and the price of one of its complements move in the *opposite direction*. For example, salsa and tortilla chips are complements, so the demand for salsa decreases when the price of tortilla chips *rises*.

Income

A good is a **normal good** if a rise in income brings an increase in demand and a fall in income brings a decrease in demand. For example, if you buy more bottled water when your income increases, then bottled water is a normal good. Most goods are normal goods (hence the name). A good is an **inferior good** if a rise in income brings a *decrease* in demand and a fall in income brings an *increase* in demand. For example, if when your income increases, you buy fewer plastic milk crates and more bookcases, then a plastic milk crate is an inferior good.

Normal good
A good for which the demand increases when income increases.

Inferior good
A good for which the demand decreases when income increases.

Expectations

Expected future income and prices influence demand. For example, you are offered a well-paid summer job, so you go to Cancun during spring break. Your demand for vacation travel has increased. Or if you expect the price of ramen to rise next week, you buy a big enough stockpile of it to get you through the rest of the school year. Your demand for ramen has increased.

Number of Buyers

The greater the number of buyers in a market, the larger is demand. For example, the demand for parking spaces, movies, bottled water, or just about anything is greater in New York City than it is in Boise, Idaho.

Preferences

Tastes or, as economists call them, *preferences* influence demand. When preferences change, the demand for one item increases and the demand for another item (or items) decreases. For example, preferences have changed as people have become better informed about the health hazards of tobacco. This change in preferences has decreased the demand for cigarettes and increased the demand for nicotine patches.

Preferences also change when new goods become available. For example, the development of MP3 technology has decreased the demand for CDs and increased the demand for Internet services and personal computers.

Demand: A Summary

Let's now summarize what you've learned about demand. A change in any influence on buyers' plans causes either a *change in the quantity demanded* or a *change in demand*. When you are thinking about the influences on demand, it is a good idea to get into the habit of asking yourself: Does this influence change the quantity demanded or does it change demand?

The distinction is crucial for figuring out how a market responds to the forces that hit it. The test for which of these two changes is occurring is simple. If the price of the good changes, other things remaining the same, there is a change in the quantity demanded and a movement along the demand curve. If any influence other than the price of the good changes, there is a change in demand and a shift of the demand curve.

Figure 4.4 illustrates and summarizes these distinctions:

- If the price of bottled water *rises* when everything else remains the same, the quantity demanded of bottled water *decreases* and there is a *movement up* the demand curve D_0. If the price *falls* when everything else remains the same, the quantity demanded *increases* and there is a *movement down* the demand curve D_0.
- If some other influence on buyers' plans changes, there is a change in demand. When the demand for bottled water *decreases*, the demand curve *shifts leftward* (to the red demand curve D_1). When the demand for bottled water *increases*, the demand curve *shifts rightward* (to the red demand curve D_2).

FIGURE 4.4

Change in Quantity Demanded Versus Change in Demand

*e*Foundations 4.1 

❶ A decrease in the quantity demanded

If the price of a good rises, *cet. par.*, the quantity demanded decreases. There is a movement up along the demand curve D_0.

❷ A decrease in demand

Demand decreases and the demand curve shifts leftward (from D_0 to D_1) if:

- The price of a substitute falls.
- The price of a complement rises.
- The price of the good is expected to fall or income is expected to fall in the future.
- Income decreases.*
- The number of buyers decreases.

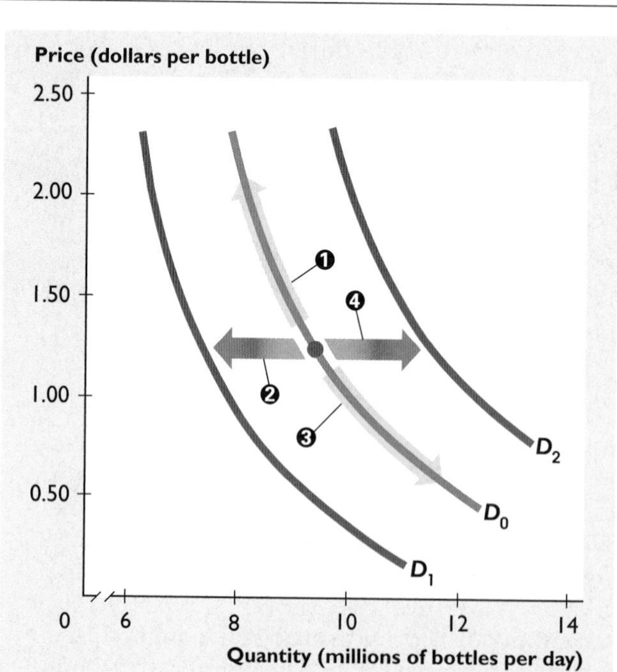

❸ An increase in the quantity demanded

If the price of a good falls, *cet. par.*, the quantity demanded increases. There is a movement down along the demand curve D_0.

❹ An increase in demand

Demand increases and the demand curve shifts rightward (from D_0 to D_2) if:

- The price of a substitute rises.
- The price of a complement falls.
- The price of the good is expected to rise or income is expected to rise in the future.
- Income increases.*
- The number of buyers increases.

* Bottled water is a normal good.

CHECKPOINT 4.1

1 Distinguish between quantity demanded and demand and explain what determines demand.

Study Guide pp. 55–58 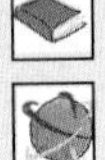

***e*Foundations 4.1**

Practice Problem 4.1

In the market for scooters, several events occur, one at a time. Explain the influence of each event on the quantity demanded of scooters and on the demand for scooters. Illustrate the effects of each event by either a movement along the demand curve or a shift in the demand curve for scooters, and say which event (or events) illustrates the law of demand in action. These events are:

a. The price of a scooter falls.
b. The price of a bicycle falls.
c. Citing rising injury rates, cities and towns ban scooters from sidewalks.
d. Average income increases.
e. Rumor has it that the price of a scooter will rise next month.
f. The number of buyers increases.

Exercise 4.1

The Internet was born in 1969, and during the first 20 years of its life, it was used mainly by scientists in universities and research laboratories. But during the 1990s, the use of Internet service increased dramatically and the price per hour of Internet service fell.

a. Are there any substitutes for Internet service? If so, provide an example.
b. Are there any complements to Internet service? If so, provide an example.
c. What are the main developments that brought about the dramatic increase in the quantity of Internet service during the 1990s?
d. Which of the developments that you have identified in (c) increased the demand for Internet service? Illustrate these effects by using the demand curve for Internet service.
e. Which of the developments that you have identified in (c) increased the quantity demanded of Internet service? Illustrate these effects by using the demand curve for Internet service.

FIGURE 1

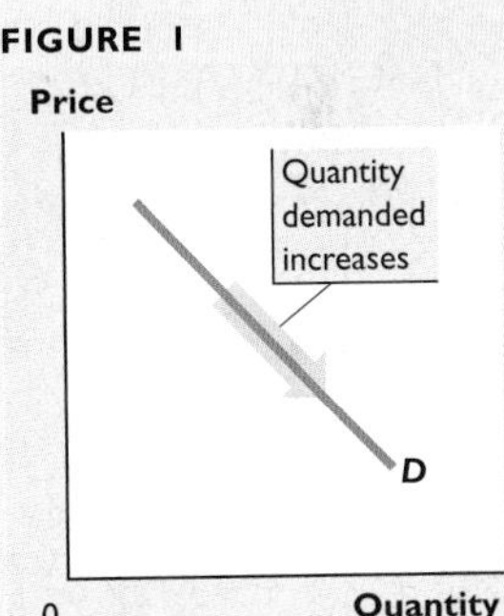

Solution to Practice Problem 4.1

a. A fall in the price of a scooter increases the quantity demanded of scooters, shown by a movement down along the demand curve for scooters (Figure 1) and is an example of the law of demand in action.
b. A bicycle is a substitute for a scooter. So when the price of a bicycle falls, the demand for scooters decreases.
c. The ban on scooters on sidewalks changes preferences and decreases the demand for scooters.

In **b** and **c**, the demand curve shifts leftward (Figure 2).

d. A scooter is (likely) a normal good. So when the average income increases, the demand for scooters increases.
e. A rise in the expected price of a scooter increases the demand for scooters now.
f. An increase in the number of buyers increases the demand for scooters.

In **d**, **e**, and **f**, the demand curve for scooters shifts rightward (Figure 2).

FIGURE 2

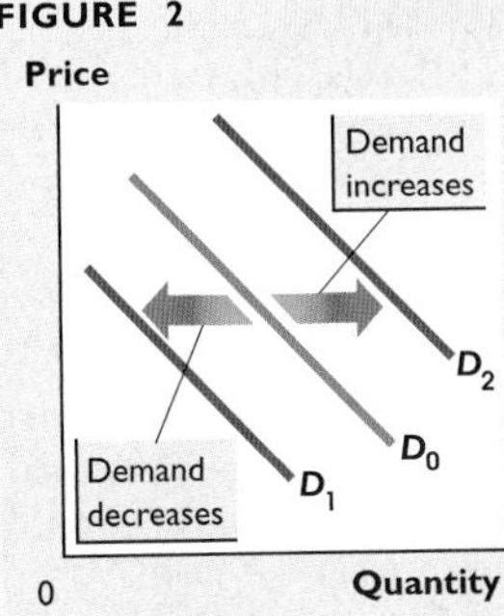

4.2 SUPPLY

A market has two sides. On one side are the buyers, or demanders, that we've just studied. On the other side of the market are the sellers, or suppliers. We now study the forces that determine suppliers' plans.

Quantity supplied
The amount of any good, service, or resource that people are willing and able to sell during a specified period at a specified price.

The **quantity supplied** of a good or service or resource is the amount that people are willing and able to sell during a specified period and at a specified price. For example, when the price of spring water is $1.50 a bottle, a spring owner decides to sell 2,000 bottles a day. The 2,000 bottles a day is the quantity supplied of spring water by this individual producer. (As in the case of demand, the quantity supplied is measured as an amount *per unit of time*.)

Many things influence selling plans, and one of them is the price. We look first at the relationship between quantity supplied of a good and its price. To study this relationship, we keep all other influences on selling plans the same. And we ask: How, other things remaining the same, does the quantity supplied of a good change as its price varies? The law of supply provides the answer.

The Law of Supply

The **law of supply** states:

> **Other things remaining the same, if the price of a good rises, the quantity supplied of that good increases; and if the price of a good falls, the quantity supplied of that good decreases.**

So the law of supply states that when all else remains the same, if the price of bottled water rises, spring owners will offer more water for sale; if the price of a CD falls, Sony Corp. will offer fewer CDs for sale.

Why, other things remaining the same, does the quantity supplied increase if the price rises and decrease if the price falls?

The basic answer is that, faced with scarce resources, suppliers have an incentive to use their resources in the way that brings the biggest return. If the price of what they sell rises and the prices of all other items remain the same, the item with the higher price brings a greater return than it did before. So suppliers will want to sell more of this item. Suppose, for example, that the price of bottled water rose from $1 a bottle to $2 a bottle while the prices of everything else, including wages and other costs, remained the same. Wouldn't the spring owners offer more water for sale? By doing so, they receive an extra $1 a bottle.

Think about the resources that you own and can offer for sale to others and ask yourself: Which of these items does *not* obey the law of supply? If the wage rate for summer jobs increased, wouldn't you be encouraged to work longer hours? If the bank offered a higher interest rate on deposits, wouldn't you be inclined to make a greater deposit in the bank? If the used book dealer offered a higher price for last year's textbooks, wouldn't you think about selling that handy math text?

Supply Schedule and Supply Curve

Supply
The relationship between the quantity supplied and the price of a good when all other influences on selling plans remain the same.

Supply is the relationship between the quantity supplied and the price of a good when all other influences on selling plans remain the same. The quantity supplied is *one* quantity at *one* price. *Supply* is a *list of quantities at different prices* illustrated by a supply schedule and a supply curve.

A **supply schedule** lists the quantities supplied at each different price when all the other influences on selling plans remain the same. The table in Figure 4.5 is one firm's (Agua's) supply schedule for bottled water. It tells us that if the price of water is 50 cents a bottle, Agua plans to sell no water. Its quantity supplied is 0 bottles a day. If the price of water is $1.00, Agua's quantity supplied is 1,000 bottles a day. Agua's quantity supplied increases to 2,000 bottles a day at a price of $1.50 a bottle and to 3,000 bottles a day at a price of $2.00 a bottle.

Supply schedule
A list of the quantities supplied at each different price when all other influences on selling plans remain the same.

A **supply curve** is a graph of the relationship between the quantity supplied of a good and its price when all the other influences on selling plans remain the same. The points on the supply curve labeled *A* through *D* represent the rows *A* through *D* of the supply schedule. For example, point *C* on the supply curve represents row C of the supply schedule and shows that the quantity supplied is 1,000 bottles a day when the price is $1.00 a bottle. Point *B* on the supply curve represents row B of the supply schedule and shows that the quantity supplied is 2,000 bottles a day when the price is $1.50 a bottle.

Supply curve
A graph of the relationship between the quantity supplied of a good and its price when all other influences on selling plans remain the same.

The upward slope of the supply curve illustrates the law of supply. Along the supply curve, when the price of the good *rises*, the quantity supplied *increases*. For example, in Figure 4.5, when the price of a bottle of water rises from $1.50 to $2.00, the quantity supplied increases from 2,000 bottles a day to 3,000 bottles a day. And when the price *falls*, the quantity supplied *decreases*. For example, when the price falls from $1.50 to $1.00 a bottle, the quantity supplied decreases from 2,000 bottles a day to 1,000 bottle a day.

FIGURE 4.5
Supply Schedule and Supply Curve

*e*Foundations 4.2 

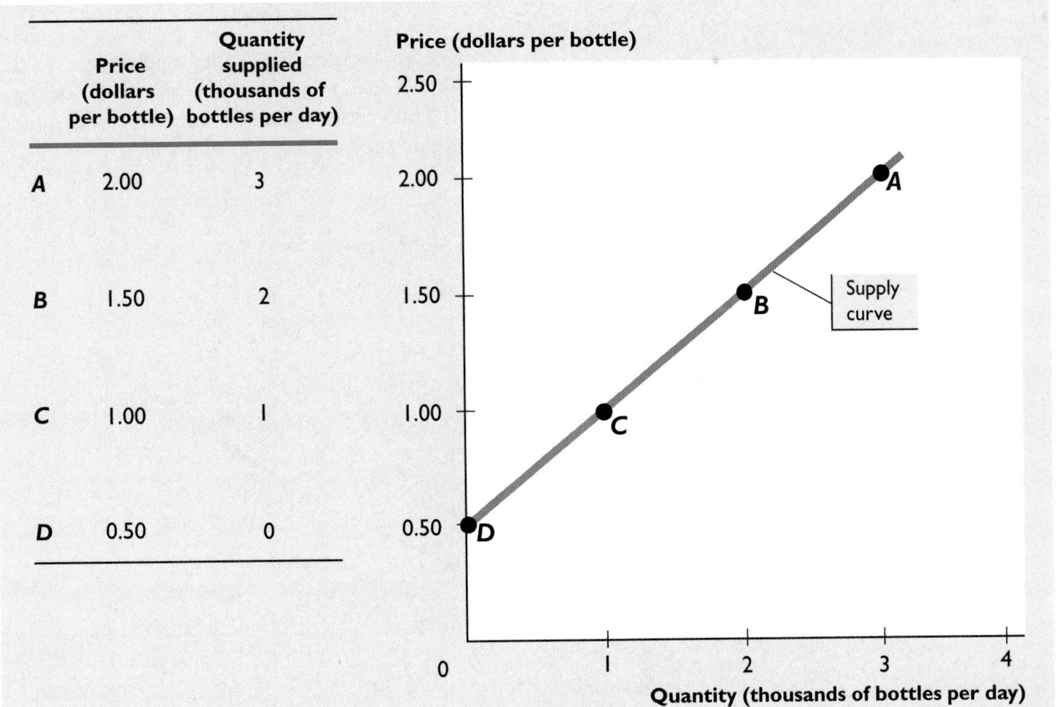

	Price (dollars per bottle)	Quantity supplied (thousands of bottles per day)
A	2.00	3
B	1.50	2
C	1.00	1
D	0.50	0

The table shows a supply schedule, which lists the quantity of water supplied at each price if all other influences on selling plans remain the same. At a price of $1.50 a bottle, the quantity supplied is 2,000 bottles a day.

The supply curve shows the relationship between quantity supplied and price, everything else remaining the same. The upward-sloping supply curve illustrates the law of supply. When the price rises, the quantity supplied increases; and when the price falls, the quantity supplied decreases.

Market supply
The sum of the supplies of all the sellers in a market.

Individual Supply and Market Supply

The supply schedule and the supply curve that you've just studied are for one seller. To study a market, we must determine the market supply.

Market supply is the sum of the supplies of all the sellers in the market. To find the market supply, imagine a market in which there are only two sellers: Agua and Prima. The table in Figure 4.6 shows three supply schedules: Agua's, Prima's, and the market supply schedule. Agua's supply schedule is the same as before. Prima's supply schedule tells us the quantity of water that Prima plans to sell at each price. To find the quantity of water supplied in the market, we sum the quantities supplied by Agua and Prima. For example, at a price of $1.00 a bottle, the quantity supplied by Agua is 1,000 bottles a day, the quantity supplied by Prima is 2,000 bottles a day, and the quantity supplied in the market is 3,000 bottles a day.

Agua's supply curve in part (a) and Prima's supply curve in part (b) are graphs of the two individual supply schedules. The market supply curve in part (c) is a graph of the market supply schedule. At a given price, the quantity supplied on the market supply curve equals the sum of the quantities supplied on the individual supply curves.

FIGURE 4.6
Individual Supply and Market Supply

*e*Foundations **4.2** 

Price (dollars per bottle)	Quantity supplied (thousands of bottles per day)		
	Agua	Prima	Market
2.00	3	4	7
1.50	2	3	5
1.00	1 +	2 =	3
0.50	0	0	0

The market supply schedule is the sum of the individual supply schedules, and the market supply curve is the horizontal sum of the individual supply curves.

At a price of $1 a bottle, the quantity supplied by Agua is 1,000 bottles a day and the quantity supplied by Prima is 2,000 bottle a day, so the total quantity supplied in the market is 3,000 bottles a day.

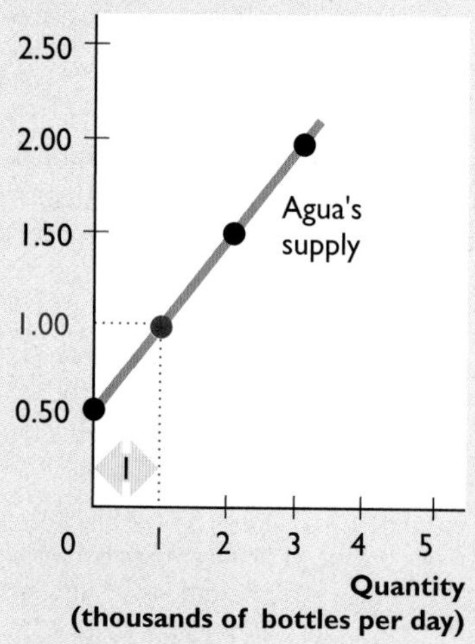

(a) Agua's supply 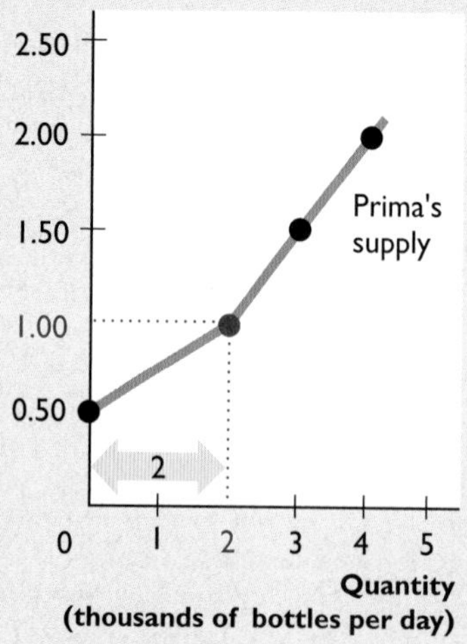 (b) Prima's supply 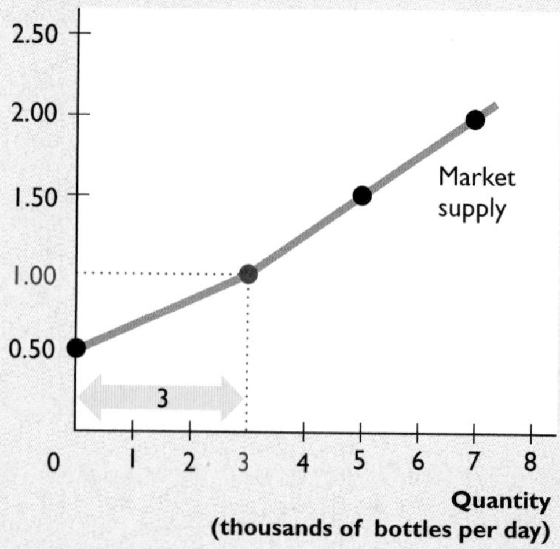 (c) Market supply

Changes in Supply

The supply curve shows how the quantity supplied changes when the price changes and *when all other influences on selling plans remain the same.* When the price changes, we call the resulting influence on selling plans the **change in the quantity supplied**, and we illustrate this change by a movement along the supply curve.

When any influence on selling plans other than the price of the good changes, there is a **change in supply**. When supply changes, *the supply curve shifts.* Figure 4.7 illustrates two changes in supply. Initially, the supply curve is S_0. When the supply of bottled water decreases, the supply curve shifts leftward to S_1. On supply curve S_1, the quantity supplied is smaller at each price. And when the supply of bottled water increases, the supply curve shifts rightward to S_2. On supply curve S_2, the quantity supplied is greater at each price.

The main influences on selling plans that change supply are:

- Prices of related goods
- Prices of resources and other inputs
- Expectations
- Number of sellers
- Productivity

Change in the quantity supplied
A change in the quantity of a good that suppliers plan to sell that results from a change in the price of the good.

Change in supply
A change in the quantity that suppliers plan to sell when any influence on selling plans other than the price of the good changes.

Prices of Related Goods

A change in the price of one good can bring a change in the supply of a related good. Related goods are either substitutes in production or complements in production. A **substitute in production** for a good is another good that can be produced in its place. Button-fly jeans are substitutes in production for cargo pants in a clothing factory, and cookie dough ice cream is a substitute in production for chocolate chip ice cream in an ice cream factory.

Substitute in production
A good that can be produced in place of another good.

FIGURE 4.7
Changes in Supply

*e*Foundations 4.2 

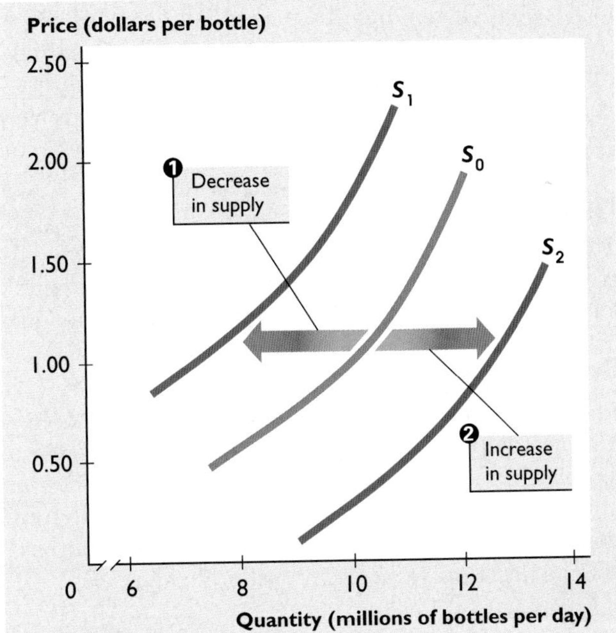

A change in any influence on sellers' plans other than a change in the price of the good itself changes supply and shifts the supply curve.

1. When supply decreases, the supply curve shifts leftward from S_0 to S_1.
2. When supply increases, the supply curve shifts rightward from S_0 to S_2.

Complement in production
A good that is produced along with another good.

A **complement in production** of a good is another good that is produced along with it. Leather is a complement in production of beef. And straw is a complement in production of wheat.

A Change in the Price of a Substitute in Production The supply of a good *decreases* if the price of one of its substitutes in production *rises;* and the supply of a good *increases* if the price of one of its substitutes in production *falls.* That is, the supply of a good and the price of one of its substitutes in production move in *opposite directions.* For example, a clothing factory can produce cargo pants or button-fly jeans, so these goods are substitutes in production. The supply of cargo pants decreases when the price of button-fly jeans rises.

A Change in the Price of a Complement in Production The supply of a good *increases* if the price of one of its complements in production *rises;* and the supply of a good *decreases* if the price of one of its complements in production *falls.* That is, the supply of a good and the price of one of its complements in production move in the *same direction.* For example, when a slaughterhouse produces beef, it also produces cowhide, so these goods are complements in production. The supply of cowhide increases when the price of beef rises.

Prices of Resources and Other Inputs

Supply changes when the price of a resource or other input used to produce the good changes. The reason is that resource and input prices influence the cost of production. And the more it costs to produce a good, the smaller is the quantity supplied of that good at each price (other things remaining the same). For example, if the wage rate of bottling-plant workers rises, it costs more to produce a bottle of water. So the supply of bottled water decreases.

Expectations

Expectations about future prices have a big influence on supply. For example, a real estate developer in Salt Lake City expects the price of a condominium to rise as the 2002 Winter Olympics approaches. So instead of selling units now, she plans to sell them later when the price is higher. This action decreases the current supply of condominiums in Salt Lake City. Expectations of future input prices also influence supply. If the developer expects builders' wages to rise sharply next year, she might build more condominiums this year before the wage increase occurs. This action increases the current supply of condominiums.

Number of Sellers

The greater the number of sellers in a market, the larger is the supply. For example, many new sellers have developed springs and water-bottling plants in the United States and the supply of bottled water has increased.

Productivity

Productivity is output per unit of input. An increase in productivity lowers costs and increases supply. A decrease in productivity has the opposite effect and decreases supply. Technological change is the main influence on productivity. For example, advances in electronic technology have lowered the cost of computers and increased their supply. Natural events such as weather patterns change farm productivity and change the supply of agricultural products.

Supply: A Summary

Let's now summarize what you've learned about supply. Changes in influences on sellers' plans cause either a *change in the quantity supplied* or a *change in supply*. Just as in the case of demand, when you are thinking about the influences on supply, try to develop the habit of asking yourself: Does this influence change the quantity supplied or does it change supply?

The test for which of these two changes is occurring is simple. If the price of the good changes, other things remaining the same, there is a change in the quantity supplied and a movement along the supply curve. If any influence other than the price of the good changes, there is a change in supply and a shift of the supply curve.

Figure 4.8 illustrates and summarizes these distinctions:

- If the price of bottled water *falls* when other things remain the same, the quantity supplied of bottled water *decreases* and there is a *movement down* the supply curve S_0. If the price *rises* when other things remain the same, the quantity supplied *increases* and there is a *movement up* the supply curve S_0.
- If any other influence on water bottlers' plans changes, there is a change in the supply of bottled water. When the supply of bottled water *decreases*, the supply curve *shifts leftward* (to the red supply curve S_1). When the supply of bottled water *increases*, the supply curve *shifts rightward* (to the red supply curve S_2).

FIGURE 4.8

Change in Quantity Supplied Versus Change in Supply

*e*Foundations 4.2 

❶ A decrease in the quantity supplied

If the price of a good falls, *cet. par.*, the quantity supplied decreases. There is a movement down along the demand curve S_0.

❷ A decrease in supply

Supply decreases and the supply curve shifts leftward (from S_0 to S_1) if:

- The price of a substitute in production rises.
- The price of a complement in production falls.
- A resource price or other input price rises.
- The price of the good is expected to rise.
- The number of sellers decreases.

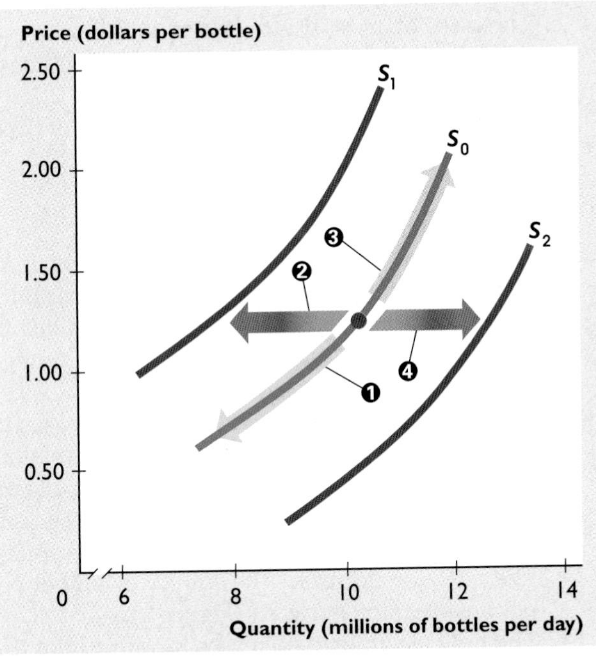

❸ An increase in the quantity supplied

If the price of a good rises, *cet. par.*, the quantity supplied increases. There is a movement up along the supply curve S_0.

❹ An increase in supply

Supply increases and the supply curve shifts rightward (from S_0 to S_2) if:

- The price of a substitute in production falls.
- The price of a complement in production rises.
- A resource price or other input price falls.
- The price of the good is expected to fall.
- The number of sellers increases.

CHECKPOINT 4.2

Study Guide pp. 58–62

*e*Foundations 4.2

2 Distinguish between quantity supplied and supply and explain what determines supply.

Practice Problem 4.2

In the market for timber beams, several events occur one at a time. Explain the influence of each event on the quantity supplied of timber beams and the supply of timber beams. Illustrate the effects of each event by either a movement along the supply curve or a shift of the supply curve of timber beams, and say which event (or events) illustrates the law of supply in action. The events are:

a. The wage rate of sawmill workers rises.
b. The price of sawdust rises.
c. The price of a timber beam rises.
d. The price of a timber beam is expected to rise next year.
e. Environmentalists convince Congress to introduce a new law that reduces the amount of forest that can be cut for timber products.
f. A new technology lowers the cost of producing timber beams.

Exercise 4.2

In the market for SUVs, several events occur one at a time. Explain the influence of each event on the quantity supplied of SUVs and the supply of SUVs. Illustrate the effects of each event by either a movement along the supply curve or a shift of the supply curve of SUVs, and say which event (or events) illustrates the law of supply in action. The events are:

a. The price of a truck rises.
b. The price of an SUV falls.
c. The price of an SUV is expected to fall next year.
d. An SUV engine defect requires a huge and costly manufacturer's recall to replace the defective engines.
e. A new robot technology lowers the cost of producing SUVs.

FIGURE 1

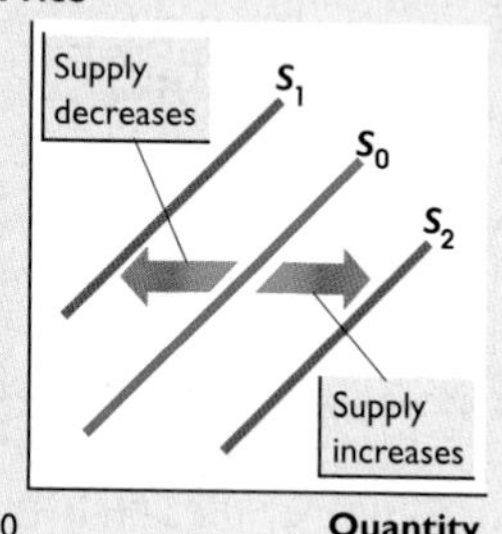

FIGURE 2

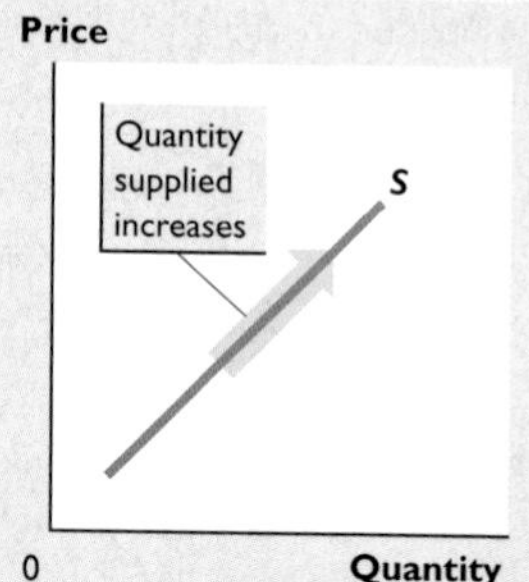

Solution to Practice Problem 4.2

a. A rise in the wage rate of sawmill workers decreases the supply of timber beams. The supply curve of timber beams shifts leftward (Figure 1).
b. Sawdust and timber beams are complements in production. An rise in the price of sawdust increases the supply of timber beams. The supply curve of timber beams shifts rightward (Figure 1).
c. A rise in the price of a timber beam increases the quantity supplied of timber beams, which is shown as a movement up along the supply curve of timber beams and is an example of the law of supply in action (Figure 2).
d. The expected rise in the price of a timber beam decreases the supply of timber beams. The supply curve of timber beams shifts leftward (Figure 1).
e. The new law decreases the supply of timber beams. The supply curve of timber beams shifts leftward (Figure 1).
f. The new technology increases the supply of timber beams and shifts the supply curve rightward (Figure 1).

4.3 MARKET EQUILIBRIUM

In everyday language, "equilibrium" means "opposing forces are in balance." In a market, the opposing forces are those of demand and supply. Buyers want the lowest possible price, and the lower the price, the greater is the quantity that they plan to buy. Sellers want the highest possible price, and the higher the price, the greater is the quantity that they plan to sell.

Market equilibrium occurs when the quantity demanded equals the quantity supplied—when buyers' and sellers' plans are consistent. The **equilibrium price** is the price at which the quantity demanded equals the quantity supplied. The **equilibrium quantity** is the quantity bought and sold at the equilibrium price.

Figure 4.9 shows the market for bottled water. The market equilibrium occurs where the demand curve and the supply curve intersect. The equilibrium price is $1 a bottle, and the equilibrium quantity is 10 million bottles a day.

At the equilibrium price, buying plans and selling plans are balanced. People would buy more water at a lower price, and bottlers would sell more water at a higher price. But at a price of $1 a bottle, the quantity that people plan to buy equals the quantity that bottlers plan to sell. The opposing forces of buying plans and selling plans are exactly balanced at a price of $1 a bottle.

An equilibrium might be stable or unstable. Balance an egg on its pointed end (if you can!) and then give it a nudge. The egg rolls over onto its side. The equilibrium was unstable. Now balance an egg on its side and give it a nudge. The egg rocks for a moment but soon settles down in its equilibrium again. Market equilibrium is like an egg balanced on its side. The market is constantly pulled toward a stable equilibrium in which neither buyers nor sellers can improve their positions by changing either the price or the quantity.

Market equilibrium
When the quantity demanded equals the quantity supplied—when buyers' and sellers' plans are consistent.

Equilibrium price
The price at which the quantity demanded equals the quantity supplied.

Equilibrium quantity
The quantity bought and sold at the equilibrium price.

FIGURE 4.9
Equilibrium Price and Equilibrium Quantity

*e*Foundations 4.3 

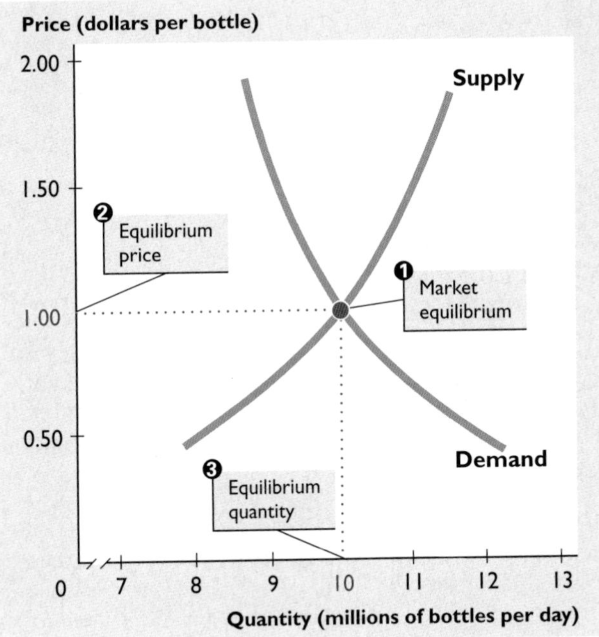

❶ Market equilibrium occurs at the intersection of the demand curve and the supply curve.

❷ The equilibrium price is $1 a bottle.

❸ At the equilibrium price, the quantity demanded and the quantity supplied are 10 million bottles a day, which is the equilibrium quantity.

Price: A Market's Automatic Regulator

When equilibrium is disturbed, market forces restore it. The **law of market forces** states:

> **When there is a shortage, the price rises; and when there is a surplus, the price falls.**

Surplus or excess supply
A situation in which the quantity supplied exceeds the quantity demanded.

Shortage or excess demand
A situation in which the quantity demanded exceeds the quantity supplied.

Price is the regulator that pulls the market toward its equilibrium. If the price is above the equilibrium price, there is a **surplus** or **excess supply**—the quantity supplied exceeds the quantity demanded—and the price falls. If the price is below the equilibrium price, there is a **shortage** or **excess demand**—the quantity demanded exceeds the quantity supplied—and the price rises.

In Figure 4.10(a), at $1.50 a bottle, suppliers plan to sell 11 million bottles but demanders buy only 9 million bottles. There is a surplus of 2 million bottles. Suppliers cut the price. As the price falls, the quantity demanded increases, the quantity supplied decreases, and the surplus decreases. The price falls until there is no surplus and comes to rest at $1 a bottle.

In Figure 4.10(b), at 75 cents a bottle, demanders plan to buy 11 million bottles but suppliers sell only 9 million bottles. There is a shortage of 2 million bottles. Suppliers raise the price. As the price rises, the quantity supplied increases, the quantity demanded decreases, and the shortage decreases. The price rises until there is no shortage and comes to rest at $1 a bottle.

FIGURE 4.10
The Forces that Achieve Equilibrium

*e*Foundations 4.3 

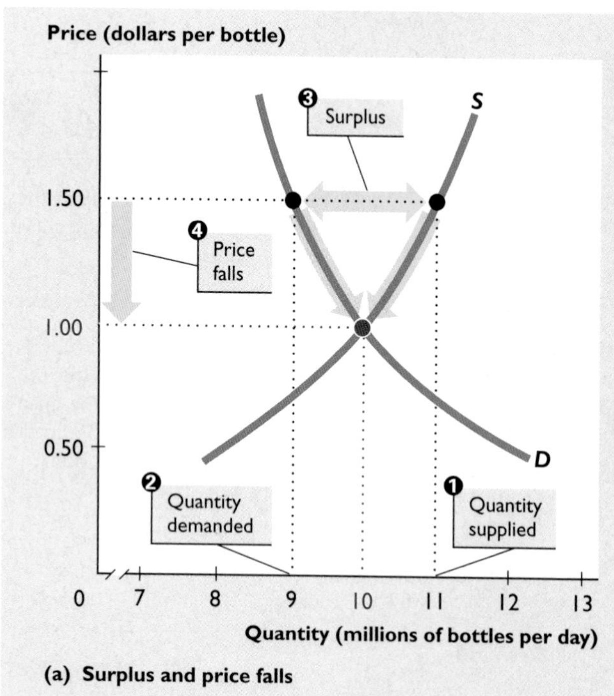

(a) Surplus and price falls

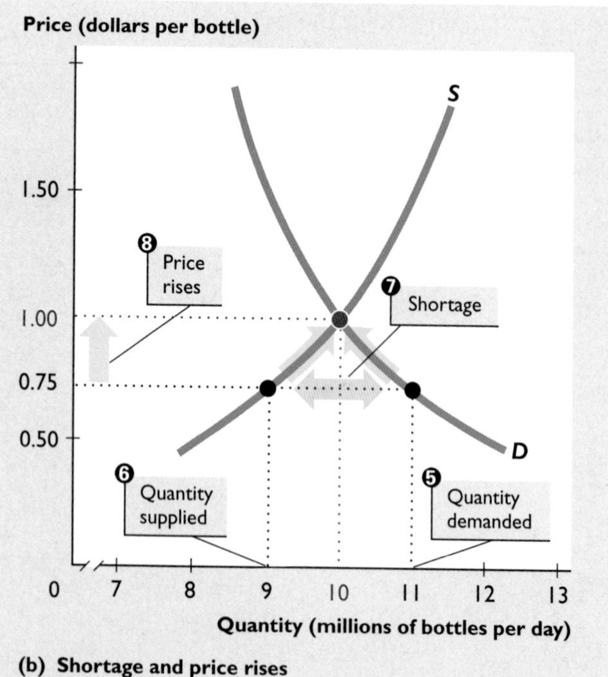

(b) Shortage and price rises

At $1.50 a bottle, ❶ the quantity supplied is 11 million bottles, ❷ the quantity demanded is 9 million bottles, ❸ the surplus is 2 million bottles, and ❹ the price falls.

At 75 cents a bottle, ❺ the quantity demanded is 11 million bottles, ❻ the quantity supplied is 9 million bottles, ❼ the shortage is 2 million bottles, and ❽ the price rises.

Effects of Changes in Demand

Markets are constantly hit by events that change demand and supply and bring changes in price and quantity. Some events change only demand, some change only supply, and some change *both* demand and supply. We'll look at all the possible cases. But we'll look first at the effects of changes in demand.

In Figure 4.11, the supply curve is *S* and, initially, the demand curve is D_0. The equilibrium price is $1 a bottle, and the equilibrium quantity is 10 million bottles.

Suppose that a new study is published that raises concerns about the safety of the public water supply. The demand for bottled water increases. In Figure 4.11(a), the demand curve *shifts rightward* to D_1. At $1 a bottle, there is now a shortage, so the price rises and the quantity supplied increases. The price rises to $1.50 a bottle, and the quantity increases to 11 million bottles a day.

Next, suppose that a new zero-calorie sports drink is invented and the demand for bottled water decreases. In Figure 4.11(b), the demand curve *shifts leftward* to D_2. At the initial price of $1 a bottle, there is now a surplus, so the price falls and the quantity supplied decreases. The price falls to 75 cents a bottle, and the quantity decreases to 9 million bottles a day.

In both cases, when demand changes, there is *no change in supply*. But there is a *change in the quantity supplied*—a movement along the supply curve.

FIGURE 4.11

The Effects of a Change in Demand

*e*Foundations 4.3 

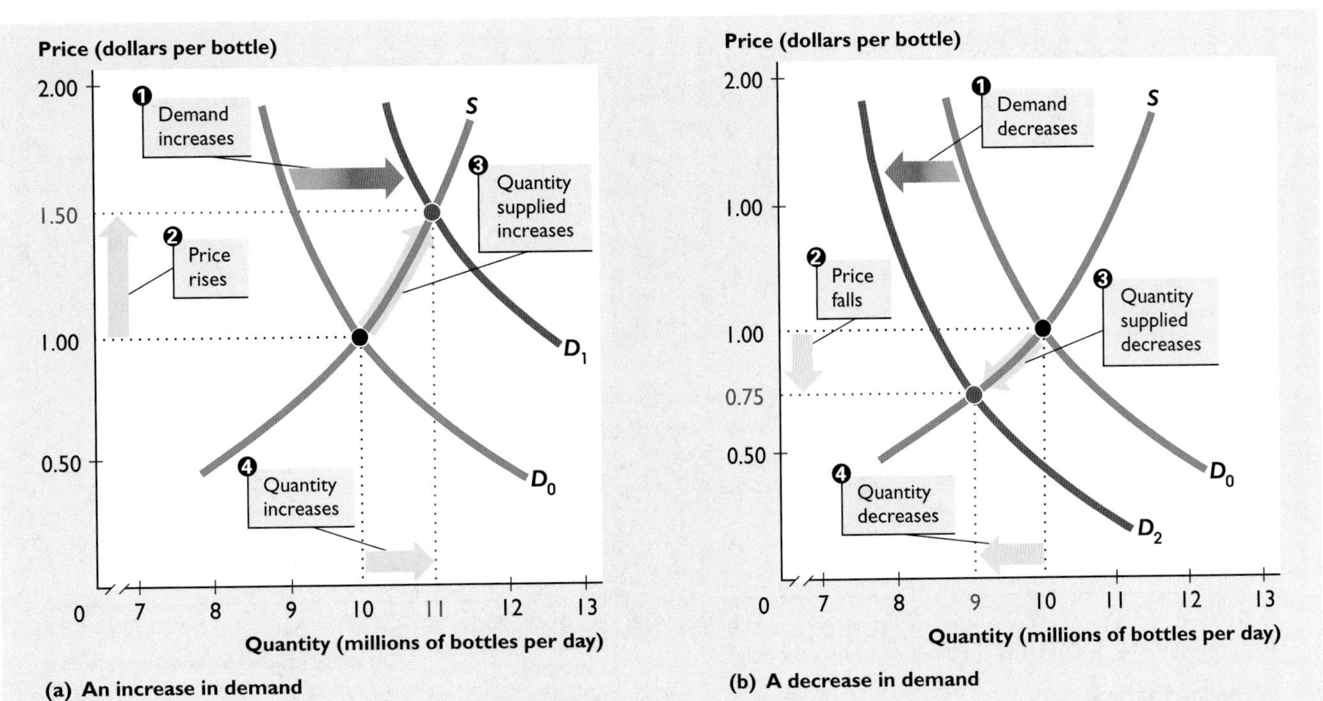

An increase in demand ❶ shifts the demand curve rightward to D_1, ❷ raises the price, ❸ increases the quantity supplied, and ❹ increases the equilibrium quantity.

A decrease in demand ❶ shifts the demand curve leftward to D_2, ❷ lowers the price, ❸ decreases the quantity supplied, and ❹ decreases the equilibrium quantity.

Effects of Changes in Supply

Let's now work out what happens when supply changes.

In Figure 4.12, the demand curve is D and, initially, the supply curve is S_0. The equilibrium price is $1 a bottle, and the equilibrium quantity is 10 million bottles.

Suppose that European water bottlers buy springs and open up bottling plants in the United States. The supply of bottled water increases. In Figure 4.12(a), the supply curve shifts rightward to S_1. At the initial price of $1 a bottle, there is now a surplus, so the price falls and the quantity demanded increases. The price falls to 75 cents a bottle, and the quantity increases to 11 million bottles a day.

When supply changes, there is *no change in demand*. But there is a *change in the quantity demanded*—a movement along the demand curve.

Next, suppose that a drought dries up some springs and the supply of bottled water decreases. In Figure 4.12(b), the supply curve shifts leftward to S_2. At the initial price of $1 a bottle, there is now a shortage, so the price rises and the quantity demanded decreases. The price rises to $1.50 a bottle, and the quantity decreases to 9 million bottles a day.

The new equilibrium price is $1.50 a bottle. Again, there is *no change in demand*. There is a *decrease in the quantity demanded* (movement along the demand curve). The equilibrium quantity decreases to 9 million bottles a day.

FIGURE 4.12
The Effects of a Change in Supply

*e*Foundations **4.3** 

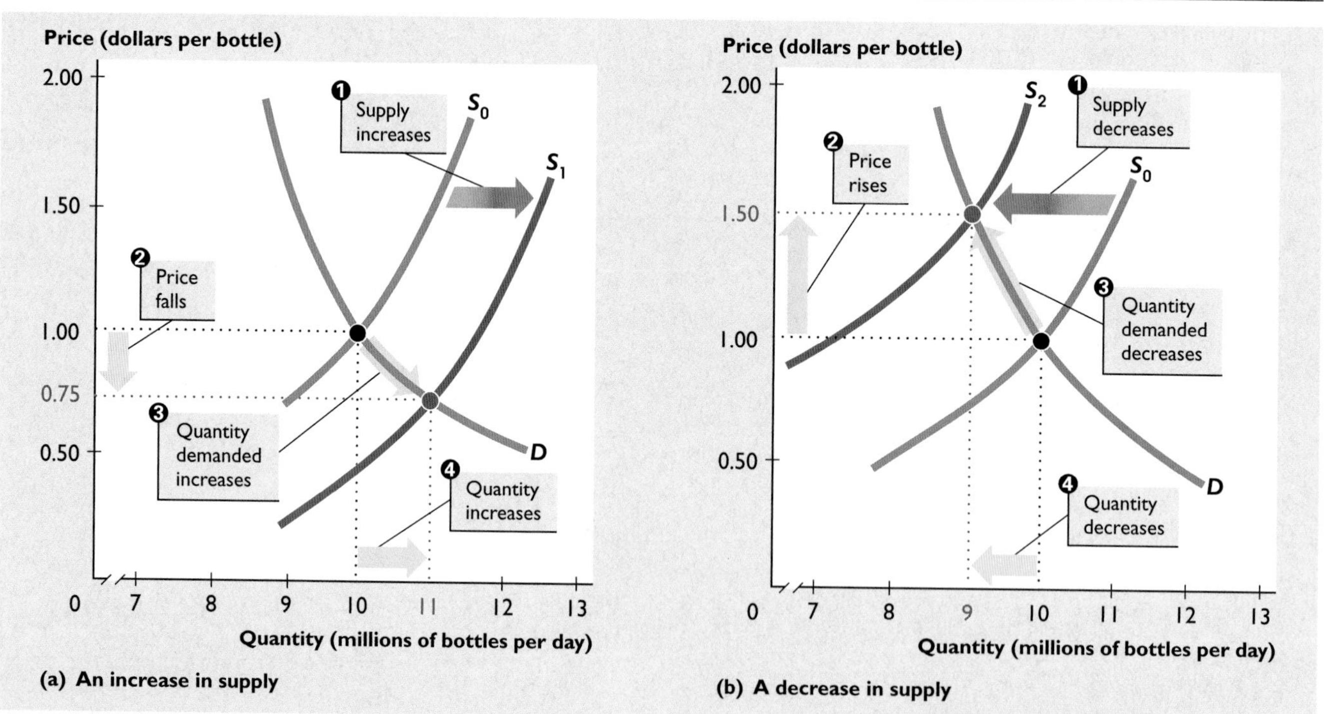

An increase in supply ❶ shifts the supply curve rightward to S_1, ❷ lowers the price, ❸ increases the quantity demanded, and ❹ increases the equilibrium quantity.

A decrease in supply ❶ shifts the supply curve leftward to S_2, ❷ raises the price, ❸ decreases the quantity demanded, and ❹ decreases the equilibrium quantity.

A Change in the Demand for Roses

Colombia and Ecuador grow most of the world's roses. On the average, the quantity of roses sold worldwide is around 6 million bunches a month. And the average price that consumers pay is around $40 a bunch.

But one month, February, is not a normal month. Each year, in February, the quantity of roses bought increases to four times that of any other month. The reason: Valentine's Day. And on Valentine's Day, the price of a bunch of roses doubles.

The demand-supply model explains these facts. The figure shows the supply curve of roses and two demand curves. The blue demand curve is the demand for roses in a normal month. This demand curve intersects the supply curve at an equilibrium price of $40 a bunch and an equilibrium quantity of 6 million bunches.

In February, the demand curve shifts rightward to the red curve. The February demand curve for roses intersects the supply curve at an equilibrium price of $80 a bunch and an equilibrium quantity of 24 million bunches.

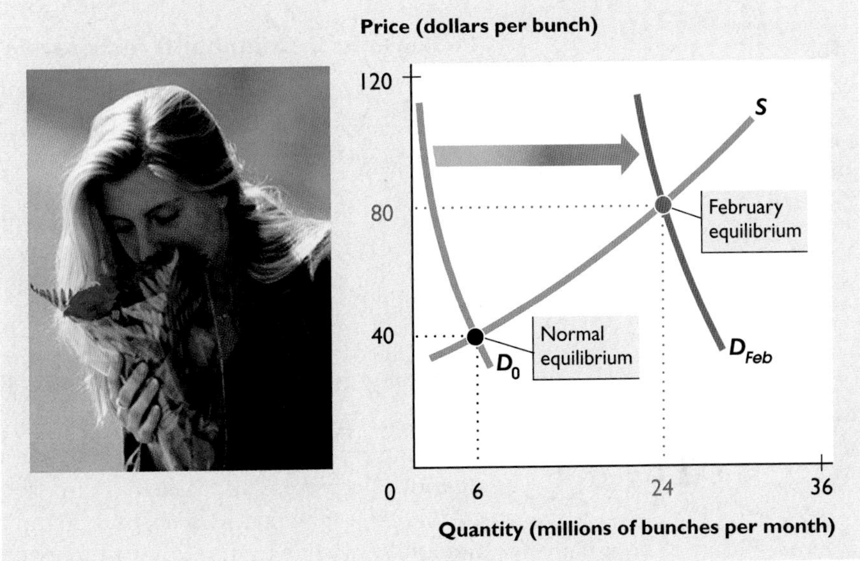

Changes in the Supply of Oil

The price of oil tumbled from $31 a barrel in 1983 to $16 a barrel in 1989. The price then jumped to $21 a barrel in 1991. The quantity of oil consumed fluctuated in the direction opposite to these price changes.

Over this period, rising income increased demand. But more fuel-efficient cars, airplanes, and furnaces offset this increase, and the demand for oil remained constant. Supply increased from 1983 through 1989 and this increase lowered the equilibrium price and increased the quantity.

The Gulf War of 1991 decreased supply, which raised the equilibrium price and decreased the quantity.

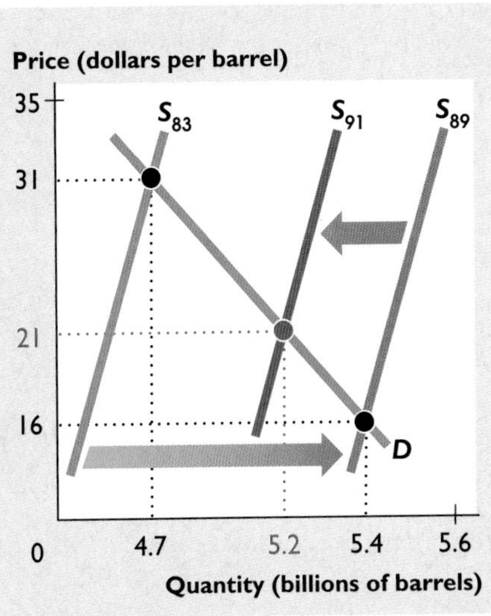

SOURCE: Energy Information Administration.

Changes in Both Demand and Supply

Often events occur that change *both* demand and supply. To study the effects of such changes on price and quantity, we combine the effects of a change in demand and a change in supply.

Increase in Demand and Increase in Supply

An increase in demand increases the quantity, and an increase in supply increases the quantity. So when demand and supply increase together, the equilibrium quantity increases. But an increase in demand raises the price, and an increase in supply lowers the price. So when demand and supply increase together, the direction of the change in the equilibrium price is ambiguous. It might rise, fall, or stay the same. Figure 4.13(a) illustrates an increase in both demand and supply in the market for personal computers. In this example, the price falls because the increase in supply is greater than the increase in demand.

Decrease in Demand and Decrease in Supply

A decrease in demand decreases the quantity, and a decrease in supply decreases the quantity. So when demand and supply decrease together, the equilibrium quantity decreases. But a decrease in demand lowers the price, and a decrease in supply raises the price. So when demand and supply decrease together, the direction of the change in the equilibrium price is ambiguous. It might rise, fall, or stay the same. Figure 4.13(b) illustrates a decrease in both demand and supply in the

FIGURE 4.13

Demand and Supply Change in the Same Direction

*e*Foundations 4.3 

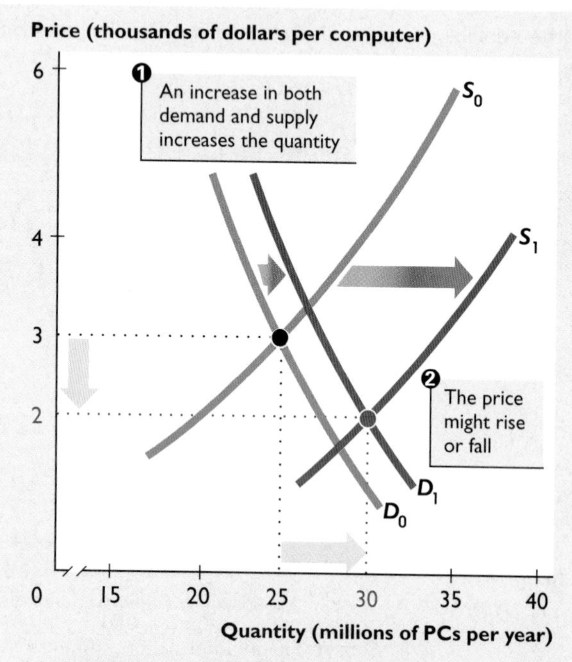

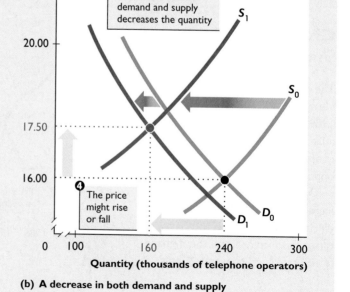

(a) An increase in both demand and supply

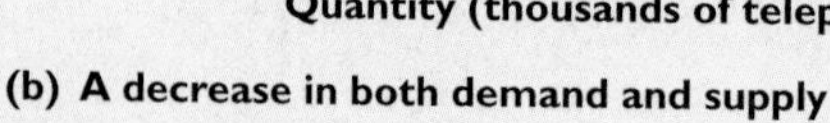

(b) A decrease in both demand and supply

market for telephone operators in the United States over the past 20 years. In this example, the price (the telephone operator's wage rate) rises because the decrease in supply exceeds the decrease in demand.

Increase in Demand and Decrease in Supply

When demand increases, the price rises. When supply decreases, the price rises. So when demand increases at the same time as supply decreases, the equilibrium price rises. But an increase in demand increases the quantity, and a decrease in supply decreases the quantity. So when demand increases and at the same time supply decreases, the equilibrium quantity can increase, decrease, or remain the same. Figure 4.14(a) illustrates this case in the market for Yahoo! stock. In this example, the quantity remains the same because the increase in demand equals the decrease in supply.

Decrease in Demand and Increase in Supply

When demand decreases, the price falls. When supply increases, the price falls. So when demand decreases at the same time as supply increases, the equilibrium price falls. But a decrease in demand decreases the quantity, and an increase in supply increases the quantity. So when demand decreases and at the same time supply increases, the equilibrium quantity can increase, decrease, or remain the same. Figure 4.14(b) illustrates this case in the market for the currency of Thailand, called the baht, in 1997. In this example, the quantity remains the same because the decrease in demand equals the increase in supply.

August 25, 2000

Expensive Winter Looms

During 2000, crude oil inventories hit a 24-year low; a pipeline exploded in New Mexico; and a hurricane in the Gulf of Mexico put natural gas supplies at risk.

A strong economy and the spread of the PC (which uses as much electricity as a refrigerator) increased the demand for energy.

Use the demand and supply model to predict how these events will change the prices and quantities in energy markets.

 *e*Foundations 4.3

FIGURE 4.14

Demand and Supply Change in Opposite Directions

*e*Foundations 4.3 

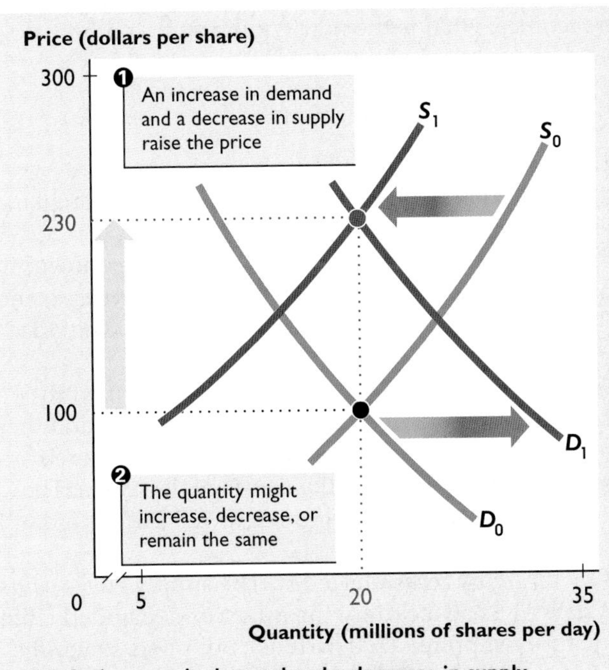

(a) An increase in demand and a decrease in supply

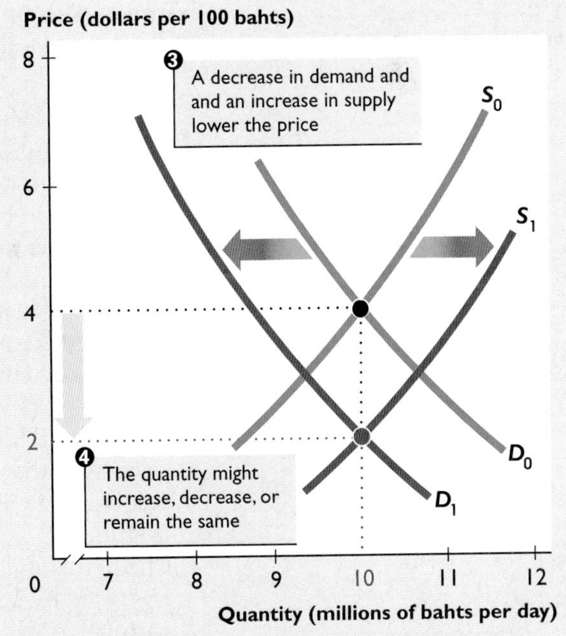

(b) A decrease in demand and an increase in supply

CHECKPOINT 4.3

Study Guide pp. 62–65 

*e*Foundations 4.3

3 **Explain how demand and supply determine price and quantity in a market and explain the effects of changes in demand and supply.**

Practice Problem 4.3

Price (dollars per carton)	Quantity demanded (cartons per day)	Quantity supplied (cartons per day)
1.00	200	110
1.25	175	130
1.50	150	150
1.75	125	170
2.00	100	190

The table shows the demand and supply schedules for milk:

a. What is the market equilibrium in the milk market?

b. Describe the situation in the milk market if the price were $1.75 a carton.

c. If the price is $1.75 a carton, explain how the market reaches equilibrium.

d. A drought decreases the quantity supplied by 45 cartons a day at each price. What is the new equilibrium and how does the market adjust to it?

e. Milk becomes more popular and the quantity demanded increases by 5 cartons a day at each price. Better feeds increase the quantity of milk supplied by 50 cartons a day at each price. If there is no drought, what is the new equilibrium, and how does the market adjust to it?

Exercise 4.3

Price (dollars per CD)	Quantity demanded (CDs per day)	Quantity supplied (CDs per day)
5.00	300	100
6.00	250	150
7.00	200	200
8.00	150	250
9.00	100	300

The table shows the demand and supply schedules for CDs:

a. What is the market equilibrium?

b. If the price of a CD is $6.00, describe the situation in the CD market. Explain how market equilibrium is restored.

c. If a rise in incomes increases the quantity of CDs demanded by 100 a day at each price, explain how the CD market adjusts to its new equilibrium.

d. A rise in the number of recording studios increases the quantity of CDs supplied by 75 a day at each price. People download more music from the Internet and the quantity demanded of CDs decreases by 25 a day at each price. With no change in incomes, what is the new equilibrium and how does the market adjust?

Solution to Practice Problem 4.3

a. Market equilibrium occurs at $1.50 a carton and 150 cartons a day.

b. At $1.75 a carton, the quantity demanded (125 cartons) is less than the quantity supplied (170 cartons), so there is a surplus of 45 cartons a day.

c. At $1.75 a carton, there is a surplus of 45 cartons a day. As suppliers lower the price, the quantity demanded increases, the quantity supplied decreases, and the surplus decreases. The price falls until the surplus disappears. The price falls to $1.50 a carton.

d. The supply curve *shifts leftward* by 45 cartons a day. At $1.50, the quantity demanded (150 cartons) exceeds the quantity supplied (105 cartons) and there is a shortage of milk. As suppliers raise the price, the quantity demanded decreases, the quantity supplied increases, and the shortage decreases. The price rises to $1.75 a carton, and the quantity decreases to 125 cartons a day (Figure 1).

e. The demand curve *shifts rightward* by 5 cartons a day. The supply curve *shifts rightward* by 50 cartons a day. At $1.50 a carton, the quantity demanded (155 cartons) is less than the quantity supplied (200 cartons). Suppliers lower the price. The price falls to $1.25 a carton, and the quantity increases to 180 cartons a day (Figure 2).

FIGURE 1

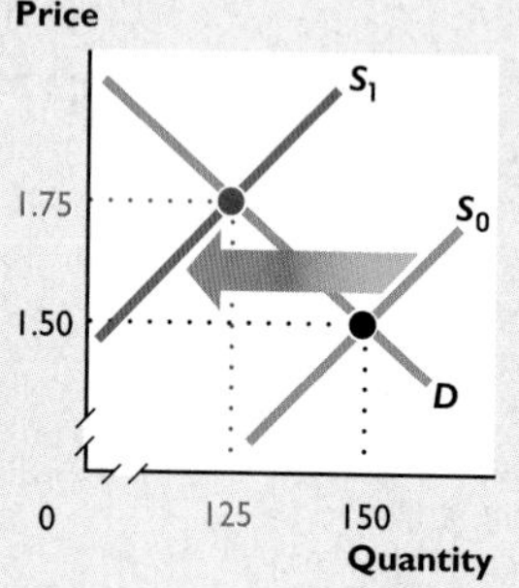

FIGURE 2

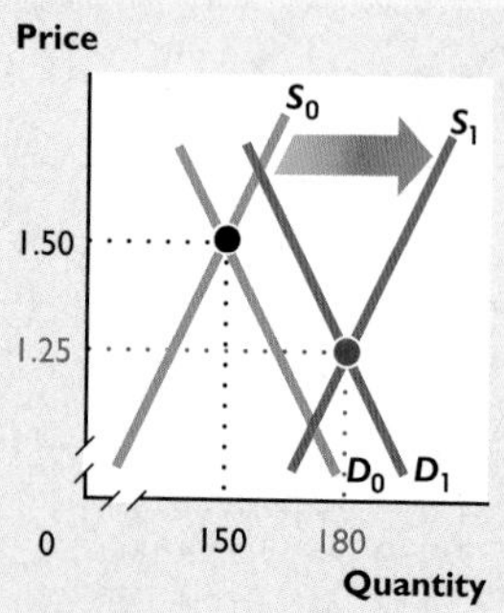

CHAPTER CHECKPOINT

Key Points

1 Distinguish between quantity demanded and demand and explain what determines demand.

- Other things remaining the same, the quantity demanded increases as the price falls and decreases as the price rises—the law of demand.
- The demand for a good is influenced by the prices of related goods, income, expectations about income and future prices, the number of buyers, and preferences. A change in any of these influences changes the demand for the good.

2 Distinguish between quantity supplied and supply and explain what determines supply.

- Other things remaining the same, the quantity supplied increases as the price rises and decreases as the price falls—the law of supply.
- The supply of a good is influenced by the prices of related goods, prices of resources and other inputs, expectations about future prices and input prices, the number of sellers, and productivity. A change in any of these influences changes the supply of the good.

3 Explain how demand and supply determine price and quantity in a market and explain the effects of changes in demand and supply.

- The law of market forces brings market equilibrium—the equilibrium price and equilibrium quantity at which buyers and sellers trade.
- The price adjusts to maintain market equilibrium—to keep the quantity demanded equal to the quantity supplied. A surplus brings a fall in the price to restore market equilibrium; a shortage brings a rise in the price to restore market equilibrium.
- Market equilibrium responds to changes in demand and supply. An increase in demand increases both the price and the quantity; a decrease in demand decreases both the price and the quantity. An increase in supply increases the quantity but decreases the price; and a decrease in supply decreases the quantity but increases the price.

Key Terms

Change in demand, 84
Change in the quantity demanded, 84
Change in the quantity supplied, 91
Change in supply, 91
Complement, 85
Complement in production, 92
Demand, 81
Demand curve, 82
Demand schedule, 82
Equilibrium price, 95
Equilibrium quantity, 95
Inferior good, 85
Law of demand, 81
Law of market forces, 96
Law of supply, 88
Market demand, 83
Market equilibrium, 95
Market supply, 90
Normal good, 85
Quantity demanded, 81
Quantity supplied, 88
Shortage or excess demand, 96
Substitute, 84
Substitute in production, 91
Supply, 88
Supply curve, 89
Supply schedule, 89
Surplus or excess supply, 96

Exercises

1. Use the link on your Foundations Web site to obtain information about the market for bottled water.
   a. How many producers are there? Does the market look competitive?
   b. Use the law of supply and demand and demand-supply diagrams to explain the changes in the price and quantity of bottled water in the past few years.
   c. Explain the effects of the bottled water market on the market for soft drinks.
   d. Explain the effects of the spread of fitness centers on the market for bottled water.
2. Use the laws of demand and supply to explain whether the following statements are true or false. In your explanation, distinguish between a change in demand and a change in the quantity demanded and between a change in supply and a change in the quantity supplied.
   a. Bananas from Africa are not sold in the United States. If they were, bananas in the United States would be cheaper.
   b. If soccer becomes more popular in the United States and basketball becomes less popular, the price of a pair of basketball shoes will rise.
   c. It is more expensive to ski in Aspen in the winter than in the spring.
   d. If the price of frozen yogurt falls, the quantity of ice cream consumed will decrease and the price of ice cream will rise.
3. What is the effect on the price and quantity of orange juice if:
   a. The price of apple juice falls?
   b. The price of apple juice falls and the wage rate paid to orange grove workers rises?
   c. Orange juice becomes more popular and a cheaper machine for picking oranges is used?
   d. Joggers switch from bottled water to orange juice?
4. Gasoline producers invent a new fuel that is cheaper and cleaner than gasoline. All new cars use the new fuel. Use a demand-supply diagram to explain the effect of this new fuel on:
   a. The price of gasoline and the quantity of gasoline bought.
   b. The price of a used car.
5. The table shows the demand and supply schedules for mouse pads:
   a. What is the market equilibrium?
   b. If the price of a mouse pad is $7.00, describe the situation in the market. Explain how the market equilibrium is restored.
   c. Explain what happens to the market equilibrium and how the market adjusts to its new equilibrium if a fall in the price of a computer changes the quantity demanded of mouse pads by 20 a week at each price.
   d. Explain what happens to the initial market equilibrium and how the market adjusts if new voice-recognition software changes the quantity demanded by 10 mouse pads a week at each price and at the same time the cost of producing a mouse pad falls and changes the quantity supplied by 30 a week at each price.

Price (dollars per pad)	Quantity demanded	Quantity supplied
	(mouse pads per week)	
3.00	160	120
4.00	150	130
5.00	140	140
6.00	130	150
7.00	120	160
8.00	110	170

6. "As more people buy computers, the demand for Internet service will increase and the price of an Internet service will fall. The fall in the price of an Internet service will decrease the supply of Internet services." Is this statement true or false? Explain your answer.

Part 2

A Closer Look at Markets

Chapter 5

Elasticities of Demand and Supply

CHAPTER CHECKLIST

When you have completed your study of this chapter, you will be able to:

1. **Define, explain the factors that influence, and calculate the price elasticity of demand.**
2. **Define, explain the factors that influence, and calculate the price elasticity of supply.**
3. **Define and explain the factors that influence the cross elasticity of demand and the income elasticity of demand.**

The equilibrium quantities and prices in the markets for goods, services, and factors of production determine *what, how,* and *for whom* goods and services are produced.

Changes in demand and supply bring changes in equilibrium quantities and prices. But by how much do prices and quantities change when demand and supply change? Does a frost in Florida bring a massive or a modest rise in the price of oranges? And does a smaller orange crop mean good news or bad news for orange growers? To answer these questions, we need to know more about demand and supply.

You are now going to learn about the *elasticity of demand* and the *elasticity of supply*—powerful ways of describing demand and supply that enable us to predict the magnitudes of price and quantity changes when either demand or supply changes.

We'll learn first about the price elasticity of demand, then about the price elasticity of supply, and finally about two other elasticities of demand.

5.1 THE PRICE ELASTICITY OF DEMAND

Price elasticity of demand
A measure of the extent to which the quantity demanded of a good changes when the price of the good changes and all other influences on buyers' plans remain the same.

The **price elasticity of demand** is a measure of the extent to which the quantity demanded of a good* changes when the price of the good changes and other influences on buyers' plans remain the same. To determine the price elasticity of demand, we compare the percentage change in the quantity demanded with the percentage change in price.

Percentage Change in Price

Suppose that Starbucks raises the price of a latte from $3 to $5 a cup. What is the percentage change in price? The change in price is the new price minus the initial price. And the percentage change is calculated as the change in price divided by the initial price, all multiplied by 100. The formula for the percentage change is:

$$\text{Percentage change in price} = \left(\frac{\text{New price} - \text{Initial price}}{\text{Initial price}}\right) \times 100.$$

In this example, the initial price is $3 and the new price is $5, so the percentage change in price is:

$$\text{Percentage change in price} = \left(\frac{\$5 - \$3}{\$3}\right) \times 100 = \left(\frac{\$2}{\$3}\right) \times 100 = 66.67 \text{ percent.}$$

Now suppose that Starbucks cuts the price of a latte from $5 to $3 a cup. What now is the percentage change in price? The initial price is now $5 and the new price is $3, so the percentage change in price is calculated as:

$$\text{Percentage change in price} = \left(\frac{\$3 - \$5}{\$5}\right) \times 100 = \left(\frac{-\$2}{\$5}\right) \times 100 = -40 \text{ percent.}$$

The same price change, $2, over the same interval, $3 to $5, is a different percentage change depending on whether the price rises or falls.

Because elasticity compares the percentage change in quantity demanded with the percentage change in price, we need a measure of percentage change that does not depend on the direction of the price change. The measure that economists use is called the *midpoint method.*

The Midpoint Method

To calculate the percentage change in price using the midpoint method, we divide the change in the price by the *average price*—the *average* of the initial price and the new price—and then multiply by 100. The average price is at the midpoint between the initial and new price, hence the name *midpoint method.*

The formula for the percentage change using the midpoint method is:

$$\text{Percentage change in price} = \left(\frac{\text{New price} - \text{Initial price}}{(\text{New price} + \text{Initial price}) \div 2}\right) \times 100.$$

* What you learn in this chapter also applies to services and factors of production.

In this formula, the numerator, (New price – Initial price), is the same as before. The denominator, (New price + Initial price) ÷ 2, is the average of the new price and the initial price.

To calculate the percentage change in the price of a Starbucks latte using the midpoint method, put $5 for new price and $3 for initial price in the formula:

$$\text{Percentage change in price} = \left(\frac{\$5 - \$3}{(\$5 + \$3) \div 2}\right) \times 100$$

$$= \left(\frac{\$2}{\$8 \div 2}\right) \times 100$$

$$= \left(\frac{\$2}{\$4}\right) \times 100 = 50 \text{ percent.}$$

Because the average price is the same regardless of whether the price rises or falls, the percentage change in price calculated by the midpoint method is the same for a price rise and a price fall.

Percentage Change in Quantity Demanded

If Starbucks raises the price of a latte, the quantity of latte demanded decreases. We calculate the percentage change in quantity demanded using the midpoint method. Suppose that when the price of a latte rises from $3 to $5 a cup, the quantity demanded decreases from 15 cups to 5 cups an hour. The percentage change in the quantity demanded using the midpoint method is:

$$\begin{array}{c}\text{Percentage change}\\ \text{in quantity}\end{array} = \left(\frac{\text{New quantity} - \text{Initial quantity}}{(\text{New quantity} + \text{Initial quantity}) \div 2}\right) \times 100$$

$$= \left(\frac{5 - 15}{(5 + 15) \div 2}\right) \times 100$$

$$= \left(\frac{-10}{20 \div 2}\right) \times 100$$

$$= \left(\frac{-10}{10}\right) \times 100 = -100 \text{ percent.}$$

Minus Sign

When the price of a good *rises*, the quantity demanded of it *decreases*—a *positive* change in price brings a *negative* change in the quantity demanded. To compare the percentage change in the price and the percentage change in the quantity demanded, we use the absolute values or magnitudes and ignore the minus sign.

Elastic and Inelastic Demand

In the Starbucks latte example, the percentage change in the quantity demanded exceeds the percentage change in price. But for other goods, the percentage change in the quantity demanded might exceed the percentage change in price, equal the percentage change in price, or be less than the percentage change in price. These three possibilities give three cases for the price elasticity of demand.

Elastic demand
When the percentage change in the quantity demanded exceeds the percentage change in price.

Unit elastic demand
When the percentage change in the quantity demanded equals the percentage change in price.

Inelastic demand
When the percentage change in the quantity demanded is less than the percentage change in price.

Perfectly elastic demand
When the quantity demanded changes by a very large percentage in response to an almost zero percentage change in price.

Perfectly inelastic demand
When the quantity demanded remains constant as the price changes.

- Demand is **elastic** if the percentage change in the quantity demanded exceeds the percentage change in price.
- Demand is **unit elastic** if the percentage change in the quantity demanded equals the percentage change in price.
- Demand is **inelastic** if the percentage change in the quantity demanded is less than the percentage change in price.

Figure 5.1 shows the different types of demand curves that illustrate the range of possible price elasticities of demand. Part (a) shows an extreme case of an elastic demand called a **perfectly elastic demand**—an almost zero percentage change in the price brings a very large percentage change in the quantity demanded. Consumers are willing to buy any quantity of the good at a given price but none at a higher price. Part (b) shows an elastic demand—the percentage change in the quantity demanded exceeds the percentage change in price. Part (c) shows a unit elastic demand—the percentage change in the quantity demanded equals the percentage change in price. Part (d) shows an inelastic demand—the percentage change in the quantity demanded is less than the percentage change in price. Finally, part (e) shows an extreme case of an inelastic demand called a **perfectly inelastic demand**—the percentage change in the quantity demanded is zero for any percentage change in price.

Influences on the Price Elasticity of Demand

What makes the demand for some things elastic and the demand for others inelastic? The influences on the price elasticity of demand fall into two groups:

- Substitution effects
- Income effects

Substitution Effects

The demand for a good is elastic if a substitute for it is easy to find. Pepsi containers can be made of either aluminum or plastic and it doesn't matter which, so the demand for aluminum is elastic.

The demand for a good is inelastic if a substitute for it is hard to find. Oil has poor substitutes (imagine a coal-fueled car), so the demand for oil is inelastic.

Three main factors influence the ability to find a substitute for a good: whether the good is a luxury or a necessity, how narrowly it is defined, and the amount of time available to find a substitute for it.

Luxury Versus Necessity We call goods such as food and housing *necessities*, and goods such as exotic vacations *luxuries*. A necessity has poor substitutes—you must eat—so the demand for a necessity is inelastic. A luxury has many substitutes—you don't absolutely have to go to Galapagos this summer—so the demand for a luxury is elastic.

FIGURE 5.1
The Range of Price Elasticities of Demand

*e*Foundations 5.1 

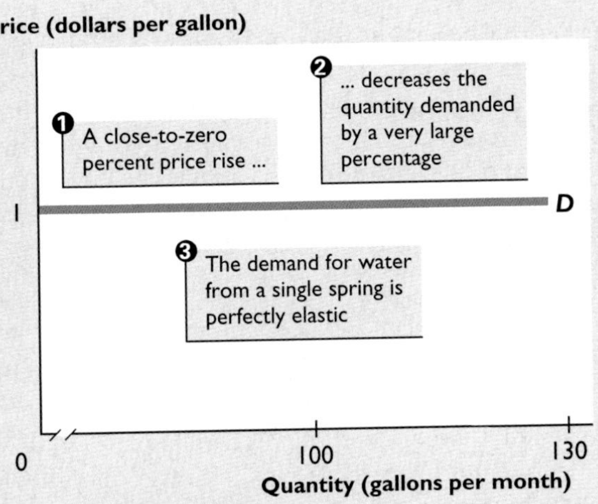

(a) Perfectly elastic demand

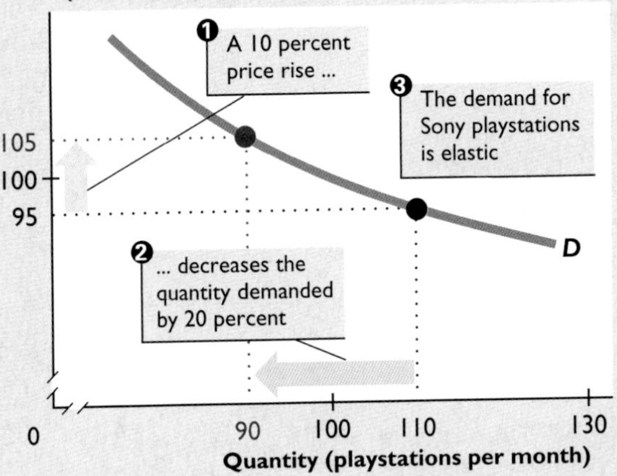

(b) Elastic demand

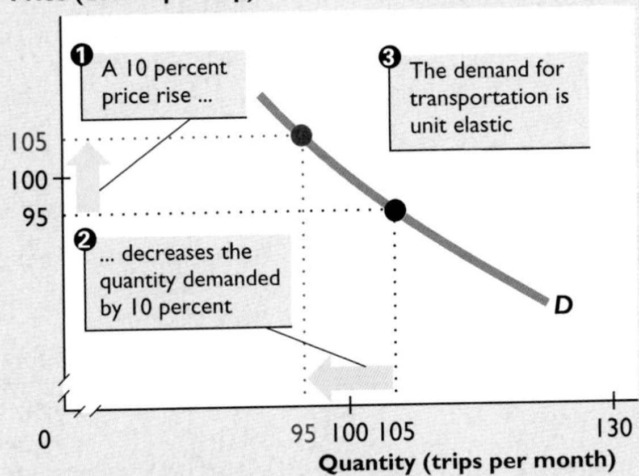

(c) Unit elastic demand

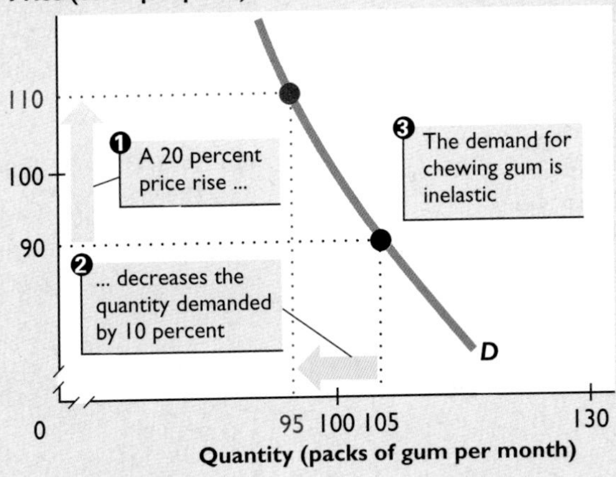

(d) Inelastic demand

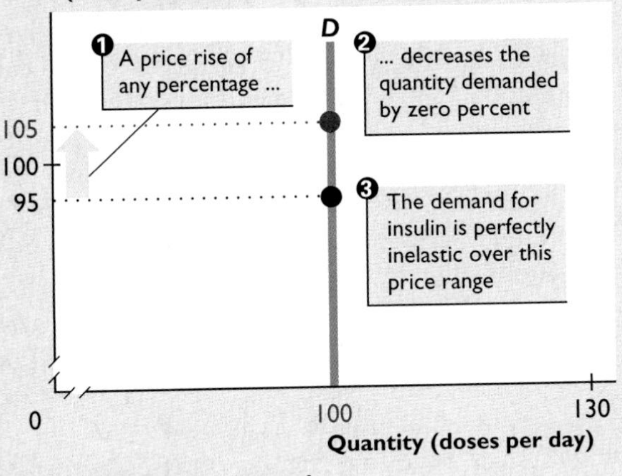

(e) Perfectly inelastic demand

❶ A price rise brings ❷ a decrease in the quantity demanded. The relationship between the percentage change in the quantity demanded and the percentage change in price determines ❸ the price elasticity of demand, which ranges from perfectly elastic (part a) to perfectly inelastic (part e).

Narrowness of Definition The demand for a narrowly defined good is elastic. For example, the demand for a Starbucks latte is elastic because a New World latte is a good substitute for it. The demand for a broadly defined good is inelastic. For example, the demand for coffee is inelastic because tea is a poor substitute for it.

Time Elapsed Since Price Change The longer the time that has elapsed since the price of a good changed, the more elastic is demand for the good. For example, when the price of gasoline increased steeply during the 1970s and 1980s, the quantity of gasoline demanded didn't change much because many people owned gas-guzzling automobiles—the demand for gasoline was inelastic. But eventually, fuel-efficient cars replaced gas guzzlers and the quantity of gasoline demanded decreased—the demand for gasoline became more elastic.

Income Effects

A price rise, like a decrease in income, means that people cannot afford to buy the same quantities of goods and services as before. The greater the proportion of income spent on a good, the greater is the impact of a rise in its price on the quantities that people can afford to buy and the more elastic is the demand for the good. Toothpaste takes a tiny proportion of your budget, and housing takes a large proportion. If the price of toothpaste doubles, you buy almost as much toothpaste as before. Your demand for toothpaste is inelastic. If an apartment rents double, you shriek and look for more roommates. Your demand for housing is more elastic than your demand for toothpaste.

Computing the Price Elasticity of Demand

To determine whether the demand for a good is elastic, unit elastic, or inelastic, we compute a numerical value for the price elasticity of demand by using the following formula:

$$\text{Price elasticity of demand} = \frac{\text{Percentage change in quantity demanded}}{\text{Percentage change in price}}.$$

- If the price elasticity of demand is greater than 1, demand is elastic.
- If the price elasticity of demand equals 1, demand is unit elastic.
- If the price elasticity of demand is less than 1, demand is inelastic.

Let's calculate the price elasticity of demand for a Starbucks latte, given the numbers we assumed above. Figure 5.2 illustrates and summarizes the calculation. Initially, the price is \$3 a cup and 15 cups an hour are sold—the initial point in the figure. Then the price rises to \$5 a cup and the quantity demanded decreases to 5 cups an hour—the new point in the figure. The price increases by \$2 a cup and the average, or midpoint, price is \$4 a cup, so the percentage change in price is 50. The quantity demanded decreases by 10 cups an hour and the average, or midpoint, quantity is 10 cups an hour, so the percentage change in quantity demanded is 100.

Using the above formula, you can see that the price elasticity of demand for a Starbucks latte is:

$$\text{Price elasticity of demand} = \frac{100 \text{ percent}}{50 \text{ percent}} = 2.$$

FIGURE 5.2
Price Elasticity of Demand Calculation

*e*Foundations 5.1 

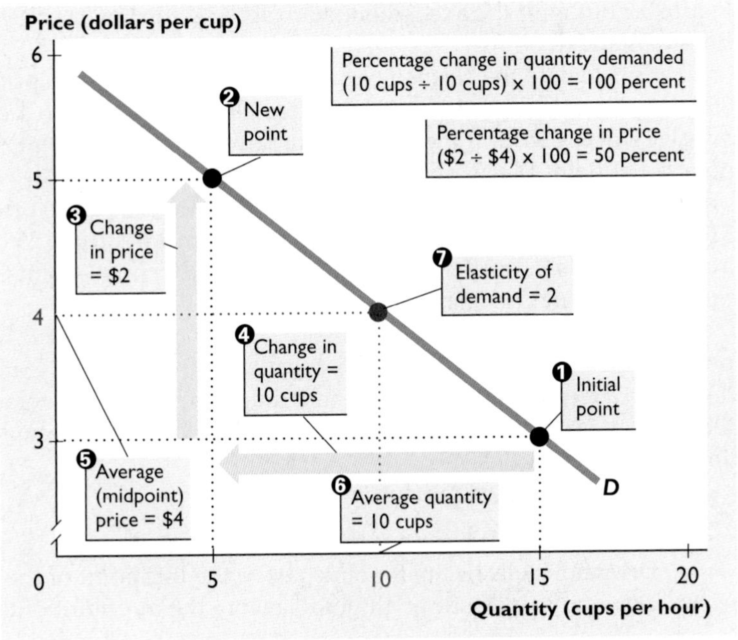

Price (dollars per cup)
6
5
4
3
0
5
10
15
20
Quantity (cups per hour)
D
Percentage change in quantity demanded (10 cups ÷ 10 cups) x 100 = 100 percent
Percentage change in price ($2 ÷ $4) x 100 = 50 percent
❷ New point
❸ Change in price = $2
❼ Elasticity of demand = 2
❹ Change in quantity = 10 cups
❶ Initial point
❺ Average (midpoint) price = $4
❻ Average quantity = 10 cups

❶ At the initial point, the price is $3 and the quantity demanded is 15 cups an hour.

❷ At the new point, the price is $5 and the quantity demanded is 5 cups an hour.

❸ The change in price is $2 a cup, and ❹ the change in the quantity demanded is 10 cups an hour.

❺ The average price is $4, and the ❻ average quantity demanded is 10 cups an hour.

The percentage change in quantity demanded is 100, the percentage change in price is 50, and ❼ the price elasticity of demand is 2.

The price elasticity of demand is 2 at the midpoint between the initial point and the new point on the demand curve. In this example, over this price range, the demand for a Starbucks latte is elastic.

Slope and Elasticity

The price elasticity of demand measures how the quantity demanded changes when the price changes along a demand curve. The *slope* of the demand curve also measures how the quantity demanded changes when the price changes (see p. 31). The slope of a relationship depends on the units of measurement. In the current example, the slope of the demand curve is in dollars per cup. In the case of the demand for coffee beans, the slope is in dollars per pound. Because the slope of the demand curve depends on the units of measurement of the good, we cannot use slope to compare the demand curves of different goods. But we *can* use elasticity.

A Units-Free Measure

Elasticity is a *units-free* measure. The percentage change in price is independent of the units in which the price is measured. It is the ratio of dollars to dollars (or cents to cents). The percentage change in quantity is also independent of the units in which the quantity is measured. For a latte, the percentage change in quantity is the ratio of cups to cups; and for coffee beans, it is the ratio of pounds to pounds. In each case, the units of measurement cancel. Better yet, when we calculate elasticity, we get a number that is the ratio of one percentage change to another percentage change—a number without units. So we can compare the demand for a latte with the demand for coffee beans.

Elasticity Along a Linear Demand Curve

Along a linear (straight-line) demand curve, the slope is constant but the elasticity varies. Figure 5.3 shows the same demand curve for a Starbucks latte as that in Figure 5.2 but with the axes extended to show some lower prices and larger quantities demanded.

Let's calculate the elasticity of demand at point *A*. If the price rises from \$3 to \$5 a cup, the quantity demanded decreases from 15 cups to 5 cups an hour. The average price is \$4, and the average quantity is 10 cups—point *A*. The elasticity of demand at point *A* is 2, and demand is elastic.

Let's calculate the elasticity of demand at point *C*. If the price falls from \$3 to \$1 a cup, the quantity demanded increases from 15 cups to 25 cups an hour. The average price is \$2, and the average quantity is 20 cups—point *C*. The elasticity of demand at point *C* is 0.5, and demand is inelastic.

Finally, let's calculate the elasticity of demand at point *B*, which is the midpoint of the demand curve. If the price rises from \$2 to \$4 a cup, the quantity demanded decreases from 20 cups to 10 cups an hour. The average price is \$3, and the average quantity is 15 cups—point *B*. The elasticity of demand at point *B* is 1, and demand is unit elastic.

Along a linear demand curve:

- Demand is unit elastic at the midpoint of the curve.
- Demand is elastic at all points above the midpoint of the curve.
- Demand is inelastic at all points below the midpoint of the curve.

FIGURE 5.3
Elasticity Along a Linear Demand Curve

*e*Foundations 5.1 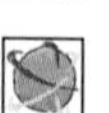

On a linear demand curve, the slope is constant but the elasticity decreases as the price falls and the quantity demanded increases.

❶ At point *A*, demand is elastic.

❷ At point *B*, which is the midpoint of the demand curve, demand is unit elastic.

❸ At point *C*, demand is inelastic.

Demand is elastic at all points above the midpoint of the demand curve and inelastic at all points below the midpoint of the demand curve.

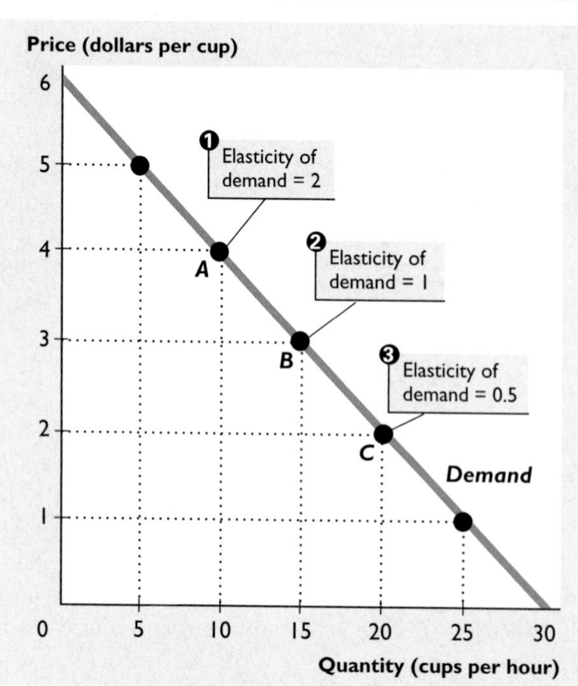

Price Elasticities of Demand

The real-world elasticities of demand in the table range from 1.52 for metals to 0.12 for food. Metals have good substitutes, such as plastics, while food has virtually no substitutes.

As we move down the list of items, they have fewer good substitutes and are more likely to be in the category of necessities.

The figure shows the proportion of income spent on food and the price elasticity of demand for food in ten countries. This figure confirms a general rule: The larger the proportion of income spent on an item, the larger is the price elasticity of demand for it.

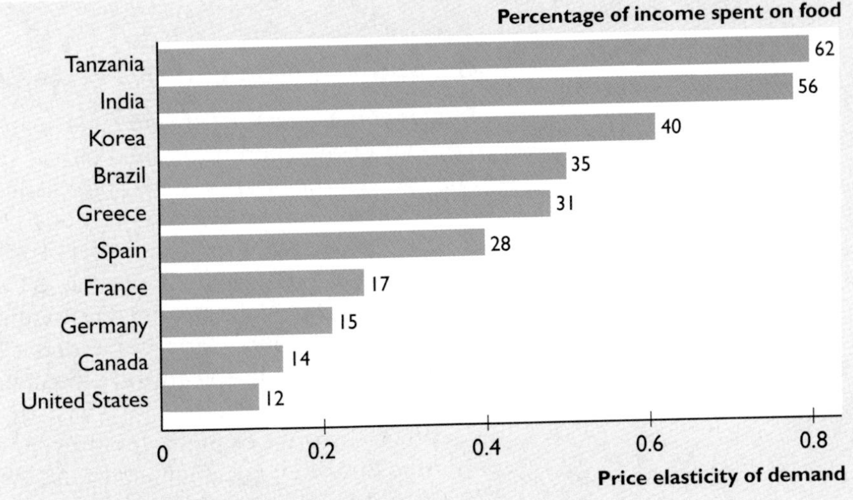

For example, in Tanzania, a low-income nation where 62 percent of income is spent on food, the price elasticity of demand for food is 0.77. In contrast, in the United States, where 12 percent of income is spent on food, the price elasticity of demand for food is 0.12.

Some Price Elasticities of Demand

Good or Service	Elasticity
Elastic Demand	
Metals	1.52
Electrical engineering products	1.39
Mechanical engineering products	1.30
Furniture	1.26
Motor vehicles	1.14
Instrument engineering products	1.10
Professional services	1.09
Transportation services	1.03
Inelastic Demand	
Gas, electricity, and water	0.92
Oil	0.91
Chemicals	0.89
Beverages (all types)	0.78
Clothing	0.64
Tobacco	0.61
Banking and insurance services	0.56
Housing services	0.55
Agricultural and fish products	0.42
Books, magazines, and newspapers	0.34
Food	0.12

SOURCES: Ahsan Mansur and John Whalley, "Numerical Specification of Applied General Equilibrium Models: Estimation, Calibration, and Data," in *Applied General Equilibrium Analysis*, eds. Herbert E. Scarf and John B. Shoven (New York: Cambridge University Press, 1984), 109; and Henri Theil, Ching-Fan Chung, and James L. Seale, Jr., *Advances in Econometrics, Supplement 1, 1989, International Evidence on Consumption Patterns* (Greenwich, Conn.: JAI Press Inc., 1989). Reprinted with permission.

Total Revenue and the Price Elasticity of Demand

Total revenue
The total revenue from the sale of a good equals the price of the good multiplied by the quantity sold.

Total revenue is the amount spent on a good and received by its sellers and equals the price of the good multiplied by the quantity of the good sold. For example, suppose that the price of a Starbucks latte is $3 and that 15 cups an hour are sold. Then total revenue is $3 a cup multiplied by 15 cups an hour, which equals $45 an hour.

We can use the demand curve for a Starbucks latte to illustrate total revenue. Figure 5.4(a) shows the total revenue from the sale of latte when the price is $3 a cup and the quantity of latte demanded is 15 cups an hour. Total revenue is shown by the blue rectangle, the area of which equals $3, its height, multiplied by 15, its length, which equals $45.

When the price changes, total revenue can change in the same direction, the opposite direction, or remain constant. Which of these outcomes occurs depends on the price elasticity of demand. By observing the change in total revenue that results from a price change (other things remaining the same), we can estimate the price elasticity of demand. This method of estimating the price elasticity of demand is called the **total revenue test**.

Total revenue test
A method of estimating the price elasticity of demand by observing the change in total revenue that results from a price change (with all other influences on the quantity sold remaining unchanged).

If demand is elastic, a given percentage rise in price brings a larger percentage decrease in the quantity demanded, so total revenue—price multiplied by quantity—decreases. Figure 5.4(a) shows this outcome. When the price of a latte is $3, the quantity demanded is 15 an hour and total revenue is $45 ($3 × 15). If the price of a latte rises to $5, the quantity demanded decreases to 5 an hour and total revenue *decreases* to $25 ($5 × 5).

If demand is inelastic, a given percentage rise in price brings a smaller percentage decrease in the quantity demanded, so total revenue increases. Figure 5.4(b) shows this outcome. When the price of a textbook is $50, the quantity demanded is 5 million a year and total revenue is $250 million ($50 × 5 million). If the price of a textbook rises to $75, the quantity demanded decreases to 4 million a year and total revenue *increases* to $300 million ($75 × 4 million).

The relationship between the price elasticity of demand and total revenue is:

- If price and total revenue change in opposite directions, demand is elastic.
- If a price change leaves total revenue unchanged, demand is unit elastic.
- If price and total revenue change in the same direction, demand is inelastic.

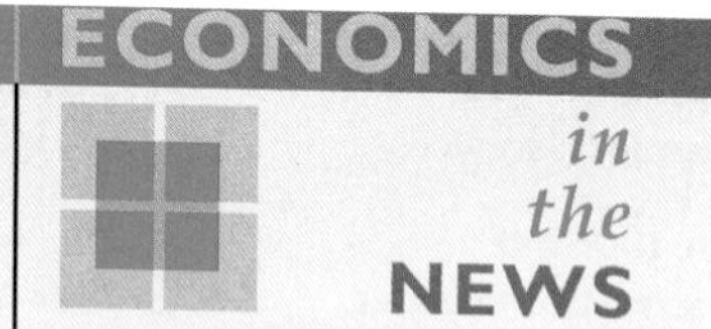

January 28, 2000

The Energy Department is puzzled by a recent sharp rise in oil prices and plans to monitor the market more closely.

Questions

1. Why do you think the price of oil has increased sharply in recent days?

2. What do you predict would be the effect on the equilibrium price and quantity of adopting the recommendation of then Texas Governor George W. Bush: that the President "jawbone" oil-producing nations and persuade them to drop prices? Explain.

3. How do you think the rise in the price of oil will affect the total revenue of oil producers? Explain.

 *e*Foundations 5.1

Your Expenditure and *Your* Elasticity of Demand

Your expenditure on a good is its price multiplied by the quantity that you buy. So expenditure for the buyer is like total revenue for the seller. When the price of a good changes, the change in your expenditure on it depends on *your* elasticity of demand. When the price of a good *rises*, your demand for that good is:

- Elastic if your expenditure on it decreases.
- Unit elastic if your expenditure on it remains constant.
- Inelastic if your expenditure on it increases.

Pay attention the next time you are confronted with a price change. Note how your expenditure on the item changes and check whether your demand for it is elastic or inelastic. Think about why it is elastic or inelastic by checking back with the list of influence on the price elasticity of demand.

FIGURE 5.4

Total Revenue and the Price Elasticity of Demand

*e*Foundations 5.1 

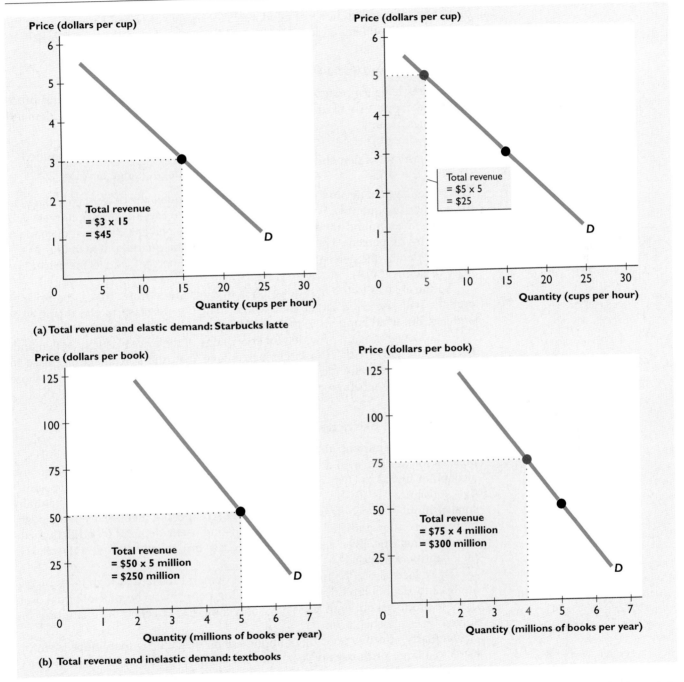

(a) Total revenue and elastic demand: Starbucks latte

(b) Total revenue and inelastic demand: textbooks

Total revenue equals price multiplied by quantity. In part (a), when the price is $3 a cup, the quantity demanded is 15 cups an hour and total revenue equals $45 an hour. When the price rises to $5 a cup, the quantity demanded decreases to 5 cups an hour and total revenue decreases to $25 an hour. Demand is elastic.

In part (b), when the price is $50 per book, the quantity demanded is 5 million books a year and total revenue equals $250 million per year. When the price rises to $75 a book, the quantity demanded decreases to 4 million books per year and total revenue increases to $300 million a year. Demand is inelastic.

Applications of the Price Elasticity of Demand

At the beginning of this chapter, we asked two questions: Does a frost in Florida bring a massive or a modest rise in the price of oranges? And does a smaller orange crop mean bad news or good news for orange growers? Knowledge of the price elasticity of demand for oranges enables us to answer these questions.

Farm Prices and Total Revenue

Economists have estimated the price elasticity of demand for agricultural products to be about 0.4—an inelastic demand. If this number applies to the demand for oranges, then:

$$\text{Price elasticity of demand} = 0.4 = \frac{\text{Percentage change in quantity demanded}}{\text{Percentage change in price}}.$$

The percentage change in the quantity demanded equals the percentage change in the equilibrium quantity. So if a frost in Florida decreases the orange harvest and decreases the equilibrium quantity of oranges by 1 percent, the price of oranges will rise by 2.5 percent. The percentage change in the quantity demanded (1 percent) divided by the percentage change in price (2.5 percent) equals the price elasticity of demand (0.4).

So the answer to the first question is that when the frost strikes, the price of oranges will rise by a larger percentage than the decrease in the quantity of oranges. But what happens to the total revenue of the orange growers?

The answer is again provided by knowledge of the price elasticity of demand. Because the price rises by a larger percentage than the percentage decrease in quantity, total revenue increases. A frost is bad news for consumers and those growers who lose their crops but good news for growers who escape the frost.

Addiction and Elasticity

We can gain important insights that might help to design potentially effective policies for dealing with addiction to drugs, whether legal (such as tobacco and alcohol) or illegal (such as crack cocaine or heroin). Nonusers' demand for addictive substances is elastic. A moderately higher price leads to a substantially smaller number of people trying a drug and so exposing themselves to the possibility of becoming addicted to it. But the existing users' demand for addictive substances is inelastic. Even a substantial price rise brings only a modest decrease in the quantity demanded.

These facts about the price elasticity of demand mean that high taxes on cigarettes and alcohol limit the number of young people who become habitual users of these products, but high taxes have only a modest effect on the quantities consumed by established users.

Similarly, effective policing of imports of an illegal drug that limits its supply leads to a large price rise and a substantial decrease in the number of new users but only a small decrease in the quantity consumed by addicts. Expenditure on the drug by addicts increases. Further, because many drug addicts finance their purchases with crime, the amount of theft and burglary increases.

Because the price elasticity of demand for drugs is low for addicts, any successful policy to decrease drug use will be one that focuses on the demand for drugs and attempts to change preferences through rehabilitation programs.

CHECKPOINT 5.1

1 Define, explain the factors that influence, and calculate the price elasticity of demand.

Study Guide pp. 70–74 

eFoundations 5.1

Practice Problem 5.1

A 10 percent increase in the price of a good has led to a 2 percent decrease in the quantity demanded of that good.

a. How would you describe the demand for this good?

b. Are substitutes for this good easy to find or does it have poor substitutes?

c. Is this good more likely to be a necessity or a luxury? Why?

d. Is the good more likely to be narrowly or broadly defined? Why?

e. Calculate the price elasticity of demand for this good.

f. Has the total revenue from the sale of the good changed? Explain your answer.

g. This good might be which of the following goods: orange juice, bread, toothpaste, theater tickets, clothing, blue jeans, Super Bowl tickets? Why?

Exercise 5.1

The price of spring water rises from $1.90 to $2.10 a bottle, and the quantity demanded decreases from 11 million to 9 million bottles a week.

a. Calculate the percentage change in the price of spring water.

b. Calculate the percentage change in the quantity demanded of spring water.

c. Is the demand for spring water elastic or inelastic?

d. Would the demand for Pepsi be more elastic or less elastic than the demand for spring water? Why?

e. Calculate the price elasticity of demand for spring water.

f. At what price is the price elasticity of demand for spring water equal to your answer in part (e)?

g. What is the change in the total revenue of sellers of spring water?

h. If the demand curve for spring water is a straight-line demand curve, is the price at which the demand for spring water is unit elastic a higher price or a lower price than your answer to part (f)? Why?

Solution to Practice Problem 5.1

Figure 1 illustrates a 10 percent increase in the price of a good that has led to a 2 percent decrease in the quantity demanded of it.

a. The percentage change in the quantity demanded is less than the percentage change in the price, so the demand for the good is inelastic.

b. A good with an inelastic demand usually has poor substitutes.

c. A good with an inelastic demand is likely to be a necessity.

d. A good with an inelastic demand is likely to be broadly defined.

e. Price elasticity of demand equals the percentage change in the quantity demanded divided by the percentage change in price, which equals $2/10$, or 0.2.

f. When demand is inelastic, a price rise increases total revenue.

g. The good might be a necessity (bread), have poor substitutes (toothpaste), or be broadly defined (clothing).

FIGURE 1

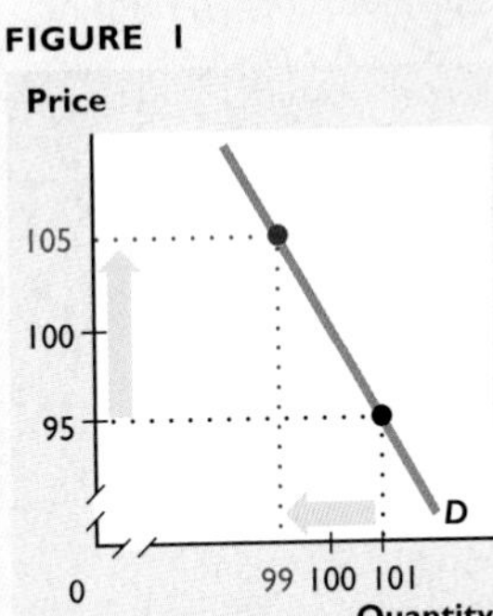

5.2 THE PRICE ELASTICITY OF SUPPLY

You know that when demand increases, the equilibrium price rises and the equilibrium quantity increases. But does the price rise by a large amount and the quantity increase by a little? Or does the price barely rise and the quantity increase by a large amount? To answer this question, we need to know the price elasticity of supply.

Price elasticity of supply
A measure of the extent to which the quantity supplied of a good changes when the price of the good changes and all other influences on sellers' plans remain the same.

The **price elasticity of supply** is a measure of the extent to which the quantity supplied of a good changes when the price of the good changes and all other influences on sellers' plans remain the same. We determine the price elasticity of supply by comparing the percentage change in the quantity supplied with the percentage change in price.

Elastic and Inelastic Supply

Supply might be:

- Elastic
- Unit elastic
- Inelastic

Perfectly elastic supply
When the quantity supplied changes by a very large percentage in response to an almost zero percentage change in price.

Elastic supply
When the percentage change in the quantity supplied exceeds the percentage change in price.

Unit elastic supply
When the percentage change in the quantity supplied equals the percentage change in price.

Inelastic supply
When the percentage change in the quantity supplied is less than the percentage change in price.

Perfectly inelastic supply
When the quantity supplied remains the same as the price changes.

Figure 5.5 illustrates the range of supply elasticities. Figure 5.5(a) shows the extreme case of a **perfectly elastic supply**—an almost zero percentage change in price brings a very large percentage change in the quantity supplied. Figure 5.5(b) shows an **elastic supply**—the percentage change in the quantity supplied exceeds the percentage change in price. Figure 5.5(c) shows a **unit elastic supply**—the percentage change in the quantity supplied equals the percentage change in price. Figure 5.5(d) shows an **inelastic supply**—the percentage change in the quantity supplied is less than the percentage change in price. And Figure 5.5(e) shows the extreme case of a **perfectly inelastic supply**—the percentage change in the quantity supplied is zero when the price changes.

Influences on the Price Elasticity of Supply

What makes the supply of some things elastic and the supply of others inelastic? The two main influences on the price elasticity of supply are:

- Production possibilities
- Storage possibilities

Production Possibilities

Some goods can be produced at a constant (or very gently rising) opportunity cost. These goods have an elastic supply. The silicon in your computer chips is an example of such a good. Silicon is extracted from sand at a tiny and almost constant opportunity cost. So the supply of silicon is perfectly elastic.

Some goods can be produced in only a fixed quantity. These goods have a perfectly inelastic supply. A beachfront home in Santa Monica can be built only on a unique beachfront lot. So the supply of these homes is perfectly inelastic.

Hotel rooms in New York City can't easily be used as office accommodation and office space cannot easily be converted into hotel rooms, so the supply of hotel rooms in New York City is inelastic. Paper and printing presses can be used to produce textbooks or magazines, and the supplies of these goods are elastic.

FIGURE 5.5
The Range of Price Elasticities of Supply

*e*Foundations 5.2

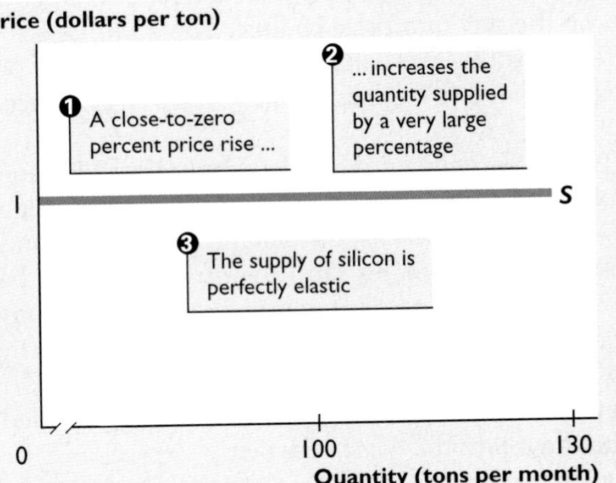

(a) Perfectly elastic supply

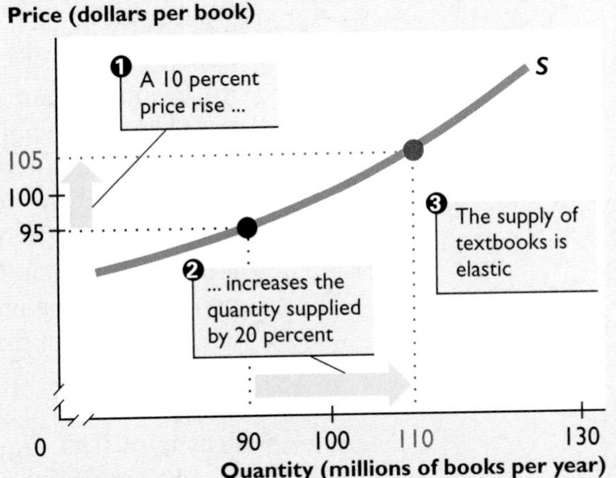

(b) Elastic supply

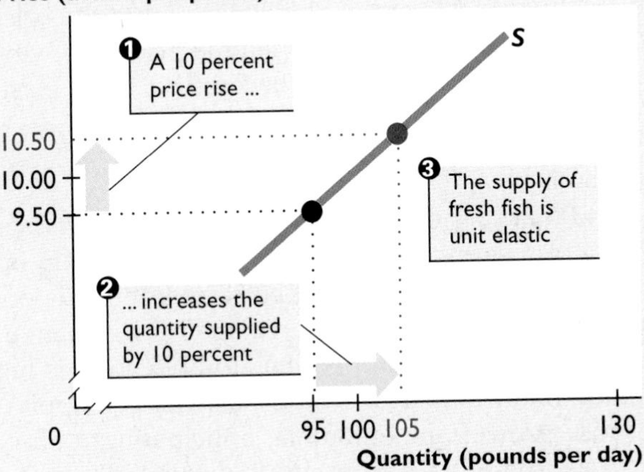

(c) Unit elastic supply

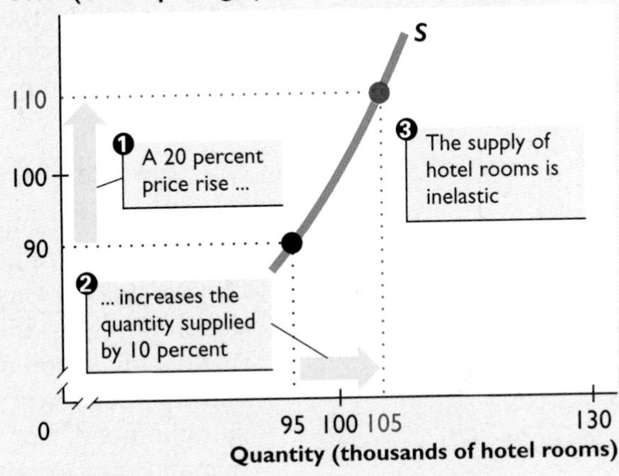

(d) Inelastic supply

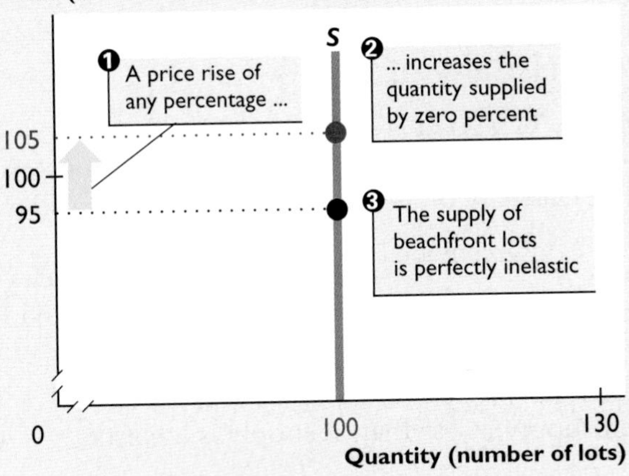

(e) Perfectly inelastic supply

❶ A price rise brings ❷ an increase in the quantity supplied. The relationship between the percentage change in the quantity supplied and the percentage change in price determines ❸ the price elasticity of supply, which ranges from perfectly elastic (part a) to perfectly inelastic (part e).

Time Elapsed Since Price Change As time passes after a price change, it becomes easier to change production plans and supply becomes more elastic. For some items—fruits and vegetables are examples—it is difficult or perhaps impossible to change the quantity supplied immediately after a price change. These goods have a perfectly inelastic supply on the day of a price change. The quantities supplied depend on crop-planting decisions that were made earlier. In the case of oranges, for example, planting decisions have to be made many years in advance of the crop being available.

Many manufactured goods also have an inelastic supply if production plans have had only a short period in which to change. For example, before it launched the PlayStation 2 in 2000, Sony made a forecast of demand, set a price, and made a production plan to supply the United States with the quantity that it believed people would be willing to buy. It turned out that demand outstripped Sony's earlier forecast. The price increased on eBay, an Internet auction market, to bring market equilibrium. At the high price that emerged, Sony would have liked to ship more PlayStations. But it could do nothing to increase the quantity supplied in the near term. The supply of the PlayStation 2 was inelastic.

As time passes, the elasticity of supply increases. After all the technologically possible ways of adjusting production have been exploited, supply is extremely elastic—perhaps perfectly elastic—for most manufactured items. By early 2001, Sony was able to step up the production rate of the PlayStation 2 and the price on eBay fell to the price at which Sony initially planned to sell the product. Over this longer time frame, the supply of the PlayStation 2 had become perfectly elastic.

Storage Possibilities

The elasticity of supply of a good that cannot be stored (for example, a perishable item such as fresh strawberries) or a service depends only on production possibilities. But the elasticity of supply of a good that can be stored depends on the decision to keep the good in storage or offer it for sale. A small price change can make a big difference to this decision, so the supply of a storable good is highly elastic. The cost of storage is the main influence on the elasticity of supply of a storable good. For example, rose growers in Colombia, anticipating a surge in demand on Valentine's Day in February, hold back supplies in late January and early February and increase their inventories of roses. They then release roses from inventory for Valentine's Day.

Computing the Price Elasticity of Supply

To determine whether the supply of a good is elastic, unit elastic, or inelastic, we compute a numerical value for the price elasticity of supply in a way similar to that used to calculate the price elasticity of demand. We use the formula:

$$\text{Price elasticity of supply} = \frac{\text{Percentage change in quantity supplied}}{\text{Percentage change in price}}.$$

- If the price elasticity of supply is greater than 1, supply is elastic.
- If the price elasticity of supply equals 1, supply is unit elastic.
- If the price elasticity of supply is less than 1, supply is inelastic.

Let's calculate the price elasticity of supply of roses. We'll use the numbers that you saw in Chapter 4 on p. 99. Figure 5.6 illustrates and summarizes the calculation. In a normal month, the price of roses is $40 a bunch and 6 million bunches are supplied—the initial point in the figure. In February, the price rises to $80 a bunch and the quantity supplied increases to 24 million bunches—the new point in the figure. The price increases by $40 a bunch and the average, or midpoint, price is $60 a bunch, so the percentage change in the price is 66.67. The quantity supplied increases by 18 million bunches and the average, or midpoint, quantity is 15 million bunches, so the percentage change in the quantity supplied is 120.

Using the above formula, you can see that the price elasticity of supply of roses is:

$$\text{Price elasticity of supply} = \frac{120 \text{ percent}}{66.67 \text{ percent}} = 1.8.$$

The price elasticity of supply is 1.8 at the midpoint between the initial point and the new point on the supply curve. In this example, over this price range, the supply of roses is elastic.

FIGURE 5.6
Price Elasticity of Supply Calculation

*e*Foundations 5.2 

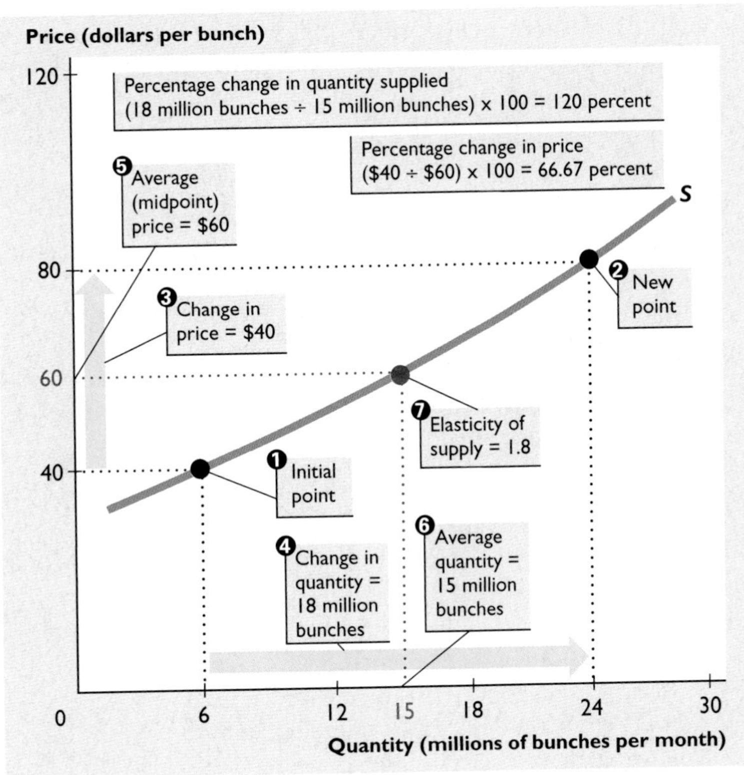

1 At the initial point, the price is $40 and the quantity supplied is 6 million bunches a month.

2 At the new point, the price is $80 and the quantity supplied is 24 million bunches a month.

3 The change in price is $40 a bunch, and 4 the change in the quantity supplied is 18 million bunches a month.

5 The average price is $60, and the 6 average quantity supplied is 15 million bunches a month.

The percentage change in quantity supplied is 120, the percentage change in price is 66.67, and 7 the price elasticity of supply is 1.8.

CHECKPOINT 5.2

Study Guide pp. 74–77

*e*Foundations 5.2

2 **Define, explain the factors that influence, and calculate the price elasticity of supply.**

Practice Problem 5.2

You are told that a 10 percent increase in the price of a good has led to a 1 percent increase in the quantity supplied of the good after one month. Use this information to answer the following questions:

a. How would you describe the supply of this good?
b. What can you say about the production possibilities of this good?
c. Calculate the price elasticity of supply.
d. If after one year, the quantity supplied has increased by 25 percent, describe how the supply has changed over the year.
e. Calculate the elasticity of supply after one year.

Exercise 5.2

The price of U.S.-produced long grain rice fell by 40 percent from January 1999 to January 2000. In response to the price fall, growers of U.S. long grain rice planted 17 percent less acreage in 2000. If the harvest also decreases by 17 percent:

a. How would you describe the supply of U.S. long grain rice?
b. How do you think production possibilities and storage possibilities influence the price elasticity of supply of long grain rice?
c. Calculate the price elasticity of supply of U.S.-produced long grain rice.
d. If the price of long grain rice remains the same, do you think the elasticity of supply will change over the coming years? Explain your answer.

FIGURE 1

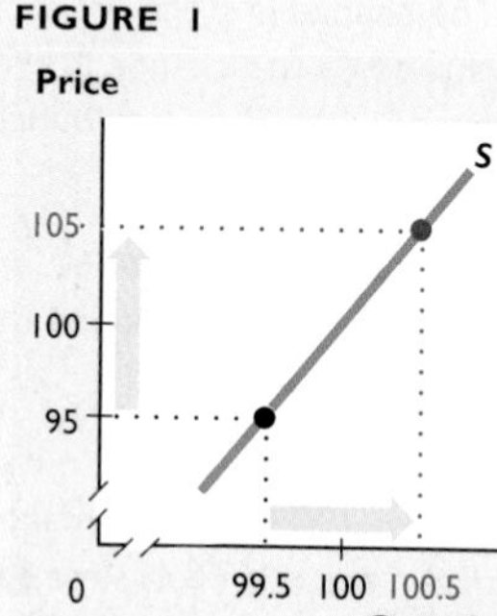

Solution to Practice Problem 5.2

Figure 1 illustrates a 10 percent increase in the price of a good that has led to a 1 percent increase in the quantity supplied of it.

a. The percentage change in the quantity supplied is less than the percentage change in the price of the good, so the supply of the good is inelastic.
b. Because the quantity supplied increases by such a small percentage after one month, the factors of production that are used to produce this good are more likely to be unique or rare.
c. The elasticity of supply equals the percentage change in the quantity supplied divided by the percentage change in the price, which is $1 \div 10$ or 0.1.
d. The supply of the good has become more elastic over the year since the price rise because other producers will have gradually started producing the good.
e. The elasticity of supply equals the percentage change in the quantity supplied divided by the percentage change in the price. After one year, the elasticity of supply is $15 \div 10$, which equals 1.5.

5.3 CROSS ELASTICITY AND INCOME ELASTICITY

Domino's Pizza in Chula Vista has a problem. Burger King has just cut its prices. Domino's manager, Pat, knows that pizzas and burgers are substitutes. He also knows that when the price of a substitute for pizza falls, the demand for pizza decreases. But by how much will the quantity of pizza bought decrease if Pat maintains his current price?

Pat also knows that pizza and soda are complements. He knows that if the price of a complement of pizza falls, the demand for pizza increases. So he wonders whether he might keep his customers by cutting the price he charges for soda. But he wants to know by how much he must cut the price of soda to keep selling the same quantity of pizza with cheaper burgers all around him.

To answer these questions, Pat needs to calculate the cross elasticity of demand. Let's examine this elasticity measure.

Cross Elasticity of Demand

The **cross elasticity of demand** is a measure of the extent to which the demand for a good changes when the price of a substitute or complement changes, other things remaining the same. It is calculated by using the formula:

Cross elasticity of demand A measure of the extent to which the demand for a good changes when the price of a substitute or complement changes, other things remaining the same.

$$\text{Cross elasticity of demand} = \frac{\text{Percentage change in quantity demanded of a good}}{\text{Percentage change in price of one of its substitutes or complements}}.$$

Suppose that when the price of a burger falls by 10 percent, the quantity of pizza demanded decreases by 5 percent.* The cross elasticity of demand for pizza with respect to the price of a burger is:

$$\text{Cross elasticity of demand} = \frac{-5 \text{ percent}}{-10 \text{ percent}} = 0.5.$$

The cross elasticity of demand for a substitute is positive. A *fall* in the price of a substitute brings a *decrease* in the quantity demanded of the good. The quantity demanded of a good and the price of one of its substitutes change in the same direction.

Suppose that when the price of soda falls by 10 percent, the quantity of pizza demanded increases by 2 percent. The cross elasticity of demand for pizza with respect to the price of soda is:

$$\text{Cross elasticity of demand} = \frac{+2 \text{ percent}}{-10 \text{ percent}} = -0.2.$$

The cross elasticity of demand for a complement is negative. A *fall* in the price of a complement brings an *increase* in the quantity demanded of the good. The quantity demanded of a good and the price of one of its complements change in opposite directions.

*As before, these percentage changes are calculated by using the midpoint method.

FIGURE 5.7
Cross Elasticity of Demand

*e*Foundations 5.3 

A burger is a *substitute* for pizza. When the price of a burger falls, the demand curve for pizza shifts leftward from D_0 to D_1. At the fixed price of pizza, the quantity demanded of pizza decreases. The cross elasticity of the demand for pizza with respect to the price of a burger is *positive*.

Soda is a *complement* of pizza. When the price of soda falls, the demand curve for pizza shifts rightward from D_0 to D_2. At the fixed price of pizza, the quantity demanded of pizza increases. The cross elasticity of the demand for pizza with respect to the price of soda is *negative*.

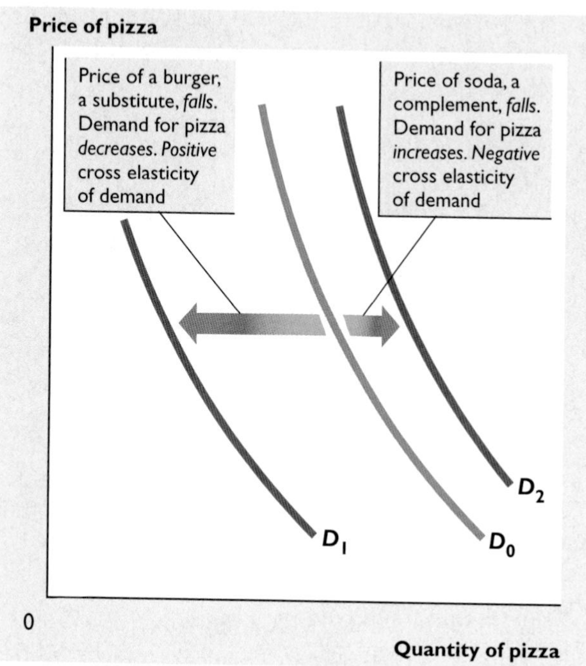

Figure 5.7 illustrates these two cross elasticities of demand for pizza. When the price of a burger falls, the demand for pizza decreases and the demand curve for pizza shifts leftward from D_0 to D_1. When the price of soda falls, the demand for pizza increases and the demand curve for pizza shifts rightward from D_0 to D_2. The magnitude of the cross elasticity determines how far the demand curve shifts.

Income Elasticity of Demand

The economy is expanding, and people are enjoying rising incomes. This prosperity is bringing an increase in the demand for all types of goods. But by how much will the demand for pizza increase?

The answer depends on the income elasticity of demand for the good. The **income elasticity of demand** is a measure of the extent to which the demand for a good changes when income changes, other things remaining the same. It is calculated by using the following formula:

Income elasticity of demand
A measure of the extent to which the demand for a good changes when income changes, other things remaining the same.

$$\text{Income elasticity of demand} = \frac{\text{Percentage change in quantity demanded}}{\text{Percentage change in income}}.$$

The income elasticity of demand falls into three ranges:

- Greater than 1 (*normal* good, income elastic)
- Between zero and 1 (*normal* good, income inelastic)
- Less than zero (*inferior* good)

In Figure 5.8(a), the quantity demanded increases more quickly than income increases. Demand is income elastic. Airline travel and jewelry are examples. In

FIGURE 5.8
Income Elasticity of Demand

*e*Foundations 5.3 

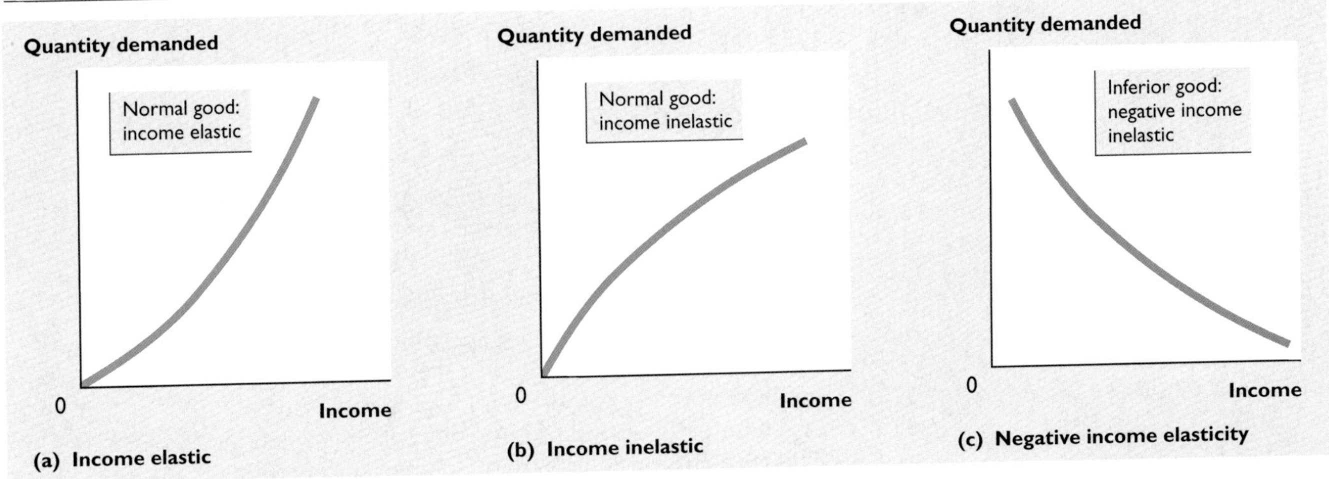

Figure 5.8(b), the quantity demanded increases less quickly than income increases. Demand is income inelastic. Food and clothing are examples. In Figure 5.8(c), the quantity demand *decreases* as income *increases*. Demand is negative income elastic. Milk crates used as bookshelves are an example.

Income Elasticities of Demand

In the United States, necessities such as food and clothing are income inelastic; luxuries such as airline and foreign travel are income elastic.

The *level* of income has a big effect on income elasticities of demand. Using data for ten countries, the figure shows that the lower the income level, the more income elastic is the demand for food.

Income (percentage of U.S. income)

Country	Income (percentage of U.S. income)
Tanzania	3.3
India	5.2
Korea	20.4
Brazil	36.8
Greece	41.3
Spain	55.9
Japan	61.6
France	81.1
Canada	99.2
United States	100

0 0.2 0.4 0.6 0.8
Income elasticity

Some Income Elasticities of Demand

Good or Service	Elasticity
Income Elastic	
Airline travel	5.82
Movies	3.41
Foreign travel	3.08
Electricity	1.94
Restaurant meals	1.61
Local buses and trains	1.38
Haircuts	1.36
Cars	1.07
Income Inelastic	
Tobacco	0.86
Alcoholic beverages	0.62
Furniture	0.53
Clothing	0.51
Newspapers	0.38
Telephone	0.32
Food	0.14

CHECKPOINT 5.3

Study Guide pp. 77–79 

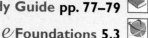

*e*Foundations 5.3

3 **Define and explain the factors that influence the cross elasticity of demand and the income elasticity of demand.**

Practice Problems 5.3

1. If the quantity demanded of good *A* increases by 5 percent when the price of good *B* rises by 10 percent and other things remain the same:
   a. Are goods *A* and *B* complements or substitutes? Why?
   b. Describe how the demand for good *A* changes.
   c. Calculate the cross elasticity of demand of good *A* with respect to good *B*.
2. If, when income rises by 5 percent and other things remain the same, the quantity demanded of good *C* increases by 1 percent:
   a. Is good *C* a normal good or an inferior good? Why?
   b. Describe how the demand for good *C* changes when income increases.
   c. Calculate the income elasticity of demand for good *C*.

Exercises 5.3

1. Suppose that when the price of a burger decreases from $2.00 to $1.75 and other things remain the same, the quantity demanded of burgers increases from 200 an hour to 400 an hour and the quantity demanded of pizza decreases from 400 an hour to 200 an hour. At the same time, the quantity demanded of soda increases from 150 an hour to 300 an hour.
   a. Calculate the cross elasticity of demand for soda with respect to burgers.
   b. Are soda and burgers substitutes or complements? Why?
   c. Calculate the cross elasticity of demand for pizza with respect to burgers.
   d. Are pizza and burgers substitutes or complements? Why?
   e. Describe how the demand for soda and the demand for pizza have changed.
2. When Jody's income increases by 10 percent and other things remain the same, Jody decreases the quantity demanded of macaroni and cheese by 20 percent and increases the quantity demanded of chicken by 5 percent.
   a. Calculate the income elasticity of demand for macaroni and cheese.
   b. Is macaroni and cheese a normal good or an inferior good? Why?
   c. Calculate the income elasticity of demand for chicken.
   d. Is chicken a normal good or an inferior good? Why?
   e. Is chicken income elastic or income inelastic?

FIGURE 1

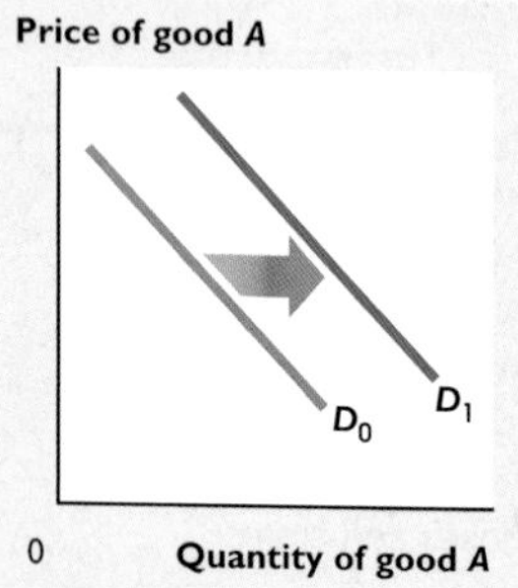

Price of good A

D_0 D_1

0 Quantity of good A

FIGURE 2

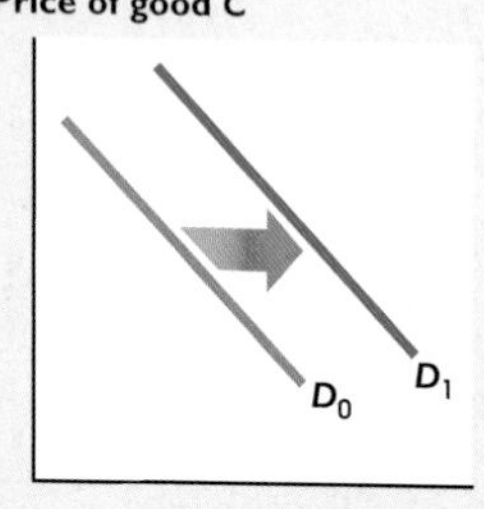

Solutions to Practice Problems 5.3

1a. Goods *A* and *B* are substitutes because when the price of good *B* rises, the quantity demanded of good *A* increases. People switch from good *B* to good *A*.

1b. The demand for good *A* increases (Figure 1).

1c. The cross elasticity of demand of good *A* with respect to good *B* equals the percentage change in the quantity demanded of good *A* divided by the percentage increase in the price of good *B*, which is 5 percent ÷ 10 percent or 0.5.

2a. Good *C* is a normal good; as income rises, the quantity demanded increases.

2b. The demand for good *C* increases (Figure 2).

2c. The income elasticity of demand of good *C* is 1 percent ÷ 5 percent = 0.2.

CHAPTER CHECKPOINT

Key Points

1 Define, explain the factors that influence, and calculate the price elasticity of demand.

- The demand for a good is elastic if when its price changes, the percentage change in the quantity demanded exceeds the percentage change in price.
- The demand for a good is inelastic if when its price changes, the percentage change in the quantity demanded is less than the percentage change in price.
- The price elasticity of demand for a good depends on how easy it is to find substitutes for the good and on the proportion of income spent on it.
- Price elasticity of demand equals the percentage change in the quantity demanded divided by the percentage change in price.
- If demand is elastic, a rise in price leads to a decrease in total revenue. If demand is unit elastic, a rise in price leaves total revenue unchanged. And if demand is inelastic, a rise in price leads to an increase in total revenue.

2 Define, explain the factors that influence, and calculate the price elasticity of supply.

- The supply of a good is elastic if when its price changes, the percentage change in the quantity supplied exceeds the percentage change in price.
- The supply of a good is inelastic if when its price changes, the percentage change in the quantity supplied is less than the percentage change in price.
- The main influences on the price elasticity of supply are the flexibility of production possibilities and storage possibilities.

3 Define and explain the factors that influence the cross elasticity of demand and the income elasticity of demand.

- Cross elasticity of demand shows how the demand for a good changes when the price of one of its substitutes or complements changes.
- Cross elasticity is positive for substitutes and negative for complements.
- Income elasticity of demand shows how the demand for a good changes when income changes. For a normal good, the income elasticity of demand is positive. For an inferior good, the income elasticity of demand is negative.

Key Terms

Exercises

1. One winter recently, the price of home heating oil increased by 20 percent and the quantity demanded decreased by 2 percent, and with no change in the price of wool sweaters, the quantity demanded of wool sweaters increased by 10 percent. Use this information to answer the following questions:
   - **a.** How would you describe the demand for home heating oil?
   - **b.** Calculate the price elasticity of demand for home heating oil.
   - **c.** Is this good more likely to be a necessity or a luxury good? Why?
   - **d.** How did the total revenue from the sale of home heating oil change? Why?
   - **e.** Calculate the cross elasticity of demand of wool sweaters with respect to the price of home heating oil.
   - **f.** Are home heating oil and wool sweaters substitutes or complements? Why?

2. The price elasticity of demand for Pete's chocolate chip cookies is 1.5. Pete wants to increase his total revenue. Would you recommend that Pete raise or lower his price of cookies? Explain your answer.

3. When heavy rain ruined the banana crop in Central America, the price of bananas rose from $1 a pound to $2 a pound. Banana sellers sold fewer bananas, but their total revenue remained unchanged.
   - **a.** By how much did the quantity demanded of bananas change?
   - **b.** Is the demand of bananas from Central America elastic or inelastic?

4. If a 10 percent increase in the demand for college places with no change in the supply of college places results in a 5 percent increase in tuition and a 2 percent increase in college places, what is the elasticity of supply of college places?

5. When income increased by 10 percent, the quantity of memberships of athletic clubs increased by 15 percent, the quantity demanded of spring water increased by 5 percent, and the quantity demanded of soft drinks decreased by 2 percent. Use the information to answer the following questions:
   - **a.** Describe the demand for memberships of athletic clubs.
   - **b.** Describe the demand for spring water.
   - **c.** Describe the demand for soft drinks.
   - **d.** The demand for which good is income elastic? Which is income inelastic?
   - **e.** Which of the three goods are normal goods? Is any good an inferior good?

6. In Pioneer Ville, the price elasticity of demand for bus rides is 0.5, the income elasticity of demand for bus rides is –0.1, and the cross elasticity of demand for bus rides with respect to gasoline is 0.2.
   - **a.** Is the demand for bus rides elastic or inelastic with respect to the price of a bus ride? Why?
   - **b.** Would an increase in bus fares increase the bus company's total revenue? Explain your answer.
   - **c.** Describe the relationship between bus rides and gasoline. Explain your answer.
   - **d.** If the price of gasoline increases by 10 percent with no change in the price of a bus ride, how will the number of bus rides change?
   - **e.** If incomes in Pioneer Ville increase by 5 percent with no change in the price of a bus ride, how will the number of bus rides change?
   - **f.** In Pioneer Ville, is a bus ride a normal good or an inferior good? Why?
   - **g.** In Pioneer Ville, are bus rides and gasoline substitutes or complements? Why?

Chapter 6

Efficiency and Fairness of Markets

CHAPTER CHECKLIST

When you have completed your study of this chapter, you will be able to:

1. **Distinguish between value and price and define consumer surplus.**
2. **Distinguish between cost and price and define producer surplus.**
3. **Explain the conditions in which markets are efficient and inefficient.**
4. **Explain the main ideas about fairness and evaluate claims that competitive markets result in unfair outcomes.**

We try to get the greatest value out of our scarce resources by comparing marginal costs and marginal benefits. You learned in Chapter 3 that when production is at a point on the *PPF* and when marginal benefit equals marginal cost, resources are being used *efficiently*.

You learned in Chapter 4 how the equilibrium quantities and prices in the market for goods, services, and factors of production determine *what*, *how*, and *for whom* goods and services are produced.

The first question that we study in this chapter brings these two sets of ideas together and asks: Are the equilibrium quantities of goods, services and factors of production the efficient quantities? In other words, are markets efficient?

The second question that we study asks: Are markets fair? Do they deliver a distribution of gains from trade that benefit both buyers and sellers in a fair way? Or do they create injustices?

We'll begin by reviewing what you learned in Chapter 3 about allocative efficiency.

EFFICIENCY: A REFRESHER

If you pay attention to the news media, you might get the impression that markets are inefficient. They make credit card interest rates too high. They make the wages of fast-food workers too low. They cause the price of coffee to go sky high every time Brazil has a serious frost. They increase the price of oil when political instability threatens the Middle East.

Are these examples of inefficiency? Or are they examples of the market doing its job and delivering an efficient outcome? To determine whether markets are efficient, we study a market that you probably participate in almost every week: the market for pizza.

To produce more pizza, we must give up some other goods and services. For example, we might give up some submarine sandwiches. To get more pizzas, we forgo submarine sandwiches. If we have fewer pizzas, we can have more submarine sandwiches. What is the efficient quantity of pizza to produce? The answer depends on the marginal benefit from pizza and its marginal cost.

Marginal Benefit

If we consume one more pizza, we receive a marginal benefit. *Marginal benefit* is the benefit that a person receives from consuming *one more unit* of a good or service. The marginal benefit from a good or service is measured as the maximum amount that a person is willing to pay for one more unit of it. So the marginal benefit from a pizza is the maximum amount of other goods and services that people are willing to give up to get one more pizza. The marginal benefit from pizza decreases as the quantity of pizza consumed increases—the principle of *decreasing marginal benefit*.

We can express the marginal benefit from pizza as the number of submarine sandwiches that people are willing to forgo to get one more pizza. But we can also express marginal benefit as the dollar value of the submarine sandwich or other goods and services that people are willing to forgo.

Figure 6.1 shows the marginal benefit from pizza expressed in this way. As the quantity of pizza increases, the dollar value of the other goods and services that people are willing to forgo to get yet one more pizza decreases—the marginal benefit of pizza curve, *MB*, slopes downward.

Marginal Cost

If we produce one more pizza, we incur a marginal cost. *Marginal cost* is the opportunity cost of producing *one more unit* of a good or service. The marginal cost of a good or service is measured as the value of the best alternative forgone. So the marginal cost of a pizza is the value of the best alternative forgone to get one more pizza. The marginal cost of a pizza increases as the quantity of pizza produced increases—the principle of *increasing marginal cost*.

We can express marginal cost as the number of submarine sandwiches we must forgo to get one more pizza. But we can also express marginal cost as the dollar value of the other goods and services we must forgo.

Figure 6.1 shows the marginal cost of pizza expressed in this way. As the quantity of pizza produced increases, the dollar value of other goods and services we must forgo to get yet one more pizza increases—the marginal cost of pizza curve, *MC*, slopes upward.

Allocative Efficiency

To determine the efficient quantity of pizza, we compare the marginal benefit from a pizza with the marginal cost of a pizza.

If the quantity of pizzas produced is 5,000 a day, the marginal benefit of a pizza at point *A* exceeds the marginal cost of a pizza at point *B*. If production increases from 4,999 to 5,000 pizzas, the benefit from the additional pizza exceeds its cost. Resources are used more efficiently—they create more value—if we produce an extra pizza and fewer other goods and services. Marginal benefit exceeds marginal cost up to the 10,000th pizza.

If the quantity produced is 15,000 pizzas a day, the marginal cost of a pizza at point *C* exceeds the marginal benefit of a pizza at point *D*. If pizza production decreases from 15,000 to 14,999, the cost saving exceeds the forgone benefit. Resources are used more efficiently—they create more value—if we produce fewer pizzas and more other goods and services. Marginal cost exceeds marginal benefit down to the 10,000th pizza.

When the quantity produced is 10,000 pizzas a day, the marginal benefit of a pizza and the marginal cost of a pizza are $10. In this situation, we cannot increase the value of the goods and services produced by either increasing or decreasing the quantity of pizza. If we increase the quantity of pizza, the 10,001st pizza costs more to produce than it is worth. And if we decrease the quantity of pizza produced, the 9,999th pizza is worth more than it costs to produce. So when marginal benefit equals marginal cost, resource use is efficient.

FIGURE 6.1
The Efficient Quantity of Pizza

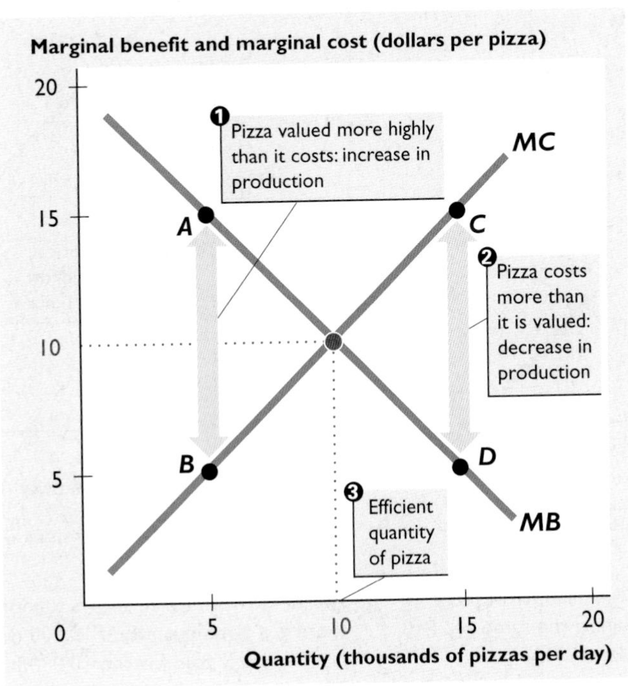

The marginal benefit curve (*MB*) shows what people *are willing to* forgo to get one more pizza. The marginal cost curve (*MC*) shows what people *must* forgo to get one more pizza.

1. If fewer than 10,000 pizzas a day are produced, marginal benefit exceeds marginal cost. Greater value can be obtained by producing more pizzas.
2. If more than 10,000 pizzas a day are produced, marginal cost exceeds marginal benefit. Greater value can be obtained by producing fewer pizzas.
3. If 10,000 pizzas a day are produced, marginal benefit equals marginal cost and the efficient quantity of pizza is available.

6.1 VALUE, PRICE, AND CONSUMER SURPLUS

To investigate whether a market is efficient, we need to understand the connection between demand and marginal benefit and between supply and marginal cost.

Demand and Marginal Benefit

In everyday life, when we talk about "getting value for money," we're distinguishing between *value* and *price*. Value is what we get, and price is what we pay. In economics, the everyday idea of value is *marginal benefit*, which we measure as the maximum price that people are willing to pay for another unit of the good or service. The demand curve tells us this price. In Figure 6.2(a), the demand curve shows the quantity demanded at a given price—when the price is $10, the quantity demanded is 10,000 pizzas a day. In Figure 6.2(b), the demand curve shows the maximum price that people are willing to pay when there is a given quantity—when 10,000 pizzas a day are available, the most that people are willing to pay for the 10,000th pizza is $10. The marginal benefit from the 10,000th pizza is $10.

A demand curve is a marginal benefit curve. The demand curve for pizza tells us the dollars' worth of other goods and services that people are willing to forgo to consume one more pizza.

FIGURE 6.2
Demand, Willingness to Pay, and Marginal Benefit

*e*Foundations **6.1** 

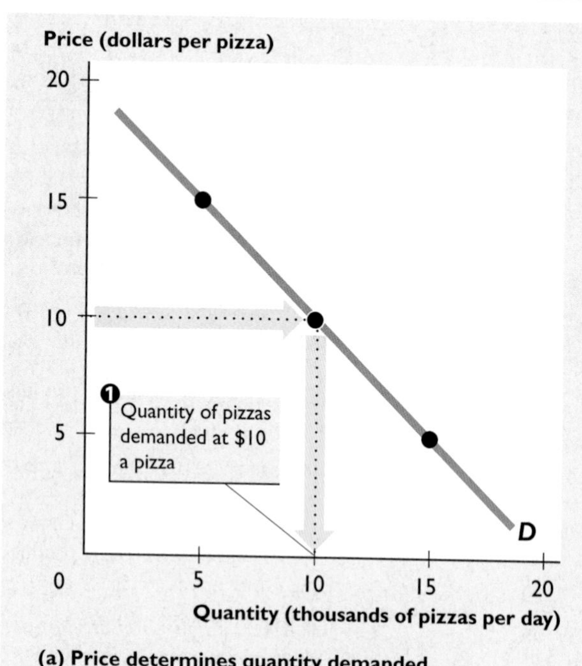

(a) Price determines quantity demanded

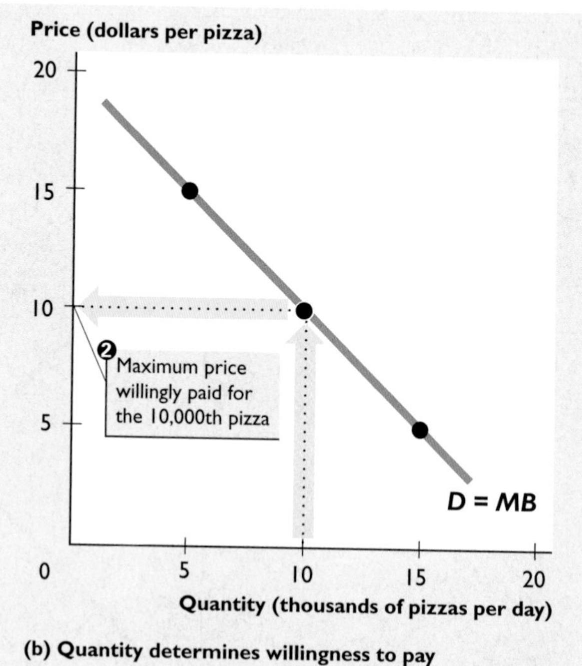

(b) Quantity determines willingness to pay

❶ The demand curve for pizza, *D*, shows the quantity of pizza demanded at each price, other things remaining the same. At $10 a pizza, the quantity demanded is 10,000 pizzas a day.

❷ The demand curve shows the maximum price willingly paid if there is a given quantity. If 10,000 pizzas are available, the maximum price willingly paid for the 10,000th pizza is $10.

Consumer Surplus

We don't always have to pay as much as we're willing to pay. When people buy something for less than it is worth to them, they receive a **consumer surplus**, which is the marginal benefit from a good minus the price paid for it.

Consumer surplus
The marginal benefit from a good or service minus the price paid for it.

Figure 6.3 illustrates consumer surplus. Lisa's demand curve for pizza tells us the quantities of pizza she plans to buy at each price and her marginal benefit from pizza at each quantity. If the price of pizza is $1.00 a slice, Lisa buys 20 slices a week. She spends $20 on pizza, which is shown by the area of the blue rectangle.

To calculate Lisa's consumer surplus, we must find her consumer surplus on each slice and add these consumer surpluses together. For the 20th slice, her marginal benefit equals $1 and she pays $1, so her consumer surplus on this slice is zero. For the 10th slice (highlighted in the figure), her marginal benefit is $1.50. So on this slice, she receives a consumer surplus of $1.50 minus $1.00, which is 50¢. For the first slice, Lisa's marginal benefit is almost $2, so on this slice she receives a consumer surplus of almost $1.

Lisa's consumer surplus—the sum of the consumer surpluses on the 20 slices she buys—is $10 a week, which is shown by the area of the green triangle. (The base of the triangle is 20 slices a week and its height is $1, so its area is 20 × $1 ÷ 2 = $10.)

Lisa's *total benefit* is the amount she pays, $20 (blue rectangle), plus her consumer surplus, $10 (green triangle), and is $30. Because Lisa must pay $20 for the pizza she consumes, her net benefit is equal to her total benefit minus what she pays. Consumer surplus is the net benefit to the consumer.

FIGURE 6.3
A Consumer's Demand and Consumer Surplus

*e*Foundations 6.1 

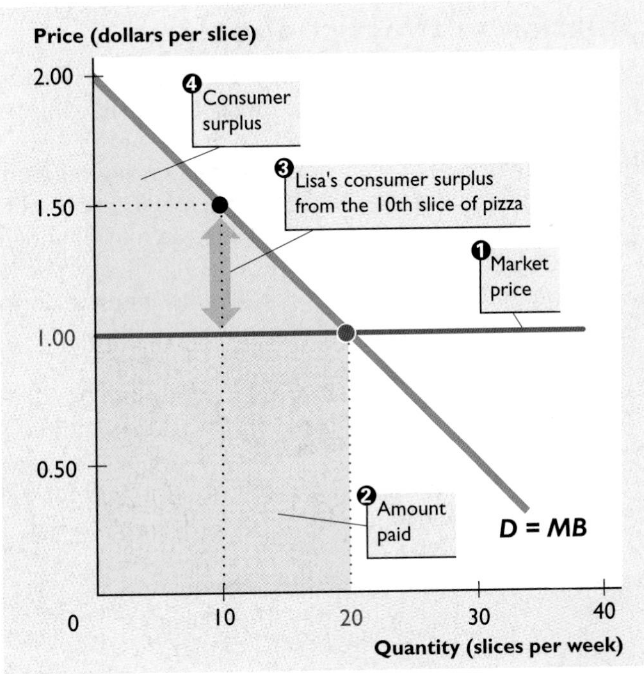

1. The market price of pizza is $1.00 a slice.
2. At the market price, Lisa buys 20 slices a week and spends $20 on pizza—the blue rectangle.
3. Lisa's demand curve tells us that she is willing to pay $1.50 for the 10th slice, so she receives a consumer surplus of 50¢ on the 10th slice.
4. Lisa's consumer surplus from the 20 slices she buys is $10—the area of the green triangle. Lisa's total benefit from pizza is the $20 she pays for it plus the $10 consumer surplus she receives, or $30.

CHECKPOINT 6.1

Study Guide pp. 84–87 

*e*Foundations 6.1

1 **Distinguish between value and price and define consumer surplus.**

Practice Problem 6.1

Figure 1 shows the demand for CDs and the market price of a CD. Use the figure to answer the following questions:

a. What is the value of the 10th CD?
b. What is the willingness to pay for the 20th CD?
c. What is the consumer surplus on the 10th CD?
d. What are the quantity of CDs bought and the consumer surplus?
e. What is the amount paid for the CDs in question (d)?
f. What is the total benefit from the CDs bought in question (d)?
g. If the price of a CD rises to $20, what is the change in the consumer surplus?

FIGURE 1

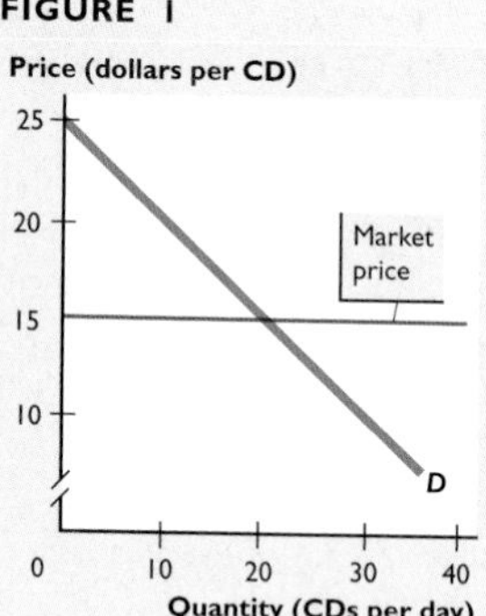

Exercise 6.1

Figure 2 shows the demand for soft drinks and the market price of a soft drink. Use the figure to answer the following questions:

a. What is the value of the 30th can of soft drink?
b. What is the willingness to pay for the 10th can of soft drink?
c. What is the consumer surplus on the 10th can of soft drink?
d. What are the quantity of soft drinks bought and the consumer surplus?
e. What is the total amount paid for the soft drinks in question (d)?
f. What is the total benefit from the soft drinks bought in question (d)?
g. If the price of a soft drink rises to $1.00 a can, what is the change in the consumer surplus?

FIGURE 2

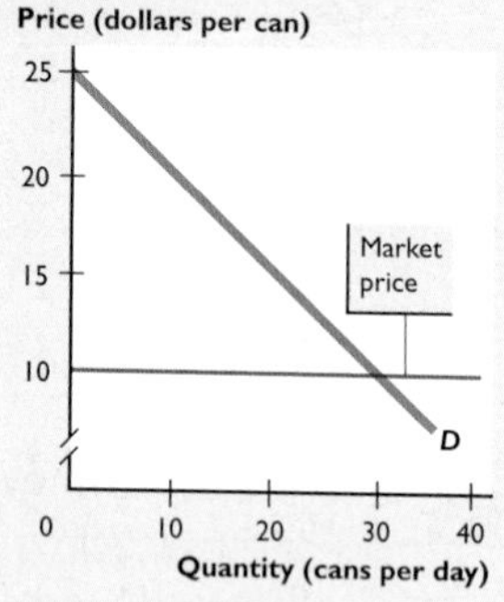

Solution to Practice Problem 6.1

a. The value of the 10th CD is the marginal benefit from the 10th CD. Value is equal to the maximum price that someone is willing to pay for the 10th CD, which is $20 (Figure 3).

b. The willingness to pay for the 20th CD is the maximum price that someone is willing to pay for the 20th CD, which is $15 (the green arrow in Figure 3).

c. Consumer surplus on the 10th CD is its marginal benefit minus the price of a CD, which is $20 – $15 = $5 (Figure 3).

d. The quantity of CDs bought is 20 a day, and the consumer surplus is ($25 – $15) × 20 ÷ 2 = $100 (the green triangle in Figure 3).

e. The amount paid for CDs is price multiplied by quantity bought, which is $15 × 20 = $300 (the blue rectangle in Figure 3).

f. The total benefit from CDs is the amount paid for CDs plus the consumer surplus on CDs, which is $300 + $100 = $400.

g. If the price of a CD rises to $20, the quantity of CDs bought decreases to 10 a day. The consumer surplus on CDs decreases to $25—($25 – $20) × 10 ÷ 2 (the smaller green triangle in Figure 4).

FIGURE 3

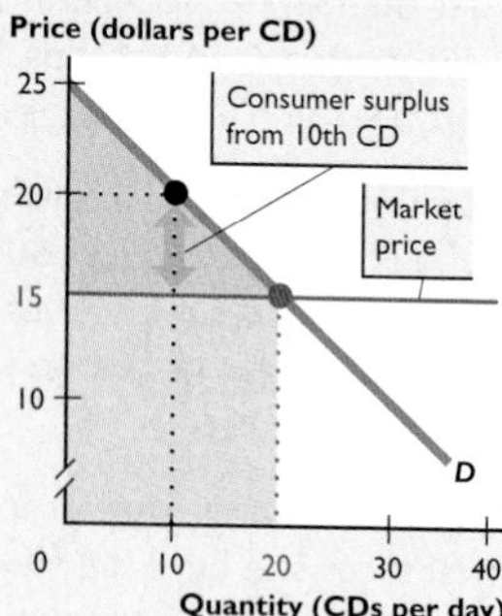

FIGURE 4

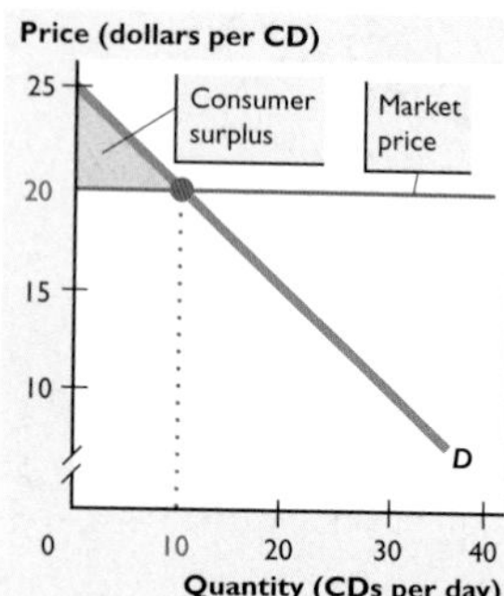

6.2 COST, PRICE, AND PRODUCER SURPLUS

What you are now going to learn about cost, price, and producer surplus parallels what you've learned about value, price, and consumer surplus.

Supply and Marginal Cost

Just as buyers distinguish between *value* and *price*, so sellers distinguish between *cost* and *price*. Cost is what a seller must give up to produce the good, and price is what a seller receives when the good is sold. The cost of producing one more unit of a good or service is its *marginal cost*. It is just worth producing one more unit of a good or service if the price for which it can be sold equals marginal cost. But the supply curve tells us this price. In Figure 6.4(a), the supply curve shows the quantity supplied at a given price—when the price of a pizza is $10, the quantity supplied is 10,000 pizzas a day. In Figure 6.4(b), the supply curve shows the minimum price that producers must receive to supply a given quantity—to supply 10,000 pizzas a day, producers must be able to get at least $10 for the 10,000th pizza. The marginal cost of the 10,000th pizza is $10. So:

A supply curve is a marginal cost curve. The supply curve of pizza tells us the dollars' worth of other goods and services that firms must forgo to produce one more pizza.

FIGURE 6.4
Supply, Minimum Supply Price, and Marginal Cost

*e*Foundations **6.2** 

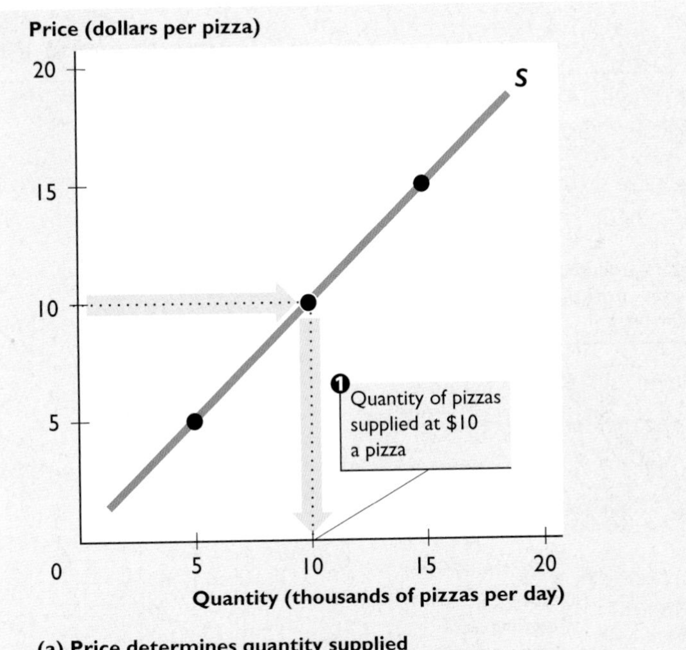

(a) Price determines quantity supplied

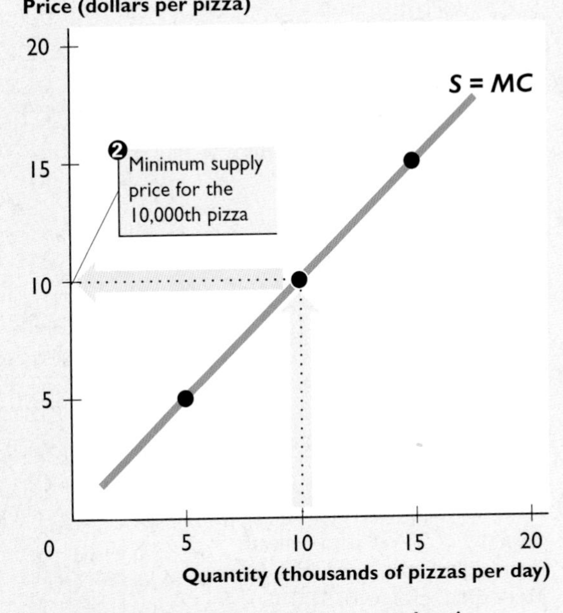

(b) Quantity determines minimum supply price

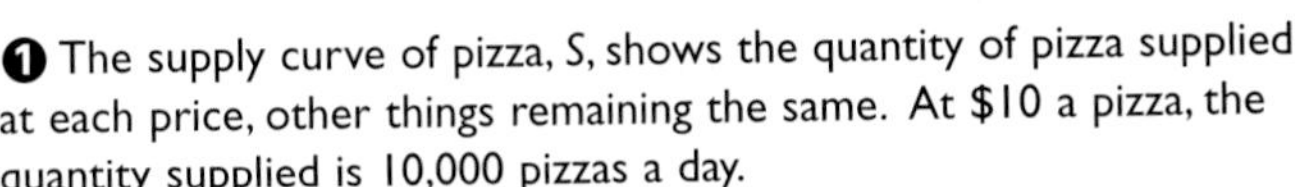
❶ The supply curve of pizza, *S*, shows the quantity of pizza supplied at each price, other things remaining the same. At $10 a pizza, the quantity supplied is 10,000 pizzas a day.

❷ The supply curve shows the minimum price that firms must be offered to supply a given quantity. The minimum supply price for the 10,000th pizza is $10.

Producer Surplus

Producer surplus
The price of a good minus the marginal cost of producing it.

When the price exceeds marginal cost, the firm obtains a **producer surplus**, which is the price of a good minus the marginal cost of producing it.

Figure 6.5 illustrates producer surplus. Max can produce pizza or bake bread. The more pizza he bakes, the less bread he can bake. His marginal cost (opportunity cost) of pizza is the value of the bread he must forgo. The marginal cost of pizza increases as Max produces more pizza.

Max's supply curve of pizza tells us the quantities of pizza that Max plans to sell at each price and his marginal cost of producing at each quantity. If the price of a pizza is \$10, Max produces 100 a day. Max's total revenue is \$1,000 a day (\$10 × 100 = \$1,000).

To calculate Max's producer surplus, we must find the producer surplus on each pizza and add these producer surpluses together. The marginal cost of the 100th pizza is \$10 and equals the \$10 he can sell it for, so his producer surplus on this pizza is zero. For the 50th pizza (highlighted in the figure), his marginal cost is \$6. So on this pizza, he receives a producer surplus of \$10 minus \$6, which is \$4. For the first pizza produced, Max's marginal cost is a bit more than \$2, so on this pizza, he receives a producer surplus of almost \$8.

Max's producer surplus—the sum of the producer surpluses on the 100 pizzas he sells—is \$400 a day, which is shown by the blue triangle. (The base of the triangle is 100 pizzas a day and its height \$8, so its area is 100 × \$8 ÷ 2 = \$400.)

The red area shows Max's cost of producing 100 pizzas a day, which is \$600. This amount equals Max's total revenue of \$1,000 a day minus his producer surplus of \$400 a day.

FIGURE 6.5
A Producer's Supply and Producer Surplus

*e*Foundations 6.2 

❶ The market price of a pizza is \$10. At this price, Max sells 100 pizzas a day and receives a total revenue of \$1,000 a day.

❷ Max's supply curve shows that the minimum that he must be offered for the 50th pizza a day is \$6, so he receives a producer surplus of \$4 on the 50th pizza.

❸ Max's producer surplus from the 100 pizzas he sells is \$400 a day—the area of the blue triangle.

❹ Max's cost of producing 100 pizzas a day is the red area beneath the marginal cost curve. It equals Max's total revenue of \$1,000 minus his producer surplus of \$400 and is \$600 a day.

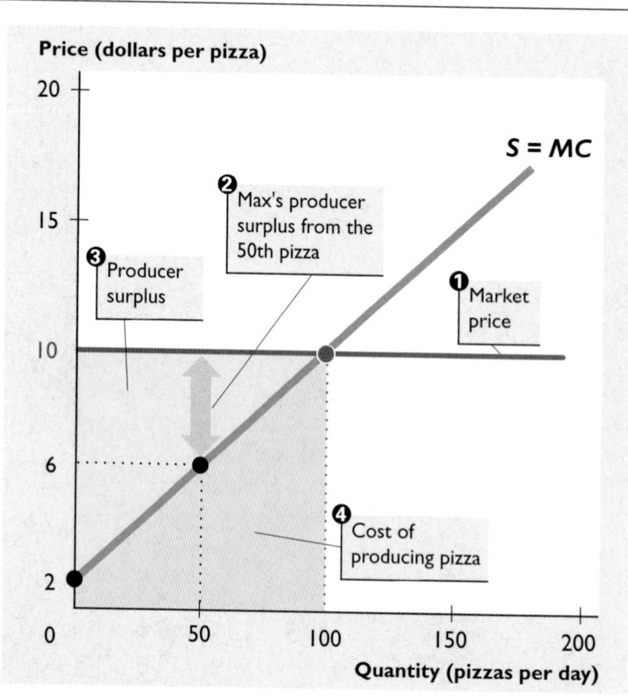

CHECKPOINT 6.2

2 **Distinguish between cost and price and define producer surplus.**

Study Guide pp. 87–90

e/**Foundations 6.2**

Practice Problem 6.2

Figure 1 shows the supply of CDs and the market price of a CD. Use the figure to answer the following questions:

a. What is the marginal cost of the 10th CD?
b. What is the minimum supply price of the 20th CD?
c. What is the producer surplus on the 10th CD?
d. What are the quantity of CDs sold and the producer surplus?
e. What is the total revenue from the CDs sold in question (d)?
f. What is the cost of producing the CDs sold in question (d)?
g. If the price of a CD falls to $10, what is the change in the producer surplus?

FIGURE 1

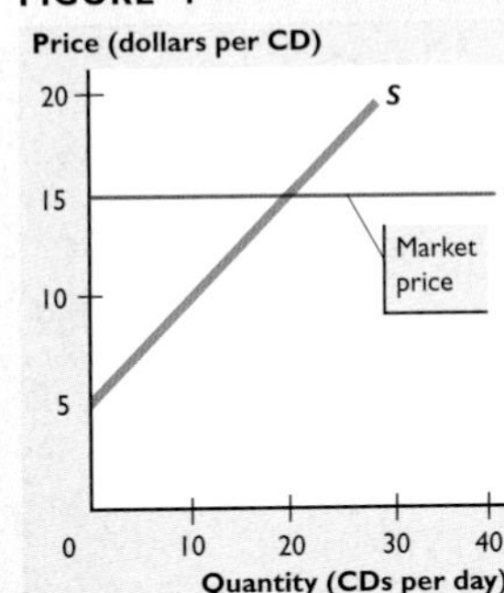

Exercise 6.2

Figure 2 shows the supply of soft drinks and the market price of a soft drink. Use the figure to answer the following questions:

a. What is the marginal cost of the 30th can of soft drink?
b. What is the minimum supply price of the 10th can of soft drink?
c. What is the producer surplus on the 10th can of soft drink?
d. What are the quantity of soft drinks sold and the producer surplus?
e. What is the total revenue from the soft drinks sold in question (d)?
f. What is the cost of producing the soft drinks sold in question (d)?
g. If the price of a soft drink falls to $1.00 a can, what is the change in the producer surplus?

FIGURE 2

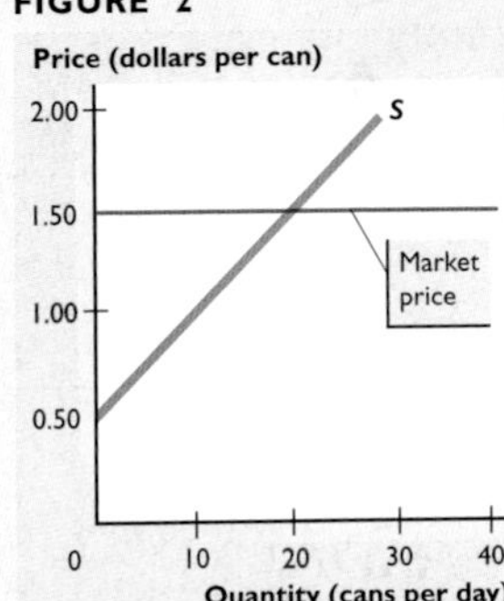

Solution to Practice Problem 6.2

a. The marginal cost of producing the 10th CD is equal to the minimum supply price for the 10th CD, which is $10 (Figure 3).
b. The minimum supply price of the 20th CD is the marginal cost of producing the 20th CD, which is $15 (Figure 3).
c. Producer surplus on the 10th CD is its market price minus its marginal cost, which is $15 – $10 = $5 (the blue arrow in Figure 3).
d. The quantity of CDs sold is 20 a day, and the producer surplus is ($15 – $5) × 20 ÷ 2 = $100 (the blue triangle in Figure 3).
e. The total revenue from CDs is the total expenditure on them, which is price multiplied by quantity sold. Total revenue is $15 × 20 = $300.
f. The cost of producing CDs equals total revenue minus producer surplus, which is $300 – $100 = $200 (the red area in Figure 3).
g. If the price of a CD falls to $10, the quantity of CDs sold decreases to 10 a day. The producer surplus on CDs decreases to ($10 – $5) × 10 ÷ 2 = $25 (the smaller blue triangle in Figure 4).

FIGURE 3

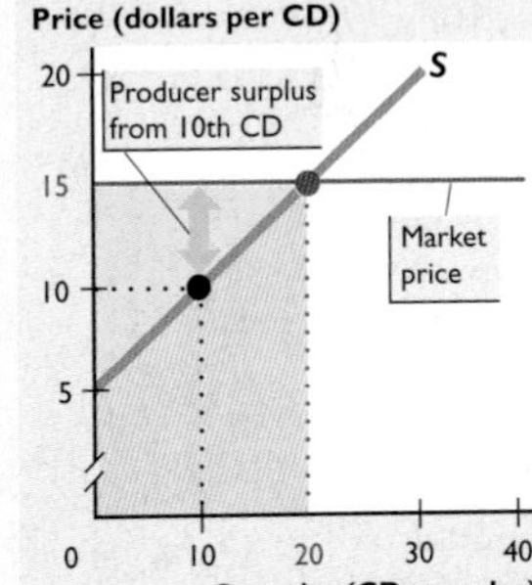

FIGURE 4

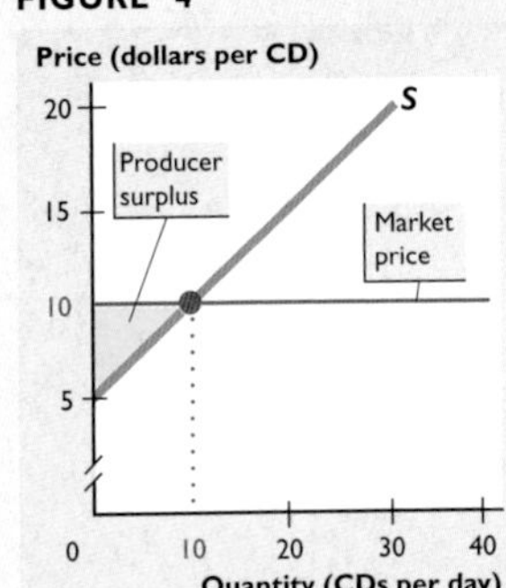

6.3 ARE MARKETS EFFICIENT?

Figure 6.6 shows the market for pizza. The demand curve, *D*, shows the demand for pizza. The supply curve, *S*, shows the supply of pizza. The equilibrium price is $10 a pizza, and the equilibrium quantity is 10,000 pizzas a day.

The market forces that you studied in Chapter 4 (pp. 95–96) will pull the pizza market to its equilibrium. If the price exceeds $10 a pizza, a surplus of pizza will force the price down. If the price is less than $10 a pizza, a shortage of pizza will force the price up. Only if the price is $10 a pizza is there neither a surplus nor a shortage of pizza and no forces operate to change its price.

So the market price and quantity are pulled toward their equilibrium values. But is this competitive equilibrium efficient? Does it produce the efficient quantity of pizza?

Efficiency of Competitive Equilibrium

The equilibrium in Figure 6.6 is efficient. Resources are being used to produce the quantity of pizza that people value most highly. It is not possible to produce more pizza without giving up some of another good or service that is valued more highly. And if a smaller quantity of pizza is produced, resources are used to produce some other good that is not valued as highly as the pizza forgone.

FIGURE 6.6
An Efficient Market for Pizza

*e*Foundations 6.3 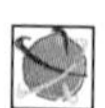

❶ Market equilibrium occurs at a price of $10 a pizza and a quantity of 10,000 pizzas a day.

❷ The supply curve is also the marginal cost curve.

❸ The demand curve is also the marginal benefit curve.

Because at the market equilibrium, marginal benefit equals marginal cost, the ❹ efficient quantity of pizza is produced. The sum of the ❺ consumer surplus and ❻ producer surplus is maximized.

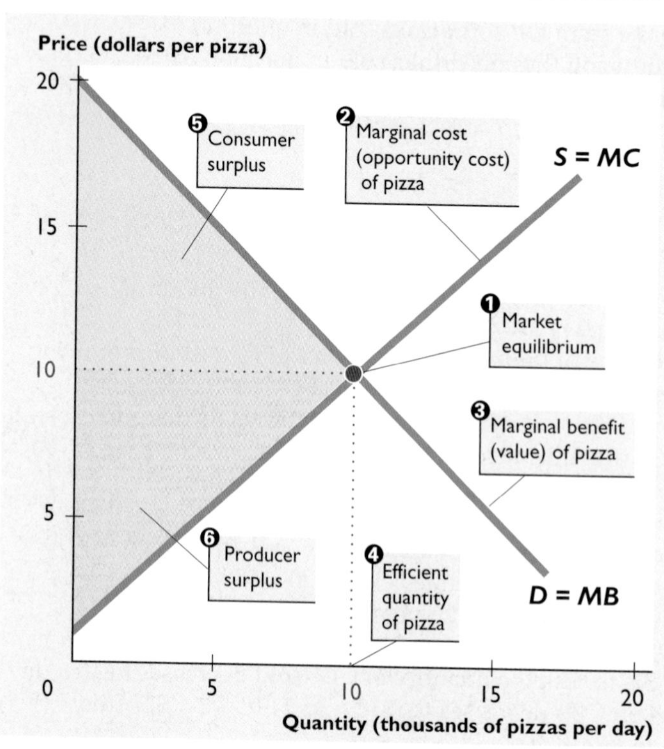

To see why the equilibrium in Figure 6.6 is efficient, think about the interpretation of the demand curve as a marginal benefit curve and the supply curve as a marginal cost curve. The demand curve tells us the marginal benefit from pizza. The supply curve tells us the marginal cost of pizza. So where the demand curve and the supply curve intersect, marginal benefit equals marginal cost.

But this condition—marginal benefit equals marginal cost—is the condition that delivers an efficient use of resources. It allocates resources to the activities that create the greatest possible value. So a competitive equilibrium is efficient.

If production is less than 10,000 pizzas a day, someone is willing to buy a pizza for more than it cost to produce. So buyers and sellers will gain if production increases. If production exceeds 10,000 pizzas a day, it costs more to produce a pizza than anyone is willing to pay for it. So buyers and sellers will gain if production decreases. Only when 10,000 pizzas a day are produced is there no unexploited gain from changing the quantity of pizza produced.

The competitive market pushes the quantity of pizza produced to its efficient level of 10,000 a day. If production is less than 10,000 pizzas a day, a shortage raises the price, which stimulates an increase in production. If production exceeds 10,000 pizzas a day, a surplus lowers the price, which decreases production.

In a competitive equilibrium, resources are used efficiently to produce the goods and services that people value most highly. And when the competitive market uses resources efficiently, the sum of consumer surplus and producer surplus is maximized.

Buyers and sellers each attempt to do the best they can for themselves, and no one plans for an efficient outcome for society as a whole. Buyers seek the lowest possible price, and sellers seek the highest possible price.

The Invisible Hand

Writing in his *Wealth of Nations* in 1776, Adam Smith was the first to suggest that competitive markets send resources to the uses in which they have the highest value. Smith believed that each participant in a competitive market is "led by an invisible hand to promote an end [the efficient use of resources] which was no part of his intention."

You can see the effects of the invisible hand at work every day. Your campus bookstore is stuffed with texts at the start of each term. It has the quantities that it predicts students will buy. The coffee shop has the variety and quantities of drinks and snacks that people plan to buy. Your local clothing shop has the sweatpants and socks and other items you plan to buy. Truckloads of textbooks, coffee and cookies, and sweatpants and socks roll along our highways and bring these items to where you and your friends want to buy them. Firms that don't know you anticipate your wants and work hard to help you satisfy them.

No government organizes all this production, and no government auditor monitors producers to ensure that they serve the public interest. The allocation of scarce resources is not planned. It happens because prices adjust to make buying plans and selling plans compatible. And it happens in a way that sends resources to the uses in which they have the highest value.

Adam Smith explained why all this amazing activity occurs. "It is not from the benevolence of the butcher, the brewer, or the baker that we expect our dinner," he wrote, "but from their regard to their own interest."

Publishing companies, coffee growers, garment manufacturers, and a host of other producers are led by their regard to their own interest to serve *your* interest.

ECONOMICS *in the* NEWS

October 1, 1999

A new Internet auction service that matches bids for and offers of college places has been launched by eCollegebid.

Questions

1. What determines the demand for college places?

2. What determines the supply of college places?

3. What determines the equilibrium price and quantity of college places?

4. Will the service provided by eCollegebid increase, decrease, or have no effect on:

- *a. The number of students who attend college?*
- *b. The average tuition rate?*
- *c. Consumer surplus?*
- *d. Producer surplus?*
- *e. Deadweight loss?*

5. Who benefits from and who bears the cost of the service provided by eCollegebid?

 *e*/**Foundations 6.3**

Eye On The U.S. Economy

The Invisible Hand and e-Commerce

You can see the influence of the invisible hand at work in the cartoon and in today's information economy.

The cold drinks vendor has both cold drinks and shade. He has an opportunity cost and a minimum supply price of each item. The park bench reader has a marginal benefit from a cold drink and from shade. The transaction that occurs tells us that the reader's marginal benefit from shade exceeds the vendor's marginal cost but the vendor's marginal cost of a cold drink exceeds the reader's marginal benefit. The transaction creates consumer surplus and producer surplus. The vendor obtains a producer surplus from selling the shade for more than its opportunity cost, and the reader obtains a consumer surplus from buying the shade for less than its marginal benefit. In the third frame of the cartoon, both the consumer and the producer are better off than they were in the first frame. The umbrella has moved to its highest value use.

The market economy relentlessly performs the activity illustrated in the cartoon to achieve an efficient allocation of resources. And rarely has the market been working as hard as it is today. Think about a few of the changes taking place in our economy and notice how the market is guiding resources toward their efficient use.

New technologies have cut the cost of producing computers. As these advances have occurred, the supply of computers has increased and the price of a computer has fallen. Lower prices have encouraged an increase in the quantity demanded of this now less costly tool. The marginal benefit from computers is brought to equality with their marginal cost.

During the past few years, hundreds of Web sites have been established that are dedicated to facilitating trading in all types of goods, services, and factors of production. One of these sites is Freeshop.com (http://www.freeshop.com/), which organizes access to hundreds of other sites that among them offer more than 1,000 "free and trial offers."

Another notable online market maker is the electronic auction site eBay (http://www.ebay.com/), where you can offer to buy or sell any of a huge variety of items.

These e-commerce innovations are increasing consumer surplus, increasing producer surplus, and achieving yet greater allocative efficiency.

Obstacles to Efficiency

Although markets generally do a good job of sending resources to where they are most highly valued, they do not always produce the efficient quantities. Sometimes markets overproduce a good or service, and sometimes they underproduce. The most significant obstacles to achieving an efficient allocation of resources in the market economy are:

- Externalities
- Public goods
- Monopoly

Externalities

An *externality* is a cost or a benefit that arises from a production activity that falls on someone other than the producer, or a cost or a benefit that arises from a consumption activity that falls on someone other than the consumer. A *spillover effect* is another name for an externality. When an electric power utility burns coal to generate electricity, it puts sulfur dioxide into the atmosphere, which falls as acid rain and damages crops. This is an example of an *external cost* of production. The utility does not consider the cost of pollution when it decides the quantity of power to produce. Its supply curve is based on its own costs, not on the costs that it inflicts on others. So too much electric power is produced.

When a homeowner maintains a beautifully landscaped yard, she benefits all the people who live around her. This is an example of an *external benefit* of consumption. The homeowner does not consider her neighbors' marginal benefit when she decides the quantity of landscaping services to buy. Her demand curve for landscaping services is based on her own marginal benefit. In this case, the quantity falls short of the efficient quantity. (We study externalities in Chapter 8.)

Public Goods

A *public good* is a good or service that is consumed simultaneously by everyone, even if they don't pay for it. Examples are national defense and law enforcement. Competitive markets would produce too small a quantity of a public good because of a *free-rider problem*—the fact that it is in each person's interest to free ride on everyone else and avoid paying for her or his share of a public good. So a competitive market produces less of a public good than the efficient quantity. (We study public goods in Chapter 9.)

Monopoly

A *monopoly* is a firm that has sole control of a market. For example, local water supply and cable television are produced by monopolies. The goal of a monopoly is to maximize profit. To achieve this goal, a monopoly produces less than the efficient quantity and raises its price. (We study monopoly in Chapter 13.)

The three types of obstacles to efficiency that we've just considered arise from some feature of the good or service or because a single producer manages to take control of an entire market. Governments influence markets in a variety of ways, and some of these can create inefficiency. They are:

- Price ceilings and price floors
- Taxes, subsidies, and quotas

Price Ceilings and Price Floors

A *price ceiling* is a regulation that makes it illegal to charge a price higher than a specified level. An example is a price ceiling on apartment rents, which some cities impose. A *price floor* is a regulation that makes it illegal to pay a price lower than a specified level. An example is the minimum wage. (We study both of these restrictions on buyers and sellers in Chapter 7.)

The presence of a price ceiling or a price floor blocks the forces of demand and supply and results in a quantity produced that might exceed or fall short of the quantity determined in an unregulated market.

Taxes, Subsidies, and Quotas

Taxes increase the prices paid by buyers and lower the prices received by sellers. So taxes decrease the quantity produced to less than the efficient quantity (for reasons that are explained in Chapter 7). All kinds of goods and services are taxed, but the highest taxes are on gasoline, alcohol, and tobacco.

Subsidies, which are payments by the government to sellers or buyers, decrease the prices paid by buyers and increase the prices received by sellers. Subsidies increase the quantity produced to more than the efficient quantity.

Quotas, which are limits to the quantity that a firm is permitted to produce, restrict output below the quantity that a competitive market would produce. Farms are sometimes subject to quotas—for example, tobacco farmers face quotas.

The impediments to efficiency that we've just reviewed and that you will study in greater detail in later chapters result in two possible outcomes:

- Underproduction
- Overproduction

Underproduction

Suppose that in the pizza market in Figure 6.6, one firm buys all the pizza outlets in the city and then cuts the quantity of pizza produced to 5,000 a day. Figure 6.7(a) shows that at this quantity, consumers are willing to pay $15 for a pizza that cost only $6 to produce. The quantity produced is inefficient.

The sum of consumer surplus and producer surplus decreases by the amount of the gray triangle in Figure 6.7(a). This triangle is called deadweight loss. **Deadweight loss** is the decrease in consumer surplus and producer surplus that results from an inefficient level of production. The deadweight loss is borne by the entire society. It is not a loss for the consumers and a gain for the producer. It is a *social* loss.

Deadweight loss
The decrease in consumer surplus and producer surplus that results from an inefficient level of production.

Overproduction

Now suppose that in the pizza market in Figure 6.6, the pizza lobby gets the government to pay the pizza producers a fat subsidy and production increases to 15,000 a day. Figure 6.7(b) shows that at this quantity, consumers are willing to pay only $5 for that marginal pizza but the marginal cost of that pizza is $4. It now costs more to produce a pizza than consumers are willing to pay for it. If we produce the 15,000th pizza, we lose $9.

Again, deadweight loss is shown by the gray triangle. The sum of consumer surplus and producer surplus is smaller than its maximum by the amount of deadweight loss.

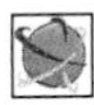

FIGURE 6.7
Underproduction and Overproduction

*e*Foundations 6.3

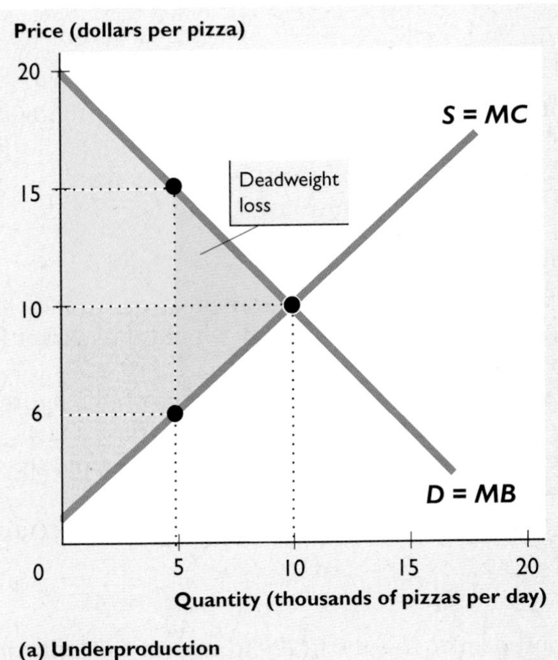

(a) Underproduction

If pizza production is restricted to 5,000 a day, a deadweight loss (the gray triangle) arises. The sum of the consumer surplus (the green area) and producer surplus (the blue area) is reduced.

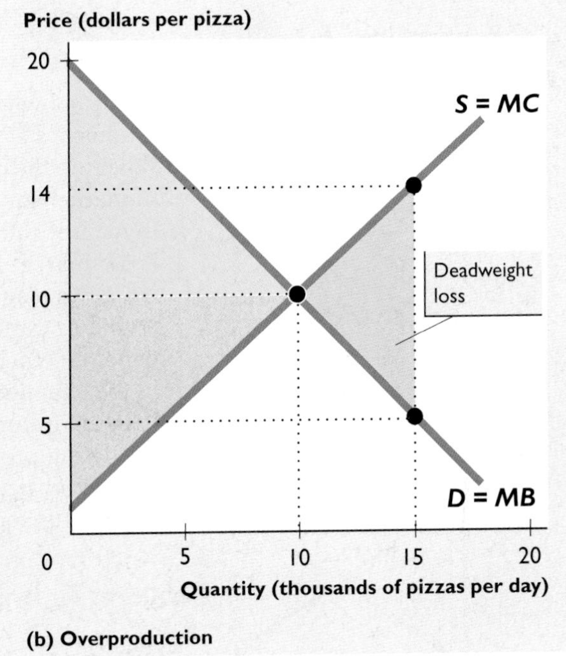

(b) Overproduction

If production increases to 15,000, a deadweight loss arises. Consumer surplus plus producer surplus equals the sum of the green and blue areas minus the gray deadweight loss triangle.

Are Mega-Mergers Efficient or Inefficient?

AOL Time Warner is a new firm that was created by merging the resources of America Online and media giant Time Warner. Time Warner itself came from a merger of Time Inc., the producer of *Time* magazine, and Warner Brothers, the moviemaker. Time-Warner also bought CNN from Ted Turner.

These mergers in the media industry are just the tip of a huge iceberg of merger activity in the U.S. and global economies. Mergers of automakers keep reducing the number of independent firms in that industry. For example, Germany's Daimler has bought Chrysler. Ford has bought Sweden's Volvo and Britain's Jaguar. Mercedes-Benz has bought Volkswagen.

In the oil industry, Exxon and Mobil have become one firm.

Mergers enable firms to avoid duplication of activities and bring resources into one organization so that they can be used more efficiently. But do mergers result in a more efficient allocation of resources? Do the bigger firms impose external costs? Do they restrict output and produce less than the efficient quantity? Do mergers need to be scrutinized by the government and sometimes blocked?

These are controversial questions that often don't have definite answers. But you can think about these questions by using what you've learned in this chapter.

Mergers are efficient if they cut costs or if they bring marginal benefit closer to marginal cost. Mergers are inefficient if they raise costs or if they widen the gap between marginal benefit and marginal cost.

CHECKPOINT 6.3

Study Guide pp. 90–93 

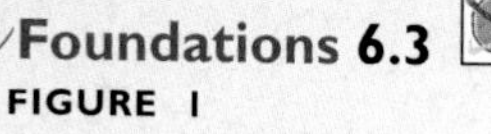

*e*Foundations 6.3

FIGURE 1

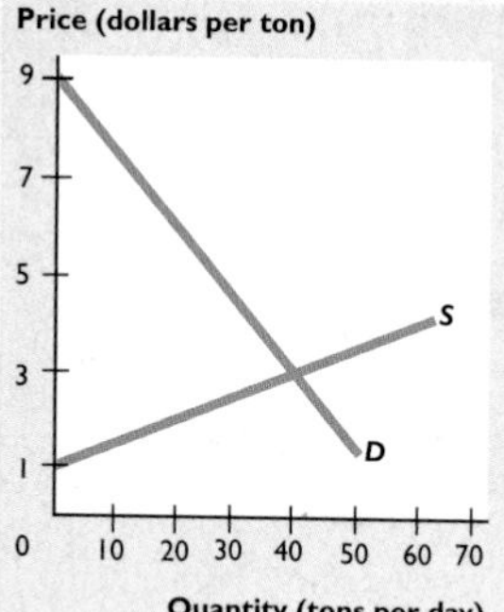

FIGURE 2

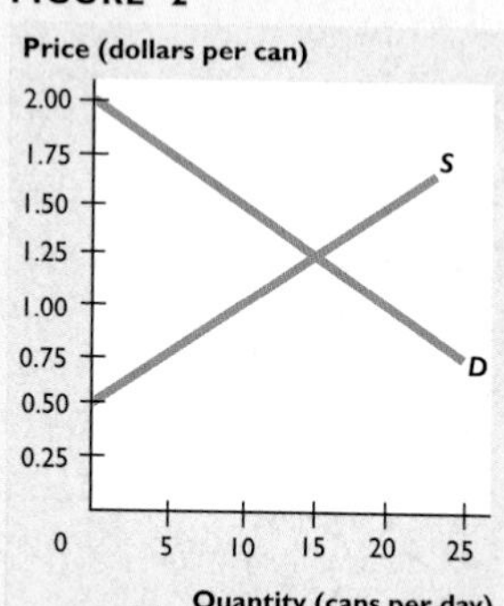

FIGURE 3

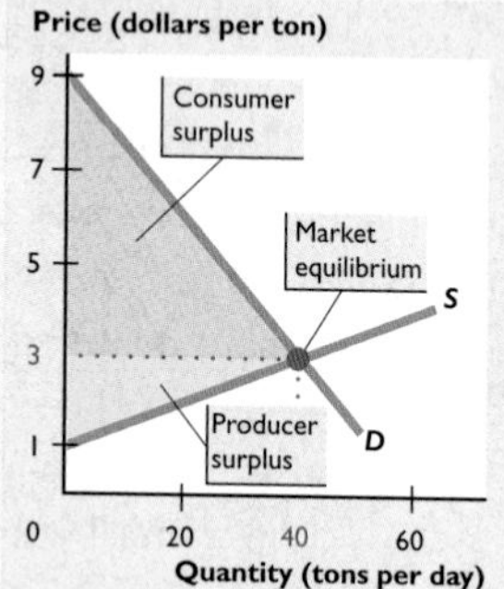

FIGURE 4

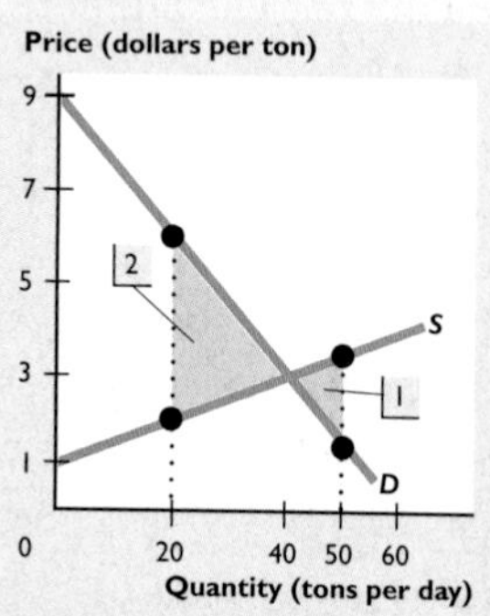

3 **Explain the conditions in which markets are efficient and inefficient.**

Practice Problem 6.3

Figure 1 shows the market for paper. Use the figure to answer the following questions:

a. What are the equilibrium price and the equilibrium quantity of paper?
b. In market equilibrium, what is the consumer surplus?
c. In market equilibrium, what is the producer surplus?
d. Is the market for paper efficient? Why or why not?
e. If a news magazine lobby group persuaded the government to pass a law requiring paper producers to sell 50 tons of paper a day, would the market for paper be efficient? Why or why not?
f. In the situation described in part (e), shade the deadweight loss on the figure.
g. If an environmental lobby group persuaded the government to pass a law restricting producers of paper to sell only 20 tons of paper a day, would the market for paper be efficient? Why or why not?
h. In the situation described in part (g), shade the deadweight loss on the figure.

Exercise 6.3

Figure 2 shows the market for soft drinks. Use the figure to answer the following questions:

a. What are the equilibrium price and equilibrium quantity of soft drinks?
b. In market equilibrium, what is the consumer surplus?
c. In market equilibrium, what is the producer surplus?
d. Is the market for soft drinks efficient? Why?
e. If the government restricted producers to 10 cans of soft drinks per day, would the market for soft drinks be efficient? Why?
f. In the situation described in part (e), what is the deadweight loss?
g. If the government passed a law requiring producers of soft drinks to sell only 20 cans a day, would the market for soft drinks be efficient? Why or why not?
h. In the situation described in part (g), what is the deadweight loss?

Solution to Practice Problem 6.3

a. Market equilibrium is 40 tons a day at a price of \$3 a ton (Figure 3).
b. Consumer surplus is (\$9 – \$3) × 40 ÷ 2 = \$120 (the green triangle in Figure 3).
c. Producer surplus is (\$3 – \$1) × 40 ÷ 2 = \$40 (the blue triangle in Figure 3).
d. The market equilibrium is efficient because marginal benefit equals marginal cost and the sum of consumer surplus and producer surplus is a maximum.
e. If the quantity produced is 50 tons a day, the market for paper is inefficient because marginal cost exceeds marginal benefit.
f. With 50 tons produced, the deadweight loss is the gray triangle labeled 1 in Figure 4.
g. If the quantity produced is 20 tons a day, the market for paper is inefficient because marginal benefit exceeds marginal cost.
h. With 20 tons produced, the deadweight loss is the gray triangle labeled 2 in Figure 4.

6.4 ARE MARKETS FAIR?

Is an efficient allocation of resources fair? Does the competitive market provide people with fair incomes for their work? And do people always pay a fair price for the things they buy? Do we need the government to step into some competitive markets to prevent the price from rising too high or falling too low?

When a natural disaster strikes, such as a severe winter storm or a hurricane, the prices of many essential items jump. The reason the prices jump is that some people have a greater demand and greater willingness to pay while at the same time, the items are in limited supply. So the higher prices achieve an efficient allocation of scarce resources. News reports of these price hikes almost never talk about efficiency. Instead, they complain about their unfairness. In Florida, there are even laws that prevent large price increases once a hurricane watch is in effect and the state has set up an Anti-Gouging Hot Line.

Similarly, when low-skilled people work for a wage that is below what most would regard as a living wage, the media and politicians talk of employers taking unfair advantage of their workers.

How do we decide whether something is fair or unfair? You know when *you* think something is unfair. But how do you know? What are the *principles* of fairness?

Economists agree about efficiency. They agree that we should make the economic pie as large as possible and to bake it at the lowest possible cost. But they do not agree about what are fair shares of the economic pie for all the people who make it. The reason is that ideas about fairness are not exclusively economic ideas. They involve politics and ethics. Here we can only provide a selective sketch of the huge literature on this subject.

All ideas about fairness are based on a fundamental principle that seems to be hard-wired into the human brain called the symmetry principle. The **symmetry principle** is the requirement that people in similar situations be treated similarly. It is the principle that lies at the center of all the main moral codes that tell us, in some form or other, to behave toward other people in the way we expect them to behave toward ourselves.

Symmetry principle
The requirement that people in similar situations be treated similarly.

Unfortunately, the symmetry principle does not deliver universally accepted prescriptions for fair arrangements and leaves a big question unanswered. To see what this unanswered question is, think of economic life as a game—a serious game. A game has an outcome or result, and it has rules. Does obeying the symmetry principle and treating people in similar situations similarly require that all the players face the same rules, or does it require that they get the same score? This question lies at the heart of disagreement about fairness in economics. Two broad and generally conflicting views of fairness are:

- It's not fair if the *result* isn't fair.
- It's not fair if the *rules* aren't fair.

It's Not Fair If the *Result* Isn't Fair

The earliest efforts to establish a principle of fairness were based on the view that the result is what matters. And the general idea was that it is unfair if people's incomes are too unequal. It is unfair that bank presidents earn millions of dollars a year while bank tellers earn only thousands of dollars a year. It is unfair that a store owner enjoys a larger profit and her customers pay higher prices in the aftermath of a winter storm.

There was a lot of excitement during the nineteenth century when economists thought they had made the incredible discovery that efficiency requires equality of incomes. To make the economic pie as large as possible, they thought, it must be cut into equal pieces, one for each person. This idea turns out to be wrong, but there is a lesson in the reason that it is wrong. So this idea is worth a closer look.

Utilitarianism

Utilitarianism
A principle that states that we should strive to achieve "the greatest happiness for the greatest number."

The nineteenth century idea that only equality brings efficiency is an extreme version of utilitarianism. **Utilitarianism** is a principle that states that we should strive to achieve "the greatest happiness for the greatest number." The people who developed this idea were known as utilitarians. They included the most eminent minds such as Jeremy Bentham and John Stuart Mill.

Some utilitarians argued that to achieve "the greatest happiness for the greatest number," income must be transferred from the rich to the poor up to the point of complete equality—to the point at which there are no rich and no poor.

They reasoned in the following way: First, everyone has the same basic wants and is similar in the capacity to enjoy life. In the technical language of economics that you've now learned to use, everyone has the same marginal benefit schedule or curve. Second, the greater a person's income, the smaller is the marginal benefit of a dollar's worth of goods and services. The millionth dollar spent by a rich person brings a smaller marginal benefit to that person than the marginal benefit of the thousandth dollar spent by a poorer person. So by transferring a dollar from the millionaire to the poorer person, more is gained than is lost, and the two people added together are better off.

But the same is true for every dollar transferred until there is no poor or rich person. Only when everyone's share of the economic pie is the same as everyone else's are we sharing resources in the most efficient way and bringing the greatest attainable total benefit. So complete equality is the only fair outcome.

The Big Tradeoff

Big tradeoff
A tradeoff between efficiency and fairness that recognizes the cost of making income transfers.

One big problem with the utilitarian idea of complete equality is that it ignores the costs of making income transfers. Recognizing the cost of making income transfers leads to what is called the **big tradeoff**, which is a tradeoff between efficiency and fairness.

The big tradeoff is based on the following facts. Income can be transferred from people with high incomes to people with low incomes only by taxing incomes. Taxing people's income from employment discourages work. It results in the quantity of labor being less than the efficient quantity. Taxing people's income from capital discourages saving. It results in the quantity of capital being less than the efficient quantity. With smaller quantities of both labor and capital, the quantity of goods and services produced is less than the efficient quantity. The economic pie shrinks.

The tradeoff is between the size of the economic pie and the degree of equality with which it is shared. The greater the amount of income redistribution through income taxes, the greater is the inefficiency—the smaller is the economic pie.

There is a second source of inefficiency. A dollar taken from a rich person does not end up as a dollar in the hands of a poorer person. Some of it is spent on administration of the tax and transfer system. The cost of tax-collecting agencies, such as the IRS, and welfare-administering agencies, such as the Health Care Financing Administration, which administers Medicaid and Medicare, must be paid with some of the taxes collected. Also, taxpayers hire accountants, auditors, and lawyers to help them ensure that they pay the correct amount of tax. These activities use skilled labor and capital resources that could otherwise be used to produce other goods and services that people value.

You can see that when all these costs are taken into account, transferring a dollar from a rich person does not give a dollar to a poor person. It is even possible that with high taxes, those with low incomes end up being worse off. Suppose, for example, that highly taxed entrepreneurs decide to work less hard and shut down some of their businesses. Low-income workers get fired and must seek other, perhaps even lower-paid work.

Because of the big tradeoff, those who say that fairness is equality propose a modified version of utilitarianism.

Make the Poorest as Well Off as Possible

A Harvard philosopher, John Rawls, proposed a modified version of utilitarianism in a classic book entitled *A Theory of Justice*, published in 1971. Rawls says that, taking all the costs of income transfers into account, the fair distribution of the economic pie is the one that makes the poorest person as well off as possible. The incomes of rich people should be taxed, and after paying the costs of administering the tax and transfer system, what is left should be transferred to the poor. But the taxes must not be so high that they make the economic pie shrink by so much that the poorest person ends up with a smaller piece. A bigger share of a smaller pie can be a smaller piece than a smaller share of a bigger pie. The goal is to make the piece enjoyed by the poorest person as big as possible. Most likely, this piece will not be an equal share.

The "fair results" ideas require a change in the results after the game is over. Some economists say that these changes are themselves unfair, and they propose a different way of thinking about fairness.

It's Not Fair If the *Rules* Aren't Fair

The idea that it's not fair if the rules aren't fair translates into *equality of opportunity*. But equality of opportunity to do what? Another Harvard philosopher, Robert Nozick, answers this question in a book entitled *Anarchy, State, and Utopia*, published in 1974.

Nozick argues that the rules must be fair and must respect two principles:

- The state must enforce laws that establish and protect private property.
- Private property may be transferred from one person to another only by voluntary exchange.

The first rule says that everything that is valuable must be owned by individuals and that the state must ensure that theft is prevented. The second rule says that the only legitimate way a person can acquire property is to buy it in exchange for something else that the person owns. If these rules—which Nozick says are the only fair rules—are followed, the result is fair. It doesn't matter how unequally the economic pie is shared, provided that it is baked by people each one of whom voluntarily provides services in exchange for the share of the pie offered in compensation.

These rules satisfy the symmetry principle. And if these rules are not followed, the symmetry principle is broken. You can see these facts by imagining a world in which the laws are not followed.

First, suppose that some resources or goods are not owned. They are common property. Then everyone is free to participate in a grab to use these resources or goods. The strongest will prevail. But when the strongest prevails, the strongest effectively *owns* the resources or goods in question and prevents others from enjoying them.

Second, suppose that we do not insist on voluntary exchange for transferring ownership of resources from one person to another. The alternative is *involuntary* transfer. In simple language, the alternative is theft.

Both of these situations violate the symmetry principle. Only the strong get to acquire what they want. The weak end up with only the resources and goods that the strong don't want.

In contrast, if the two rules of fairness are followed, everyone—strong and weak—is treated in a similar way. Everyone is free to use their resources and human skills to create things that are valued by themselves and others and to exchange the fruits of their efforts with each other. This is the only set of arrangements that obeys the symmetry principle.

If private property rights are enforced and if voluntary exchange takes place in a competitive market, then resources will be allocated efficiently if there are no external costs and external benefits, public goods, monopolies, price ceilings and price floors, taxes, subsidies, or quotas.

According to the Nozick rules, the resulting distribution of income and wealth will be fair. Let's study a concrete example to examine the claim that if resources are allocated efficiently they are also allocated fairly.

A Price Hike in a Natural Disaster

An earthquake has broken the pipes that deliver drinking water to a city. The price of bottled water jumps from $1 to $8 a bottle in the 30 or so shops that have water for sale.

First, let's agree that the water is being used *efficiently*. There is a fixed amount of bottled water in the city, and given the quantity available, some people are willing to pay $8 to get a bottle. The water goes to the people who value it most highly. Marginal benefit equals marginal cost, and consumer surplus plus producer surplus is maximized.

So the water resources are being used efficiently. But are they being used fairly? Shouldn't people who can't afford to pay $8 a bottle get some of the available water for a lower price that they can afford? Isn't the fair solution for the shops to sell water for a lower price that people can afford? Or perhaps it might be fairer if the government bought the water and then made it available to people through a government store at a "reasonable" price. Let's think about these alternative solutions to the water problem of this city.

The first answer that jumps into your mind is that the water should somehow be made available at a more reasonable price. But is this the correct answer?

Shop Offers Water for $5 Suppose that Chip, a shop owner, offers water at $5 a bottle. Who will buy it? There are two types of buyers. Larry is an example of one type. He values water at $8—is willing to pay $8 a bottle. Recall that given the quantity of water available, the equilibrium price is $8 a bottle. If Larry buys the water, he consumes it. Larry ends up with a consumer surplus of $3 on the bottle, and Chip receives $3 *less* of producer surplus.

Mitch is an example of the second type of buyer. Mitch would not pay $8 for a bottle. In fact, he wouldn't even pay $5 to consume a bottle of water. But he buys a bottle for $5. Why? Because he plans to sell the water to someone who is willing to pay $8 to consume it. When Mitch buys the water, Chip again receives a producer surplus of $3 less than he would receive if he charged the going market price. Mitch now becomes a water dealer. He sells the water to Larry for the going price of $8 and earns a producer surplus of $3.

So by being public-spirited and offering water for less than the market price, Chip ends up $3 a bottle worse off and the people who buy from him end up $3 a bottle better off. Larry consumes the water in both situations because he values the water at $8 a bottle. But the distribution of consumer surplus and producer surplus is different in the two cases. When Chip offers the water for $5 a bottle, he ends up with a smaller producer surplus and either Larry gets a larger consumer surplus or Mitch gets a larger producer surplus.

So which is the fair arrangement: the one that favors Chip or the one that favors Larry or Mitch? The fair-rules view is that both arrangements are fair. Chip voluntarily sells the water for $5, so in effect, he is helping the community to cope with its water problem. It is fair that he should help. But the choice is his. He owns the water. It is not fair that he should be compelled to help.

Government Buys Water Now suppose instead that the government buys all the water. The going price is $8 a bottle, so that's what the government pays. Now the government offers the water for sale for $1 a bottle, its "normal" price.

The quantity of water supplied is exactly the same as before. But now, at $1 a bottle, the quantity demanded is much larger than the quantity supplied. There is a shortage of water.

Because there is a water shortage, the government must use some mechanism to ration the available quantity. We'll assume that the government allocates everyone a lottery ticket. But only 50 percent of the tickets are winners and entitle the holder to one bottle of water. Suppose that Mitch is a winner and Larry is a loser. So Mitch, who is willing to pay less than $5, gets a bottle for $1, and Larry, who is willing to pay $8 a bottle, misses out.

What does Mitch do? Does he drink his bottle? He does not. He sells it to Larry, who values the water at $8. And Mitch enjoys a $7 producer surplus from his temporary water trading business.

The main difference between the government scheme and Chip's private charitable contributions lies in the fact that to buy the water for $8 and sell it for $1, the government must tax someone $7 for each bottle sold. So whether this arrangement is fair depends on whether the taxes are fair.

Taxes are an involuntary transfer of private property, so, according to the fair-rules view, they are unfair. But most economists, and most people, think that there is such a thing as a fair tax. So it seems that the fair-rules view needs to be weakened a bit. Agreeing that there is such a thing as a fair tax is the easy part. Agreeing on what is a fair tax brings endless disagreement and debate.

CHECKPOINT 6.4

Study Guide pp. 93–95

*e*Foundations 6.4

4 **Explain the main ideas about fairness and evaluate claims that competitive markets result in unfair outcomes.**

Practice Problem 6.4

A winter storm cuts the power supply and isolates a small town in the mountains. The people rush to buy candles from the town store, which is the only source of supply of candles. The store owner decides to ration the candles to one per family but keep the price of a candle unchanged.

a. Who gets to consume the candles?
b. Who receives the consumer surplus on candles?
c. Who receives the producer surplus on candles?
d. Is the outcome efficient?
e. Is the outcome fair according to the utilitarian principle?
f. Is the process fair according to the symmetry principle?
g. If the town government declares a state of emergency and gives every family $100 to cope with the crisis, does this produce a more efficient and fairer outcome?

Exercise 6.4

A drought has drastically reduced the water available in a desert town. The only store decides to sell the bottled water it has at the highest price that people are willing to pay.

a. Who gets to consume the water?
b. Who receives the consumer surplus on water?
c. Who receives the producer surplus on water?
d. Is the outcome efficient?
e. Is this outcome fair or unfair?
f. By what principle of fairness is the outcome fair or unfair?

Solution to Practice Problem 6.4

a. The people who buy candles from the town store are not necessarily the people who consume the candles. A buyer from the town store can sell a candle and will do so if the price exceeds her or his marginal benefit. The people who value them most—who are willing to pay the most—will consume the candles.
b. Only the consumers—the people who are willing to pay the most for candles—receive the consumer surplus on candles.
c. The town store owner receives the same producer surplus as normal. People who sell the candles they buy from the store receive additional producer surplus.
d. The outcome is efficient.
e. The outcome is unfair according to the utilitarian principle because candles are shared unequally.
f. The process is fair according to the symmetry principle because only voluntary transactions occur.
g. Providing every family with $100 increases the equilibrium price of candles. But it doesn't change the quantity of candles available. And to pay the $100, the town government must raise taxes, which might be fair or unfair.

CHAPTER CHECKPOINT

Key Points

1 Distinguish between value and price and define consumer surplus.

- Marginal benefit is measured by the maximum price that consumers are willing to pay for a good or service.
- A demand curve is a marginal benefit curve.
- Value is what people are *willing to* pay; price is what people *must* pay.
- Consumer surplus equals marginal benefit minus price, summed over the quantity consumed.

2 Distinguish between cost and price and define producer surplus.

- Marginal cost is measured by the minimum price producers must be offered to increase production by one unit.
- A supply curve is a marginal cost curve.
- Opportunity cost is what producers pay; price is what producers receive.
- Producer surplus equals price minus marginal cost, summed over the quantity produced.

3 Explain the conditions in which markets are efficient and inefficient.

- In a competitive equilibrium, marginal benefit equals marginal cost and resource allocation is efficient.
- The market provides more than the efficient quantity of goods and services that have external costs and less than the efficient quantity of goods and services that have external benefits.
- The market provides less than the efficient quantity of public goods because of the free-rider problem.
- A monopoly produces less than the efficient quantity.
- Price ceilings and price floors decrease the quantity produced to less than the efficient quantity.
- Taxes and quotas decrease the quantity produced to less than the efficient quantity, and subsidies increase the quantity produced to more than the efficient quantity.
- Both underproduction and overproduction create a deadweight loss.

4 Explain the main ideas about fairness and evaluate claims that competitive markets result in unfair outcomes.

- Ideas about fairness divide into two groups: fair *results* and fair *rules*.
- Fair-results ideas require income transfers from the rich to the poor.
- Fair-rules ideas require property rights and voluntary exchange.

Key Terms

Big tradeoff, 148
Consumer surplus, 135
Deadweight loss, 144
Producer surplus, 138
Symmetry principle, 147
Utilitarianism, 148

TABLE 1

Price (dollars per sandwich)	Quantity demanded (sandwiches per hour)	Quantity supplied (sandwiches per hour)
0	400	0
1	350	50
2	300	100
3	250	150
4	200	200
5	150	250
6	100	300
7	50	350
8	0	400

TABLE 2

Price (dollars per bag)	Quantity demanded before flood (thousands of bags)	Quantity demanded during flood (thousands of bags)	Quantity supplied (thousands of bags)
0	40	70	0
1	35	65	5
2	30	60	10
3	25	55	15
4	20	50	20
5	15	45	25
6	10	40	30
7	5	35	35
8	0	30	40

Exercises

1. Table 1 shows the demand and supply schedules for sandwiches. Use the table to answer the following questions:
   a. What is the efficient quantity of sandwiches?
   b. What is the consumer surplus if the efficient quantity of sandwiches is produced?
   c. What is the producer surplus if the efficient quantity of sandwiches is produced?
   d. If Sandwiches To Go, Inc. buys all the sandwich producers and cuts production to 100 sandwiches an hour, what is the deadweight loss that is created?
   e. If in question (d), Sandwiches To Go, Inc. rations sandwiches to two per person, is this distribution of sandwiches fair? By what principle of fairness would the distribution be unfair?

2. Table 2 shows the demand and supply schedules for sandbags before and during a major flood. Use the table to answer the following questions:
   a. What happens to consumer surplus and producer surplus during the flood?
   b. Is the allocation of resources efficient (i) before the flood and (ii) during the flood?
   c. If, during the flood, the government rationed sandbags and gave all families an equal quantity of them, what would happen to the consumer surplus, producer surplus, quantity, and price of sandbags?
   d. Is the outcome described in part (c) more efficient than it would be if the government took no action?
   e. Is the outcome described in part (c) fairer than it would be if the government took no action?

3. Students can visit science centers and art museums at a discount. Is this arrangement efficient? Is it fair? Explain.

4. The winner of the men's tennis singles at the U.S. Open is paid much more than the runner-up, but it takes two to have a singles final. Is this compensation arrangement efficient? Is it fair? Explain why it might illustrate the big tradeoff.

5. The winner of the men's tennis singles at the U.S. Open is paid the same as the winner of the women's singles. But the winners of men's golf tournaments are paid much more than the winners of the women's golf tournaments. Are these compensation arrangements efficient? Are they fair? Explain.

6. Is it fair that Tiger Woods wins so many golf competitions? Would it be fair if a rule were adopted saying that after three wins in a season, a golfer could not compete for the rest of the season? Explain.

Part 3

How Governments Influence the Economy

Chapter 7

Government Influences on Markets

CHAPTER CHECKLIST

When you have completed your study of this chapter, you will be able to:

1 **Explain the effects of taxes on goods and labor and determine who pays the taxes.**

2 **Explain how a rent ceiling creates a housing shortage, inefficiency, and unfairness.**

3 **Explain how the minimum wage creates unemployment, inefficiency, and unfairness.**

Governments influence markets when they collect the tax revenues that finance public expenditures on such items as national defense, education, welfare, police, and fire protection. Governments also influence markets when they control prices in an attempt to redistribute income toward those who are at the lower end of the economic ladder.

Can Congress target taxes at businesses so that workers pay the least tax? And can governments help low-income people by holding down their cost of housing or by boosting their wages and employment benefits?

This chapter studies these questions. It expands your study of demand, supply, and market equilibrium in Chapter 4, elasticity in Chapter 5, and efficiency and fairness in Chapter 6.

First, we look at the effects of taxes. We then look at rent ceilings. And finally, we study minimum wage laws.

7.1 TAXES

Almost everything you buy, from a new futon frame to a plane ticket home to a late-night order of chow mein, is taxed. But who really pays the tax? Because the sales tax is added to the price of a good or service when it is sold, isn't it obvious that *you* pay the tax? Isn't the price higher than it otherwise would be by an amount equal to the tax? It can be, but usually it isn't. And it is even possible that you actually pay none of the tax!

When you work, you pay income tax on your wage income. And you and your employer each pay a half of a tax called FICA (Federal Insurance Contribution Act). Who really pays these taxes? Again, isn't it obvious that you pay the income tax and you and your employer split the FICA tax equally? The answer again is no!

To see how we can make sense of these apparently absurd statements, we first define the concept of *tax incidence.*

Tax Incidence

Tax incidence
The division of the burden of a tax between the buyer and the seller.

Tax incidence is the division of the burden of a tax between the buyer and the seller. When the government imposes a tax on the sale of a good, the price of the good might rise by the full amount of the tax, by some lesser amount, or not at all. If the price rises by the full amount of the tax, then the burden of the tax falls entirely on the buyer. If the price rises by a lesser amount than the tax, then the burden of the tax falls partly on the buyer and partly on the seller. And if the price doesn't change, then the burden of the tax falls entirely on the seller.

To see the determinants of tax incidence, suppose the government puts a $10 tax on CD players. What are the effects of this tax on the price and quantity of CD players? To answer this question, we need to work out what happens to demand and supply in the market for CD players.

Figure 7.1 shows this market. With no tax on CD players, the equilibrium price of a CD player is $100 and 5,000 players are bought and sold each week.

When a good is taxed, it has two prices: a price that excludes the tax and a price that includes the tax. Buyers respond only to the price that includes the tax, because that is the price they pay. Sellers respond only to the price that excludes the tax, because that is the price they receive. The tax is like a wedge between these two prices.

Let's make the price on the vertical axis of Figure 7.1 the price paid by the buyer—the price that *includes* the tax. When a tax is imposed and the price changes, there is a change in the quantity demanded but no change in demand. That is, there is a movement along the demand curve and no shift of the demand curve.

But the supply changes and the supply curve shifts. The tax is like an increase in the suppliers' cost, so supply decreases and the supply curve shifts leftward to the curve labeled *S + tax.* To determine the position of this new supply curve, we add the tax to the minimum price that sellers are willing to accept for each quantity. For example, with no tax, sellers are willing to offer 5,000 CD players a week for $100 each. So with a $10 tax, sellers would be willing to offer 5,000 CD players a week for $110 each—a price that includes the tax. The *S + tax* curve describes the terms on which sellers are willing to offer CD players for sale now that there is a $10 tax.

FIGURE 7.1
A Tax on CD Players

*e*Foundations 7.1 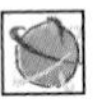

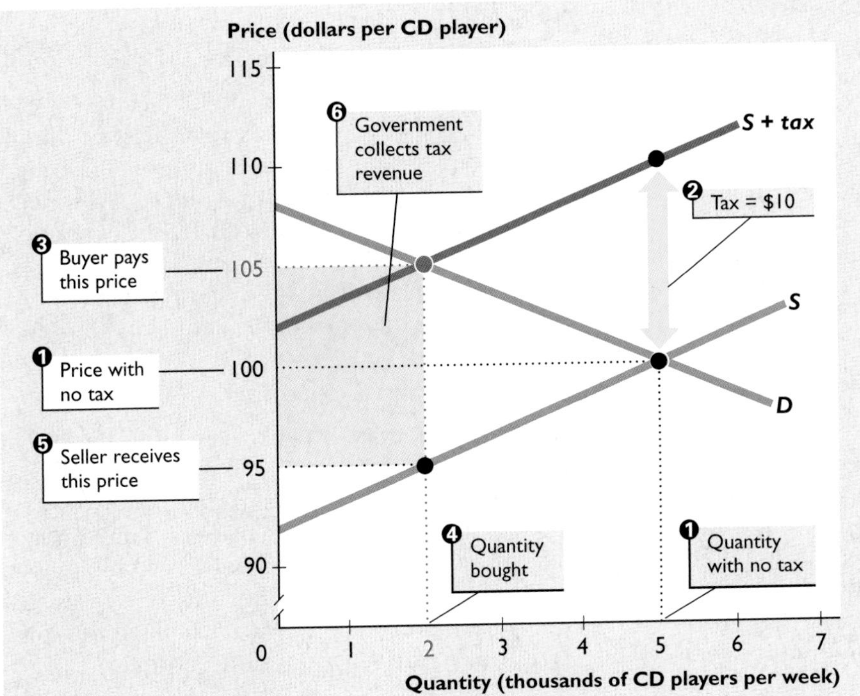

❶ With no tax, the price of a CD player is $100 and 5,000 CD players a week are bought.

❷ A $10 tax on CD players shifts the supply curve to *S* + *tax*.

❸ The price rises to $105—an increase of $5 a CD player.

❹ The quantity decreases to 2,000 CD players a week.

❺ Sellers receive $95—a decrease of $5 a CD player.

❻ The government collects tax revenue of $20,000 a week—the purple rectangle.

The burden of the tax is split equally between the buyer and the seller—each pays $5 per CD player.

Equilibrium occurs where the new supply curve intersects the demand curve—at a price of $105 and a quantity of 2,000 CD players a week. The $10 tax increases the price paid by the buyer by $5—from $100 to $105 a player. And it decreases the price received by the seller by $5—from $100 to $95 a player. The buyer and the seller share the $10 tax equally.

This tax brings in tax revenue to the government equal to the tax per CD player ($10) multiplied by the number of CD players sold (2,000 a week), which is $20,000 a week. The purple rectangle in Figure 7.1 illustrates the tax revenue.

Tax Incidence and Elasticities of Demand and Supply

In the example that you've just studied, the buyer and the seller split the tax equally. This equal sharing of the tax is a special case and does not usually occur. But some sharing of the tax between the buyer and seller is usual. Also, there are other special cases in which either the buyer or the seller pays the entire tax.

The division of the burden of the tax between the buyer and the seller depends on the elasticities of demand and supply:

- For a given elasticity of supply, the buyer pays a larger share of the tax the more inelastic is the demand for the good.
- For a given elasticity of demand, the seller pays a larger share of the tax the more inelastic is the supply of the good.

Tax Incidence and Elasticity of Demand

To see how the division of a tax between the buyer and the seller depends on the elasticity of demand, we'll look at two extreme cases.

Perfectly Inelastic Demand: Buyer Pays Entire Tax

Figure 7.2(a) shows the market for insulin, a vital daily medication of diabetics. Demand is perfectly inelastic at 100,000 doses a week regardless of the price, as shown by the vertical demand curve. (Demand is not likely to be perfectly inelastic at every price, but over some low price range, it might be.) With no tax, the price is $2 a dose and the quantity is 100,000 doses a week. If the government taxes insulin at 20¢ a dose, the price rises to $2.20 a dose but the quantity does not change. The 20¢ tax leaves the price received by the seller unchanged but raises the price paid by the buyer by 20¢. The buyer pays the entire tax.

Perfectly Elastic Demand: Seller Pays Entire Tax

Figure 7.2(b) shows the market for pink marker pens. Demand is perfectly elastic at $1 a pen, as shown by the horizontal demand curve. If pink pens are less expensive than other pens, everyone uses pink. If pink pens are more expensive than other pens, no one uses a pink pen. With no tax, the price of a pink marker is $1 and the quantity is 4,000 pens a week. If the government taxes pink marker pens at 10¢ a pen, the price remains at $1 a pen and the quantity decreases to 1,000 a week. The 10¢ tax leaves the price paid by the buyer unchanged but lowers the amount received by the seller by 10¢. The seller pays the entire tax.

Tax Incidence and Elasticity of Supply

To see how the division of a tax between the buyer and the seller depends on the elasticity of supply, we'll again look at two extreme cases.

Perfectly Inelastic Supply: Seller Pays Entire Tax

Figure 7.2(c) shows the market for water from a mineral spring that flows at a constant rate that can't be controlled. Supply is perfectly inelastic at 100,000 bottles a week, as shown by the vertical supply curve. With no tax, the price is 50¢ a bottle and the 100,000 bottles that flow from the spring are bought. If the government taxes spring water at 5¢ a bottle, the supply curve does not change. Spring owners still produce 100,000 bottles a week regardless of the price they receive. But buyers are willing to buy the 100,000 bottles only if the price is 50¢ a bottle. So the price remains at 50¢ a bottle. The tax lowers the price received by the seller by 5¢ a bottle. The seller pays the entire tax.

Perfectly Elastic Supply: Buyer Pays Entire Tax

Figure 7.2(d) shows the market for sand from which computer-chip makers extract silicon. Supply of this sand is perfectly elastic at a price of 10¢ a pound as shown by the horizontal supply curve. With no tax, the price is 10¢ a pound and 5,000 pounds a week are bought. If the government taxes sand at 1¢ a pound, the price rises to 11¢ a pound and the quantity decreases to 3,000 pounds a week. The tax increases the price paid by the buyer by 1¢ a pound. The buyer pays the entire tax.

FIGURE 7.2
Tax Incidence and the Elasticities of Demand and Supply

*e*Foundations 7.1 

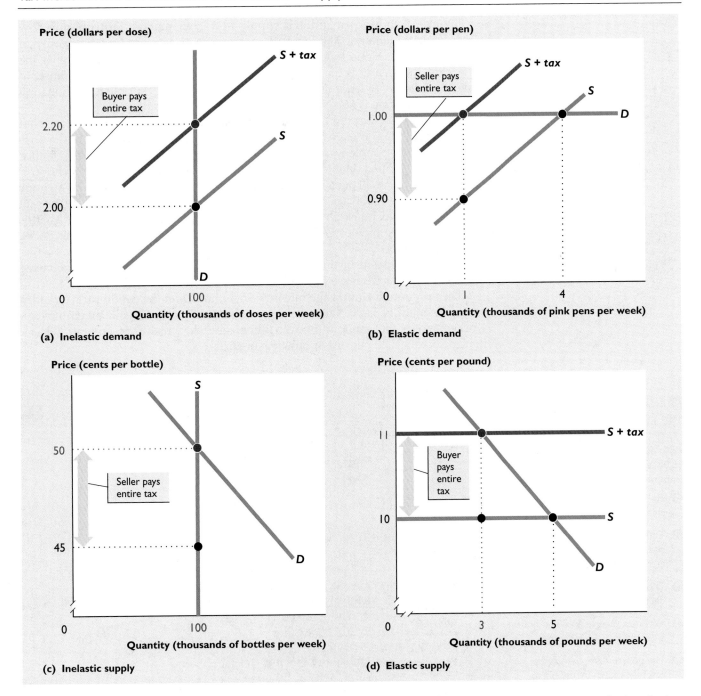

(a) Inelastic demand

(b) Elastic demand

(c) Inelastic supply

(d) Elastic supply

In part (a), the demand for insulin is perfectly inelastic. A tax of 20¢ a dose raises the price by 20¢, and the buyer pays all the tax.

In part (b), the demand for pink marker pens is perfectly elastic. A tax of 10¢ a pen lowers the price received by the seller by 10¢, and the seller pays all the tax.

In part (c), the supply of mineral spring water is perfectly inelastic. A tax of 5¢ a bottle lowers the price received by the seller by 5¢, and the seller pays all the tax.

In part (d), the supply of sand is perfectly elastic. A tax of 1¢ a pound increases the price by 1¢ a pound, and the buyer pays all the tax.

Taxes on Income and Employment

The principles that you've just learned apply to all types of taxes. Let's see how they apply to the income tax and the payroll tax.

Figure 7.3 shows demand and supply in a labor market. Firms decide how much labor to demand. The lower the wage rate, the greater is the quantity of labor demanded. Households decide how much labor to supply. The higher the wage rate, the greater is the quantity of labor supplied. The wage rate adjusts to make the quantity of labor demanded equal to the quantity supplied. Without any taxes, the wage rate is \$6 an hour and 4,000 people are employed.

Now suppose that the government introduces a 20 percent income tax. That is, for every dollar of wage income earned, people must pay 20 cents to the government. If 4,000 people were willing to work for \$6 an hour, this quantity of labor will now be supplied only if people can earn an after-tax income of \$6 an hour.

If the tax rate is 20 percent, the pre-tax wage rate will need to be \$7.50 an hour to deliver an after-tax wage rate of \$6 an hour. (Check that if the pre-tax wage rate is \$7.50 and the tax rate is 20 percent, the amount of tax paid out of \$7.50 is \$1.50—20 percent or one fifth of \$7.50—so the wage rate after tax is \$7.50 minus \$1.50, which equals \$6.)

With a 20 percent income tax, the supply of labor curve shifts to the curve labeled *S* + *tax*—a decrease in supply.

The new equilibrium wage rate is \$6.25 an hour, and the equilibrium quantity of employment is 3,000. With a wage rate of \$6.25 an hour paid by employers, workers *receive* that amount minus a 20 percent tax, which is \$5 an hour. (Check that \$1.25 equals 20 percent or one fifth of \$6.25.)

FIGURE 7.3

The Income Tax

e/Foundations **7.1** 

With no income tax, the wage rate is \$6.00 an hour and 4,000 people are employed.

1. An income tax of 20 percent shifts the supply curve to *S* + *tax*.
2. The wage rate paid by employers rises to \$6.25 an hour—an increase of 25 cents an hour.
3. The number of people employed decreases to 3,000.
4. Workers receive \$5.00 an hour—a decrease of \$1 an hour.
5. The government collects tax revenue shown by the purple rectangle.

Workers pay most of the tax because the supply of labor is more inelastic than the demand for labor.

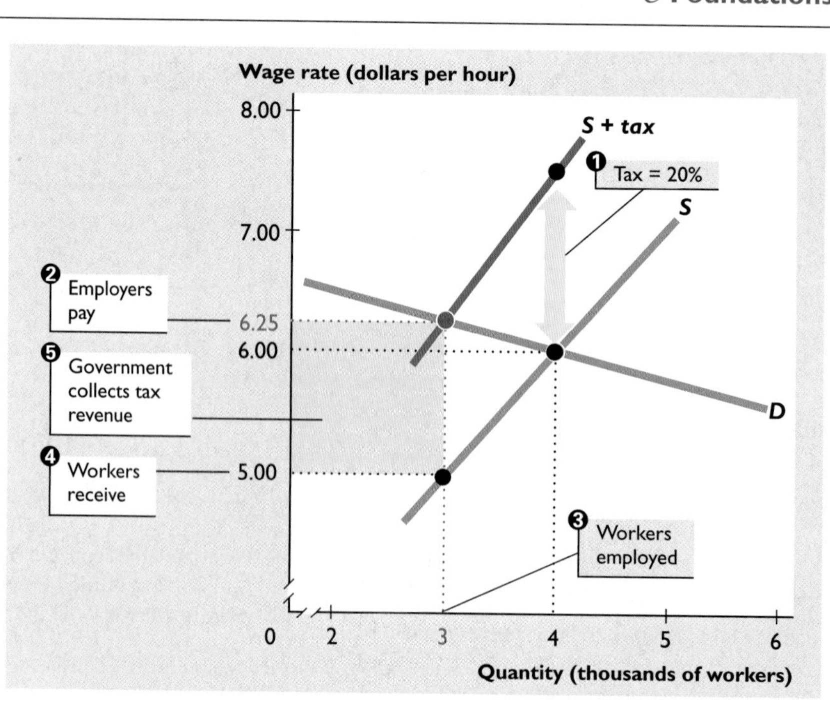

So with the income tax, the tax paid is $1.25 an hour. Of this amount, the employer pays 25 cents and the worker pays $1. This division of the burden arises because the demand for labor is more elastic than the supply of labor.

Suppose that people are annoyed because workers pay $1 and firms pay only 25 cents of the income tax. And suppose that Congress decides to make the employers pay more. Congress abolishes the income tax and replaces it with a payroll tax. A **payroll tax** is a tax on employers based on the wages they pay their workers.

Payroll tax
A tax on employers based on the wages they pay their workers.

To make it easy to compare the payroll tax and the income tax, suppose that the new payroll tax is set at $1.25 an hour, which is equivalent to the 20 percent income tax paid in previous example.

Figure 7.4 shows the effects of this new tax. As before, with no taxes, the equilibrium wage rate is $6 an hour and 4,000 people are employed. With a $1.25 an hour payroll tax, firms are no longer willing to hire 4,000 people at a $6 an hour wage rate. Because firms must pay $1.25 an hour to the government, they will hire 4,000 people at a wage rate of $6 minus $1.25, which is $4.75 an hour. The demand for labor decreases, and the demand for labor curve shifts to *D – tax*. The equilibrium wage rate falls to $5 an hour, and 3,000 people are employed.

The total cost of labor to the firm is $6.25 an hour, the $5 an hour wage rate plus the $1.25 an hour tax. The purple rectangle shows the tax paid.

Notice that the payroll tax delivers the same outcome as the income tax. Workers receive the same take-home wage, and firms pay the same total wage. Congress has tried to get employers to pay the tax that workers were previously paying, but the law has failed. When the laws of Congress come into conflict with the laws of economics, economics wins. This fact is not surprising. No one thinks that Congress can repeal the law of gravity. And Congress can't repeal the laws of supply and demand either.

FIGURE 7.4
A Payroll Tax

*e*Foundations **7.1** 

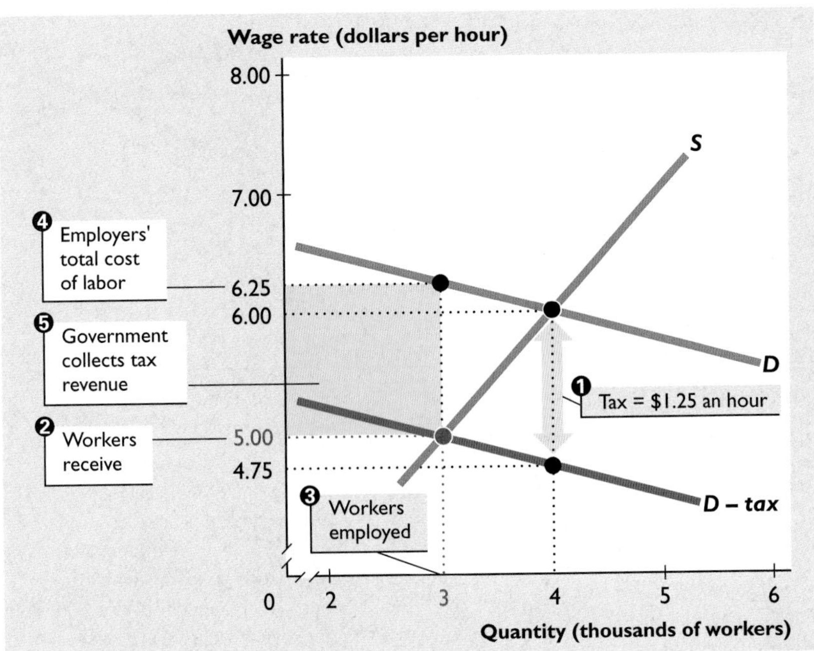

With no taxes, the wage rate is $6.00 an hour and 4,000 people are employed.

1. A payroll tax of $1.25 an hour shifts the demand curve to *D – tax*.
2. The wage rate falls to $5 an hour—a decrease of $1.00 an hour.
3. The number of workers employed decreases to 3,000.
4. Employers' total cost of labor rises to $6.25 an hour—the $5.00 wage rate plus the $1.25 payroll tax.
5. The government collects tax revenue shown by the purple rectangle.

Taxes and Efficiency

You've seen that a tax places a wedge between the price paid by buyers and the price received by sellers. The price paid by buyers equals marginal benefit, and the price received by sellers equals marginal cost. Because a tax places a wedge between the buyers' price and the sellers' price, it also puts a wedge between marginal benefit and marginal cost. The equilibrium quantity is less than the efficient quantity and a deadweight loss arises.

Figure 7.5 shows the inefficiency of taxes. In part (a), with no tax, marginal benefit equals marginal cost and the market is efficient. In part (b), with a tax, marginal benefit exceeds marginal cost. Consumer surplus and producer surplus shrink. Part of each surplus goes to the government as tax revenue—the purple area—and part of each surplus becomes a deadweight loss—the gray area.

Excess burden
The deadweight loss from a tax—the amount by which the burden of a tax exceeds the tax revenue received by the government.

Because a tax creates a deadweight loss, the burden of the tax exceeds the tax revenue. To remind us of this fact, we call the deadweight loss that arises from a tax the **excess burden** of the tax. But because the government uses the tax revenue to provide goods and services that people value, only the excess burden is the cost of the tax. And even this excess burden might be worth bearing to obtain the benefits of government-provided services. We'll examine this issue further when we study public goods and the tax system in Chapter 9.

FIGURE 7.5
Taxes and Efficiency

*e*Foundations 7.1 

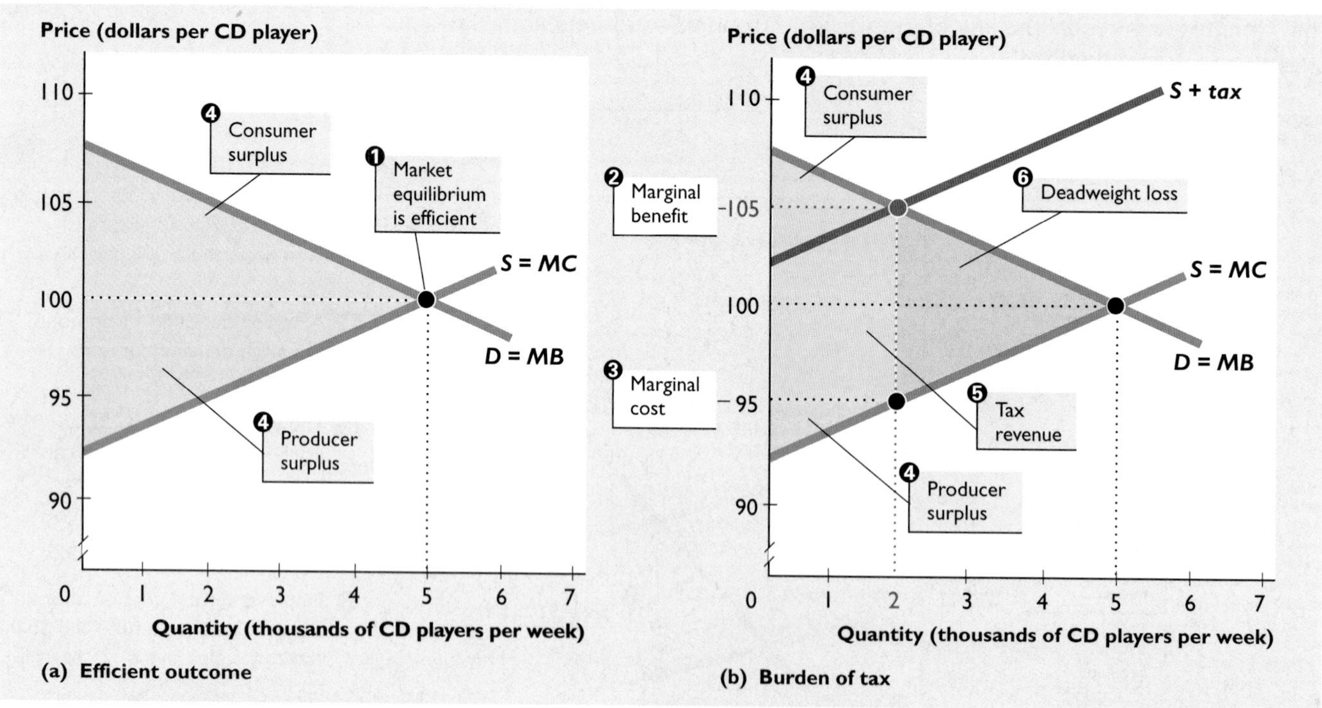

In part (a), ❶ the market is efficient with marginal benefit equal to marginal cost.

In part (b), a $10 tax drives a wedge between ❷ marginal benefit and ❸ marginal cost. ❹ Consumer surplus (green area) and producer surplus (blue area) shrink by the amount of the ❺ tax revenue (purple rectangle) and ❻ deadweight loss (gray area). The loss of consumer surplus and producer surplus is the burden of the tax, which equals the tax revenue plus the deadweight loss.

CHECKPOINT 7.1

1 Explain the effects of taxes on goods and labor and determine who pays the taxes.

Study Guide pp. 102–107

*e*Foundations 7.1

Practice Problems 7.1

1. Figure 1 shows the market for golf balls. If the government imposes a sales tax on golf balls at 60 cents a ball:
   a. What is the increase in the price that buyers pay for golf balls?
   b. What is the decrease in the price that sellers receive?
   c. What is the decrease in the quantity of golf balls?
   d. What is the tax revenue from golf ball sales?
   e. Which is the more inelastic: the demand for golf balls or the supply of golf balls? How can you tell?
   f. What is the excess burden of the sales tax on golf balls?
2. The supply of labor in Hawaii is elastic, and the demand for labor is inelastic.
   a. Does the employer or the worker pay more of the tax on labor income?
   b. If a payroll tax replaces the income tax in (a), does the employer or the worker pay more of the tax?

FIGURE 1

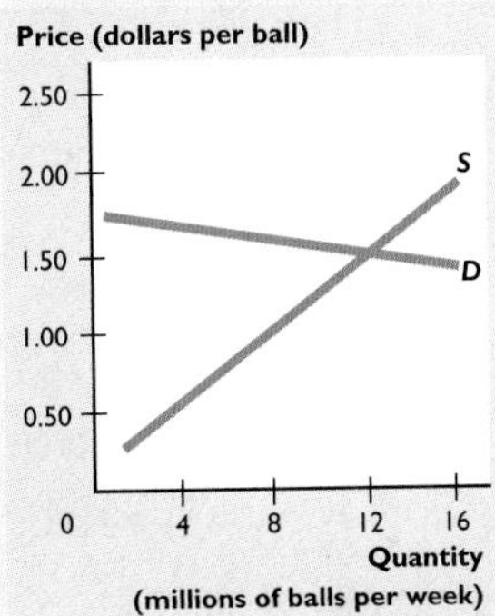

Exercises 7.1

1. With the growth in telephone calls in recent years, the government decides to tax calls at 20 cents each. If the supply of telephone calls is perfectly elastic and the demand for telephone calls is elastic:
   a. How much of the tax would the buyer pay on a call?
   b. Would the tax reduce the number of calls?
   c. Would the market for telephone calls be efficient?
   d. What is the excess burden of the tax?
2. Under what circumstances would the buyer pay all of a sales tax?
3. Under what circumstances would the employer pay all of a payroll tax? In this case, would the labor market be efficient?

Solutions to Practice Problems 7.1

Figure 2 illustrates the solutions to Practice Problem 1.

1a. When golf balls are taxed at 60 cents each, the price rises from \$1.50 to \$1.60.
1b. The price that sellers receive falls from \$1.50 to \$1.00.
1c. The quantity of golf balls decreases from 12 million to 8 million a week.
1d. The tax revenue from golf ball sales is \$0.60 multiplied by 8 million, which equals \$4.8 million a week.
1e. Supply is the more inelastic because the seller pays more of the tax.
1f. The excess burden of the sales tax on golf balls is \$1.2 million. Excess burden equals the deadweight loss, which is (\$4 million balls × 60 cents) ÷ 2 (the gray triangle in Figure 2).

2a. The employer pays more of the income tax.
2b. It makes no difference.

FIGURE 2

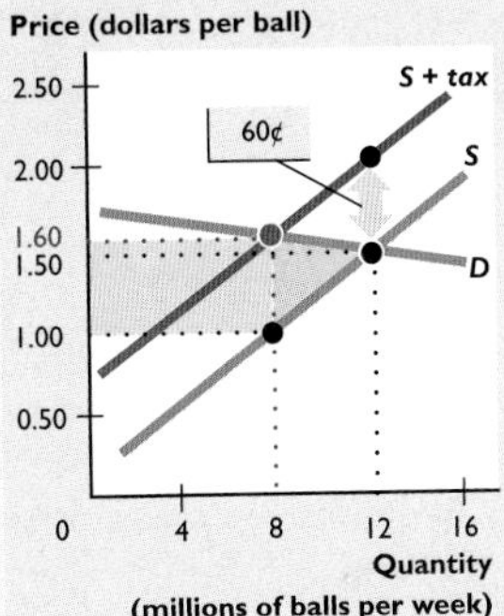

7.2 PRICE CEILINGS

People with low incomes would be able to buy more goods and services if prices were lower. One price that looms large in everyone's budget is that of housing. The price of housing is the rent that people pay for a house or apartment. This rent is determined by demand and supply in the housing market.

Figure 7.6 shows the apartment rental market in Biloxi, Mississippi. The rent is $550 a month, and 4,000 apartments are rented.

A Rent Ceiling

Rent ceiling
A government regulation that makes it illegal to charge more than a specified rent for housing.

Price ceiling
The highest price at which it is legal to trade a particular good, service, or factor of production. A rent ceiling is an example of a price ceiling.

Biloxi apartment rents have increased by $100 a month in just two years. Suppose that concerned citizens ask the mayor to impose a **rent ceiling**—a government regulation that makes it illegal to charge more than a specified rent for housing. A rent ceiling is an example of a **price ceiling**, which is the highest price at which it is legal to trade a particular good, service, or factor of production. How would a rent ceiling affect the Biloxi housing market?

The effect of a rent ceiling depends on whether it is imposed at a level above or below the equilibrium rent. In Figure 7.6, the equilibrium rent is $550 a month. If Biloxi introduced a rent ceiling above $550 a month, nothing would change. The reason is that people are already paying $550 a month, and because this rent is below the rent ceiling, the rent paid doesn't change.

But a rent ceiling that is set *below* the equilibrium rent has powerful effects on the market. The reason is that it attempts to prevent the rent from rising high enough to regulate the quantities demanded and supplied. The law and the market are in conflict, and one (or both) of them must yield.

FIGURE 7.6
A Housing Market

*e*Foundations 7.2 

The demand for and supply of housing determine the equilibrium rent of $550 a month and the equilibrium quantity of 4,000 units of housing.

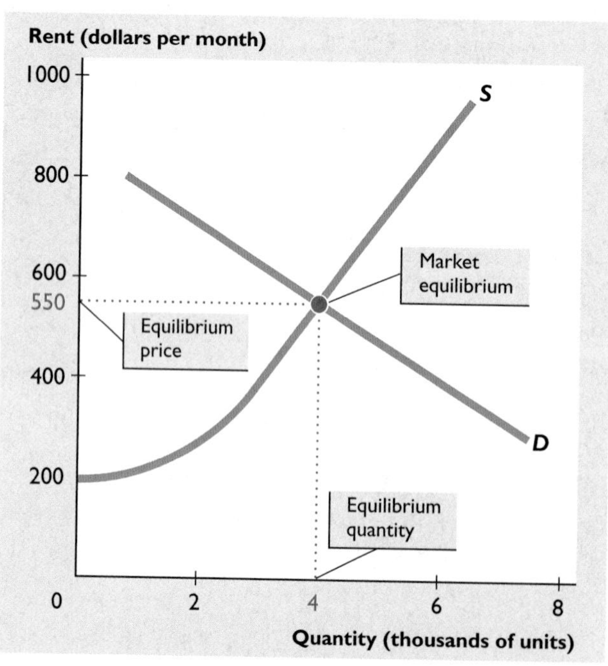

Figure 7.7 shows one effect of a rent ceiling that is set below the equilibrium rent. The rent ceiling is $400 a month. We've shaded the area *above* the rent ceiling because a rent in this region is illegal. At a rent of $400 a month, the quantity of housing supplied is 3,000 units and the quantity demanded is 6,000 units. So there is a shortage of 3,000 units of housing.

The first effect, then, of a rent ceiling is a housing shortage. People are seeking a larger amount of housing than builders and the owners of existing buildings have an incentive to make available.

But the story does not end here. Somehow the 3,000 units of housing that owners are willing to make available must be allocated among people who are seeking 6,000 units. How is this allocation achieved? When a rent ceiling creates a housing shortage, two developments occur:

- A black market
- Increased search activity

A Black Market

A **black market** is an illegal market that operates alongside a government-regulated market. A rent ceiling sometimes creates a black market in housing as frustrated renters and landlords try to find ways of raising the rent above the legally imposed ceiling. Landlords want higher rents because they know that renters are willing to pay more for the existing quantity of housing. Renters are willing to pay more to jump to the head of the queue.

Black market
An illegal market that operates alongside a government-regulated market.

Because raising the rent is illegal, landlords and renters use creative tricks for getting around the law. One of these tricks is for a new tenant to pay a high price

FIGURE 7.7
A Rent Ceiling Creates a Shortage

*e*Foundations 7.2 

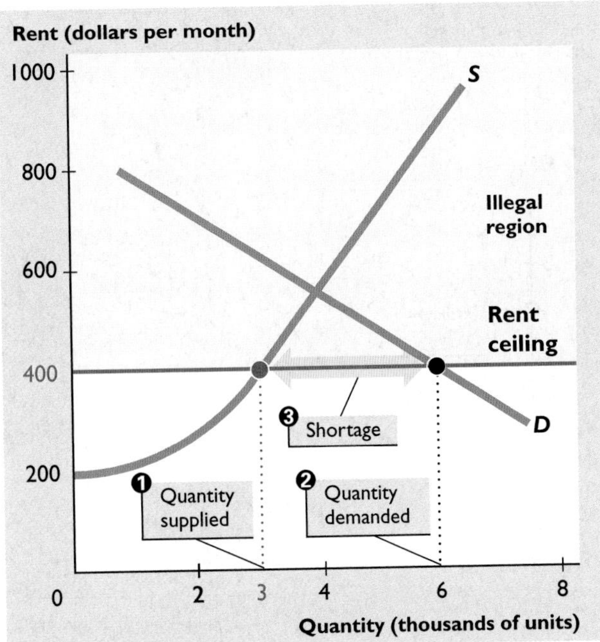

A rent ceiling is imposed below the equilibrium rent. In this example, the rent ceiling is $400 a month.

1. The quantity of housing supplied decreases to 3,000 units.
2. The quantity of housing demanded increases to 6,000 units.
3. A shortage of 3,000 units arises.

for worthless fittings—perhaps paying $2,000 for threadbare drapes. Another is for the tenant to pay a high price for new locks and keys—called "key money."

Figure 7.8 shows how high the black market rent might go in Biloxi. With strict enforcement of the rent ceiling, the quantity of housing available is 3,000 units. But at this quantity, renters are willing to offer as much as $625 a month—the amount determined on the demand curve.

So a small number of landlords illegally offer housing for rents up to $625 a month. The black market rent might be at any level between the rent ceiling of $400 and the maximum that a renter is willing to pay of $625.

Increased Search Activity

Search activity
The time spent looking for someone with whom to do business.

The time spent looking for someone with whom to do business is called **search activity**. We spend some time in search activity almost every time we buy something. You want the latest hot CD, and you know 4 stores that stock it. But which store has the best deal? You need to spend a few minutes on the telephone finding out. In some markets, we spend a lot of time searching. An example is the used car market. People spend a lot of time checking out alternative dealers and cars.

But when a price ceiling creates a shortage of housing, search activity *increases*. In a rent-controlled housing market, frustrated would-be renters scan the newspapers, not only for housing ads but also for death notices! Any information about newly available housing is useful. And they race to be first on the scene when news of a possible apartment breaks.

The *opportunity cost* of a good is equal to its price *plus* the value of the search time spent finding the good. So the opportunity cost of housing is equal to the rent plus the value of the search time spent looking for an apartment. Search activity is costly. It uses time and other resources, such as telephones, automobiles, and

FIGURE 7.8
A Rent Ceiling Creates a Black Market and Housing Search

*e*Foundations 7.2 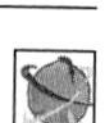

With a rent ceiling of $400 a month,

1. 3,000 units of housing are available.
2. Someone is willing to pay $625 a month for the 3,000th unit of housing.
3. Black market rents might be as high as $625 a month and resources get used up in costly search activity.

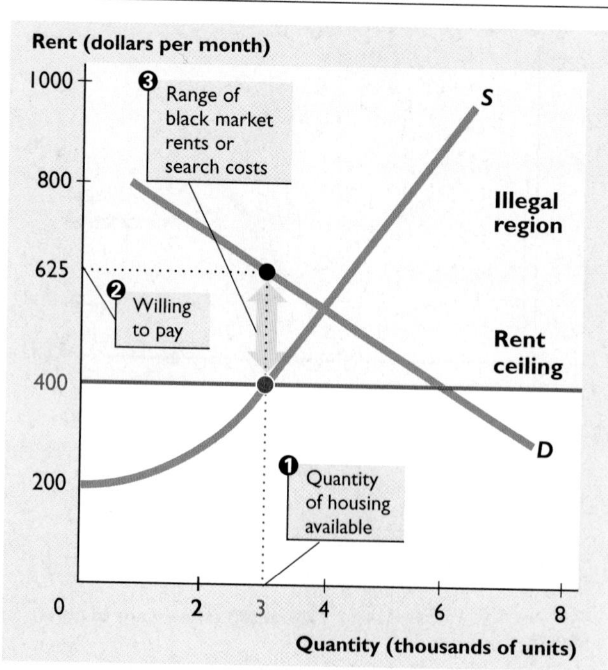

gasoline that could have been used in other productive ways. In Figure 7.8, to find accommodation at $400 a month, someone who is willing to pay a rent of $625 a month would be willing to spend on search an amount that is equivalent to adding $225 a month to the rent. For a one-year lease, this amount is enormous.

A rent ceiling controls the rent portion of the cost of housing, but it does not control the search cost. So when the search cost is added to the rent, some people end up paying a higher opportunity cost for housing than they would if there were no rent ceiling.

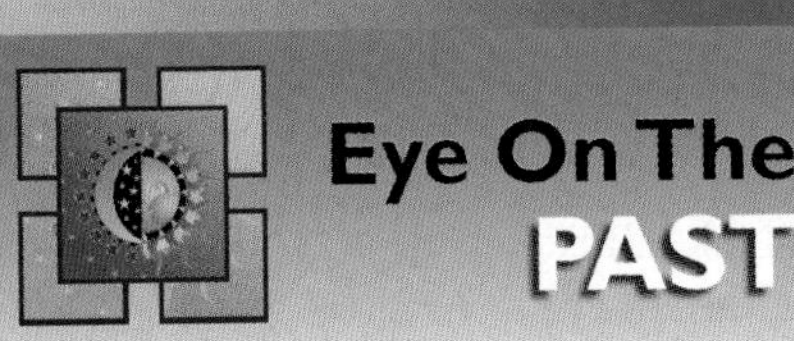

An Earthquake and a Rent Ceiling: A Tale of Two Eras in One City

Let's transport ourselves to San Francisco in April 1906, as the city is suffering from a massive earthquake and

fire. You can sense the enormity of San Francisco's problems from a headline in the *New York Times* on April 19, 1906 describing the first days of the crisis:

Over 500 Dead, $200,000,000 Lost in San Francisco Earthquake: Nearly Half the City Is in Ruins and 50,000 Are Homeless

The commander of federal troops in charge of the emergency described the magnitude of the problem:

> Not a hotel of note or importance was left standing. The great apartment houses had vanished ... two-hundred-and-twenty-five thousand people were ... homeless.[1]

In a single day, more than half the people in a city of 400,000 had lost their homes. Temporary shelters and camps alleviated some of the problem, but the apartment buildings and houses left standing had to accommodate 40 percent more people than they had before the earthquake.

The *San Francisco Chronicle* was not published for more than a month after the earthquake. When it reappeared on May 24, 1906, the city's housing shortage—what would seem to be a major news item that would still be of grave importance—was not even mentioned. Milton Friedman and George Stigler describe the situation:

> *There is not a single mention of a housing shortage!* The classified advertisements listed sixty-four offers of flats and houses for rent, and nineteen of houses for sale, against five advertisements of flats or houses wanted. Then and thereafter a considerable number of all types of accommodation ... were offered for rent.[2]

How did San Francisco cope with such a devastating decrease in the supply of housing? The answer is that a free market brought a rise in the rent and an increase in the intensity of use of the buildings that remained. People rented out rooms that they had previously used themselves. The high rents were an incentive for owners to rebuild as quickly as possible.

At the end of World War II (in 1945), the population of San Francisco grew by 30 percent. At the same time, a large-scale building program increased the number of houses and apartments by 20 percent. So each dwelling unit had to accommodate 10 percent more people. San Francisco had a housing "problem" about a quarter of the magnitude of that following the 1906 earthquake. Yet in 1946, the city's housing shortage was a huge political problem. Newspaper advertisements seeking apartments outnumbered those offering apartments by more than seven to one. Why? San Francisco had rent ceilings in 1946. It had a free housing market in 1906.

[1] Milton Friedman and George J. Stigler, "Roofs or Ceilings? The Current Housing Problem," in *Popular Essays on Current Problems*, Vol. 1, No. 2 (New York: Foundation for Economic Education, 1946), 3–159.

[2] Friedman and Stigler, p. 3.

Are Rent Ceilings Efficient?

A housing market with no rent ceiling determines the rent at which the quantity demanded equals the quantity supplied. In this situation, scarce housing resources are allocated efficiently because the marginal cost of housing equals the marginal benefit. Figure 7.9(a) shows this efficient outcome in the Biloxi apartment rental market. In this efficient market, the sum of *consumer surplus* (the green area) and *producer surplus* (the blue area) is maximized at the equilibrium rent and quantity of housing (see Chapter 6, p. 138).

Figure 7.9(b) shows that with a rent ceiling, the outcome is inefficient. Marginal benefit exceeds marginal cost. Producer surplus and consumer surplus shrink, and a deadweight loss (the gray area) arises. This loss is borne by the people who can't find housing and by landlords who can't offer housing at the lower rent ceiling.

But the total loss exceeds the deadweight loss. Resources get used in costly search activity and in evading the law in the black market. The value of these resources might be as large as the red rectangle. There is yet a further loss: the cost of enforcing the rent ceiling law. This loss, which is borne by taxpayers, is not visible in the figure.

FIGURE 7.9

The Inefficiency of a Rent Ceiling

*e*Foundations 7.2 

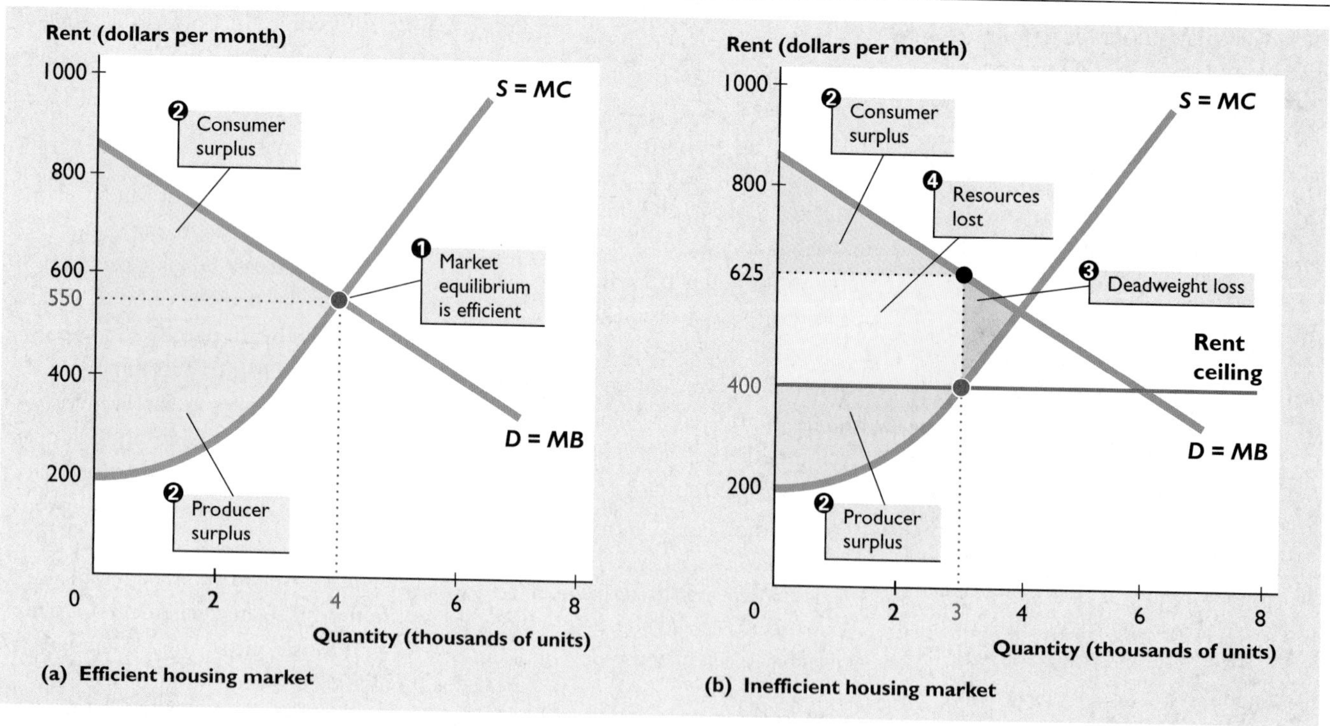

In part (a), ❶ the market is efficient with marginal benefit equal to marginal cost.

In part (b), a rent ceiling restricts the quantity supplied and marginal benefit exceeds marginal cost. ❷ Consumer surplus (green area) and producer surplus (blue area) shrink by the amount of ❸ the deadweight loss (gray area) and ❹ the resources lost in search activity and evading the rent ceiling law (red area). Resource use is inefficient.

While a rent ceiling causes inefficiency, not everyone loses. Those people who live in apartments at the rent ceiling get an increase in consumer surplus. And landlords who charge a black market rent get an increase in producer surplus.

The costs of a rent ceiling that we've just considered are only the initial costs. With the rent below the market rent, landlords have no incentive to maintain their buildings in a good state of repair. So over time, the quality and quantity of housing supplied *decrease* and the loss arising from a rent ceiling increases.

The size of the loss from a rent ceiling depends on the elasticities of supply and demand. If supply is inelastic, a rent ceiling brings a small decrease in the quantity of housing supplied. And if demand is inelastic, a rent ceiling brings a small increase in the quantity of housing demanded. So the more inelastic the supply or the demand, the smaller is the shortage of housing and the smaller is the deadweight loss.

Are Rent Ceilings Fair?

We've seen that rent ceilings prevent scarce resources from being allocated efficiently—resources do not flow to their highest-valued use. But don't they ensure that scarce housing resources are allocated more fairly?

You learned in Chapter 6 (pp. 142–144) that fairness is a complex idea about which there are two broad views: fair *results* versus fair *rules*. Rent controls violate the fair rules view of fairness because they block voluntary exchange. But do they deliver a fair result? Do rent ceilings ensure that scarce housing goes to the poor people whose need is greatest?

Blocking rent adjustments that bring the quantity of housing demanded into equality with the quantity supplied doesn't end scarcity. So when the law prevents the rent from adjusting and blocks the price mechanism from allocating scarce housing, some other allocation mechanism must be used. If that mechanism were one that provided the housing to the poorest, then the allocation might be regarded as fair.

But the mechanisms that get used do not usually achieve such an outcome. First-come-first-served is one allocation mechanism. Discrimination based on race, ethnicity, or sex is another. And discrimination against young newcomers and in favor of old established families is yet another. None of these mechanisms delivers a fair outcome.

Rent ceilings in New York City provide examples of these mechanisms at work. The main beneficiaries of rent ceilings in New York City are families that have lived in the city for a long time—including some rich and famous ones. These families enjoy low rents while newcomers pay high rents for hard-to-find apartments.

If Rent Ceilings Are So Bad, Why Do We Have Them?

The economic case against rent ceilings is now widely accepted, so *new* rent ceiling laws are rare. But when governments try to repeal rent control laws, as the New York City government did in 1999, current renters lobby politicians to maintain the ceilings. Also, people who are prevented from finding housing would be happy if they got lucky and managed to find a rent-controlled apartment. So there is plenty of political support for rent ceilings.

Apartment owners who oppose rent ceilings are a minority, so their views are not a powerful influence on politicians. Because more people support rent ceilings than oppose them, politicians are sometimes willing to support them too.

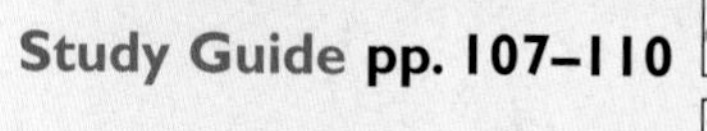

CHECKPOINT 7.2

Study Guide pp. 107–110

*e*Foundations 7.2

2 **Explain how a rent ceiling creates a housing shortage, inefficiency, and unfairness.**

Practice Problem 7.2

Figure 1 shows the rental market for apartments in a Chicago suburb:

a. What is the rent in this suburb and how many apartments are rented?
b. If the city of Chicago imposes a rent ceiling of $900 a month, what is the rent in this suburb and how many apartments are rented?
c. If the city of Chicago imposes a rent ceiling of $600 a month, what is the rent in this suburb and how many apartments are rented?
d. With a strictly enforced $600 rent ceiling, is the housing market efficient? Explain why or why not.
e. If the city strictly enforces the rent ceiling, is the housing market fair? Explain why or why not.
f. If a black market develops, how high could the black market rent be? Explain your answer.

FIGURE 1

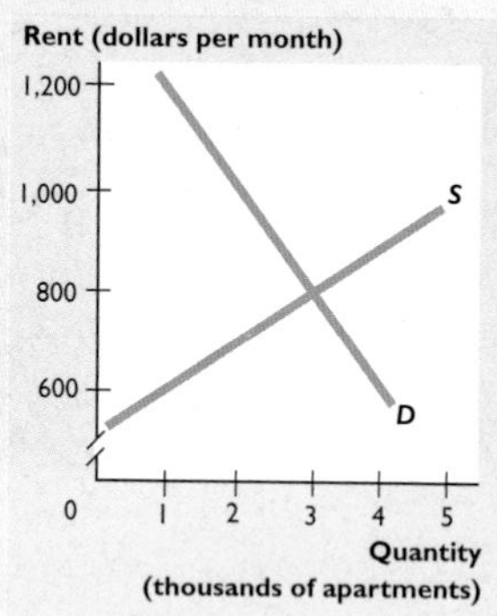

Exercise 7.2

Figure 2 shows the demand for on-campus student housing at Fort Lewis College, Durango. The college has 1,400 rooms for rent.

a. What are the equilibrium rent and the equilibrium quantity of rooms rented?
b. If the city imposed a rent ceiling on on-campus housing of $100 a week, how would you describe the on-campus housing market? Would the allocation of housing be efficient? Would it be fair?
c. If the rent ceiling of $100 a week were strictly enforced and there were no black market, who would gain and who would lose?
d. If with the $100 a week rent ceiling a black market developed, what rent would be offered for a room? Would the allocation of housing be efficient? Would it be fair?

FIGURE 2

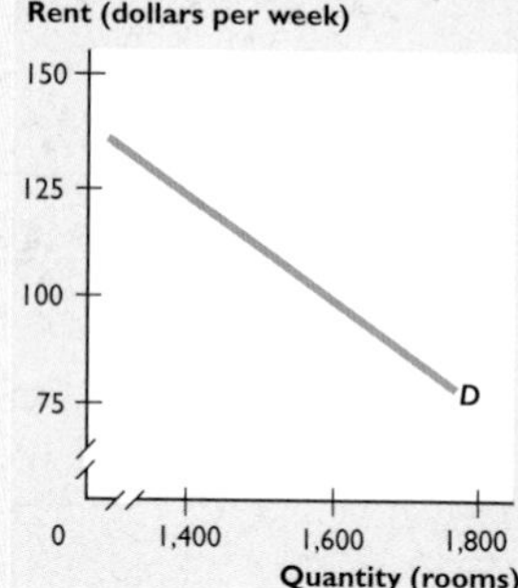

Solution to Practice Problem 7.2

a. The equilibrium rent is $800 a month, and 3,000 apartments are rented.
b. A rent ceiling of $900 a month is above the equilibrium rent, so the outcome is the market equilibrium rent of $800 a month with 3,000 apartments rented.
c. With the rent ceiling at $600 a month, the number of apartments rented is 1,000 and the rent is $600 a month (Figure 3).
d. The housing market is not efficient. With 1,000 apartments rented, marginal benefit exceeds marginal cost and a deadweight loss arises (Figure 3).
e. The rent ceiling makes the allocation of housing less fair in both views of fairness: It blocks voluntary transactions, and it does not provide more housing to those in most need.
f. In a black market, some people will be willing to rent an apartment for more than the rent ceiling. The highest rent that someone would offer is $1,200 a month. This rent equals the willingness of someone to pay for the 1,000th apartment (Figure 3).

FIGURE 3

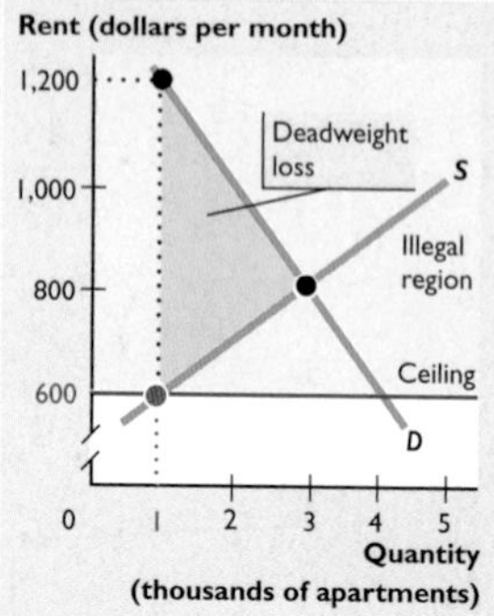

7.3 PRICE FLOORS

The labor market influences the jobs we get and the wages we earn. Firms hire labor, so they decide how much labor to demand. The lower the wage rate, the greater is the quantity of labor that firms demand. Households decide how much labor to supply. The higher the wage rate, the greater is the quantity of labor households are willing to supply. The wage rate adjusts to make the quantity of labor demanded equal to the quantity supplied.

The equilibrium wage rate might be high or low. Figure 7.10 shows a market in which the equilibrium wage rate is low. It is the market for fast-food servers in Yuma.

In this market, the demand for labor curve is *D*. On this demand curve, at a wage rate of $10 an hour, the quantity of fast-food servers demanded is zero. If A&W, Burger King, Taco Bell, McDonald's, Wendy's, and the other fast-food places had to pay servers $10 an hour, they wouldn't hire any. They would replace them with vending machines! But at wage rates below $10 an hour, they would hire servers. At a wage rate of $5 an hour, they would hire 5,000 servers.

On the supply side of the market, no one is willing to work for $2 an hour. To attract servers, the firms must pay more than $2 an hour.

Equilibrium in this market occurs at a wage rate of $5 an hour with 5,000 people employed as servers.

Suppose that the government thinks that no one should have to work for a wage rate as low as $5 an hour and decides it wants to increase the wage rate. Can the government improve conditions for these workers by passing a minimum wage law? Let's find out.

FIGURE 7.10
A Market for Fast-Food Servers

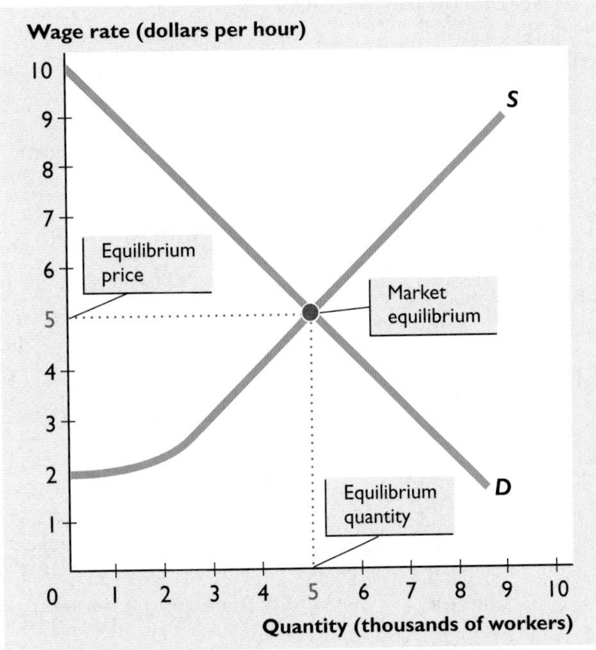

The demand for and supply of fast-food servers determine the equilibrium wage rate of $5 an hour and the equilibrium quantity of 5,000 servers employed.

The Minimum Wage

Minimum wage law
A government regulation that makes hiring labor for less than a specified wage illegal.

Price floor
The lowest price at which it is legal to trade a particular good, service, or factor of production. The minimum wage is an example of a price floor.

A **minimum wage law** is a government regulation that makes hiring labor for less than a specified wage illegal. Firms are free to pay a wage rate that exceeds the minimum wage but may not pay less than the minimum. A minimum wage is an example of a **price floor**, which is the lowest price at which it is legal to trade a particular good, service, or factor of production.

The effect of a price floor depends on whether it is set below or above the equilibrium price. In Figure 7.10, the equilibrium wage rate is \$5 an hour and at this wage rate, firms hire 5,000 workers. If the government introduced a minimum wage below \$5 an hour, nothing would change. The reason is that firms are already paying \$5 an hour, and because this wage exceeds the minimum wage, the wage rate paid doesn't change. Firms continue to hire 5,000 workers.

But the aim of a minimum wage is to boost the incomes of low-wage earners. So in the markets for the lowest-paid labor, the minimum wage will exceed the equilibrium wage.

Suppose that the government introduces a minimum wage of \$7 an hour. Figure 7.11 shows the effects of this law. Wage rates below \$7 an hour are illegal, so we've shaded the illegal region *below* the minimum wage. Firms and workers are no longer permitted to operate at the equilibrium point in this market because it is in the illegal region. Market forces and political forces are in conflict.

The government can set a minimum wage. But it can't tell employers how many workers to hire. If firms must pay \$7 an hour for labor, they will hire only 3,000 workers. At the equilibrium wage rate of \$5 an hour, they hired 5,000 workers. So when the minimum wage is introduced, firms fire 2,000 workers.

FIGURE 7.11
A Minimum Wage Creates Unemployment

*e*Foundations 7.3 

A minimum wage is introduced above the equilibrium wage rate. In this example, the minimum wage rate is \$7 an hour.

❶ The quantity of labor demanded decreases to 3,000 workers.

❷ The quantity of labor supplied increases to 7,000 people.

❸ 4,000 people are unemployed.

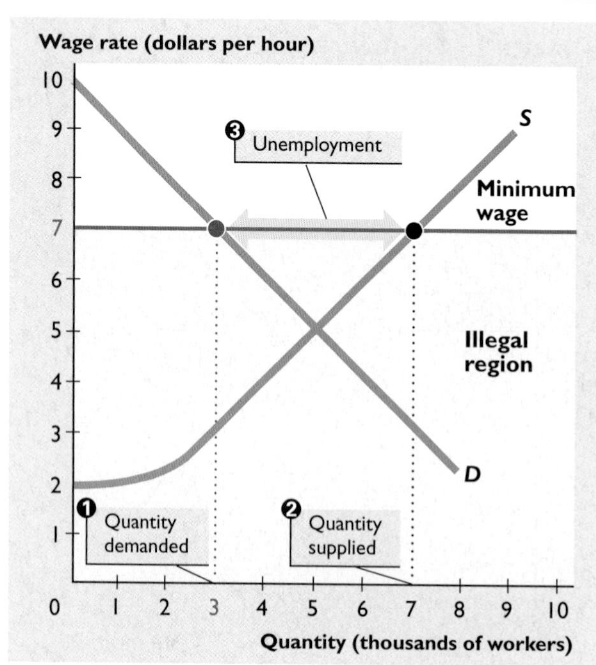

But at a wage rate of $7 an hour, another 2,000 people who didn't want to work for $5 an hour now try to find work as servers—at $7 an hour, the quantity supplied is 7,000 workers. With 2,000 workers fired and another 2,000 looking for work at the higher wage rate, 4,000 people who would like to work as servers are unemployed.

Somehow, the 3,000 jobs available must be allocated among the 7,000 people who are available for and willing to work. How is this allocation achieved? The answer is by increased job-search activity and illegal hiring.

Increased Job Search Activity

People spend a good deal of time and resources finding a good job. But with a minimum wage, more people are looking for jobs than the number of jobs available. Frustrated unemployed workers spend time and other resources searching for hard-to-find jobs. In Figure 7.12, to find a job at $7 an hour, someone who is willing to work for $3 an hour would be willing to spend on search an amount that is equivalent to subtracting $4 an hour from the wage rate. For a job that might last a year or more, this amount is large.

Illegal Hiring

With more people looking for work than the number of jobs available, some firms and workers might agree to do business at an illegal wage rate below the minimum wage—a black market in which the illegal wage is below the minimum wage.

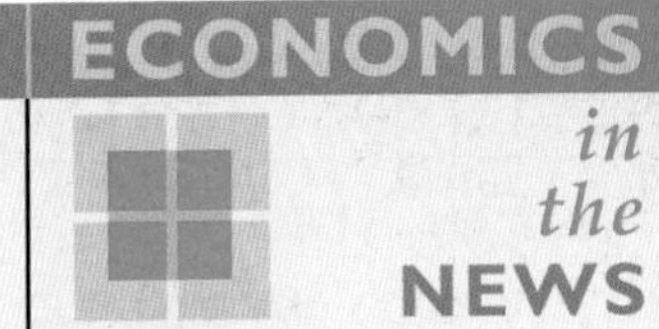

August, 2000

Deal possible in Congress on minimum wage increase

A deal is being struck that will raise the minimum wage by $1 over two years and, at the same time, provide tax breaks for business to cushion the cost increase.

Questions

1. How would a $1 increase in the minimum wage affect a labor market?

2. Would the unemployment rate increase, decrease, or remain unchanged? Explain.

3. How do you think that tax breaks for business would influence the effects of a higher minimum wage? Explain.

 *e*Foundations 7.3

FIGURE 7.12

A Minimum Wage Increases Job Search

*e*Foundations 7.3 

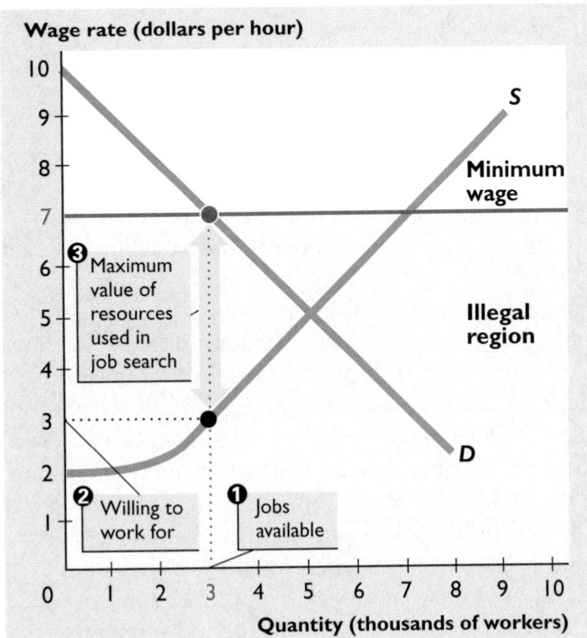

The minimum wage rate is set at $7 an hour:

❶ 3,000 jobs are available.

❷ The minimum wage rate for which someone is willing to work is $3 an hour.

❸ Illegal wage rates might range from just below the legal minimum of $7 an hour to the minimum that someone is willing to accept of $3 an hour.

The maximum people are willing to spend on job search is an amount equivalent to subtracting $4 an hour—the $7 they would receive if they found a job minus the $3 they are willing to work for—from the wage rate.

The Federal Minimum Wage

The federal government's *Fair Labor Standards Act* sets the minimum wage, which was last changed in 1997 when it was raised to $5.15 an hour.

The minimum wage creates unemployment. But how much unemployment does it create? Until recently, most economists believed that a 10 percent increase in the minimum wage rate decreased teenage employment by between 1 and 3 percent.

David Card of the University of California at Berkeley and Alan Krueger of Princeton University, have challenged this view. They claim that following a rise in the minimum wage in California, New Jersey, and Texas, the *employment* rate of low-income workers *increased*. They suggest three reasons why a rise in the wage rate might increase employment:

(1) Workers become more conscientious and productive.

(2) Workers are less likely to quit, so costly labor turnover is reduced.

(3) Managers make a firm's operations more efficient.

Most economists are skeptical about these ideas. They say that if higher wages make workers more productive and reduces labor turnover, firms will freely pay workers a higher wage. And they argue that there are other explanations for the employment increase that Card and Krueger found.

Daniel Hamermesh of the University of Texas at Austin says that they got the timing wrong. Firms *anticipated* the minimum wage rise and so cut employment *before* it occurred. Looking at employment changes *after* the minimum wage increased missed its main effect. Finis Welch of Texas A&M University and Kevin Murphy of the University of Chicago say the employment effects that Card and Krueger found are caused by regional differences in economic growth, not changes in the minimum wage.

Also, looking only at employment misses the supply-side effect of the minimum wage. It brings an increase in the number of people who drop out of high school to look for work.

Is the Minimum Wage Efficient?

The efficient allocation of a factor of production is similar to that of a good or service, which you studied in Chapter 6. The demand for labor tells us about the marginal benefit of labor to the firms that hire it. Firms benefit because the labor they hire produces the goods or services that they sell. Firms are willing to pay a wage rate equal to the benefit they receive from an additional hour of labor. So in Figure 7.13(a), the demand curve for labor tells us the marginal benefit that the firms in Yuma receive from hiring fast-food servers. The marginal benefit minus the wage rate is a surplus for the firms.

The supply of labor tells us about the marginal cost of working. To work, people must forgo leisure or working in the home, activities that they value. The wage rate received minus the marginal cost of working is a surplus for workers.

An efficient allocation of labor occurs when the marginal benefit to firms equals the marginal cost borne by workers. Such an allocation occurs in the labor market in Figure 7.13(a). Firms enjoy a surplus (the blue area), and workers enjoy a surplus (the green area). The sum of these surpluses is maximized.

Figure 7.13(b) shows the loss from a minimum wage. With a minimum wage of $5 an hour, 3,000 workers are hired. Marginal benefit exceeds marginal cost. The firms' surplus and workers' surplus shrink, and a deadweight loss (the gray area) arises. This loss is borne by firms that cut back employment and by people who can't find jobs at the higher wage rate.

But the total loss exceeds the deadweight loss. Resources get used in costly job-search activity as each unemployed person keeps looking for a job—writing letters, making phone calls, going for interviews, and so on. The value of these resources might be as large as the red rectangle.

FIGURE 7.13
The Inefficiency of the Minimum Wage

*e*Foundations 7.3 

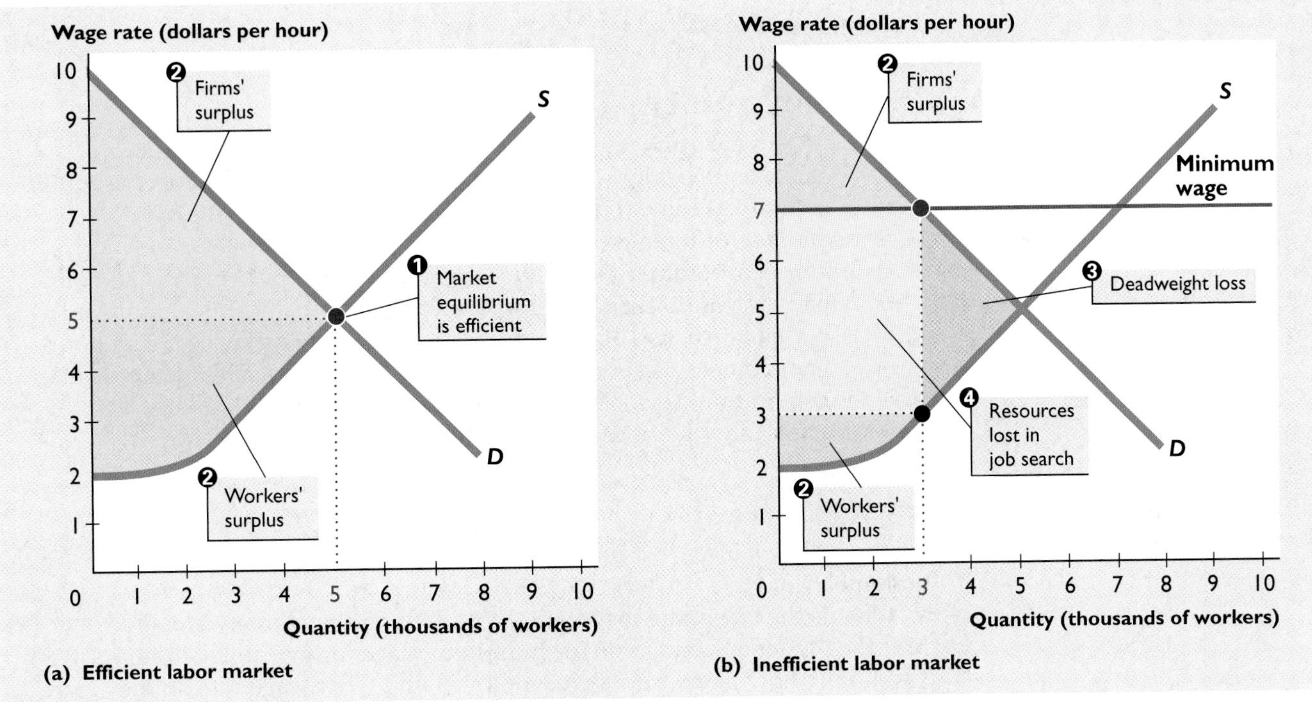

❶ In part (a), the market equilibrium is efficient.
In part (b), a minimum wage restricts the quantity demanded and ❷ the workers' surplus (green area) and firms' surplus (blue area) shrink by the amount of ❸ the deadweight loss (gray area) and ❹ the resources lost in job-search activity (red area). Resource use is inefficient.

Is the Minimum Wage Fair?

The minimum wage is unfair on both views of fairness—it delivers an unfair *result* and imposes unfair *rules*. The *result* is unfair because only those people who find jobs benefit. The unemployed end up worse off than with no minimum wage. And those who get jobs are probably not the least well off. When the wage rate doesn't allocate jobs, discrimination, another source of unfairness, increases. The minimum wage imposes unfair *rules* because it blocks voluntary exchange. Firms are willing to hire more labor and people are willing to work more. But they are not permitted by the minimum wage law to do so.

If the Minimum Wage Is So Bad, Why Do We Have It?

Although the minimum wage is inefficient, not everyone loses from it. The people who find jobs at the minimum wage rate are better off. Other supporters of the minimum wage believe that the elasticities of demand and supply in the labor market are low, so not much unemployment results. Labor unions support the minimum wage because it puts upward pressure on all wage rates including those of union workers. Nonunion labor is a substitute for union labor, so when the minimum wage rises, the demand for union labor increases.

CHECKPOINT 7.3

Study Guide pp. 110–113 

*e*Foundations 7.3

3 **Explain how the minimum wage creates unemployment, inefficiency, and unfairness.**

FIGURE 1

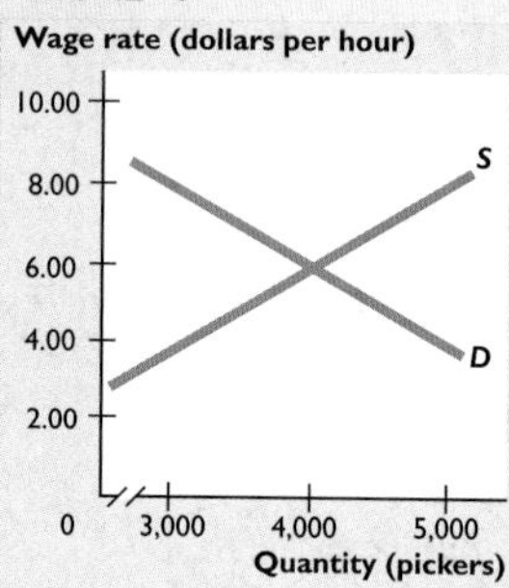

Practice Problem 7.3

Figure 1 shows the market for tomato pickers in southern California.

a. What is the equilibrium wage rate of tomato pickers and what is the equilibrium quantity of tomato pickers employed?
b. Is the market for tomato pickers efficient?
c. If California introduces a minimum wage for tomato pickers of $4 an hour, how many tomato pickers are employed and how many are unemployed?
d. If California introduces a minimum wage for tomato pickers of $8 an hour, how many tomato pickers are employed and how many are unemployed?
e. Is the minimum wage of $8 an hour efficient? Is it fair?
f. Who gains and who loses from the minimum wage of $8 an hour?

FIGURE 2

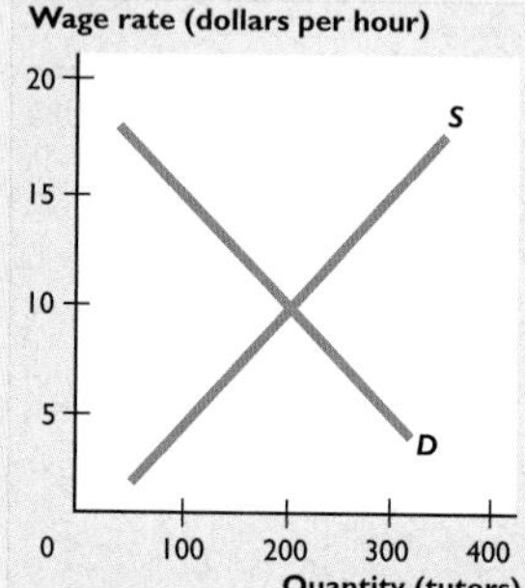

Exercise 7.3

Figure 2 shows a market for private math tutors in Madison organized by the Students' Union.

a. What is the wage rate that math tutors earn and how many are hired?
b. If the Students' Union sets the minimum wage for private math tutors at $8 an hour, how many tutors are employed and what wage rate do they earn?
c. If the Students' Union sets the minimum wage for private math tutors at $15 an hour, how many tutors are employed and what wage rate do they earn?
d. Is the minimum wage of $15 an hour efficient? Is it fair?
e. If a black market gets going and the Students' Union cannot enforce the minimum wage, what wage rate might some unscrupulous tutors earn?

Solution to Practice Problem 7.3

a. The equilibrium wage rate is $6 an hour, and 4,000 pickers are employed.
b. The market for tomato pickers is efficient because the marginal benefit to tomato growers equals the marginal cost borne by the pickers.
c. The minimum wage of $4 an hour is below the equilibrium wage rate, so 4,000 tomato pickers are employed and none are unemployed.
d. The minimum wage of $8 an hour is above the equilibrium wage rate, so 3,000 pickers are employed (determined by the demand for tomato pickers) and 5,000 people would like to work as pickers for $8 an hour (determined by the supply curve), so 2,000 are unemployed (Figure 3).
e. The minimum wage of $8 an hour is not efficient because it creates a deadweight loss—the marginal benefit to growers (on the demand curve) exceeds the marginal cost to pickers (on the supply curve). An additional loss arises as unemployed tomato pickers search for jobs. The minimum wage is unfair by both of the fairness criteria.
f. Tomato pickers who find work at $8 an hour gain. Tomato growers and unemployed pickers lose.

FIGURE 3

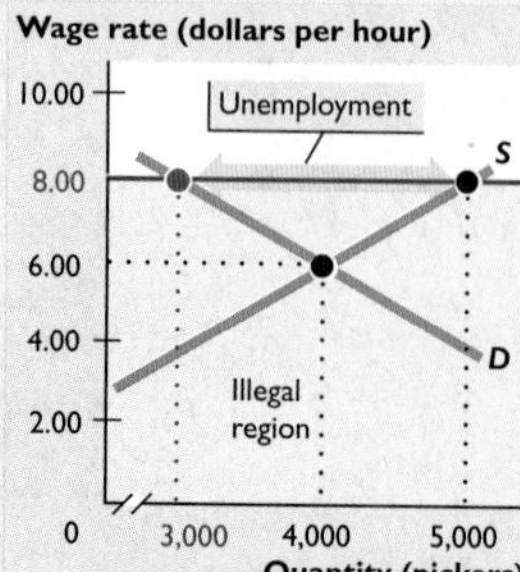

CHAPTER CHECKPOINT

Key Points

1 Explain the effects of taxes on goods and labor and determine who pays the taxes.

- A tax on a good raises the price of the good but usually by less than the tax.
- The shares of a tax paid by the buyer and by the seller depend on the elasticity of demand and the elasticity of supply.
- The less elastic the demand and the more elastic the supply, the greater is the price increase, the smaller is the quantity decrease, and the larger is the share of the tax paid by the buyer.
- If demand is perfectly elastic or supply is perfectly inelastic, the seller pays all the tax. And if demand is perfectly inelastic or supply is perfectly elastic, the buyer pays all the tax.
- The elasticities of demand and supply, not Congress, determine who pays the income tax and who pays a payroll tax.
- Taxes create inefficiency by driving a wedge between marginal benefit and marginal cost and creating a deadweight loss.

2 Explain how a rent ceiling creates a housing shortage, inefficiency, and unfairness.

- A price ceiling set above the equilibrium price has no effects.
- A price ceiling set below the equilibrium price creates a shortage, costly search, and a black market.
- A price ceiling is inefficient and unfair.
- A rent ceiling is an example of a price ceiling.

3 Explain how the minimum wage creates unemployment, inefficiency, and unfairness.

- A price floor set below the equilibrium price has no effects.
- A price floor set above the equilibrium price creates a surplus, costly search, and illegal trading.
- A price floor is inefficient and unfair.
- The minimum wage is an example of a price floor.

Key Terms

Black market, 167
Excess burden, 164
Minimum wage law, 174
Payroll tax, 163
Price ceiling, 166
Price floor, 174
Rent ceiling, 166
Search activity, 168
Tax incidence, 158

Exercises

1. The government decides to put a tax of 20 percent on luxury boats. If the average price of a luxury boat is $1 million, will the government get $200,000 in tax revenue for each boat sold? Who will pay most of this tax: boat sellers or boat buyers? Will this tax be efficient? Will it be fair? Explain your answers.
2. In Florida, sunscreen and sunglasses are necessities. If the tax on these items is doubled, who will pay most of the sales tax increase: buyers or sellers. Will the tax increase halve the quantity of sunscreen and sunglasses bought? Is the tax fair? Explain your answers.
3. To encourage inner-city youths to spend more time playing sports, the government introduces a super income tax of 10 percent on professional basketball players and plans to use the revenue to improve inner-city sports facilities. Will the super income tax raise much revenue for the government? Who will pay most of the tax: the players or the team owners?
4. In question 3, would a payroll tax of 10 percent bring in the same amount of revenue for the government as the super income tax? Who pays the payroll tax: the players or the team owners?
5. During the 1996 Olympic Games, many residents of Atlanta left the city and rented out their homes. Despite the increase in the quantity of housing available, rents soared. If the city of Atlanta had imposed a rent ceiling at the time of the 1996 Olympic Games, describe how the housing market would have functioned.
6. Concerned about the political fallout from rising gas prices, the government decides to impose a ceiling on the price of gasoline of $1.00 a gallon. Explain how the market for gasoline would react to this price ceiling if:
   a. The oil-producing nations increased production and drove the equilibrium price of gasoline to 90 cents a gallon.
   b. A global shortage of oil sent the equilibrium price of gasoline to $2.00 a gallon.

   Explain which of these two situations would result in an efficient use of resources and why.
7. Bakers earn $10 an hour, gas pump attendants earn $4 an hour, and copy shop workers earn $5 an hour. If the government introduces a minimum wage of $5 an hour, explain how the markets for bakers, gas pump attendants, and copy shop workers will respond initially to the minimum wage.
8. The equilibrium retail price of beef falls to $2 a pound, a price at which cattle ranchers can't survive. To help the struggling ranchers, the government declares that it is illegal to buy beef for less than $5 a pound. The government also appoints a large number of observers to keep a close watch on the beef market and ensure that the law is observed to the letter. Black market traders are effectively eliminated. Describe the situation in the beef market, and explain why the cattle ranchers want the government to abandon the price floor.

Chapter 8

Externalities

CHAPTER CHECKLIST

When you have completed your study of this chapter, you will be able to:

1 **Explain why negative externalities lead to inefficient overproduction and how property rights, pollution charges, or taxes can achieve a more efficient outcome.**

2 **Explain why positive externalities lead to inefficient underproduction and how public provision, subsidies, vouchers, and patents can achieve a more efficient outcome.**

You learned in Chapter 6 that markets are not always efficient. And you saw in Chapter 7 some government actions that create inefficiency. In this chapter, we study markets in which governments help to achieve a more efficient outcome. In these markets, the actions of buyers and sellers affect other people, for ill or good, in ways that are ignored by the market participants.

We burn huge quantities of coal and oil that bring acid rain and global warming, and we dump toxic waste into rivers, lakes, and oceans. These environmental issues are simultaneously everybody's problem and nobody's problem. How can we create incentives that make us consider the damage that we inflict on others every time we turn on our heating or air conditioning?

Almost every day, we hear about a new discovery in medicine, engineering, chemistry, physics, and even economics. Advances in knowledge bring benefits to all, not just to the scientists who make the advances. How much should we spend on the education and research that make these advances possible?

EXTERNALITIES IN OUR DAILY LIVES

Externality
A cost or a benefit that arises from production that falls on someone other than the producer; or a cost or benefit that arises from consumption that falls on someone other than the consumer.

Negative externality
A production or consumption activity that creates an external cost.

Positive externality
A production or consumption activity that creates an external benefit.

An **externality** is a cost or a benefit that arises from production that falls on someone other than the producer; or a cost or a benefit that arises from consumption that falls on someone other than the consumer. Before we embark on the two main tasks of this chapter, we're going to review the range of externalities, classify them, and give some everyday examples.

First, an externality can arise from either a production activity or a consumption activity. Second, it can be either a **negative externality**, which imposes an external cost, or a **positive externality**, which provides an external benefit. So there are four types of externalities:

- Negative production externalities
- Positive production externalities
- Negative consumption externalities
- Positive consumption externalities

Negative Production Externalities

When the U.S. Open tennis tournament is being played at Flushing Meadows, players, spectators, and television viewers around the world share a negative production externality that many New Yorkers experience every day—the noise of airplanes taking off from Kennedy Airport. Aircraft noise imposes a large cost on millions of people who live under the flight paths to airports in every major city.

Logging and the clearing of forests is the source of another negative production externality. These activities destroy the habitat of wildlife and influence the amount of carbon dioxide in the atmosphere, which has a long-term effect on temperature. So these external costs are borne by everyone and by future generations.

Pollution, which we examine in more detail in the next section, is another and a major example of this type of externality.

Positive Production Externalities

To produce orange blossom honey, Honey Run Honey of Chico, California, locates beehives next to an orange orchard. The honeybees collect pollen and nectar from the orange blossom to make the honey. At the same time, they transfer pollen between the blossoms, which helps to fertilize them. Two positive production

externalities are present in this example. Honey Run Honey gets a positive production externality from the owner of the orange orchard. And the orange grower gets a positive production externality from Honey Run.

Negative Consumption Externalities

Negative consumption externalities are a source of irritation for most of us. Smoking tobacco in a confined space creates fumes that many people find unpleasant and that pose a health risk. So smoking in restaurants and on airplanes generates a negative externality. To avoid this negative externality, many restaurants and all airlines ban smoking. But while a smoking ban avoids a negative consumption externality for most people, it imposes a negative consumption externality on smokers. The majority, for whom the ban is in place, impose a cost on the minority—the smokers who would prefer to enjoy the consumption of tobacco while dining or taking a plane trip.

Noisy parties and outdoor rock concerts are other examples of negative consumption externalities. And they are also examples of the fact that a simple ban on an activity is not a solution. Banning noisy parties avoids the external cost on sleep-seeking neighbors, but it results in the sleepers imposing an external cost on the fun-seeking partygoers.

Permitting dandelions to grow in lawns, not picking up leaves in the fall, allowing a dog to bark loudly or to foul a neighbor's lawn, and letting your cell phone ring in class are other examples of negative consumption externalities.

Positive Consumption Externalities

When you get a flu vaccination, you lower your risk of being infected during the winter. But if you avoid the flu, your neighbor, who didn't get vaccinated, has a better chance of remaining healthy. Flu vaccinations generate positive consumption externalities.

When its owner restores a historic building, everyone who sees the building gets pleasure from it. Similarly, when someone erects a spectacular home—such as those built by Frank Lloyd Wright during the 1920s and 1930s—or other exciting building—such as the Chrysler and Empire State Buildings in New York or the Wrigley Building in Chicago—an external consumption benefit flows to everyone who has an opportunity to view it.

Education, which we examine in more detail in this chapter, is another and a major example of this type of externality.

8.1 NEGATIVE EXTERNALITIES: POLLUTION

You've just seen that pollution is an example of a negative externality. Both production and consumption activities create pollution. But here, we'll focus on pollution as a negative production externality. When a chemical factory dumps waste into a river, the people who live by the river and use it for fishing and boating bear the cost of the pollution. The chemical factory does not consider the cost of pollution when it decides the quantity of chemicals to produce. Its supply curve is based on its own costs, not on the costs that it inflicts on others. You're going to discover that when external costs are present, we produce more output than the efficient quantity and we get more pollution than the efficient quantity.

Pollution and other environmental problems are not new. Preindustrial towns and cities in Europe had severe sewage disposal problems that created cholera epidemics and plagues that killed millions. Nor is the desire to find solutions to environmental problems new. The development in the fourteenth century of a pure water supply and the hygienic disposal of garbage and sewage are examples of early contributions to improving the quality of the environment.

Popular discussions about pollution and the environment often pay little attention to economics. They focus on physical aspects of the environment, not on costs and benefits. A common assumption is that activities that damage the environment are morally wrong and must cease. In contrast, an economic study of the environment emphasizes costs and benefits. Economists talk about the efficient amount of pollution or environmental damage. This emphasis on costs and benefits does not mean that economists, as citizens, don't share the same goals as others and value a healthy environment. Nor does it mean that economists have the right answers and everyone else has the wrong ones. Rather, economics provides a set of tools and principles that help to clarify the issues.

The starting point for an economic analysis of the environment is the distinction between private costs and social costs.

Private Costs and Social Costs

Marginal private cost
The cost of producing an additional unit of a good or service that is borne by the producer of that good or service.

Marginal external cost
The cost of producing an additional unit of a good or service that falls on people other than the producer.

Marginal social cost
The marginal cost incurred by the entire society—by the producer and by everyone else on whom the cost falls. It is the sum of marginal private cost and marginal external cost.

A *private cost* of production is a cost that is borne by the producer of a good or service. *Marginal cost* is the cost of producing an *additional unit* of a good or service. So **marginal private cost** (*MC*) is the cost of producing an additional unit of a good or service that is borne by the producer of that good or service.

You've seen that an *external cost* is a cost of producing a good or service that is *not* borne by the producer but borne by other people. A **marginal external cost** is the cost of producing an additional unit of a good or service that falls on people other than the producer.

Marginal social cost (*MSC*) is the marginal cost incurred by the entire society—by the producer and by everyone else on whom the cost falls—and is the sum of marginal private cost and marginal external cost. That is,

$$MSC = MC + \text{Marginal external cost.}$$

We express costs in dollars. But we must always remember that a cost is an opportunity cost—what we give up to get something. A marginal external cost is what someone other than the producer of a good or service must give up when the producer makes one more unit of the item. Something real, such as a clean river or clean air, is given up.

Valuing an External Cost

Economists use market prices to put a dollar value on the cost of pollution. For example, suppose that there are two similar rivers, one polluted and the other clean. Five hundred identical homes are built along the side of each river. The homes on the clean river rent for $2,500 a month, and those on the polluted river rent for $1,500 a month. If the pollution is the only detectable difference between the two rivers and the two locations, the rent decrease of $1,000 per month is the cost of the pollution. For the 500 homes, the external cost is $500,000 a month.

External Cost and Output

Figure 8.1 shows an example of the relationship between output and cost in a chemical industry that pollutes. The marginal cost curve, *MC*, describes the private marginal cost borne by the firms that produce the chemical. Marginal cost increases as the quantity of chemical produced increases. If the firms dump waste into a river, they impose an external cost that increases with the amount of the chemical produced. The marginal social cost curve, *MSC*, is the sum of marginal private cost and marginal external cost. For example, when output is 4,000 tons per month, marginal private cost is $100 a ton, marginal external cost is $125 a ton, and marginal social cost is $225 a ton.

In Figure 8.1, as the quantity of chemicals produced increases, the amount of pollution increases and the external cost of pollution increases. The quantity of chemicals produced and the amount of pollution created depend on how the market for chemicals operates. First, we'll see what happens when the industry is free to pollute.

FIGURE 8.1
An External Cost

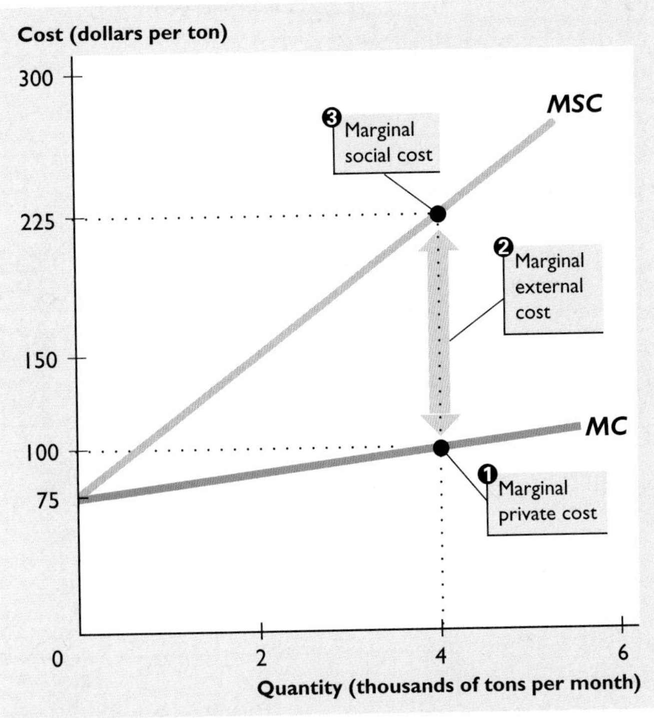

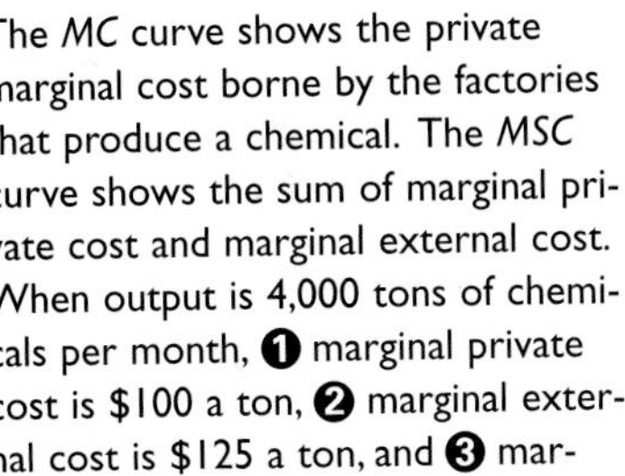
The *MC* curve shows the private marginal cost borne by the factories that produce a chemical. The *MSC* curve shows the sum of marginal private cost and marginal external cost. When output is 4,000 tons of chemicals per month, ❶ marginal private cost is $100 a ton, ❷ marginal external cost is $125 a ton, and ❸ marginal social cost is $225 a ton.

Production and Pollution: How Much?

When an industry is unregulated, the amount of pollution it creates depends on the market equilibrium price and quantity of the good produced. Figure 8.2 illustrates the outcome in the market for a pollution-creating chemical.

The demand curve for the chemical is *D*. This curve also measures the marginal benefit, *MB*, to the buyers of the chemical (see Chapter 6, p. 134). The supply curve is *S*. This curve also measures the marginal private cost, *MC*, of the producers (see Chapter 6, p. 137). The supply curve is the marginal private cost curve because when firms make their production and supply decisions, they consider only the costs that they will bear. Market equilibrium occurs at a price of $100 a ton and a quantity of 4,000 tons a month.

This equilibrium is inefficient. You learned in Chapter 6 that the allocation of resources is efficient when marginal benefit equals marginal cost. But we must count all the costs—private and external—when we compare marginal benefit and marginal cost. So with an external cost, the allocation is efficient when marginal benefit equals marginal *social* cost. This outcome occurs when the quantity of chemicals produced is 2,000 tons a month. The market equilibrium overproduces by 2,000 tons a month and creates a deadweight loss, the gray triangle.

How can the people who live by the polluted river get the chemical factories to decrease their output of chemicals and create less pollution? If some method can be found to achieve this outcome, everyone—the owners of the chemical factories and the residents of the riverside homes—can gain. Let's explore some solutions.

FIGURE 8.2

Inefficiency with an External Cost

*e*Foundations **8.1** 

The market supply curve is the marginal private cost curve, *S* = *MC*. The demand curve is the marginal benefit curve, *D* = *MB*.

1. Market equilibrium at a price of $100 a ton and 4,000 tons a month is inefficient because 2 marginal social cost exceeds 3 marginal benefit.
4. The efficient quantity is 2,000 tons a month.
5. The gray triangle shows the deadweight loss created by the pollution externality.

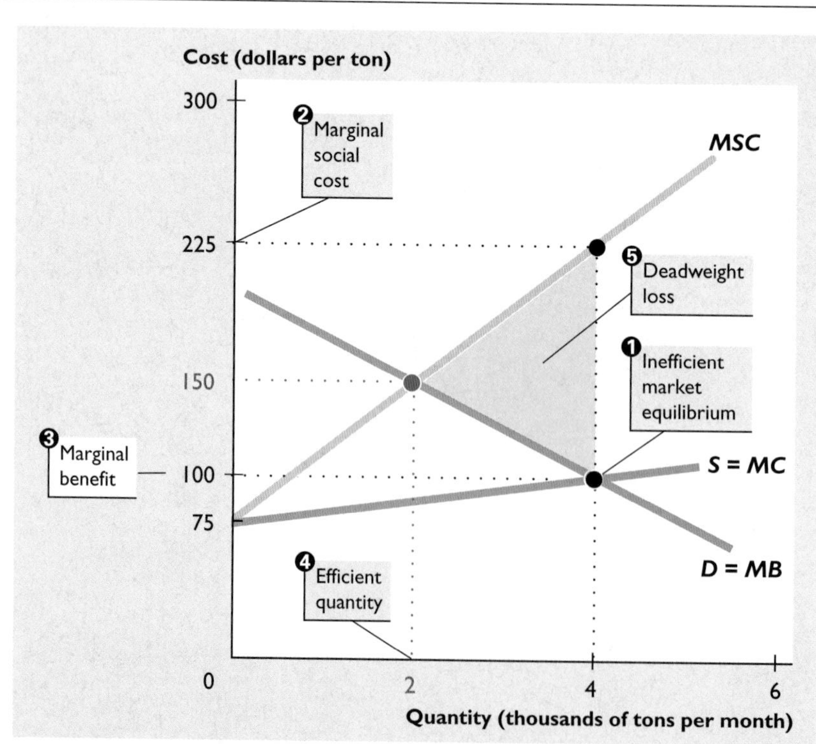

Property Rights

Sometimes it is possible to reduce the inefficiency arising from an externality by establishing a property right where one does not currently exist. **Property rights** are legally established titles to the ownership, use, and disposal of factors of production and goods and services that are enforceable in the courts.

Property rights
Legally established titles to the ownership, use, and disposal of factors of production and goods and services that are enforceable in the courts.

Suppose that the chemical factories own the river and the 500 homes alongside it. The rent that people are willing to pay depends on the amount of pollution. Using the earlier example, people are willing to pay \$2,500 a month to live alongside a pollution-free river but only \$1,500 a month to live with the pollution created by 4,000 tons of chemicals a month. If the factories produce this quantity, they lose \$1,000 a month for each home and a total of \$500,000 a month.

The chemical factories are now confronted with the cost of their pollution decision. They might still decide to pollute, but if they do, they face the opportunity cost of their actions—forgone rent from the people who live by the river.

Figure 8.3 illustrates the outcome by using the same example as in Figure 8.2. With property rights in place, the original marginal cost curve no longer measures all the costs that the factories face in producing the chemical. It excludes the pollution costs that they must now bear. The former *MSC* curve now becomes the marginal private cost curve *MC*. All the costs fall on the factories, so the market supply curve is based on all the marginal costs and is the curve labeled *S* = *MC*.

Market equilibrium now occurs at a price of \$150 a ton and a quantity of 2,000 tons a month. This outcome is efficient. The factories still produce some pollution, but it is the efficient quantity.

FIGURE 8.3
Property Rights Achieve an Efficient Outcome

*e*Foundations 8.1 

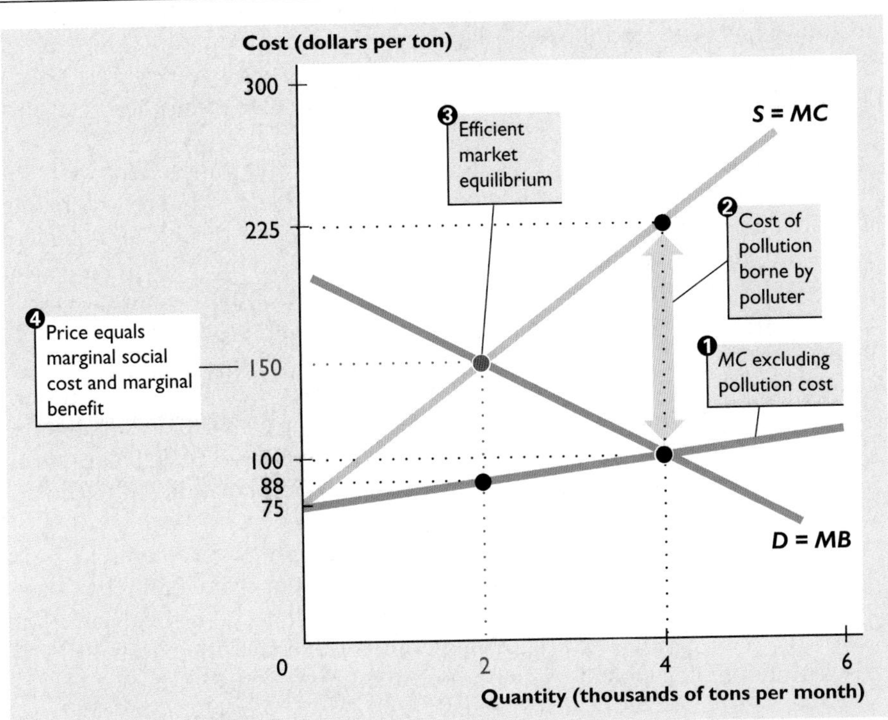

1. With property rights, the marginal cost curve that excludes pollution costs shows only part of the producers' marginal cost.
2. The marginal private cost curve includes the cost of pollution, and the supply curve is *S* = *MC*.
3. Market equilibrium is at a price of \$150 a ton and a quantity of 2,000 tons a month and is efficient because 4 marginal social cost equals marginal benefit.

The Coase Theorem

Does it matter how property rights are assigned? Does it matter whether the polluter or the victim of the pollution owns the resource that might be polluted? Until 1960, everyone—including economists who had thought long and hard about the problem—thought that it did matter. But in 1960, Ronald Coase had a remarkable insight, now called the Coase theorem.

Coase theorem
The proposition that if property rights exist, only a small number of parties are involved, and transactions costs are low, then private transactions are efficient and the outcome is not affected by who is assigned the property right.

The **Coase theorem** is the proposition that if property rights exist, only a small number of parties are involved, and transactions costs are low, then private transactions are efficient. There are no externalities because the transacting parties take all the costs and benefits into account. Furthermore, it doesn't matter who has the property rights.

Application of the Coase Theorem

Let's apply the Coase theorem to the polluted river. In the example that we've just studied, the factories own the river and the homes. Suppose that instead, the residents own their homes and the river. Now the factories must pay a fee to the homeowners for the right to dump their waste. The greater the quantity of waste dumped into the river, the more the factories must pay. So again, the factories face the opportunity cost of the pollution they create. The quantity of chemicals produced and the amount of waste dumped are the same whoever owns the homes and the river. If the factories own them, they bear the cost of pollution because they receive a lower income from home rents. And if the residents own the homes and the river, the factories bear the cost of pollution because they must pay a fee to the homeowners. In both cases, the factories bear the cost of their pollution and dump the efficient amount of waste into the river.

Transactions costs
The opportunity costs of conducting a transaction.

The Coase solution works only when transactions costs are low. **Transactions costs** are the opportunity costs of conducting a transaction. For example, when you buy an apartment, you incur a series of transactions costs. You might pay a realtor to help you find the best place and a financial planner to help you get the best loan, and you pay a lawyer to run checks that assure you that the seller owns the property and that after you've paid for it, the ownership has been properly transferred to you.

In the example of the homes alongside a river, the transactions costs that are incurred by a small number of chemical factories and a few homeowners might be low enough to enable them to negotiate the deals that produce an efficient outcome. But in many situations, transactions costs are so high that it would be inefficient to incur them. In these situations, the Coase solution is not available.

Suppose, for example, that everyone owns the airspace above their homes up to, say, 10 miles. If someone pollutes your airspace, you can charge a fee. But to collect the fee, you must identify who is polluting your airspace and persuade them to pay you. Imagine the costs of negotiating and enforcing agreements with the 50 million people who live in your part of the United States (and perhaps in Canada or Mexico) and the several thousand factories that emit sulfur dioxide and create acid rain that falls on your property!

In this situation, we use public choices through governments to cope with externalities. But the transactions costs that prevent us from using the Coase solution are opportunity costs, and governments can't wave a magician's wand to eliminate them. So attempts by the government to deal with externalities offer no easy solution. Let's look at some of these attempts.

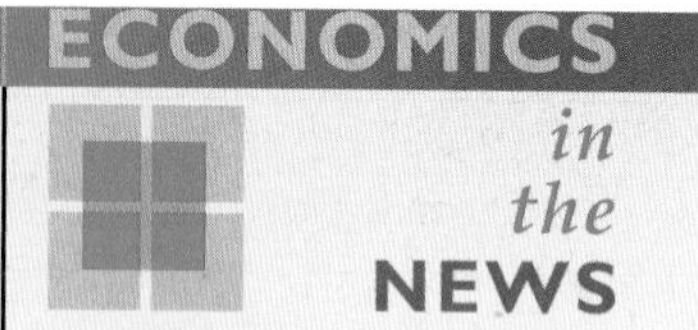

May 19, 2000

Golf Club Squeals over Pig Farm Neighbor

As golfers play the 15th hole at the Florida Club, the air is filled with the sounds of country music—and the stench from Paul Thompson's pig farm.

Questions

1. What economic problem does this news article describe?

2. What is the Coase solution to the problem?

3. Why can't the Coase solution be implemented?

4. Can you devise a solution to the problem that makes the pig farmer and the golfers better off?

e/**Foundations 8.1**

Government Actions in the Face of External Costs

The three main methods that governments use to cope with externalities are:

- Emission charges
- Marketable permits
- Taxes

Emission Charges

Emission charges confront a polluter with the external cost of pollution and provide an incentive to seek new technologies that are less polluting. In the United States, the Environmental Protection Agency (EPA) sets emission charges, which are, in effect, a price per unit of pollution. The more pollution a firm creates, the more it pays in emission charges. This method of dealing with environmental externalities has been used only modestly in the United States, but it is common in Europe. For example, in France, Germany, and the Netherlands, water polluters pay a waste disposal charge.

To work out the emission charge that achieves efficiency, the regulator must determine the marginal external cost of pollution at different levels of output and levy a charge on polluters that equals that cost. The polluter then incurs a marginal cost that includes both private and external costs. But to achieve the efficient outcome, the regulator needs a lot of information about the polluting industry that, in practice, is not available.

Another way of overcoming excess pollution is to issue firms with pollution quotas that they can buy and sell—with marketable permits. Let's look at this alternative.

Marketable Permits

Instead of imposing emission charges on polluters, each potential polluter might be assigned a pollution limit. To achieve efficiency, marginal benefit and marginal cost must be assessed, just as in the case of emission charges. Provided that these benefit-cost calculations are correct, the same efficient outcome can be achieved with quantitative limits as with emission charges. But in the case of quantitative limits, a cap must be set for each polluter.

Marketable permits are a clever way of overcoming the need for the regulator to know every firm's marginal cost schedule. The government issues each firm a permit to emit a certain amount of pollution, and firms can buy and sell these permits. Firms that have a low marginal cost of reducing pollution sell their permits, and firms that have a high marginal cost of reducing pollution buy permits. The market in permits determines the price at which firms trade permits. And firms buy or sell permits until their marginal cost of pollution equals the market price.

This method of dealing with pollution provides an even stronger incentive than do emission charges to find technologies that pollute less because the price of a permit to pollute rises as the demand for permits increases.

Taxes

The government can use taxes as an incentive for producers to cut back on an activity that creates an external cost. By setting the tax rate equal to the marginal external cost, firms can be made to behave in the same way as they would if they bore the cost of the externality directly.

Pollution Trends

Air quality in the United States is getting better. Lead has been almost eliminated, and sulfur dioxide, carbon monoxide, and suspended particulates have been reduced substantially. But nitrogen dioxide and ozone have persisted at close to their 1975 levels.

The earth's average temperature has increased over the past 100 years, and most of the increase occurred before 1940. No one knows why this temperature increase has occurred, but some scientists believe the cause to be carbon dioxide emissions from road transportation and electric utilities, methane created by cows and other livestock, nitrous oxide emissions of electric utilities and from fertilizers, and chlorofluorocarbons (CFCs) from refrigeration equipment and (in the past) aerosols.

The ozone layer in the earth's atmosphere protects us from cancer-causing ultraviolet rays from the sun. A hole in the ozone layer over Antarctica is getting bigger. How our industrial activity influences the ozone layer is not well understood, but some scientists think that CFCs are one source of ozone layer depletion.

The largest sources of water pollution are the dumping of industrial waste and treated sewage in lakes and rivers and the runoff from fertilizers. A more dramatic source is the

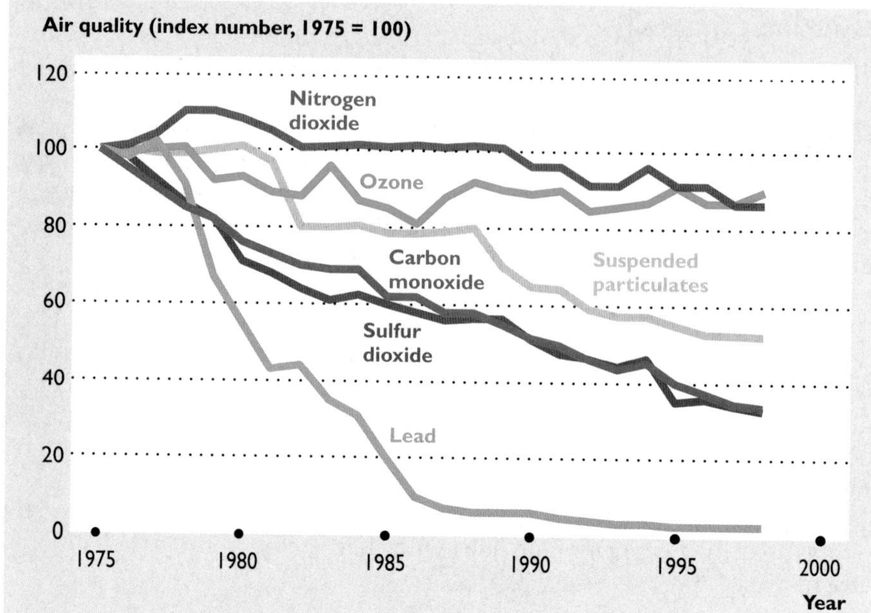

SOURCE: U.S. Environmental Protection Agency, *National Air Quality and Emissions Trend Report*, 1999.

Effects of Government Actions

To see how government actions can change market outcomes in the face of externalities, let's return to the example of the chemical factories and the river.

Assume that the government has assessed the cost of the marginal externality cost accurately and imposes a tax on the factories that exactly equals this cost.

Figure 8.4 illustrates the effects of this tax. The demand curve and marginal benefit curve $D = MB$ and the firms' marginal cost curve MC are the same as in Figure 8.3. The pollution tax equals the marginal external cost of the pollution. We add this tax to marginal cost to find the market supply curve. This curve is the one labeled $S = MC + tax = MSC$. This curve is the market supply curve because it tells us the quantities supplied at each price given the firms' marginal cost and the tax they must pay. This curve is also the marginal social cost curve because the pollution tax has been set equal to the marginal external cost.

Demand and supply now determine the market equilibrium price at $150 a ton and the equilibrium quantity at 2,000 tons a month. At this scale of chemical production, the marginal social cost is $150 and the marginal benefit is $150, so the outcome is efficient. The firms incur a marginal cost of $88 a ton and pay a tax of $62 a ton. The government collects tax revenue of $176,000 a month.

accidental spilling of crude oil into the oceans such as the *Exxon Valdez* spill in Alaska in 1989 and an even larger spill in the Russian Arctic in 1994. The most frightening is the dumping of nuclear waste into the ocean by the former Soviet Union.

Land pollution arises from dumping toxic waste products. Ordinary household garbage does not pose a pollution problem unless dumped garbage seeps into the water supply. This possibility increases as less suitable landfill sites are used. It is estimated that 80 percent of existing landfills in the United States will be full by 2010.

Some densely populated regions (such as New York, New Jersey, and other East Coast states) and densely populated countries (such as Japan and the Netherlands), where land costs are high, are seeking less costly alternatives to landfill, such as recycling and incineration. Recycling is an apparently attractive alternative, but it requires an investment in new technologies to be effective. Incineration is a high-cost alternative to landfill, and it produces air pollution. These alternatives become efficient only when the cost of using landfills is high, as it is in densely populated regions and countries.

FIGURE 8.4
A Pollution Tax

*e*Foundations **8.1** 

❶ A pollution tax is imposed that is equal to the marginal external cost of pollution. The supply curve becomes the marginal private cost curve, *MC*, plus the tax—the curve labeled $S = MC + tax$.

❷ Market equilibrium is at a price of $150 a ton and a quantity of 2,000 tons a month and is efficient because ❸ marginal social cost equals marginal benefit.

❹ The government collects tax revenue shown by the purple rectangle.

A Carbon Fuel Tax?

Most countries tax gasoline at a much higher rate than does the United States. Why don't we have a higher gas tax to encourage a large reduction in emissions?

The question becomes even more pressing when we consider not only the current levels of greenhouse gases but also their projected future levels. In 1990, annual carbon emissions worldwide were a staggering 6 billion tons. By 2050, with current policies, that annual total is predicted to be 24 billion tons.

Part of the reason we do not have a higher gas tax is that many people do not accept the scientific evidence that emissions produce global warming. Climatologists are uncertain about how carbon emissions translate into atmospheric concentrations—about how the flow of emissions translates into a stock of pollution. The main uncertainty arises because carbon drains from the atmosphere into the oceans and vegetation at a rate that is not well understood. Climatologists are also uncertain about the connection between carbon concentration and temperature. And economists are uncertain about how a temperature increase translates into economic costs and benefits. Some economists believe that the costs and benefits are almost zero, while others believe that a temperature increase of 5.4 degrees Fahrenheit by 2090 will reduce the total output of goods and services by 20 percent.

Another factor weighing against a large change in fuel use is that the costs would be borne now, while the benefits, if any, would come many years in the future. To compare future benefits with current costs, we must use an interest rate. If the interest rate is 1 percent a year, a dollar today becomes $2.70 in 100 years. If the interest rate is 5 percent a year, a dollar today becomes more than $131.50 in 100 years. So at an interest rate of 1 percent a year, it is worth spending $1 million in 2000 on pollution control to avoid $2.7 million in environmental damage in 2100. At an interest rate of 5 percent a year, it is worth spending $1 million today only if this expenditure avoids $131.5 million in environmental damage in 100 years from now.

Because large uncertain future benefits are needed to justify small current costs, a general tax on carbon fuels is not a high priority on the political agenda.

A final factor working against a large change in fuel use is the international pattern of the use of carbon fuels. Right now, carbon pollution comes in even doses from the industrial countries and the developing countries. But by 2050, three quarters of the carbon pollution will come from the developing countries (if the trends persist).

One reason for the high pollution rate in some developing countries (notably China, Russia, and other Eastern European countries) is that their governments subsidize the use of coal or oil. These subsidies lower producers' marginal costs and encourage the greater use of these fuels. The result is that the quantity of carbon fuels used exceeds the efficient quantity—and by a large amount. It is estimated that by 2050, these subsidies will induce annual global carbon emissions of some 10 billion tons—about two fifths of total emissions. If the subsidies were removed, global emissions in 2050 would be 10 billion tons a year less.

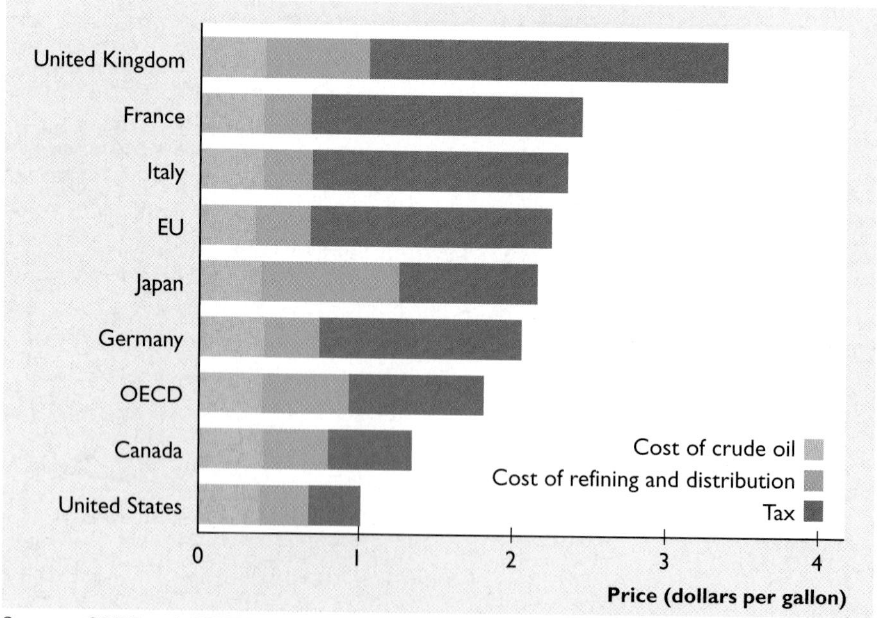

Sources: OPEC and OECD, 1999.

CHECKPOINT 8.1

1 **Explain why negative externalities lead to inefficient overproduction and how property rights, pollution charges, or taxes can achieve a more efficient outcome.**

Study Guide pp. 118–122 
eFoundations 8.1 

Practice Problem 8.1

Figure 1 illustrates the unregulated market for pesticide. When the factories produce pesticide, they also create waste, which they dump into a lake on the outskirts of the town. The marginal external cost of the dumped waste is equal to the marginal private cost of producing the pesticide, so the marginal social cost of producing the pesticide is double the marginal private cost.

a. What is the quantity of pesticide produced if no one owns the lake?
b. What is the efficient quantity of pesticide?
c. If the residents of the town own the lake, what is the quantity of pesticide produced and how much do the pesticide factories pay to residents of the town?
d. If the pesticide factories own the lake, how much pesticide is produced and how much does the town pay the factories to produce the efficient quantity of pesticide?
e. Suppose that no one owns the lake but that the government levies a pollution tax. What is the tax per ton of pesticide that will achieve the efficient outcome?

FIGURE 1

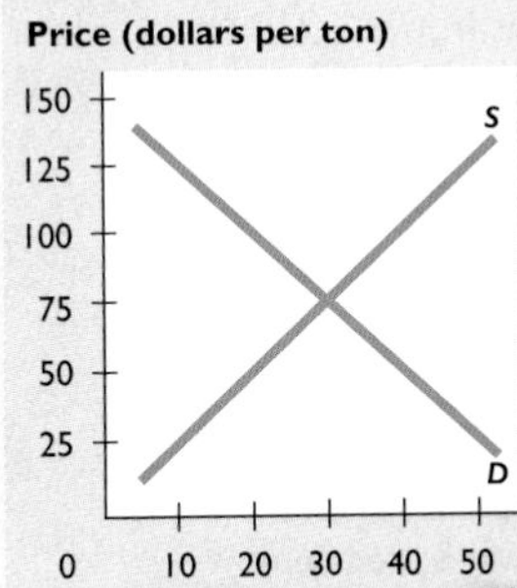

Exercise 8.1

Suppose that, in Practice Problem 8.1, no property rights are assigned to the lake but the government issues marketable pollution permits that are just sufficient to enable the factories to produce the efficient output of pesticide. The permits are divided equally between the townspeople and the factories.

a. What is the efficient amount of pesticide?
b. What is the price of a marketable permit?
c. Who buys permits and who sells permits?
d. How would the outcome differ if all the permits were allocated to the factories?
e. How would the outcome differ if all the permits were allocated to the townspeople?

Solution to Practice Problem 8.1

a. The quantity of pesticide produced is 30 tons a week (Figure 2).
b. The efficient quantity of pesticide is 20 tons a week. At the efficient quantity, the marginal benefit to the factories equals the marginal social cost, which is the sum of the marginal private cost and the marginal external cost. When the factories produce 20 tons a week, the marginal social cost is \$100 a ton and the marginal private benefit is \$100 a ton.
c. The quantity of pesticide produced is the efficient quantity, 20 tons a week, and the factories pay the townspeople the marginal external cost of \$50 a ton.
d. The town pays the factories \$50 a ton for an agreement that they will not produce more than 20 tons of pesticide a week.
e. A tax of \$50 a ton will achieve the efficient quantity of pesticide produced.

FIGURE 2

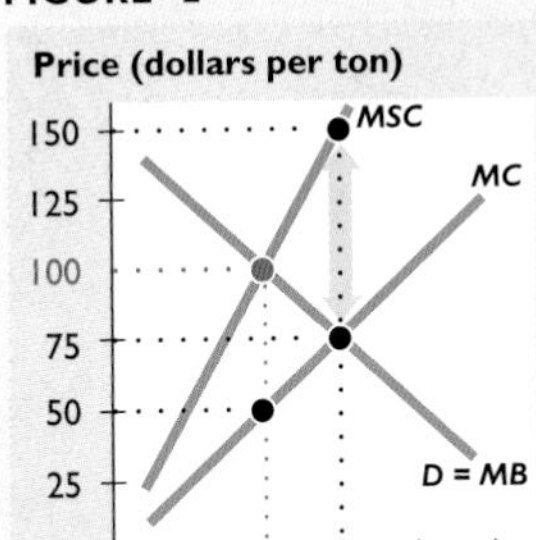

8.2 POSITIVE EXTERNALITIES: KNOWLEDGE

Knowledge comes from education and research. To study the economics of knowledge, we must distinguish between private benefits and social benefits.

Private Benefits and Social Benefits

Marginal private benefit
The benefit from an additional unit of a good or service that the consumer of that good or service receives.

Marginal external benefit
The benefit from an additional unit of a good or service that people other than the consumer of the good or service enjoy.

Marginal social benefit
The marginal benefit enjoyed by society—by the consumers of a good or service and by everyone else who benefits from it. It is the sum of marginal private benefit and marginal external benefit.

A *private benefit* is a benefit that the consumer of a good or service receives. *Marginal benefit* is the benefit from an *additional unit* of a good or service. So **marginal private benefit** (*MB*) is the benefit from an additional unit of a good or service that the consumer of that good or service receives.

You've seen that an *external benefit* is a benefit from a good or service that someone other than the consumer receives. A **marginal external benefit** is the benefit from an additional unit of a good or service that people other than the consumer enjoy.

Marginal social benefit (*MSB*) is the marginal benefit enjoyed by society—by the consumer of a good or service (marginal private benefit) plus the marginal benefit enjoyed by others (the marginal external benefit). That is,

$$MSB = MB + \text{Marginal external benefit.}$$

Figure 8.5 shows an example of the relationship between marginal private benefit, marginal external benefit, and marginal social benefit. The marginal benefit curve, *MB*, describes the marginal private benefit—such as expanded job opportunities and higher incomes—enjoyed by college graduates. Marginal private benefit decreases as the quantity of education increases.

FIGURE 8.5
An External Benefit

*e*Foundations 8.2 

The *MB* curve shows the private marginal benefit enjoyed by the people who receive a college education. The *MSB* curve shows the sum of marginal private benefit and marginal external cost. When 15 million students attend college, ❶ marginal private benefit is $10,000 per student, ❷ marginal external benefit is $15,000 per student, and ❸ marginal social benefit is $25,000 per student.

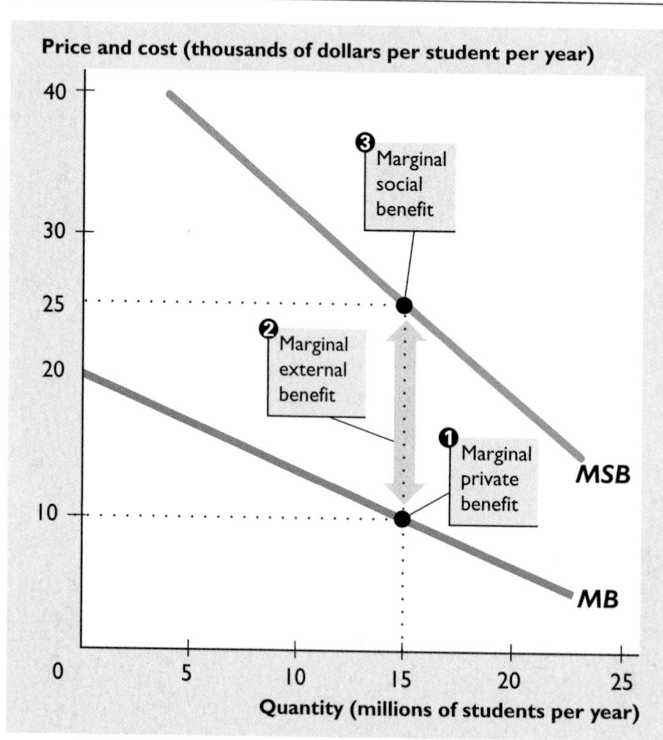

But college graduates generate external benefits. On the average, college graduates communicate more effectively with others and tend to be better citizens. Their crime rates are lower, and they are more tolerant of the views of others. And a society with a large number of college graduates can support activities such as high-quality newspapers and television channels, music, theater, and other organized social activities.

In the example in Figure 8.5, the marginal external benefit is $15,000 per student per year when 15 million students enroll in college. The marginal social benefit curve *MSB* is the sum of marginal private benefit and marginal external benefit. For example, when 15 million students a year enroll in college, the marginal private benefit is $10,000 per student and the marginal external benefit is $15,000 per student, so the marginal social benefit is $25,000 per student.

When people make decisions about how much schooling to undertake, they undervalue its external benefits and place most emphasis on its private benefits. The result is that if education were provided by private schools that charged full-cost tuition, we would produce too few college graduates.

Figure 8.6 illustrates the underproduction if the government left education to the private market. The supply curve is the marginal cost curve of the private schools, *S* = *MC*. The demand curve is the marginal private benefit curve, *D* = *MB*. Market equilibrium is at a tuition of $15,000 per student per year and 7.5 million students per year. At this equilibrium, marginal social benefit is $38,000 per student, which exceeds marginal cost by $23,000. There are too few students in college. The efficient number is 15 million, where marginal social benefit equals marginal cost. The gray triangle shows the deadweight loss created by the underproduction.

FIGURE 8.6
Inefficiency with an External Benefit

*e*Foundations 8.2 

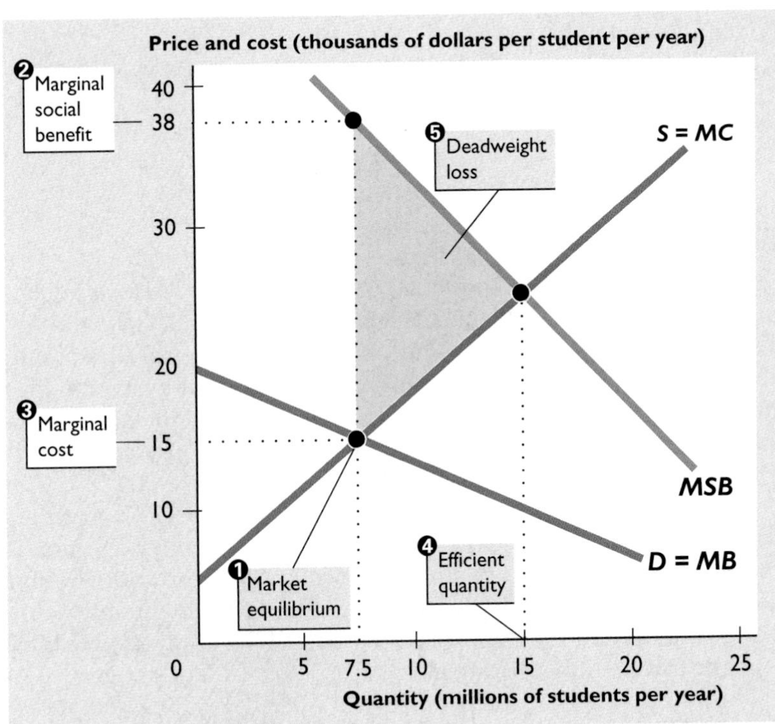

The market demand curve is the marginal private benefit curve, *D* = *MB*. The supply curve is the marginal cost curve, *S* = *MC*.

1. Market equilibrium is at a tuition of $15,000 a year and 7.5 million students and is inefficient because 2 marginal social benefit exceeds 3 marginal cost.
4. The efficient quantity is 15 million students.
5. The gray triangle shows the deadweight loss created by the external benefits of college education.

Underproduction similar to that in Figure 8.6 would occur at other levels of education—grade school and high school—if an unregulated market produced it. When children learn basic reading, writing, and number skills, they receive the private benefit of increased earning power. But even these basic skills bring the external benefit of developing better citizens.

External benefits also arise from research that leads to the discovery of new knowledge. When Isaac Newton worked out the formulas for calculating the rate of response of one variable to another—calculus—everyone was free to use his method. When a spreadsheet program called VisiCalc was invented, Lotus Corporation and Microsoft were free to copy the basic idea and create 1-2-3 and Excel. When the first shopping mall was built and found to be a successful way of arranging retailing, everyone was free to copy the idea, and malls spread like mushrooms.

Once someone has discovered how to do something, others can copy the basic idea. They do have to work to copy an idea, so they face an opportunity cost. But they do not usually have to pay the person who made the discovery to use it. When people make decisions about how much research to undertake, they undervalue its external benefits and place most emphasis on its private benefits.

When people make decisions about the quantity of education or the amount of research to undertake, they balance the marginal private cost against the marginal private benefit. They undervalue the external benefit. As a result, if we left education and research to unregulated market forces, we would get too little of these activities.

To get closer to producing the efficient quantity of a good or service that generates an external benefit, we make public choices, through governments, to modify the market outcome.

Government Actions in the Face of External Benefits

Four devices that governments can use to achieve a more efficient allocation of resources in the presence of external benefits, such as those that arise from education and research, are:

- Public provision
- Private subsidies
- Vouchers
- Patents and copyrights

Public Provision

Public provision
The production of a good or service by a public authority that receives the bulk of its revenue from the government.

Public provision is the production of a good or service by a public authority that receives the bulk of its revenue from government. The education services produced by the public universities, colleges, and schools are examples of public provision.

Figure 8.7(a) shows how public provision might overcome the underproduction that arises in Figure 8.6. Public provision cannot lower the cost of production, so marginal cost is the same as before. Marginal private benefit and marginal external benefit are also the same as before.

The efficient quantity occurs where marginal social benefit equals marginal cost. In Figure 8.7(a), this quantity is 15 million students. Tuition is set to ensure that the efficient number of students enrolls. That is, tuition is set at the level that equals the marginal private benefit at the efficient quantity. In Figure 8.7(a), tuition is $10,000 a year. The rest of the cost of the public university is borne by the taxpayers and, in this example, is $15,000 per student per year.

Private Subsidies

A **subsidy** is a payment that the government makes to private producers. By making the subsidy depend on the level of output, the government can induce private decision makers to consider external benefits when they make their choices.

Subsidy
A payment that the government makes to private producers that depends on the level of output.

Figure 8.7(b) shows how a subsidy to private colleges works. In the absence of a subsidy, the marginal cost curve is the market supply curve of private college education, $S = MC$. The marginal benefit is the demand curve, $D = MB$. In this example, the government provides a subsidy to colleges of $15,000 per student per year. We must subtract the subsidy from the marginal cost of education to find the colleges' supply curve. That curve is $S = MC - subsidy$ in the figure. The equilibrium tuition (market price) is $10,000 a year, and the equilibrium quantity is 15 million students. To educate 15 million students, colleges incur a marginal cost of $25,000 a year. The marginal social benefit is also $25,000 a year. So with marginal cost equal to marginal social benefit, the subsidy has achieved an efficient outcome. The tuition and the subsidy just cover the colleges' marginal cost.

Whether a public school operating on government-provided funds or a private school receiving a subsidy does a better job is a difficult question to resolve.

FIGURE 8.7
Public Provision or Private Subsidy to Achieve an Efficient Outcome

*e*Foundations 8.2

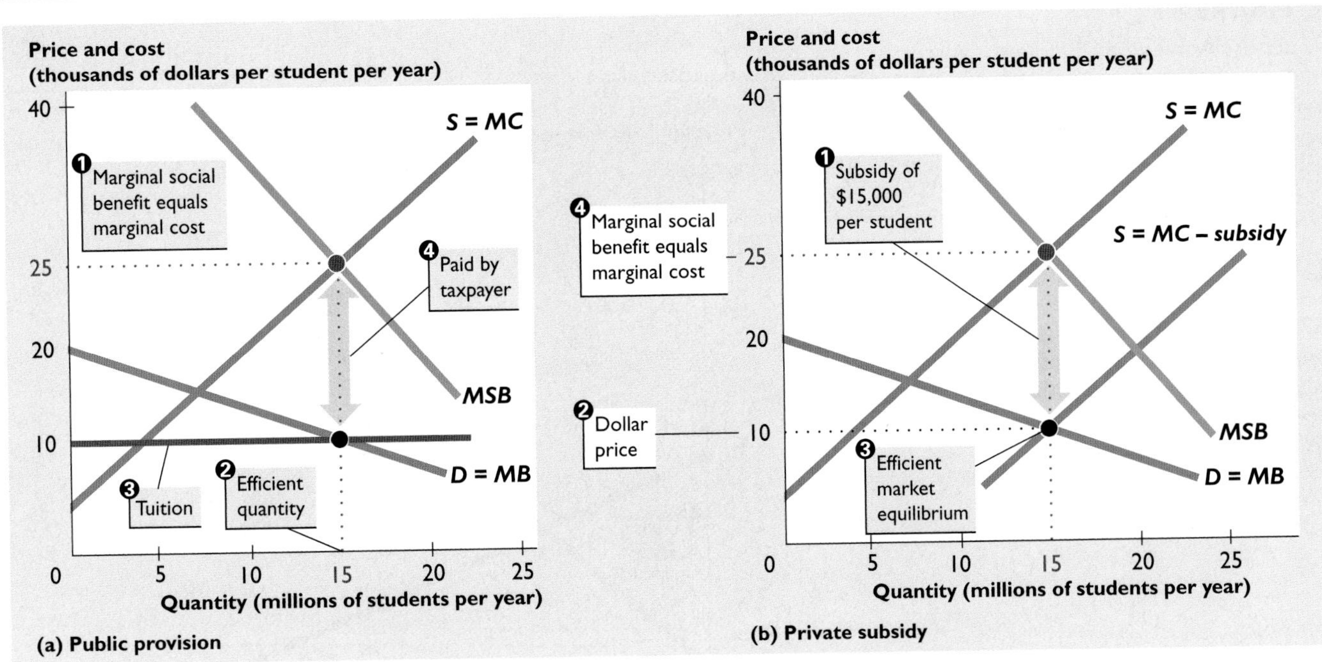

❶ Marginal social benefit equals marginal cost with 15 million students enrolled in college, the ❷ efficient quantity.

❸ Tuition is set at $10,000 per year, and ❹ the taxpayers cover the remaining $15,000 of marginal cost per student.

With a ❶ subsidy of $15,000 per student, the supply curve is $S = MC - subsidy$. ❷ The equilibrium price is $10,000, and ❸ the market equilibrium is efficient with 15 million students enrolled in college. ❹ Marginal social benefit equals marginal cost.

It turns on the efficiency of alternative mechanisms for monitoring school performance and on the strength of the incentives that school boards and private school operators have to deliver a high-quality service.

Vouchers

Voucher
A token that the government provides to households that can be used to buy specified goods or services.

A **voucher** is a token that the government provides to households, which they can use to buy specified goods or services. Food stamps that the U.S. Department of Agriculture provides under a federal Food Stamp Program are examples of vouchers. The vouchers (stamps) can be spent only on food and are designed to improve the diet and health of extremely poor families.

School vouchers have been advocated as a means of improving the quality of education and have been used in Cleveland and Milwaukee, though a proposition to introduce school vouchers in Michigan was defeated in the 2000 election.

A school voucher allows parents to choose the school their children will attend and to use the voucher to pay part of the cost. The school cashes the vouchers to pay its bills. A voucher could be provided to a college student in a similar way, and although technically not a voucher, a federal Pell Grant has a similar effect.

Because vouchers can be spent only on a specified item, they increase the willingness to pay for that item and so increase the demand for it. Figure 8.8 shows how a voucher system works. The government provides vouchers worth $15,000 per student per year. Parents (or students) use these vouchers to supplement the dollars they pay for college education. The marginal social benefit curve becomes the demand for college education $D = MSB$. The market equilibrium occurs at a

FIGURE 8.8
Vouchers Achieve an Efficient Outcome

*e*Foundations 8.2 

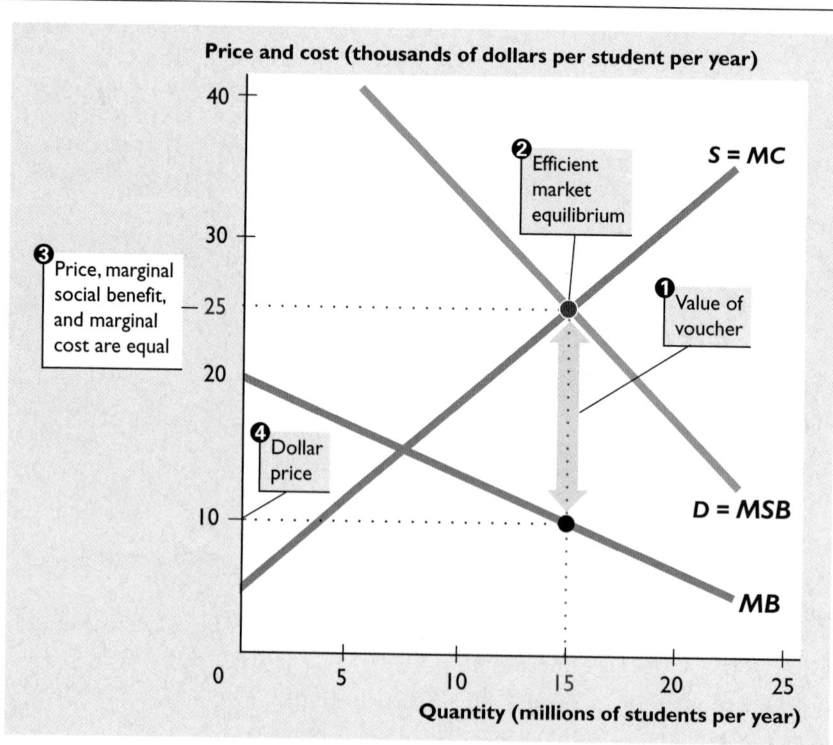

With vouchers, buyers are willing to pay *MB* plus ❶ the value of the voucher, so the marginal social benefit curve becomes the demand curve *D* = *MSB*.

❷ Market equilibrium is efficient with 15 million students enrolled in college because ❸ price, marginal social benefit, and marginal cost are equal. The tuition consists of ❹ the dollar price of $10,000 per year and ❶ the value of the voucher.

price of $25,000 per student per year and 15 million students attend college. Each student pays $10,000 tuition, and schools collect an additional $15,000 per student from the voucher.

If the government estimates the value of the external benefit correctly and makes the value of the voucher equal the marginal external benefit, the outcome from the voucher scheme is efficient. Marginal cost equals marginal social benefit, and the deadweight loss is eliminated.

Vouchers are similar to subsidies, but they provide the consumer rather than the producer with the financial resources. Advocates of vouchers say that they offer a more efficient outcome than subsidies do because the consumer can monitor school performance more effectively than the government can.

Patents and Copyrights

Knowledge might be an exception to the principle of diminishing marginal benefit. Additional knowledge (about the right things) makes people more productive. And there seems to be no tendency for the additional productivity from additional knowledge to diminish.

For example, in just 15 years, advances in knowledge about computers have given us increasingly powerful processor chips. Each advance in knowledge about how to design and manufacture a processor chip has brought ever-larger increments in performance and productivity. Similarly, each advance in knowledge about how to design and build an airplane has brought ever larger increments in performance: Orville and Wilbur Wright's "Flyer 1" was a one-seat plane that could hop a farmer's field. The Lockheed Constellation was an airplane that could fly 120 passengers from New York to London, but with two refueling stops in Newfoundland and Ireland, not much space, and a lot of noise and vibration. The latest version of the Boeing 747 can carry 450 people nonstop from Los Angeles to Sydney, Australia, or from New York to Tokyo—flights of 7,500 miles that take 14 hours. Examples such as these can be found in fields as diverse as agriculture, biogenetics, communications, engineering, entertainment, medicine, and publishing.

Because knowledge is productive and generates external benefits, it is necessary to use public policies to ensure that those who develop new ideas have incentives to encourage an efficient level of effort. The main way of providing the right incentives uses the central idea of the Coase theorem and assigns property rights—called **intellectual property rights**—to creators. The legal device for establishing intellectual property rights is the patent or copyright. A **patent** or **copyright** is a government-sanctioned exclusive right granted to the inventor of a good, service, or productive process to produce, use, and sell the invention for a given number of years. A patent enables the developer of a new idea to prevent others from benefiting freely from an invention for a limited number of years. But to obtain the protection of the law, an inventor must make knowledge of the invention public.

Intellectual property rights
The property rights of the creators of knowledge and other discoveries.

Patent or copyright
A government-sanctioned exclusive right granted to the inventor of a good, service, or productive process to produce, use, and sell the invention for a given number of years.

Although patents encourage invention and innovation, they do so at an economic cost. While a patent is in place, its holder has a monopoly. And monopoly is another source of inefficiency (which is explained in Chapter 13). But without a patent, the effort to develop new goods, services, or processes is diminished and the flow of new inventions is slowed. So the efficient outcome is a compromise that balances the benefits of more inventions against the cost of temporary monopoly in newly invented activities.

CHECKPOINT 8.2

Study Guide pp. 122–126 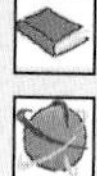

*e*Foundations 8.2

2 **Explain why positive externalities lead to inefficient underproduction and how public provision, subsidies, vouchers, and patents can achieve a more efficient outcome.**

Practice Problem 8.2

Figure 1 shows the marginal private benefit from college education. The marginal cost of a college education is a constant $6,000 a year. The marginal external benefit from a college education is $4,000 per student per year.

a. If colleges are private and government has no involvement in college education, how many people will undertake a college education and what will be the tuition?

b. What is the efficient number of students?

c. If the government decides to provide public colleges, what tuition will these colleges charge to achieve the efficient number of students? How much will taxpayers have to pay?

d. If the government decides to subsidize private colleges, what subsidy will achieve the efficient number of college students?

e. If the government offers vouchers to those who enroll at a college and no subsidy, what is the value of the voucher that will achieve the efficient number of students?

FIGURE 1

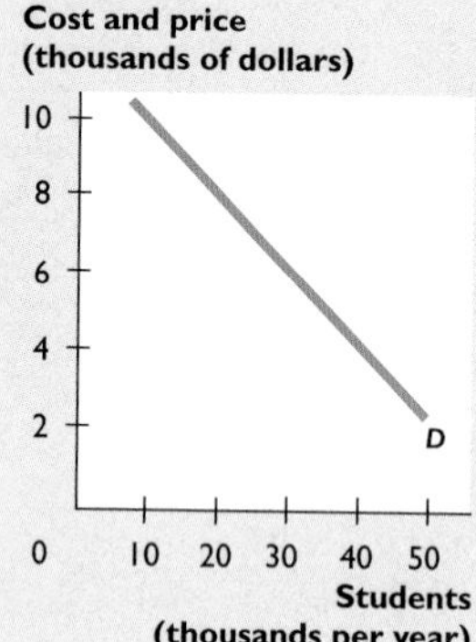

Exercise 8.2

Figure 2 shows the marginal private benefit from a business degree and the marginal cost of obtaining a business degree. The marginal external benefit is $18,000 per business graduate per year.

a. If colleges are private and there is no government involvement in business education, how many people take a business degree and what is the tuition?

b. What is the efficient number of business students?

c. If the government decides to provide public business schools, what tuition will the public schools charge to achieve the efficient number of students?

d. If the government decides to subsidize private business colleges, what subsidy will achieve the efficient number of students?

e. If the government offers vouchers to business students and no subsidy, what is the value of the voucher that will achieve the efficient number of students?

FIGURE 2

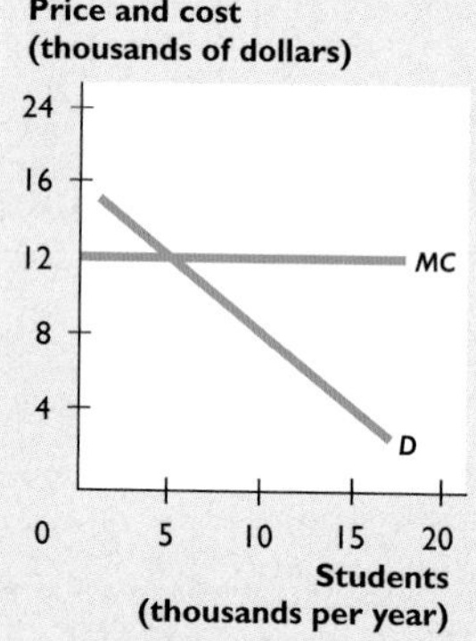

Solution to Practice Problem 8.2

a. The tuition will be $6,000 a year, and 30,000 students will enroll—the intersection of the *MB* and *MC* curves (Figure 3).

b. The efficient number of students is 50,000 a year—the intersection of the *MSB* and *MC* curves (Figure 3).

c. To enroll 50,000 students, public colleges would charge $2,000 per student and taxpayers would pay $4,000 per student (Figure 3).

d. The subsidy would be $4,000 per student, which is equal to the marginal external benefit.

e. The value of the voucher will be $4,000 per student. The enrollment will be 50,000 if the tuition is $2,000. But the private college tuition is $6,000, so to get 50,000 students to enroll, the value of the voucher will have to be $4,000.

FIGURE 3

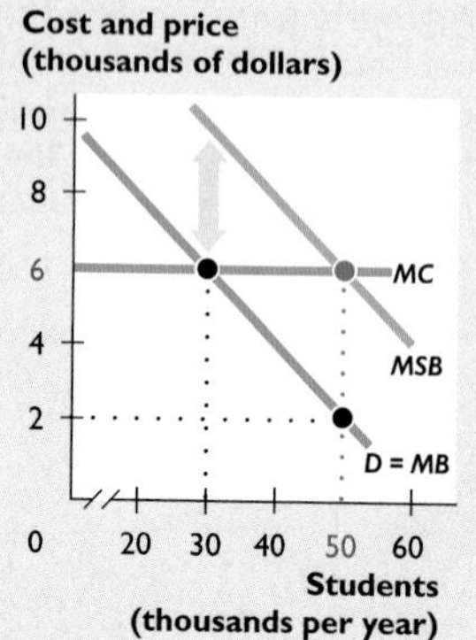

CHAPTER CHECKPOINT

Key Points

1 Explain why negative externalities lead to inefficient overproduction and how property rights, pollution charges, or taxes can achieve a more efficient outcome.

- External costs are costs of production that fall on people other than the producer of a good or service. Marginal social cost equals marginal private cost plus marginal external cost.
- Producers take account only of marginal private cost and overproduce when there is a marginal external cost.
- Sometimes it is possible to overcome a negative externality by assigning a property right.
- When property rights cannot be assigned, governments might overcome externalities by using emission charges, marketable permits, or taxes.

2 Explain why positive externalities lead to inefficient underproduction and how public provision, subsidies, vouchers, and patents can achieve a more efficient outcome.

- External benefits are benefits that are received by people other than the consumer of a good or service. Marginal social benefit equals marginal private benefit plus marginal external benefit.
- External benefits from education arise because better-educated people are better citizens, commit fewer crimes, and support social activities.
- External benefits from research arise because once someone has worked out a basic idea, others can copy.
- Vouchers or subsidies to private schools or the provision of public education below cost can achieve a more efficient provision of education.
- Patents and copyrights create intellectual property rights and an incentive to innovate. But they do so by creating a temporary monopoly, the cost of which must be balanced against the benefit of more inventive activity.

Key Terms

Coase theorem, 188
Copyright, 199
Externality, 182
Intellectual property rights, 199
Marginal external benefit, 194
Marginal external cost, 184
Marginal private benefit, 194
Marginal private cost, 184
Marginal social benefit, 194
Marginal social cost, 184
Negative externality, 182
Patent, 199
Positive externality, 182
Property rights, 187
Public provision, 196
Subsidy, 197
Transactions costs, 188
Voucher, 198

Exercises

1. Tom and Larry are working on a project that makes it necessary for them to spend a day together. Tom likes to smoke, and his marginal benefit from one cigar a day is $20. The price of a cigar is $2. Larry dislikes cigar smoke, and his marginal benefit from a smoke-free environment is $25 a day. What is the outcome if they:
   a. Meet at Tom's home?
   b. Meet at Larry's home?

2. If in Exercise 1, Tom's marginal benefit from one cigar a day is $25 and Larry's marginal benefit from a smoke-free environment is $20 a day, what is the outcome if they:
   a. Meet at Tom's home?
   b. Meet at Larry's home?

3. The urban sprawl of a city has increased so much that it borders on a steel mill. Table 1 shows the cost of cutting the pollution generated by the steel mill. It also shows the property taxes that people are willing to pay at different levels of pollution. Assume that the property taxes that people are willing to pay measure the total benefit from cleaner air that results from the percentage cut in pollution.
   a. With no pollution control, how much pollution will there be?
   b. What is the efficient percentage decrease in pollution?
   c. If the city owns the steel mill, how much pollution will there be?
   d. If the city is a company town owned by the steel mill, how much pollution will there be?

4. The marginal cost of educating a college student is $5,000 a year. Table 2 shows the marginal private benefit schedule from a college education. The marginal external benefit for college education is $2,000 per student per year.
   a. With no public colleges and no government involvement in college education, how many students will enroll and what is the tuition?
   b. If the government subsidizes private colleges and sets the subsidy so that the efficient number of students will enroll in college, what is the subsidy per student? How many students will enroll?
   c. If the government offers vouchers to students (but no subsidy to private colleges) and values the vouchers so that the efficient number of students will enroll in college, what is the value of the voucher? How many students will enroll?

5. For many people, distance education has cut the cost of a college education. If in Exercise 4, an Internet course cuts the cost to $3,500 a year and increases the marginal external benefit to $3,000 student per year, what now are your answers to Exercise 4?

6. Explain why the quantity of research undertaken would be less if researchers could not obtain patents and copyrights for their discoveries.

7. Use the link on your Foundations Web site to visit the EPA Web site. At the EPA home page, click on the map of the United States to go to stories about your region. Find a story about a negative production externality and explain which of the tools reviewed in this chapter the government is using to address the externality. Explain how the government's action will work or why you think it will not work.

TABLE 1

Pollution cut (percentage)	Property taxes willingly paid (dollars per day)	Total cost of pollution on cut (dollars per day)
0	0	0
10	150	10
20	285	25
30	405	45
40	510	70
50	600	100
60	675	135
70	735	175
80	780	220
90	810	270

TABLE 2

Students (millions per year)	Marginal private benefit (dollars per student per year)
1	5,000
2	3,000
3	2,000
4	1,500
5	1,200
6	1,000
7	800
8	500

Chapter 9

Public Goods and the Tax System

CHAPTER CHECKLIST

When you have completed your study of this chapter, you will be able to:

1 Distinguish between public goods and private goods, explain the free-rider problem, and explain how the quantity of public goods is determined.

2 Explain the effects of income taxes and review the main ideas about the fairness of the tax system.

You learned a lot about the influence of government on markets in Chapters 7 and 8. You saw in Chapter 7 that taxes can drive a wedge between marginal benefit and marginal cost and create a deadweight loss; the total burden of a tax exceeds the revenue that it raises. In contrast to this inefficient outcome, you saw in Chapter 8 that in the markets for goods that create an externality, the government might levy a tax to make an otherwise inefficient market efficient.

In this chapter, we study two more aspects of government influence on economic life. First, we look at the services that the government provides. These services include the enforcement of law and order and the provision of national defense. Why does the government provide these services and what determines the scale on which they are provided? Second, we look at the tax system—the taxes that pay for government services and redistribute income among families and individuals. Why does most of the government's tax revenue come from income taxes? Why are income taxes progressive? Is the tax system fair?

9.1 PUBLIC GOODS AND THE FREE-RIDER PROBLEM

Why does the government provide goods and services such as national defense and public health? Why don't we buy our national defense from a private firm that competes for our dollars in the marketplace in the same way that McDonald's and Coca-Cola do? To answer these questions, we need to explain what is special about public goods.

Public Goods

Public good
A good or service that can be consumed simultaneously by everyone and from which no one can be excluded.

Private good
A good or service that can be consumed by only one person at a time and only by those people who have bought it or own it.

Nonrival
If the consumption of a good or service by one person does not decrease the quantity of the good available for someone else.

Rival
If the consumption of a good or service by one person decreases the quantity of the good that is available for others.

Nonexcludable
If it is technologically impossible, or extremely costly, to prevent a person from enjoying the benefits of a good or service.

Excludable
If it is technologically possible to prevent a person from enjoying the benefits of a good or service.

A **public good** is a good or service that can be consumed simultaneously by everyone and from which no one can be excluded. National defense is an example of a public good. Everyone enjoys the benefits of the national defense system, and no one can be excluded from receiving its benefits.

A public good contrasts with a **private good**—a good or service that can be consumed by only one person at a time and only by those who have bought it or own it. A can of Coke is an example of a private good. Only the person who drinks the can of Coke enjoys its benefits, and everyone except that person is excluded from consuming it.

Public goods and private goods are distinguished along two dimensions. The first dimension is rivalry. A good is **nonrival** if consumption by one person does not decrease the quantity of the good available for someone else. An example is watching a television show. Everyone who is tuned to a station can view a show, and when one additional person switches on the TV, no other viewer is affected. National defense is another example of a nonrival good. One person's consumption of the security provided by the national defense system does not decrease the security of fellow citizens. A good is **rival** if consumption by one person decreases the quantity of the good that is available for others. An example is drinking a can of Coke or eating a hotdog. If you drink a can of Coke or eat a hotdog, but no one can drink the same can of Coke or eat the same hotdog.

The second dimension is excludability. A good is **nonexcludable** if it is technologically impossible, or extremely costly, to prevent someone from benefiting from it. An example is a lighthouse. It would be difficult to restrict a boat owner's view of the light emitted by a lighthouse. If the light is on, everyone who wants to see it can do so and no one can be excluded from enjoying its benefits. National defense is another example of a nonexcludable good. The military cannot select whom it will protect in a country and whom it will not. A good is **excludable** if it is technologically possible to prevent a person from enjoying its benefits. An example is pay-per-view television. Using the available scrambler technology, cable companies can ensure that only the people who have paid the program fee receive them.

Figure 9.1 classifies goods along these two dimensions and gives some examples. A good that is both nonrival and nonexcludable is called a *pure public good*. A good that is both rival and excludable is called a *pure private good*.

Many goods have a public element but are not pure public goods. They are called *mixed goods*. An example is a tunnel. A tunnel is nonrival until it becomes congested. One more car in a tunnel with plenty of space does not reduce anyone else's consumption of transportation services. But once the tunnel becomes congested, an extra vehicle lowers the quality of the tunnel for everyone else—it becomes rival like a private good. Also, users can be excluded from a tunnel by

FIGURE 9.1
Public Goods and Private Goods

e/Foundations 9.1 

	Nonexcludable	Excludable
Nonrival	**Pure public goods** National defense The law Lighthouse	**Excludable and nonrival** Cable television Website Bridge or tunnel (not congested)
Rival	**Nonexcludable and rival** Parking at a shopping mall A crosswalk Fish in the ocean	**Pure private goods** Food Car House

SOURCE: Adapted from and inspired by E. S. Savas, *Privatizing the Public Sector* (Chatham, NJ: Chatham House Publishers, 1982), p. 34.

A pure public good (top left) is one for which consumption is nonrival and from which it is impossible to exclude a consumer. A pure private good (bottom right) is one for which consumption is rival and from which consumers can be excluded. Some goods are nonexcludable but are rival (bottom left), and some goods are nonrival but are excludable (top right).

tollgates. Another example is fish in the ocean. Ocean fish are rival because a fish taken by one person is not available for others. Ocean fish are also nonexcludable because it is difficult to prevent people from catching them.

The Free-Rider Problem

Free rider
A person who enjoys the benefits of a good or service without paying for it.

Public goods create a free-rider problem. A **free rider** is a person who enjoys the benefits of a good or service without paying for it. Because everyone can consume the same quantity of a public good and no one can be excluded from enjoying its benefits, no one has an incentive to pay for it. Everyone has an incentive to free ride. Because of the free-rider problem, the market would provide too small a quantity of a public good. To produce the efficient quantity, government action is required.

To see how a private market would provide too little of a public good and how government might provide the efficient quantity, we need to learn how to determine the marginal benefit of a public good.

The Marginal Benefit of a Public Good

To learn about the marginal benefit of a public good, we'll study a concrete example. Suppose that for its defense, a country is considering launching some surveillance satellites. What is the value or benefit of these satellites? The benefit that a satellite provides is the value of its services. Because the services provided by a satellite are nonrival and nonexcludable—because they are a public good—everyone must consume the same quantity of them. To find the economy-wide value of the satellites, we must somehow add together the marginal benefits of everyone in the economy.

For a private good, everyone faces the same price and chooses the quantity to buy. To obtain the economy's marginal benefit curve for a private good, we need to find the economy-wide quantity demanded at each price—the sum of the quantities demanded at each price (see Chapter 4, p. 83). In contrast, for a public good, everyone must consume the same quantity. But each individual has a private valuation of that quantity. To obtain the economy's marginal benefit curve for a public good, we need to find the economy-wide willingness to pay at each quantity—the sum of the marginal benefits of all individuals at each quantity.

Figure 9.2 shows the marginal benefit that arises from defense satellites for an economy of two people: Lisa and Max. The principle that we learn in this artificial case applies to our actual economy with its 276 million people.

Lisa's and Max's marginal benefits are graphed as MB_L and MB_M, respectively, in parts (a) and (b) of Figure 9.2. The marginal benefit from a public good is similar to the marginal benefit from a private good: Its magnitude diminishes as the quantity of the good increases. For Lisa, the marginal benefit from the first satellite is $80, and from the second it is $60. By the time 5 satellites are deployed, Lisa's marginal benefit is zero. For Max, the marginal benefit from the first satellite is $50, and from the second it is $40. By the time 5 satellites are deployed, Max perceives only $10 worth of marginal benefit.

Part (c) shows the economy's marginal benefit curve, *MB*. An individual's marginal benefit curve for a public good is similar to an individual's demand curve for a private good. But the economy's marginal benefit curve for a public good is different from the market demand curve for a private good. To obtain the market demand curve for a private good, we sum the quantities demanded by all individuals at each *price*—we sum the individual demand curves horizontally. But to find the economy's marginal benefit curve of a public good, we sum the marginal benefits of all individuals at each *quantity*—we sum the individual marginal benefit curves vertically. The resulting marginal benefit for the economy made up of Lisa and Max is the economy's marginal benefit curve graphed in part (c)—the curve *MB*. Lisa's marginal benefit from the first satellite is added to Max's marginal benefit from the first satellite because they both benefit from the first satellite.

The Marginal Cost of a Public Good

The marginal cost of a public good is determined in the same way as that of a private good. What you learned about marginal cost in Chapters 3 and 6 applies to this case. So the marginal cost of a satellite is similar to the marginal cost of a pizza. Marginal cost increases as the quantity of satellites produced increases—the principle of *increasing marginal cost*. And the marginal cost curve of satellites slopes upward.

FIGURE 9.2
Marginal Benefit of a Public Good

*e*Foundations 9.1 

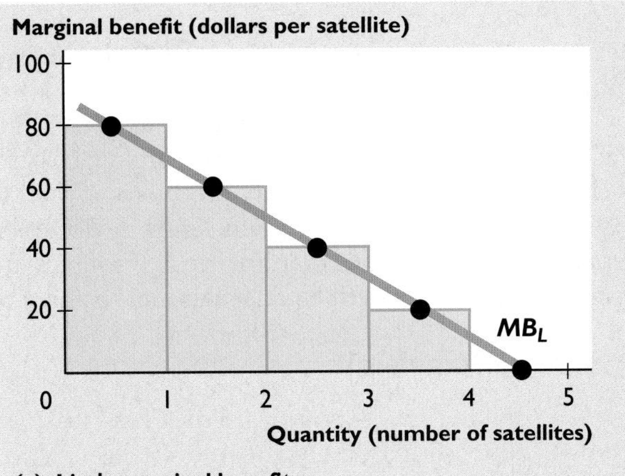

(a) Lisa's marginal benefit

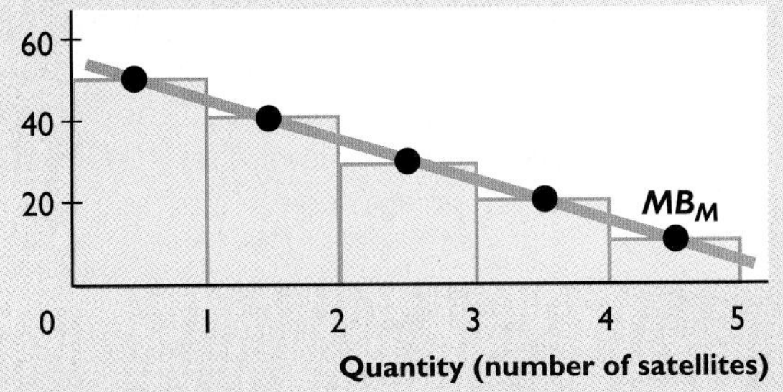

(b) Max's marginal benefit

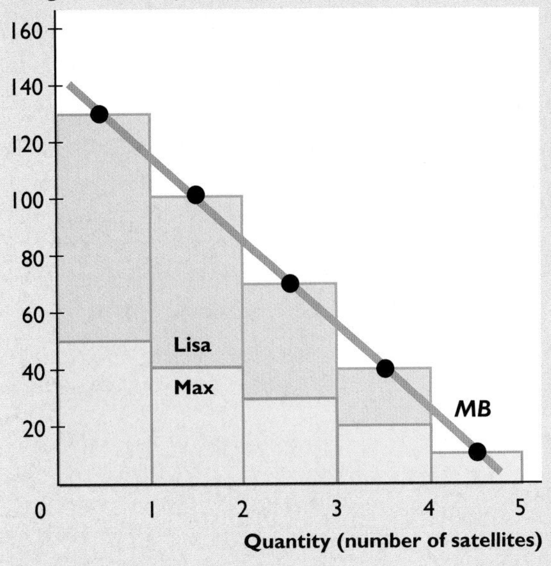

(c) Economy's marginal benefit

The marginal benefit curves for a public good are MB_L for Lisa and MB_M for Max. The marginal benefit of the public good for the economy is the sum of the marginal benefits of all individuals at each quantity. The marginal benefit curve for the economy is *MB*.

November 7, 2000

The U.S. Election Is About Missiles

For Asia, the hottest issue in the U.S. presidential election isn't Social Security. It's not education. It's not health care. It's missiles.

Questions

1. What are the two broad views about deploying missile defenses?

2. What are the factors that influence the social costs and social benefits of missile defenses?

3. Is a missile defense system a public good or a private good?

 *e*Foundations **9.1**

The Efficient Quantity of a Public Good

In the real world, an economy with two people would not buy any satellites—because the total benefit falls far short of the cost. But the 276 million people in the United States might. To determine the efficient quantity, we use the same principles that you first learned in Chapter 6 and that you used repeatedly in Chapters 7 and 8: We find the quantity at which marginal benefit equals marginal cost.

Figure 9.3 shows the marginal benefit curve *MB* and marginal cost curve *MC* of satellites. If marginal benefit exceeds marginal cost, resources can be used more efficiently by increasing the quantity produced. If marginal cost exceeds marginal benefit, resources can be used more efficiently by decreasing the quantity produced. And if marginal benefit equals marginal cost, resources are being used efficiently. In this example, marginal benefit equals marginal cost when 200 satellites are provided.

Private Provision

Could a private firm—say, North Pole Protection, Inc.—deliver the efficient quantity of satellites? Most likely, it couldn't because no one would have an incentive to buy his or her share of the satellite system. Everyone would reason as follows: "The number of satellites provided by North Pole Protection, Inc., is not affected by my decision to pay my share or not. But my own private consumption will be greater if I free ride and do not pay my share of the cost of the satellite system. If I do not pay, I enjoy the same level of security and I can buy more private goods. I will spend my money on private goods and free ride on the public good." Such reasoning is the free-rider problem. And if everyone reasons the same way, North Pole Protection, Inc., has no revenue and so provides no satellites.

FIGURE 9.3

The Efficient Quantity of a Public Good

*e*Foundations **9.1** 

❶ With fewer than 200 satellites, marginal benefit *MB* exceeds marginal cost *MC*. An increase in the quantity will make resource use more efficient.

❷ With more than 200 satellites, marginal cost exceeds marginal benefit. A decrease in the quantity will make resource use more efficient.

❸ With 200 satellites, marginal benefit *MB* equals marginal cost *MC*. Resource use is efficient.

❹ The efficient quantity is 200 satellites.

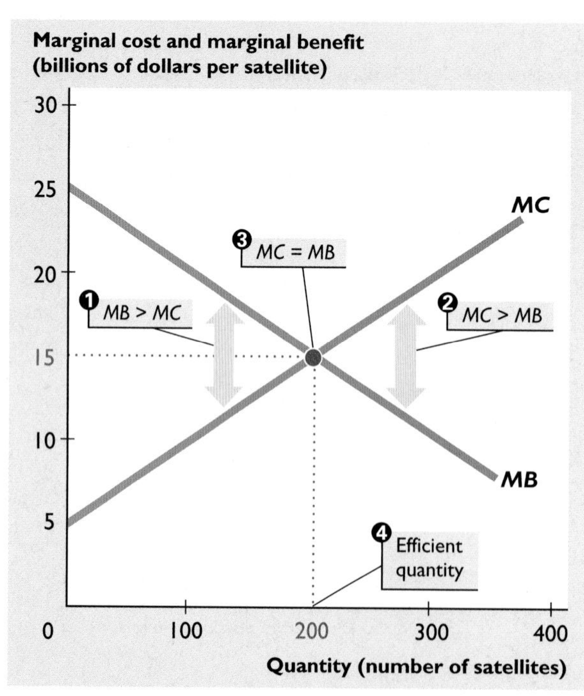

Public Provision

The political process determines the quantity of a public good. Suppose that there are two political parties, the Hawks and the Doves, which agree on all issues except for the quantity of defense satellites. The Hawks want 300 satellites, and the Doves want 100 satellites. But both parties want to get elected, so they run a voter survey and discover the marginal benefit curve of Figure 9.3. They also consult with satellite producers to establish the marginal cost schedule. The parties then do a "what-if" analysis. If the Hawks propose 300 satellites and the Doves propose 100 satellites, the voters will be equally unhappy with both parties. Compared to the efficient quantity, the Doves want an underprovision of 100 satellites and the Hawks want an overprovision of 100 satellites. The deadweight losses are equal. So the election would be too close to call.

Contemplating this outcome, the Hawks realize that they are too hawkish to get elected. They figure that if they scale back to 250 satellites, they will win the election if the Doves propose 100 satellites. The Doves reason in a similar way and figure that if they increase the number of satellites to 150, they can win the election if the Hawks propose 300 satellites. But both parties know how the other is reasoning. And they each realize that they must provide 200 satellites, or they will lose the election. So they both propose 200 satellites. The voters are indifferent between the parties, and each party receives 50 percent of the vote.

FIGURE 9.4
An Efficient Political Outcome

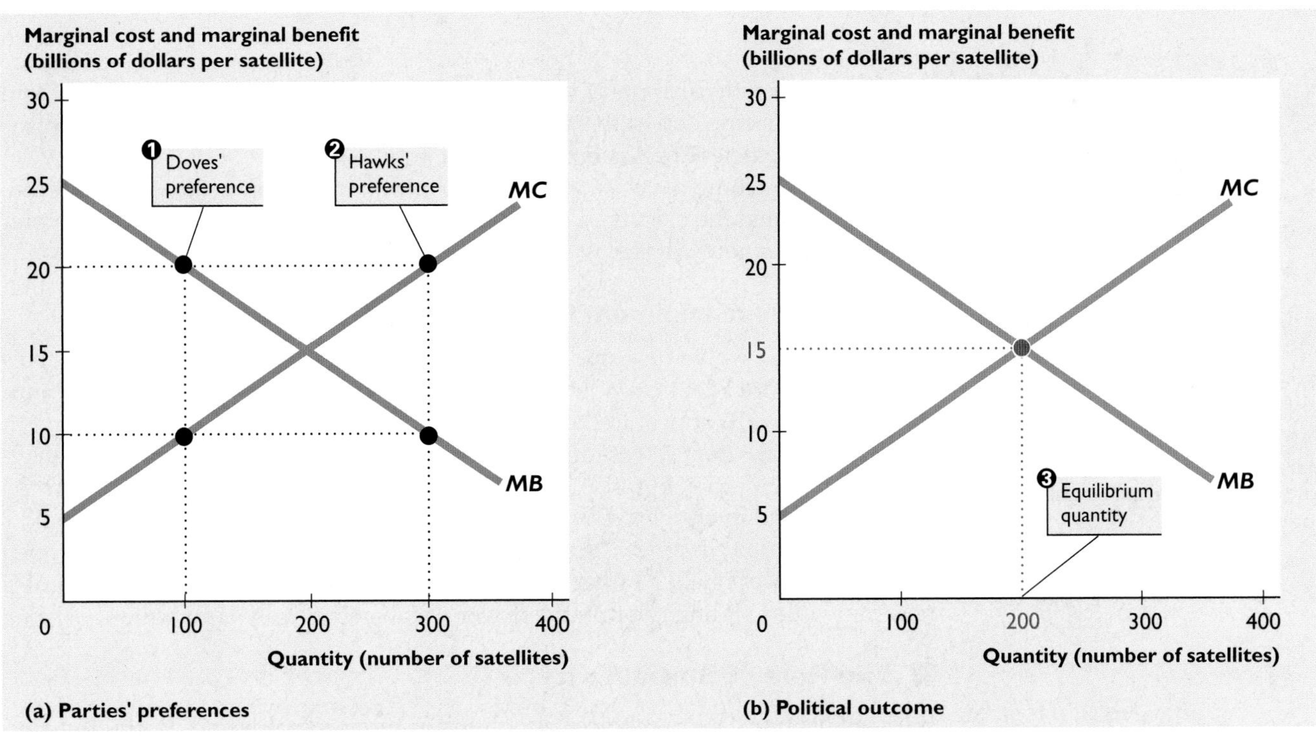

1. The Doves would like to provide 100 satellites.
2. The Hawks would like to provide 300 satellites.
3. The political outcome is 200 satellites because unless each party proposes 200 satellites, the other party can beat it in an election.

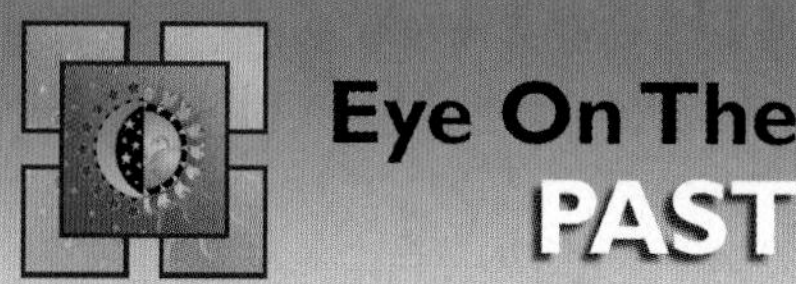

Defense Spending in the United States

National defense is a public good. And its marginal benefit changes as global events change the demands placed on the military.

During the 1960s, the United States was embroiled in the Vietnam War. This controversial war ultimately became too unpopular to sustain. But at its height, during the late 1960s, it commanded large military resources and total U.S. defense spending reached almost 9 percent of total income.

After the Vietnam War ended, during the early 1970s, public opinion supported opening a dialog with China and seeking arms reduction agreements with the Soviet Union as the most effective ways to minimize military threats. So U.S. defense spending decreased as a percentage of total income.

Opinion changed yet again during the early 1980s, and the Reagan administration increased defense spending.

The end of the Cold War brought further defense spending cuts during the 1990s.

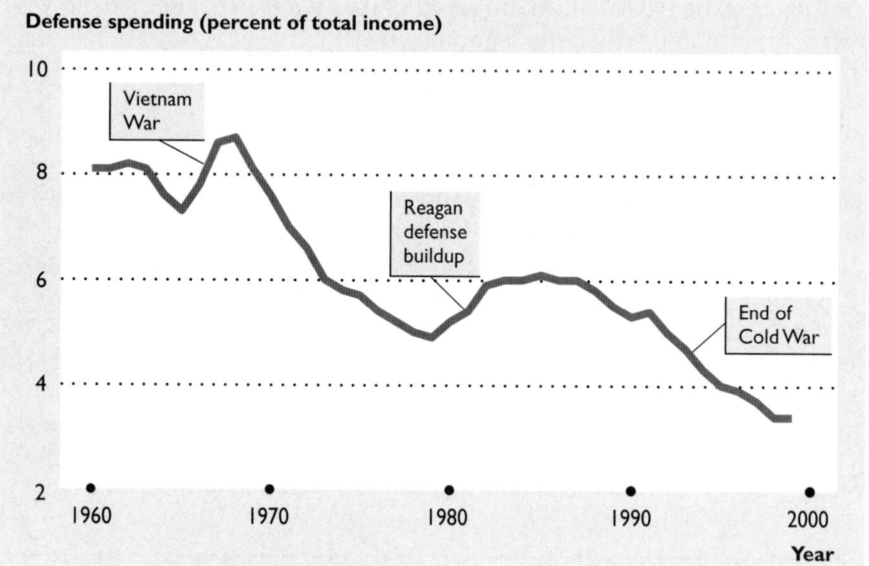

SOURCE: *Economic Report of the President*, 2001.

Regardless of which party wins the election, 200 satellites are provided. And this quantity is efficient. In this example, competition in the political marketplace results in the efficient provision of a public good.

For this outcome to occur, voters must be well informed, evaluate the alternatives, and vote in the election. Political parties must be well informed about voter preferences. As you will see, we can't expect to achieve this outcome.

The Principle of Minimum Differentiation

Principle of minimum differentiation
The tendency for competitors to make themselves identical to appeal to the maximum number of clients or voters.

In the example we've just studied, both parties propose identical policies. This tendency toward identical policies is an example of the **principle of minimum differentiation**: To appeal to the maximum number of clients or voters, competitors tend to make themselves identical. This principle not only describes the behavior of political parties but also explains why fast-food restaurants cluster in the same block and even why new car models have similar features. If McDonald's opens a restaurant in a new location, it is more likely that Burger King will open next door to McDonald's rather than a mile down the road. If Chrysler designs a new van with a sliding door on the driver's side, most likely Ford will too.

The Role of Bureaucrats

Bureaucrats translate the choices of politicians into programs and control the day-to-day activities that deliver public goods. The behavior of bureaucrats modifies the outcome of the political process in a way that we'll now examine.

The End of the Cold War

From the end of World War II to the beginning of the 1990s, a Cold War raged between NATO and the Warsaw Pact nations. NATO (the North Atlantic Treaty Organization) consists of the United States and most of the nations of Western Europe. The Warsaw Pact nations were the Soviet Union (of which Russia was the largest part) and other Eastern European nations.

In 1991, the Soviet Union collapsed. This collapse brought economic turmoil, and the defense spending on what military planners call the "potential threat states" shrank.

The figure shows the numbers. Measured in 2000 dollars, defense spending in the potential threat states decreased from around $600 billion a year during the 1980s to $180 billion a year during the mid-1990s—a 70 percent cut.

Faced with a much smaller threat, the marginal benefit of national defense decreased in the United States and the rest of NATO. The political marketplace responded to this decreased marginal benefit by cutting defense spending. In the United States, the cut was about 20 percent. In the rest of NATO, it was only 8 percent. The different degrees of cutting reflect differing national assessments of the marginal benefit of national defense.

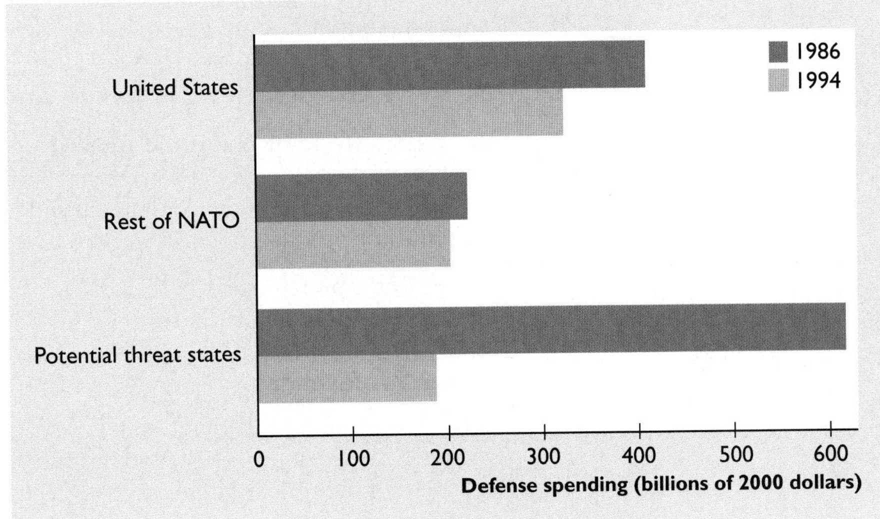

SOURCE: Commonwealth Institute, Cambridge, MA.

Sticking with the previous satellite example, if competition between two political parties delivers the efficient quantity of satellites, will the Defense Department—the Pentagon—cooperate and accept this outcome?

The Pentagon's objective is to maximize the defense budget. To increase its budget, the Pentagon might do two things: First, try to persuade the politicians that 200 satellites cost more than the originally budgeted amount. Second, and pressing its position more strongly, argue for more than 200 satellites. Won't the politicians block the Pentagon because not providing the efficient number of satellites will cost future votes? They will if voters are well informed and know what is best for them. But voters might not be well informed. If not, well-informed interest groups might enable the Pentagon to achieve its objective.

Rational Ignorance

Rational choice balances marginal benefit and marginal cost. An implication of rational choice is that it is rational for a voter to be ignorant about an issue unless that issue has a perceptible effect on the voter's well-being. **Rational ignorance** is the decision not to acquire information because the marginal cost of doing so exceeds the expected marginal benefit. For example, each voter in the United States knows that he or she can make virtually no difference to the defense policy of the U.S. government. Each voter also knows that it would take an enormous amount of time and effort to become even moderately well informed about alternative defense technologies. So voters remain relatively uninformed about the technicalities of

Rational ignorance
The decision not to acquire information because the marginal cost of doing so exceeds the expected marginal benefit.

defense issues. (Although we are using defense policy as an example, the same principle applies to all aspects of government economic activity.)

All voters consume national defense. But not all voters produce national defense—only a small number work in the defense industry. Voters who own or work for firms that produce satellites have a direct personal interest in defense because it affects their incomes. These voters have an incentive to become well informed about defense issues and to lobby politicians to further their own interests. In collaboration with the defense bureaucracy, these voters exert a larger influence on public policy than do the relatively uninformed voters who only consume this public good.

Why Government Is Large and Grows

Now that we know how the quantity of public goods is determined, we can explain part of the reason for the growth of government. Government grows in part because the demand for some public goods increases at a faster rate than the demand for private goods. There are two possible reasons for this growth:

- Voter preferences
- Inefficient overprovision

Voter Preferences

The growth of government can be explained by voter preferences. As voters' incomes increase (as they usually do), the demand for many public goods increases more quickly than income. Technically, the income elasticity of demand for many public goods is greater than 1. (See Chapter 5, pp. 126–127.) Many public goods, and particularly the most expensive ones, are in this category. They include transportation systems such as highways, airports, and air-traffic control systems; public health; education; and national defense. If politicians did not support increased expenditures on these items, they would not get elected.

Inefficient Overprovision

Inefficient overprovision explains why government might be large. Once a bureaucracy is established, the goal of budget maximization combined with voters' rational ignorance might explain why governments take an increasing proportion of total income.

Voter Backlash

If government grows too large relative to what voters are willing to accept, there might be a backlash against government programs and a large bureaucracy. This viewpoint prevailed in the United States during the 1990s at the state and federal level, and it forced politicians of all parties to embrace smaller and leaner government.

Another way in which voters—and politicians—can try to counter the tendency toward expanding government budgets is to privatize the production of public goods. Public goods must be provided by government and paid for by taxes to overcome the free-rider problem. But a government-operated agency need not produce public goods. Private firms can produce the goods and sell them to governments. For example, private firms often provide services such as garbage collection, and experiments are being conducted with private fire departments and even private prisons.

CHECKPOINT 9.1

1 **Distinguish between public goods and private goods, explain the free-rider problem, and explain how the quantity of public goods is determined.**

Study Guide pp. 132–136 

*e*Foundations 9.1 

Practice Problems 9.1

1. Classify the following goods as public goods or private goods. With each good, is there a free-rider problem? If not, how is it avoided? The goods are:
   a. Measles vaccination
   b. Fire protection
   c. Interstate 80 in rural Wyoming
2. Table 1 provides information about a mosquito control program.
   a. What quantity of spraying would a private mosquito control program provide?
   b. What is the efficient quantity of spraying?
   c. In a single-issue election on the quantity of spraying, what quantity would the political outcome deliver?

TABLE 1

Quantity (square miles per day)	Marginal cost (dollars per day)	Marginal benefit (dollars per day)
0	0	0
1	1,000	5,000
2	2,000	4,000
3	3,000	3,000
4	4,000	2,000
5	5,000	1,000

Exercises 9.1

1. Classify the following goods as public goods or private goods. With each good, is there a free-rider problem? If not, how is it avoided? The goods are:
   a. The Grand Canyon
   b. Street lighting in urban areas
   c. Flood control in the Mississippi watershed
   d. The beach at Santa Monica
2. Table 2 gives information about fire protection in Jacksonville, North Carolina.
   a. What is the quantity of fire protection that a private company would provide?
   b. What is the efficient quantity of fire protection?
   c. In a single-issue election on the quantity of fire protection, what quantity would the political outcome deliver?

TABLE 2

Quantity (number of fire stations)	Marginal cost (cents per $100 of property per year)	Marginal benefit (cents per $100 of property per year)
0	0	0
1	2.08	60.00
2	3.04	30.00
3	4.00	10.00
4	4.06	4.06
5	5.12	3.00

Solutions to Practice Problems 9.1

1a. Measles vaccination is a private good—whoever wants it buys it.

1b. Fire protection is a public good. Private provision would create a free-rider problem. Public provision avoids the free-rider problem by collecting the cost of provision via property taxes.

1c. Interstate 80 in rural Wyoming is a public good. The public good creates a free-rider problem that is avoided because the governments collect various taxes—on gas and through vehicle registration fees.

2a. A private mosquito control program would provide zero spraying because the free-rider problem would prevail.

2b. The efficient quantity of spraying is 3 square miles a day—the quantity at which the marginal benefit equals the marginal cost.

2c. The political outcome would deliver is the efficient quantity: 3 square miles a day.

9.2 THE TAX SYSTEM

Taxes generate the financial resources that federal, state, and local governments use to provide public goods and to redistribute income. Governments use five types of taxes:

- Income taxes
- Social Security taxes
- Sales taxes
- Property taxes
- Excise tax

Figure 9.5 shows the relative amounts raised by these five types of tax in 2000. Personal income taxes are the biggest revenue source and raised 43 percent of tax revenues. Social Security taxes are the next biggest revenue source at 22 percent of total taxes. State sales taxes and other taxes raised 16 percent of total taxes, corporate income taxes 8 percent, local government property taxes 8 percent, and excise taxes 3 percent. Although they raise a small amount of revenue, excise taxes have big effects on some markets. You saw these effects in Chapter 7 (pp. 158–164). Here, we focus on the biggest tax source, income taxes.

Income Taxes

Income taxes are paid on personal incomes and corporate profits. In 2000, the personal income tax raised $1 trillion for the federal government and another $270 billion for state and local governments. Corporate profits taxes raised $207 billion for the federal government and $41 billion for the state governments. We'll look first at the effects of personal income taxes and then at corporate profits taxes.

FIGURE 9.5
Government Tax Revenues

*e*Foundations 9.2 

Income taxes generate 51 percent (43 percent personal and 8 percent corporate) of government total tax revenue. Social Security taxes generate 22 percent of total tax revenue. Property taxes generate 8 percent and excise taxes bring in only 3 percent of total tax revenue.

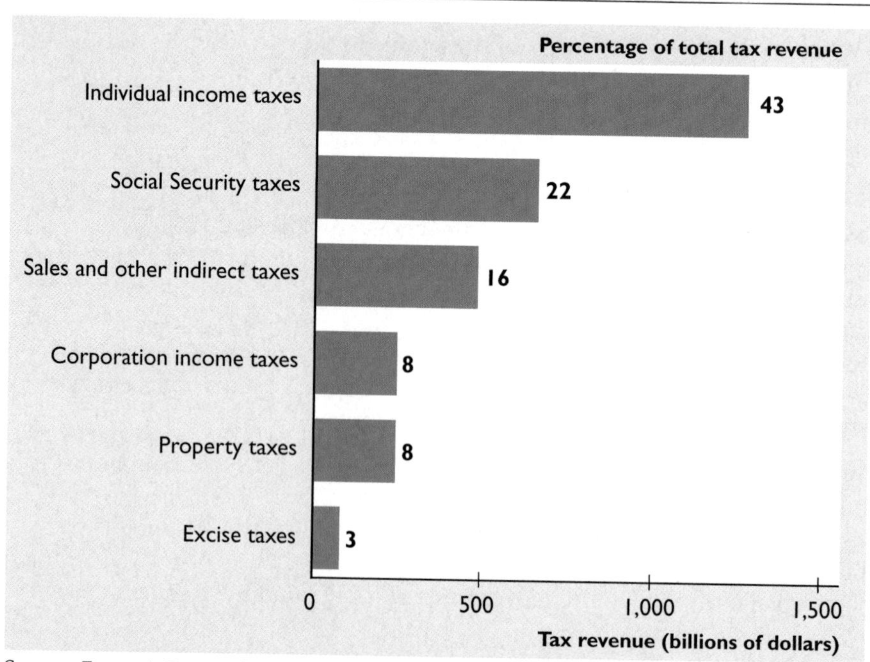

SOURCE: *Economic Report of the President*, 2001.

Personal Income Tax

The amount of income tax that a person pays depends on her or his **taxable income**, which equals total income minus a *personal exemption* and a *standard deduction* or other allowable deductions. In 2000, the personal exemption was $2,800 and the standard deduction was $4,400 for a single person. So for such a person, taxable income equals total income minus $7,200.

Taxable income
Total income minus personal exemption and a standard deduction or other allowable deductions.

The tax rate depends on the income level, and Figure 9.6 shows the tax rate for a single person. The percentages in the table are marginal tax rates. A **marginal tax rate** is the percentage of an additional dollar of income that is paid in tax. For example, if taxable income increases from $26,250 to $26,251, the additional tax paid is 28 cents and the marginal tax rate is 28 percent. If taxable income increases from $288,350 to $288,351, the additional tax paid is 39.6 cents and the marginal tax rate is 39.6 percent. The marginal tax rate increases with income.

Marginal tax rate
The percentage of an additional dollar of income that is paid in tax.

The **average tax rate** is the percentage of income that is paid in tax. The average tax rate is less than the marginal tax rate. For example, suppose a single person earns $50,000 in a year. Tax paid is zero on the first $7,200, plus $3,938 (15 percent) on the next $26,250, plus $4,634 (28 percent) on the remaining $16,550. Total taxes equal $8,572, which is 17.1 percent of $50,000. So that person's average tax rate is 17.1 percent.

Average tax rate
The percentage of income that is paid in tax.

If the average tax rate increases as income increases, the tax is a **progressive tax**. In most countries, the personal income tax is a progressive tax. To see this feature of the U.S. income tax, calculate the average tax rate for someone whose income is $100,000 a year. Tax paid is zero on the first $7,200, plus $3,938 (15 percent) on the next $26,250, plus $10,444 (28 percent) on the next $37,300, plus $9,068 on the remaining $29,250. Total taxes are $23,449, which is 23.4 percent of $100,000. So a person who earns $100,000 has an average tax rate of 23.4 percent.

Progressive tax
An increase in the average tax rate as income increases.

FIGURE 9.6
Marginal Tax Rates and Average Tax Rates

*e*Foundations 9.2 

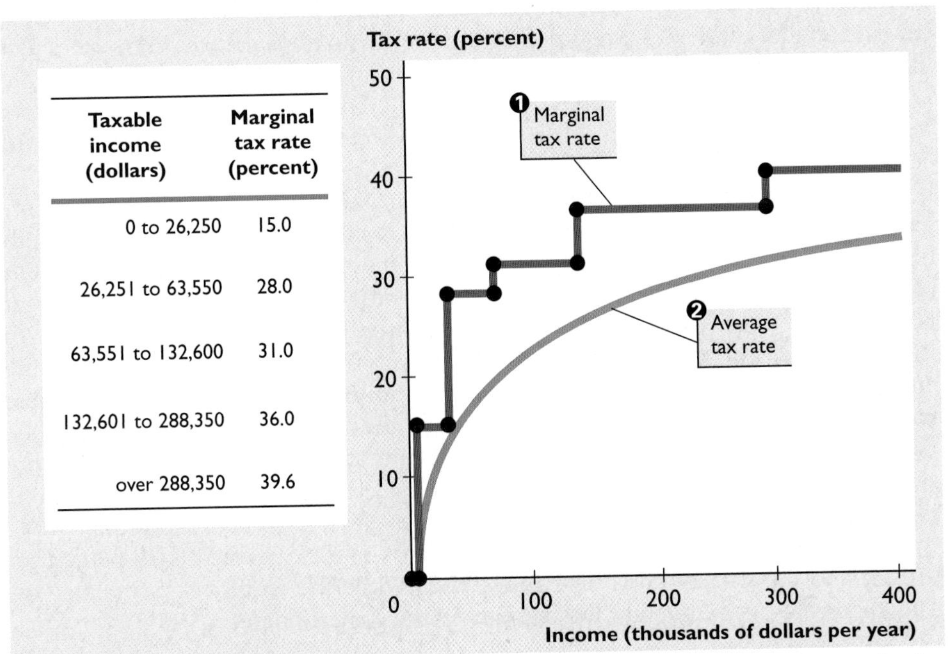

Taxable income (dollars)	Marginal tax rate (percent)
0 to 26,250	15.0
26,251 to 63,550	28.0
63,551 to 132,600	31.0
132,601 to 288,350	36.0
over 288,350	39.6

❶ Marginal tax rates increase with income—the table gives the data.

❷ Average tax rates increase with income, but the average rate is less than the marginal rate.

SOURCE: Internal Revenue Service.

Proportional tax
A constant average tax rate at all income levels.

Regressive tax
A decrease in the average tax rate as income increases.

A progressive tax contrasts with a **proportional tax**, which has the same average tax rate at all income levels, and a **regressive tax**, which has a decreasing average tax rate as income increases.

Corporate Income Tax

The corporate income tax is a tax on the profits of corporations. In popular discussions of taxes, the corporate income tax is seen as a free source of revenue for the government. Taxing people's income is bad, but taxing corporations' income is just fine. However, it turns out that taxing corporations is even more inefficient than taxing people. The corporate income tax actually taxes corporate income twice—once as the profit of the corporation that earns it and a second time as the income of the people who receive dividends on the stock they own.

The Effects of Income Taxes

You already know quite a lot about the effects of taxes on markets because you studied this topic in Chapter 7 (pp. 158–164). In that chapter, you learned about two effects of taxes: *tax incidence* and *excess burden*. Tax incidence is the place where the burden of the tax rests. You learned that tax incidence depends on the elasticities of demand and supply. The total burden of a tax is the amount of tax paid plus the deadweight loss. Excess burden is deadweight loss that a tax generates because it drives a wedge between marginal benefit and marginal cost.

Here, we'll probe the incidence and excess burden of income taxes. The effects of income taxes depend on the source of income that is taxed because the elasticities of supply vary across the different factors of production whose incomes are taxed. We'll look in turn at taxes on three sources of income: labor, capital, and land and other unique resources.

Taxes on Labor Income

Figure 9.7 shows how the income tax affects labor markets. Part (a) shows the market for low-wage workers, and part (b) shows the market for high-wage workers. These labor markets are competitive, and with no income taxes, they work just like all the other competitive markets you have studied. The demand curves are *LD*, and the supply curves are *LS* (in both parts of the figure). Low-wage workers would earn $10 an hour and work 40 hours a week. High-wage workers would earn $360 an hour and work 36 hours a week.

With an income tax, the supply curves shift. Low-wage workers face a marginal tax rate of 15 percent. If low-wage workers are willing to supply the 40th hour a week for $10 when there is no tax, then they are willing to supply the 40th hour when there is a 15 percent tax only if the wage rises to $11.76 an hour. That is, they want to get the $10 they received before plus $1.76 (15 percent of $11.76) that they now must pay in taxes. So the supply of labor decreases because the amount workers receive is lowered by the amount of tax paid. The acceptable wage rate at each level of employment rises by the amount of the tax that must be paid. For low-wage workers who face a tax rate of 15 percent, the supply curve shifts to *LS* + *tax*. The equilibrium wage rate rises to $10.35 an hour, but the after-tax wage rate falls to $8.80 an hour. Employment falls to 35 hours a week.

In this example, the tax on an hour of work is $1.55 (which is 15 percent of $10.35) and the worker ends up paying $1.20 while the employer pays 35 cents. The tax creates a deadweight loss shown by the gray triangle.

FIGURE 9.7
A Tax on Labor Income

*e*Foundations 9.2

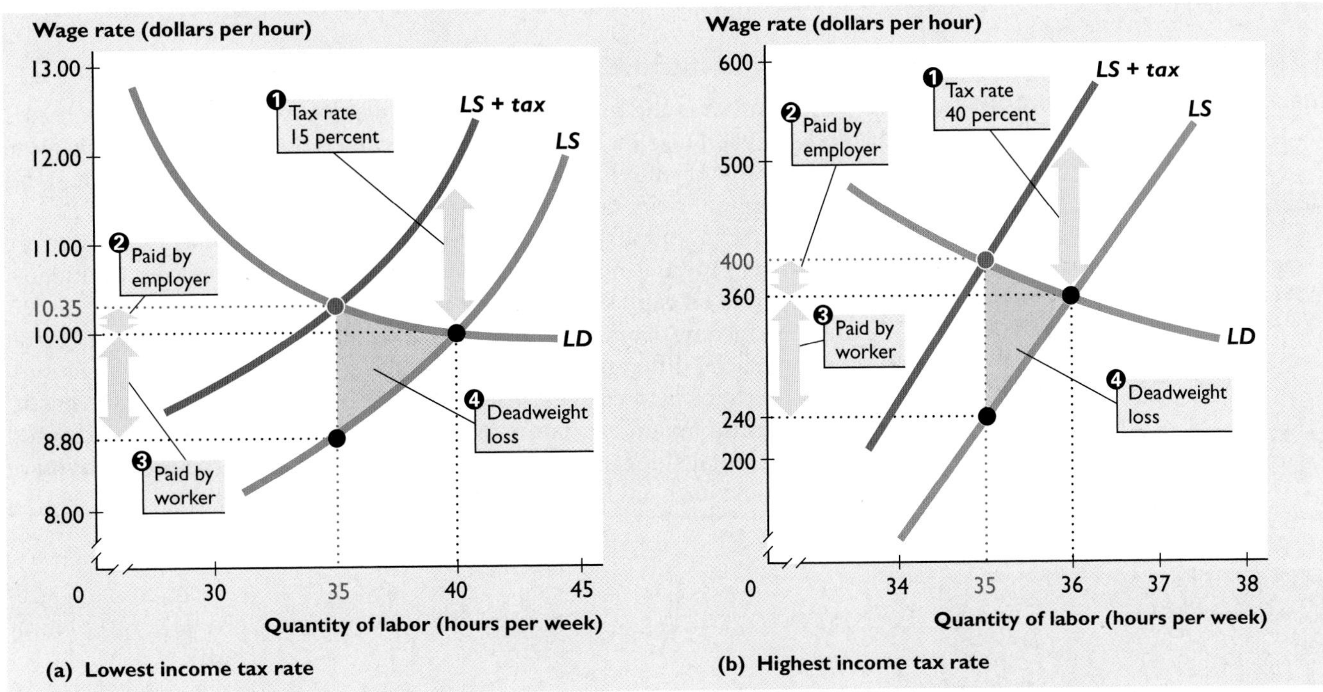

❶ Low-wage workers face a 15 percent marginal income tax rate (part a), and high-wage workers face a 40 percent marginal income tax rate (part b). The income tax decreases the supply of labor, raises the wage rate, and lowers the after-tax wage rate.

In each case, the tax ❷ paid by the employer is less than that ❸ paid by the worker.

❹ A deadweight loss arises in each case.

High-wage workers face an income tax rate of 40 percent (we've rounded the actual highest marginal rate of 39.6 percent). The supply of these workers is probably less elastic than that of lower-paid workers. Many high-paid workers do jobs that they enjoy, and they would likely work a similar number of hours a week no matter what they were paid over some range of hourly compensation. Figure 9.7(b) is based on this assumption. When a 40 percent marginal tax rate is imposed, the supply curve shifts to *LS* + *tax* in part (b). The equilibrium wage rate rises from \$360 to \$400 an hour, and the after-tax wage rate falls to \$240 an hour. Employment falls to 35 hours a week. Despite the much higher marginal tax rate faced by high-paid workers, the decrease in employment of high-wage workers is smaller than that of low-wage workers because the elasticity of supply of high-wage labor is less than that for low-wage labor.

In this example, the tax on an hour of work is \$160 (which is 40 percent of \$400). The worker ends up paying \$120, and the employer pays \$40. The tax creates a deadweight loss shown by the gray triangle.

The deadweight loss is much larger for the high-wage workers than for the low-wage workers. The area of the gray triangle measures it. For the low-paid worker, the deadweight loss is (\$1.55 × 5) ÷ 2 = \$3.88 a week. For the high-paid worker, the deadweight loss is (\$160 × 1) ÷ 2 = \$80 a week.

These examples of the effects of taxes on labor income illustrate the large deadweight loss (and excess burden) of the high rates of income tax that high-wage workers face. Even assuming, as we have done here, that the elasticity of supply of these workers is low, the tax brings a high cost in lost efficiency.

Taxes on Capital Income

Income from capital is the interest that people receive on savings such as bonds and bank deposits. It also includes dividends received on stocks that people own. The capital income of individuals is added to their other sources of income and taxed at the marginal rates set out in Table 9.1.

In addition, corporations pay an income tax on their profits. These profits are also income from capital. And because people pay income tax on their dividends, the income tax rate on capital exceeds the rates on personal incomes.

Taxing the income from capital works like taxing the income from labor, except for one crucial difference: Because capital is internationally mobile, its supply is highly (perhaps perfectly) elastic. If the supply of capital is perfectly elastic, firms pay the entire tax on capital income and the quantity of capital decreases. With a smaller capital stock than firms would otherwise have, the productivity of labor and labor incomes are lower than they would otherwise be.

TABLE 9.1 U.S. PERSONAL INCOME TAX RATES IN 2000

Taxable income	Marginal tax rate
$0 to $26,250	15.0 percent
$26,251 to $63,550	28.0 percent
$63,551 to $132,600	31.0 percent
$132,601 to $288,350	36.0 percent
Over $288,350	39.6 percent

Taxes Around the World

Total tax revenue in the United States is 30 percent of total income. The Australians and Japanese pay similar percentages of their total incomes in taxes.

Taxes are much lower in Korea and Mexico than in the United States. Taxes in Mexico are only around one half of U.S. taxes.

But most of the world pays a much higher level of tax than Americans pay. In Sweden, the highest-taxed nation, total taxes are almost 55 percent of total income. In most of Europe, taxes exceed 40 percent of income.

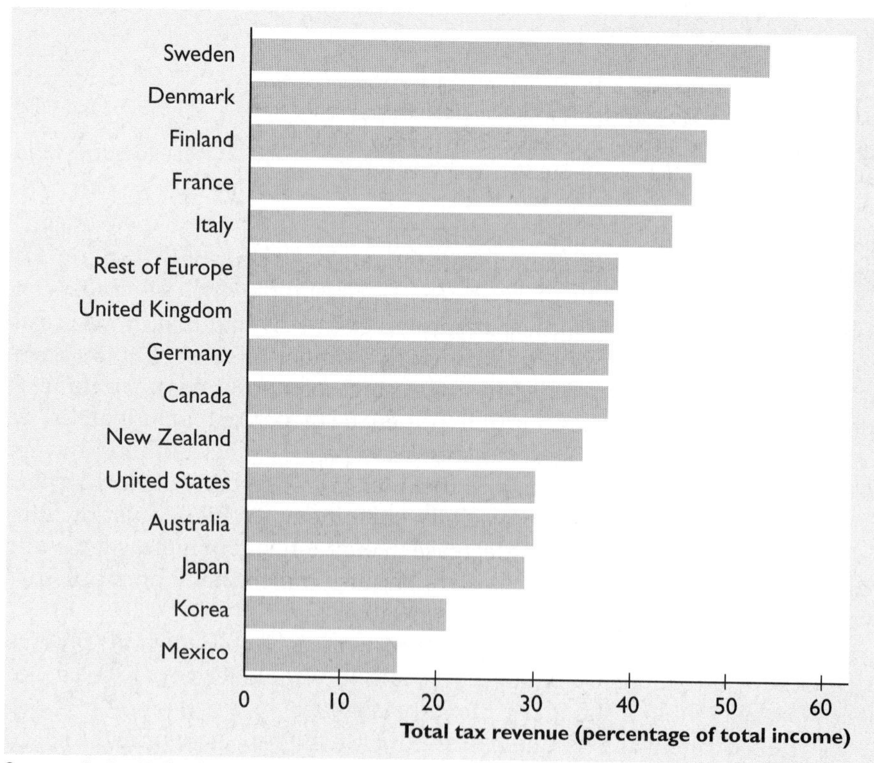

SOURCE: Swiss Federal Tax Administration.

FIGURE 9.8
A Tax on Capital Income

*e*Foundations 9.2 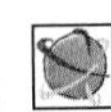

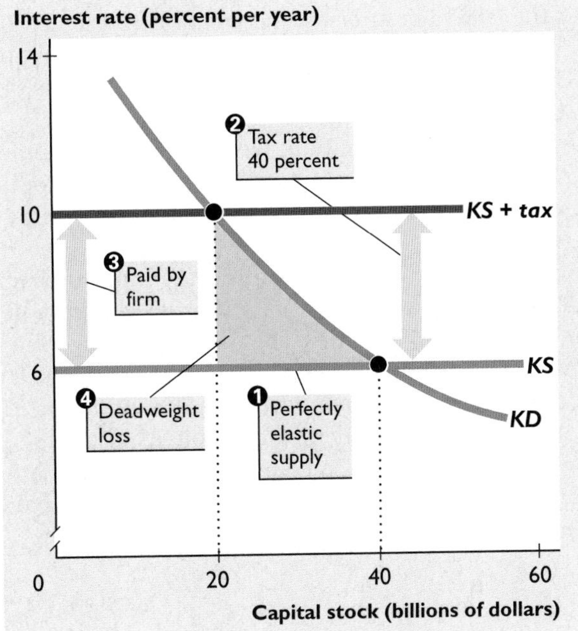

1 The supply of capital is highly elastic (here, perfectly elastic).

With a 2 40 percent tax on income from capital, the supply curve becomes *KS + tax*.

The interest rate rises to 10 percent a year, and 3 the firm pays the entire tax.

4 A large deadweight loss arises.

Figure 9.8 illustrates the effects of the tax on capital income. A firm's demand curve for capital is *KD*. The firm can obtain all the capital it wishes at an interest rate of 6 percent a year. So the supply curve of capital is *KS*. With no tax on capital income, the firm uses $40 billion worth of capital. With an income tax rate of 40 percent, the supply of capital changes and the supply curve shifts to *KS + tax*. The suppliers now want to receive an additional 4 percent a year in interest to pay their capital income tax. They are not willing to offer capital for less than 10 percent a year.

In the new equilibrium, the quantity of capital decreases and the interest rate rises. Firms pay the entire capital income tax, and suppliers of capital receive the same after-tax interest rate that they would have received in the absence of a capital income tax.

The magnitude of the deadweight loss (and excess burden) of the capital income tax depends on the elasticity of demand for capital. Here, we've assumed that the elasticity of demand for capital is 1.33, which is a likely value for this elasticity and which creates a large excess burden of the tax on capital income.

Taxes on Land and Other Unique Resources

The income that people earn from land is taxed as part of their total income. Taxing the income from land works in the same way as taxing the income from other sources except for one crucial difference: The supply of land is highly (perhaps perfectly) *inelastic*. For this reason, the tax on land income is fully borne by the landowners and the quantity of land is unaffected by the tax. With no change in the quantity of land, the tax on land income creates no deadweight loss or excess burden and is efficient.

Figure 9.9(a) illustrates a tax on land income. A fixed amount of land is supplied regardless of the rent. The demand for land determines the rent. In this example, the quantity of land is 250 billion acres and the equilibrium rent is $1,000 an acre. When a 40 percent tax is imposed on rent income, the landowners pay all of the tax. Their after-tax income falls to $600 an acre.

This tax is efficient because the equilibrium quantity of land does not change. The tax generates no deadweight loss or excess burden. A tax on land is an ideal tax from the perspective of efficiency.

The principle that applies to a tax on income from land also applies to the income from any unique resource that has a perfectly inelastic supply. Another example of such a resource is the talent of an outstanding movie star or television personality.

Figure 9.9(b) illustrates this case. Suppose that Barbara Walters is willing to do 24 big television interviews a year. Her supply of interview services is perfectly inelastic at that quantity. The networks compete for her services, and the demand curve reflects their willingness to pay for them. The equilibrium price is $250,000 per interview, or an annual fee of $6 million for 24 interviews a year.

If Barbara Walters pays income tax at a rate of 40 percent on this income, she receives an after-tax income of $150,000 per interview, or $3.6 million a year. Barbara Walters pays the entire tax. The price paid by the networks is unaffected

FIGURE 9.9

A Tax on Land and Other Unique Resource Income

*e*Foundations 9.2 

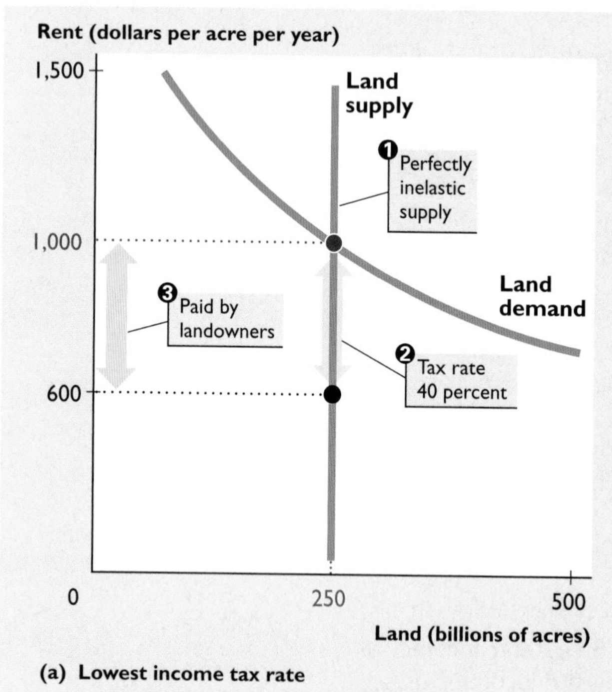

(a) Lowest income tax rate

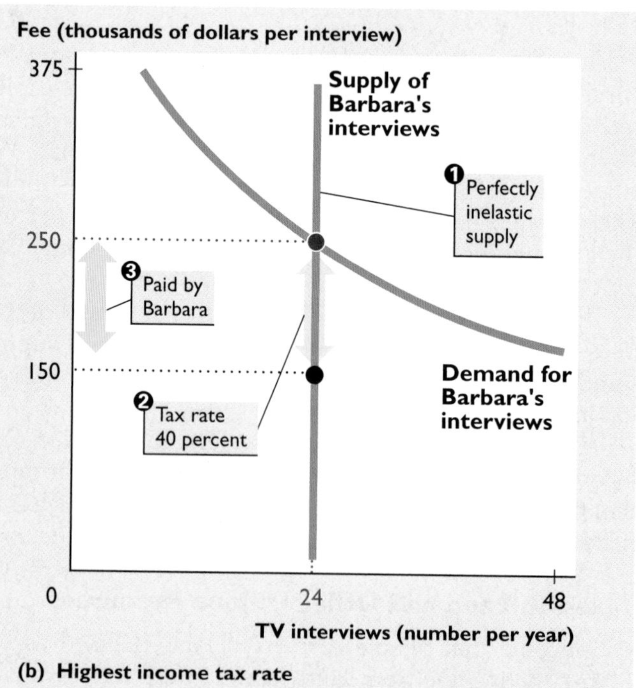

(b) Highest income tax rate

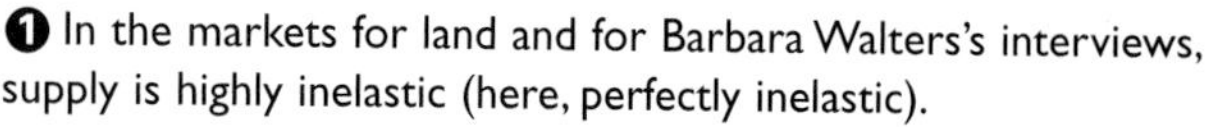
❶ In the markets for land and for Barbara Walters's interviews, supply is highly inelastic (here, perfectly inelastic).

With a ❷ 40 percent tax on income from these resources, the supply curves and the market prices remain unchanged and ❸ the landlord and Barbara Walters pay the entire tax. There is no deadweight loss, and the tax is efficient.

by this tax, and the efficient number of interviews is performed. There is no deadweight loss or excess burden created by the tax on Barbara Walters's income.

Why We Have a Progressive Income Tax

We have a progressive income tax because a majority of voters support it and so the politicians who support it get elected. The economic model that predicts progressive income taxes is called the *median voter model*. The core idea of the median voter model is that political parties pursue the policies that are most likely to attract the support of the median voter. The median voter is the one in the middle of the range of opinion—one half of the voter population lies on one side and one half on the other.

To see how the median voter model predicts a progressive income tax, first imagine that government programs benefit everyone equally and are paid for by a proportional income tax. Everyone pays the same percentage of his or her income. In this situation, there is redistribution from high-income voters to low-income voters. Everyone benefits equally from the programs, but because they have higher incomes, the high-income voters pay a larger amount of taxes.

Is this situation the best one possible for the median voter? No, it is not. Let's see why. Suppose that instead of using a proportional tax, the marginal tax rate is lowered for low-income voters and increased for high-income voters—a progressive tax. Low-income voters are now better off, and high-income voters are worse off. Low-income voters will support this change, and high-income voters will oppose it. But there are many more low-income voters than high-income voters, so the low-income voters will win.

The median voter is a low-income voter. In fact, because the distribution of income is skewed, the median voter has a smaller income than the average income. This fact raises the question: Why doesn't the median voter support taxes that skim off all income above the average and redistribute it to everyone with a below-average income so that everyone ends up with the same income?

The answer is that the income tax would be so progressive that it would discourage work effort and saving by high-income voters, and the median voter would be worse off with such a radical redistribution than under the arrangements that prevail today.

■ Is the Tax System Fair?

We've examined the efficiency of different types of taxes, and explained why the political system delivers a progressive tax system. These topics have occupied most of this chapter because they are the central issues about the tax system that economics can address. But they are not the topics that occupy most of the political discussion and media comment on taxes. Whenever political leaders debate tax issues, it is fairness, not efficiency, that looms above all other considerations. Democrats complain that Republican tax cuts are unfair because they end up giving most of the benefits of lower taxes to the rich. Republicans counter that when taxes are cut, it is fair that those who pay most of the taxes get the biggest breaks. Because the rich pay most of the taxes, it is fair that they get most of the tax cuts.

We discussed fairness in Chapter 6 (pp. 147–151) when we considered whether markets deliver a fair outcome. You saw there that economists do not agree about fairness and that it is not an exclusively economic issue. You also saw that the *symmetry principle*—the principle that people in similar situations should be treated similarly—lies at the center of all discussions of fairness.

This same principle is applied in discussions about the fairness of the tax system. But as before, it does not provide a unique and universally accepted prescription for a fair tax system. There are two conflicting principles of fairness of taxes:

- The benefits principle
- The ability-to-pay principle

The Benefits Principle

Benefits principle
The proposition that people should pay taxes equal to the benefits they receive from public services.

The **benefits principle** is the proposition that people should pay taxes equal to the benefits they receive from public services. This arrangement is fair because it means that those who benefit most pay the most. It makes tax payments and the consumption of public goods similar to private expenditures and the consumption of private goods. If taxes are based on the benefits principle, the people who enjoy the largest marginal benefit from the legal system pay the most for it, just as the people who enjoy the largest marginal benefit from playing video games have the greatest demand for games and spend the most on them.

To implement the benefits principle, it would be necessary to have an objective method of measuring each individual's marginal benefit from public goods. In the absence of such a method, the principle can be used to justify a wide range of different, and obviously not all fair, arrangements.

For example, the benefits principle can justify high fuel taxes to pay for public highways. Here, the argument would be that those who value the highways most use them most and so should pay most of the cost of providing them. Similarly, the benefits principle can justify high taxes on alcoholic beverages and tobacco products. Here, the argument would be that those who drink and smoke the most impose the largest burden on public health care services and so should pay the greater part of the cost of those services.

The benefits principle can also be used to justify a progressive income tax. Here, the argument would be that the rich receive a disproportionately large share of the benefit from law and order and from living in a secure environment, so they should pay the largest share of providing these items.

The Ability-to-Pay Principle

Ability-to-pay principle
The proposition that people should pay taxes according to how easily they can bear the burden.

The **ability-to-pay principle** is the proposition that people should pay taxes according to how easily they can bear the burden. A rich person can more easily bear the burden of providing public goods than a poor person can, so the rich should pay higher taxes than the poor. The ability-to-pay principle involves comparing people along two dimensions: vertically and horizontally.

Horizontal equity
The requirement that taxpayers with the same ability to pay, pay the same taxes.

Horizontal Equity If taxes are based on ability to pay, taxpayers with the same ability to pay should pay the same taxes—a situation called **horizontal equity**. While horizontal equity is easy to agree with in principle, it is difficult to implement in practice. If two people are identical in every respect, horizontal equity is easy to apply. But how do we compare people who are similar but not identical? The greatest difficulty arises in working out differences in ability to pay that arise from the state of a person's health and from a person's family responsibilities. The U.S. income tax has many special deductions and other rules that aim to achieve horizontal equity.

Vertical Equity If horizontal comparisons are difficult, vertical comparisons are impossible. **Vertical equity** is the requirement that taxpayers with a greater ability to pay bear a greater share of the taxes. This proposition easily translates into the requirement that people with higher incomes should pay higher taxes. But it provides no help in determining how steeply taxes should increase as income increases. Should taxes be proportional to income? Should they be regressive? Should they be progressive? All of these arrangements have higher-income people paying higher taxes, so they all satisfy the basic idea of vertical equity. But most people have stronger views that include the extent to which the rich pay more.

Vertical equity
The requirement that taxpayers with a greater ability to pay bear a greater share of the taxes.

You've seen that the U.S. tax code uses progressive income taxes—marginal tax rates and average tax rates that increase with income. Progressive taxes can be justified as fair on the basis of the principle of vertical equity. But their use to achieve vertical equity produces a problem for the attainment of horizontal equity. The problem shows up most clearly in the U.S. tax code in its treatment of single persons and married couples.

The Marriage Tax Problem In the U.S. tax code, a married couple is considered a single taxpayer. This arrangement means that when a man and a woman get married, they stop paying income tax as two individuals and instead pay as one individual. To see the marriage tax problem, suppose the tax code (simpler than in the United States) is as follows: no deductions or exemptions; incomes up to $20,000 a year bear no tax; incomes in excess of $20,000 are taxed at 10 percent. Now think about Al and Judy, two struggling young journalists who each earn $20,000 a year and who get married. As single people, they paid no tax. Married, their income is $40,000, so they pay $2,000 a year in tax (10 percent of $20,000). Their marriage tax is $2,000 a year. (This example is *much* more severe than the marriage tax in the United States, but it serves to highlight the source of the problem.)

We could make a simple change to the tax law to overcome this problem for Al and Judy: Tax married couples as two single persons. That is what is done in most countries and what some economists say should be done in the United States. If we make this change in the tax law, Al and Judy pay no tax after their marriage just as before. We've solved the marriage tax problem.

Before we conclude that this small change to the tax code would clean up a source of unfairness, let's think about its effect on Denise and Frank. Frank is a painter whose work just doesn't sell. He has no income. Denise is a successful artist whose work is in steady demand and earns her $40,000 a year. As two single artists, Frank pays no tax and Denise pays $2,000 a year (10 percent of $20,000). If they marry, under the arrangement that taxes a married couple as a single taxpayer, they still pay $2,000 in tax.

Now compare Frank and Denise with Al and Judy. If we tax married couples as a single taxpayer, both couples earn $40,000 a year and both pay income tax of $2,000 a year. But if we tax them as single persons, Frank and Denise pay $2,000 a year and Al and Judy pay nothing. So which is fair? Horizontal equity requires Frank and Denise to be treated like Al and Judy. Taxing them as couples rather than as individuals achieves this outcome. But it taxes marriage, which seems unfair. The problem arises from the progressive tax. It would not arise if taxes were proportional. Because horizontal equity conflicts with progressive taxes, some people say that only proportional taxes are fair.

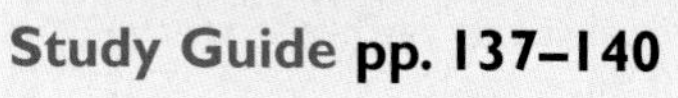

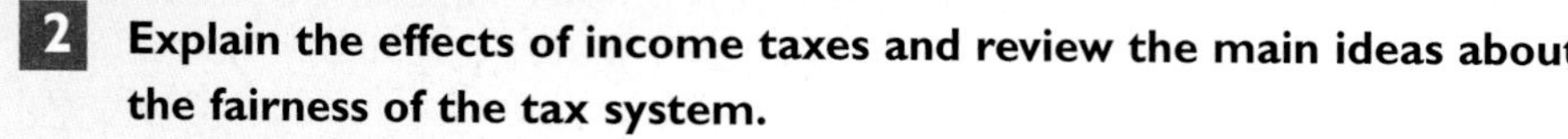

CHECKPOINT 9.2

Study Guide pp. 137–140

*e*Foundations 9.2

2 **Explain the effects of income taxes and review the main ideas about the fairness of the tax system.**

Practice Problems 9.2

1. Florida levies the following taxes: a 5.5 percent corporate income tax, a 6 percent sales tax, a 13.3 percent excise tax on gasoline, a 33.9 cents a pack excise tax on cigarettes, a 48 cents a gallon excise tax on beer, a $2.25 a gallon excise tax on wine, and property taxes that vary across the counties and range from 1.4 percent to 2.0 percent of property values.
   Classify Florida's taxes into progressive, proportional, and regressive taxes.
2. In Hong Kong, the marginal tax rates on salaries ranges from 2 percent to 20 percent with a maximum average tax of 15 percent, which is reached on incomes of about $59,000. Compare the tax rates in Hong Kong with the U.S. federal tax rate. In which country is the personal income tax (tax on salaries) more progressive? Why?

Exercises 9.2

1. California taxes personal incomes, and in 1999, there were 6 tax brackets that ranged from 1.0 percent on a taxable income of $5,264 to 9.3 percent on taxable incomes above $434,548. Personal income taxes raised 42.5 percent of the state's tax revenue. An 8.84 percent corporate income tax raised 7.5 percent of state tax revenue. A 6 percent sales tax raised almost 31.3 percent of state tax revenue. Excise taxes, which included an 18 percent tax on gasoline, an 87 cents a pack tax on cigarettes, and a 20 cents a gallon tax on beer and wine, raised 7.8 percent of revenue.

   Classify these Californian taxes into progressive, proportional, and regressive taxes.

TABLE 1

Taxable income	Marginal tax rate
$1 to $5,400	0 percent
$5,401 to $20,700	20 percent
$20,701 to $38,000	34 percent
$38,001 to $50,000	43 percent
$50,001 and over	47 percent

2. Table 1 shows the marginal tax rates in Australia in 2000.
   a. Draw a graph of the marginal tax rates in Australia.
   b. Compare your graph with Figure 9.6. Which country has the more progressive taxes on personal income?
   c. Calculate the average tax rate for each range of taxable income. Is the average Australian tax higher or lower than in the United States?

Solutions to Practice Problems 9.2

1. Florida's property taxes are probably progressive if counties with the higher tax rates are those with higher property values. The corporate income tax does not vary with income, so this tax is a proportional tax. Saving increases with income, so expenditure as a fraction of incomes decreases as income increases. As a result, the flat sales tax and excise taxes are regressive taxes.
2. The U.S. federal tax on personal incomes is more progressive because the average tax rate rises from 0 to about 30 percent, while in Hong Kong the average tax rate rises from 2 percent to 15 percent.

CHAPTER CHECKPOINT

Key Points

1 Distinguish between public goods and private goods, explain the free-rider problem, and explain how the quantity of public goods is determined.

- A public good is a good or service that is consumed by everyone and that is nonrival and nonexcludable.
- A public good creates a free-rider problem—no one has a private incentive to pay her or his share of the cost of providing a public good.
- The efficient level of provision of a public good is that at which marginal benefit equals marginal cost.
- Competition between political parties, each of which tries to appeal to the maximum number of voters, can lead to the efficient scale of provision of a public good and to both parties proposing the same policies—the principle of minimum differentiation.
- Bureaucrats try to maximize their budgets, and if voters are rationally ignorant, they might vote to support taxes that provide public goods in quantities that exceed the efficient quantity.

2 Explain the effects of income taxes and review the main ideas about the fairness of the tax system.

- Government revenue comes from income taxes, payroll taxes, sales taxes, property taxes, and excise taxes.
- Income taxes decrease the level of employment and create a deadweight loss.
- Taxes can be progressive (the average tax rate rises with income), proportional (the average tax rate is constant), or regressive (the average tax rate falls with income).
- Income taxes are progressive because this arrangement is in the interest of the median voter.
- The two main principles of fairness of taxes—the benefits principle and the ability-to-pay principle—do not deliver universally accepted standards of fairness, and vertical equity and horizontal equity can come into conflict.

Key Terms

Exercises

1. Classify each of the following goods as either a public good or a private good. With each good, is there a free-rider problem? If not, how is the free-rider problem avoided?
   a. Millennium celebrations in Times Square, New York
   b. The Santa Monica freeway on a Friday afternoon
   c. The city's sewerage system
   d. The railway network
   e. The Great Lakes

FIGURE I

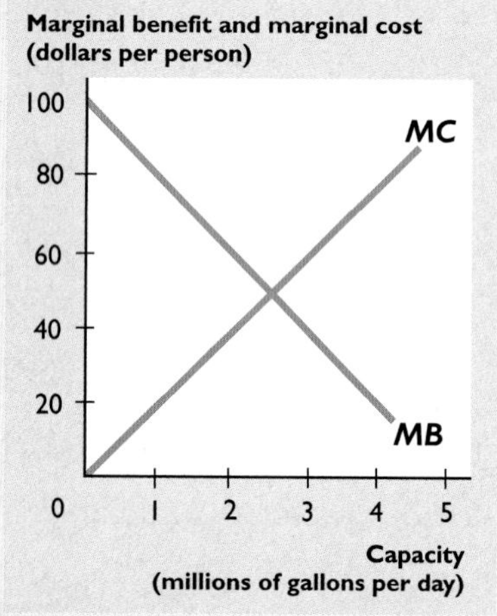

2. Figure 1 shows the marginal benefit and marginal cost of a sewerage disposal system in a city of 1 million people.
   a. What is the efficient capacity of the sewerage disposal system?
   b. How much would each person have to pay in taxes if the city installed the efficient capacity?
   c. If voters are well-informed about the costs and benefits of the sewerage disposal system, what capacity will voters choose in a referendum?
   d. If voters are rationally ignorant, will bureaucrats install the efficient capacity? Explain your answer.
3. Both a progressive state income tax and a proportional state income tax create a deadweight loss. Use the link on your Foundations Web site to see what type of personal income tax the residents of your state pay. Compare your state's income tax rate with that of neighboring states.
4. In 1999, Ohio had a personal income tax rate that ranged from 0.716 percent on incomes up to $5,000 to 7.228 percent on incomes above $200,000. There are nine income tax brackets in Ohio and the median income in 1999 was around $60,000. Connecticut's personal income tax rate has two tax brackets: 3 percent tax on income up to $10,000 and 4.5 percent on income above $10,000. The median income in 1999 was around $76,000.
   a. Which of these states has the more progressive income tax?
   b. If a referendum were held today on the personal income tax structure in each of these states, what outcome would the median voter model predict?
   c. If the elasticities of the supplies of low-income labor in both states were the same and if the elasticities of the supplies of high-income labor in both states were the same, which tax structure would create the larger deadweight loss? Explain your answer.
5. Is it fair that some states such as Texas and Florida have no state income tax while other states tax personal income? Give reasons.
6. Use the data on Florida and California in Checkpoint 9.2 (p. 224) to compare the types of income and excise taxes that these two states levy.

Part 4

A Closer Look at Decision Makers

Chapter 10

Consumer Choice and Demand

CHAPTER CHECKLIST

When you have completed your study of this chapter, you will be able to:

1 **Calculate and graph a budget line that shows the limits to a person's consumption possibilities.**

2 **Explain marginal utility theory and use it to derive a consumer's demand curve.**

3 **Use marginal utility theory to explain the paradox of value: Why water is vital but cheap while diamonds are relatively useless but expensive.**

This chapter studies the consumption choices of people like you and your friends. It presents a model of consumer choice based on the concept of marginal utility and the fundamental idea of economics that people make rational choices.

We presented the law of demand in Chapter 4 as an intuitive proposition. But exactly *why* does the quantity demanded of a good increase when its price falls, other things remaining the same? Also, *why* is the demand for one good influenced by the prices of other goods? And *why* does income influence demand?

You learned in Chapter 5 that the demand for some goods is elastic while the demand for others is inelastic. Why? What makes demand elastic or inelastic?

Marginal utility theory answers these questions. It also provides a stronger foundation for the interpretation of the demand curve as the willingness-to-pay curve and marginal benefit curve that you saw in Chapter 6 and applied in Chapters 7 through 9.

10.1 CONSUMPTION POSSIBILITIES

We begin our study of consumption choices by learning about the limits to what a person can afford to buy. Your consumption choices are limited by your income and by the prices that you must pay. We summarize these influences on buying plans in the budget line.

The Budget Line

Budget line
A line that describes the limits to consumption choices and that depends on a consumer's budget and the prices of goods and services.

A **budget line** describes the limits to consumption possibilities. Tina has already committed most of her income to renting an apartment, buying textbooks, paying her campus meal plan, and saving a few dollars each month. Having made these decisions, Tina has a remaining budget of $4 a day, which she spends on two goods: bottled water and chewing gum. The price of water is $1 a bottle, and the price of gum is 50¢ a pack. If Tina spends all of her available budget, she reaches the limits of her consumption of bottled water and gum.

Figure 10.1 illustrates Tina's possible consumption of bottled water and gum. Rows *A* through *E* in the table show five possible ways of spending $4 on these two goods. If Tina spends all of her $4 on gum, she can buy 8 packs a day. In this case, she has nothing available to spend on bottled water. Row *A* shows this possibility. At the other extreme, if Tina spends her entire $4 on bottled water, she can buy 4 bottles a day and no gum. Row *E* shows this possibility. Rows *B*, *C*, and *D* show three other possible combinations that Tina can afford.

FIGURE 10.1
Consumption Possibilities

*e*Foundations **10.1** 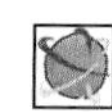

Tina's budget line shows the boundary between what she can and cannot afford. The rows of the table list Tina's affordable combinations of bottled water and chewing gum when her budget is $4 a day, the price of water is $1 a bottle, and the price of chewing gum is 50¢ a pack. For example, row *A* tells us that Tina exhausts her $4 budget when she buys 8 packs of gum and no water.

The figure graphs Tina's budget line. Points *A* through *E* on the graph represent the rows of the table.

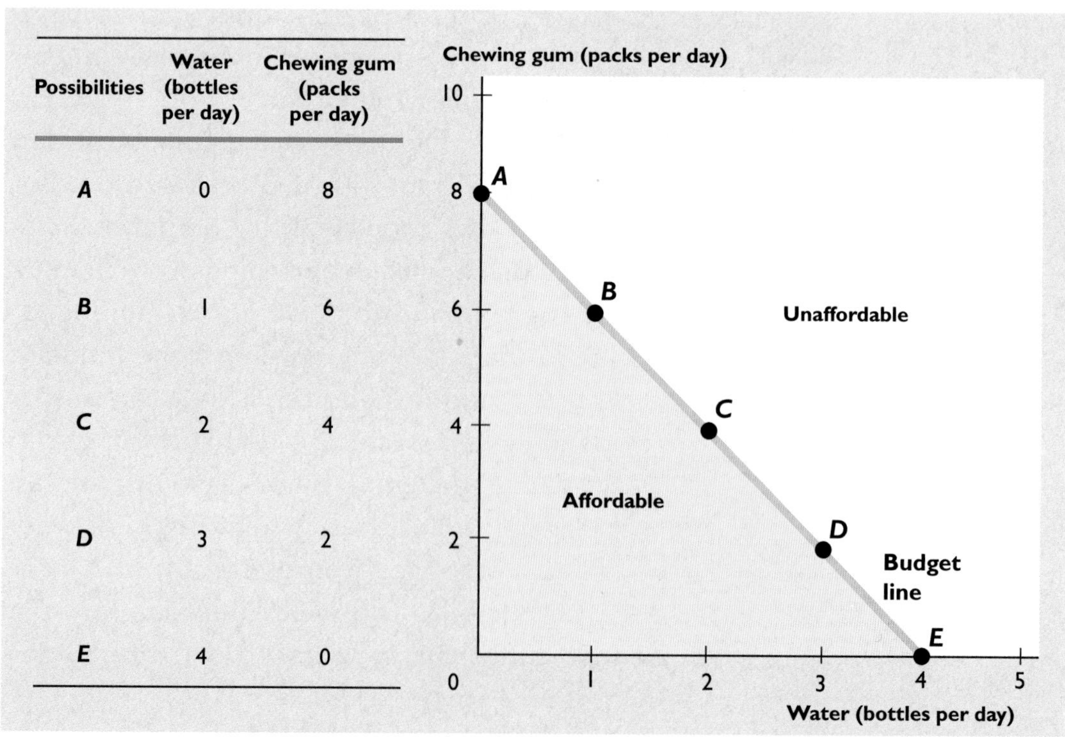

Possibilities	Water (bottles per day)	Chewing gum (packs per day)
A	0	8
B	1	6
C	2	4
D	3	2
E	4	0

Points *A* through *E* in the figure illustrate the possibilities in the table. The line passing through these points is Tina's budget line. Tina's budget line limits her choices. It marks the boundary between what she can and cannot afford. She can afford any combination on the budget line and inside it (in the orange area). She cannot afford any combination outside the budget line (in the white area).

Notice that the budget line in Figure 10.1 is similar to the *production possibilities frontier*, or *PPF*, in Chapter 3 (p. 57). Both curves show a limit to what is feasible. The *PPF* is a technological limit that does not depend on prices. But the budget line does depend on prices. Consumption possibilities change when prices or the available budget change. Let's see how Tina's consumption possibilities change when the price of water or gum changes or her budget changes.

Changes in Prices

If the price of one good rises when the prices of other goods and the budget remain the same, consumption possibilities shrink. If the price of one good falls when the prices of other goods and the budget remain the same, consumption possibilities expand. To see these changes in consumption possibilities, let's see what happens to Tina's budget line when the price of a bottle of water changes.

A Fall in the Price of Water

Figure 10.2 shows the effect on Tina's budget line of a fall in the price of bottled water from $1 to 50¢ when the price of gum and her budget remain unchanged. If Tina spends all her budget on bottled water, she can now afford 8 bottles a day.

FIGURE 10.2
A Fall in the Price of Water

*e*Foundations 10.1 

Possibilities	Water (bottles per day) $1 a bottle	Water (bottles per day) 50¢ a bottle	Chewing gum (packs per day)
A	0	0	8
B	1	2	6
C	2	4	4
D	3	6	2
E	4	8	0

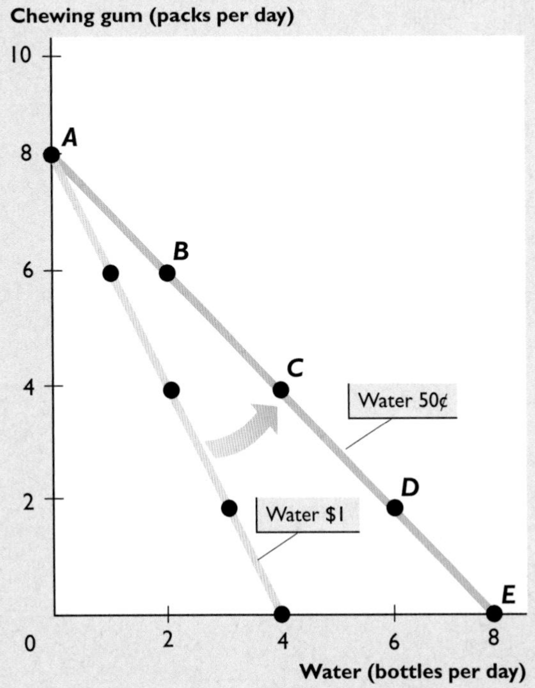

When the price of water falls from $1 a bottle to 50¢ a bottle, the budget line rotates outward and becomes less steep.

Her consumption possibilities have expanded. But because the price of gum is unchanged, if she spends all her budget on gum, she can still afford only 8 packs of gum a day. Her budget line has rotated outward.

A Rise in the Price of Water

Figure 10.3 shows the effect on Tina's budget line of a rise in the price of bottled water from \$1 to \$2 when the price of gum and her budget remain unchanged. If Tina spends all her budget on bottled water, she can now afford only 2 bottles a day. Tina's consumption possibilities have shrunk. But again, because the price of gum is unchanged, if Tina spends all her budget on gum, she can still afford 8 packs of gum a day. Her budget line has rotated inward.

Prices and the Slope of the Budget Line

Notice that when the price of bottled water changes and the price of gum remains unchanged, the slope of the budget line changes. In Figure 10.2, when the price of bottled water falls, the budget line becomes less steep. In Figure 10.3, when the price of bottled water rises, the budget line becomes steeper.

Recall that "slope equals rise over run." The rise is an *increase* in the quantity of gum, and the run is a *decrease* in the quantity of bottled water. The slope of the budget line is negative, which means that there is a tradeoff between the two goods. Along the budget line, consuming more of one good implies consuming less of the other good. The slope of the budget line is an *opportunity cost*. It is like the slope of the production possibilities frontier. It tells us what the consumer must give up to get one more unit of a good.

FIGURE 10.3
A Rise in the Price of Water

*e*Foundations **10.1** 

When the price of water rises from \$1 a bottle to \$2 a bottle, the budget line rotates inward and becomes steeper.

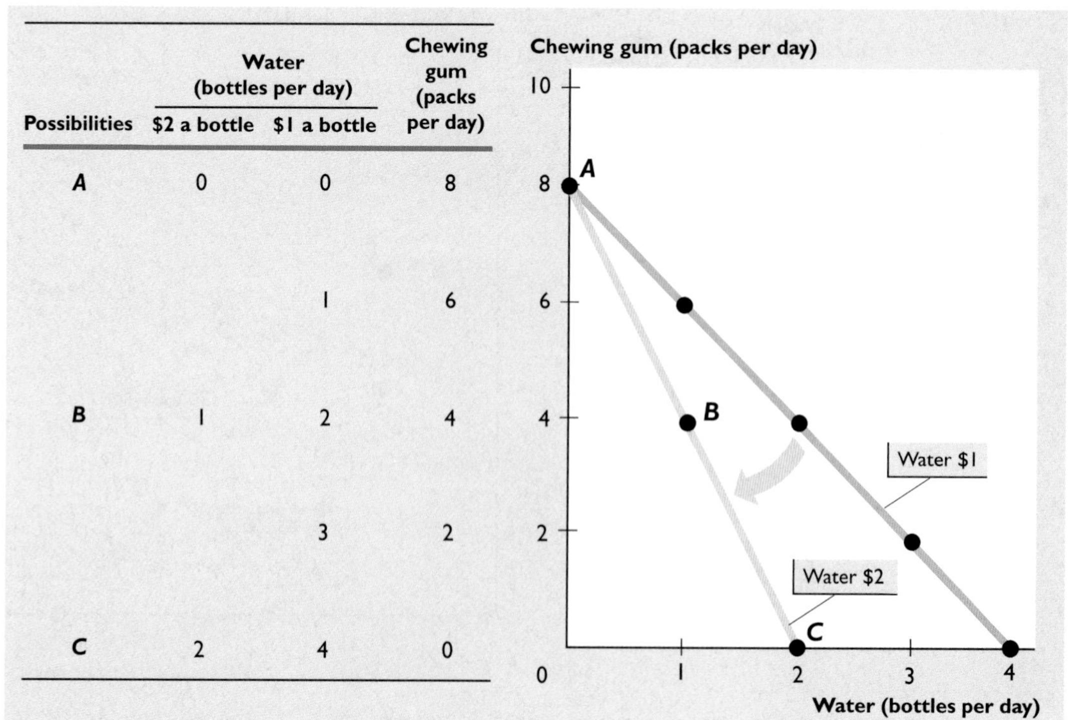

Possibilities	Water (bottles per day) \$2 a bottle	\$1 a bottle	Chewing gum (packs per day)
A	0	0	8
		1	6
B	1	2	4
		3	2
C	2	4	0

Let's calculate the slopes of the three budget lines in Figures 10.2 and 10.3.

- When the price of bottled water is \$1, the slope of the budget line is 8 packs of gum divided by 4 bottles of water, which equals 2 packs of gum per bottle.
- When the price of bottled water is 50¢, the slope of the budget line is 8 packs of gum divided by 8 bottles water, which equals 1 pack of gum per bottle.
- When the price of bottled water is \$2, the slope of the budget line is 8 packs of gum divided by 2 bottles of water, which equals 4 packs of gum per bottle.

Think about what these slopes mean as opportunity costs. When the price of water is \$1 a bottle and the price of gum is 50¢ a pack, it costs 2 packs of gum to buy a bottle of water. When the price of water is 50¢ a bottle and the price of gum is 50¢ pack, it costs 1 pack of gum to buy a bottle of water. And when the price of water is \$2 a bottle and the price of gum is 50¢ a pack, it costs 4 packs of gum to buy a bottle of water.

Another name for an opportunity cost is a relative price. A **relative price** is the price of one good in terms of another good. If the price of gum is 50¢ a pack and the price of water is \$1 a bottle, the relative price of bottled water is 2 packs per bottle. It is calculated as the price of water divided by the price of gum (\$1 a bottle ÷ 50¢ a pack = 2 packs per bottle).

Relative price
The price of one good in terms of another good—an opportunity cost. It equals the price of one good divided by the price of another good.

When the price of the good plotted on the x-axis falls, other things remaining the same, the budget line becomes less steep, and the opportunity cost and relative price of the good on the x-axis falls.

Eye On The U.S. ECONOMY

Relative Prices on the Move

Over a number of years, relative prices change a great deal. Some of the most dramatic changes occur in high-technology products such as computers. But many other relative prices change, and many fall.

The figure shows the price changes of 10 items that feature in most people's budgets between 1980 and 2000. Fruits and vegetables have had some of the largest relative price increases, along with housing.

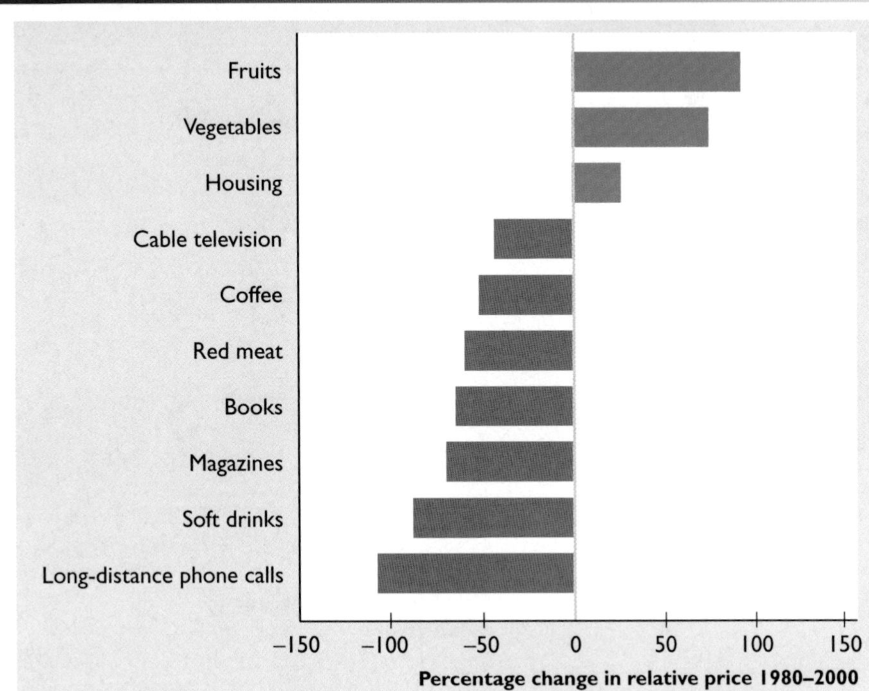

The largest relative price declines are in long-distance phone calls. But books, magazines, and a host of other items have relatively lower prices today than they did 20 years ago.

These changes in relative prices change people's budget lines and change the choices that they make.

A Change in the Budget

Figure 10.4 shows the effect of a change in Tina's budget on her consumption possibilities. When Tina's budget changes, the prices that she pays don't change. So the relative price of the items she buys doesn't change. But when her budget increases, her consumption possibilities expand, and her budget line shifts outward. When her budget decreases, her consumption possibilities shrink and her budget line shifts inward. Because prices don't change, the slope of the budget line does not change.

The initial budget line is the same one that we began with in Figure 10.1 when Tina's budget is $4. Suppose that on one day, Tina loses her purse that has $2 in it. On this day, she has only $2 to spend. Tina's new budget line in Figure 10.4 shows how much she can consume with a budget of $2. She can buy either 4 packs of gum and no bottled water or 2 bottles of water and no gum, or any other combinations on the $2 budget line.

Suppose that on another day, Tina sells an old CD for $2. On this day, she has $6 available and her budget line shifts rightward. She can now buy 12 packs of gum and no bottled water or 6 bottles of water and no gum or any other combination on the $6 budget line.

The three budget lines in Figure 10.4 have the same slope because the prices of the two goods have not changed; the relative price is the same on all three budget lines.

FIGURE 10.4
Changes in a Consumer's Budget

*e*Foundations **10.1** 

An increase in the budget shifts the budget line rightward, and a decrease in the budget shifts the budget line leftward. The slope of the budget line doesn't change because prices have not changed.

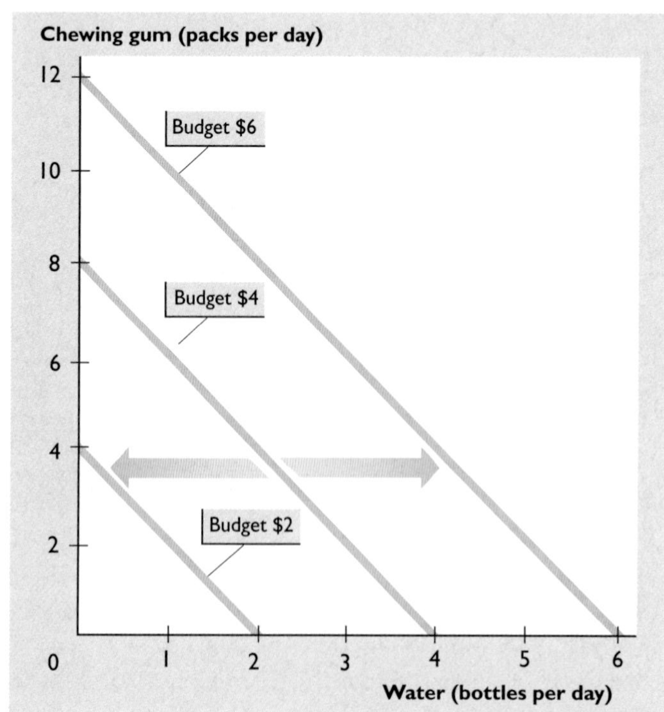

CHECKPOINT 10.1

1 Calculate and graph a budget line that shows the limits to a person's consumption possibilities.

Study Guide pp. 146–149
eFoundations 10.1

Practice Problem 10.1

Jerry's burger and magazine budget is \$12 a week. The price of a burger is \$2, and the price of a magazine is \$4.

a. List the combinations of burgers and magazines that Jerry can afford.
b. Draw a graph of Jerry's budget line with the quantity of burgers plotted on the x-axis.
c. What is the relative price of a magazine? Explain your answer.
d. Describe how the budget line in (b) changes if the following events occur one at a time and other things remain the same:
   - The price of a magazine falls.
   - The price of a burger rises.
   - Jerry's budget for burgers and magazines increases.

FIGURE 1

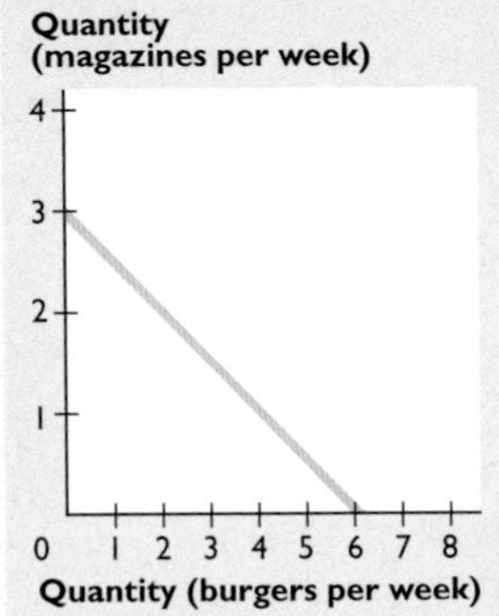

Exercise 10.1

Martha's cake and pasta budget is \$24 a week. The price of a cake is \$4, and the price of a dish of pasta is \$6.

a. List the combinations of cake and pasta that Martha can afford.
b. Draw a graph of Martha's budget line with pasta plotted on the x-axis.
c. If the price of a dish of pasta is halved, what is the change in the relative price of a cake? Explain your answer.
d. Describe how Martha's budget line in (b) changes if the following events occur one at a time and other things remain the same:
   - The price of a dish of pasta falls.
   - The price of a cake rises.
   - Martha's cake and pasta budget decreases.

FIGURE 2

Solution to Practice Problem 10.1

a. Jerry can afford the following combinations, all of which cost the \$12 in his budget: 3 magazines and no burgers; 2 magazines and 2 burgers; 1 magazine and 4 burgers; no magazines and 6 burgers.
b. The budget line is a straight line running from 3 magazines on the y-axis to 6 burgers on the x-axis (Figure 1).
c. The relative price of a magazine is the opportunity cost of a magazine—the number of burgers that Jerry must forgo to get 1 magazine. The relative price of a magazine also equals the price of a magazine divided by the price of a burger, which is \$4 per magazine ÷ \$2 per burger = 2 burgers per magazine.
d. With a lower price of a magazine, the number of magazines that Jerry can buy with \$12 increases. The budget line rotates outward (Figure 2).
   With a higher price of a burger, the number of burgers that Jerry can buy with \$12 decreases. The budget line rotates inward (Figure 2).
   With a bigger budget, Jerry can buy more of both magazines and burgers. The budget line shifts outward (Figure 3).

FIGURE 3

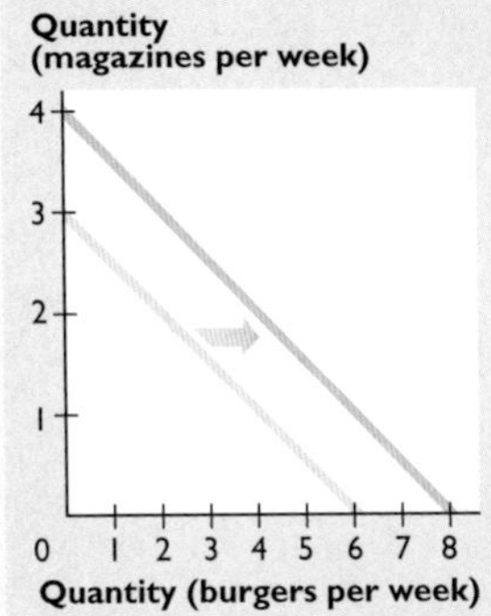

10.2 MARGINAL UTILITY THEORY

The budget line tells us about consumption *possibilities*, but it doesn't tell us a person's consumption *choice*. The quantities of goods and services that people choose depend on consumption possibilities and *preferences*. Economists use the concept of utility* to describe preferences. You are going to learn how economists use the concept of utility to explain the quantities that people choose to buy and predict how those quantities change when prices change. You will see how economists derive a consumer's demand curve from utility-maximizing choices.

Utility

Utility
The benefit or satisfaction that a person gets from the consumption of a good or service.

The benefit or satisfaction that a person gets from the consumption of a good or service is called **utility**. In everyday language, "utility" means "usefulness." In economics, it is an index of how much a person wants something. Utility is a bit like temperature. It is a useful but abstract concept measured in arbitrary units.

Temperature: An Analogy

You know when you feel hot, and you know when you feel cold. But you can't *observe* temperature itself. It is an abstract concept. You can observe water turning to steam if it is hot enough or turning to ice if it is cold enough. And you can use a thermometer to predict when such changes will occur.

The scale on the thermometer is what we call temperature. But the units in which we measure temperature are arbitrary. For example, we can accurately predict that when a Celsius thermometer shows a temperature of 0, water will turn to ice. But the units of measurement do not matter because this same event also occurs when a Fahrenheit thermometer shows a temperature of 32. Similarly, when a Celsius thermometer shows a temperature of 100, water will boil. But this same event also occurs when a Fahrenheit thermometer shows a temperature of 212.

The concept of utility helps us make predictions about consumption choices in much the same way that the concept of temperature helps us make predictions about physical phenomena. But marginal utility theory is not as precise as the theory that enables us to predict when water will turn to ice or steam. The main reason is that people's preferences sometimes change.

Let's now see how we can use the concept of utility to describe preferences.

Total Utility

Total utility
The total benefit that a person gets from the consumption of a good or service. Total utility generally increases as the quantity consumed of a good increases.

Total utility is the total benefit that a person gets from the consumption of a good or service. Total utility depends on the quantity of the good consumed—more consumption generally gives more total utility. Table 10.1 shows Tina's total utility from bottled water and chewing gum. If she consumes no bottled water and no gum, she gets no utility. If she consumes 1 bottle of water a day, she gets 15 units of utility. If she consumes 1 pack of gum a day, it provides her with 32 units of utility. As Tina increases the quantity of bottled water and packs of gum she consumes, her total utility from each increases.

*Economists also use an alternative method of describing preferences called indifference curves, which are described in the optional appendix to this chapter.

Tina's total utility numbers tell us that she gets a lot of pleasure from chewing gum. The first pack a day gives her more than twice the utility that her first bottle of water provides. But by the time Tina has consumed 7 packs of gum in a day, the 8th pack gives her no more utility. An 8th bottle of water, on the other hand, does increase her total utility.

Marginal Utility

Marginal utility is the change in total utility that results from a one-unit increase in the quantity of a good consumed. Table 10.1 shows the calculation of Tina's marginal utility from bottled water and chewing gum. Let's find Tina's marginal utility from a 3rd bottle of water a day (highlighted in the table). Her total utility from 3 bottles is 36 units, and her total utility from 2 bottles is 27 units. So for Tina, the marginal utility from drinking a 3rd bottle of water each day is:

Marginal utility
The change in total utility that results from a one-unit increase in the quantity of a good consumed.

Marginal utility of 3rd bottle = 36 units – 27 units = 9 units.

In the table, marginal utility appears midway between the quantities because the *change* in consumption produces the *marginal* utility. The table displays the marginal utility for each quantity of water and gum consumed.

Notice that Tina's marginal utility decreases as her consumption of water and gum increases. For example, her marginal utility from bottled water decreases from 15 units for the first bottle to 12 units from the second and 9 units from the third. Similarly, her marginal utility from chewing gum decreases from 32 units for the first pack to 16 units from the second and 8 units from the third. We call this decrease in marginal utility as the quantity of a good consumed increases the principle of **diminishing marginal utility**.

Diminishing marginal utility
The general tendency for marginal utility to decrease as the quantity of a good consumed increases.

To see why marginal utility diminishes, think about the following situations: In one, you've been studying all day and have had nothing to drink. Someone offers you a bottle of water. The marginal utility you get from that water is large—with Tina's numbers, it provides 15 units of utility. In the second situation, you've

TABLE 10.1
Tina's Total Utility and Marginal Utility

*e*Foundations 10.2 

Bottled water			Chewing gum		
Quantity (bottles per day)	Total utility	Marginal utility	Quantity (packs per day)	Total utility	Marginal utility
0	0		0	0	
		15			32
1	15		1	32	
		12			16
2	27		2	48	
		9			8
3	36		3	56	
		6			6
4	42		4	62	
		5			4
5	47		5	66	
		4			2
6	51		6	68	
		3			1
7	54		7	69	
		2			0
8	56		8	69	

been on a bottled water binge. You've drunk 7 bottles during the day. Now someone offers you another bottle of water, and you say thanks very much and sip it slowly. You enjoy the 8th bottle of the day, but the marginal utility from the 8th bottle is only 2 units.

Similarly, suppose you've been unable to buy a pack of gum for more than a day. A friend offers you a pack. Relief! You chew and receive 32 units of utility. On another day, you've chewed until your jaws ache and have gone through 7 packs. You're offered an 8th, and this time you say thanks very much but I'll pass on that one. You know that the 8th pack of gum would bring you no marginal utility.

For Tina, the marginal utility of gum diminishes more rapidly than does the marginal utility of bottled water.

We can illustrate the features of a consumer's preferences that we've just described with a total utility curve and a marginal utility curve. Figure 10.5 shows Tina's total utility and marginal utility from bottled water. You can see the principle of diminishing marginal utility in this figure. Part (a) shows us that as Tina drinks more bottled water, her total utility from it increases. It also shows that total utility increases at a decreasing rate. You can see diminishing marginal utility in part (a) because the step increases in utility get smaller as the quantity of water consumed increases.

Part (b) graphs Tina's marginal utility. Each of the steps in part (a) is placed side by side in part (b). We've enlarged the scale of the y-axis in part (b) to emphasize the diminishing marginal utility. The curve that passes through the midpoints of the bars in part (b) is Tina's marginal utility curve.

The numbers in Table 10.1 and the graphs in Figure 10.5 describe Tina's preferences and, along with her budget line, enable us to predict the choices that she makes. That is our next task.

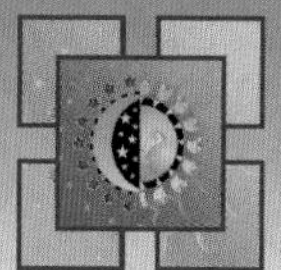

Eye On The PAST

Jeremy Bentham, William Stanley Jevons, and the Birth of Utility

The concept of utility was revolutionary when Jeremy Bentham (1748–1832) proposed it in the early 1800s. He used the idea to advance his then radical support for free education, free medical care, and social security. It took another fifty years before William Stanley Jevons (1835–1882) developed the concept of *marginal* utility and used it to predict people's consumption choices. Jevons's main claim to fame in his own day was his suggestion—wrong as it turned out—that sunspots cause business cycles. But his lasting legacy is the marginal utility theory that you're learning in this chapter.

FIGURE 10.5
Total Utility and Marginal Utility

*e*Foundations 10.2 

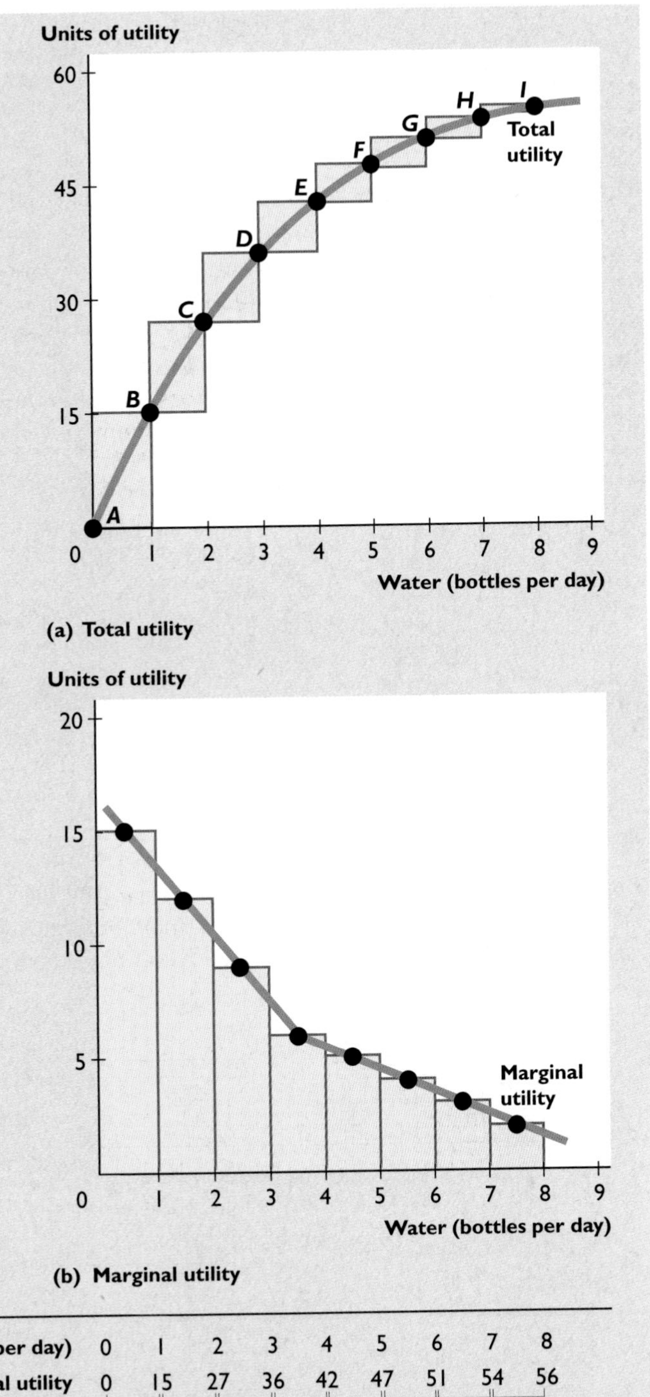

Water (bottles per day)	0	1	2	3	4	5	6	7	8
Total utility	0	15	27	36	42	47	51	54	56
Marginal utility	15	12	9	6	5	4	3	2	
	A	B	C	D	E	F	G	H	I

Part (a) graphs Tina's total utility from bottled water. It also shows as a bar the extra total utility she gains from each additional bottle of water—her marginal utility—as the steps along the total utility curve.

Part (b) shows how Tina's marginal utility from bottled water diminishes by placing the bars shown in part (a) side by side as a series of declining steps.

Maximizing Total Utility

Utility-maximizing rule
The rule that leads to the greatest total utility from all the goods and services consumed. The rule is:
1. Allocate the entire available budget.
2. Make the marginal utility per dollar spent the same for all goods.

The goal of a consumer is to allocate the available budget in a way that maximizes total utility. The consumer achieves this goal by choosing the point on the budget line at which the *sum* of the utilities obtained from all goods is as large as possible. This outcome occurs when a person follows the **utility-maximizing rule**:

1. Allocate the entire available budget.
2. Make the marginal utility per dollar spent the same for all goods.

Allocate the Available Budget

Because we face scarcity, we want more than we can afford. So we use the entire available budget. Using the entire budget doesn't mean not saving anything. The available budget is the amount available after choosing how much to save, and in Tina's case, after deciding how much to spend on some other goods. The principles that you are learning here apply to the choice of how much of total income to save and spend on other goods just as they apply to the choice of how to allocate the currently available budget between chewing gum and water.

Equalize the Marginal Utility Per Dollar Spent

Spending the entire available budget doesn't automatically maximize utility. The budget might be spent in the wrong way. Making the marginal utility per dollar spent the same for all goods gets the most out of a budget. To see why, let's look at Tina's choice between water and gum.

Tina's Utility-Maximizing Choice We're going to see how the utility-maximizing rule works for Tina as she allocates $4 a day between bottled water and chewing gum when the price of water is $1 a bottle and the price of gum is 50¢ a pack.

The first step is to make a table in which each row shows a combination of water and gum that costs $4. Table 10.2 shows such a table.

Notice that as we move down the rows of the table, the quantities of bottled water and the expenditure on water increase and the quantities of chewing gum and the expenditure on chewing gum decrease. The reason is that the quantities in each row describe one point that is on Tina's budget line (in Figure 10.1), which means that she can just afford to buy each combination. For example, if she buys 1

TABLE 10.2
Tina's Affordable Combinations of Water and Gum

*e*Foundations **10.2** 

	Quantity of water (bottles per day)	Quantity of gum (packs per day)	Expenditure on water at $1 per bottle	Expenditure on gum at 50¢ per pack	Total expenditure
			(dollars per day)		
A	0	8	0	4	4
B	1	6	1	3	4
C	2	4	2	2	4
D	3	2	3	1	4
E	4	0	4	0	4

bottle of water and 6 packs of gum (row *B*), she spends $1 on water and $3 on gum, and her total expenditure equals her entire $4 budget.

Marginal Utility per Dollar Spent The **marginal utility per dollar spent** is the increase in total utility that comes from the last dollar spent on a good. We calculate marginal utility per dollar spent by dividing the marginal utility from a good by the price of the good. For example, if Tina buys 1 bottle of water a day, her marginal utility from the 1 bottle of water is 15 units. The price of bottled water is $1, so the marginal utility per dollar spent on bottled water is 15 units divided by $1, which equals 15 units of utility per dollar. Similarly, if Tina buys 1 pack of gum a day, her marginal utility from the 1 pack is 32 units. The price of a pack of gum is 50¢, so the marginal utility per dollar spent on gum is 32 units divided by 50¢, which equals 64 units of utility per dollar.

Marginal utility per dollar spent
The increase in total utility that comes from the last dollar spent on a good.

Table 10.3 shows Tina's marginal utility per dollar spent for bottled water and gum for all the affordable combinations in Table 10.2. Table 10.3 also shows the marginal utilities of gum for quantities between the affordable combinations.

Suppose that Tina spends all her budget on water—she is on row *E* of Table 10.4. She has 15 units of utility from the first bottle, 12 from the second, 9 from the third, and 6 from the fourth. Her total utility is 15 + 12 + 9 + 6 = 42 units. The utility that she gets from the last dollar spent on water—her marginal utility per dollar spent on water—is 6 units.

Now suppose that she decreases her consumption of water by 1 bottle a day and buys 2 packs of gum. She moves from row *E* to row *D* of Table 10.3. Her utility from water decreases by 6 units. But her utility from gum increases. She gains 32 units of utility from the first pack of gum and 16 units from the second. So the utility gain from gum (16 units) exceeds the utility loss from water (6 units). When Tina consumes 2 packs of gum a day, her marginal utility from gum is 16 units. The price of gum is 50¢ a pack, so her marginal utility per dollar spent on gum is 16 units ÷ 50¢ = 32 units per dollar. Her marginal utility from the third bottle of water is 9 units. The price of water is $1 a bottle, so the marginal utility per dollar spent on water is 9. That is, when Tina buys 3 bottles of water and 2 packs of gum (row *D*), the marginal utility per dollar spent on water (9) is less than the marginal utility per dollar spent on gum (32).

TABLE 10.3
Tina's Marginal Utilities per Dollar Spent

*e*Foundations **10.2** 

	Bottled water			Chewing gum		
	Quantity (bottles per day)	**Marginal utility**	**Marginal utility per dollar spent**	**Quantity (packs per day**	**Marginal utility**	**Marginal utility per dollar spent**
A	0			8	0	0
				7	1	2
B	1	15	15	6	2	4
				5	4	8
C	2	12	12	4	6	12
				3	8	16
D	3	9	9	2	16	32
				1	32	64
E	4	6	6	0		

Suppose that Tina decreases her consumption of water by another bottle a day to 2 bottles and spends an additional dollar on gum, taking her consumption of gum to 4 packs a day. She moves from row *D* to row *C* of Table 10.3. Tina's total utility from water decreases by 9 units. But she gains more than 9 units of utility from gum. Her marginal utility from the 3rd pack of gum is 8 units, and her marginal utility from the 4th pack is 6 units. So her total utility from gum increases by 14 units. When Tina consumes 4 packs of gum a day, her marginal utility from gum is 6 units. The price of gum is 50¢ a pack, so her marginal utility per dollar spent on gum is 6 units ÷ 50¢ = 12 units per dollar. Her marginal utility from the second bottle of water is 12 units. The price of water is $1 a bottle, so the marginal utility per dollar spent on water is 12. When Tina consumes 2 bottles of water and 4 packs of gum a day, on row *C*, her marginal utility per dollar spent is equal for the two goods.

As we've increased Tina's consumption of gum and decreased her consumption of water, her total utility has increased. But we have now reached the point at which Tina has allocated her budget in the best possible way. She cannot obtain more total utility than she has in this situation because her marginal utility per dollar spent is equal for water and gum. If she now buys less water and more gum, her total utility will decrease.

To be convinced of this fact, suppose that she decreases her consumption of water by 1 more bottle and spends an additional dollar on gum, taking her consumption of gum to 6 packs a day. She moves from row *C* to row *B* of Table 10.3. Tina now loses 12 units of utility from water. She gains less than 12 units from gum. Her marginal utility from the 5th pack of gum is 4 units, and her marginal utility from the 6th pack is 2 units. So her total utility from gum increases by only 6 units while her total utility from water decreases by 12 units. When Tina consumes 1 bottle of water and 6 packs of gum a day on row *B*, her marginal utility per dollar spent on water is 15 and her marginal utility per dollar spent on gum is 4.

So if Tina buys 2 bottles of water and 4 packs of gum (row *C* of Table 10.3), her marginal utility per dollar spent is equal for both goods and her total utility is maximized.

Units of Utility

In calculating Tina's utility-maximizing choice in Table 10.3, we have not used the concept of *total* utility. All our calculations use *marginal utility* and *price*. By making the marginal utility per dollar spent equal for both goods, we know that Tina maximizes her total utility.

This way of viewing maximum utility is important: it means that the units in which utility is measured do not matter. We could double or halve all the numbers measuring utility, or multiply them by any other positive number, or square them, or take their square roots. None of these changes in the units used to measure utility makes any difference to the outcome. Just as changing from degrees Celsius to degrees Fahrenheit doesn't affect a prediction about the freezing point of water, so changing the units of utility doesn't affect our prediction about the consumption choice that maximizes total utility.

Finding the Demand Curve

We can use marginal utility theory to find a demand schedule and demand curve. In fact, we've just found one entry in Tina's demand schedule and one point on her demand curve for bottled water. When the price of bottled water is $1 (and the price of gum is 50¢ and her budget is $4 a day), the quantity of water that Tina buys is 2 bottles a day. Figure 10.6 records this outcome as row *A* on Tina's demand schedule and point *A* on her demand curve.

Let's find the second point, *B*, which shows the quantity of water Tina buys when the price of water falls to 50¢ a bottle and other things remain the same. The table in Figure 10.6 shows Tina's new affordable combinations and marginal utilities per dollar spent.

You can tell right away that Tina will increase her consumption of bottled water. Why? Because at her current consumption levels, the marginal utility per dollar spent on bottled water now exceeds the marginal utility per dollar spent on gum. In fact, the marginal utility per dollar spent on bottled water at each quantity has doubled because the price of bottled water has halved. Also, with a lower price of bottled water, Tina can afford to consume more bottled water each day.

If Tina continued to consume 2 bottles of water and 4 packs of gum, her marginal utility per dollar spent on bottled water would be 24, which is twice the marginal utility per dollar spent on gum. Also, Tina would be spending only $3, so she would have another $1 available. Suppose that she spent the spare $1 on bottled water. She would then be consuming 4 bottles of water a day.

FIGURE 10.6

Tina's Demand for Bottled Water

*e*Foundations **10.2** 

	Bottled water		Chewing gum	
	Quantity (bottles per day)	Marginal utility per dollar spent	Quantity (packs per day)	Marginal utility per dollar spent
A	0		8	0
B	1	30	7	2
C	2	24	6	4
D	3	18	5	8
E	4	12	4	12
F	5	10	3	16
G	6	8	2	32
H	7	6	1	64
I	8	4	0	

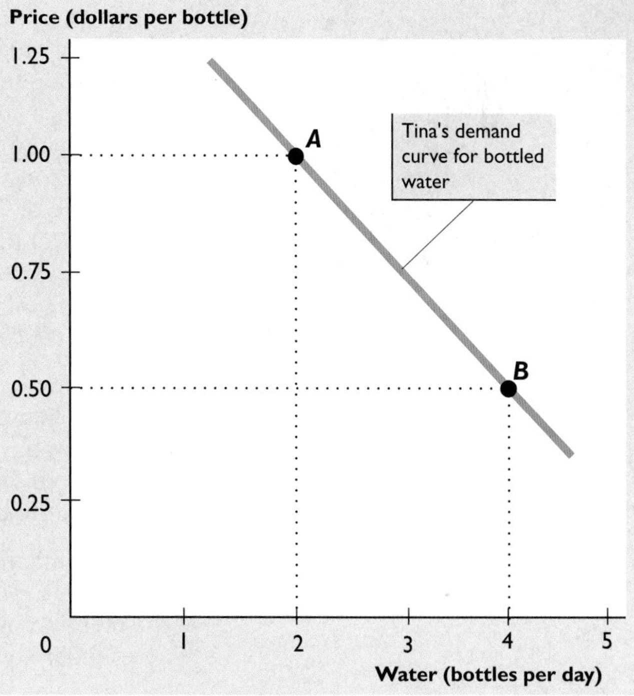

When the price of water is $1 a bottle (and her budget is $4 and the price of a pack of gum is 50¢), Tina buys 2 bottles of water and 4 packs of gum a day. She is at point *A* on her demand curve for water.

When the price of water falls to 50¢ (and other things remain the same), Tina buys 4 bottles of water and 4 packs of gum a day and moves to point *B* on her demand curve for bottled water.

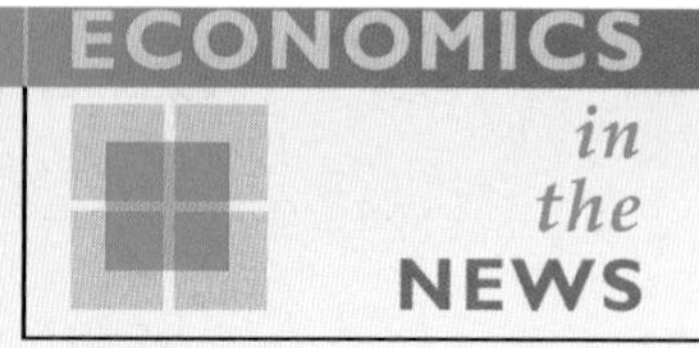

February 20, 1999

Coca-Cola Sells Bottled Water in the United States

Water. It's the real thing. Coca-Cola Company began selling bottled water in the United States in 1999.

It is called ***Dasani***....

THE DETROIT NEWS

Questions

1. Why do you think Coca-Cola Company entered the bottled water market?

2. Use marginal utility theory to explain why the demand for bottled water increased during the 1990s.

 *e*Foundations **10.2**

Her marginal utility per dollar spent on bottled water would now be 12. You can see this number on row *E* of the table in Figure 10.6. But the marginal utility per dollar that Tina gets from gum is 12. So Tina now maximizes her total utility by consuming 4 bottles of water and 4 packs of gum. You've now found a second point on Tina's demand curve for bottled water: When the price of bottled water is 50¢ (other things remaining the same), Tina buys 4 bottles of water a day.

In this example, Tina increases the quantity of water consumed and does not change her consumption of gum. This outcome is special to this numerical example and doesn't usually happen. With different marginal utility numbers, when the price of water falls, Tina might increase or decrease her consumption of gum, but she will increase her consumption of water because marginal utility of water diminishes.

Marginal Utility and the Elasticity of Demand

You saw in Chapter 5 that the demand for some goods is elastic and the demand for other goods is inelastic. Demand is elastic when the percentage change in the quantity demanded exceeds the percentage change in price. Demand is inelastic when the percentage change in the quantity demanded is less than the percentage change in price.

The price elasticity of demand is related to marginal utility. If, as the quantity consumed of a good increases, marginal utility decreases quickly, the demand for the good is inelastic. The reason is that for a given change in the price, only a small change in the quantity consumed of the good is needed to bring its marginal utility per dollar spent back to equality with that on all the other items in the consumer's budget.

But if, as the quantity consumed of a good increases, marginal utility decreases slowly, the demand for that good is elastic. In this case, for a given change in the price, a large change in the quantity consumed of the good is needed to bring its marginal utility per dollar spent back to equality with that on all the other items in the consumer's budget.

In the example of Tina's demand for bottled water, we fixed the numbers to make her elasticity of demand special. Can you work out what it is? (Hint: Use the total revenue test described on p. 116.)

The Power of Marginal Analysis

The method that we've used to find Tina's utility-maximizing choice of bottled water and gum is an example of the power of marginal analysis. By comparing the marginal gain from having more of one good with the marginal loss from having less of another good, Tina gets the maximum attainable utility.

The rule to follow is simple:

- If the marginal utility per dollar spent on water exceeds the marginal utility per dollar spent on gum, buy more water and less gum;
- If the marginal utility per dollar spent on gum exceeds the marginal utility per dollar spent on water, buy more gum and less water.

More generally, if the marginal gain from an action exceeds the marginal loss, take the action. You have met this principle before, and you will meet it time and again in your study of economics. Soon, you will find yourself using it when you make your own choices, especially when you must make a big decision.

CHECKPOINT 10.2

2 Explain marginal utility theory and use it to derive a consumer's demand curve.

Study Guide pp. 149–153 

*e*Foundations 10.2 

Practice Problem 10.2

Table 1 shows Jerry's total utility from burgers and magazines.

a. Calculate Jerry's marginal utility from the second burger in the week.
b. If the price of a burger is $2, calculate the marginal utility per dollar spent on burgers when Jerry buys 2 burgers a week.
c. Calculate Jerry's marginal utility from the second magazine in the week.
d. If the price of a magazine is $4, calculate the marginal utility per dollar spent on magazines when Jerry buys 2 magazines.
e. When the price of a burger is $2, the price of a magazine is $4, and Jerry has $12 a week to spend, Jerry buys 2 burgers and 2 magazines. Does he maximize his total utility? Explain your answer.

TABLE 1

Burgers		Magazines	
Quantity per week	Total utility	Quantity per week	Total utility
0	0	0	0
1	14	1	100
2	24	2	120
3	32	3	134
4	38	4	144

Exercise 10.2

Table 2 shows Wendy's total utility from tacos and movies. The price of a taco is $2, the price of a movie is $8, and Wendy has $22 a week to spend on tacos and movies.

a. Calculate Wendy's marginal utility from the third movie in the week.
b. Calculate the marginal utility per dollar spent on movies when Wendy sees 3 movies a week.
c. Calculate Wendy's marginal utility from the fourth taco in the week.
d. Calculate the marginal utility per dollar spent on tacos when Wendy buys 2 tacos a week.
e. If Wendy sees 2 movies and buys 2 tacos a week, is she maximizing total utility? Explain your answer. If Wendy is not maximizing total utility, explain how she would adjust her consumption choice to do so.

TABLE 2

Tacos		Movies	
Quantity per week	Total utility	Quantity per week	Total utility
0	0	0	0
1	11	1	32
2	20	2	60
3	27	3	84
4	30	4	104
5	31	5	120
6	31	6	132

Solution to Practice Problem 10.2

a. The marginal utility from the second burger equals the total utility from 2 burgers minus the total utility from 1 burger and is 24 – 14 = 10 units of utility.
b. The marginal utility per dollar spent on burgers when Jerry buys 2 burgers equals the marginal utility of the second burger (10) divided by the price of a burger ($2), which equals 5.
c. The marginal utility from the second magazine equals the total utility from 2 magazines minus the total utility from 1 magazine and is 120 – 100 = 20 units.
d. The marginal utility per dollar spent on magazines when Jerry buys 2 magazines equals the marginal utility of the second magazine (20) divided by the price of a magazine ($4), which equals 5.
e. When a burger costs $4 and a magazine costs $8, Jerry buys 2 burgers and 2 magazines. Jerry has $12 to spend, so he spends his entire budget. The marginal utility per dollar spent on burgers (5, answer **b**) equals marginal utility per dollar spent on magazines (5, answer **d**), so Jerry maximizes his total utility.

10.3 EFFICIENCY, PRICE, AND VALUE

Marginal utility theory helps us to deepen our understanding of the concept of efficiency and to see more clearly the distinction between *value* and *price*. Let's see how.

Consumer Efficiency

When Tina allocates her limited budget to maximize total utility, she is using her resources efficiently. Any other allocation of her budget would leave her able to attain a higher level of total utility.

But when Tina has allocated her budget to maximize total utility, she is *on* her demand curve for each good. A demand curve describes the quantity demanded at each price *when total utility is maximized*. When we studied efficiency in Chapter 6, we learned that a demand curve is also a willingness-to-pay curve. It tells us a consumer's *marginal benefit*—the benefit from consuming an additional unit of a good. You can now give the idea of marginal benefit a deeper meaning.

Marginal benefit is the maximum price a consumer is willing to pay for an extra unit of a good or service when total utility is maximized.

The Paradox of Value

For centuries, philosophers were puzzled by the paradox of value. Water is more valuable than a diamond because water is essential to life itself. Yet water is much cheaper than a diamond. Why? Adam Smith tried to solve this paradox, but it was not until marginal utility theory had been developed that anyone could give a satisfactory answer.

You can solve this puzzle by distinguishing between *total* utility and *marginal* utility. Total utility tells us about relative value; marginal utility tells us about relative price. The total utility from water is enormous. But remember, the more we consume of something, the smaller is its marginal utility. We use so much water that its marginal utility—the benefit we get from one more glass of water—diminishes to a small value. Diamonds, on the other hand, have a small total utility relative to water, but because we buy few diamonds, they have a large marginal utility. When a household has maximized its total utility, it has allocated its budget so that the marginal utility per dollar spent is equal for all goods. Diamonds have a high price and a high marginal utility. Water has a low price and a low marginal utility. When the high marginal utility of diamonds is divided by the high price of a diamond, the result is a number that equals the low marginal utility of water divided by the low price of water. The marginal utility per dollar spent is the same for diamonds as for water.

Consumer Surplus

Consumer surplus measures value in excess of the amount paid. In Figure 10.7, the demand for and supply of water (part a) determine the price of water P_W and the quantity of water consumed Q_W. The demand for and supply of diamonds (part b) determine the price of a diamond P_D and the quantity of diamonds Q_D. Water is cheap but provides a large consumer surplus, while diamonds are expensive but provide a small consumer surplus.

FIGURE 10.7
The Paradox of Value

*e*Foundations **10.3** 

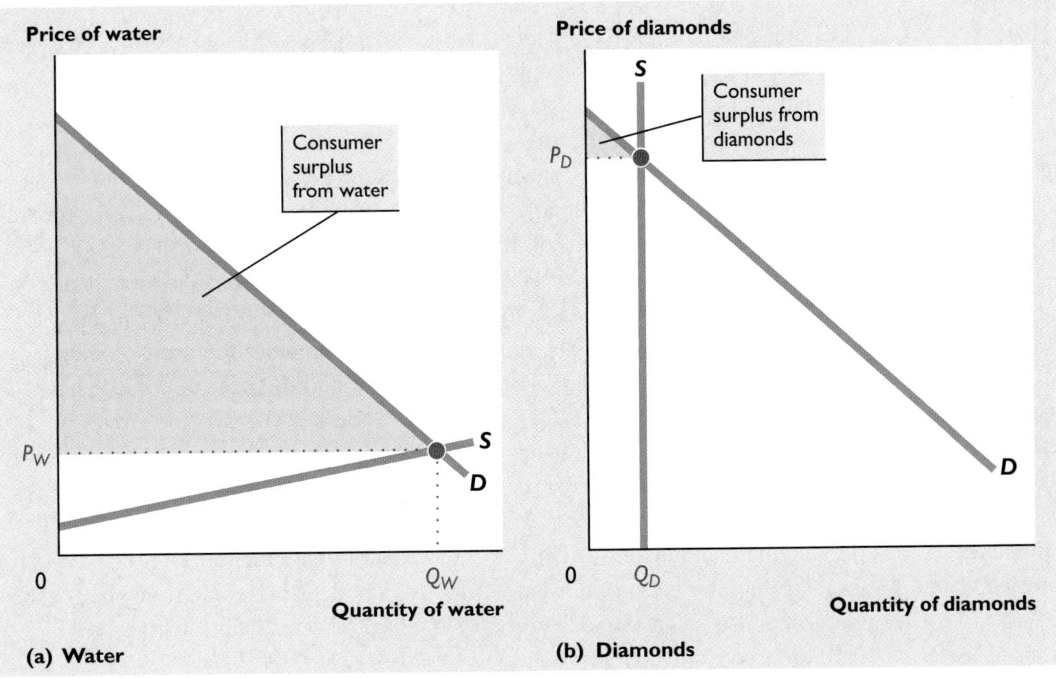

Part (a) shows the demand for water, *D*, and the supply of water, *S*. Demand and supply determine the price of water at P_W and the quantity at Q_W. The consumer surplus from water is the large green triangle.

Part (b) shows the demand for diamonds, *D*, and the supply of diamonds, *S*. Demand and supply determine the price of a diamond at P_D and the quantity at Q_D. The consumer surplus from diamonds is the small green triangle.

Water is valuable—has a large consumer surplus—but cheap. Diamonds are less valuable than water—have a smaller consumer surplus—but are expensive.

CHECKPOINT 10.3

3 **Use marginal utility theory to explain the paradox of value: Why water is vital but cheap while diamonds are relatively useless but expensive.**

Study Guide pp. 153–155
*e*Foundations **10.3** 

Practice Problem 10.3

Tony rents 500 videos a year at $3 each and buys 10,000 gallons of tap water a year, for which he pays $50. Tony is maximizing total utility. If Tony's marginal utility from water is 0.5 unit per gallon, what is his marginal utility from a video rental? Which good is the more valuable to Tony: water or videos? Why?

Exercise 10.3

Which good is more valuable to you: water or your economics text?

Solution to Practice Problem 10.3

Marginal utility per dollar spent is the same for video rentals and water. Marginal utility of a video divided by $3 equals the marginal utility of water divided by 0.5¢. So the marginal utility of a video equals 600 times the marginal utility of a gallon of water, which is $600 \times 0.5 = 300$ units.

Water most likely generates more total utility for Tony, but videos generate more marginal utility.

Rational Choices in Beverage Markets

Bottled water sales grew from $2.65 billion in 1990 to $4.3 billion in 1998. They grew by almost 10 percent during 1998. Soda sales were much greater, at $56.3 billion in 1998, but they grew by only 3 percent during the year.

PepsiCo (makers of Pepsi-Cola) started selling bottled water in 1993 and became the market leader. Coca-Cola Company, which traditionally tried to encourage people to drink Coke, Sprite, and its other sodas, entered the sports drink market some years ago and the bottled water market in 1999.

Consumption patterns change over time, and the figure shows some trends in the consumption of beverages in the United States during the 1990s. The quantities of bottled water and soda consumed have increased. The quantities of coffee and beer consumed have decreased. You can understand these trends by using marginal utility theory.

People receive utility from consuming bottled water, soda, coffee, and beer. To maximize total utility, people make the marginal utility per dollar spent equal for all goods. So people consume bottled water, soda, coffee, and beer in quantities that make the marginal utilities per dollar spent on all of them equal, as shown by the equation at the bottom of the page.

If the price of a good rises, other things remaining the same, the marginal utility of that good must increase to maintain maximum possible utility. But marginal utility increases as the quantity consumed of the good decreases. So other things remaining the same, when the price of a good rises, the quantity consumed of that good decreases. If changes in prices explain the consumption trends in the figure, then it must be that the prices of water and soda have fallen relative to the prices of beer and coffee.

The price of bottled water has fallen as high-cost spring water has been replaced with lower-cost water purified by reverse osmosis and carbon filtering. The price of bottled water has also fallen as more firms have entered the water market.

Similarly, the price of soda has fallen as more firms have entered the soda market and generic sodas have taken off.

The price of coffee increased through the 1990s because of low crop yields in some growing regions (Brazil experienced a very severe frost and drought in 1994) and because of export restrictions by major producers.

The true price of beer, or opportunity cost of beer, also increased. The money price of beer didn't change much, but improved policing and stiffer penalties for drunk driving have increased the cost of drinking beer.

You can see that the trends in what people drink can be understood as the responses to changes in prices. The trends are not a mystery or a social phenomenon. They are the consequences of people trying to get the highest value from their scarce resources.

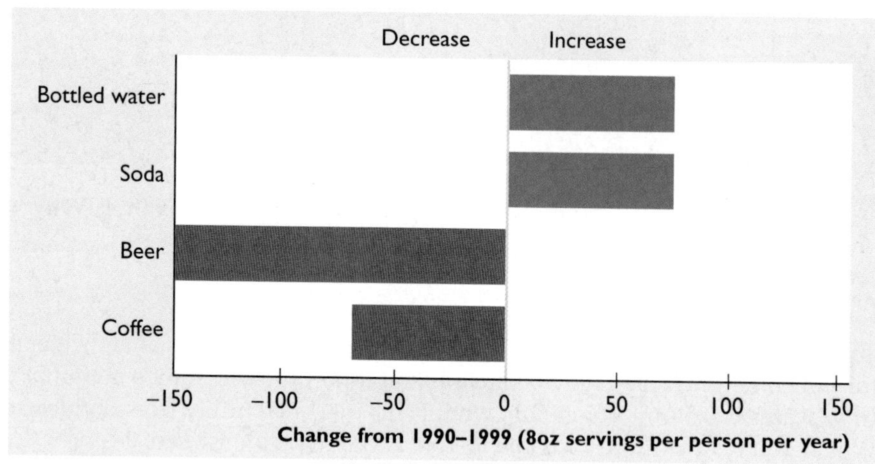

SOURCE: *Detroit News.*

$$\frac{MU_{water}}{P_{water}} = \frac{MU_{soda}}{P_{soda}} = \frac{MU_{coffee}}{P_{coffee}} = \frac{MU_{beer}}{P_{beer}}$$

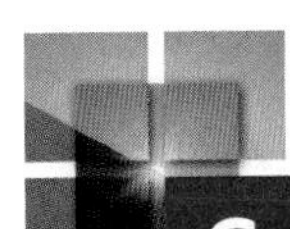

CHAPTER CHECKPOINT

Key Points

1 Calculate and graph a budget line that shows the limits to a person's consumption possibilities.

- Consumption possibilities and preferences determine consumption choices.
- Consumption possibilities are constrained by the budget and prices. Some combinations of goods are affordable, and some are not affordable.
- The budget line is the boundary between what a person can and cannot afford with a given budget and given prices.
- The slope of the budget line determines the relative price of the good measured on the x-axis in terms of the good measured on the y-axis.
- A change in one price changes the slope of the budget line. A change in the budget shifts the budget line but does not change its slope.

2 Explain marginal utility theory and use it to derive a consumer's demand curve.

- Total utility is maximized when the entire budget is spent and marginal utility per dollar spent is equal for all goods.
- If the marginal utility per dollar spent on good *A* exceeds that on good *B*, total utility increases if the quantity purchased of good *A* increases and the quantity purchased of good *B* decreases.
- Diminishing marginal utility theory implies the law of demand. That is, other things remaining the same, the higher the price of a good, the smaller is the quantity demanded of that good.

3 Use marginal utility theory to explain the paradox of value: Why water is vital but cheap while diamonds are relatively useless but expensive.

- When consumers maximize total utility, they use resources efficiently.
- Marginal utility theory resolves the paradox of value.
- When we talk loosely about value, we are thinking of *total* utility or consumer surplus. But price is related to *marginal* utility.
- Water, which we consume in large amounts, has a high total utility and a large consumer surplus but a low price and low marginal utility.
- Diamonds, which we consume in small amounts, have a low total utility and a small consumer surplus but a high price and a high marginal utility.

Key Terms

Budget line, 230
Diminishing marginal utility, 237
Marginal utility, 237
Marginal utility per dollar spent, 241
Relative price, 233
Total utility, 236
Utility, 236
Utility-maximizing rule, 240

Exercises

1. Use the numbers in Table 10.1 on p. 237 to make graphs of Tina's total utility and marginal utility from chewing gum.
   - **a.** Compare Tina's marginal utility from chewing gum with that from bottled water. Which marginal utility diminishes more rapidly?
   - **b.** On the basis of her marginal utility for bottled water (shown in Figure 10.5 on p. 239) and her marginal utility for chewing gum, is Tina's demand for chewing gum more elastic or less elastic than her demand for bottled water?
   - **c.** If Tina's budget increases, which good will she buy more of: bottled water or chewing gum? Why?
   - **d.** If Tina's budget increases and, at the same time, the price of a bottle of water rises, what can you say about how Tina's consumption of bottled water and chewing gum will change?

TABLE 1

Cake		Pasta	
Quantity per week	Total utility	Dishes per week	Total utility
0	0	0	0
1	10	1	20
2	18	2	36
3	25	3	48
4	31	4	56
5	36	5	60
6	40	6	60

2. Table 1 shows Martha's total utility from cakes and pasta.
   - **a.** Calculate Martha's total utility when she buys 4 cakes and 1 dish of pasta a week.
   - **b.** Calculate Martha's marginal utility from the third cake in the week.
   - **c.** If the price of a cake is $4 and Martha buys 3 cakes a week, calculate the marginal utility per dollar spent on cake.
   - **d.** Calculate Martha's marginal utility from the second dish of pasta in the week.
   - **e.** If the price of pasta is $8 a dish and Martha buys 2 dishes a week, calculate the marginal utility per dollar spent on pasta.
   - **f.** When the price of cake is $4, the price of pasta is $8 a dish, and Martha has $24 a week to spend, she buys 2 cakes and 2 dishes of pasta. Does she maximize her total utility? Explain your answer.
3. Use the information in Table 1 to answer the following questions:
   - **a.** When the price of a cake is $4, Martha has $24 to spend, and the price of pasta falls from $8 to $4, what quantities of cake and pasta does Martha buy?
   - **b.** What are two points on Martha's demand curve for pasta?
   - **c.** Is Martha's demand for pasta elastic or inelastic?
   - **d.** When the price of a cake is $4, the price of pasta is $8 a dish, and Martha's available budget increases to $40 a week, what quantities of cake and pasta does Martha buy?
4. Tim buys 2 cans of cola and 1 pizza when he has $6 to spend on lunch, cola is $1 a can, and pizzas $4 each.
   - **a.** What is the relative price of a pizza?
   - **b.** If the price of a pizza falls to $2:
     - **i.** How will Tim's consumption possibilities change? Explain.
     - **ii.** Will Tim change what he has for lunch? Explain your answer.
     - **iii.** How will the fall in the price of pizza affect Tim's consumption of pizza?
5. Every day, Josie buys 2 cups of coffee and 1 sandwich for lunch. The price of a cup of coffee is $3, and the price of a sandwich is $5. Josie's choice of lunch is a rational choice, and she spends only $11 on lunch.
   - **a.** Compare Josie's marginal utility from coffee with her marginal utility from the sandwich.
   - **b.** Is Josie's allocation of her $11 efficient? Explain.

APPENDIX: INDIFFERENCE CURVES

You are going to discover a neat idea—that of drawing a map of a person's preferences. A preference map is based on the intuitively appealing assumption that people can sort all the possible combinations of goods into three groups: preferred, not preferred, and indifferent. To make this idea concrete, let's ask Tina to tell us how she ranks combinations of bottled water and chewing gum.

An Indifference Curve

Figure A10.1(a) shows part of Tina's answer. She tells us that she currently consumes 2 bottles of water and 2 packs of gum a day at point C. She then lists all the combinations of bottled water and chewing gum that she says are as acceptable to her as her current consumption. When we plot these combinations of water and gum, we get the green curve. This curve is the key element in a map of preferences and is called an indifference curve.

An **indifference curve** is a line that shows combinations of goods among which a consumer is *indifferent*. The indifference curve in Figure A10.1(a) tells us that Tina is just as happy to consume 2 bottles of water and 4 packs of gum a day at point *C* as to consume the combination of water and gum at any other point along the indifference curve. Tina also says that she prefers all the combinations of bottled water and gum above the indifference curve—the yellow area—to those on the indifference curve. These combinations contain more water, more gum, or more of both. She also prefers any combination on the indifference curve to any combination in the gray area below the indifference curve. These combinations contain less water, less gum, or less of both.

Indifference curve
A line that shows combinations of goods among which a consumer is indifferent.

FIGURE A10.1
A Preference Map

*e*Foundations **A10.1** 

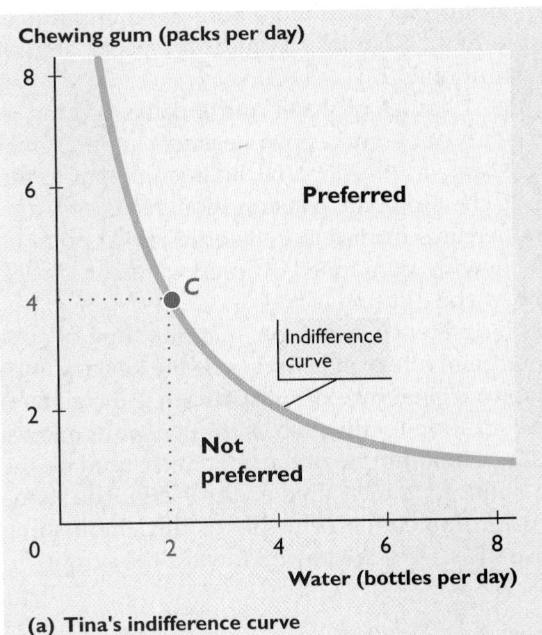

(a) Tina's indifference curve

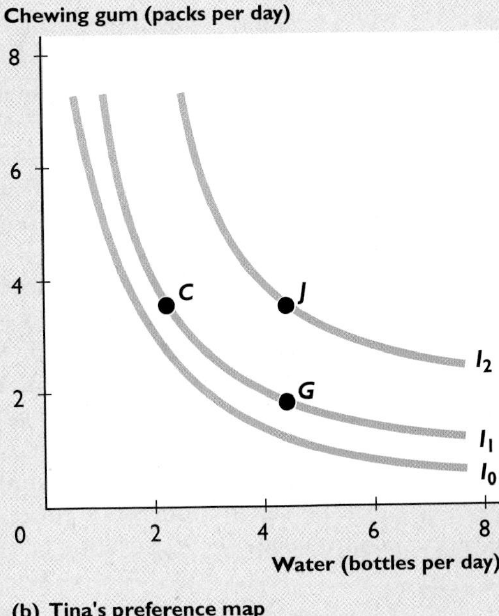

(b) Tina's preference map

In part (a), Tina consumes 2 bottles of water and 4 packs of chewing gum a day at point *C*. She is indifferent between all the points on the green indifference curve. She prefers any point above the indifference curve (yellow area) to any point on it, and she prefers any point on the indifference curve to any point below it (gray area).

Part (b) shows three indifference curves of Tina's preference map. She prefers point *J* to point *C* or *G*, so she prefers any point on I_2 to any point on I_1.

The indifference curve in Figure A10.1(a) is just one of a whole family of such curves. This indifference curve appears again in Figure A10.1(b) labeled I_1. The curves labeled I_0 and I_2 are two other indifference curves. Tina prefers any point on indifference curve I_2, such as point *J*, to any point on indifference curve I_1, such as points *C* or *G*. She prefers any point on I_1 to any point on I_0. We refer to I_2 as being a higher indifference curve than I_1 and I_1 as being higher than I_0.

A preference map is a series of indifference curves that resemble the contour lines on a map. By looking at the shape of the contour lines on a map, we can draw conclusions about the terrain. Similarly, by looking at the shape of the indifference curves, we can draw conclusions about a person's preferences.

Marginal Rate of Substitution

Marginal rate of substitution
The rate at which a person will give up good *y* (the good measured on the *y*-axis) to get more of good *x* (the good measured on the *x*-axis) and at the same time remain on the same indifference curve.

The concept of the marginal rate of substitution is the key to "reading" a preference map. The **marginal rate of substitution** (*MRS*) is the rate at which a person will give up good *y* (the good measured on the *y*-axis) to get more of good *x* (the good measured on the *x*-axis) and at the same time remain indifferent (remain on the same indifference curve). The marginal rate of substitution is measured by the magnitude of the slope of an indifference curve.

If the indifference curve is *steep*, the marginal rate of substitution is *high*. The person is willing to give up a large quantity of good *y* to get a small quantity of good *x* while remaining indifferent. But if the indifference curve is *flat*, the marginal rate of substitution is *low*. The person is willing to give up only a small amount of good *y* to get a large amount of good *x* to remain indifferent.

Figure A10.2 shows you how to calculate the marginal rate of substitution. Suppose that Tina consumes 2 bottles of water and 4 packs of gum at point *C* on indifference curve I_1. We calculate her marginal rate of substitution by measuring the magnitude of the slope of the indifference curve at point *C*. To measure this magnitude, place a straight line against, or tangent to, the indifference curve at point *C*. Along that line, as gum consumption decreases from 8 packs to zero packs, water consumption increases from zero bottles to 4 bottles. So at point *C*, Tina is willing to give up 8 packs of gum for 4 bottles of water, or 2 packs of gum per bottle. Her marginal rate of substitution is 2.

Now suppose that Tina consumes 4 bottles of water and 2 packs of gum at point *G*. The slope of the indifference curve at point *G* now measures her marginal rate of substitution. That slope is the same as the slope of the line tangent to the indifference curve at point *G*. Here, as chewing gum consumption decreases from 4 packs to zero, water consumption increases from zero to 8 bottles. So at point *G*, Tina is willing to give up 4 packs of chewing gum for 8 bottles of water, or ½ pack of gum per bottle. Her marginal rate of substitution is ½.

Diminishing marginal rate of substitution
The general tendency for the marginal rate of substitution to decrease as the consumer moves down along the indifference curve, increasing consumption of good *x* and decreasing consumption of good *y*.

As Tina moves down along her indifference curve, her marginal rate of substitution diminishes. Diminishing marginal rate of substitution is the key assumption of consumer theory. **Diminishing marginal rate of substitution** is the general tendency for the marginal rate of substitution to diminish as the consumer moves along an indifference curve, increasing consumption of the good measured on the *x*-axis and decreasing consumption of the good measured on the *y*-axis. The shape of a person's indifference curves incorporates the principle of the diminishing marginal rate of substitution because the curves are bowed toward the origin.

FIGURE A10.2
The Marginal Rate of Substitution

*e*Foundations **A10.1** 

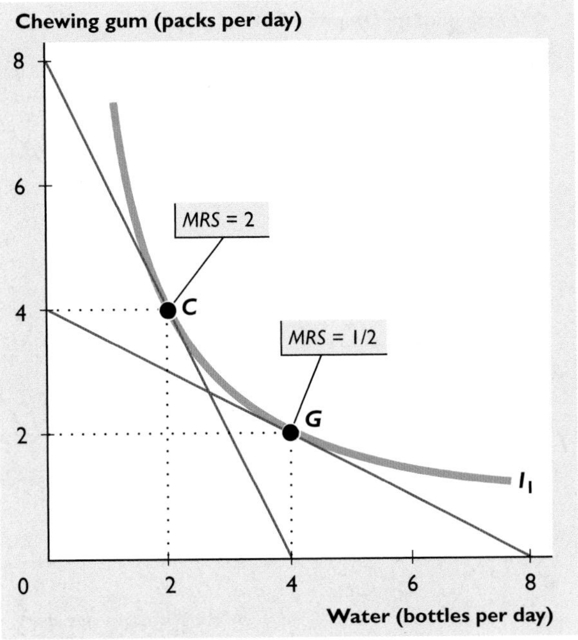

The magnitude of the slope of an indifference curve is called the marginal rate of substitution (*MRS*). The red line at point *C* tells us that Tina is willing to give up 8 packs of gum to consume 4 bottles of water. Her marginal rate of substitution at point *C* is 8 divided by 4, which equals 2. The red line at point *G* tells us that Tina is willing to give up 4 packs of gum to get 8 bottles of water. Her marginal rate of substitution at point *G* is 4 divided by 8, which equals ½.

Consumer Equilibrium

The goal of the consumer is to buy the affordable quantities of goods that make the consumer as well off as possible. The indifference curves describe the consumer's preferences, and they tell us that the higher the indifference curve, the better off is the consumer. So the consumer's goal can be restated as being to allocate her budget in a way to get onto the highest attainable indifference curve.

The consumer's budget and the prices of the goods limit the consumer's choices. The budget line illustrated in Figure 10.1 (p. 230) summarizes the limits on the consumer's choice. We combine the indifference curves of Figure A10.2 with the budget line of Figure 10.1 to work out the consumer's choice and find the consumer equilibrium.

Figure A10.3 shows Tina's budget line from Figure 10.1 and her indifference curves from Figure A10.1(b). Tina's best affordable point is 2 bottles of water and 4 packs of gum—at point *C*. Here, Tina:

- Is on her budget line
- Is on her highest attainable indifference curve
- Has a marginal rate of substitution between water and gum equal to the relative price of water and gum.

For every point inside the budget line, such as point *J*, there are points *on* the budget line that Tina prefers. For example, she prefers any point on the budget line between *F* and *H* to point *J*. So she chooses a point on the budget line.

FIGURE A10.3
Consumer Equilibrium

*e*Foundations **A10.1** 

Tina's best affordable point is *C*. At that point, she is on her budget line and also on the highest attainable indifference curve. At a point such as *H*, Tina is willing to give up more bottled water in exchange for chewing gum than she has to. She can move to point *J*, which is just as good as point *H*, and have some unspent budget. She can spend that budget and move to *C*, a point that she prefers to point *J*.

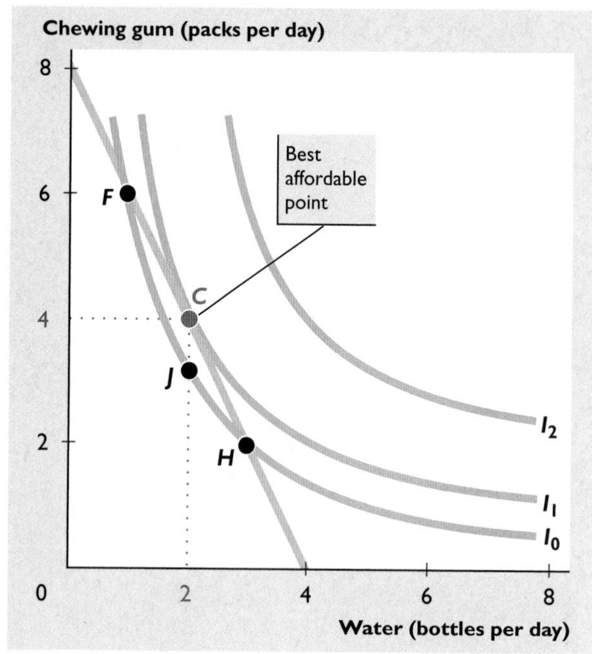

Every point on the budget line lies on an indifference curve. For example, point H lies on the indifference curve I_0. At point H, Tina's marginal rate of substitution (the magnitude of the slope of the indifference curve I_0) is less than the relative price (the magnitude of the slope of the budget line). Tina is willing to give up more bottled water in exchange for chewing gum than the budget line says she must. So she moves along her budget line from H toward C. As she does so, she passes through a number of indifference curves (not shown in the figure) located between indifference curves I_0 and I_1. All of these indifference curves are higher than I_0, and therefore Tina prefers any point on them to point H. But when Tina gets to point C, she is on the highest attainable indifference curve. If she keeps moving along the budget line, she starts to encounter indifference curves that are lower than I_1. So Tina chooses point C—her best affordable point.

At the chosen point, the marginal rate of substitution (the magnitude of the slope of the indifference curve) equals the relative price (the magnitude of the slope of the budget line).

We can now use this model of consumer choice to predict the effect of a change in the price of water on the quantity of water demanded. That is, we can use this model to generate the demand curve for bottled water.

Deriving the Demand Curve

To derive Tina's demand curve for bottled water, we change the price of water, shift the budget line, and work out the new best affordable point. Figure A10.4(a) shows the change in the budget line and the change in consumer equilibrium when the price of water falls from \$1 a bottle to 50¢ a bottle.

Initially when the price of water is \$1 a bottle, Tina consumes at point *C* (part a). When the price of a bottle of water falls from \$1 to 50¢, her budget line rotates outward and she can now get onto a higher indifference curve. Her best affordable point is now point *K*. Tina increases the quantity of water she buys from 2 to 4 bottles a day. She continues to buy 4 packs of gum a day.

Figure A10.4(b) shows Tina's demand curve for bottled water. When the price of water is \$1, she buys 2 bottles a day, at point *A*. When the price of water falls to 50¢, she buys 4 bottles a day, at point *B*. Tina's demand curve traces out her best affordable quantity of bottled water as the price of a bottle of water varies.

FIGURE A10.4

Deriving Tina's Demand Curve

*e*Foundations **A10.1** 

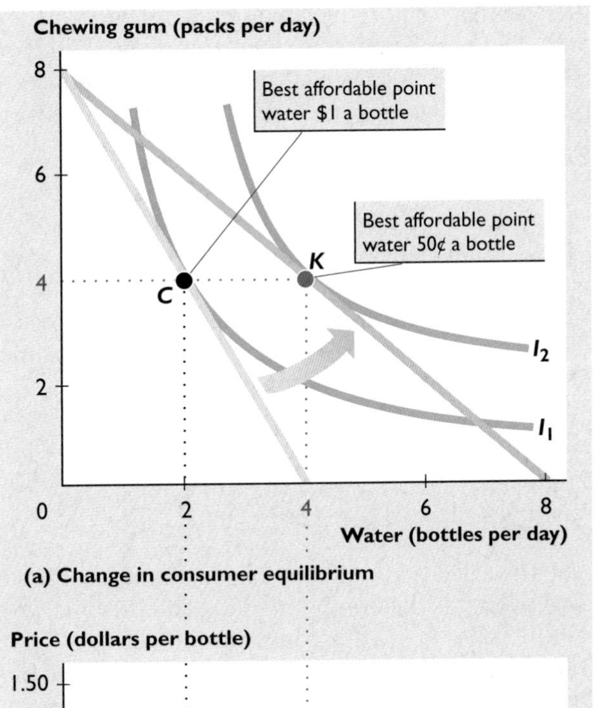

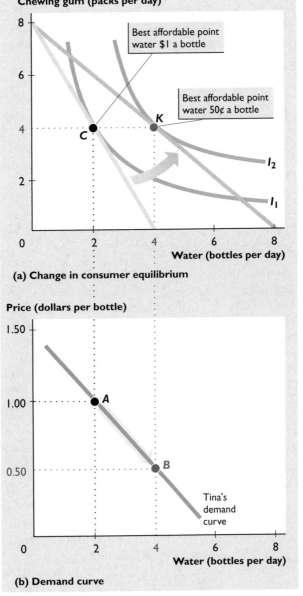

In part (a), Tina initially consumes at point *C*. When the price of water falls from \$1 to 50¢ a bottle, she consumes at point *K*.

In part (b), when the price of water falls from \$1 to 50¢ a bottle, Tina moves along her demand curve for bottled water from point *A* to point *B*.

APPENDIX CHECKPOINT

Study Guide pp. 162–164

eFoundations A10.1

FIGURE 1

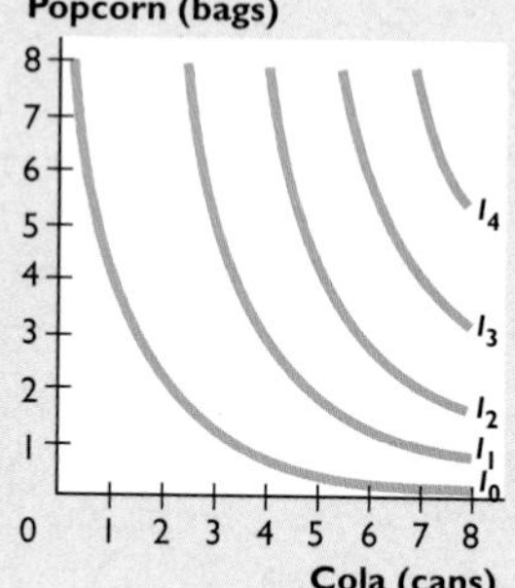

FIGURE 2

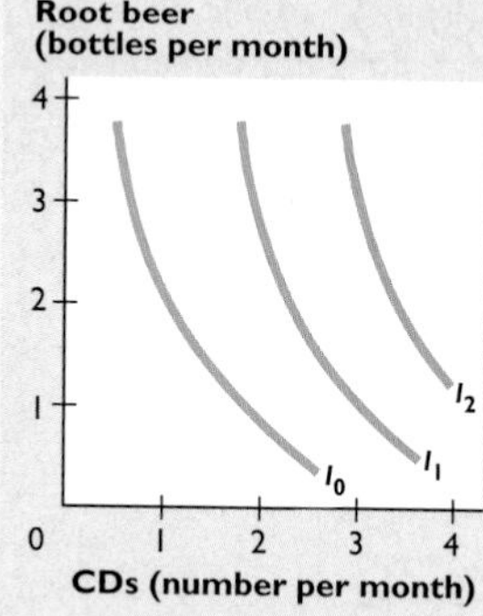

Exercises

1. Sara has a budget of $12 a week. Popcorn costs $3 a bag, and cola costs $3 a can. Figure 1 illustrates Sara's preferences.
   a. What is the relative price of cola in terms of popcorn?
   b. What is the opportunity cost of a can of cola?
   c. Draw a graph of Sara's budget line with cola on the *x*-axis.
   d. What are the quantities of popcorn and cola that Sara buys?
   e. What is Sara's marginal rate of substitution of popcorn for cola at the point at which she consumes?

2. Suppose that in the situation described in Exercise 1, the price of cola falls to $1.50 per can and the price of popcorn and Sara's budget remain constant.
   a. Find the new quantities of cola and popcorn that Sara buys.
   b. Find two points on Sara's demand curve for cola.

3. Marc has a budget of $20 per week. Root beer costs $5 a can, and CDs cost $10 each. Figure 2 illustrates his preferences.
   a. What is the relative price of root beer in terms of CDs?
   b. What is the opportunity cost of a can of root beer?
   c. Draw a graph of Marc's budget line with CDs on the *x*-axis.
   d. What quantities of root beer and CDs does Marc buy?
   e. Calculate Marc's marginal rate of substitution of CDs for root beer at the point at which he consumes.

4. Now suppose that in the situation described in Exercise 3, the price of a CD falls to $5 and the price of root beer and Marc's budget remain constant.
   a. Find the new quantities of root beer and CDs that Marc buys.
   b. Find two points on Marc's demand curve for CDs.

5. The sales tax is a tax on goods. Some people say that a consumption tax, a tax that is paid on both goods and services, would be better. If we replaced the sales tax with a consumption tax:
   a. What would happen to the relative price of floppy disks and haircuts?
   b. What would happen to the budget line showing the quantities of floppy disks and haircuts you can afford to buy?
   c. How would you change your purchases of floppy disks and haircuts?
   d. Which type of tax is best for the consumer and why?

6. Jim spends all his income on apartment rent, food, clothing, and vacations. He gets a pay raise from $3,000 a month to $4,000 a month. At the same time, airfares and other vacation related costs increase by 50 percent.
   a. How do you think Jim will change his spending pattern as a result of the changes in his income and prices?
   b. Can you say whether Jim is better off or worse off in his new situation?
   c. If all prices rise by 50 percent, how does Jim change his purchases? And can you now say whether he is better off or worse off?
   d. Show in a figure the changes in Jim's choices that the change in income and changes in prices induce.

Chapter 11

Production and Cost

CHAPTER CHECKLIST

When you have completed your study of this chapter, you will be able to:

1. **Explain how economists measure a firm's cost of production and profit.**
2. **Explain the relationship between a firm's output and labor employed in the short run.**
3. **Explain the relationship between a firm's output and costs in the short run.**
4. **Derive and explain a firm's long-run average cost curve.**

In Chapter 10, you saw how consumer choices lead to the law of demand. In this chapter, you're going to lay the foundation for understanding how firms' decisions in competitive markets lead to the law of supply. We continue to use the big ideas that define the economic way of thinking. But we now apply these ideas to the decisions of firms. Firms face scarcity and make *rational* choices; the *cost* of something is what a firm *must give up* to produce it; and firms respond to *incentives*.

You're now going to see how these principles lead firms to make decisions that minimize the cost of producing a given output. In this chapter, you'll learn how a firm's costs are determined and how they vary as the firm varies its output.

What you learn in this chapter you will use again and again in the four chapters of the next part, so it is very important that you thoroughly understand the content of this chapter before moving forward to Chapter 12.

11.1 ECONOMIC COST AND PROFIT

The 20 million firms in the United States differ in size and in what they produce. But they all perform the same basic economic function: They hire factors of production and organize them to produce and sell goods and services. To understand the behavior of a firm, we need to know its goals.

The Firm's Goal

If you asked a group of entrepreneurs what they are trying to achieve, you would get many different answers. Some would talk about making a high-quality product, others about business growth, others about market share, and others about workforce job satisfaction. All of these goals might be pursued, but they are not the fundamental goal. They are means to a deeper goal.

The firm's goal is to *maximize profit*. A firm that does not seek to maximize profit is either eliminated or bought by firms that *do* seek that goal. To calculate a firm's profit, we must determine its total revenue and total cost. Economists have a special way of defining and measuring cost and profit, which we'll explain and illustrate by looking at Sam's Smoothies, a firm that is owned and operated by Samantha.

Accounting Cost and Profit

In 2001, Sam's Smoothies' total revenue from the sale of smoothies was $150,000. The firm paid $20,000 for fruit, yogurt, and honey; $22,000 in wages for the labor it hired; and $3,000 in interest to the bank. These expenses totalled $45,000.

Sam's accountant said that the depreciation of the firm's blenders, refrigerators, and shop during 2001 was $10,000. Depreciation is the fall in the value of the firm's capital, and accountants calculate it by using the Internal Revenue Service's rules, which are based on standards set by the Financial Accounting Standards Board. So the accountant reported Sam's Smoothies' total cost for 2001 as $55,000 and the firm's profit as $95,000—$150,000 of total revenue minus $55,000 of total costs.

Sam's accountant measures cost and profit to ensure that the firm pays the correct amount of income tax and to show the bank how Sam's has used its bank loan. Economists have a different purpose: to predict the decisions that a firm makes to maximize its profit. These decisions respond to *opportunity cost* and *economic profit*.

Opportunity Cost

To produce its output, a firm employs factors of production: land, labor, capital, and entrepreneurship. Another firm could have used these same resources to produce alternative goods or services. In Chapter 3 (pp. 62–64), resources can be used to produce either bottled water or CDs, so the opportunity cost of producing a bottle of water is the number of CDs forgone. Pilots who fly passengers for United Airlines can't at the same time fly freight for Federal Express. Construction workers who are building an office tower can't simultaneously build apartments. A communication satellite operating at peak capacity can carry television signals or e-mail messages but not both at the same time. A journalist writing for the *New*

York Times can't at the same time create Web news reports for CNN. And Samantha can't simultaneously run her smoothies business and a flower shop.

The highest-valued alternative forgone is the opportunity cost of a firm's production. From the viewpoint of the firm, this opportunity cost is the amount that the firm must pay the owners of the factors of production it employs to attract them from their best alternative use. So a firm's opportunity cost of production is the cost of the factors of production it employs.

To determine these costs, let's return to Sam's and look at the opportunity cost of producing smoothies.

Explicit Costs and Implicit Costs

The amount that a firm pays to attract resources from their best alternative use is either an explicit cost or an implicit cost. A cost paid in money is an **explicit cost**. Because the amount spent could have been spent on something else, an explicit cost is an opportunity cost. The wages that Samantha pays labor, the interest she pays the bank, and her expenditure on fruit, yogurt, and honey are explicit costs.

Explicit cost
A cost paid in money.

A firm incurs an **implicit cost** when it uses a factor of production but does not make a direct money payment for its use. The two categories of implicit cost are economic depreciation and the cost of the firm owner's resources.

Implicit cost
An opportunity cost incurred by a firm when it uses a factor of production for which it does not make a direct money payment.

Economic depreciation is the opportunity cost of the firm using capital that it owns. It is measured as the change in the *market value* of capital—the market price of the capital at the beginning of a period minus its market price at the end of a period. Suppose that Samantha could have sold her blenders, refrigerators, and shop on December 31, 2000, for $250,000. If she can sell the same capital on December 31, 2001, for $246,000, her economic depreciation during 2001 is $4,000. This is the opportunity cost of using her capital during 2001, not the $10,000 depreciation calculated by Sam's accountant.

Economic depreciation
An opportunity cost of a firm using capital that it owns—measured as the change in the *market* value of capital over a given period.

Interest is another cost of capital. When the firm's owner provides the funds used to buy capital, the opportunity cost of those funds is the interest income forgone by not using them in the best alternative way. If Sam loaned her firm funds that could have earned her $1,000 in interest, this amount is an implicit cost of producing smoothies.

When a firm's owner supplies labor, the opportunity cost of the owner's time spent working for the firm is the wage income forgone by not working in the best alternative job. For example, instead of working at her next best job that pays $34,000 a year, Sam supplies labor to her smoothies business. This implicit cost of $34,000 is part of the opportunity cost of producing smoothies.

Finally, a firm's owner often supplies entrepreneurship, the factor of production that organizes the business and bears the risk of running it. The return to entrepreneurship is **normal profit**. Normal profit is part of a firm's opportunity cost because it is the cost of a forgone alternative—running another firm. Instead of running Sam's Smoothies, Sam could earn $16,000 a year running a flower shop. This amount is an implicit cost of production at Sam's Smoothies.

Normal profit
The return to entrepreneurship. Normal profit is part of a firm's opportunity cost because it is the cost of not running another firm.

Economic Profit

A firm's **economic profit** equals total revenue minus total cost. Total revenue is the amount received from the sale of the product. It is the price of the output multiplied by the quantity sold. Total cost is the sum of the explicit costs and implicit costs and is the opportunity cost of production.

Economic profit
A firm's total revenue minus total cost.

TABLE 11.1
Economic Accounting

*e*Foundations 11.1 

Item		
Total Revenue		**$150,000**
Explicit Costs		
Cost of fruit, yogurt, and honey	$20,000	
Wages	$22,000	
Interest	$3,000	
Implicit Costs		
Samantha's forgone wages	$34,000	
Samantha's forgone interest	$1,000	
Economic depreciation	$4,000	
Normal profit	$16,000	
Opportunity Cost		**$100,000**
Economic Profit		**$50,000**

Because one of the firm's implicit costs is *normal profit*, the return to the entrepreneur equals normal profit plus economic profit. If a firm incurs an economic loss, the entrepreneur receives less than normal profit.

Table 11.1 summarizes the economic cost concepts, and Figure 11.1 compares the economic view and the accounting view of cost and profit. The total revenue received by Sam's Smoothies is $150,000; the opportunity cost of the resources that Sam uses is $100,000; and Sam's economic profit is $50,000.

FIGURE 11.1
Two Views of Cost and Profit

*e*Foundations 11.1 

Economists measure economic profit as total revenue minus opportunity cost. Opportunity cost includes explicit costs and implicit costs. Normal profit is an implicit cost. Accountants measure profit as total revenue minus explicit costs—costs paid in money—and depreciation.

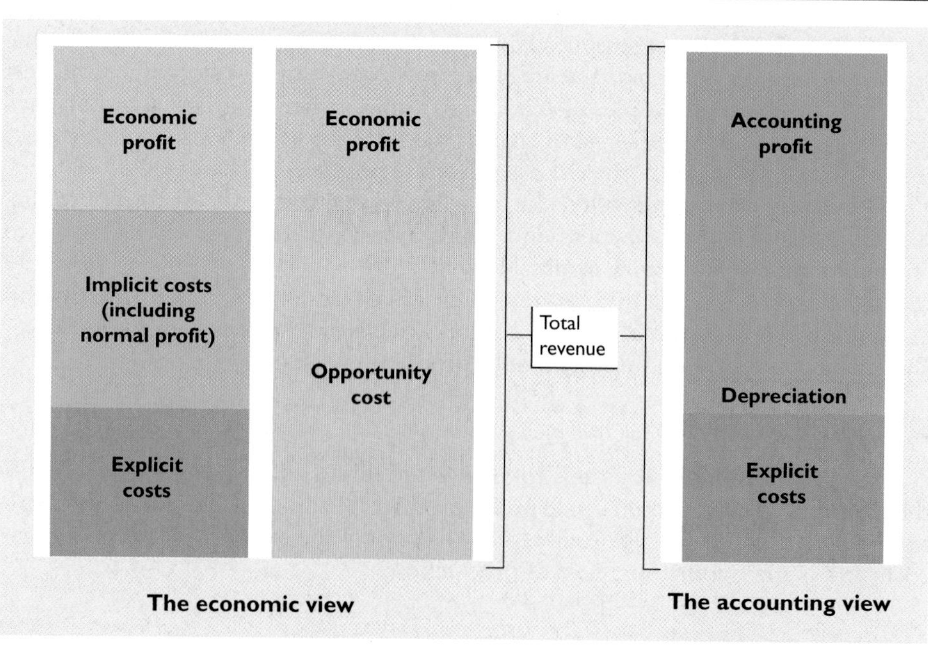

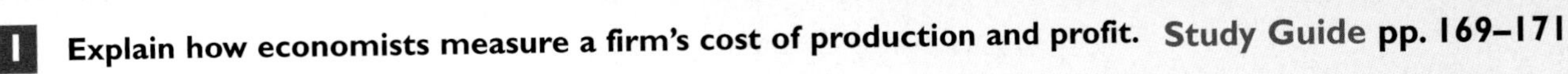

CHECKPOINT 11.1

1 Explain how economists measure a firm's cost of production and profit. Study Guide **pp. 169–171**

*e*Foundations **11.1**

Practice Problem 11.1

Lee is a computer programmer who earned $35,000 in 1999. But with the new millennium, Lee decided to try a new career. He loves water sports, and in 2000 he opened a body board manufacturing business. At the end of the first year of operation, he submitted the following information to his accountant:

- **i.** He stopped renting out his seaside cottage for $3,500 a year and used it as his factory.
- **ii.** He spent $50,000 on materials, phone, utilities, and the like.
- **iii.** He leased machines for $10,000 a year.
- **iv.** He paid $15,000 in wages.
- **v.** He used $10,000 from his savings account at the bank, which pays 5 percent a year interest.
- **vi.** He borrowed $40,000 at 10 percent a year from the bank.
- **vii.** He sold $160,000 worth of body boards.
- **viii.** Normal profit is $25,000 a year.

a. Calculate Lee's explicit costs.
b. Calculate Lee's implicit costs.
c. What does the accountant calculate for Lee's profit?
d. Calculate Lee's economic profit.

Exercise 11.1

In 1999, Roma was a schoolteacher and earned $40,000. But she enjoys creating cartoons, so at the beginning of 2000, Roma quit teaching and set to work as a cartoonist. She stopped renting out her basement for $5,000 a year and began to use it as her office. She used $5,000 from her savings account to buy a new computer, and she leased a printer for $150 a year. During 2000, Roma paid $1,250 for paper, utilities, and postage; the bank paid 5 percent a year on savings account balances; and Roma sold $50,000 of cartoons. Normal profit is $3,000 a year. At the end of 2000, Roma was offered $4,000 for her computer. For 2000, calculate Roma's:

a. Explicit costs.
b. Implicit costs.
c. Economic profit.

Solution to Practice Problem 11.1

a. Explicit costs are costs paid with money. Explicit costs are items (ii), (iii), (iv), and (vi). Explicit costs equal $50,000 + $10,000 + $15,000 + $4,000, or $79,000.

b. A firm incurs implicit costs when it forgoes alternative actions but does not make a payment. Implicit costs are Lee's wages forgone and items (i), (v), and (viii). That is, implicit costs equal $35,000 + $3,500 + $500 + $25,000, or $64,000.

c. The accountant measures Lee's profit as total revenue minus explicit costs. That is, profit equals $160,000 – $79,000, which equals $81,000.

d. Economic profit equals total revenue minus total costs. Total cost is the sum of explicit costs plus implicit costs. Total costs is $79,000 + $64,000, which equals $143,000. So Lee's economic profit equals $160,000 – $143,000, which is $17,000.

SHORT RUN AND LONG RUN

The main goal of this chapter is to explore the influences on a firm's cost. The key influence is the quantity of output that the firm produces per period. The greater the output rate, the higher is the total cost of production. But the effect of a change in production on cost depends on how soon the firm wants to act. A firm that plans to change its output rate tomorrow has fewer options than a firm that plans ahead and intends to change its production six months from now.

To study the relationship between a firm's output decision and its costs, we distinguish two decision time frames:

- The short run
- The long run

The Short Run: Fixed Plant

Short run
The time frame in which the quantities of some resources are fixed. In the short run, a firm can usually change the quantity of labor it uses but not the quantity of capital.

The **short run** is a time frame in which the quantities of some resources are fixed. For most firms, the fixed resources are the firm's technology and capital—its equipment and buildings. The management organization is also fixed in the short run. We call the fixed resources that the firm uses its *fixed inputs* and those that it can vary its *variable inputs*. The collection of fixed resources is the firm's *plant*. So in the short run, a firm's plant is fixed.

Sam's Smoothies' plant is its blenders, refrigerators, and shop. Sam's cannot change these inputs in the short run. An electric power utility can't change the number of generators it uses in the short run. An airport can't change the number of runways, terminal buildings, and traffic control facilities in the short run.

To increase output in the short run, a firm must increase the quantity of variable factors it uses. Labor is usually the variable factor of production. To produce more smoothies, Sam must hire more labor. Similarly, to increase the production of electricity, a utility must hire more engineers and run its generators for longer hours. To increase the volume of traffic it handles, an airport must hire more check-in clerks, cargo handlers, and air-traffic controllers.

Short-run decisions are easily reversed. A firm can increase or decrease output in the short run by increasing or decreasing the labor hours it hires.

The Long Run: Variable Plant

Long run
The time frame in which the quantities of all resources can be changed.

The **long run** is a time frame in which the quantities of *all* resources can be varied. That is, the long run is a period in which the firm can change its *plant*.

To increase output in the long run, a firm can increase the size of its plant. Sam's Smoothies can install more blenders and refrigerators and increase the size of its shop. An electric power utility can install more generators. And an airport can build more runways, terminals, and traffic-control facilities.

Long-run decisions are *not* easily reversed. Once a firm buys a new plant, its resale value is usually much less than the amount the firm paid for it. The difference between the cost of the plant and its resale value is a *sunk cost*. A sunk cost is irrelevant to the firm's decisions (see Chapter 1, p. 14). The only costs that influence the firm's decisions are the short-run cost of changing its labor inputs and the long-run cost of changing its plant.

We're going to study costs in the short run and the long run. We begin with the short run and describe the limits to the firm's production possibilities.

11.2 SHORT-RUN PRODUCTION

To increase the output of a fixed plant, a firm must increase the quantity of labor it employs. We describe the relationship between output and the quantity of labor employed by using three related concepts:

- Total product
- Marginal product
- Average product

Total Product

Total product (*TP*) is the total quantity of a good produced in a given period. Total product is an output *rate*—the number of units produced per unit of time (for example, per hour, day, or week). Total product increases as the quantity of labor employed increases, and we illustrate this relationship as a total product schedule and total product curve like those in Figure 11.2. The total product schedule (the table below the graph) lists the maximum quantities of smoothies per hour that Sam can produce with her existing plant at each quantity of labor. Points *A* through *H* on the *TP* curve correspond to the columns in the table.

Total product
The total output produced in a given period.

FIGURE 11.2
Total Product Schedule and Total Product Curve

*e*Foundations 11.2 

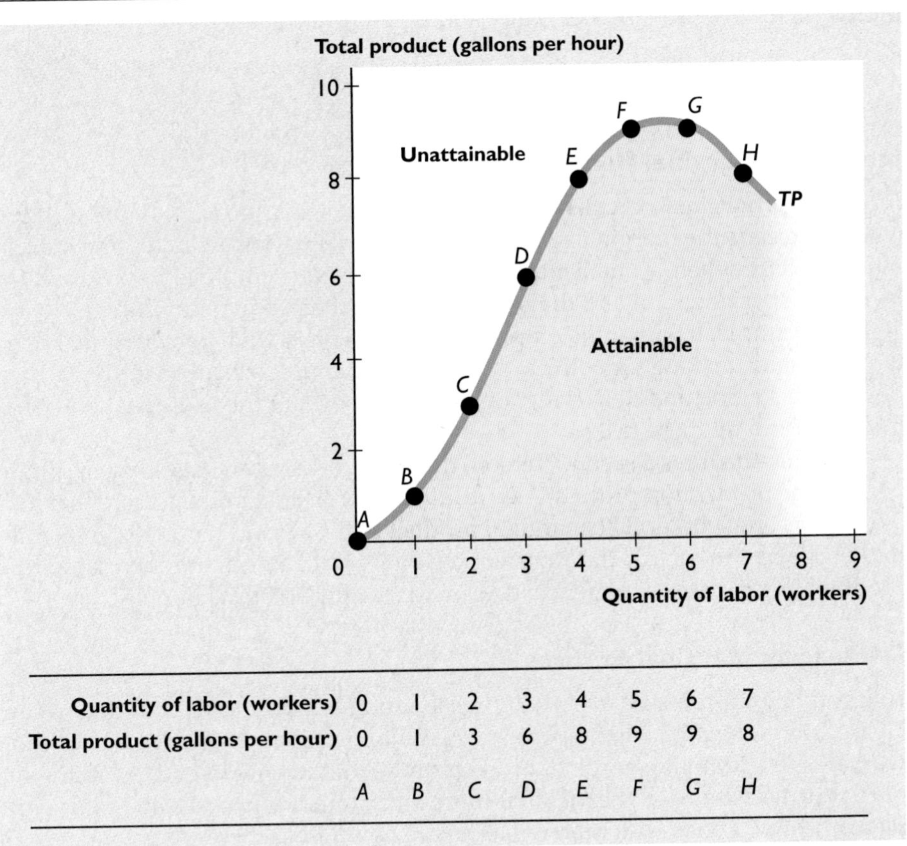

Quantity of labor (workers)	0	1	2	3	4	5	6	7
Total product (gallons per hour)	0	1	3	6	8	9	9	8
	A	B	C	D	E	F	G	H

The total product schedule shows how the quantity of smoothies that Sam's can produce changes as the quantity of labor employed changes. In column *C*, Sam's employs 2 workers and can produce 3 gallons of smoothies an hour.

The total product curve, *TP*, graphs the data in the table. Points *A* through *H* on the curve correspond to the columns of the table. The total product curve separates attainable outputs from unattainable outputs. Points below the *TP* curve are inefficient. Points on the *TP* curve are efficient.

Like the *production possibilities frontier* (see Chapter 3, p. 58), the total product curve separates attainable outputs from unattainable outputs. All the points that lie above the curve are unattainable. Points that lie below the curve, in the orange area, are attainable. But they are inefficient: They use more labor than is necessary to produce a given output. Only the points *on* the total product curve are efficient.

Marginal Product

Marginal product
The change in total product that results from a one-unit increase in the quantity of labor employed.

Marginal product (*MP*) is the change in total product that results from a one-unit increase in the quantity of labor employed. It tells us the contribution to total product of adding one additional worker. When the quantity of labor increases by more (or less) than one worker, we calculate marginal product as:

Marginal product = Change in total product ÷ Change in quantity of labor.

Figure 11.3 shows Sam's Smoothies' marginal product curve, *MP*, and its relationship with the total product curve. You can see that as the quantity of labor increases from 1 to 3 workers, marginal product increases. But as yet more workers are employed, marginal product decreases. When the 7th worker is employed, marginal product is negative.

Notice that the steeper the slope of the total product curve in part (a), the greater is marginal product in part (b). And when the total product curve turns downward in part (a), marginal product is negative in part (b).

The total product curve and marginal product curve in Figure 11.3 incorporate a feature that is shared by all production processes in firms as different as the Ford Motor Company, Jim's Barber Shop, and Sam's Smoothies:

- Increasing marginal returns initially
- Decreasing marginal returns eventually

Increasing Marginal Returns

Increasing marginal returns
When the marginal product of an additional worker exceeds the marginal product of the previous worker.

Increasing marginal returns occur when the marginal product of an additional worker exceeds the marginal product of the previous worker. Increasing marginal returns occur when a small number of workers are employed and arise from increased specialization and division of labor in the production process.

For example, if Samantha employs just one worker, that person must learn all the aspects of making smoothies: running the blender, cleaning it, fixing breakdowns, packaging and delivering, buying and checking the fruit. That one person must perform all these tasks.

If Samantha hires a second person, the two workers can specialize in different parts of the production process. As a result, two workers produce more than twice as much as one worker. The marginal product of the second worker is greater than the marginal product of the first worker. Marginal returns are increasing. Most production processes experience increasing marginal returns initially.

Decreasing Marginal Returns

Decreasing marginal returns
When the marginal product of an additional worker is less than the marginal product of the previous worker.

All production processes eventually reach a point of *decreasing* marginal returns. **Decreasing marginal returns** occur when the marginal product of an additional worker is less than the marginal product of the previous worker. Decreasing marginal returns arise from the fact that more and more workers use the same equipment and work space. As more workers are employed, there is less and less that is productive for the additional worker to do. For example, if Samantha hires a

FIGURE 11.3
Total Product and Marginal Product

*e*Foundations 11.2 

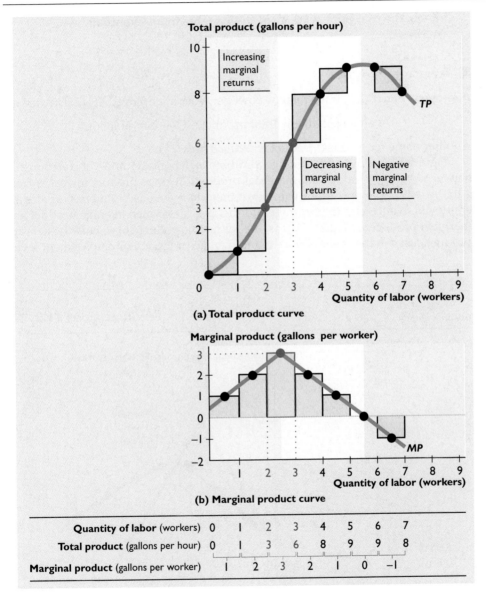

(a) Total product curve

(b) Marginal product curve

Quantity of labor (workers)	0	1	2	3	4	5	6	7
Total product (gallons per hour)	0	1	3	6	8	9	9	8
Marginal product (gallons per worker)	1	2	3	2	1	0	−1	

The table calculates marginal product and the orange bars illustrate it. When labor increases from 2 to 3 workers, total product increases from 3 gallons to 6 gallons an hour. So marginal product is the orange bar whose height is 3 gallons (in both parts of the figure).

In part (b), marginal product is graphed midway between the labor inputs to emphasize that it is the result of *changing* inputs. Marginal product increases to a maximum (when 3 workers are employed in this example) and then declines—diminishing marginal product.

fourth worker, output increases but not by as much as it did when she hired the third worker. In this case, three workers exhaust all the possible gains from specialization and the division of labor. By hiring a fourth worker, Sam's produces more smoothies per hour, but the equipment is being operated closer to its limits. Sometimes the fourth worker has nothing to do because the machines are running without the need for further attention.

Hiring yet more workers continues to increase output but by successively smaller amounts until Samantha hires the sixth worker, at which point total product stops rising. Add a seventh worker and the workplace is so congested that the workers get in each other's way and total product falls.

Decreasing marginal returns are so pervasive that they qualify for the status of a law: the **law of decreasing returns**, which states that:

> **As a firm uses more of a variable input, with a given quantity of fixed inputs, the marginal product of the variable input eventually decreases.**

Average Product

Average product
Total product divided by the quantity of an input. The average product of labor is total product divided by the quantity of labor employed.

Average product (*AP*) is the total product per worker employed. It is calculated as:

Average product = Total product ÷ Quantity of labor.

Another name for average product is *productivity*.

Figure 11.4 shows the average product of labor, *AP*, and the relationship between average product and marginal product. Average product increases from 1 to 3 workers (its maximum value) but then decreases as yet more workers are employed. Notice also that average product is largest when average product and marginal product are equal. That is, the marginal product curve cuts the average product curve at the point of maximum average product. For employment levels

FIGURE 11.4

Average Product and Marginal Product

*e*Foundations **11.2** 

The table calculates average product. For example, when the quantity of labor is 3 workers, total product is 6 gallons per hour, so average product is 6 ÷ 3 = 2 gallons per worker.

The average product curve is *AP*. When marginal product exceeds average product, average product is increasing. When marginal product is less than average product, average product is decreasing.

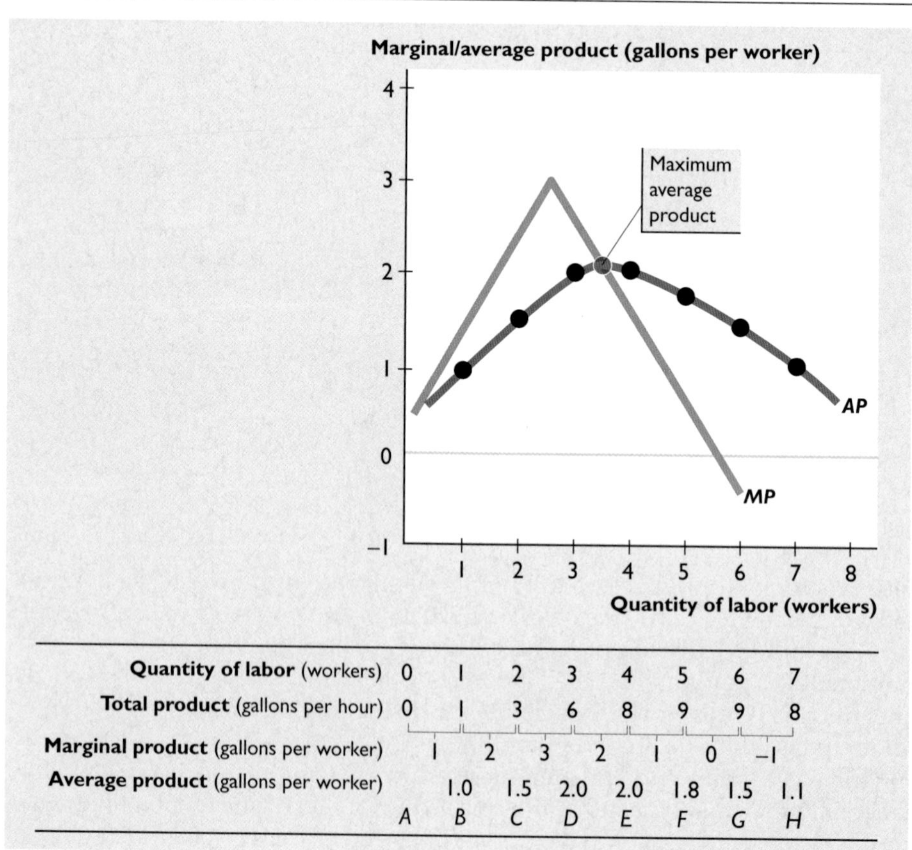

	A		B		C		D		E		F		G		H
Quantity of labor (workers)	0		1		2		3		4		5		6		7
Total product (gallons per hour)	0		1		3		6		8		9		9		8
Marginal product (gallons per worker)		1		2		3		2		1		0		–1	
Average product (gallons per worker)			1.0		1.5		2.0		2.0		1.8		1.5		1.1

at which marginal product exceeds average product, the average product curve slopes upward and average product increases as more labor is employed. For employment levels at which marginal product is less than average product, the average product curve is downward sloping and average product decreases as more labor is employed.

The relationship between average product and marginal product is a general feature of the relationship between the average value and the marginal value of any variable. Let's look at a familiar example.

Marginal Grade and Grade Point Average Samantha is a part-time student who takes just one course each semester. To understand the relationship between average product and marginal product, think about the relationship between Sam's average grade and her marginal grade over five semesters, shown in Figure 11.5. In the first semester, Samantha takes French and her grade is a C (2). This grade is her marginal grade—the grade on the last course taken. It is also her average grade—her GPA. In the next semester, Samantha takes calculus and gets a B (3). Calculus is Sam's marginal course, and her marginal grade is 3. Her GPA rises to 2.5. Because her marginal grade exceeds her average grade, it pulls her average up. In the third semester, Samantha takes economics and gets an A (4)—her new marginal grade. Because her marginal grade exceeds her GPA, it again pulls her average up. Sam's GPA is now 3, the average of 2, 3, and 4. The fourth semester, she takes history and gets a B (3). Because her marginal grade is equal to her average, her GPA does not change. In the fifth semester, Samantha takes English and gets a D (1). Because her marginal grade of 1 is below her GPA of 3, her GPA falls.

This everyday relationship between average and marginal values is similar to the relationship between average and marginal product. Sam's GPA increases when her marginal grade exceeds her GPA. Her GPA falls when her marginal grade is below her GPA. And her GPA is constant when her marginal grade equals her GPA. The relationship between marginal product and average product is exactly the same as that between Sam's marginal and average grades.

FIGURE 11.5
Marginal Grade and Grade Point Average

*e*Foundations 11.2 

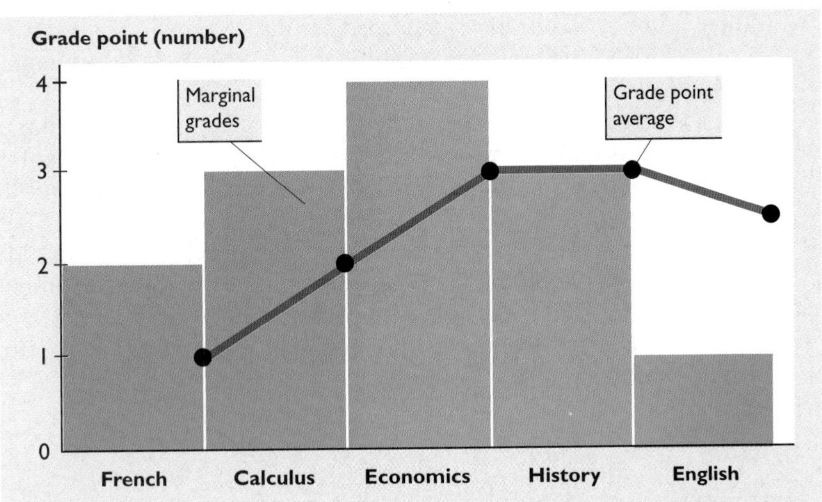

Sam's first course is French, for which she gets a C (2). Her marginal grade is 2, and her GPA is 2. She then gets a B (3) in calculus, which pulls her average up to 2.5. Next, she gets an A (4) in economics, which pulls her GPA up to 3. In her next course, history, she gets a B (3), which maintains her GPA. In her final course, English, she gets a D (1), which pulls her average down.

CHECKPOINT 11.2

Study Guide pp. 171–173

eFoundations 11.2

2 **Explain the relationship between a firm's output and labor employed in the short run.**

Practice Problem 11.2

Tom leases a farmer's field and grows pineapples. Tom hires students to pick and pack the pineapples. Table 1 sets out Tom's total product schedule.

a. Calculate the marginal product of the third student.
b. Calculate the average product of three students.
c. Over what numbers of students does marginal product increase?
d. When marginal product increases, compare average product and marginal product.

TABLE 1

Labor (students per day)	Total product (pineapples per day)
0	0
1	100
2	220
3	300
4	360
5	400
6	420
7	430

Exercise 11.2

Lisa has a lawn-mowing business. Lisa hires students to mow the lawns. Table 2 sets out Lisa's total product schedule.

a. Calculate the marginal product of the fourth student.
b. Calculate the average product of four students.
c. Over what numbers of students does marginal product decrease?
d. When marginal product decreases, compare average product and marginal product.

TABLE 2

Labor (students per day)	Total product (lawns cut per day)
0	0
1	20
2	44
3	70
4	94
5	114
6	120

Solution to Practice Problem 11.2

a. Marginal product of the third student is the change in total product that results from hiring the third student. When Tom hires 2 students, total product is 220 pineapples a day. When Tom hires 3 students, total product is 300 pineapples a day. Marginal product of the third worker is the total product of 3 workers minus the total product of 2 workers, which is 300 pineapples a day minus 220 pineapples a day, or 80 pineapples a day.
b. Average product equals total product divided by the number of students. When Tom hires 3 students, total product is 300 pineapples a day, so average product is 300 pineapples a day divided by 3 students, which equals 100 pineapples a day.
c. Marginal product of the first student is 100 pineapples a day, that of the second student is 120 pineapples a day, and that of the third student is 80 pineapples a day. So marginal product increases when Tom hires the first and second students.
d. When Tom hires 1 student, marginal product is 100 pineapples a day and average product is 100 pineapples a day. When Tom hires 2 students, marginal product is 120 pineapples a day and average product is 110 pineapples a day. That is, when Tom hires the second student, marginal product exceeds average product.

11.3 SHORT-RUN COST

To produce more output in the short run, a firm must employ more labor, which means that it must increase its costs. We describe the relationship between output and cost using three cost concepts:

- Total cost
- Marginal cost
- Average cost

Total Cost

A firm's **total cost** (*TC*) is the cost of all the factors of production used by the firm. Total cost divides into two parts: total fixed cost and total variable cost. **Total fixed cost** (*TFC*) is the cost of a firm's fixed factors of production: land, capital, and entrepreneurship. Because in the short run, the quantities of these inputs don't change as output changes, total fixed cost doesn't change as output changes. **Total variable cost** (*TVC*) is the cost of a firm's variable factor of production—labor. To change its output in the short run, a firm must change the quantity of labor it employs, so total variable cost changes as output changes.

Total cost
The cost of all the factors of production used by a firm.

Total fixed cost
The cost of the fixed factors of production used by a firm—the cost of land, capital, and entrepreneurship.

Total variable cost
The cost of the variable factor of production used by a firm—the cost of labor.

Total cost is the sum of total fixed cost and total variable cost. That is,

$$TC = TFC + TVC.$$

Table 11.2 shows Sam's Smoothies' total costs. Sam's fixed costs are $10 an hour regardless of whether it operates or not—*TFC* is $10 an hour. To produce smoothies, Samantha hires labor, which costs $6 an hour. *TVC*, which increases as output increases, equals the number of workers per hour multiplied by $6. For example, to produce 6 gallons an hour, Samantha hires 3 workers, so *TVC* is $18 an hour. *TC* is the sum of *TFC* and *TVC*. So to produce 6 gallons an hour, *TC* is $28. Check the calculation in each row and note that to produce some quantities—2 gallons an hour, for example—Sam hires a worker for only part of the hour.

TABLE 11.2
Sam's Smoothies' Total Costs

*e*Foundations 11.3 

Labor (workers per hour)	Output (gallons per hour)	Total fixed cost	Total variable cost	Total cost
		(dollars per hour)		
0	0	10	0.00	10.00
1.00	1	10	6.00	16.00
1.60	2	10	9.60	19.60
2.00	3	10	12.00	22.00
2.35	4	10	14.10	24.10
2.70	5	10	16.20	26.20
3.00	6	10	18.00	28.00
3.40	7	10	20.40	30.40
4.00	8	10	24.00	34.00
5.00	9	10	30.00	40.00

Figure 11.6 illustrates Sam's total cost curves. The green total fixed cost curve (*TFC*) is horizontal because total fixed cost does not change when output changes. It is a constant at $10 an hour. The purple total variable cost curve (*TVC*) and the blue total cost curve (*TC*) both slope upward because variable cost increases as output increases. The arrows highlight total fixed cost as the vertical distance between the *TVC* and *TC* curve.

Let's now look at Sam's Smoothies' marginal cost.

Marginal Cost

In Figure 11.6, total variable cost and total cost increase at a decreasing rate at small levels of output and then begin to increase at an increasing rate as output increases. To understand these patterns in the changes in total cost, we need to use the concept of *marginal cost.*

Marginal cost
The change in total cost that results from a one-unit increase in output.

A firm's **marginal cost** is the change in total cost that results from a one-unit increase in output. Table 11.3 calculates the marginal cost for Sam's Smoothies. When, for example, output increases from 5 gallons to 6 gallons an hour, total cost increases from $26.20 to $28. So the marginal cost of this gallon of smoothies is $1.80 ($28 – $26.20).

Marginal cost tells us how total cost changes as output changes. The final cost concept tells us what it costs, on the average, to produce a unit of output. Let's now look at Sam's average costs.

FIGURE 11.6
Total Cost Curves at Sam's Smoothies

*e*Foundations 11.3 

Total fixed cost (*TFC*) is constant—it graphs as a horizontal line—and total variable cost (*TVC*) increases as output increases. Total cost (*TC*) also increases as output increases. The vertical distance between the total cost curve and the total variable cost curve is total fixed cost, as illustrated by the two arrows.

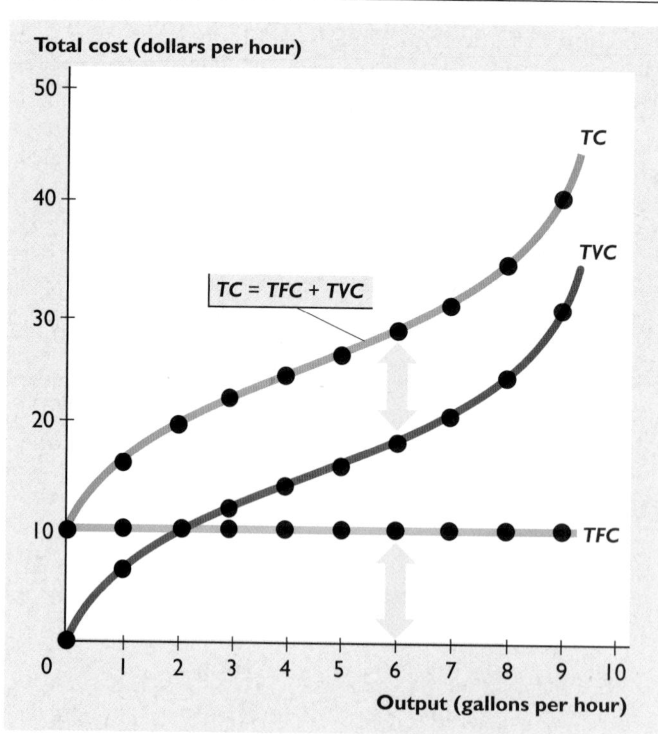

Average Cost

There are three average cost concepts:

- Average fixed cost
- Average variable cost
- Average total cost

Average fixed cost (AFC) is total fixed cost per unit of output. **Average variable cost** (AVC) is total variable cost per unit of output. **Average total cost** (ATC) is total cost per unit of output. The average cost concepts are calculated from the total cost concepts as follows:

Average fixed cost
Total fixed cost per unit of output.

Average variable cost
Total variable cost per unit of output.

Average total cost
Total cost per unit of output, which equals average fixed cost plus average variable cost.

$$TC = TFC + TVC.$$

Divide each total cost term by the quantity produced, Q, to give:

$$\frac{TC}{Q} = \frac{TFC}{Q} + \frac{TVC}{Q},$$

or

$$ATC = AFC + AVC.$$

Table 11.3 shows these average costs. For example, when output is 3 gallons an hour, average fixed cost is ($10 ÷ 3), which equals $3.33; average variable cost is ($12 ÷ 3), which equals $4.00; and average total cost is ($22 ÷ 3), which equals $7.33. Note that average total cost ($7.33) equals average fixed cost ($3.33) plus average variable cost ($4.00).

TABLE 11.3
Sam's Smoothies' Marginal Cost and Average Cost

*e*Foundations 11.3 

Output (gallons per hour)	Total cost (dollars per hour)	Marginal cost (dollars per worker)	Average fixed cost (dollars per gallon)	Average variable cost (dollars per gallon)	Average total cost (dollars per gallon)
0	10.00		–	–	–
		6.00			
1	16.00		10.00	6.00	16.00
		3.60			
2	19.60		5.00	4.80	9.80
		2.40			
3	22.00		3.33	4.00	7.33
		2.10			
4	24.10		2.50	3.53	6.03
		2.10			
5	26.20		2.00	3.24	5.24
		1.80			
6	28.00		1.67	3.00	4.67
		2.40			
7	30.40		1.43	2.91	4.34
		3.60			
8	34.00		1.25	3.00	4.25
		6.00			
9	40.00		1.11	3.33	4.44

Figure 11.7 graphs the marginal cost and average cost data in Table 11.3. The red marginal cost curve (*MC*) is U-shaped because of the way in which marginal product changes. Recall that when Samantha hires a second or a third worker, marginal product increases. Over this range, output increases and marginal cost decreases. But when Samantha hires a fourth or more workers, marginal product decreases. Over this range, output increases and marginal cost increases.

The green average fixed cost curve (*AFC*) slopes downward. As output increases, the same constant total fixed cost is spread over a larger output. The blue average total cost curve (*ATC*) and the purple average variable cost curve (*AVC*) are U-shaped. The vertical distance between the average total cost and average variable cost curves is equal to average fixed cost—as indicated by the two arrows. That distance shrinks as output increases because average fixed cost decreases with increasing output.

The marginal cost curve intersects the average variable cost curve and the average total cost curve at their minimum points. That is, when marginal cost is less than average cost, average cost is decreasing; and when marginal cost exceeds average cost, average cost is increasing. This relationship holds for both the *ATC* curve and the *AVC* curve and is another example of the relationship you saw in Figure 11.4 for average product and marginal product and in Sam's course grades.

FIGURE 11.7

Average Cost Curves and Marginal Cost Curve at Sam's Smoothies

*e*Foundations 11.3 

Average fixed cost (*AFC*) decreases as output increases. The average total cost curve (*ATC*) and average variable cost curve (*AVC*) are U-shaped. The vertical distance between these two curves is equal to average fixed cost, as illustrated by the two arrows.

Marginal cost is the change in total cost when output increases by one unit. The marginal cost curve (*MC*) is U-shaped and intersects the average variable cost curve and the average total cost curve at their minimum points.

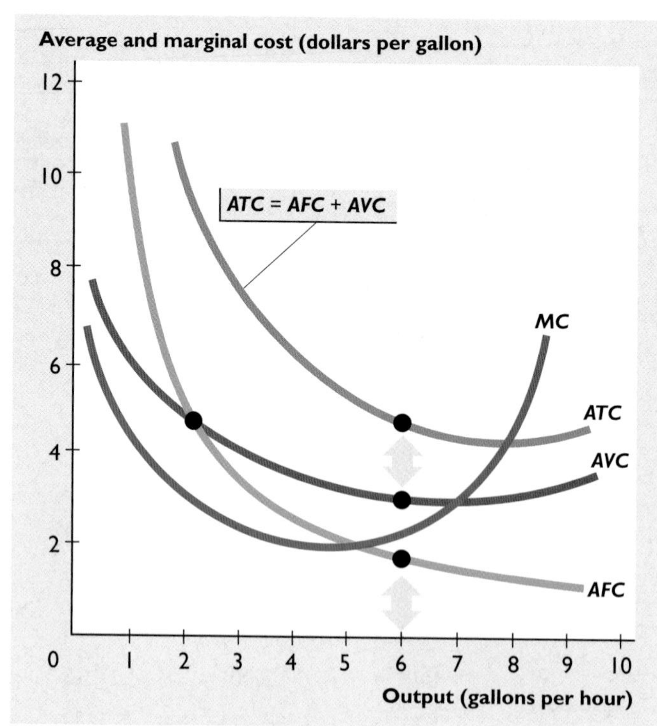

Why the Average Total Cost Curve Is U-Shaped

Average total cost, *ATC*, is the sum of average fixed cost, *AFC*, and average variable cost, *AVC*. So the shape of the *ATC* curve combines the shapes of the *AFC* and *AVC* curves. The U-shape of the average total cost curve arises from the influence of two opposing forces:

- Spreading total fixed cost over a larger output
- Decreasing marginal returns

When output increases, the firm spreads its total fixed costs over a larger output and its average fixed cost decreases—its average fixed cost curve slopes downward.

Decreasing marginal returns means that as output increases, ever larger amounts of labor are needed to produce an additional unit of output. So average variable cost eventually increases, and the *AVC* curve eventually slopes upward.

The shape of the average total cost curve combines these two effects. Initially, as output increases, both average fixed cost and average variable cost decrease, so average total cost decreases and the *ATC* curve slopes downward. But as output increases further and decreasing marginal returns set in, average variable cost begins to increase. Eventually, average variable cost increases more quickly than average fixed cost decreases, so average total cost increases and the *ATC* curve slopes upward.

All the short-run cost concepts that you've met are summarized in Table 11.4.

TABLE 11.4
A Compact Glossary of Costs

*e*Foundations 11.3 

Term	Symbol	Definition	Equation
Fixed cost		The cost of a fixed factor of production that is independent of the quantity produced	
Variable cost		The cost of a variable factor of production that varies with the quantity produced	
Total fixed cost	*TFC*	Cost of the fixed factors of production	
Total variable cost	*TVC*	Cost of the variable factor of production	
Total cost	*TC*	Cost of all factors of production	$TC = TFC + TVC$
Total product	*TP*	Total quantity produced (output *Q*)	
Marginal cost	*MC*	Change in total cost resulting from a one-unit increase in output*	$MC = \Delta TC \div \Delta Q$
Average fixed cost	*AFC*	Total fixed cost per unit of output	$AFC = TFC \div Q$
Average variable cost	*AVC*	Total variable cost per unit of output	$AVC = TVC \div Q$
Average total cost	*ATC*	Total cost per unit of output	$ATC = AFC + AVC$

*In this equation, the Greek letter delta (Δ) stands for "change in."

Cost Curves and Product Curves

A firm's cost curves and product curves are linked, and Figure 11.8 shows how. The top figure shows the average product curve and the marginal product curve—like those in Figure 11.4. The bottom figure shows the average variable cost curve and the marginal cost curve—like those in Figure 11.7.

The figure highlights the links between the product and costs. At low levels of employment and output, as the firm hires more labor, marginal product and average product rise and output increases faster than costs. So marginal cost and average variable cost fall. Then, at the point of maximum marginal product, marginal cost is a minimum. As the firm hires more labor, marginal product decreases and marginal cost increases. But average product continues to rise, and average variable cost continues to fall. Then, at the point of maximum average product, average variable cost is a minimum. As the firm hires even more labor, average product decreases and average variable cost increases.

Shifts in the Cost Curves

The position of a firm's short-run cost curves in Figures 11.6 and 11.7 depend on two factors:

- Technology
- Prices of factors of production

Technology

A technological change that increases productivity shifts the total product curve upward. It also shifts the marginal product curve and the average product curve upward. With a better technology, the same inputs can produce more output, so an advance in technology lowers the average and marginal costs and shifts the short-run cost curves downward.

For example, advances in robotic technology have increased productivity in the automobile industry. As a result, the product curves of DaimlerChrysler, Ford, and GM have shifted upward, and their average and marginal cost curves have shifted downward. But the relationships between their product curves and cost curves have not changed. The curves are still linked, as in Figure 11.8.

Often a technological advance results in a firm using more capital, a fixed input, and less labor, a variable input. For example, today telephone companies use computers to connect long-distance calls instead of the human operators they used in the 1980s. When a telephone company makes this change, total variable cost decreases and total cost decreases, but total fixed cost increases. This change in the mix of fixed cost and variable cost means that at small output levels, average total cost might increase, but at large output levels, average total cost decreases.

Prices of Factors of Production

An increase in the price of a factor of production increases costs and shifts the cost curves. But how the curves shift depends on which resource price changes. An increase in rent or some other component of *fixed* cost shifts the fixed cost curves (*TFC* and *AFC*) upward and shifts the total cost curve (*TC*) upward but leaves the variable cost curves (*AVC* and *TVC*) and the marginal cost curve (*MC*) unchanged.

FIGURE 11.8
Product Curves and Cost Curves

*e*Foundations 11.3 

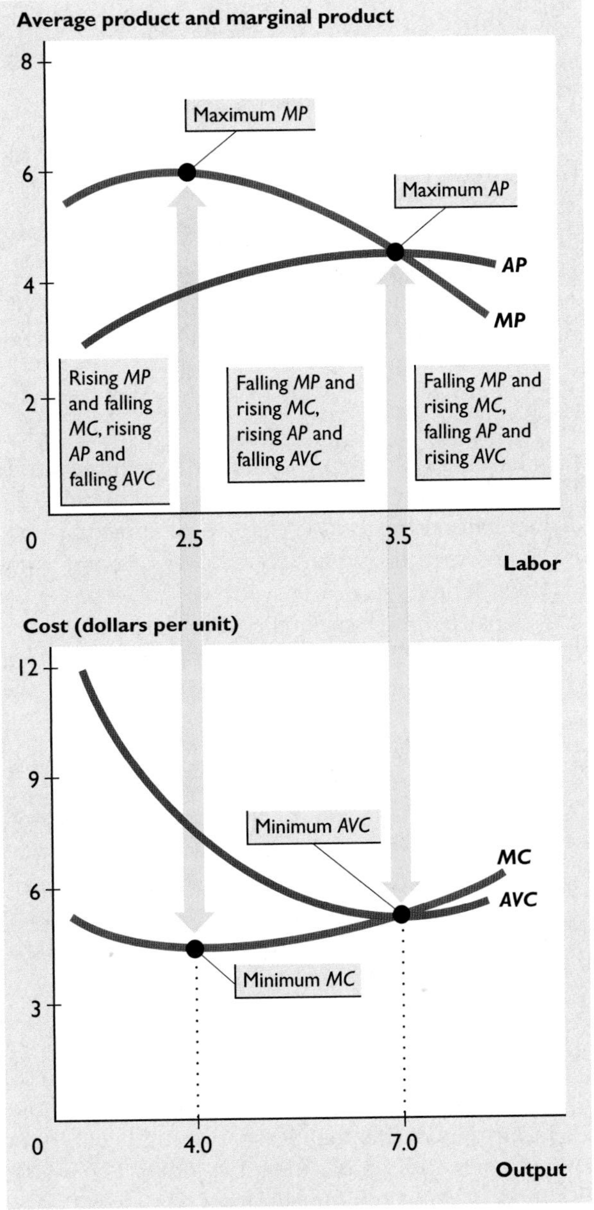

A firm's marginal cost curve is linked to its marginal product curve. If marginal product rises, marginal cost falls. If marginal product is a maximum, marginal cost is a minimum. If marginal product diminishes, marginal cost rises.

A firm's average variable cost curve is linked to its average product curve. If average product rises, average variable cost falls. If average product is a maximum, average variable cost is a minimum. If average product diminishes, average variable cost rises.

An increase in wage rates or some other component of *variable* cost shifts the variable curves (*TVC* and *AVC*) and the marginal cost curve (*MC*) upward but leaves the fixed cost curves (*AFC* and *TFC*) unchanged. So, for example, if the interest expense paid by a trucking company increases, the fixed cost of transportation services increases, but if the wage rate paid to truck drivers increases, the variable cost and marginal cost of transportation services increase.

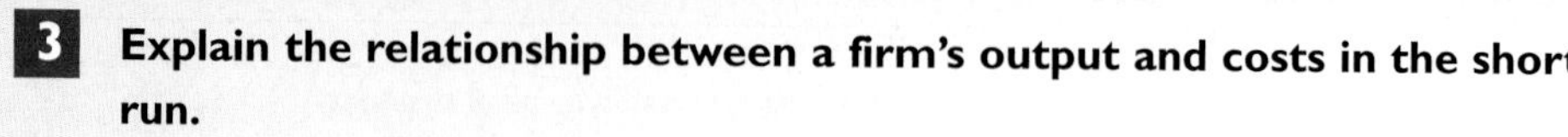

CHECKPOINT 11.3

Study Guide pp. 173–176

***e*Foundations 11.3**

3 **Explain the relationship between a firm's output and costs in the short run.**

Practice Problem 11.3

Tom leases a farmer's field for $120 a day and grows pineapples. Tom pays students $100 a day to pick and pack the pineapples. Tom leases capital at $80 a day. Table 1 gives the daily output.

a. Construct the total cost schedule.
b. Construct the average total cost schedule.
c. Construct the marginal cost schedule.
d. At what output is Tom's average total cost a minimum?

TABLE 1

Labor (students per day)	Output (pineapples per day)
0	0
1	100
2	220
3	300
4	360
5	400
6	420
7	430

Exercise 11.3

Lisa has a lawn-mowing business. Lisa hires students at $40 a day to mow lawns. Lisa leases 5 lawn mowers for $200 a day. Table 2 gives the daily output.

a. Construct the total variable cost and total cost schedules.
b. Construct the average fixed cost, average variable cost, and average total cost schedules.
c. Construct the marginal cost schedule.
d. Check that the gap between total cost and total variable cost is the same at all outputs. Explain why.

TABLE 2

Labor (students per day)	Output (lawns cut per day)
0	0
1	20
2	44
3	70
4	94
5	114
6	120

Solution to Practice Problem 11.3

a. Total cost is the sum of total fixed cost and total variable cost. Tom leases the farmer's field for $120 a day and leases capital for $80 a day, so Tom's total fixed cost is $200 a day. Total variable cost is the wages of the students. For example, when Tom hires 3 students, the total variable cost is $300 a day. So when Tom hires 3 students, total cost is $500 a day. The *TC* column of Table 3 shows the total cost schedule.

b. Average total cost is the total cost divided by total product. For example, when Tom hires 3 students, they pick and pack 300 pineapples a day, and Tom's total cost is $500 a day. Average total cost is $1.67 a pineapple. The *ATC* column of Table 3 shows the average total cost schedule.

c. Marginal cost is the increase in total cost that results from picking and packing one additional pineapple a day. The total cost (from Table 1) of picking and packing 100 pineapples a day is $300. The total cost of picking and packing 220 pineapples a day is $400. The increase in the number of pineapples is 120, and the increase in total cost is $100. So the marginal cost is the increase in total cost divided by the increase in the number of pineapples. Marginal cost equals $100/120 pineapples, which is $0.83 per pineapple. The *MC* column of Table 3 shows the marginal cost schedule.

d. At the minimum of average total cost, average total cost and marginal cost are equal. Minimum average total cost is $1.67 a pineapple.

TABLE 3

Labor	*TP*	*TC*	*MC*	*ATC*
0	0	200		–
			1.00	
1	100	300		3.00
			0.83	
2	220	400		1.82
			1.25	
3	300	500		1.67
			1.67	
4	360	600		1.67
			2.50	
5	400	700		1.75
			5.00	
6	420	800		1.91
			10.00	
7	430	900		2.09

11.4 LONG-RUN COST

In the long run, a firm can vary both the quantity of labor and the quantity of capital. A small firm, such as Sam's Smoothies, can increase its plant by moving into a larger building and installing more machines. A big firm such as General Motors can decrease its plant by closing down some production lines.

We are now going to see how costs vary in the long run when a firm varies its plant—the quantities of labor and capital it uses.

The first thing that happens is that the distinction between fixed cost and variable cost disappears. All costs are variable in the long run.

Plant Size and Cost

When a firm changes its plant size, its cost of producing a given output changes. In Figure 11.7 (p. 272), the lowest average total cost that Sam can achieve is $4.25 a gallon, which occurs when she produces 8 gallons of smoothies an hour. Samantha wonders what would happen to her average total cost if she increased the size of her plant by renting a bigger building and installing a larger number of blenders and refrigerators. Will the average total cost of producing a gallon of smoothie fall, rise, or remain the same?

Each of these three outcomes is possible, and they arise because when a firm changes the size of its plant, it might experience:

- Economies of scale
- Diseconomies of scale
- Constant returns to scale

Economies of Scale

If when a firm increases its plant size and labor employed by the same percentage, its output increases by a larger percentage, the firm's average total cost decreases. The firm experiences **economies of scale**. The main source of economies of scale is greater specialization of both labor and capital.

Specialization of Labor If GM produced 100 cars a week, each production line worker would have to perform many different tasks. But if GM produces 10,000 cars a week, each worker can specialize in a small number of tasks and become highly proficient at them. The result is that the average product of labor increases and the average total cost of producing a car falls.

Specialization also occurs off the production line. For example, a small firm usually does not have a specialist sales manager, personnel manager, and production manager. One person covers all these activities. But when a firm is large enough, specialists perform these activities. Average product increases, and the average total cost falls.

Specialization of Capital At a small output rate, firms often must employ general-purpose machines and tools. For example, with an output of a few gallons an hour, Sam's Smoothies uses regular blenders like the one in your kitchen. But if Sam's produces hundreds of gallons an hour, it uses custom blenders that fill, empty, and clean themselves. The result is that the output rate is larger and the average total cost of producing a gallon of smoothie is lower.

Economies of scale
A condition in which, when a firm increases its plant size and labor employed by the same percentage, its output increases by a larger percentage and its average total cost decreases.

ECONOMICS *in the* NEWS

January 29, 2001

Chrysler to Cut 26,000 Jobs

DaimlerChrysler announced a cut in Chrysler's work force of 26,000 as part of a restructuring plan aimed at bringing the North American car producer back to profitability. The cuts include indefinitely closing a plant and reducing production from 3 shifts to 2 shifts in some other plants.

Questions

1. How does indefinitely closing a plant influence DaimlerChrysler's costs? Sketch the effects on the firm's cost curves (ATC, AVC, AFC, and MC).
2. How does reducing production to two shifts influence DaimlerChrysler's costs? Sketch the effects on the firm's cost curves (ATC, AVC, AFC, and MC).
3. Which of these changes, if any, are short-run changes and which, if any, are long-run changes?

 *e*Foundations 11.4

Diseconomies of Scale

Diseconomies of scale
A condition in which, when a firm increases its plant size and labor employed by the same percentage, its output increases by a smaller percentage and its average total cost increases.

If when a firm increases its plant size and labor employed by the same percentage, output increases by a smaller percentage, the firm's average total cost increases. The firm experiences **diseconomies of scale**. Diseconomies of scale arise from the difficulty of coordinating and controlling a large enterprise. The larger the firm, the greater is the cost of communicating both up and down the management hierarchy and among managers. Eventually, management complexity brings rising average cost. Diseconomies of scale occur in all production processes but in some, perhaps, only at a very large output rate.

Constant Returns to Scale

Constant returns to scale
A condition in which, when a firm increases its plant size and labor employed by the same percentage, its output increases by the same percentage and its average total cost remains constant.

If when a firm increases its plant size and labor employed by the same percentage, output increases by that same percentage, the firm's average total cost remains constant. The firm experiences **constant returns to scale**. Constant returns to scale occur when a firm is able to replicate its existing production facility including its management system. For example, General Motors might double its production of Cavaliers by doubling its production facility for those cars. It can build an identical production line and hire an identical number of workers. With the two identical production lines, GM produces exactly twice as many cars. The average cost of producing a Cavalier is identical in the two plants. So when production increases, average total cost remains constant.

The Long-Run Average Cost Curve

Long-run average cost curve
A curve that shows the lowest average cost at which it is possible to produce each output when the firm has had sufficient time to change both its plant size and labor employed.

The **long-run average cost curve** shows the lowest average cost at which it is possible to produce each output when the firm has had sufficient time to change both its labor force and its plant.

Figure 11.9 shows Sam's Smoothies' long-run average cost curve *LRAC*. This long-run average cost curve is derived from the short-run average total cost curves for different possible plant sizes.

With its current small plant, Sam's Smoothies operates on the average total cost curve ATC_1 in Figure 11.9. The other three average total cost curves are for successively bigger plants. In this example, for outputs up to 5 gallons an hour, the existing plant with average total cost curve ATC_1 produces smoothies at the lowest attainable average cost. For outputs between 5 and 10 gallons an hour, average total cost is lowest on ATC_2. For outputs between 10 and 15 gallons an hour, average total cost is lowest on ATC_3. And for outputs in excess of 15 gallons an hour, average total cost is lowest on ATC_4.

The segment of each of the four average total cost curves for which that plant has the lowest average total cost is highlighted in dark blue in Figure 11.9. The scallop-shaped curve made up of these four segments is Sam's Smoothies' long-run average cost curve.

Economies and Diseconomies of Scale

When economies of scale are present, the *LRAC* curve slopes downward. The *LRAC* curve in Figure 11.9 shows that Sam's Smoothies experiences economies of scale for output rates up to 9 gallons an hour. At output rates between 9 and 12 gallons an hour, the firm experiences constant returns to scale. And at output rates that exceed 12 gallons an hour, the firm experiences diseconomies of scale.

FIGURE 11.9
Long-run Average Cost Curve

*e*Foundations **11.4** 

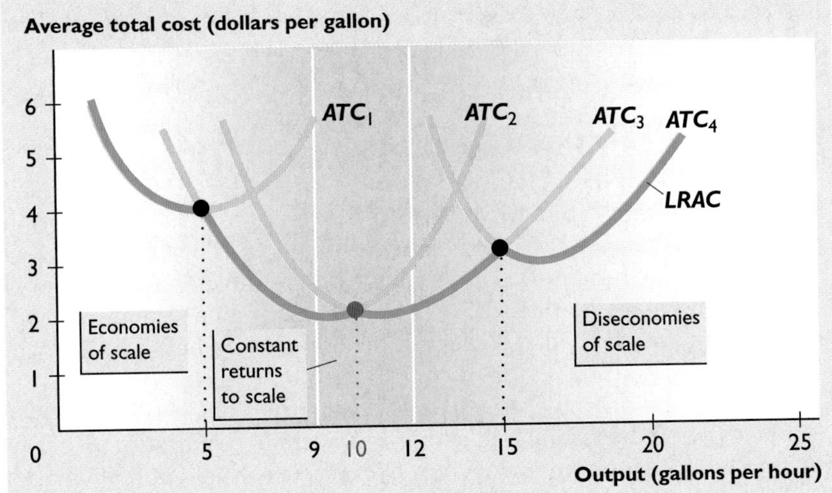

In the long run, Samantha can vary both capital and labor inputs. The long-run average cost curve traces the lowest attainable average total cost of producing each output.

Sam's experiences economies of scale as output increases to 9 gallons an hour, constant returns to scale for outputs between 9 gallons and 12 gallons an hour, and diseconomies of scale for outputs that exceed 12 gallons an hour.

The ATM and the Cost of Getting Cash

Most banks use automated teller machines—ATMs—to dispense cash. But small credit unions don't have ATMs. Instead, they employ tellers.

Gemini Consulting of Morristown, New Jersey, estimates that the average total cost of a transaction is $1.07 for a teller and 27¢ for an ATM. Given these numbers, why don't small credit unions install ATMs and lay off their tellers?

The answer is scale. At a small number of transactions per month, it costs less to use a teller than an ATM. In the figure, the average total cost curve for transactions done with a teller is ATC_T. The average total cost curve for transactions done with an ATM is ATC_A. You can see that if the number of transactions is Q per month, the average total cost per transaction is the same for both methods. For a bank that does more than Q transactions per month, the least-cost method is the ATM. For a credit union that does fewer than Q transactions per month, its least-cost method is the teller. More technology is not always more efficient.

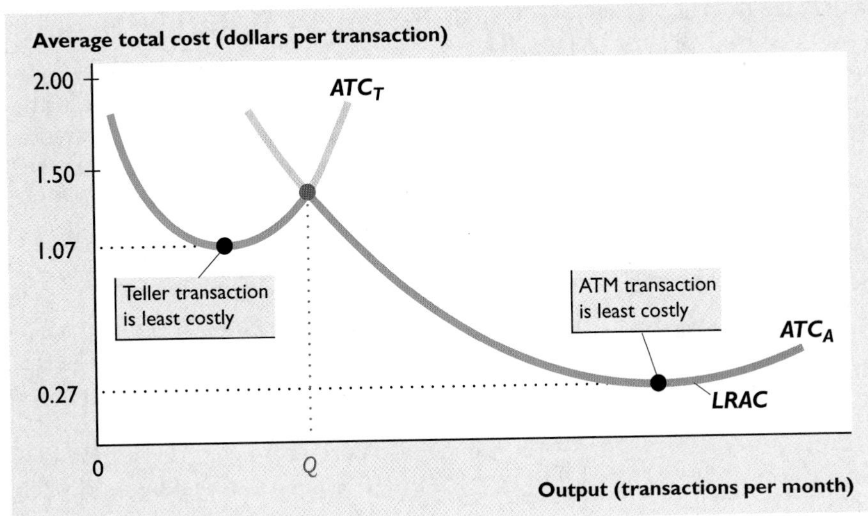

CHECKPOINT 11.4

Study Guide pp. 177–179 

e/Foundations 11.4

4 **Derive and explain a firm's long-run average cost curve.**

Practice Problem 11.4

Tom grows pineapples. He leases a farmer's field for $120 a day and capital for $80 a day. He hires students at $100 a day. Suppose that Tom now leases two fields for $240 a day and twice as much capital for $160 a day. Tom discovers that his output is the numbers in the third column of Table 1. The numbers in the second column are his output with 1 field and the original amount of capital.

a. Find Tom's average total cost curve schedule when he operates with two fields.

b. Make a graph of Tom's average total cost curves using 1 field and 2 fields, and show on the graph Tom's long-run average cost curve.

c. Over what output range will Tom operate with 1 field and at what output rate will he operate with 2 fields?

d. What happens to Tom's average total cost curve if he farms 2 fields and doubles his capital?

e. Does Tom experience economies of scale or diseconomies of scale?

TABLE 1

Labor (students per day)	Output with 1 field (pineapples per day)	Output with 2 fields (pineapples per day)
0	0	0
1	100	220
2	220	460
3	300	620
4	360	740
5	400	820
6	420	860
7	430	880

Exercise 11.4

Lisa has a lawn-mowing business. Lisa hires students at $5 an hour to mow the lawns. Lisa leases 5 lawn mowers for $200 a day. Suppose that Lisa doubles the number of students she hires and doubles the number of lawn mowers that she rents. If Lisa experiences diseconomies of scale:

a. Explain what has happened to her average total cost curve.

b. What might be the source of the diseconomies of scale?

TABLE 2

TP (1 field)	*ATC* (1 field)	*TP* (2 fields)	*ATC* (2 fields)
100	3.00	220	2.27
220	1.82	460	1.30
300	1.67	620	1.13
360	1.67	740	1.08
400	1.75	820	1.10
420	1.91	860	1.16
430	2.09	880	1.25

Solution to Practice Problem 11.4

a. Total cost is fixed cost of $400 a day plus $100 a day for each student hired. Average total cost is the total cost divided by output. The "*ATC* with 2 fields" column of Table 2 shows Tom's average total cost schedule.

b. Figure 1 shows Tom's average total cost curves using 1 field at ATC_1. This curve graphs the data on *ATC* and total product in Table 3 on p. 276. Using 2 fields, the average total cost curve is ATC_2. Tom's long-run average cost curve is the lower segments of these two *ATC* curves, highlighted in Figure 1.

c. If Tom produces up to 300 pineapples a day, he will operate with 1 field. If he produces more than 300 pineapples a day, he will operate with 2 fields.

d. When Tom farms 2 fields and doubles his capital, average total cost increases at low outputs (up to 300 a day) and decreases at high outputs (greater than 300 a day).

e. Tom experiences economies of scale because as he has increased his plant, the average total cost of picking and packing a pineapple decreases.

FIGURE 1

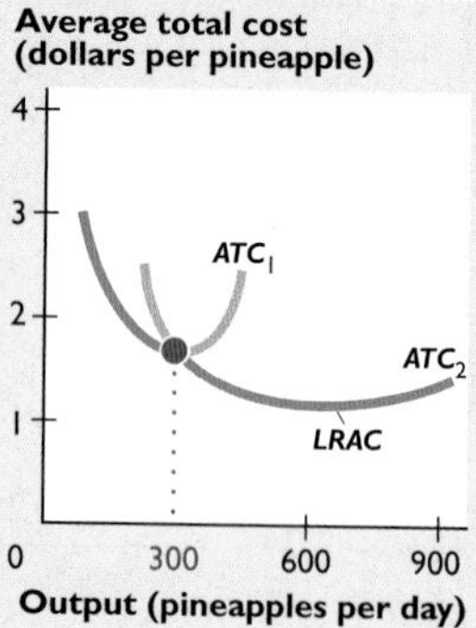

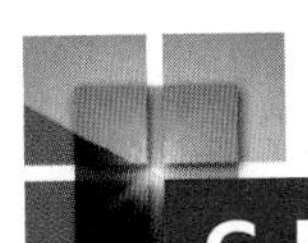

CHAPTER CHECKPOINT

Key Points

1 Explain how economists measure a firm's cost of production and profit.

- Firms seek to maximize economic profit, which is total revenue minus total cost.
- Total cost equals opportunity cost—the sum of explicit costs plus implicit costs and includes normal profit.

2 Explain the relationship between a firm's output and labor employed in the short run.

- In the short run, the firm can change the output it produces by changing labor only.
- A total product curve shows the limits to the output that the firm can produce with a given quantity of capital and different quantities of labor.
- As the quantity of labor increases, the marginal product of labor increases initially but eventually decreases—the law of decreasing returns.

3 Explain the relationship between a firm's output and costs in the short run.

- As total product increases, total fixed cost is constant, and total variable cost and total cost increase.
- As total product increases, average fixed cost decreases and average variable cost, average total cost, and marginal cost decrease at small outputs and increase at large outputs. Their curves are U-shaped.

4 Derive and explain a firm's long-run average cost curve.

- In the long run, the firm can change the size of its plant.
- Long-run cost is the cost of production when all inputs have been adjusted to produce at the lowest attainable cost.
- The long-run average cost curve traces out the lowest attainable average total cost at each output when both capital and labor inputs can be varied.
- The long-run average cost curve slopes downward with economies of scale and upward with diseconomies of scale.

Key Terms

Exercises

1. Sonya used to sell real estate and earn \$25,000 a year, but she now sells greetings cards. Normal profit for the retailers of greeting cards is \$14,000. Over the past year, Sonya bought \$10,000 worth of cards from manufacturers of cards. She sold these cards for \$58,000. Sonya rents a shop for \$5,000 a year and spends \$1,000 on utilities and office expenses. Sonya owns a cash register, which she bought for \$2,000 from her savings account. Her bank pays 3 percent a year on savings accounts. At the end of the year, Sonya was offered \$1,600 for her cash register machine. Calculate Sonya's:
   a. Explicit costs
   b. Implicit costs
   c. Economic profit

TABLE 1

Labor (workers per day)	Total product (body boards per day)
0	0
1	20
2	44
3	60
4	72
5	80
6	84
7	86

2. Len's body board factory rents equipment for shaping boards at \$300 a week. Len hires students for \$1,000 a week. Table 1 sets out the total product schedule of Len's body board factory.
   a. Construct the marginal product and average product schedules.
   b. After how many workers employed do marginal returns decrease?
   c. Construct the total variable cost and total cost schedules.
   d. Calculate total cost minus total variable cost at each output rate. What does this quantity equal? Why?
   e. Construct the average fixed cost, average variable cost, and average total cost schedules.
   f. Construct the marginal cost schedule.
   g. At what output is Len's average total cost a minimum?
   h. At what output is Len's average variable cost a minimum?
   i. Explain why the output at which average variable cost is a minimum is smaller than the output at which average total cost is a minimum.

3. Table 2 sets out the quantity of labor (*L*), total product, and the various costs incurred at Bill's factory. Calculate the values of *A*, *B*, *C*, *D*, and *E*. Show your work.

TABLE 2

L	*TP*	*TVC*	*TC*	*AFC*	*AVC*	*ATC*	*MC*
1	100	350	850	**C**	3.50	**D**	
							2.50
2	240	700	**B**	2.08	2.92	5.00	
							E
3	380	**A**	1,550	1.32	2.76	4.08	
							5.83
4	440	1,400	1,900	1.14	3.18	4.32	
							11.67
5	470	1,750	2,250	1.06	3.72	4.79	

4. Explain what the long-run average cost curve shows and how it is derived.

5. Explain the sources of economies of scale and diseconomies of scale, and illustrate these two situations in a figure.

6. Provide examples of industries in which you think economies of scale exist and explain why you think they are present in these industries.

7. Provide examples of industries in which you think diseconomies of scale exist and explain why you think they are present in these industries.

Prices, Profits, and Industry Performance

Chapter

12

Perfect Competition

CHAPTER CHECKLIST

When you have completed your study of this chapter, you will be able to:

1 **Explain a perfectly competitive firm's profit-maximizing choices and derive its supply curve.**

2 **Explain how output, price, and profit are determined in the short run.**

3 **Explain how output, price, and profit are determined in the long run.**

Some markets are highly competitive, and firms find it hard to earn profits. Other markets appear to be almost free from competition, and firms earn large profits. Some markets are dominated by fierce advertising campaigns in which each firm seeks to persuade buyers that it has the best products. And some markets display a warlike character. In this chapter, we study the first of the above market types, known as perfect competition.

What you learned in the previous chapter gets its first big workout in this chapter. If your understanding of a firm's cost curves is still a bit shaky, check back to Chapter 11 when you need to.

You're going to see how the principles of rational choice, balancing costs and benefits at the margin, and responding to incentives enable us to understand and predict the decisions that firms make in competitive markets.

MARKET TYPES

The four market types are:

- Perfect competition
- Monopoly
- Monopolistic competition
- Oligopoly

Perfect Competition

Perfect competition
A market in which there are many firms, each selling an identical product; many buyers; and no restrictions on the entry of new firms into the industry.

Perfect competition exists when:

- Many firms sell an identical product to many buyers.
- There are no restrictions on entry into (or exit from) the market.
- Established firms have no advantage over new firms.
- Sellers and buyers are well informed about prices.

These conditions that define perfect competition arise when the market demand for the product is large relative to the output of a single producer. And this situation arises when economies of scale are absent so the efficient scale of each firm is small. But a large market and the absence of economies of scale are not sufficient to create perfect competition. In addition, each firm must produce a good or service that has no characteristics that are unique to that firm so that consumers don't care from which firm they buy. Firms in perfect competition all look the same to the buyer.

Wheat farming, fishing, wood pulping and paper milling, the manufacture of paper cups and plastic shopping bags, lawn service, dry cleaning, and the provision of laundry services are all examples of highly competitive industries.

Other Market Types

Monopoly
A market for a good or service that has no close substitutes and in which there is one supplier that is protected from competition by a barrier preventing the entry of new firms.

Monopolistic competition
A market in which a large number of firms compete by making similar but slightly different products.

Oligopoly
A market in which a small number of firms compete.

Monopoly arises when one firm sells a good or service that has no close substitutes and a barrier blocks the entry of new firms. In some places, the phone, gas, electricity, and water suppliers are local monopolies—monopolies that are restricted to a given location. For many years, a global firm called DeBeers had a near international monopoly in diamonds.

Monopolistic competition arises when a large number of firms compete by making similar but slightly different products. Each firm is the sole producer of the particular version of the good in question. For example, in the market for running shoes, Nike, Reebok, Fila, Asics, New Balance, and many others make their own versions of the perfect shoe. The term "monopolistic competition" reminds us that each firm has a monopoly on a particular brand of shoe but the firms compete with each other.

Oligopoly arises when a small number of firms compete. Airplane manufacture is an example of oligopoly. Oligopolies might produce almost identical products, such as Kodak and Fuji film. Or they might produce differentiated products such as the colas produced by Coke and Pepsi.

We study perfect competition in this chapter, monopoly in Chapter 13, and monopolistic competition and oligopoly in Chapter 14.

12.1 A FIRM'S PROFIT-MAXIMIZING CHOICES

A firm's objective is to maximize *economic profit*, which is equal to *total revenue* minus the *total cost* of production. *Normal profit*, the return that the firm's entrepreneur can obtain in the best alternative business, is part of the firm's cost.

In the short run, a firm achieves its objective by deciding the quantity to produce. This quantity influences the firm's total revenue, total cost, and economic profit. In the long run, a firm achieves its objective by deciding whether to enter or exit a market.

These are the key decisions that a firm in perfect competition makes. Such a firm does *not* choose the price at which to sell its output. The firm in perfect competition is a **price taker**—it cannot influence the price of its product.

Price taker
A firm that cannot influence the price of the good or service that it produces.

Price Taker

To see why a firm in perfect competition is a price taker, imagine that you are a wheat farmer in Kansas. You have a thousand acres under cultivation—which sounds like a lot. But then you go on a drive through Colorado, Oklahoma, Texas, and back up to Nebraska and the Dakotas. You find unbroken stretches of wheat covering millions of acres. And you know that there are similar vistas in Canada, Argentina, Australia, and Ukraine. Your thousand acres are a drop in the ocean. Nothing makes your wheat any better than any other farmer's, and all the buyers of wheat know the price they must pay. If the going price of wheat is \$4 a bushel, you are stuck with that price. You can't get a higher price than \$4, and you have no incentive to offer it for less than \$4 because you can sell your entire output at that price.

The producers of most agricultural products are price takers. We'll illustrate perfect competition with another agriculture example: the market for maple syrup. The next time you pour syrup on your pancakes, think about the competitive market that gets this product from the sap of the maple tree to your table!

Dave's Maple Syrup is one of the more than 10,000 similar firms in the maple syrup market of North America. Dave is a price taker. Like the Kansas wheat farmer, he can sell any quantity he chooses at the going price but none above that price. Dave faces a *perfectly elastic* demand. The demand for Dave's syrup is perfectly elastic because syrup from Casper Sugar Shack and all the other maple farms in the United States and Canada are *perfect substitutes* for Dave's syrup.

We'll explore Dave's decisions and their implications for the way a competitive market works. We begin by defining some revenue concepts.

Revenue Concepts

In perfect competition, market demand and market supply determine the price. A firm's *total revenue* equals this given price multiplied by the quantity sold. A firm's **marginal revenue** is the change in total revenue that results from a one-unit increase in the quantity sold. In perfect competition, marginal revenue equals price. The reason is that the firm can sell any quantity it chooses at the going market price. So if the firm sells one more unit, it sells it for the market price and total revenue increases by that amount. But this increase in total revenue is marginal revenue. So marginal revenue equals price.

Marginal revenue
The change in total revenue that results from a one-unit increase in the quantity sold.

The table in Figure 12.1 illustrates the equality of marginal revenue and price. The price of syrup is \$8 a can. Total revenue is equal to the price multiplied by the quantity sold. So if Dave sells 10 cans, his total revenue is $10 \times \$8 = \$80$. If the quantity sold increases from 10 cans to 11 cans, total revenue increases from \$80 to \$88, so marginal revenue is \$8 a can, the same as the price.

Figure 12.1 illustrates price determination and revenue in the perfectly competitive market. Market demand and market supply in part (a) determine the market price. Dave is a price taker, so he sells his syrup for the market price. The demand curve for Dave's syrup is the horizontal line at the market price in part (b). Because price equals marginal revenue, the demand curve for Dave's syrup is Dave's marginal revenue curve (*MR*). The total revenue curve (*TR*), in part (c), shows the total revenue at each quantity sold. Because he sells each can for the market price, the total revenue curve is an upward-sloping straight line.

Profit-Maximizing Output

As output increases, total revenue increases. But total cost also increases. And because of *decreasing marginal returns* (see pp. 264–266), total cost eventually increases faster than total revenue. There is one output level that maximizes economic profit, and a perfectly competitive firm chooses this output level.

FIGURE 12.1

Demand, Price, and Revenue in Perfect Competition

*e*Foundations 12.1 

Price (dollars per can)
16
8
0
Market supply curve
S
Market demand curve
D
100
150
Quantity (thousands of cans per day)

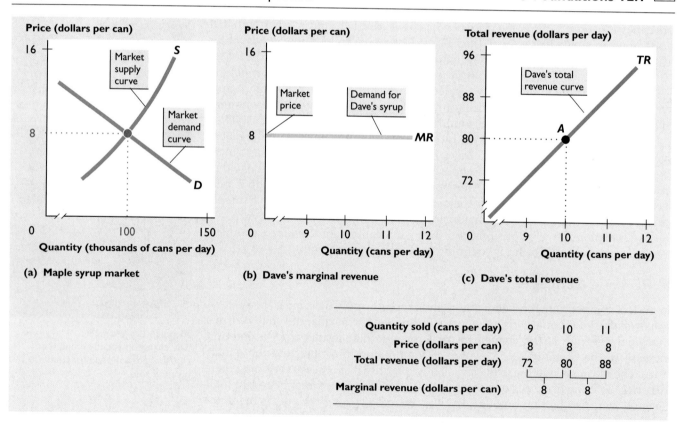

(a) Maple syrup market

Price (dollars per can)
16
8
0
Market price
Demand for Dave's syrup
MR
9
10
11
12
Quantity (cans per day)

(b) Dave's marginal revenue

Total revenue (dollars per day)
96
88
80
72
0
Dave's total revenue curve
TR
A
9
10
11
12
Quantity (cans per day)

(c) Dave's total revenue

Quantity sold (cans per day)	9	10	11
Price (dollars per can)	8	8	8
Total revenue (dollars per day)	72	80	88
Marginal revenue (dollars per can)	8		8

Part (a) shows the market for maple syrup. The market price is \$8 a can. The table calculates total revenue and marginal revenue.

Part (b) shows the demand curve for Dave's syrup, which is Dave's marginal revenue curve (*MR*).

Part (c) shows Dave's total revenue curve (*TR*). Point *A* corresponds to the second column of the table.

One way to find the profit-maximizing output is to use a firm's total revenue and total cost curves. Profit is maximized at the output level at which total revenue exceeds total cost by the largest amount. Figure 12.2 shows how to do this for Dave's Maple Syrup.

The table lists Dave's total revenue, total cost, and economic profit at different output levels. Figure 12.2(a) shows the total revenue and total cost curves. These curves are graphs of the numbers shown in the first three columns of the table. The total revenue curve (*TR*) is the same as that in Figure 12.1(c). The total cost curve (*TC*) is similar to the one that you met in Chapter 11 (p. 270). Figure 12.2(b) is an economic profit curve.

Dave makes an economic profit on outputs between 4 and 13 cans a day. At outputs of less than 4 cans a day and more than 13 cans a day, he incurs an economic loss. At outputs of 4 cans and 13 cans a day, total cost equals total revenue and Dave's economic profit is zero—Dave's *break-even points*.

The profit curve is at its highest when the vertical distance between *TR* and *TC* is greatest. In this example, profit maximization occurs at an output of 10 cans a day. At this output, Dave's economic profit is $29 a day.

FIGURE 12.2

Total Revenue, Total Cost, and Economic Profit

*e*Foundations 12.1 

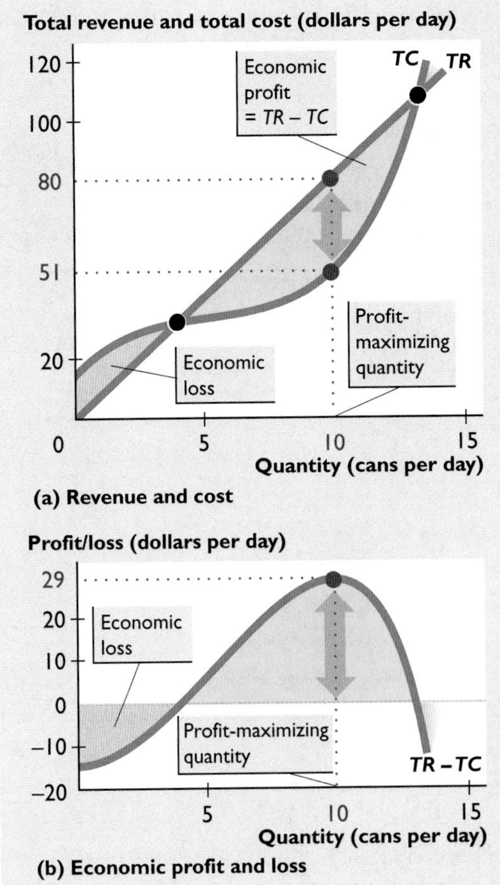

(a) Revenue and cost

(b) Economic profit and loss

Quantity (Q) (cans per day)	Total revenue (TR)	Total cost (TC)	Economic profit (TR – TC)
	(dollars per day)		
0	0	15	–15
1	8	22	–14
2	16	27	–11
3	24	30	–6
4	32	32	0
5	40	33	7
6	48	34	14
7	56	36	20
8	64	39	25
9	72	44	28
10	80	51	29
11	88	60	28
12	96	76	20
13	104	104	0
14	112	144	–32

In part (a), economic profit is the vertical distance between the total cost and total revenue curves. Dave's maximum economic profit is $29 a day ($80 – $51) when output is 10 cans a day.

In part (b), economic profit is the height of the profit curve.

Marginal Analysis and the Supply Decision

Another way to find the profit-maximizing output is to use *marginal analysis,* which compares marginal revenue, *MR,* with marginal cost, *MC.* As output increases, marginal revenue remains constant but marginal cost increases.

If marginal revenue exceeds marginal cost (if $MR > MC$), then the extra revenue from selling one more unit exceeds the extra cost incurred to produce it. Economic profit increases if output *increases.* If marginal revenue is less than marginal cost (if $MR < MC$), then the extra revenue from selling one more unit is less than the extra cost incurred to produce it. Economic profit increases if output *decreases.* If marginal revenue equals marginal cost (if $MR = MC$), economic profit is maximized. The rule $MR = MC$ is a prime example of marginal analysis.

Figure 12.3 illustrates these propositions. The table records Dave's marginal revenue and marginal cost. If Dave increases output from 9 cans to 10 cans a day, marginal revenue is $8 and marginal cost is $7. Because marginal revenue exceeds marginal cost, economic profit increases. The last column of the table shows that economic profit increases from $28 to $29. The blue area in the figure shows this economic profit from the tenth can.

If Dave increases output from 10 cans to 11 cans a day, marginal revenue is still $8 but marginal cost is $9. Because marginal revenue is less than marginal cost, economic profit decreases. The last column of the table shows that economic profit decreases from $29 to $28. The red area in the figure shows this economic loss from the eleventh can.

Dave maximizes economic profit by producing 10 cans a day, the quantity at which marginal revenue equals marginal cost.

FIGURE 12.3
Profit-Maximizing Output

e/**Foundations 12.1** 

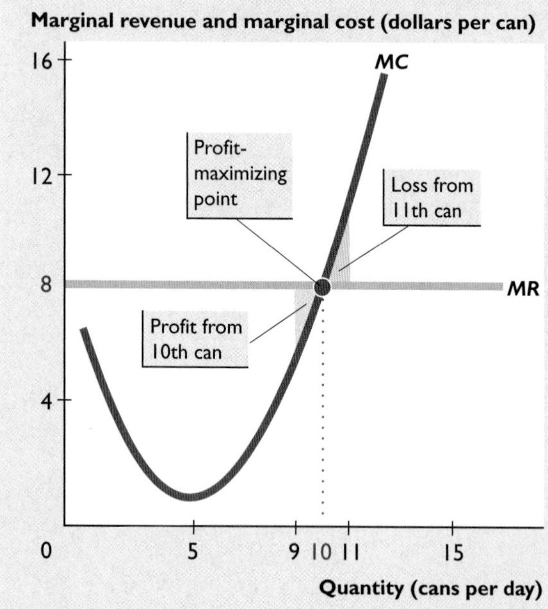

Quantity (Q) (cans per day)	Total revenue (TR) (cans per day)	Marginal revenue (MR) (dollars per can)	Total cost (TC) (cans per day)	Marginal cost (MC) (dollars per can)	Economic profit (TR – TC) (cans per day)
8	64		39		25
		8		5	
9	72		44		28
		8		7	
10	80		51		29
		8		9	
11	88		60		28
		8		16	
12	96		76		20

Profit is maximized when marginal revenue equals marginal cost at 10 cans a day. If output increases from 9 to 10 cans a day, marginal cost is $7, which is less than the marginal revenue of $8, and profit increases. If output increases from 10 to 11 cans a day, marginal cost is $9, which exceeds the marginal revenue of $8, and profit decreases.

In the example that we've just worked through, Dave's profit-maximizing output is 10 cans a day. This quantity is Dave's *quantity supplied* at a price of $8 a can. If the price were higher than $8 a can, he would increase production. If the price were lower than $8 a can, he would decrease production. These profit-maximizing responses to different prices are the foundation of the law of supply: *Other things remaining the same, the higher the price of a good, the greater is the quantity supplied of that good.*

Exit and Temporary Shutdown Decisions

Sometimes, the price falls so low that a firm cannot cover its costs. What does the firm do in such a situation? The answer depends on whether the firm expects the low price to be permanent or temporary.

If a firm is incurring an economic loss that it believes is permanent and sees no prospect of ending, the firm exits the market. We'll study the consequences of this action later in this chapter where we look at the long run (pp. 299–301).

If a firm is incurring an economic loss that it believes is temporary, it will remain in the market, and it might produce some output or temporarily shut down. To decide whether to produce or to shut down, the firm compares the loss it would incur in the two situations.

If the firm shuts down, it incurs an economic loss equal to total fixed cost. If the firm produces some output, it incurs an economic loss equal to total fixed cost *plus* total variable cost *minus* total revenue. If total revenue exceeds total variable cost, the firm's economic loss is less than total fixed cost. So it pays the firm to produce. But if total revenue were less than total variable cost, the firm's economic loss would exceed total fixed cost. So the firm would shut down temporarily. Total fixed cost is the largest economic loss that the firm will incur.

The firm's economic loss equals total fixed cost when price equals average variable cost. So the firm produces if price exceeds average variable cost and shuts down if average variable cost exceeds price.

The Firm's Short-Run Supply Curve

A perfectly competitive firm's short-run supply curve shows how the firm's profit-maximizing output varies as the price varies, other things remaining the same. This supply curve is based on the marginal analysis and shutdown decision that we've just explored.

Figure 12.4 derives Dave's supply curve. Part (a) shows the marginal cost and average variable cost curves, and part (b) shows the supply curve. There is a direct link between the marginal cost and average variable cost curves and the supply curve. Let's see what that link is.

If the price is above minimum average variable cost, Dave maximizes profit by producing the output at which marginal cost equals price. We can determine the quantity produced at each price from the marginal cost curve. At a price of $8 a can, the marginal revenue curve is MR_1 and Dave maximizes profit by producing 10 cans. If the price rises to $12 a can, the marginal revenue curve is MR_2 and Dave increases production to 11 cans a day.

The firm shuts down if the price falls below the minimum of average variable cost. The **shutdown point** is the output and price at which the firm just covers its total variable cost. In Figure 12.4(a), if the price is $3 a can, the marginal revenue curve is MR_0, and the profit-maximizing output is 7 cans a day at the shutdown

Shutdown point
The output and price at which price equals minimum average variable cost.

point. But both price and average variable cost equal $3 a can, so total revenue equals total variable cost and Dave incurs an economic loss equal to total fixed cost. At a price below $3 a can, if Dave produces any positive quantity, average *variable* cost exceeds price and the firm's loss exceeds total fixed cost. So at a price below $3 a can, Dave shuts down and produces nothing.

Dave's short-run supply curve, shown in Figure 12.4(b), has two separate parts: First, at prices that exceed minimum average variable cost, the supply curve is the same as the marginal cost curve above the shutdown point (*S*). Second, at prices below minimum average variable cost, Dave shuts down and produces nothing. His supply curve runs along the vertical axis. At a price of $3 a can, Dave is indifferent between shutting down and producing 7 cans a day. Either way, he incurs a loss of $15 a day, which equals his total fixed cost.

So far, we have studied one firm in isolation. We have seen that the firm's profit-maximizing actions depend on the price, which the firm takes as given. In the next section, you'll learn how market supply is determined.

FIGURE 12.4

Dave's Supply Curve

*e*Foundations 12.1 

Part (a) shows that at $8 a can, Dave produces 10 cans a day; at $12 a can, he produces 11 cans a day; and at $3 a can, he produces 7 cans a day. At any price below $3 a can, Dave produces nothing. The minimum average variable cost is the shutdown point.

Part (b) shows Dave's supply curve, which is made up of the marginal cost curve (part a) at all points *above* the shutdown point *S* (minimum average variable cost) and the vertical axis at all prices *below* the shutdown point.

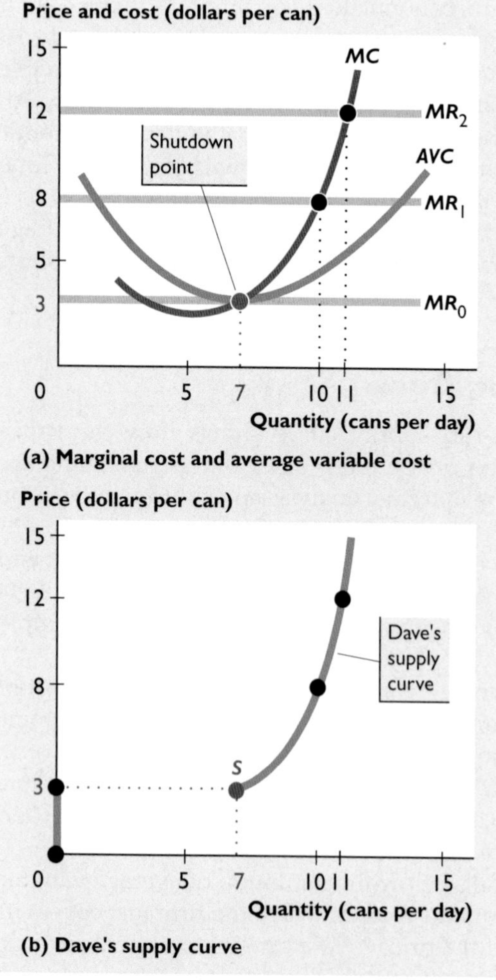

CHECKPOINT 12.1

1 **Explain a perfectly competitive firm's profit-maximizing choices and derive its supply curve.**

Study Guide pp. 186–190 
e/Foundations 12.1 

Practice Problems 12.1

1. Sarah's Salmon Farm produces 1,000 fish a week. The marginal cost is $30 a fish, average variable cost is $20 a fish, and the market price is $25 a fish. Is Sarah maximizing profit? Explain why or why not. If Sarah is not maximizing profit, to do so, will she increase or decrease the number of fish she produces in a week?

2. Trout farming is a perfectly competitive industry, and all trout farms have the same cost curves. The market price is $25 a fish. To maximize profit, each farm produces 200 fish a week. Average total cost is $20 a fish, and average variable cost is $15 a fish. Minimum average variable cost is $12 a fish.
   a. If the price falls to $20 a fish, will trout farms continue to produce 200 fish a week? Explain why or why not.
   b. If the price falls to $12 a fish, what will the trout farmer do?
   c. What is one point on the trout farm's supply curve?

Exercise 12.1

Roy is a potato farmer, and the world potato market is perfectly competitive. The market price is $25 a bag. Roy sells 40 bags a week, and his marginal cost is $20 a bag.

a. Calculate Roy's total revenue.
b. Calculate Roy's marginal revenue.
c. Is Roy maximizing profit? Explain your answer.
d. The price falls to $18 a bag, and Roy cuts his output to 25 bags a week. His average variable cost and marginal cost fall to $18 a bag. Is Roy maximizing profit? Is he making an economic profit or incurring an economic loss?
e. What is one point on Roy's supply curve?

Solutions to Practice Problems 12.1

1. Profit is maximized when marginal cost equals marginal revenue. In perfect competition, marginal revenue equals the market price and is $25 a fish. Because marginal cost exceeds marginal revenue, Sarah is not maximizing profit. To maximize profit, she will decrease her output until marginal cost falls to $25 a fish (see Figure 1).

2a. The farm will produce fewer than 200 fish a week. The marginal cost increases as the farm produces more fish. So to reduce its marginal cost from $25 to $20, the farm cuts production.

2b. If the price falls to $12 a fish, farms cut production to where marginal cost equals $12. But because $12 is minimum average variable cost, this price puts farms at the shutdown point. Farms will be indifferent between producing the profit-maximizing output and producing nothing. Either way, they incur an economic loss equal to total fixed cost.

2c. At $25 a fish, the quantity supplied is 200 fish; at $12 a fish, the quantity supplied might be zero; at a price below $12 a fish, the quantity supplied is zero.

FIGURE 1

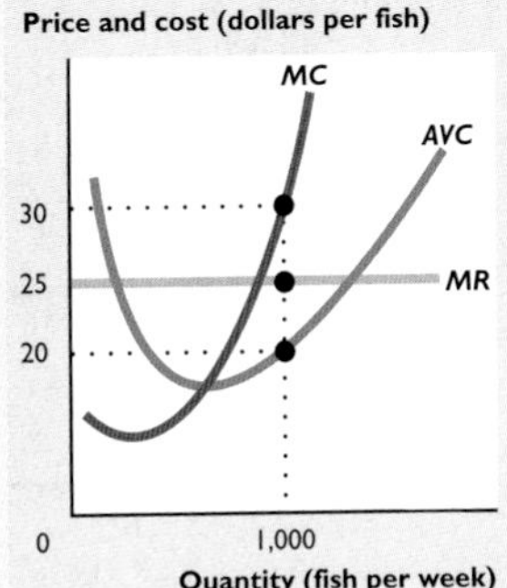

12.2 OUTPUT, PRICE, AND PROFIT IN THE SHORT RUN

To determine the price and quantity in a perfectly competitive market, we need to know how market demand and supply interact. We begin by studying a perfectly competitive market in the short run when the number of firms is fixed.

Market Supply in the Short Run

The market supply curve in the short run shows the quantity supplied at each price by a fixed number of firms. The quantity supplied at a given price is the sum of the quantities supplied by all firms at that price.

Figure 12.5 shows the supply curve for the competitive syrup market. In this example, the market consists of 10,000 firms exactly like Dave's Maple Syrup. The table shows how the market supply schedule is constructed. At prices below \$3, every firm in the market shuts down; the quantity supplied is zero. At a price of \$3, each firm is indifferent between shutting down and producing nothing or operating and producing 7 cans a day. The quantity supplied by each firm is *either* 0 or 7 cans, and the quantity supplied in the market is *between* 0 (all firms shut down) and 70,000 (all firms produce 7 cans a day each). At prices above \$3, we sum the quantities supplied by the 10,000 firms, so the quantity supplied in the market is 10,000 times the quantity supplied by one firm.

At prices below \$3, the market supply curve runs along the price axis. Supply is perfectly inelastic. At a price of \$3, the market supply curve is horizontal. Supply is perfectly elastic. At prices above \$3, the supply curve is upward sloping.

FIGURE 12.5
The Market Supply Curve

*e*Foundations 12.2 

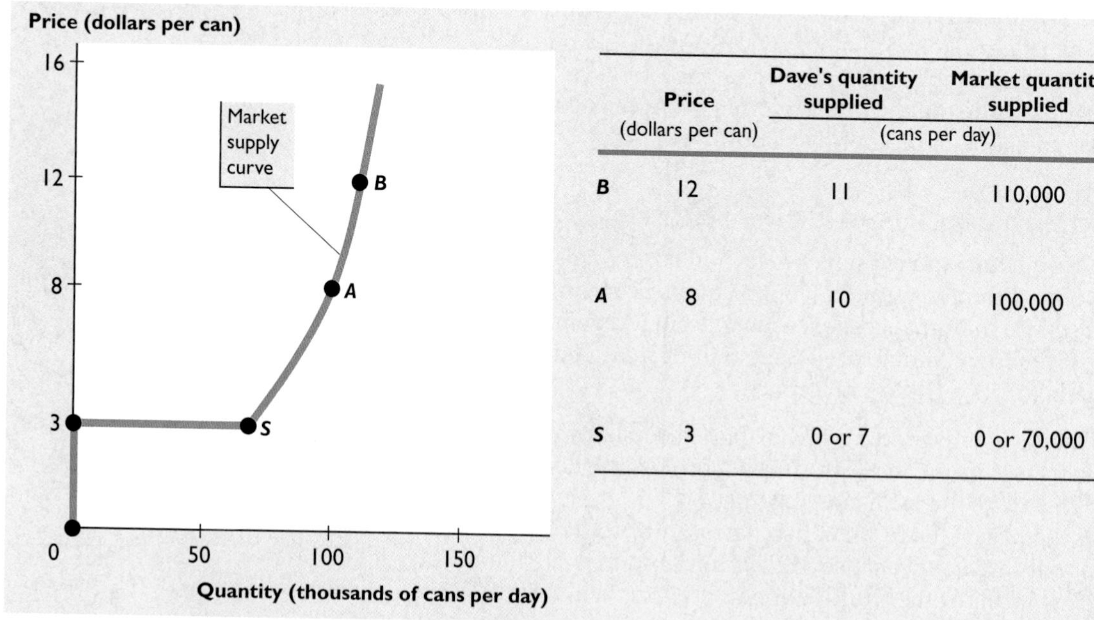

	Price (dollars per can)	Dave's quantity supplied (cans per day)	Market quantity supplied (cans per day)
B	12	11	110,000
A	8	10	100,000
S	3	0 or 7	0 or 70,000

A market with 10,000 identical firms has a supply schedule similar to that of the individual firm, but the quantity supplied is 10,000 times greater. At the shutdown price of \$3 a can, each firm produces either 0 or 7 cans a day, but the market supply curve is perfectly elastic at that price.

Short-Run Equilibrium in Good Times

Market demand and market supply determine the price and quantity bought and sold. Figure 12.6(a) shows a short-run equilibrium in the syrup market. The supply curve S is the same as that in Figure 12.5.

If the demand curve D_1 shows market demand, the equilibrium price is $8 a can. Although market demand and market supply determine this price, each firm takes the price as given and produces its profit-maximizing output, which is 10 cans a day. Because the market has 10,000 firms, market output is 100,000 cans a day.

Figure 12.6(b) shows the situation that the Dave faces. The price is $8 a can, so Dave's marginal revenue is constant at $8 a can. Dave maximizes profit by producing 10 cans a day.

Figure 12.6(b) also shows Dave's average total cost curve (*ATC*). Recall that average total cost is the cost per unit produced. It equals total cost divided by the quantity of output produced.

Here, when Dave produces 10 cans a day, his average total cost is $5.10 a can. So the price of $8 a can exceeds average total cost by $2.90 a can. This amount is Dave's economic profit per can.

If we multiply the economic profit per can of $2.90 by the number of cans, 10 a day, we arrive at Dave's economic profit, which is $29 a day.

The blue rectangle shows this economic profit. The height of that rectangle is the profit per can, $2.90, and the length is the quantity of cans, 10 a day, so the area of the rectangle measures Dave's economic profit of $29 a day.

FIGURE 12.6
Economic Profit in the Short Run

e **Foundations 12.2** 

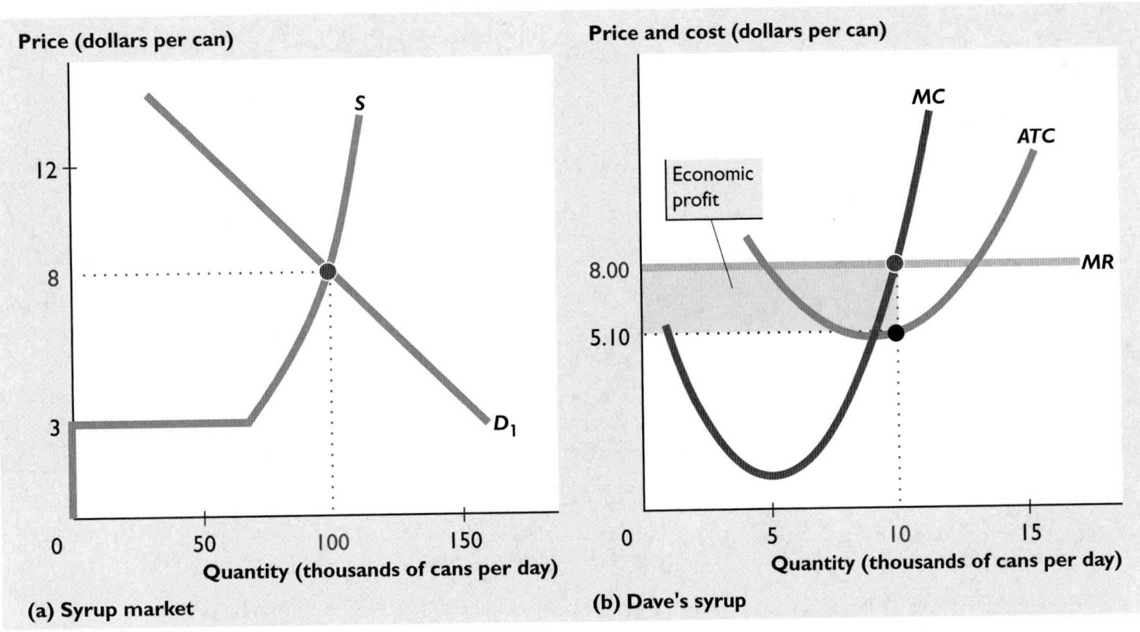

In part (a), with market demand curve D_1 and market supply curve S, the price is $8 a can.

In part (b), Dave's marginal revenue is $8 a can, so he produces 10 cans a day. At this quantity, price ($8) exceeds average total cost ($5.10), so Dave makes an economic profit shown by the blue rectangle.

Short-Run Equilibrium in Bad Times

In the short-run equilibrium that we've just examined, Dave is enjoying an economic profit. But such an outcome is not inevitable. Figure 12.7 shows the syrup market in a less happy state. The market demand curve is now D_2. The market still has 10,000 firms, and the costs of these firms are the same as before. So the market supply curve, S, is the same as before.

With the demand and supply curves shown in Figure 12.7(a), the equilibrium price of syrup is $3 a can and the equilibrium quantity is 70,000 cans a day.

Figure 12.7 (b) shows the situation that Dave faces. The price is $3 a can, so Dave's marginal revenue is constant at $3 a can. Dave maximizes profit by producing 7 cans a day.

Figure 12.7(b) also shows Dave's average total cost curve (*ATC*), and you can see that when Dave produces 7 cans a day, his average total cost is $5.14 a can. So the price of $3 a can is less than average total cost by $2.14 a can. This amount is Dave's economic loss per can.

If we multiply the economic loss per can of $2.14 by the number of cans, 7 a day, we arrive at Dave's economic loss, which is $14.98 a day.

The red rectangle shows this economic loss. The height of that rectangle is the loss per can, $2.14, and the length is the quantity of cans, 7 a day, so the area of the rectangle measures Dave's economic loss of $14.98 a day.

FIGURE 12.7

Economic Loss in the Short Run

*e*Foundations 12.2 

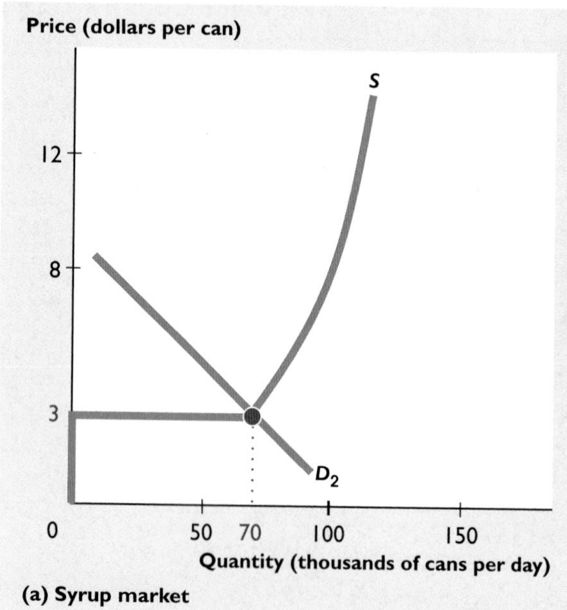

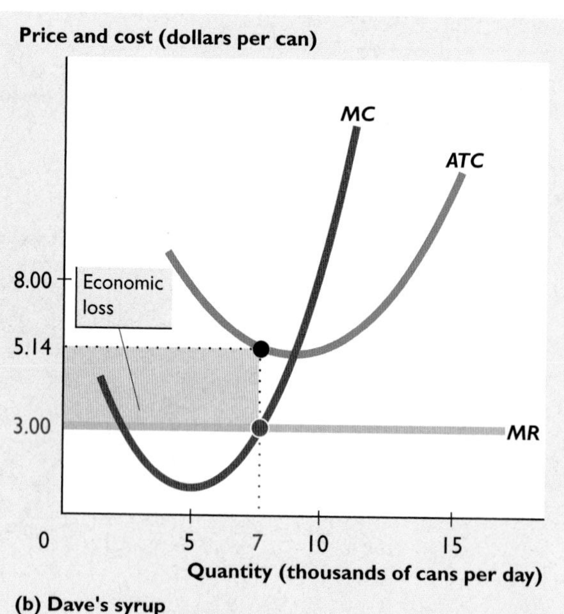

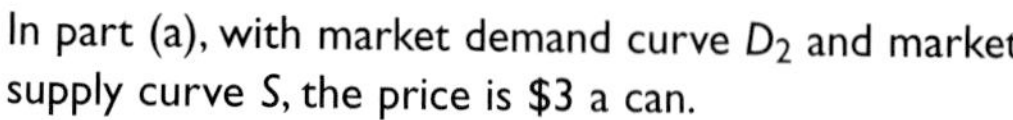
In part (a), with market demand curve D_2 and market supply curve S, the price is $3 a can.

In part (b), Dave's marginal revenue is $3 a can, so he produces 7 cans a day. At this quantity, price ($3) is less than average total cost ($5.14), so Dave incurs an economic loss shown by the red rectangle.

CHECKPOINT 12.2

2 **Explain how output, price, and profit are determined in the short run.**

Study Guide pp. 190–193 

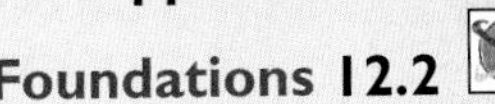

Practice Problem 12.2

Tulip growing is a perfectly competitive industry, and all tulip growers have the same cost curves. The market price of tulips is $25 a bunch, and each grower maximizes profit by producing 2,000 bunches a week. The average total cost of producing tulips is $20 a bunch, and the average variable cost is $15 a bunch. Minimum average variable cost is $12 a bunch.

a. What is the economic profit that each grower is making in the short run?
b. What is the price at the grower's shutdown point?
c. What is the each grower's profit at the shutdown point?

Exercises 12.2

1. Lisa's Lawn Company is a lawn-mowing business in a perfectly competitive market for lawn-mowing services. Table 1 sets out Lisa's costs. If the market price is $30 a lawn:
   a. How many lawns an hour does Lisa's Lawn Company mow?
   b. What is Lisa's profit in the short run?
2. In Exercise 1, if the market price falls to $20 a lawn:
   a. How many lawns an hour does Lisa's Lawn Company mow?
   b. What is Lisa's profit in the short run?
3. In Exercise 1:
   a. At what market price will Lisa shut down?
   b. When Lisa shuts down, what will be her economic loss?

TABLE 1

Quantity (lawns per hour)	Total cost (dollars per lawn)
0	30
1	40
2	55
3	75
4	100
5	130
6	165

Solution to Practice Problem 12.2

a. The market price ($25) exceeds the average total cost ($20), so tulip growers are making an economic profit of $5 a bunch. Each grower produces 2,000 bunches a week, so each grower makes an economic profit of $10,000 a week (Figure 1).

b. The price at which a grower will shut down is equal to the minimum average variable cost—$12 a bunch (Figure 1).

c. At the shutdown point, the grower incurs an economic loss equal to total fixed cost. *ATC* = *AFC* + *AVC*. When 2,000 bunches a week are grown, *ATC* is $20 a bunch and *AVC* is $15 a bunch, so *AFC* is $5 a bunch. Total fixed cost equals $10,000 a week—$5 a bunch × 2,000 bunches a week. So at the shutdown point, the grower incurs an economic loss equal to $10,000 a week.

FIGURE 1

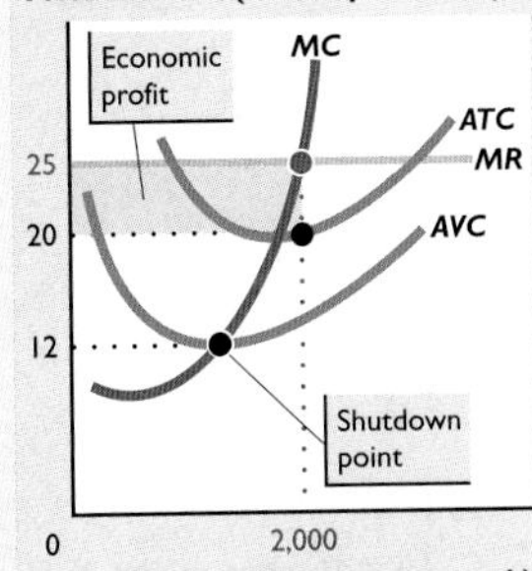

12.3 OUTPUT, PRICE, AND PROFIT IN THE LONG RUN

Neither good times nor bad times last forever in perfect competition. In the long run, a firm in perfect competition earns normal profit. It earns zero economic profit and incurs no economic loss.

Figure 12.8 shows the syrup market in a long-run equilibrium. The market demand curve is now D_3. The market still has 10,000 firms, and the costs of these firms are the same as before. So the market supply curve, *S*, is the same as before.

With the demand and supply curves shown in Figure 12.8(a), the equilibrium price of syrup is $5 a can and the equilibrium quantity is 90,000 cans a day.

Figure 12.8(b) shows the situation that Dave faces. The price is $5 a can, so Dave's marginal revenue is constant at $5 a can and Dave maximizes profit by producing 9 cans a day.

Figure 12.8(b) also shows Dave's average total cost curve (*ATC*), and you can see that when Dave produces 9 cans a day, his average total cost is $5 a can, which is also the minimum average total cost. That is, Dave can't produce syrup at an average total cost that is less than $5 a can no matter what his output is.

The price of $5 a can equals average total cost, so Dave has neither an economic profit nor an economic loss. He breaks even. But because his average total cost includes normal profit, Dave earns normal profit.

FIGURE 12.8

Long-run Equilibrium

*e*Foundations 12.3 

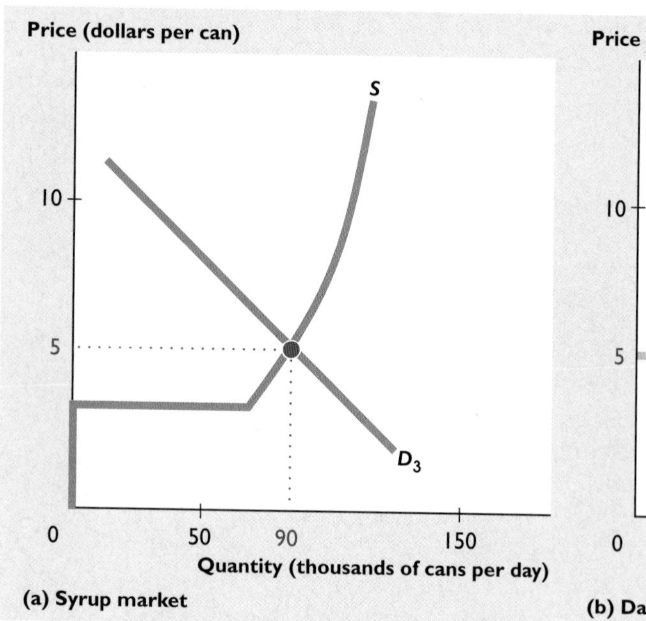

(a) Syrup market

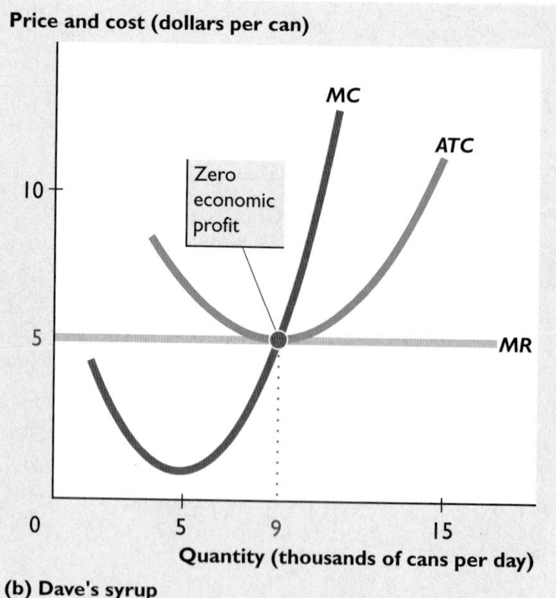

(b) Dave's syrup

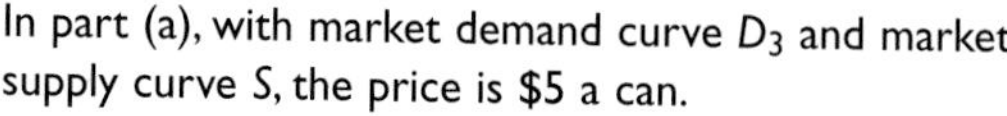
In part (a), with market demand curve D_3 and market supply curve *S*, the price is $5 a can.

In part (b), Dave's marginal revenue is $5 a can, so he produces 9 cans a day, where marginal cost equals marginal revenue. At this profit-maximizing quantity, price equals average total cost ($5), so Dave earns no economic profit. He earns normal profit.

Entry and Exit

In the short run, a perfectly competitive firm might make an economic profit (Figure 12.6) or incur an economic loss (Figure 12.7). But in the long run, a firm earns normal profit (Figure 12.8).

In the long run, firms respond to economic profit and economic loss by either entering or exiting a market. New firms enter a market in which the existing firms are making an economic profit. And existing firms exit a market in which they are incurring an economic loss. Temporary economic profit or temporary economic loss, like a win or loss at a casino, does not trigger entry and exit. But the prospect of persistent economic profit or loss does.

Entry and exit influence price, the quantity produced, and economic profit. The immediate effect of the decision to enter or exit is to shift the market supply curve. If more firms enter a market, supply increases and the market supply curve shifts rightward. If firms exit a market, supply decreases and the market supply curve shifts leftward.

Let's see what happens when new firms enter a market.

The Effects of Entry

Figure 12.9 shows the effects of entry. Initially, the market is in long-run equilibrium. Demand is D_0, supply is S_0, the price is $5 a can, and the quantity is 90,000 cans a day. A surge in the popularity of syrup increases demand, and the demand curve shifts to D_1. The price rises to $8 a can, and the firms in the syrup market increase output and make an economic profit.

Times are good for syrup producers like Dave, so other potential syrup producers want some of the action. New firms begin to enter the market. As they do so, supply increases and the market supply curve shifts rightward to S_1. With the

FIGURE 12.9
The Effects of Entry

*e*Foundations 12.3 

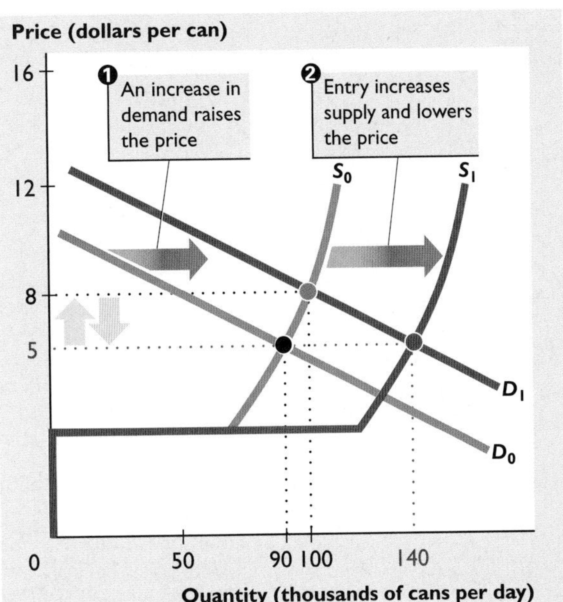

Starting in long-run equilibrium, ❶ demand increases from D_0 to D_1 and the price rises from $5 to $8 a can.

Economic profit brings entry. ❷ As firms enter the market, the supply curve shifts rightward, from S_0 to S_1. The equilibrium price falls from $8 to $5 a can, and the quantity produced increases from 100,000 to 140,000 cans a day.

greater supply and unchanged demand, the price falls from $8 to $5 a can and the quantity increases to 140,000 cans a day.

Market output increases, but because the price falls, Dave and the other producers decrease output, back to its original level. But because the number of firms in the market increases, the market as a whole produces more.

As the price falls, each firm's economic profit decreases. When the price falls to $5, economic profit disappears and each firm makes a normal profit. The entry process stops, and the market is again in long-run equilibrium.

You have just discovered a key proposition:

Economic profit is an incentive for new firms to enter a market, but as they do so, the price falls and the economic profit of each existing firm decreases.

The Effects of Exit

Figure 12.10 shows the effects of exit. Again we begin on demand curve D_0 and supply curve S_0 in long-run equilibrium. Now suppose that the development of a new high-nutrition, low-fat breakfast food decreases the demand for pancakes, and as a result, the demand for maple syrup decreases to D_2. Firms' costs are the same as before, so the market supply curve is S_0, just as it was before.

With demand at D_2 and supply at S_0, the price falls to $3 a can and 70,000 cans a day are produced. The firms in the syrup market incur economic losses.

Times are tough for syrup producers, and Dave must seriously think about leaving his dream business and finding some other way of making a living. But other producers are in the same situation as Dave. And some start to exit the market while Dave is still thinking through his options.

FIGURE 12.10
The Effects of Exit

*e*Foundations 12.3 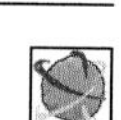

Starting in long-run equilibrium, ❶ demand decreases from D_0 to D_2 and the price falls from $5 to $3 a can.

Economic loss brings exit. ❷ As firms exit the market, the supply curve shifts leftward, from S_0 to S_2. The equilibrium price rises from $3 to $5 a can, and the quantity produced decreases from 70,000 to 40,000 cans a day.

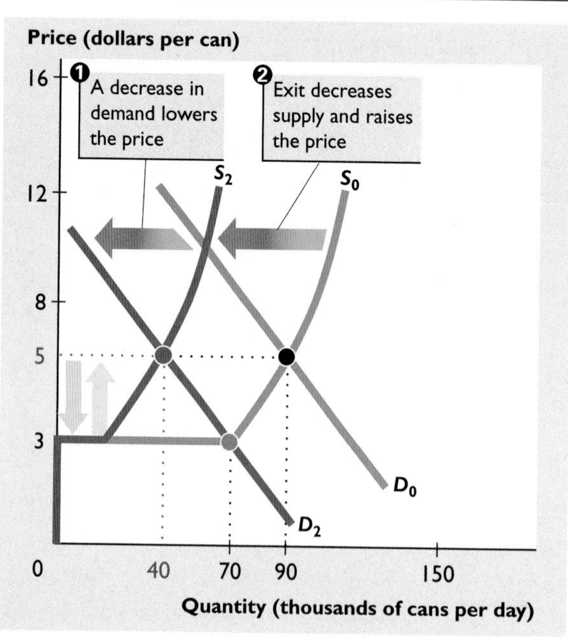

As firms exit, the market supply curve shifts leftward to S_2. With the decrease in supply, output decreases from 70,000 to 40,000 cans and the price rises from $3 to $5 a can.

As the price rises, Dave and each other firm that remains in the market move up along their supply curves and increase output. That is, for each firm that remains in the market, the profit-maximizing output *increases*. As the price rises and each firm sells more, economic loss decreases. When the price rises to $5, each firm makes a normal profit. Dave is happy that he can still make a living producing syrup.

You have just discovered a second key proposition:

Economic loss is an incentive for firms to exit a market, but as they do so, the price rises and the economic loss of each remaining firm decreases.

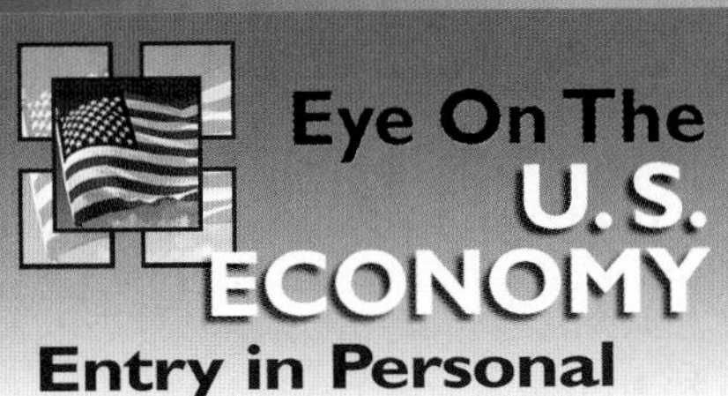

Entry in Personal Computers, Exit in Farm Machines

An example of entry and falling prices occurred during the 1980s and 1990s in the personal computer market. When IBM introduced its first PC in 1981, there was little competition; the price was $7,000 (a bit more than $14,000 in today's money) , and IBM earned a large economic profit on the new machine. But new firms such as Compaq, NEC, Dell, and a host of others entered the market with machines that were technologically identical to IBM's. In fact, they were so similar that they came to be called "clones." The massive wave of entry into the personal computer market shifted the supply curve rightward and lowered the price and the economic profit for all firms. Today, a $1,000 computer is much more powerful than its 1981 ancestor that cost 14 times as much.

An example of a firm leaving a market is International Harvester, a manufacturer of farm equipment. For decades, people associated the name "International Harvester" with tractors, combines, and other farm machines. But International Harvester wasn't the only maker of farm equipment. The market became intensely competitive, and the firm began to incur an economic loss. Now the company has a new name, Navistar International, and it doesn't make tractors any more. After years of economic losses and shrinking revenues, it got out of the farm-machine business in 1985 and started to make trucks.

International Harvester exited because it was incurring an economic loss. Its exit decreased supply and made it possible for the remaining firms in the market to earn a normal profit.

February 21, 2000

Music Schools Scaling Up

Adults aged 25 to 55 are the fastest-growing group of piano students. This trend has Jinean Florom of the Discover Music Learning Center in Littleton, Colorado, thrilled. Enrollment at her music school took off six years ago. Her profits have doubled every year since then. She has hired 10 new piano teachers, 2 guitar teachers, and a horn instructor and is searching for a larger studio.

Adapted from CNNfn.com

Questions

1. Is the music education industry competitive? Why or why not?

2. Make a diagram that shows a firm's costs and the demand for its product and use the diagram to illustrate the situation at the Discover Music Center.

3. Do you predict that firms are entering or exiting the music education business? Explain your answer.

 **e/Foundations 12.3**

A Permanent Change in Demand

The long-run adjustments in the maple syrup market that we've just explored apply to all competitive markets. The market begins in long-run equilibrium. Price equals the minimum of average total cost, and firms are making normal profit. Then demand increases permanently. The increase in demand raises the price above minimum average total cost, so firms make economic profits. To maximize profit, firms increase output to keep marginal cost equal to price.

The market is now in short-run equilibrium but not long-run equilibrium. It is in short-run equilibrium because the number of firms is fixed. But it is not in long-run equilibrium because each firm is making an economic profit.

The economic profit is an incentive for new firms to enter the market. As they do so, market supply starts to increase and the price starts to fall. At each lower price, a firm's profit-maximizing output is less, so each firm decreases its output. That is, as firms enter the market, market output increases but the output of each firm decreases. Eventually, enough firms enter for market supply to have increased by enough to return the price to its original level. At this price, the firms produce the same quantity that they produced before the increase in demand and they earn normal profit again. The market is again in long-run equilibrium.

The difference between the initial long-run equilibrium and the final long-run equilibrium is the number of firms in the market. A permanent increase in demand increases the number of firms. Each firm produces the same output in the new long-run equilibrium as initially and earns a normal profit. In the process of moving from the initial equilibrium to the new one, firms make economic profits.

The demand for airline travel in the world economy has increased permanently in recent years, and the deregulation of the airlines has freed up firms to seek profit opportunities in this market. The result has been a massive rate of entry of new airlines. The process of competition and change in the airline market, although not a perfectly competitive market, is similar to what we have just studied.

A permanent decrease in demand triggers a similar response, except in the opposite direction. The decrease in demand brings a lower price, economic loss, and exit. Exit decreases market supply and eventually raises the price to its original level.

One feature of the predictions that we have just generated seems odd: In the long run, regardless of whether demand increases or decreases, the price returns to its original level. Is this outcome inevitable? In fact, it is not. It is possible for the long-run equilibrium price to remain the same, rise, or fall.

External Economies and Diseconomies

External economies
Factors beyond the control of an individual firm that lower its costs as the *market* output increases.

External diseconomies
Factors outside the control of a firm that raise the firm's costs as *market* output increases.

The change in the long-run equilibrium price depends on external economies and external diseconomies. **External economies** are factors beyond the control of an individual firm that lower its costs as the *market* output increases. **External diseconomies** are factors outside the control of a firm that raise the firm's costs as *market* output increases. With no external economies or external diseconomies, a firm's costs remain constant as the *market* output changes.

Figure 12.11 illustrates these three cases and introduces a new supply concept: the long-run market supply curve.

FIGURE 12.11
Long-run Changes in Price and Quantity

*e*Foundations 12.3 

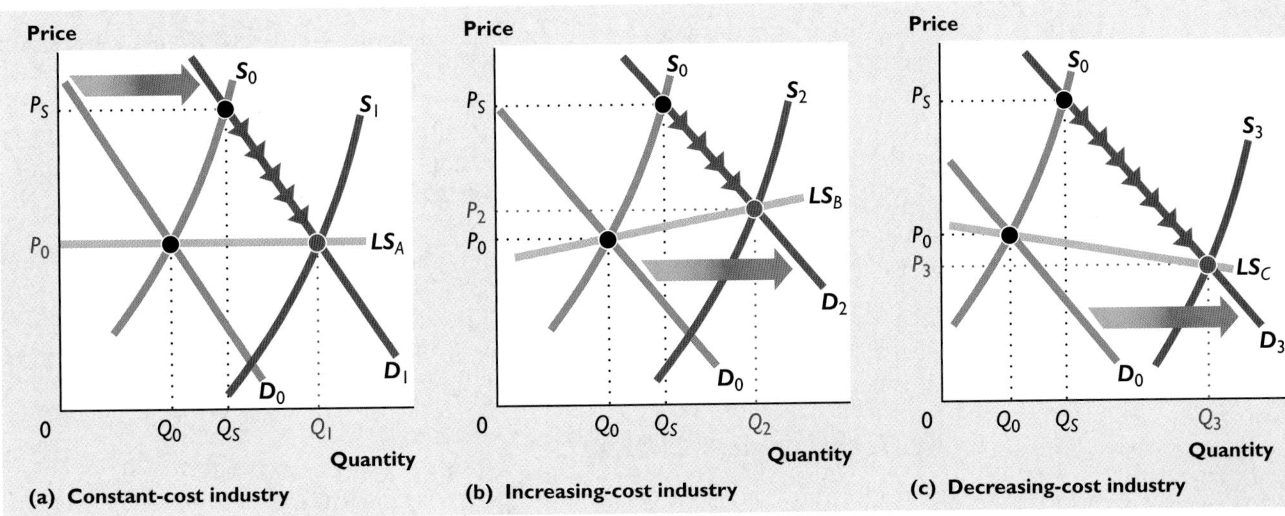

When demand increases from D_0 to D_1, entry occurs and the market supply curve shifts from S_0 to S_1. The long-run market supply curve, LS_A, is horizontal.

The long-run market supply curve is LS_B; the price rises to P_2, and the quantity increases to Q_2. This case occurs in industries with external diseconomies.

The long-run market supply curve is LS_C; the price falls to P_3, and the quantity increases to Q_3. This case occurs in an industry with external economies.

A **long-run market supply curve** shows the relationship between the quantity supplied and the price as the number of firms adjusts to achieve zero economic profit.

Long-run market supply curve
A curve that shows how the quantity supplied by a market varies as the price varies and the number of firms in the market varies to achieve zero economic profit.

Part (a) shows the case we have just studied: no external economies or diseconomies. The long-run market supply curve (LS_A) is perfectly elastic. In this case, a permanent increase in demand from D_0 to D_1 has no effect on the price in the long run. The increase in demand initially increases the price to P_S and increases the quantity to Q_S. Entry increases supply from S_0 to S_1, which lowers the price to its original level, P_0, and increases the quantity to Q_1.

Part (b) shows the case of external diseconomies. The long-run market supply curve (LS_B) slopes upward. A permanent increase in demand from D_0 to D_2 increases the price in both the short run and the long run. As in the previous case, the increase in demand initially increases the price to P_S and increases the quantity to Q_S. Entry increases supply from S_0 to S_2, which lowers the price to P_2 and increases the quantity to Q_2.

One source of external diseconomies is congestion. The airline market provides a good example. With bigger airline market output, there is more congestion of airports and airspace, which results in longer delays and extra waiting time for passengers and airplanes. These external diseconomies mean that as the output of air transportation services increases (in the absence of technological advances), average cost increases. As a result, the long-run supply curve is upward sloping. So a permanent increase in demand brings an increase in quantity and a rise in the price.

Part (c) shows the case of external economies. In this case, the long-run market supply curve (LS_C) slopes downward. A permanent increase in demand from D_0 to D_3 increases the price in the short run and lowers it in the long run. Again, the increase in demand initially increases the price to P_S, and increases the quantity to Q_S. Entry increases supply from S_0 to S_3, which lowers the price to P_3 and increases the quantity to Q_3.

One of the best examples of external economies is the growth of specialist support services for a market as it expands. As farm output increased in the nineteenth and early twentieth centuries, the services available to farmers expanded and average farm costs fell. For example, new firms specialized in the development and marketing of farm machinery and fertilizers. As a result, average farm costs decreased. Farms enjoyed the benefits of external economies. As a consequence, as the demand for farm products increased, the output increased but the price fell.

Over the long term, the prices of many goods and services have fallen. Some have fallen because of external economies. But prices in markets with external diseconomies have also fallen. The reason in both cases is that technological advances increase supply and shift the long-run supply curve rightward. Let's now study this influence on a competitive market.

Technological Change

Firms are constantly discovering lower-cost techniques of production. For example, the cost of producing personal computers has tumbled. So have the costs of producing CD players, DVD players, and most other electronic products. Most cost-saving production techniques cannot be implemented without investing in new plants. Consequently, it takes time for a technological advance to spread through a market. Some firms whose plants are on the verge of being replaced will be quick to adopt the new technology, while other firms whose plants have recently been replaced will continue to operate with an old technology until they can no longer cover their average variable cost. Once average variable cost cannot be covered, a firm will scrap even a relatively new plant (embodying an old technology) in favor of a plant with a new technology.

New technology allows firms to produce at a lower cost. As a result, as firms adopt a new technology, their cost curves shift downward. With lower costs, firms are willing to supply a given quantity at a lower price or, equivalently, they are willing to supply a larger quantity at a given price. In other words, market supply increases, and the market supply curve shifts rightward. With a given demand, the quantity produced increases and the price falls.

Two forces are at work in a market undergoing technological change. Firms that adopt the new technology make an economic profit. So new-technology firms have an incentive to enter. Firms that stick with the old technology incur economic losses. They either exit the market or switch to the new technology.

As old-technology firms exit and new-technology firms enter, the price falls and the quantity produced increases. Eventually, the market arrives at a long-run equilibrium in which all the firms use the new technology and each firm makes zero economic profit (a normal profit). Because competition eliminates economic profit in the long run, technological change brings only temporary gains to firms. But the lower prices and better products that technological advances bring are permanent gains for consumers.

The process that we've just described is one in which some firms experience economic profits and others experience economic losses—a period of dynamic change for a market. Some firms do well, and others do badly. Often, the process has a geographical dimension: The expanding new-technology firms bring prosperity to what was once the boondocks, and with old-technology firms going out of business, traditional industrial regions decline. Sometimes, the new-technology firms are in a foreign country, while the old-technology firms are in the domestic economy. The information revolution of the 1990s has produced many examples of changes like these. Commercial banking (a competitive but less than perfectly competitive industry), which was traditionally concentrated in New York, San Francisco, and other large cities, now flourishes in Charlotte, North Carolina, which has become the nation's number three commercial banking city. Television shows and movies, traditionally made in Los Angeles and New York, are now made in large numbers in Orlando and Toronto.

Technological advances are not confined to the information and entertainment market. Food production is undergoing a major technological change because of genetic engineering.

The North American Market in Maple Syrup

North American maple syrup production runs at about 8 million gallons a year. Most of this syrup is produced in Canada, but farms in Vermont, New York, Maine, Wisconsin, New Hampshire, Ohio, and Michigan together produce close to 20 percent of the total output.

The number of firms that produce maple syrup can only be estimated, because some are tiny and sell their output to a small local market. But there are around 9,500 producers in Canada and approaching 2,000 in the United States.

Maple syrup is not quite a homogeneous product. And at the retail level, people have preferences about brands and sources of supply. But at the wholesale level, the market is highly competitive and a good example of perfect competition.

All of the events that can occur in a perfectly competitive market and that we've studied in this chapter have actually occurred in the maple syrup market over the past 20 years.

During the 1980s, the technology for extracting sap advanced as more taps were installed that use a plastic tube vacuum technology. During this period, farms exited the market and the average farm increased in scale. In 1980, the average farm had 1,400 taps; by 1990, this number was 2,000; and by 1996, the number of taps had increased to 2,400.

During the 1990s, with a steady growth in the demand for maple syrup, new farms entered the market.

Through the past 20 years, total production has increased and the price has held remarkably stable at around $8 per half-gallon can. So increasing demand has brought economic profit, which in turn has brought entry and an increase in supply.

CHECKPOINT 12.3

Study Guide pp. 193–196
*e*Foundations 12.3

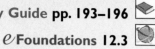

3 **Explain how output, price, and profit are determined in the long run.**

Practice Problem 12.3

Tulip growing is a perfectly competitive industry, and all tulip growers have the same cost curves. The market price of tulips is \$15 a bunch, and each grower maximizes profit by producing 1,500 bunches a week. The average total cost of producing tulips is \$21 a bunch. Minimum average variable cost is \$12 a bunch, and the minimum average total cost is \$18 a bunch. Tulip growing is a constant cost industry.

a. What is a tulip grower's economic profit in the short run?
b. How does the number of tulip growers change in the long run?
c. What is the price in the long run?
d. What is the economic profit in the long run?

Exercise 12.3

Lisa's Lawn Company is a lawn-mowing business in a perfectly competitive market for lawn-mowing services. Table 1 sets out Lisa's costs.

a. If the market price is \$30 a lawn, what is Lisa's economic profit?
b. If the market price is \$30 a lawn, do new firms enter or do existing firms exit the industry in the long run?
c. What is the price of the lawn service in the long run?
d. How many lawns does Lisa mow in the long run?
e. What is Lisa's economic profit in the long run?

TABLE 1

Quantity (lawns per hour)	Total cost (dollars per lawn)
0	30
1	40
2	55
3	75
4	100
5	130
6	165

FIGURE 1

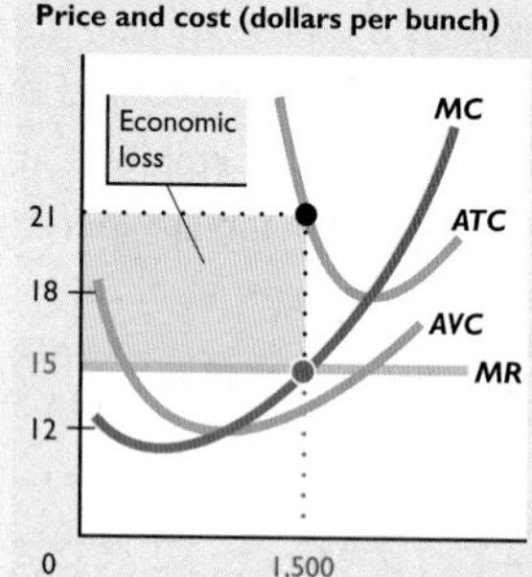

FIGURE 2

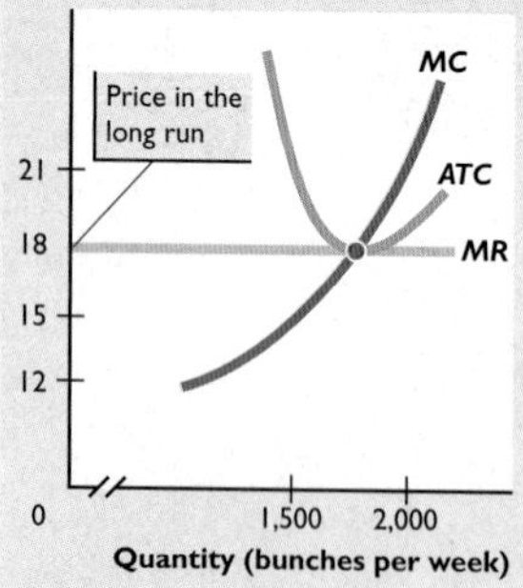

Solution to Practice Problem 12.3

a. The price is less than average total cost, so the tulip grower is incurring an economic loss in the short run. Because the price exceeds minimum average total cost, the tulip grower continues to produce. The economic loss equals the loss per bunch (\$21 minus \$15) multiplied by the number of bunches (1,500), which equals \$9,000 (Figure 1).

b. Because firms in the industry are incurring a loss, some firms will exit in the long run. So the number of tulip growers will decrease.

c. The price in the long run will be such that economic profit is zero. That is, as tulip growers exit, the price will rise until it equals the minimum average total cost. Because tulip growing is a constant cost industry, the long-run price will be \$18 a bunch (Figure 2).

d. Profit in the long run will be zero. Tulip growers will make normal profit (Figure 2).

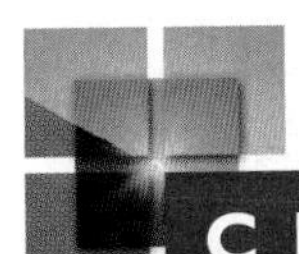

CHAPTER CHECKPOINT

Key Points

1 Explain a perfectly competitive firm's profit-maximizing choices and derive its supply curve.

- A perfectly competitive firm is a price taker.
- Marginal revenue equals price.
- The firm produces the output at which price equals marginal cost.
- If price is less than minimum average variable cost, the firm temporarily shuts down.
- A firm's supply curve is the upward-sloping part of its marginal cost curve above minimum average variable cost.

2 Explain how output, price, and profit are determined in the short run.

- Market demand and market supply determine price.
- Firms choose the quantity to produce that maximizes profit, which is the quantity at which marginal cost equals price.
- In short-run equilibrium, a firm can make an economic profit or incur an economic loss.

3 Explain how output, price, and profit are determined in the long run.

- Economic profit induces entry, which increases supply and lowers price and profit. Economic loss induces exit, which decreases supply and raises price and profit.
- In the long run, economic profit is zero and there is no entry or exit.
- The long-run effect of a change in demand on price depends on whether there are external economies (price falls) or external diseconomies (price rises) or neither (price remains constant).
- New technologies increase supply and in the long run lower the price and increase the quantity.

Key Terms

External diseconomies, 302
External economies, 302
Long-run market supply curve, 303
Marginal revenue, 287
Monopolistic competition, 286
Monopoly, 286
Oligopoly, 286
Perfect competition, 286
Price taker, 287
Shutdown point, 291

Exercises

1. In what type of market is each of the following goods and services sold? Explain your answers.
   a. Sugar
   b. Jeans
   c. Camera film
   d. Toothpaste
   e. Taxi rides in a town with one taxi company
2. Explain why in a perfectly competitive market, the firm is a price taker. Why can't the firm choose the price at which it sells its good?
3. Imagine that the restaurant industry is perfectly competitive. Joe's Diner is always packed in the evening but rarely has a customer at lunchtime. Why doesn't Joe's Diner close at lunchtime—temporarily shut down?
4. Explain why a perfectly competitive firm's supply curve is only part of its marginal cost curve.
5. 3M created Post-it Notes, also known as sticky notes. Soon many other firms entered the sticky note market and started to produce sticky notes.
   a. What was the incentive for these firms to enter the sticky note market?
   b. As time goes by, do you expect more firms to enter this market? Explain why or why not?
   c. Can you think of any reason why any of these firms might exit the sticky note market?
6. When Rod Laver completed his first grand slam in tennis in 1962, all rackets were made of wood. Today, tennis players use graphite rackets. As the demand for wooden tennis rackets decreased permanently, how did the profits of the firms producing wooden tennis rackets change? As some of these firms switched to producing graphite rackets, how did their economic profits change?

7. Use the link on your Foundations Web site to obtain information about the world market for wheat and then answer the following questions:
   a. Is the world market for wheat perfectly competitive? Why or why not?
   b. What has happened to the price of wheat during the 1990s?
   c. What has happened to the quantity of wheat produced during the 1990s?
   d. What do you think have been the main influences on the demand for wheat during the 1990s?
   e. What do you think have been the main influences on the supply of wheat during the 1990s?
   f. Do you think farmers entered or exited the wheat market during the 1990s? Explain your answer.
8. Small aluminum scooters have become popular in past few years. Explain the evolution of the market for scooters. Sketch the cost and revenue curves of a typical firm in the scooter industry:
   a. When the scooter fashion began.
   b. When the scooter fashion was two years old.
   c. When the scooter fashion faded.

Chapter 13

Monopoly

CHAPTER CHECKLIST

When you have completed your study of this chapter, you will be able to:

1. **Explain how monopoly arises and distinguish between single-price monopoly and price-discriminating monopoly.**
2. **Explain how a single-price monopoly determines its output and price.**
3. **Compare the performance of single-price monopoly with that of perfect competition.**
4. **Explain how price discrimination increases profit.**
5. **Explain how monopoly regulation influences output, price, economic profit, and efficiency.**

If you live in University City, Missouri, you buy your electricity from Union Electric or light your home with candles. If you live in Gainesville, Florida, and want cable TV service, you have only one option: buy from Cox Cable. These are examples of monopoly. Such firms can choose their own price. How do such firms choose the quantity to produce and the price at which to sell it? Do they charge too much?

Some firms—hairdressers, museums, and movie theaters are examples—give discounts to students. Are these firms run by generous folk to whom the model of profit-maximizing firms doesn't apply? Aren't these firms throwing profit away by cutting ticket prices and offering discounts?

In this chapter, we study monopoly. We learn how a monopoly behaves, and we discover whether monopoly is efficient and fair.

13.1 MONOPOLY AND HOW IT ARISES

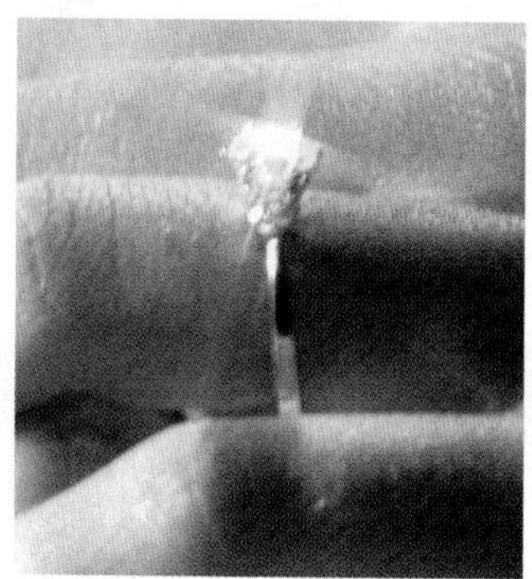

A *monopoly* is a market with a single supplier of a good or service that has no close substitutes and in which natural or legal barriers to entry prevent competition.

Markets for local telephone service, gas, electricity, and water are examples of local monopoly. GlaxoSmithKline has a monopoly on AZT, a drug that is used to treat AIDS. DeBeers, a South African firm, controls 80 percent of the world's production of raw diamonds—close to being a monopoly but not quite one.

How Monopoly Arises

Monopoly arises when there are:

- No close substitutes
- Barriers to entry

No Close Substitutes

If a good has a close substitute, even though only one firm produces it, that firm effectively faces competition from the producers of substitutes. Water supplied by a local public utility is an example of a good that does not have close substitutes. While it does have a close substitute for drinking—bottled spring water—it has no effective substitutes for doing the laundry, taking a shower, or washing a car.

Sometimes the arrival of a new product weakens a monopoly. For example, Federal Express, UPS, the fax machine, and e-mail have weakened the monopoly of the U.S. Postal Service; broadband fiber-optic phone lines and the satellite dish have weakened the monopoly of cable television companies.

The arrival of a new product can also create a monopoly. For example, the IBM PC of the early 1980s gave a monopoly in PC operating systems to Microsoft's DOS.

Barriers to Entry

Barrier to entry
A natural or legal constraint that protects a firm from competitors.

Anything that protects a firm from the arrival of new competitors is a **barrier to entry**. There are two types of barrier to entry:

- Natural
- Legal

Natural monopoly
A monopoly that arises because one firm can meet the entire market demand at a lower price than two or more firms could.

Natural Barriers to Entry A **natural monopoly** exists when the technology for producing a good or service enables one firm to meet the entire market demand at a lower price than two or more firms could. One electric power distributor can meet the market demand for electricity at a lower cost than two or more firms could. Imagine two or more sets of wires running to your home so that you could choose your electric power supplier.

Figure 13.1 illustrates a natural monopoly in the distribution of electric power. Here, the demand curve for electric power is *D* and the long-run average cost curve is *LRAC*. Economies of scale prevail over the entire length of this *LRAC* curve, indicated by the fact that the curve slopes downward. One firm can produce 4 million kilowatt-hours at 5 cents a kilowatt-hour. At this price, the quantity demanded is 4 million kilowatt-hours. So if the price was 5 cents, one firm could supply the entire market. If two firms shared the market, it would cost each

FIGURE 13.1
Natural Monopoly

*e*Foundations 13.1 

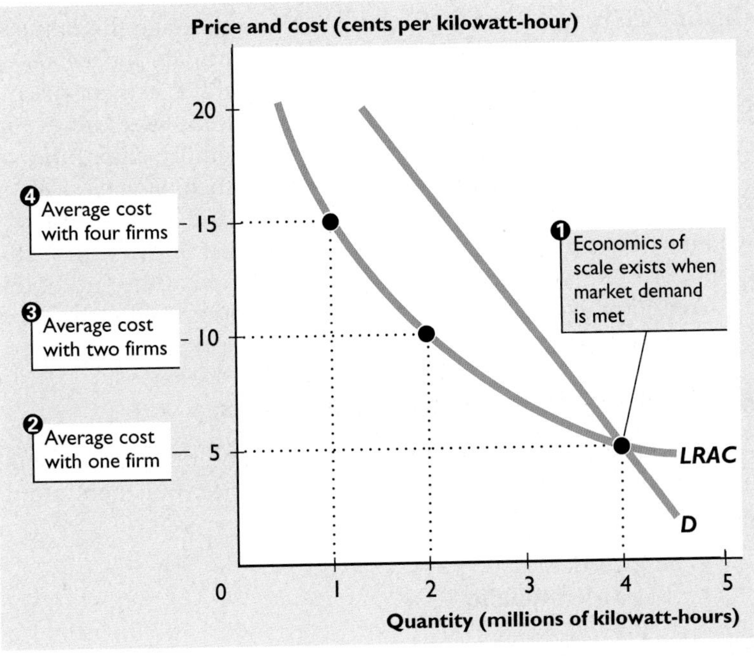

The demand curve for electric power is *D*, and the long-run average cost curve is *LRAC*.

❶ Economies of scale exist over the entire *LRAC* curve. One firm can distribute 4 million kilowatt-hours at a ❷ cost of 5 cents a kilowatt-hour. This same total output ❸ costs 10 cents a kilowatt-hour with two firms and ❹ 15 cents a kilowatt-hour with four firms. So one firm can meet the market demand at a lower cost than two or more firms can, and the market is a natural monopoly.

of them 10 cents a kilowatt-hour to produce a total of 4 million kilowatt-hours. If four firms shared the market, it would cost each of them 15 cents a kilowatt-hour to produce a total of 4 million kilowatt-hours. So in conditions like those shown in Figure 13.1, one firm can supply the entire market at a lower cost than two or more firms can.

The distribution of water and natural gas are two other examples of natural monopoly.

Legal Barriers to Entry Legal barriers to entry create legal monopoly. A **legal monopoly** is a market in which competition and entry are restricted by the concentration of ownership of a natural resource or by the granting of a public franchise, government license, patent, or copyright.

Legal monopoly
A market in which competition and entry are restricted by the concentration of ownership of a natural resource or by the granting of a public franchise, government license, patent, or copyright.

A firm can create its own barrier to entry by buying up a significant portion of a natural resource. DeBeers, which controls more than 80 percent of the world's production of raw diamonds, is an example of this type of monopoly. There is no natural barrier to entry in diamonds. Even though the diamond is a relatively rare mineral, its sources of supply could have many owners who compete in a global competitive auction market. DeBeers was able to prevent such competition by being a dominant player and effectively controlling entry.

A *public franchise* is an exclusive right granted to a firm to supply a good or service, an example of which is the U.S. Postal Service's exclusive right to deliver first-class mail. A *government license* controls entry into particular occupations, professions, and industries. An example is Michael's Texaco in Charleston, Rhode Island, which is the only firm in the area licensed to test for vehicle emissions.

A *patent* is an exclusive right granted to the inventor of a product or service. A *copyright* is an exclusive right granted to the author or composer of a literary, musical, dramatic, or artistic work. Patents and copyrights are valid for a limited time period that varies from country to country. In the United States, a patent is valid for 20 years. Patents are designed to encourage the *invention* of new products and production methods. They also stimulate *innovation*—the use of new inventions—by encouraging inventors to publicize their discoveries and offer them for use under license. Patents have stimulated innovations in areas as diverse as soybean seeds, pharmaceuticals, memory chips, and video games.

Most monopolies are regulated by government agencies. We can better understand why governments regulate monopolies and what effects regulations have if we know how unregulated monopoly behaves. So we'll first study unregulated monopoly and then look at monopoly regulation at the end of this chapter.

A monopoly sets its own price, but in doing so, it faces a market constraint. Let's see how the market limits a monopoly's pricing choices.

Monopoly Price-Setting Strategies

A monopolist faces a tradeoff between price and the quantity sold. To sell a larger quantity, the monopolist must set a lower price. But there are two price-setting possibilities that create different tradeoffs:

- Single price
- Price discrimination

Single Price

Single-price monopoly
A monopoly that must sell each unit of its output for the same price to all its customers.

A **single-price monopoly** is a firm that must sell each unit of its output for the same price to all its customers. DeBeers sells diamonds (of a given size and quality) for the same price to all its customers. If it tried to sell at a higher price to some customers than to others, only the low-price customers would buy from DeBeers. Others would buy from DeBeers's low-price customers. So DeBeers is a *single-price* monopoly.

Price Discrimination

Price-discriminating monopoly
A monopoly that is able to sell different units of a good or service for different prices.

A **price-discriminating monopoly** is a firm that is able to sell different units of a good or service for different prices. Many firms price discriminate. Airlines offer a dizzying array of different prices for the same trip. Pizza producers charge one price for a single pizza and almost give away a second one. Different customers might pay different prices (like airfares), or one customer might pay different prices for different quantities bought (like the bargain price for a second pizza).

When a firm price discriminates, it appears to be doing its customers a favor. In fact, it is charging the highest possible price for each unit sold and making the largest possible profit.

Not all monopolies can price discriminate. The main obstacle to the practice of price discrimination is resale by the customers who buy for a low price. Because of resale possibilities, price discrimination is limited to monopolies that sell services that cannot be resold.

CHECKPOINT 13.1

1 **Explain how monopoly arises and distinguish between single-price monopoly and price-discriminating monopoly.**

Study Guide pp. 202–204

*e*Foundations 13.1

Practice Problems 13.1

1. Monopoly arises in which of the following situations?
   a. Coca-Cola cuts its price below that of Pepsi-Cola in an attempt to increase its market share.
   b. A single firm, protected by a barrier to entry, produces a personal service that has no close substitutes.
   c. A barrier to entry exists, but some close substitutes for the good exist.
   d. A firm offers discounts to students and seniors.
   e. A firm can sell any quantity it chooses at the going price.
   f. The government issues Tiger Woods, Inc. an exclusive license to produce golf balls.
   g. A firm experiences economies of scale even when it produces the quantity that meets the entire market demand.
2. Which of the cases in Problem 1 are natural monopolies and which are legal monopolies? Which can price discriminate, which cannot, and why?

Exercises 13.1

1. Which of the following situations is a monopoly?
   a. The supermarket that stocks the best-quality products
   b. The supermarket that charges the highest prices
   c. The firm that has the largest share of the market sales
   d. The truck stop in the Midwest, miles from anywhere
   e. A firm that produces a good that has an inelastic demand
   f. The only airline that flies from St. Louis to Kansas City
2. Which of the cases in Exercise 1 are natural monopolies and which are legal monopolies? Which can price discriminate, which cannot, and why?

Solutions to Practice Problems 13.1

1. Monopoly arises when a single firm produces a good or services that has no close substitutes and a barrier to entry exists. Monopoly arises in (b), (f), and (g). In (a), there is more than one firm. In (c), the good has some close substitutes. In (d), a monopoly might be able to price discriminate, but other types of firms (for example, pizza producers and art museums) price discriminate and they are not monopolies. In (e), the demand for the good that the firm produces is perfectly elastic and there is no limit to what the firm could sell if it wished. Such a firm is in perfect competition.
2. Natural monopoly exists when one firm can meet the entire market demand at a lower price than two or more firms could. So (g) is a natural monopoly, but (b) could be also. Legal monopoly exists when the granting of a right creates a barrier to entry. So (f) is a legal monopoly, but (b) could be also. Monopoly (b) could price discriminate because a personal service cannot be resold. Monopoly (f) could not price discriminate because golf balls can be resold.

13.2 SINGLE-PRICE MONOPOLY

To understand how a single-price monopoly makes its output and price decisions, we must first study the link between price and marginal revenue.

Price and Marginal Revenue

Because in a monopoly there is only one firm, the firm's demand curve is the market demand curve. Let's look at Bobbie's Barbershop, the sole supplier of haircuts in Cairo, Nebraska. The table in Figure 13.2 shows the demand schedule for Bobbie's haircuts. For example, at $12, consumers demand 4 haircuts per hour (row *E*).

Total revenue is the price multiplied by the quantity sold. For example, in row *D*, Bobbie sells 3 haircuts at $14 each, so total revenue is $42. *Marginal revenue* is the change in total revenue resulting from a one-unit increase in the quantity sold. For example, if the price falls from $16 (row *C*) to $14 (row *D*), the quantity sold increases from 2 to 3 haircuts. Total revenue rises from $32 to $42, so the change in total revenue is $10. Because the quantity sold increases by 1 haircut, marginal revenue equals the change in total revenue and is $10. Marginal revenue is placed between the two rows to emphasize that marginal revenue relates to the *change* in the quantity sold.

Figure 13.2 shows Bobbie's demand curve and marginal revenue curve (*MR*) and also illustrates the calculation that we've just made. Notice that at each output, marginal revenue is less than price—the marginal revenue curve lies below the demand curve. Why is marginal revenue less than price? It is because when the price is lowered to sell one more unit, two opposing forces affect total revenue.

FIGURE 13.2
Demand and Marginal Revenue

*e*Foundations 13.2 

The table shows Bobbie's demand, total revenue, and marginal revenue schedules.

If the price falls from $16 to $14, the quantity sold increases from 2 to 3. ❶ Total revenue lost on 2 haircuts is $4; ❷ total revenue gained on 1 haircut is $14; and ❸ marginal revenue is $10.

	Price (dollars per haircut)	Quantity demanded (haircuts per hour)	Total revenue (dollars)	Marginal revenue (dollars per haircut)
A	20	0	0	
				18
B	18	1	18	
				14
C	16	2	32	
				10
D	14	3	42	
				6
E	12	4	48	
				2
F	10	5	50	

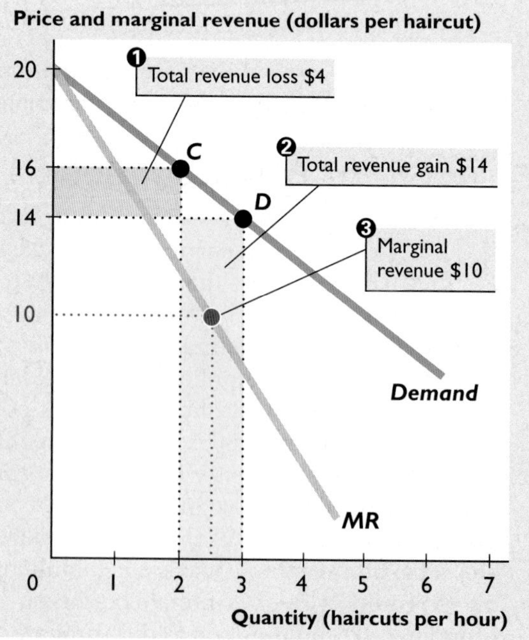

The lower price results in a revenue loss, and the increased quantity sold results in a revenue gain. For example, at a price of $16, Bobbie sells 2 haircuts (point C). If she lowers the price to $14, she sells 3 haircuts and has a revenue gain of $14 on the third haircut. But she now receives only $14 on the first two—$2 less than before. As a result, she loses $4 of revenue on the first 2 haircuts. To calculate marginal revenue, she must deduct this amount from the revenue gain of $14. So he marginal revenue is $10, which is less than the price.

Marginal Revenue and Elasticity

In Chapter 5 (p. 116), you learned about the *total revenue test*, which determines whether demand is elastic or inelastic. Recall that if a price fall increases total revenue, demand is elastic, but if it decreases total revenue, demand is inelastic.

We can use the total revenue test to see the relationship between marginal revenue and elasticity. Figure 13.3 illustrates this relationship. As the price falls from $20 to $10, the quantity demanded increases from 0 to 5 an hour. Total revenue increases (part b), so demand is elastic and marginal revenue is positive (part a). As the price falls from $10 to $0, the quantity demanded increases from 5 to 10 an hour. Total revenue decreases (part b), so demand is inelastic and marginal revenue is

FIGURE 13.3
Marginal Revenue and Elasticity

*e*Foundations 13.2 

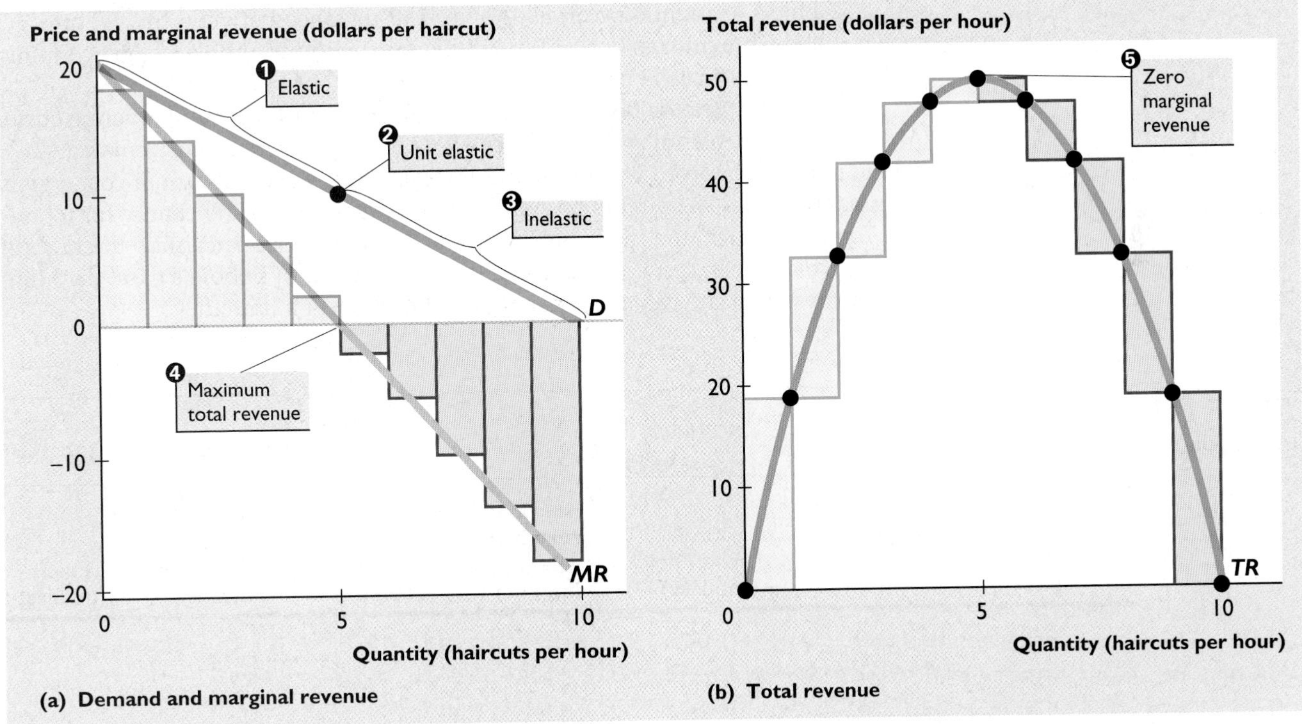

Over the range from 0 to 5 haircuts an hour, marginal revenue is positive and ❶ demand is elastic. At 5 haircuts an hour, marginal revenue is zero and ❷ demand is unit elastic. Over the range 5 to 10 haircuts an hour, marginal revenue is negative and ❸ demand is inelastic. At zero marginal revenue in part (a), ❹ total revenue is maximized. And at maximum total revenue in part (b), ❺ marginal revenue is zero.

negative (part a). When the price is $10, total revenue is a maximum, demand is unit elastic, and marginal revenue is zero.

The relationship between marginal revenue and elasticity implies that a monopoly never profitably produces an output in the inelastic range of its demand curve. It could charge a higher price, produce a smaller quantity, and increase its profit. Let's look at a monopoly's output and price decision.

Output and Price Decision

To determine the output level and price that maximize a monopoly's profit, we study the behavior of both revenue and costs as output varies.

Table 13.1 summarizes the information we need about Bobbie's revenue, costs, and economic profit. Economic profit, which equals total revenue minus total cost, is maximized at $12 an hour when Bobbie sells 3 haircuts an hour for $14 each. If she sold 2 haircuts for $16 each, her economic profit would be only $9. And if she sold 4 haircuts for $12 each, her economic profit would be only $8.

You can see why 3 haircuts is Bobbie's profit-maximizing output by looking at the marginal revenue and marginal cost. When Bobbie increases output from 2 to 3 haircuts, her marginal revenue is $10 and her marginal cost is $7. Profit increases by the difference, $3 an hour. If Bobbie increases output yet further, from 3 to 4 haircuts, her marginal revenue is $6 and her marginal cost is $10. In this case, marginal cost exceeds marginal revenue by $4, so profit decreases by $4 an hour.

Figure 13.4 shows the information contained in Table 13.1 graphically. Part (a) shows Bobbie's total revenue curve (*TR*) and her total cost curve (*TC*). It also shows Bobbie's economic profit as the vertical distance between the *TR* and *TC* curves. Bobbie maximizes her profit at 3 haircuts an hour and earns an economic profit of $12 an hour ($42 of total revenue minus $30 of total cost).

Figure 13.4(b) shows Bobbie's demand curve (*D*) and marginal revenue curve (*MR*) along with her marginal cost curve (*MC*) and average cost curve (*ATC*). Bobbie maximizes profit by producing the output at which marginal cost equals marginal revenue—3 haircuts an hour. But what price does she charge for a haircut? To set the price, the monopoly uses the demand curve and finds the highest price at which it can sell the profit-maximizing output. In Bobbie's case, the highest price at which she can sell 3 haircuts an hour is $14 a haircut.

TABLE 13.1

A Monopoly's Output and Price Decision

*e*Foundations 13.2 

	Price (dollars per haircut)	Quantity demanded (haircuts per hour)	Total revenue (dollars)	Marginal revenue (dollars per haircut)	Total cost (dollars)	Marginal cost (dollars per haircut)	Profit (dollars)
A	20	0	0		12		−12
				18		5	
B	18	1	18		17		1
				14		6	
C	16	2	32		23		9
				10		7	
D	**14**	**3**	**42**		**30**		**12**
				6		10	
E	12	4	48		40		8
				2		15	
F	10	5	50		55		−5

When Bobbie produces 3 haircuts an hour, her average cost is $10 (read from the *ATC* curve) and her price is $14 (read from the *D* curve). Her profit per haircut is $4 ($14 minus $10). Bobbie's economic profit is shown by the blue rectangle, which equals the profit per haircut ($4) multiplied by the number of haircuts (3 an hour), for a total of $12 an hour.

A positive economic profit is an incentive for firms to enter a market. But barriers to entry prevent that from happening in a monopoly. So in a monopoly, the firm can make a positive economic profit and continue to do so indefinitely.

A monopoly charges a price that exceeds marginal cost, but does it always make an economic profit? The answer is no! Bobbie makes a positive economic profit in Figure 13.4. But suppose that Bobbie's landlord increases the rent she pays for her barbershop. If Bobbie pays an additional $12 an hour in shop rent, her fixed cost increases by that amount. Her marginal cost and marginal revenue don't change, so her profit-maximizing output remains at 3 haircuts an hour. Her profit decreases by $12 an hour to zero. If Bobbie pays more than an additional $12 an hour for her shop rent, she incurs an economic loss. If this situation were permanent, Bobbie would go out of business. But monopoly entrepreneurs are creative, and Bobbie might find another shop at a lower rent.

FIGURE 13.4
A Monopoly's Profit-Maximizing Output and Price

*e*Foundations 13.2 

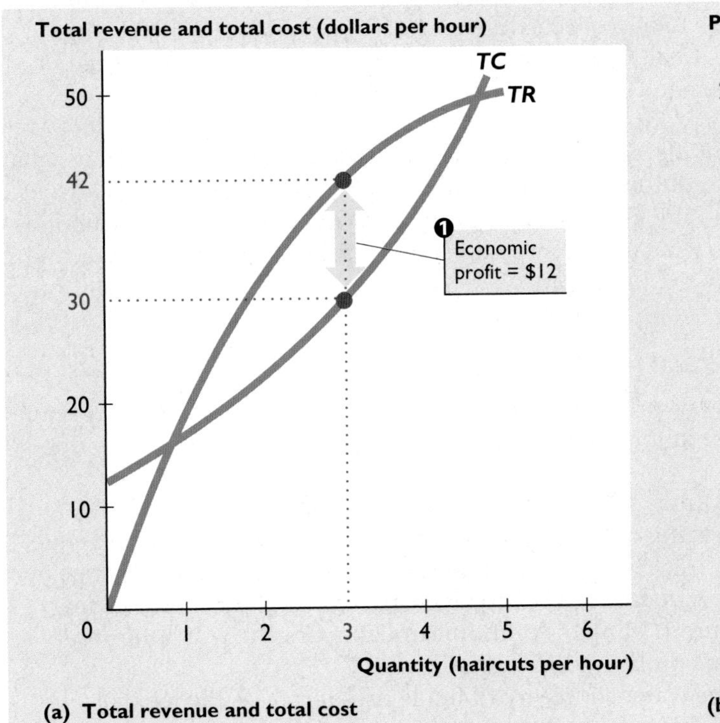

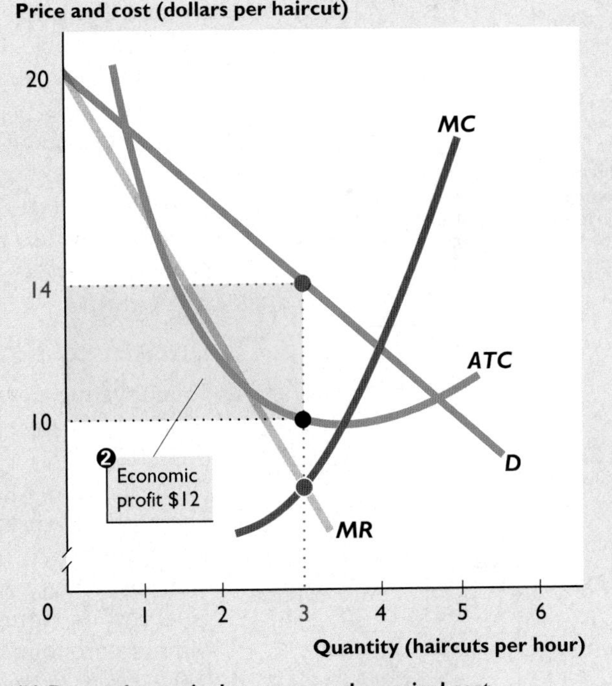

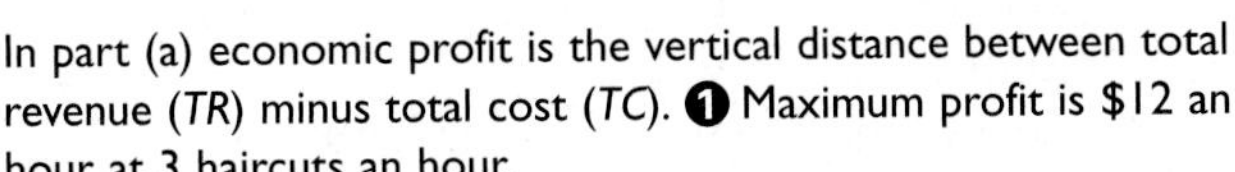
In part (a) economic profit is the vertical distance between total revenue (*TR*) minus total cost (*TC*). ❶ Maximum profit is $12 an hour at 3 haircuts an hour.

In part (b), economic profit is maximized when marginal cost (*MC*) equals marginal revenue (*MR*). The price is determined by the demand curve (*D*) and is $14. ❷ Economic profit, the blue rectangle, is $12—the profit per haircut ($4) multiplied by 3 haircuts.

CHECKPOINT 13.2

Study Guide **pp. 204–207** 

*e*Foundations **13.2**

2 **Explain how a single-price monopoly determines its output and price.**

Practice Problem 13.2

Minnie's Mineral Springs is a single-price monopoly. The first two columns of Table 1 show the demand schedule for Minnie's spring water, and the middle and third columns show the firm's total cost schedule.

a. Calculate Minnie's total revenue schedule and marginal revenue schedule.
b. Sketch Minnie's demand curve and marginal revenue curve.
c. Calculate Minnie's profit-maximizing output, price, and economic profit.
d. If the owner of the water source that Minnie uses increases the fee that Minnie pays by $15.5 an hour, what are Minnie's new profit-maximizing output, price, and economic profit?
e. If instead of increasing the fee that Minnie pays by $15.5 an hour, the owner of the water source increases the fee that Minnie pays by $4 a bottle, what are Minnie's new profit-maximizing output, price, and economic profit?

TABLE 1

Price (dollars per bottle)	Quantity (bottles per hour)	Total cost (dollars per hour)
10	0	1.0
9	1	1.5
8	2	2.5
7	3	5.5
6	4	10.5
5	5	17.5

Exercise 13.2

Dolly's Diamond is a single-price monopoly. The first two columns of Table 2 show the demand schedule for Dolly's Diamond, and the middle and third column show the firm's total cost schedule.

a. Calculate Dolly's total revenue schedule and marginal revenue schedule.
b. Sketch Dolly's demand curve and marginal revenue curve.
c. Calculate Dolly's profit-maximizing output, price, and economic profit.
d. If the government places a fixed tax on Dolly's Diamond of $1,000 a day, what are Dolly's new profit-maximizing output, price, and economic profit?
e. If instead of imposing a fixed tax on Dolly's, the government taxes diamonds at $600 per carat, what are Dolly's new profit-maximizing output, price, and economic profit?

TABLE 2

Price (dollars per carat)	Quantity (carats per day)	Total cost (dollars per day)
2,200	0	800
2,000	1	1,600
1,800	2	2,600
1,600	3	3,800
1,400	4	5,200
1,200	5	6,800

Solution to Practice Problem 13.2

a. Total revenue equals price multiplied by quantity sold, and marginal revenue equals the change in total revenue when the quantity sold increases by one unit (Table 3).

TABLE 3

Quantity (bottles per hour)	Total revenue dollars per hour)	Marginal revenue (dollars per bottle)
0	0	
		8
1	8	
		4
2	12	
		0
3	12	
		–4
4	8	
		–8
5	0	

b. Figure 1 shows Minnie's demand curve and marginal revenue curve.
c. The profit-maximizing output is 3 bottles per hour, where marginal revenue equals marginal cost. To calculate Minnie's marginal cost, find the change in total cost when the quantity produced increases by 1 bottle. Then plot marginal cost on Figure 1. Minnie's profit-maximizing price is $7 a bottle, and Minnie's economic profit is $15.5 an hour.
d. If the owner of the water source that Minnie uses increases the fee that Minnie pays by $15.5 an hour, Minnie's fixed cost increases but her marginal cost doesn't change. Her profit-maximizing output and price are unchanged, but she now earns no economic profit.
e. If Minnie pays an extra $4 a bottle, her marginal cost increases by this amount. Her new profit-maximizing output is 2 bottles per hour; the price is $8 per bottle; and economic profit is $5.50.

FIGURE 1

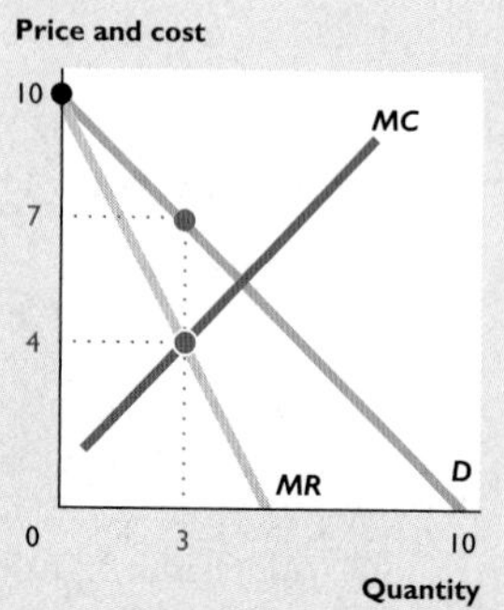

13.3 MONOPOLY AND COMPETITION COMPARED

Imagine a market in which many small firms operate in perfect competition. Then a single firm buys out all these small firms and creates a monopoly. What happens in this market to the quantity produced, the price, and efficiency?

Output and Price

Figure 13.5 shows the market that we'll study. The market demand curve is D. Initially, with many small firms in the market, the market supply curve is S, which is the sum of the supply curves—and marginal cost curves—of the individual firms. The equilibrium price is P_C, which makes the quantity demanded equal the quantity supplied. The equilibrium quantity is Q_C. Each firm takes the price P_C and maximizes its profit by producing the output at which its own marginal cost equals the price.

A single firm now buys all the firms in this market. Consumers don't change, so the demand curve doesn't change. But the monopoly recognizes this demand curve as a constraint on its sales and knows that its marginal revenue curve is MR.

The market supply curve in perfect competition is the sum of the marginal cost curves of the firms in the industry. So the monopoly's marginal cost curve is the market supply curve of perfect competition—labeled $S = MC$. The monopoly maximizes profit by producing the quantity at which marginal revenue equals marginal cost, which is Q_M. This output is smaller than the competitive output, Q_C. And the monopoly charges the price P_M, which is higher than P_C. So:

Compared to a perfect competition, a single-price monopoly produces a smaller output and charges a higher price.

FIGURE 13.5
Monopoly's Smaller Output and Higher Price

*e*Foundations 13.3 

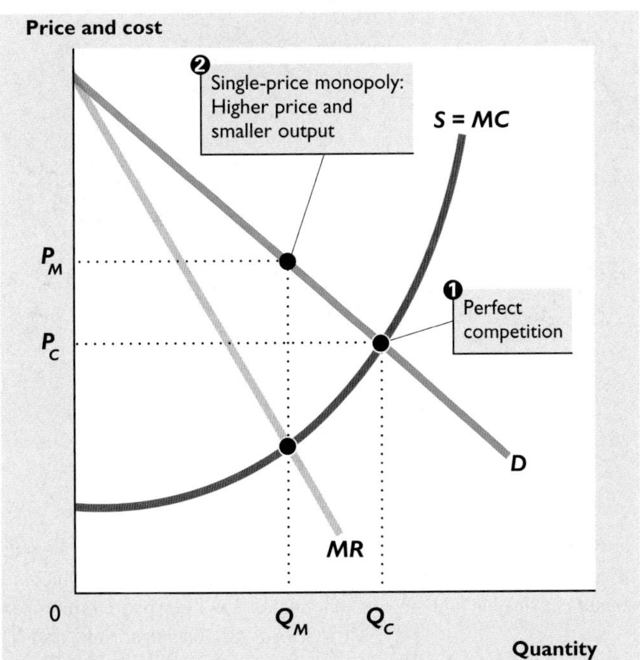

1. A competitive industry produces the quantity Q_C at price P_C.
2. A single-price monopoly produces the quantity Q_M at which marginal revenue equals marginal cost and sells that quantity for the price P_M. Compared to perfect competition, a single-price monopoly restricts output and raises the price.

Is Monopoly Efficient?

You learned in Chapter 6 that resources are used efficiently when marginal benefit equals marginal cost. Figure 13.6(a) shows that perfect competition achieves this efficient use of resources. The demand curve ($D = MB$) shows the marginal benefit to consumers. The supply curve ($S = MC$) shows the marginal cost (opportunity cost) to producers. At the competitive equilibrium, the price is P_C and the quantity is Q_C. Marginal benefit equals marginal cost and resource use is efficient. The sum of *consumer surplus* (Chapter 6, p. 135), the green triangle, and *producer surplus* (Chapter 6, p. 138), the blue area, is maximized.

Figure 13.6(b) shows that monopoly is inefficient. Monopoly output is Q_M and price is P_M. Price (marginal benefit) exceeds marginal cost and the underproduction creates a *deadweight loss* (Chapter 6, p. 144–145), shown by the gray area. Consumers lose partly by getting less of the good, shown by the gray triangle above P_C, and partly by paying more for the good. Consumer surplus shrinks to the smaller green triangle. Producers lose by selling less of the good, shown by the part of the gray area below P_C, but gain by selling their output for a higher price, shown by the dark blue rectangle. Producer surplus expands and is larger in monopoly than in perfect competition.

FIGURE 13.6

The Inefficiency of Monopoly

*e*Foundations 13.3 

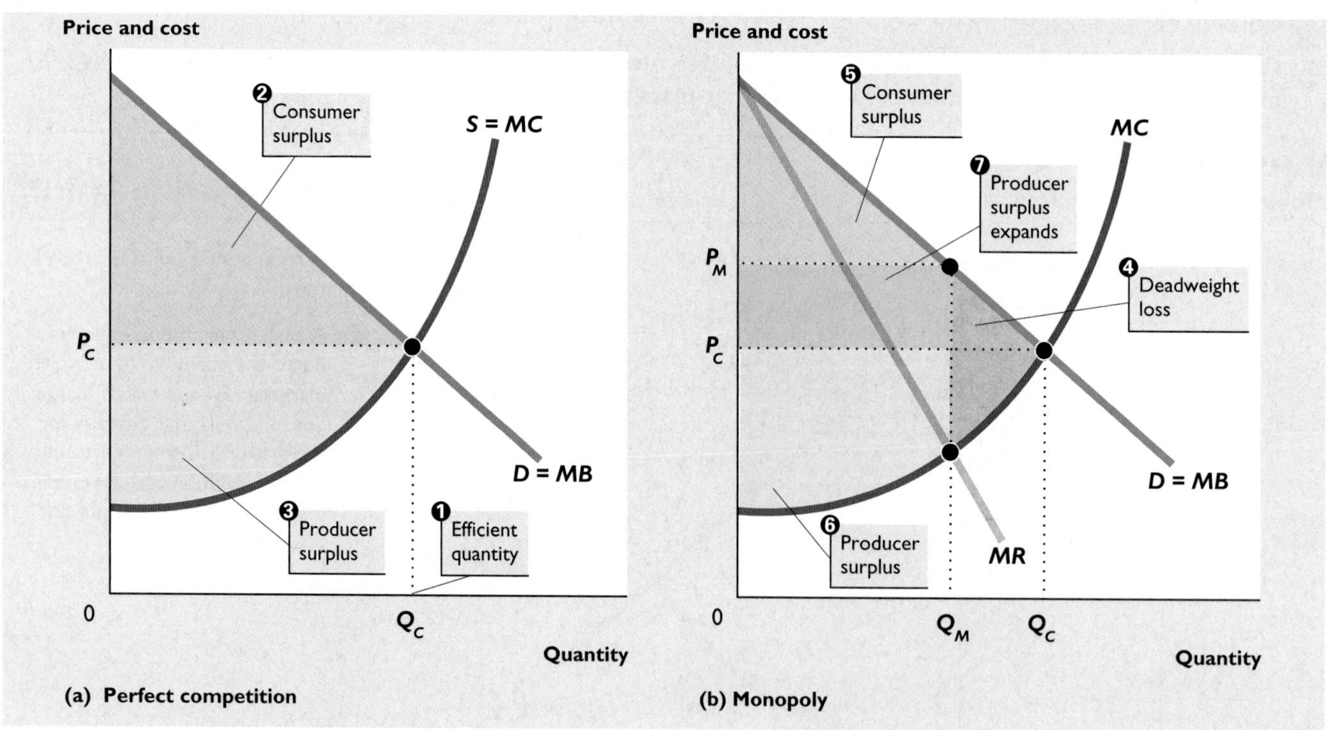

In perfect competition, ❶ the equilibrium quantity is the efficient quantity, Q_C, because at that quantity, the price, P_C, equals marginal benefit and marginal cost. The sum of ❷ consumer surplus and ❸ producer surplus is maximized.

In a single-price monopoly, the equilibrium quantity, Q_M, is inefficient because the price, P_M, which equals marginal benefit, exceeds marginal cost. Underproduction creates a ❹ deadweight loss. ❺ Consumer surplus shrinks and ❻ producer surplus ❼ expands.

Is Monopoly Fair?

Monopoly is inefficient because it creates a deadweight loss. But monopoly also *redistributes* consumer surplus. The producer gains, and the consumers lose.

Figure 13.6 shows this redistribution. The monopoly gets the difference between the higher price, P_M, and the competitive price, P_C, on the quantity sold, Q_M. So the dark blue rectangle shows the part of the consumer surplus taken by the monopoly. This portion of the loss of consumer surplus is not a loss to society. It is redistribution from consumers to the monopoly producer.

Is the gain for the monopoly and loss for consumers fair? You learned about two standards of fairness in Chapter 6: fair *results* and fair *rules*. Redistribution from the rich to the poor is consistent with the fair results view. So on this view of fairness, whether monopoly redistribution is fair or unfair depends on who is richer: the monopolist or the consumers of its product. It might be either. Whether the *rules* are fair depends on whether the monopoly has benefited from a protected position that is not available to anyone else. If everyone is free to acquire the monopoly, then the rules are fair. So monopoly is inefficient and it might be, but is not always, unfair.

The pursuit of monopoly profit leads to an additional costly activity that we'll now describe: rent seeking.

Rent Seeking

Rent seeking is the act of obtaining special treatment by the government to create economic profit or to divert consumer surplus or producer surplus away from others. ("Rent" is a general term in economics that includes all forms of surplus such as consumer surplus, producer surplus, and economic profit.) Rent seeking does not always create a monopoly, but it always restricts competition and often creates a monopoly.

Rent seeking
The act of obtaining special treatment by the government to create economic profit or to divert consumer surplus or producer surplus away from others.

Scarce resources can be used to produce the goods and services that people value or they can be used in rent seeking. Rent seeking is potentially profitable for the rent seeker but costly to society because it uses scarce resources purely to transfer wealth from one person or group to another person or group rather than to produce the things that people value.

To see why rent seeking occurs, think about the two ways that a person might become the owner of a monopoly:

- Buy a monopoly
- Create a monopoly by rent seeking

Buy a Monopoly

A person might try to earn a monopoly profit by buying a firm (or a right) that is protected by a barrier to entry. Buying a taxicab medallion in New York is an example. The number of medallions is restricted, so their owners are protected from unlimited entry into the industry. A person who wants to operate a taxi must buy a medallion from someone who already has one. But anyone is free to enter the bidding for a medallion. So competition among buyers drives the price up to the point at which they earn only normal profit. For example, competition for the right to operate a taxi in New York City has led to a price of more than $165,000 for a taxi medallion, which is sufficiently high to eliminate economic profit for taxi operators and leave them with normal profit.

Create a Monopoly by Rent Seeking

Because buying a monopoly means paying a price that soaks up the economic profit, creating a monopoly by rent seeking is an attractive alternative to buying one. Rent seeking is a political activity. It takes the form of lobbying and trying to influence the political process to get laws that create legal barriers to entry. Such influence might be sought by making campaign contributions in exchange for legislative support or by indirectly seeking to influence political outcomes through publicity in the media or by direct contacts with politicians and bureaucrats. An example of a rent created in this way is the law that restricts the quantities of textiles that can be imported into the United States. Another is a law that limits the quantity of tomatoes that can be imported in the United States. These laws restrict competition, which decreases the quantity for sale and increases prices.

Rent Seeking Equilibrium

Rent seeking is a competitive activity. If an economic profit is available, a rent seeker will try to get some of it. Competition among rent seekers pushes up the cost of rent seeking until it leaves the monopoly earning only a normal profit after paying the rent-seeking costs.

Figure 13.7 shows a rent-seeking equilibrium. The cost of rent seeking is a fixed cost that must be added to a monopoly's other costs. The average cost curve, which includes the fixed cost of rent seeking, shifts upward until it just touches the demand curve. Consumer surplus is unaffected. But the deadweight loss of monopoly now includes the original deadweight loss triangle plus the economic profit consumed by rent seeking, which the enlarged gray area shows.

FIGURE 13.7
Rent-Seeking Equilibrium

*e*Foundations 13.3 

❶ Rent seeking costs exhaust economic profit. The firm's rent-seeking costs are fixed costs. They add to total fixed cost and to average total cost. The *ATC* curve shifts upward until, at the profit-maximizing price, the firm breaks even.

❷ Consumer surplus shrinks.

❸ The deadweight loss increases.

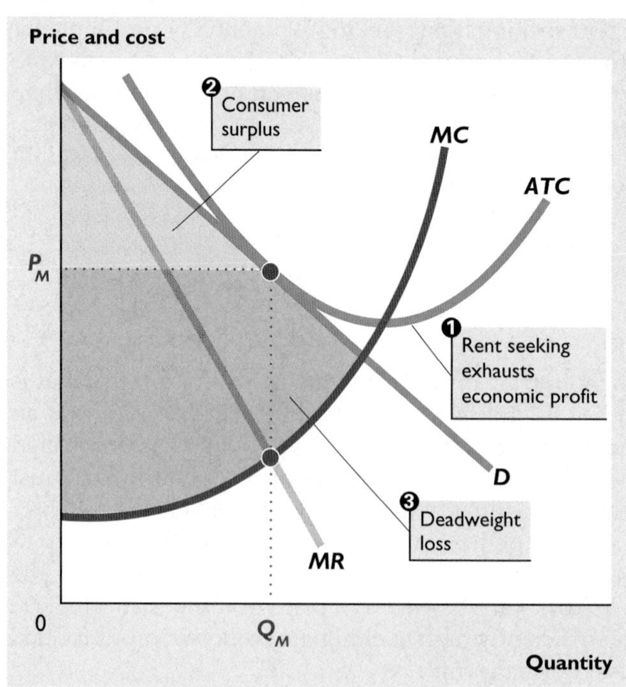

CHECKPOINT 13.3

3 **Compare the performance of single-price monopoly with that of perfect competition.**

Study Guide pp. 208–210 

e/Foundations 13.3 

Practice Problem 13.3

Township is a small isolated community served by one newspaper that can meet the market demand at a lower cost than two or more newspapers could. There is no local radio or TV station and no Internet access. The *Township Gazette* is the only source of news. Figure 1 shows the marginal cost of printing the *Township Gazette* and the demand for it. The *Township Gazette* is a profit-maximizing, single-price monopoly.

a. How many copies of the *Township Gazette* are printed each day?
b. What is the price of the *Township Gazette*?
c. What is the efficient number of copies of the *Township Gazette*?
d. What is the price at which the efficient number of copies could be sold?
e. Is the number of copies printed the efficient quantity? Explain why or why not.
f. On the graph, show the consumer surplus that is redistributed from consumers to the *Township Gazette*.
g. On the graph, show the deadweight loss that arises from the monopoly of the *Township Gazette*.

FIGURE 1

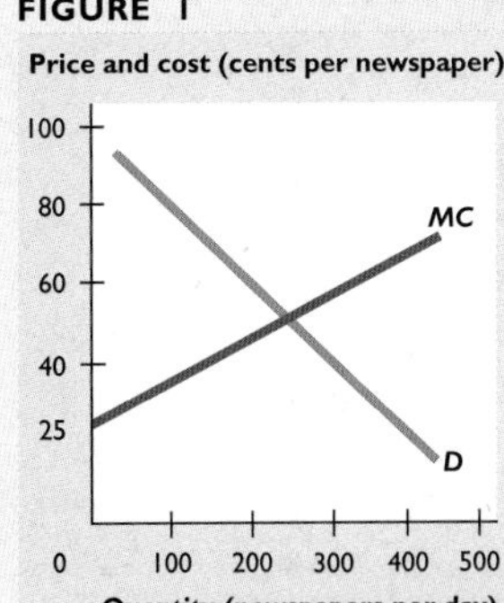

Exercise 13.3

Is Bobbie's Barbershop in Cairo, Nebraska, (on pp. 316–317) efficient? What is the consumer surplus that is transferred to Bobbie? What is the deadweight loss that she generates? How much would someone be willing to pay to buy Bobbie's monopoly?

Solution to Practice Problem 13.3

a. The profit-maximizing quantity of newspapers for the *Township Gazette* is 150 a day, where marginal revenue equals marginal cost (Figure 2).
b. The price is 70¢ a copy (Figure 2).
c. The efficient quantity of copies is 250, where demand (marginal benefit) equals marginal cost (Figure 2).
d. The efficient quantity would be bought at 50¢ a copy (Figure 2).
e. The number of copies printed is not efficient because the marginal benefit of the 150th copy exceeds its marginal cost (Figure 2).
f. The blue rectangle ❶ in Figure 2 shows the consumer surplus transferred from the consumers to the *Township Gazette*.
g. The gray triangle ❷ in Figure 2 shows the deadweight loss.

FIGURE 2

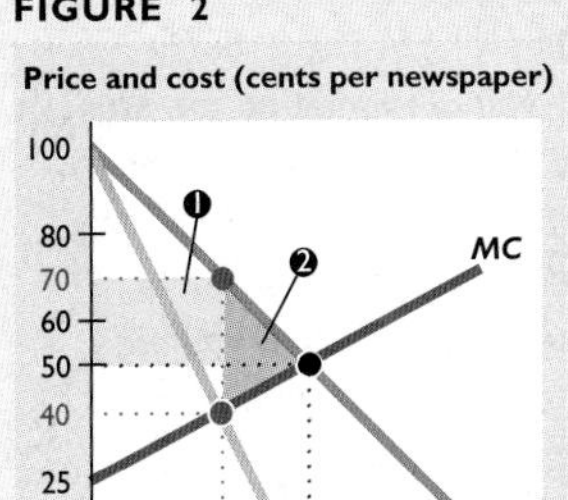

13.4 PRICE DISCRIMINATION

Price discrimination—selling a good or service at a number of different prices—is widespread. You encounter it when you travel, go to the movies, get your hair cut, buy pizza, or visit an art museum. At first sight, it appears that price discrimination contradicts the assumption of profit maximization. Why would a movie operator allow children to see movies at half price? Why would a hairdresser charge students and senior citizens less? Aren't these firms losing profit by being nice to their customers?

Deeper investigation shows that far from lowering profit, price discriminators make a bigger profit than they would otherwise. So a monopoly has an incentive to find ways of discriminating and charging each buyer the highest possible price. Some people pay less with price discrimination, but others pay more.

Most price discriminators are *not* monopolies, but monopolies do price discriminate when they can. To be able to price discriminate, a firm must:

- Identify and separate different types of buyers.
- Sell a product that cannot be resold.

Price discrimination is charging different prices for a single good or service because the willingness to pay varies across buyers. Not all price *differences* are price *discrimination*. Some goods that are similar but not identical have different prices because they have different production costs. For example, the cost of producing electricity depends on time of day. If an electric power company charges a higher price for consumption between 7:00 and 9:00 in the morning and between 4:00 and 7:00 in the evening than it does at other times of the day, it is not price discriminating.

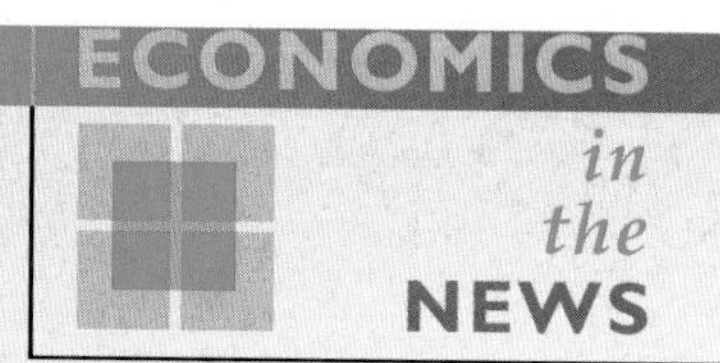

November 4, 1999

Drug Price Hikes

Drug prices in the United States increased last year at a rate that was four times the rate of price increases on the average.

Questions

1. In what type of market do the drug companies operate: perfect competition, monopolistic competition, oligopoly, or monopoly?

2. Why do you think drug prices are increasing at a faster rate than prices on the average?

3. What, if anything, do you think the U.S. federal government should do about rising drug prices?

 **eFoundations 13.4**

Price Discrimination and Consumer Surplus

The key idea behind price discrimination is to convert consumer surplus into economic profit. To extract every dollar of consumer surplus from every buyer, the monopoly would have to offer each individual customer a separate price schedule based on that customer's own willingness to pay. Such price discrimination cannot be carried out in practice because a firm does not have enough information about each consumer's demand curve. But firms try to extract as much consumer surplus as possible, and to do so, they discriminate in two broad ways:

- Among groups of buyers
- Among units of a good

Discriminating Among Groups of Buyers

To price discriminate among groups of buyers, the firm offers different prices to different types of buyers, based on things like age, employment status, or some other easily distinguished characteristic. This type of price discrimination works when each group has a different average willingness to pay for the good or service.

For example, a face-to-face sales meeting with a customer might bring a large and profitable order. For salespeople and other business travelers, the marginal benefit from an airplane trip is large and the price that such a traveler will pay for a trip is high. In contrast, for a vacation traveler, any of several different trips or even no vacation trip are options. So for vacation travelers, the marginal benefit of a trip is small and the price that such a traveler will pay for a trip is low. Because business travelers are willing to pay more than vacation travelers are, it is possible for an airline to profit by price discriminating between these two groups.

Discriminating Among Units of a Good

To price discriminate among units of a good, the firm charges the same prices to all its customers but offers a lower price per unit for a larger number of units bought. When Pizza Hut charges $10 for one home-delivered pizza and $14 for two, it is using this type of price discrimination. In this example, the price of the second pizza is only $4.

Let's see how an airline exploits the differences in demand by business and vacation travelers and increases its profit by price discriminating.

Profiting by Price Discriminating

Global Air has a monopoly on an exotic route. Figure 13.8 shows the demand curve (*D*) for travel on this route and Global Air's marginal revenue curve (*MR*). It also shows Global Air's marginal cost curve (*MC*) and average cost curve (*ATC*).

Initially, Global is a single-price monopoly and maximizes its profit by producing 8,000 trips a year (the quantity at which *MR* equals *MC*). The price is $1,200 per trip. The average cost of a trip is $600, so economic profit is $600 a trip. On 8,000 trips, Global's economic profit is $4.8 million a year, shown by the blue rectangle. Global's customers enjoy a consumer surplus shown by the green triangle.

FIGURE 13.8
A Single Price of Air Travel

*e*Foundations 13.4 

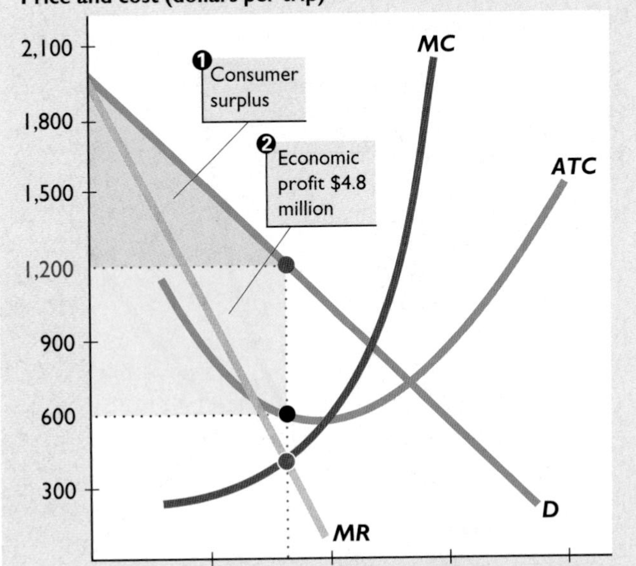

Global Air has a monopoly on an air route. The demand curve for travel on this route is *D*, and Global's marginal revenue curve is *MR*. Its marginal cost curve is *MC*, and its average total cost curve is *ATC*.

As a single-price monopoly, Global maximizes profit by selling 8,000 trips a year at $1,200 a trip. ❶ Global's customers enjoy a consumer surplus—the green triangle—and ❷ Global's economic profit is $4.8 million a year—the blue rectangle.

Global is struck by the fact that many of its customers are business travelers, and Global suspects that they are willing to pay more than $1,200 a trip. So Global does some market research, which tells Global that some business travelers are willing to pay as much as $1,800 a trip. Also, these customers almost always change their travel plans at the last moment. Another group of business travelers is willing to pay $1,600. These customers know a week ahead when they will travel and they never want to stay over a weekend. Yet another group are willing to pay up to $1,400 and these travelers know two weeks ahead when they will travel and don't want to stay away over a weekend.

So Global announces a new fare schedule. No restrictions, $1,800; 7-days advance purchase, no cancellation, $1,600; 14-days advance purchase, no cancellation, $1,400; 14-days advance purchase must stay over weekend, $1,200.

Figure 13.9 shows the outcome with this new fare structure and also shows why Global is pleased with its new fares. It sells 2,000 trips at each of its four prices. Global's economic profit increases by the blue steps in the figure. Its economic profit is now its original $4.8 million a year plus an additional $2.4 million from its new higher fares. Consumer surplus has shrunk to the smaller green area.

Perfect Price Discrimination

Perfect price discrimination
Price discrimination that extracts the entire consumer surplus by charging the highest price that consumers are willing to pay for each unit.

But Global reckons that it can do even better. It plans to achieve **perfect price discrimination**, which extracts the entire consumer surplus. To do so, Global must get creative and come up with a host of additional business fares ranging between $2,000 and $1,200, each one of which appeals to a small segment of the business market and that together extract the entire consumer surplus from the business travelers.

FIGURE 13.9
Price Discrimination

*e*Foundations 13.4 

Global revises its fare structure. It now offers no restrictions at $1,800, 7-day advance purchase at $1,600, 14-day advance purchase at $1,400, and must stay over the weekend at $1,200. Global sells 2,000 units at each of its four new fares. It economic profit increases by $2.4 million a year to $7.2 million a year, which is shown by the original blue rectangle plus the blue steps. Global's customers' consumer surplus shrinks.

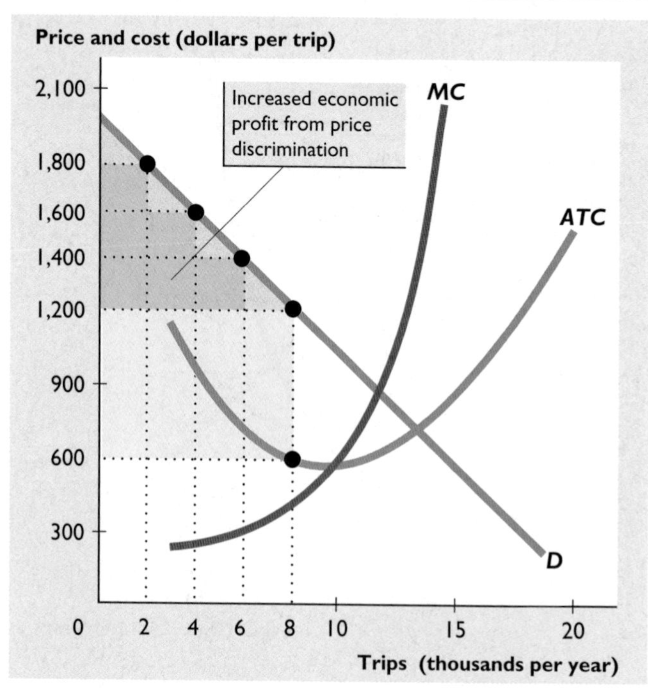

Once Global is discriminating finely between different customers and getting from each the maximum they are willing to pay, something special happens to marginal revenue. Recall that for the single-price monopoly, marginal revenue is less than price. The reason is that when the price is cut to sell a larger quantity, the price is lower on all units sold. But with perfect price discrimination, Global sells only the marginal seat at the lower price. All the other customers continue to buy for the highest price they are willing to pay. So for the perfect price discriminator, marginal revenue equals price and the demand curve becomes the marginal revenue curve.

With marginal cost equal to price, Global can obtain yet greater profit by increasing output up to the point at which price (and marginal revenue) is equal to marginal cost.

So Global now seeks additional travelers who will not pay as much as $1,200 a trip but who will pay more than marginal cost. More creative pricing comes up with vacation specials and other fares that have combinations of advance reservation, minimum stay, and other restrictions that make these fares unattractive to its existing customers but attractive to a further group of travelers. With all these fares and specials, Global extracts the entire consumer surplus and maximizes economic profit.

Figure 13.10 shows the outcome with perfect price discrimination. The dozens of fares paid by the original travelers who are willing to pay between $1,200 and $2,000 have extracted the entire consumer surplus from this group and converted it into economic profit for Global. The new fares between $900 and $1,200 have attracted 3,000 additional travelers but have taken their entire consumer surplus also. Global is earning an economic profit of more than $9 million a year.

FIGURE 13.10
Perfect Price Discrimination

*e*Foundations 13.4 

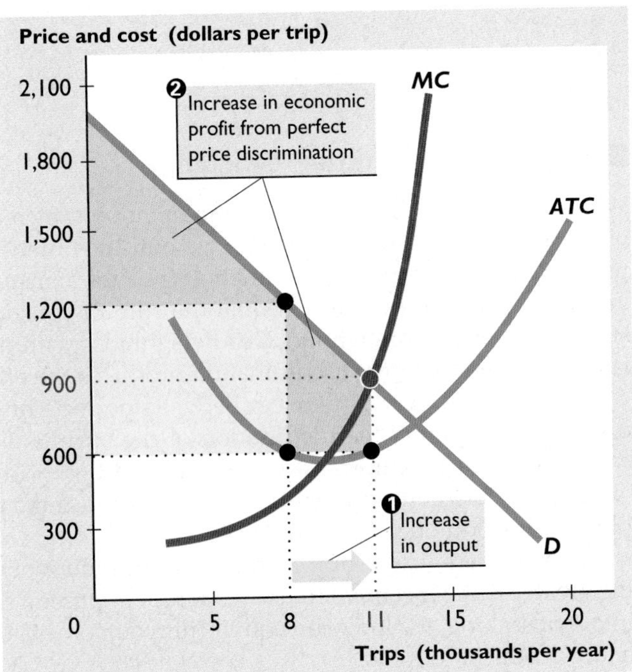

With perfect price discrimination, the demand curve becomes Global's marginal revenue curve. Economic profit is maximized when the lowest price equals marginal cost.

❶ Output increases to 11,000 passengers a year, and ❷ Global's economic profit increases to $9.35 million a year.

Airline Price Discrimination

The normal coach fare from San Francisco to Washington, D.C., is $1,200. Book 14 days in advance, and this fare is $500. On a typical flight, United Airlines or American Airlines might have passengers paying as many as 20 different fares.

The airlines sort their customers according to their willingness to pay by offering a maze of advance-purchase and stayover restrictions that attract price-sensitive leisure travelers but don't get bought by business travelers.

Despite the sophistication of the airlines' pricing schemes, about 30 percent of seats fly empty. The marginal cost of filling an empty seat is close to zero, so a ticket sold at a few dollars would be profitable.

Extremely low prices are now feasible, thanks to Priceline.com. Shopping around airlines with bids from travelers, Priceline brokers about 1,000 tickets a day and gets the lowest possible fares.

Would it bother you to hear how little I paid for this flight?

From William Hamilton, "Voodoo Economics," © 1992 by the Chronicle Publishing Company, p. 3. Reprinted with permission of Chronicle Books.

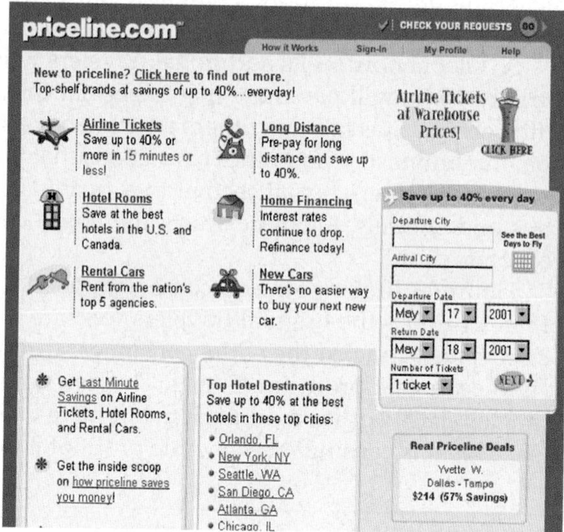

Price Discrimination Efficiency

With perfect price discrimination, the monopoly increases output to the point at which price equals marginal cost. This output is identical to that of perfect competition. Perfect price discrimination pushes consumer surplus to zero but increases producer surplus to equal the sum of consumer surplus and producer surplus in perfect competition. Deadweight loss with perfect price discrimination is zero. So perfect price discrimination produces the efficient quantity.

But there are two differences between perfect competition and perfect price discrimination. First, the distribution of the surplus is different. It is shared by consumers and producers in perfect competition while the producer gets it all with perfect price discrimination. Second, because the producer grabs all the surplus, rent seeking becomes profitable.

Rent seekers use resources in pursuit of monopoly, and the bigger the rents, the greater is the incentive to use resources to pursue those rents. With free entry into rent seeking, the long-run equilibrium outcome is that rent seekers use up the entire producer surplus.

CHECKPOINT 13.4

4 Explain how price discrimination increases profit.

Study Guide pp. 210–212 

e/**Foundations 13.4** 

Practice Problem 13.4

Village, a small isolated town, has one doctor. For a 30-minute consultation, the doctor charges a rich person twice as much as a poor person.

a. Does the doctor practice price discrimination?
b. Does the doctor's pricing system redistribute consumer surplus? If so, explain how.
c. Is the doctor using resources efficiently? Explain your answer.
d. If the doctor decided to charge everyone the maximum price that he or she would be willing to pay, what would be the consumer surplus?
e. In part (d), is the market for medical service in Village efficient?

Exercises 13.4

1. What is price discrimination? Give some real-world examples of price discrimination.
2. What conditions are necessary for price discrimination to occur?
3. Which of the following situations is price discrimination?
   a. The local drug store offers senior citizens a discount on all purchases made on Tuesdays.
   b. Airline offers standby fares at a 75 percent discount.
   c. Domino's offers "Buy 1 pizza for $15 and get a second one for only $1."
   d. A bank charges a higher interest rate on a loan to a student to buy a motorcycle than it charges on a loan to a doctor to buy an identical motorcycle.
   e. Farmers in Southern California pay a lower price for water than do the residents of Los Angeles.
   f. The U.S. Postal Service charges a lower price to mail a postcard than to mail a letter.

Solution to Practice Problem 13.4

a. The doctor practices price discrimination because rich people and poor people pay a different price for the same service: a 30-minute consultation.
b. With price discrimination, the doctor takes some of the consumer surplus. So yes, consumer surplus is reduced and redistributed to the doctor as economic profit.
c. No, the doctor creates a deadweight loss and so is not using resources efficiently.
d. The doctor now practices perfect price discrimination. To maximize profit, the doctor increases the number of consultations to make the lowest price charged equal to marginal cost. The doctor takes the entire consumer surplus. So consumer surplus is zero.
e. The doctor no longer creates a deadweight loss, so resources are being used efficiently.

13.5 MONOPOLY POLICY ISSUES

The comparison of monopoly and competition makes monopoly look bad. Monopoly is inefficient, and it captures consumer surplus and converts it into economic profit or pure waste in the form of rent-seeking costs. If monopoly is so bad, why do we put up with it? Why don't we have laws that crack down on monopoly so hard that it never rears its head? We do indeed have laws that limit monopoly and regulate the prices that monopolies are permitted to charge. But monopoly also brings some benefits. We begin this review of monopoly policy issues by looking at the benefits of monopoly. We then look at the regulation of monopoly. (Chapter 15 reviews monopoly regulation and antitrust law.)

Gains from Monopoly

The main reason why monopoly exists is that it has potential advantages over a competitive alternative. These advantages arise from:

- Economies of scale
- Incentives to innovate

Economies of Scale

Economies of scale can lead to *natural monopoly*—a situation in which a single firm can produce at a lower average cost than a larger number of smaller firms can. Examples of industries in which economies of scale are so significant that they lead to a natural monopoly are becoming more rare. Public utilities such as gas, electric power, local telephone service, and garbage collection once were natural monopolies. But technological advances now enable us to separate the *production* of electric power and natural gas from their *distribution*. The provision of water though, remains a natural monopoly. Where significant economies of scale exist, it would be wasteful not to have a monopoly. So creating competition in a market that is a natural monopoly would be wasteful.

Incentives to Innovate

Invention leads to a wave of innovation as new knowledge is applied to the production process. Do large firms with monopoly power or small competitive firms lacking monopoly power innovate most? The evidence is mixed. Large firms do more research and development than do small firms, and they are usually the first to use a new technology. But their rate of productivity growth is no greater than that of small firms.

Regulating Natural Monopoly

Figure 13.11 shows the demand curve, *D*, the marginal revenue curve, *MR*, the long-run average cost curve, *ATC*, and the marginal cost curve, *MC*, for a gas distribution company. The firm's marginal cost is constant at 10 cents per cubic foot. Average cost decreases as output increases. This firm is a natural monopoly.

If the firm is not regulated and maximizes profit, it produces only 2 million cubic feet a day, the quantity at which marginal cost equals marginal revenue. The firm prices gas at 20 cents a cubic foot and makes an economic profit of 2 cents a cubic foot, or $40,000 a day. This outcome is inefficient. Gas costs 20 cent a cubic

FIGURE 13.11
Regulating a Natural Monopoly

*e*Foundations 13.5 

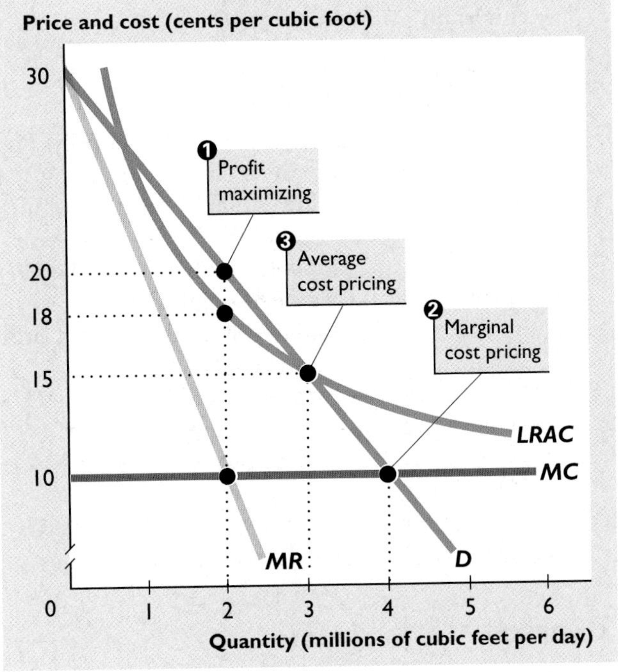

The demand curve for gas is the curve *D*. The natural monopoly's marginal cost, *MC*, is constant at 10 cents per cubic foot and its long-run average cost curve is *LRAC*.

1. The unregulated natural monopoly produces 2 million cubic feet and sets the price at 20 cents a cubic foot.
2. With a marginal cost pricing rule, the price is 10 cents per cubic foot and the quantity produced is 4 million cubic feet per day. The firm incurs an economic loss.
3. With an average cost pricing rule, the price is 15 cents per cubic foot and the quantity produced is 3 million cubic feet per day. The firm makes a normal profit.

foot when marginal cost is only 10 cents a cubic foot. Also, the gas company is making an economic profit. What can regulation do to change this outcome?

An efficient use of resources is achieved when marginal benefit equals marginal cost. You can see in Figure 13.11 that this outcome occurs if the price is regulated at 10 cents per cubic foot and if 4 million cubic feet per day are produced. A **marginal cost pricing rule** that sets price equal to marginal cost achieves this outcome.

Marginal cost pricing rule
A price rule for a natural monopoly that sets price equal to marginal cost.

The marginal cost pricing rule is efficient, but it leaves the natural monopoly incurring an economic loss. How can a firm cover its costs and, at the same time, obey a marginal cost pricing rule? One possibility is to use a two-part price (called a two-part tariff). For example, the gas company might charge a monthly fixed fee that covers its fixed cost and then charge for gas consumed at marginal cost. But a natural monopoly cannot always cover its costs in this way.

Regulators almost never use marginal cost pricing because of its consequences for the firm's profit. Instead, they use an **average cost pricing rule**, which sets the price equal to average cost and enables the firm to cover its costs and earn a normal profit.

Average cost pricing rule
A price rule for a natural monopoly that sets the price equal to average cost and enables the firm to cover its costs and earn a normal profit.

Figure 13.11 shows the average cost pricing outcome. The firm charges 15 cents a cubic foot and sells 3 million cubic feet per day. This outcome is better for consumers than the unregulated profit-maximizing outcome. The price is 5 cents a cubic foot lower, and the quantity consumed is 1 million cubic feet per day more. And the outcome is better for the producer than the marginal cost pricing rule outcome. The firm earns normal profit. The outcome is inefficient but less so than the unregulated profit-maximizing outcome.

CHECKPOINT 13.5

Study Guide pp. 212–214

*e*Foundations 13.5

5 **Explain how monopoly regulation influences output, price, economic profit, and efficiency.**

Practice Problem 13.5

The local water company is a natural monopoly. Figure 1 shows the demand for water and the water company's cost of providing water.

FIGURE 1

a. If the company is an unregulated profit-maximizer:
   i. What is the price of water?
   ii. What quantity of water would be supplied?
   iii. What would be the deadweight loss?
b. If the company is regulated to make normal profit:
   i. What is the price of water?
   ii. What quantity of water would be supplied?
   iii. What would be the deadweight loss?
c. If the company is regulated to be efficient:
   i. What is the price of water?
   ii. What quantity of water would be supplied?
   iii. What would be the deadweight loss?

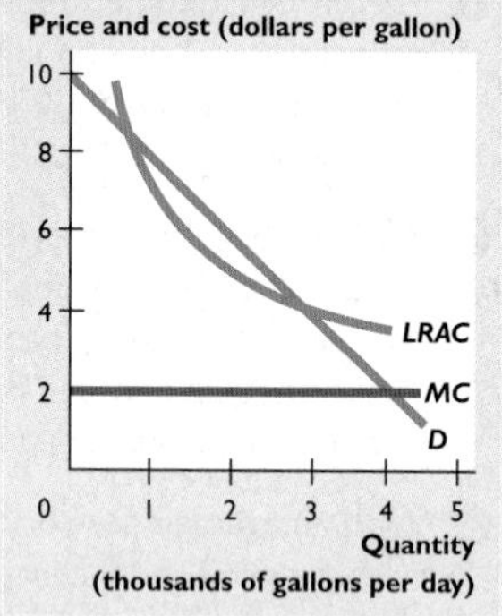

Exercise 13.5

DeBeers has a monopoly in the production of diamonds. If world governments got together and regulated the price so that:

a. Diamond production was efficient:
   i. Would the price of a diamond change? If so, explain how and why?
   ii. Would DeBeers make an economic profit, normal profit, or an economic loss?
   iii. Would the consumer surplus change? If so, explain how and why.
b. DeBeers made normal profit:
   i. Would the price of a diamond change? If so, explain how and why?
   ii. Would the deadweight loss created by DeBeers change? If so, explain how and why?
   iii. Would the consumer surplus change? If so, explain how and why.

FIGURE 2

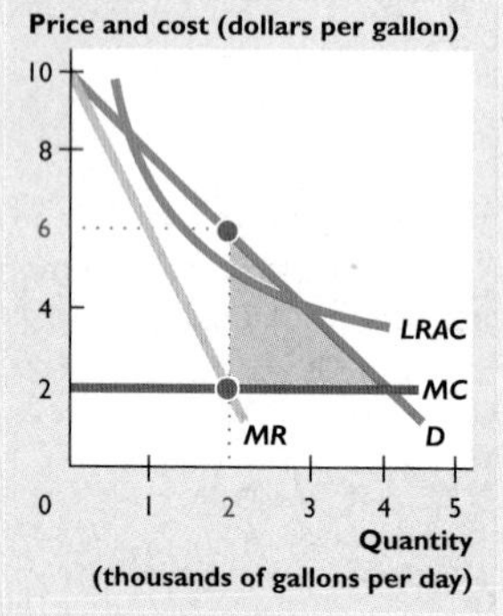

Solution to Practice Problem 13.5

FIGURE 3

a. The price of water is $6 a gallon, the quantity produced is 2,000 gallons a day, and the deadweight loss is $4,000 a day (the shaded triangle in Figure 2).
b. To make normal profit, the monopoly is regulated to set the price equal to average cost. Water is $4 a gallon, the quantity produced is 3,000 gallons a day, and the deadweight loss is $1,000 a day (the shaded triangle in Figure 3).
c. To be efficient, the monopoly is regulated to set the price (marginal benefit) equal to marginal cost. Water is $2 a gallon, the quantity produced is 4,000 gallons a day, and the deadweight loss is zero (Figure 4.)

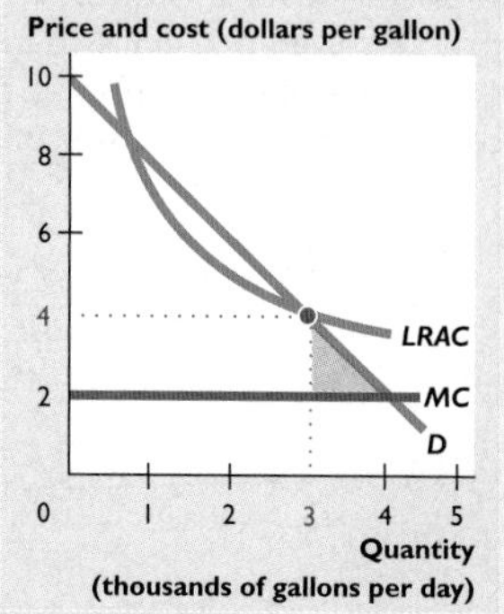

FIGURE 4

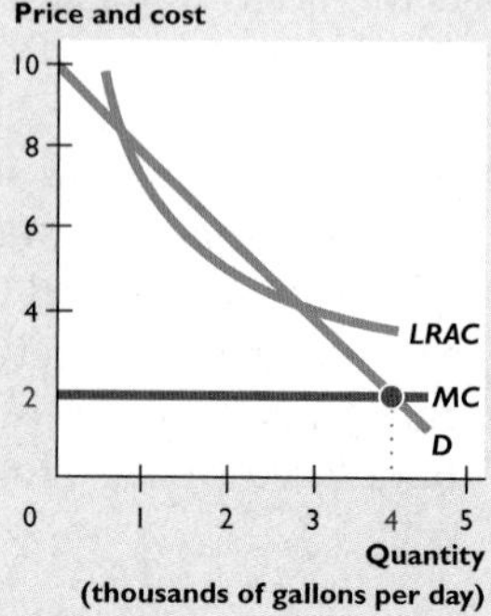

CHAPTER CHECKPOINT

Key Points

1 Explain how monopoly arises and distinguish between single-price monopoly and price-discriminating monopoly.

- A monopoly is a market with a single supplier of a good or service that has no close substitutes and in which legal or natural barriers to entry prevent competition.
- A monopoly can price discriminate when there is no resale possibility.
- Where resale is possible, a firm charges a single price.

2 Explain how a single-price monopoly determines its output and price.

- The demand for a monopoly's output is the market demand, and a single-price monopoly's marginal revenue is less than price.
- A monopoly maximizes profit by producing the output at which marginal revenue equals marginal cost and by charging the maximum price that consumers are willing to pay for that output.

3 Compare the performance of single-price monopoly with that of perfect competition.

- A single-price monopoly charges a higher price and produces a smaller quantity than does a perfectly competitive market and creates a deadweight loss.
- Monopoly imposes a loss on society that equals its deadweight loss plus the cost of the resources devoted to rent seeking.

4 Explain how price discrimination increases profit.

- Perfect price discrimination charges a different price for each unit sold, obtains the maximum price that each consumer is willing to pay for each unit, and redistributes the entire consumer surplus to the monopoly.
- With perfect price discrimination, the monopoly produces the same output as would a perfectly competitive market, but rent seeking uses some of the surplus.

5 Explain how monopoly regulation influences output, price, economic profit, and efficiency.

- Natural monopolies can produce at a lower price than competitive firms can, and monopolies might be more innovative than competitive firms.
- Efficient regulation requires that price equal marginal cost, but for a natural monopoly, such a price is less than average cost.
- Average cost pricing is a rule that covers a firm's costs and provides a normal profit but is inefficient.

Key Terms

Exercises

1. The Big Top is the only circus in the nation. The table sets out the demand schedule for circus tickets and the cost schedule for producing the circus:

Price (dollars per ticket)	Quantity demanded (hundreds of tickets per week)	Quantity supplied (hundreds of tickets per week)	Total cost (dollars per week)
20	0	0	2,000
18	100	100	2,600
16	200	200	3,200
14	300	300	3,800
12	400	400	4,400
10	500	500	5,000
8	600	600	5,600
6	700	700	6,200
4	800	800	6,800

   a. Calculate Big Top's total revenue and marginal revenue from the sale of tickets.
   b. Calculate Big Top's profit-maximizing price, output, and economic profit.
   c. In Exercise 2, what is the consumer surplus and producer surplus?
   d. When Big Top maximizes profit, is the circus efficient? Explain why or why not.
   e. If the circus industry was competitive, how many tickets would be sold and what would be the price of a ticket?
   f. Big Top offers children a discount of 50 percent. How will this discount change the consumer surplus and producer surplus? Will Big Top be more efficient?
   g. Circus lovers lobby the government to regulate the price of a circus ticket. If the government regulates circus tickets such that Big Top makes normal profit, what will be the price of a ticket, how many tickets will be sold, and what will be the deadweight loss?
   h. Circus lovers lobby the government to regulate the price of a circus ticket. If the government regulates circus tickets such that Big Top is to operate efficiently, what will be the price of a ticket, how many tickets will be sold, and what will be its economic profit?

2. Your local art museum, which is a local monopoly, is worried that it is not generating enough revenue to cover its costs and the city government is cutting its budget. The museum charges $1 admission and $5 for special exhibitions. The museum director asks you to help him solve his problem. Can you suggest a pricing scheme that will bring in more revenue? At the same time, can you help the museum to get even more people visiting it?

3. Call around a few travel agents, and get some prices for a trip from the major airport nearest you to anywhere in the world that interests you. Get the best fare possible, and establish the restrictions on its use. Compare it with the normal fare. Explain how the restrictions increase the total revenue of the airline.

Chapter 14

Monopolistic Competition and Oligopoly

CHAPTER CHECKLIST

When you have completed your study of this chapter, you will be able to:

1. **Explain how price and quantity are determined in monopolistic competition.**
2. **Explain why selling costs are high in monopolistic competition.**
3. **Explain the dilemma faced by firms in oligopoly.**
4. **Use game theory to explain how price and quantity are determined in oligopoly.**

Every week, we receive newspapers stuffed with fliers and coupons to grab our attention and to persuade us that Albertsons, Kroger, Safeway, and Shop 'n' Save have the best deals in town. In perfect competition, there are no best deals or fliers. Each firm produces an identical product and is a price taker. How do firms that offer slightly different deals from other firms set their prices?

Until recently, only Intel Corporation made the chips that drive PCs. In 1994, the prices of PCs powered by Intel's fast Pentium chips collapsed. The reason: Intel faced competition from two new entrants, Advanced Micro Devices Inc. and Cyrix Corp. But with only three chip producers, we don't have much competition. How is the price of a computer chip determined?

To understand fliers, coupons, and the price of a computer chip, we need the richer models of monopolistic competition and oligopoly, which are explained in this chapter.

14.1 MONOPOLISTIC COMPETITION

You have studied two market structures: perfect competition and monopoly. In perfect competition, a large number of firms produce identical goods, there are no barriers to entry, and each firm is a price taker. In the long run, there is no economic profit. In monopoly, a single firm protected from competition by barriers to entry might earn an economic profit, even in the long run.

Many real-world markets are competitive, but not as fiercely so as perfect competition. Firms in these markets possess some power to set their prices as monopolies do. We call this type of market monopolistic competition.

Monopolistic competition is a market structure in which:

- A large number of firms compete.
- Each firm produces a differentiated product.
- Firms compete on product quality, price, and marketing.
- Firms are free to enter and exit.

Large Number of Firms

In monopolistic competition, as in perfect competition, the industry consists of a large number of firms. The presence of a large number of firms has three implications for the firms in the industry.

Small Market Share

Each firm supplies a small part of the market. Consequently, although each firm can influence the price of its own product, it has little power to influence the market average price.

No Market Dominance

Each firm must be sensitive to the average market price of the product. But it does not pay attention to any one individual competitor. Because all the firms are relatively small, no single firm can dictate market conditions, so no one firm's actions directly affect the actions of the other firms.

Collusion Impossible

Firms sometimes try to profit from illegal collusion with other firms to fix prices and not undercut each other. Collusion is impossible when the market has a large number of firms, as it does in monopolistic competition.

Product Differentiation

Product differentiation
Making a product that is slightly different from the products of competing firms.

Product differentiation is making a product that is slightly different from the products of competing firms. A differentiated product has close substitutes, but it does not have perfect substitutes. When the price of one firm's product rises, the quantity demanded of it decreases. For example, Adidas, Asics, Diadora, Etonic, Fila, New Balance, Nike, Puma, and Reebok all make differentiated running shoes. Other things remaining the same, if the price of Adidas running shoes rises and the prices of the other shoes remain constant, some people will switch from Adidas to another brand and Adidas will sell fewer shoes.

Competing on Quality, Price, and Marketing

Product differentiation enables a firm to compete with other firms in three areas: quality, price, and marketing.

Quality

The quality of a product is the physical attributes that make it different from the products of other firms. Quality includes design, reliability, the service provided to the buyer, and the buyer's ease of access to the product. Quality lies on a spectrum that runs from high to low. Go to the J. D. Power Consumer Center at jdpower.com, and you'll see the many dimensions on which this rating agency describes the quality of autos, financial services, travel and accommodation services, telecommunication services, and new homes—all examples of products that have a large range of quality variety.

Price

Because of product differentiation, a firm in monopolistic competition faces a downward-sloping demand curve. So, like a monopoly, the firm can set both its price and its output. But there is a tradeoff between the product's quality and price. A firm that makes a high-quality product can charge a higher price than a firm that makes a low-quality product can.

Marketing

Because of product differentiation, a firm in monopolistic competition must market its product. Marketing takes two main forms: advertising and packaging. A firm that produces a high-quality product wants to sell it for a suitably high price. To be able to do so, the firm must advertise and package its product in a way that convinces buyers that they are getting the higher quality for which they are paying. For example, drug companies advertise and package their brand-name drugs to persuade buyers that these items are superior to the lower-priced generic alternatives. Similarly, a firm that produces a low-quality product uses advertising and packaging to persuade buyers that although the quality is low, the low price more than compensates for this fact.

Entry and Exit

In monopolistic competition, there are no barriers to entry. Consequently, a firm cannot make an economic profit in the long run. When firms make economic profits, new firms enter the industry. This entry lowers prices and eventually eliminates economic profits. When economic losses are incurred, some firms leave the industry. Exit increases prices and profits and eventually eliminates the economic losses. In long-run equilibrium, firms neither enter nor leave the industry and the firms in the industry make zero economic profit.

Identifying Monopolistic Competition

To identify monopolistic competition, economists use two indexes of the extent to which a market is dominated by a small number of firms. These indexes are:

- The four-firm concentration ratio
- The Herfindahl-Hirschman Index

Four-firm concentration ratio The percentage of the value of sales accounted for by the four largest firms in an industry.

The **four-firm concentration ratio** is the percentage of the value of sales accounted for by the four largest firms in an industry. The range of the concentration ratio is from almost zero for perfect competition to 100 percent for monopoly. The boundary between oligopoly and monopolistic competition is generally regarded as being around 40: A four-firm concentration ratio that exceeds 40 percent is regarded as an indication of oligopoly and a ratio of less than 40 percent is regarded as an indication of monopolistic competition.

Herfindahl-Hirschman Index The square of the percentage market share of each firm summed over the largest 50 firms (or summed over all the firms if there are fewer than 50) in a market.

The **Herfindahl-Hirschman Index**—also called the HHI—is the square of the percentage market share of each firm summed over the largest 50 firms (or summed over all the firms if there are fewer than 50) in a market. For example, if there are four firms in a market and the market shares of the firms are 50 percent, 25 percent, 15 percent, and 10 percent, the Herfindahl-Hirschman Index is

$$\text{HHI} = 50^2 + 25^2 + 15^2 + 10^2 = 3{,}450.$$

In perfect competition, the HHI is small. For example, if each of the largest 50 firms in an industry has a market share of 0.1 percent, the HHI is $0.1^2 \times 50 = 0.5$. In a monopoly, the HHI is 10,000—the firm has 100 percent of the market: $100^2 = 10{,}000$.

The HHI became a popular measure of the degree of competition during the 1980s, when the Justice Department used it to classify markets. A market in which the HHI is less than 1,000 is regarded as being competitive. A market in which the HHI lies between 1,000 and 1,800 is regarded as being moderately competitive. But a market in which the HHI exceeds 1,800 is regarded as being uncompetitive. The Justice Department scrutinizes any merger of firms in a market in which the HHI exceeds 1,000, and it is likely to challenge a merger if the HHI exceeds 1800.

A market with a high concentration ratio or HHI might nonetheless be competitive because the few firms in a market face competition from many firms that can easily enter the market and will do so if economic profits are available.

Examples of Monopolistic Competition

These 10 industries are all examples of monopolistic competition. They have a large number of firms, shown in brackets after the name of the industry. The bars measure the percentage of industry total revenue received by the 20 largest firms. The number on the right is the Herfindahl-Hirschman Index.

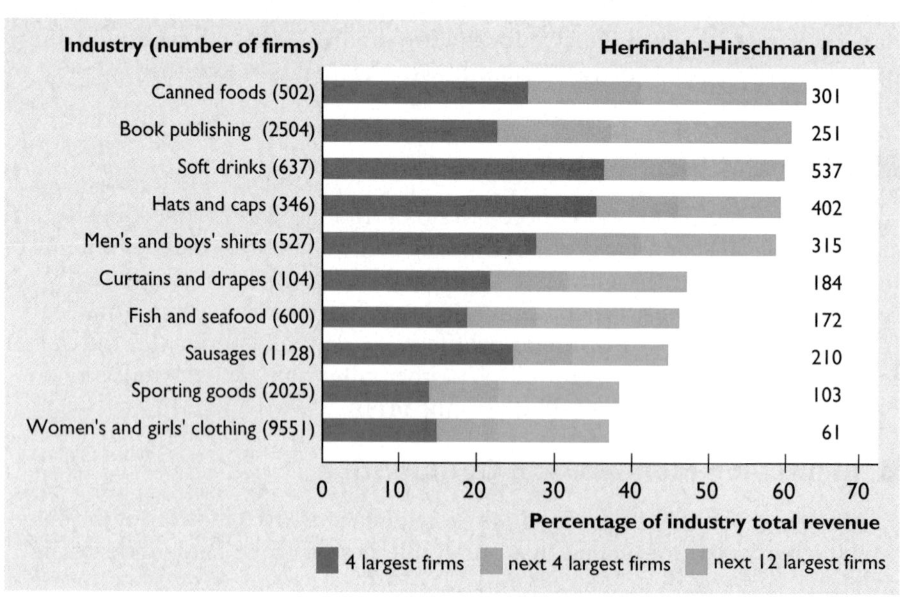

SOURCE: U.S. Census Bureau.

Output and Price in Monopolistic Competition

Think about the decisions that Tommy Hilfiger must make about Tommy jeans. First, the firm must decide on the design and quality of its jeans and on its marketing program. We'll suppose that Tommy Hilfiger has already made these decisions so that we can concentrate on the firm's output and pricing decision. But we'll study quality and marketing decisions in the next section.

For a given quality of jeans and a given amount of marketing activity, Tommy Hilfiger faces given costs and market conditions. How, given its costs and the demand for its jeans, does Tommy Hilfiger decide the quantity of jeans to produce and the price at which to sell them?

The Firm's Profit-Maximizing Decision

A firm in monopolistic competition makes its output and price decision just as a monopoly firm does. Figure 14.1 illustrates this decision for Tommy jeans. The demand curve for Tommy jeans is *D*. The *MR* curve shows the marginal revenue curve associated with this demand curve. It is derived just like the marginal revenue curve of a single-price monopoly that you studied in Chapter 13. The *ATC* curve shows the average total cost of producing Tommy jeans and *MC* is the marginal cost curve.

Tommy Hilfiger maximizes profit by producing the output at which marginal revenue equals marginal cost. In Figure 14.1, this output is 150 pairs of jeans a day. Tommy Hilfiger charges the price that buyers are willing to pay for this quantity, which is determined by the demand curve. This price is $70 a pair. When it produces 150 pairs of jeans a day, Tommy Hilfiger's average total cost is $20 a pair, and it makes an economic profit of $7,500 a day ($50 a pair multiplied by 150 pairs of jeans a day). The blue rectangle shows Tommy Hilfiger's economic profit.

FIGURE 14.1
Output and Price in Monopolistic Competition

*e*Foundations **14.1** 

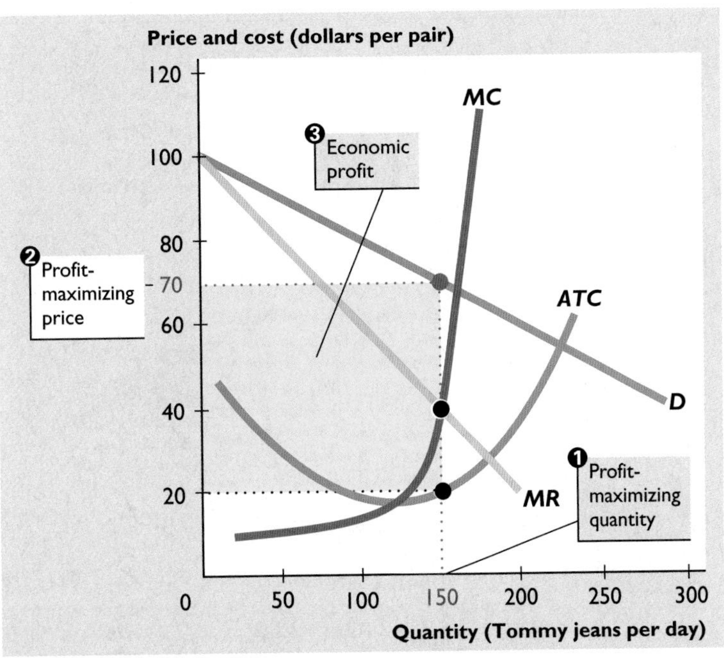

The firm maximizes its economic profit by producing the quantity at which marginal revenue equals marginal cost and charging the highest price possible for that quantity.

❶ The profit-maximizing output is 150 pairs of Tommy jeans per day, and ❷ the profit-maximizing price is $70 per pair.

Average total cost is $20 per pair, so the firm makes ❸ an economic profit of $7,500 a day ($50 per pair multiplied by 150 pairs).

So far, the firm in monopolistic competition looks just like a single-price monopoly. It produces the quantity at which marginal revenue equals marginal cost and then charges the price that buyers are willing to pay for that quantity, as determined by the demand curve. The key difference between monopoly and monopolistic competition lies in what happens next.

Long Run: Zero Economic Profit

There is no restriction on entry in monopolistic competition, so if firms in an industry are making an economic profit, other firms have an incentive to enter that industry.

As the Gap and Calvin Klein start to make jeans similar to Tommy jeans, some people will switch to these other brands and the demand for Tommy jeans will decrease. The demand curve for Tommy jeans and the marginal revenue curve start to shift leftward. At each point in time, the firm maximizes its profit by producing the quantity at which marginal revenue equals marginal cost and by charging the highest price that buyers are willing to pay for this quantity. As the demand curve shifts leftward, the profit-maximizing quantity and price fall.

Figure 14.2 shows the long-run equilibrium. The demand curve for Tommy jeans has shifted leftward to *D*', and the marginal revenue curve has shifted leftward to *MR*'. The firm produces 50 pairs of jeans a day and sells them for $30 each. At this output level, average total cost is also $30 a pair. So Tommy Hilfiger is making zero economic profit on its jeans. When all the firms in the industry are earning zero economic profit, there is no incentive for new firms to enter.

If demand is so low relative to costs that firms incur economic losses, exit will occur. As firms leave an industry, the demand for the products of the remaining firms increases and their demand curves shift rightward. The exit process ends when all the firms in the industry are making zero economic profit.

FIGURE 14.2
Output and Price in the Long Run

*e*Foundations 14.1 

Economic profit encourages new entrants, and the entry of new firms decreases the demand for each firm's product. The demand curve and marginal revenue curve shift leftward.

When the demand curve has shifted to *D*', the marginal revenue curve is *MR*' and the firm is in long-run equilibrium.

❶ The output that maximizes profit is 50 pairs of Tommy jeans a day, and ❷ the price is $30 per pair. Average total cost is also $30 per pair, so ❸ economic profit is zero.

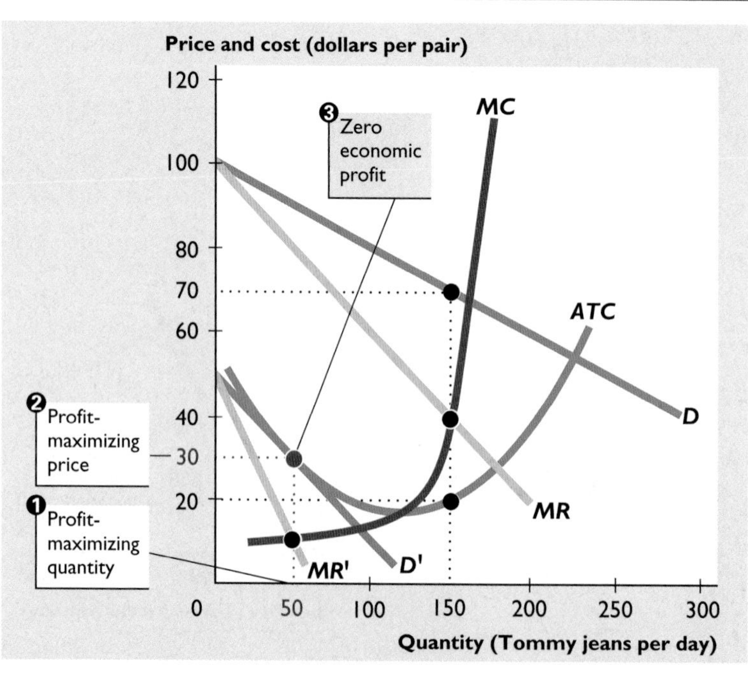

Monopolistic Competition and Efficiency

Efficiency requires that the marginal benefit of the consumer equal the marginal cost of the producer. Price measures marginal benefit, so efficiency requires price to equal marginal cost. In monopolistic competition, price exceeds marginal revenue and marginal revenue equals marginal cost, so price exceeds marginal cost—a sign of inefficiency.

But this inefficiency arises from product differentiation—variety—that consumers value and for which they are willing to pay. So the loss that arises because marginal benefit exceeds marginal cost must be weighed against the gain that arises from greater product variety. It is almost inconceivable that consumers would be better off with no variety and price equal to marginal cost. So in a broader view of efficiency, monopolistic competition brings gains for consumers.

Another interesting feature of firms in monopolistic competition is that they always have excess capacity in long-run equilibrium.

Excess Capacity

A firm's **capacity output** is the output at which average total cost is a minimum—the output at the bottom of the U-shaped *ATC* curve. This output is 125 pairs of jeans a day in Figure 14.3. Firms in monopolistic competition always have *excess capacity* in the long run. In Figure 14.3, Tommy Hilfiger produces 50 pairs of jeans a day and has excess capacity of 75 pairs of jeans a day. That is, Tommy Hilfiger produces a smaller output than that which minimizes average total cost. Consequently, the consumer pays a price that exceeds minimum average total cost. This result arises from the fact that the firm faces a downward-sloping demand curve. The demand curve slopes downward because of product differentiation, so product differentiation creates excess capacity.

Capacity output
The output at which average total cost is a minimum.

FIGURE 14.3
Excess Capacity

*e*Foundations 14.1 

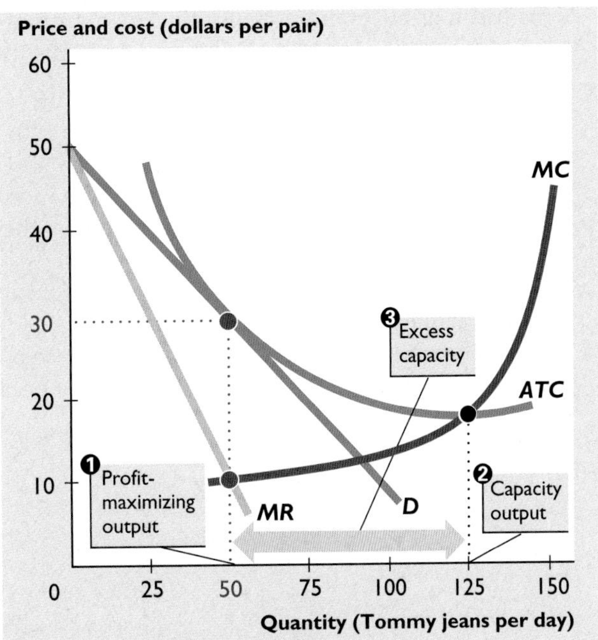

In long-run equilibrium, entry decreases the demand for one firm's output to the point at which the firm makes zero economic profit.

❶ The firm produces 50 pairs of jeans a day.

❷ The firm's capacity output is the output at which average total cost is a minimum—125 pairs a day.

Because the demand curve in monopolistic competition slopes downward, the output that maximizes profit is always less than capacity output in long-run equilibrium.

❸ In long-run equilibrium, the firm operates with excess capacity.

CHECKPOINT 14.1

Study Guide pp. 220–223 

*e*Foundations 14.1

1 Explain how price and quantity are determined in monopolistic competition.

Practice Problem 14.1

Natti is a dot.com entrepreneur who has established a Web site at which people can design and buy a pair of cool sunglasses. Natti pays $4,000 a month for her Web server and Internet connection. The glasses that her customers design are made to order by another firm, and Natti pays this firm $50 a pair. Natti has no other costs. Table 1 shows the demand schedule for Natti's sunglasses.

a. Calculate Natti's profit-maximizing output, price, and economic profit.
b. Do you expect other firms to enter the Web sunglasses business and compete with Natti?
c. What happens to the demand for Natti's sunglasses in the long run?
d. What happens to Natti's economic profit in the long run?

TABLE 1

Price (dollars per pair)	Quantity demanded (pairs per month)
250	0
200	50
150	100
100	150
50	200
0	250

Exercise 14.1

Lorie restrings tennis racquets. Her fixed costs are $1,000 a month, and it costs her $15 of labor time to restring one racquet. Table 2 shows the demand schedule for Lorie's restringing services.

a. Calculate Lorie's profit-maximizing output, price, and economic profit.
b. Do you expect other firms to enter the tennis racquet restringing business and compete with Lorie?
c. What happens to the demand for Lorie's restringing services in the long run?
d. What happens to Lorie's economic profit in the long run?

TABLE 2

Price (dollars per racquet)	Quantity demanded (racquets per month)
25	0
20	10
15	20
10	30
5	40
0	50

Solution to Practice Problem 14.1

FIGURE 1

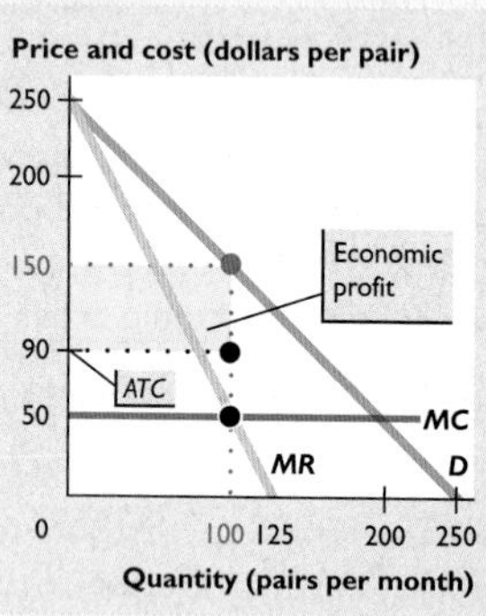

a. Marginal cost, *MC*, is $50 a pair—the price that Natti pays her supplier of glasses. To find marginal revenue, plot the demand curve using the numbers in the demand schedule provided (see Figure 1). Note that the demand curve cuts to *x*-axis at 250 pairs a month. The marginal revenue, *MR*, curve has a slope twice that of the demand curve and cuts the *x*-axis at 125 pairs a month.

Profit is maximized when *MC* = *MR* and Natti sells 100 pairs a month. The price is $150, and average total cost, *ATC*, is $90—$50 marginal cost (and average variable cost) and $40 average fixed cost. Economic profit is $60 a pair on 100 pairs a month, which is $6,000 a month.

b. Because Natti is making an economic profit, other firms have an incentive to enter and will do so.
c. As firms enter Natti's market, the demand for Natti's sunglasses will decrease and the demand curve will shift leftward.
d. As the demand for Natti's sunglasses decreases, her economic profit also decreases. In the long run, she will earn zero economic profit.

14.2 PRODUCT DEVELOPMENT AND MARKETING

When we studied a firm's output and price decision, we supposed that it had already made its product quality and marketing decisions. We're now going to study these decisions and the impact they have on the firm's output, price, and economic profit.

Innovation and Product Development

To enjoy economic profits, firms in monopolistic competition must be continuously developing new products. The reason is that wherever economic profits are earned, imitators emerge and set up business. So to maintain its economic profit, a firm must seek out new products that will provide it with a competitive edge, even if only temporarily. A firm that manages to introduce a new and differentiated product will temporarily have a less elastic demand for its product and will be able to increase its price temporarily. It will make an economic profit. Eventually, new firms that make close substitutes for the innovative product will enter and compete away the economic profit arising from this initial advantage. So to restore economic profit, the firm must again innovate.

Cost Versus Benefit of Product Innovation

The decision to innovate is based on the same type of profit-maximizing calculation that you've already studied. Innovation and product development are costly activities, but they bring in additional revenues. The firm must balance the cost and benefit at the margin. At a low level of product development, the marginal revenue from a better product exceeds the marginal cost. When the marginal dollar spent on product development (its marginal cost) brings in an additional dollar of revenue (its marginal benefit), the firm is spending the profit-maximizing amount on product development.

For example, when Eidos Interactive released Tomb Raider III, it was probably not the best game that Eidos could have created. Rather, it was the game that balanced the marginal benefit and willingness of the consumer to pay for further game enhancements against the marginal cost of these enhancements.

Efficiency and Product Innovation

Is product innovation an efficient activity? Does it benefit the consumer? There are two views about the answers to these questions. One view is that monopolistic competition brings to market many improved products that bring great benefits to the consumer. Clothing, kitchen and other household appliances, computers, computer programs, cars, and many other products keep getting better every year, and the consumer benefits from these improved products.

But many so-called improvements amount to little more than changing the appearance of a product or giving a different look to the packaging. In these cases, there is little objective benefit to the consumer.

But regardless of whether a product improvement is real or imagined, its value to the consumer is its marginal benefit, which equals the amount the consumer is willing to pay. In other words, the value of product improvements is the increase in price that the consumer is willing to pay. The marginal benefit to the producer is marginal revenue, which in equilibrium equals marginal cost. Because price exceeds marginal cost in monopolistic competition, product improvement is not pushed to its efficient level.

February 22, 2000

Airlines Back Off Price Rise

With jet fuel prices at their highest levels since the Gulf War, American Airlines, Delta Air Lines, Continental Airlines, and United Airlines proposed higher fares on domestic routes. But Northwest Airlines held to its existing prices, and in the face of this decision, the other four airlines backed off their earlier plan.

Adapted from CNNfn.com

Questions

1. What is the structure of the market for domestic air travel in the United States?

2. Why do some airlines want higher prices?

3. Why is one airline unwilling to raise its prices?

4. Why don't the airlines just get together and negotiate a deal on prices?

5. Why can't each airline just set and stick to the price that would maximize profit as if the industry were a monopoly?

 *e*Foundations **14.2**

Marketing

Designing and developing products that are actually different from those of other firms are ways to achieve some product differentiation. But firms also attempt to create a consumer perception of product differentiation even when actual differences are small. Advertising and packaging are the principal means that firms use to achieve this end. An American Express card is a different product from a Visa card. But the actual differences are not the main ones that American Express emphasizes in its marketing. The deeper message is that if you use an American Express card, you can be like Tiger Woods (or another highly successful person).

Marketing Expenditures

Firms in monopolistic competition incur huge costs to ensure that buyers appreciate and value the differences between their own products and those of their competitors. So a large proportion of the prices that we pay cover the cost of selling a good. Advertising in newspapers and magazines and on radio, television, and the Internet is the main selling cost. But it is not the only one. Selling costs include the cost of shopping malls that look like movie sets; glossy catalogs and brochures; and the salaries, airfares, and hotel bills of salespeople.

The total scale of selling costs is hard to estimate, but some components can be measured. A survey conducted by a commercial agency suggests that for cleaning supplies and toys, around 15 percent of the price of an item is spent on advertising. Figure 14.4 shows some estimates for these and other industries.

FIGURE 14.4
Advertising Expenditures

*e*Foundations 14.2 

Advertising expenditures are a large part of total revenue for producers of cleaning supplies, toys, confectionery, and cosmetics.

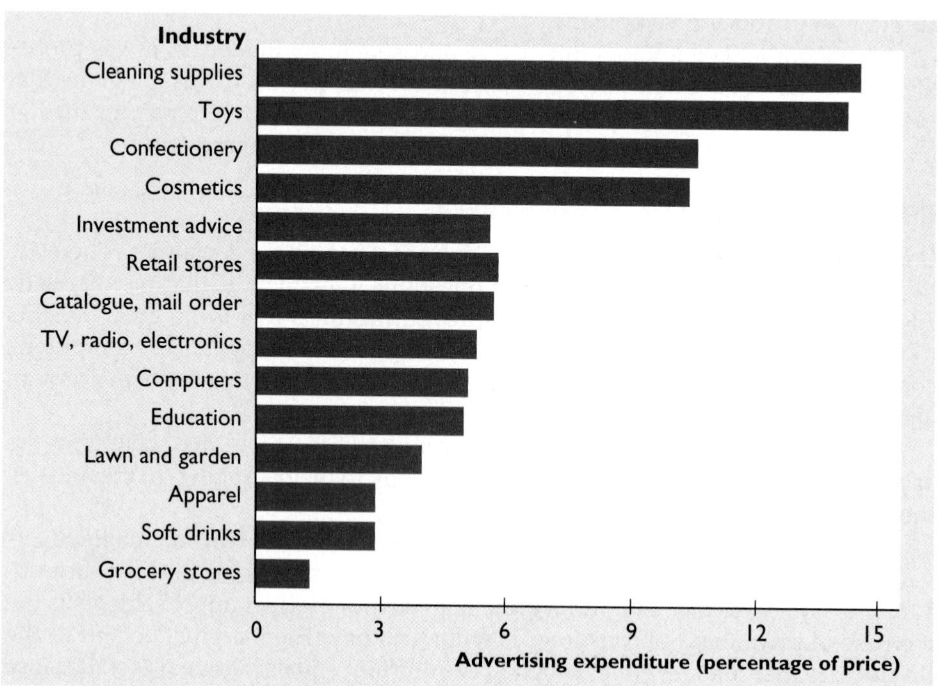

SOURCE: Schoenfeld & Associates, Lincolnwood, Illinois , reported at http://www.toolkit.cch.com/text/p03_7006.stm

For the U.S. economy as a whole, there are some 20,000 advertising agencies, which employ more than 200,000 people and have sales of $45 billion. But these numbers are only part of the total cost of advertising because firms have their own internal advertising departments, the costs of which we can only guess.

Advertising expenditures and other selling costs affect the profits of firms in two ways. They increase costs, and they change demand. Let's look at these effects.

Selling Costs and Total Costs

Selling costs such as advertising expenditures increase the costs of a monopolistically competitive firm above those of a perfectly competitive firm or a monopoly. Advertising costs and other selling costs are fixed costs. They do not vary as total output varies. So, just like fixed production costs, advertising costs per unit decrease as production increases.

Figure 14.5 shows how selling costs and advertising expenditures change a firm's average total cost. The blue curve shows the average total cost of production. The red curve shows the firm's average total cost of production plus advertising. The height of the red area between the two curves shows the average fixed cost of advertising. The *total* cost of advertising is fixed. But the *average* cost of advertising decreases as output increases.

The figure shows that if advertising increases the quantity sold by a large enough amount, it can lower average total cost. For example, if the quantity sold increases from 25 pairs of jeans a day with no advertising to 125 pairs of jeans a day with advertising, average total cost falls from $30 a pair to $20 a pair. The reason is that although the *total* fixed cost has increased, the greater fixed cost is spread over a greater output, so average total cost decreases.

FIGURE 14.5
Selling Costs and Total Costs

*e*Foundations **14.2** 

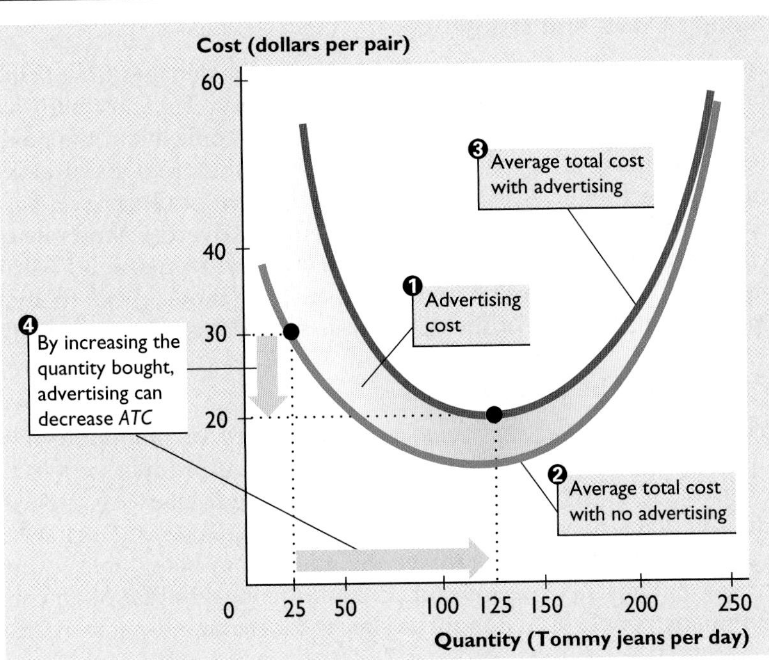

Selling costs such as the cost of advertising are fixed costs.

1. When advertising costs are added to 2 the average total cost of production, 3 average total cost increases by a greater amount at small outputs than at large outputs.

4. If advertising enables sales to increase from 25 pairs of jeans a day to 125 pairs a day, it *lowers* the average total cost from $30 a pair to $20 a pair.

The Selling Cost of a Pair of Running Shoes

Have you ever wondered what you're paying for when you buy a new pair of running shoes? Your new Nikes cost you $70. But who got that money?

The figure shows you the answer. The plastic and other materials from which the shoe is made cost $9. The producer, in Asia, paid $8 in wages and capital costs and normal profit. The U.S. government collected $3 when the shoes were imported into the United States. These items total $20. The remaining $50 is selling cost. It is the cost (including normal profit) of Nike's marketing its shoes and of the retailer from whom you bought them. The table provides a more detailed breakdown of these costs.

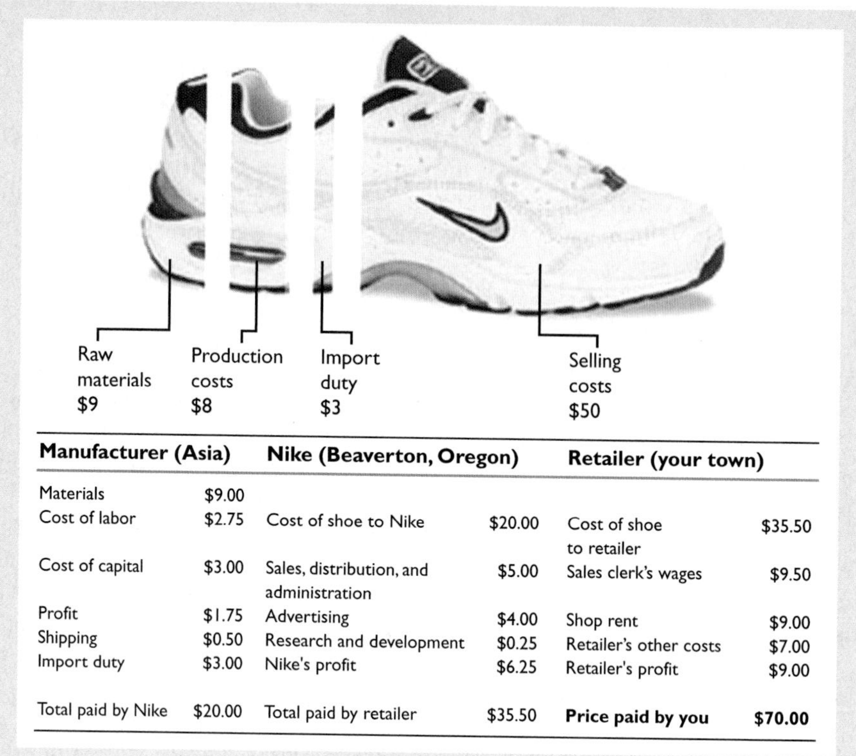

Manufacturer (Asia)		Nike (Beaverton, Oregon)		Retailer (your town)	
Materials	$9.00				
Cost of labor	$2.75	Cost of shoe to Nike	$20.00	Cost of shoe to retailer	$35.50
Cost of capital	$3.00	Sales, distribution, and administration	$5.00	Sales clerk's wages	$9.50
Profit	$1.75	Advertising	$4.00	Shop rent	$9.00
Shipping	$0.50	Research and development	$0.25	Retailer's other costs	$7.00
Import duty	$3.00	Nike's profit	$6.25	Retailer's profit	$9.00
Total paid by Nike	$20.00	Total paid by retailer	$35.50	**Price paid by you**	**$70.00**

Selling Costs and Demand

Advertising and other selling efforts change the demand for a firm's product. But how? Does demand increase, or does it decrease? The most natural answer is that advertising increases demand. By informing people about the quality of its product or by persuading people to switch from the products of other firms, a firm might expect to increase the demand for its own product.

But all firms in monopolistic competition advertise. And all seek to persuade customers that they have the best deal. If advertising enables a firm to survive, it might increase the number of firms in the market. And to the extent that it increases the number of firms, it *decreases* the demand faced by any one firm.

Efficiency: The Bottom Line

The bottom line on the question of efficiency of monopolistic competition is ambiguous. In some cases, the gains from extra product variety unquestionably offset the selling costs and the extra cost arising from excess capacity. The tremendous varieties of books and magazines, clothing, food, and drinks are examples of such gains. It is less easy to see the gains from being able to buy brand-name drugs that have a chemical composition identical to that of a generic alternative. But many people do willingly pay more for the brand-name alternative.

CHECKPOINT 14.2

2 **Explain why selling costs are high in monopolistic competition.**

Study Guide pp. 223–225 
*e*Foundations 14.2 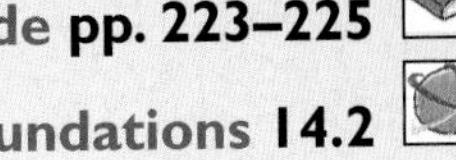

Practice Problem 14.2

Bianca bakes delicious cookies. Her total fixed cost is $40 a day, and her average variable cost is $1 a bag. Few people know about Bianca's Cookies, and she is maximizing her profit by selling 10 bags a day for $5 a bag. Bianca thinks that if she spends $50 a day on advertising, she can increase her market and sell 25 bags a day for $5 a bag.

a. If Bianca's belief about the effect of advertising is correct, can she increase her economic profit by advertising?

b. If she advertised, would her average total cost increase or decrease at the quantity produced?

c. If Bianca's belief about the effect of advertising is correct, would she continue to sell her cookies for $5 a bag, or would she raise or lower her price?

Exercise 14.2

Bianca—the same Bianca as in the Practice Problem—changes the recipe that she uses and now bakes even more delicious cookies. Bianca's costs don't change, but people love her new cookies and think that they are much better than those of the other cookie producers.

a. How will the change described here affect Bianca's price, quantity produced, and economic profit?

b. Can she still increase her economic profit by advertising?

Solution to Practice Problem 14.2

a. With no advertising, Bianca's total revenue is $50 (10 bags at $5 a bag) and her total cost is $50 (total fixed cost $40 and total variable cost $10). So her economic profit is zero.

With $50 a day advertising expenditure, Bianca has a total revenue of $125 (25 bags at $5) and total cost of $115 (total fixed cost is now $90, and total variable cost is now $25). Her economic profit with no price change is $10. So Bianca can increase her economic profit by advertising.

b. If Bianca advertises, her average total cost decreases. With no advertising, her average total cost is $5 a bag ($50 ÷ 10). With advertising, her average total cost is $4.60 a bag ($115 ÷ 25 bags).

c. We can't say whether she would continue to sell her cookies for $5 a bag. It would depend on how her demand curve shifts. Advertising costs are fixed costs, so they don't change marginal cost, which remains at $1 a bag. She will sell the profit-maximizing quantity (the quantity at which marginal revenue equals marginal cost) for the highest price she can.

14.3 OLIGOPOLY

Another type of market that stands between the extremes of perfect competition and monopoly is oligopoly. *Oligopoly* is a market structure in which:

- A small number of firms compete.
- Natural or legal barriers prevent the entry of new firms.

Oligopoly is a market with a small number of firms, and each firm is large and can influence the market price. In any market, the price depends on the total quantity supplied. In monopoly, one firm controls this quantity and so also controls the price. In perfect competition, no firm is big enough to influence the total quantity supplied, so no firm can influence the price. Oligopoly is unlike both of these cases. More than one firm controls the quantity supplied, so no *one* firm controls the price. But each firm is large, and the quantity produced by each firm influences the price.

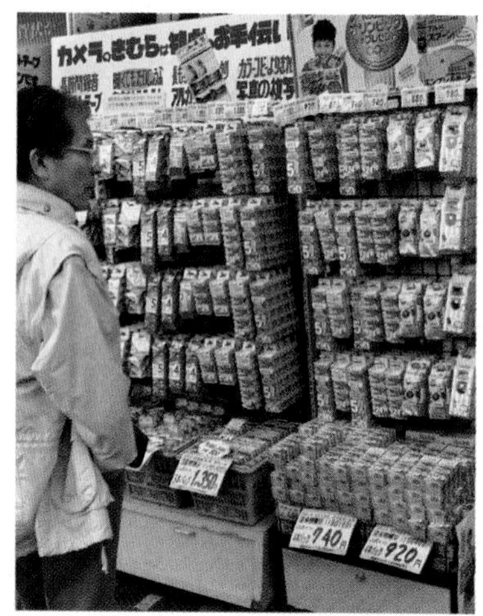

Like monopoly, the firms in an oligopoly operate behind a barrier to entry. And also like monopoly, the barriers to entry can arise for either natural reasons or legal reasons. A natural oligopoly is a market in which economies of scale exist but the output of a few firms is required to meet the market demand at the lowest possible cost. One firm could not meet the market demand at as low a price as a few firms could. But economies of scale are sufficiently large that more than a few firms could not survive and earn a normal profit.

A legal oligopoly arises when a legal barrier to entry protects the small number of firms in a market. A city might license two taxi firms, or two bus companies, for example.

Firms in an oligopoly might produce identical or differentiated products.

The problem for a firm in oligopoly is that its own profit-maximizing actions might decrease the profits of its competitors. But if each firm's actions decrease the profits of the other firms, all the firms end up with a lower profit.

Collusion

Cartel
A group of firms acting together to limit output, raise price, and increase economic profit.

One possible way of avoiding a self-defeating outcome is for the firms in an oligopoly to form a cartel. A **cartel** is a group of firms acting together—in collusion—to limit output, raise price, and increase economic profit. Cartels are illegal in the United States (and in most other countries) and are undertaken in secret. Firms in an oligopoly would like to be able to agree with each other to fix the price at a level that maximizes their joint profit.

Duopoly
A market in which there are only two producers.

It turns out that collusion usually breaks down. To understand why, and to learn how price and output are determined in an oligopoly, we're going to study a special case called duopoly. **Duopoly** is a market in which there are only two producers. You can probably see some examples of duopoly where you live. Many cities have only two local newspapers, two taxi companies, two copy centers, or two college bookstores. In the global economy, there are only two major producers of photographic film—Kodak and Fuji—and of commercial jet aircraft—Boeing in the United States and Airbus Industrie in Europe.

Although duopoly is common, the main reason for studying it is not its realism. We study it because it captures the essence of oligopoly and reveals the mutual interdependence of firms most effectively. Also, if collusion is difficult for a duopoly, it is even more difficult for an oligopoly with three or more firms.

Duopoly In Airplanes

Airbus and Boeing are the only makers of large commercial jet aircraft. Suppose that they have identical production costs. To keep things simple, we'll assume that the marginal cost of an airplane is $1 million and that total fixed cost is zero.

Figure 14.6 shows the market demand schedule and demand curve for airplanes. Airbus and Boeing must share this market. The total quantity of aircraft sold (and the quantities sold by each firm) depends on the price.

Competitive Outcome

If this industry had a large number of firms and was perfectly competitive, the marginal cost curve would be the industry supply curve. The equilibrium is where the industry supply curve (marginal cost curve) intersects the demand curve—12 airplanes a week would be sold for $1 million each. Total cost would be $12 million and total revenue would also be $12 million, so economic profit would be zero—a long-run equilibrium in perfect competition.

Monopoly Outcome

If this industry had only one firm, the firm would be a single-price monopoly because an airplane is a durable good that can be resold. The marginal revenue curve would be the one shown in Figure 14.6. Marginal revenue equals marginal cost when 6 airplanes a week are produced and the price is $13 million per airplane. Total cost would be $6 million and total revenue would be $78 million, so economic profit would be $72 million a week.

FIGURE 14.6
A Market for Airplanes

*e*Foundations 14.3 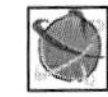

Quantity (airplanes per week)	Price	Marginal revenue	Marginal cost
	(millions of dollars per airplane)		
0	25	25	1
1	23	21	1
2	21	17	1
3	19	13	1
4	17	9	1
5	15	5	1
6	13	1	1
7	11		1
8	9		1
9	7		1
10	5		1
11	3		1
12	1		1

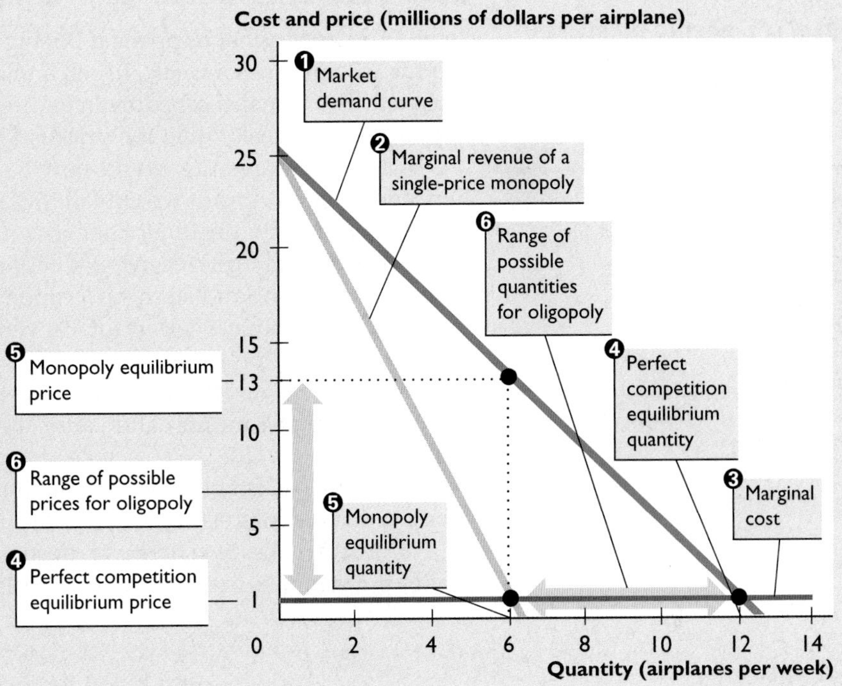

Cost and price (millions of dollars per airplane)
1 Market demand curve
2 Marginal revenue of a single-price monopoly
6 Range of possible quantities for oligopoly
4 Perfect competition equilibrium quantity
3 Marginal cost
5 Monopoly equilibrium price
6 Range of possible prices for oligopoly
4 Perfect competition equilibrium price
5 Monopoly equilibrium quantity
Quantity (airplanes per week)

Range of Possible Oligopoly Outcomes

Because oligopoly is a market structure that lies between perfect competition and monopoly, these extremes that we've just found provide the maximum range within which the oligopoly outcome might lie. If Airbus and Boeing persistently cut their prices to increase their production and quantity sold, they might drive the price down all the way to the perfectly competitive price and end up with no economic profit. In contrast, if the two firms were able to collude and set the monopoly price, they could end up sharing the maximum available monopoly profit.

The Duopolists' Dilemma

TABLE 14.1 MONOPOLY OUTCOME

	Boeing	Airbus	Market total
Quantity (airplanes a week)	3	3	6
Price ($ million per airplane)	13	13	13
Total revenue ($ million)	39	39	78
Total cost ($ million)	3	3	6
Economic profit ($ million)	36	36	72

You've just seen that if this industry had only one firm, 6 airplanes a week would be produced and the price of an airplane would be $13 million. Economic profit would be $72 million a week. If this same outcome could be achieved with two firms in the industry, Airbus and Boeing might each produce 3 airplanes a week and make an economic profit of $36 million each (see Table 14.1).

Because this outcome is the one that maximizes monopoly profit, we know that there is no better outcome for the two firms in total. That is, their joint profits cannot be any higher than the $72 million a week that a monopoly can achieve.

But can one firm make a larger profit than $36 million a week at the expense of the other firm? To answer this question, we need to see what happens if one of the firms increases output by 1 airplane a week. Because the two firms in this example are identical, we can explore this question with either Boeing or Airbus increasing production by 1 airplane a week and the other holding output at 3 a week. We'll suppose that Boeing increases output to 4 airplanes a week and Airbus at first continues to produce 3 airplanes a week.

Boeing Increases Output to 4 Airplanes a Week

TABLE 14.2 BOEING INCREASES OUTPUT TO 4 AIRPLANES A WEEK

	Boeing	Airbus	Market total
Quantity (airplanes a week)	4	3	7
Price ($ million per airplane)	11	11	11
Total revenue ($ million)	44	33	77
Total cost ($ million)	4	3	7
Economic profit ($ million)	40	30	70

Table 14.2 shows what happens if Boeing produces 4 airplanes a week and Airbus produces 3 airplanes a week. To sell a total output of 7 airplanes a week, the price must fall. The demand schedule in Figure 14.6 tells us that the quantity demanded is 7 airplanes a week when the price is $11 million per airplane.

Market total revenue would now be $77 million, total cost would be $7 million, and economic profit would fall to $70 million. But the distribution of this economic profit is now unequal. Boeing would gain, and Airbus would lose.

Boeing would now receive $44 million a week in total revenue, have a total cost of $4 million, and earn an economic profit of $40 million. Airbus would receive $33 million a week in total revenue, incur a total cost of $3 million, and earn an economic profit of $30 million.

So by increasing its output by 1 airplane a week, Boeing can increase its economic profit by $4 million and cause the economic profit of Airbus to fall by $6 million.

This situation is better for Boeing, but would Airbus go along with it? Would it be in Airbus's interest to hold its output at 3 airplanes a week?

To answer this question, we need to compare the economic profit Airbus makes if it maintains its output at 3 airplanes a week with the profit it makes if it produces 4 airplanes a week. How much economic profit does Airbus make if it produces 4 airplanes a week with Boeing also producing 4 a week?

Airbus Increases Output to 4 Airplanes a Week

With both firms producing 4 airplanes a week, total output is 8 airplanes a week. To sell 8 airplanes a week, the price must fall further. The demand schedule in Figure 14.6 tells us that the quantity demanded is 8 airplanes a week when the price is $9 million per airplane.

Table 14.3 keeps track of the data. Market total revenue would now be $72 million, total cost would be $8 million, and economic profit would fall to $64 million. With both firms producing the same output, the distribution of this economic profit is now equal.

Both firms would now receive $36 million a week in total revenue, have a total cost of $4 million, and earn an economic profit of $32 million. For Airbus, this outcome is an improvement on the previous one by $2 million a week. For Boeing, this outcome is worse than the previous one by $8 million a week.

This situation is better for Airbus, but would Boeing go along with it? You know that Boeing would be worse off if it decreased its output to 3 airplanes a week because it would get the outcome that Airbus has in Table 14.2—an economic profit of only $30 million a week. But would Boeing be better off if it increased output to 5 airplanes a week?

TABLE 14.3 AIRBUS INCREASES OUTPUT TO 4 AIRPLANES A WEEK

	Boeing	Airbus	Market total
Quantity (airplanes a week)	4	4	8
Price ($ million per airplane)	9	9	9
Total revenue ($ million)	36	36	72
Total cost ($ million)	4	4	8
Economic profit ($ million)	32	32	64

Boeing Increases Output to 5 Airplanes a Week

To answer the question we've just posed, we need to calculate Boeing's economic profit if Airbus maintains its output at 4 airplanes a week and Boeing increases output to 5 a week.

Table 14.4 keeps track of the data. Total output is now 9 airplanes a week. To sell this quantity, the price must fall to $7 million per airplane. Market total revenue is $63 million and total cost is $9 million, so economic profit for the two firms is $54 million. The distribution of this economic profit is again unequal. But now both firms would lose.

Boeing would now receive $35 million a week in total revenue, have a total cost of $5 million, and earn an economic profit of $30 million—$2 million less than if it maintained its output at 4 airplanes a week (in Table 14.3). Airbus would receive $28 million a week in total revenue, incur a total cost of $4 million, and earn an economic profit of $24 million—$8 million less than before.

So neither firm can gain by increasing output beyond 4 airplanes a week. But there is a dilemma. If both firms stick to the monopoly output, they both produce 3 airplanes and make $36 million. If they both increase production to 4 airplanes a week, they both make $32 million. If only one of them increases production to 4 airplanes a week, that firm makes an economic profit of $40 million while the one that keeps production constant at 3 airplanes makes a lower economic profit of $30 million. So what will the firms do?

We can speculate about what they will do. But to work out the answer, we need to use some game theory. We'll leave the question that we've just asked dangling and return to it after we've learned the basic ideas about game theory that we need.

TABLE 14.4 BOEING INCREASES OUTPUT TO 5 AIRPLANES A WEEK

	Boeing	Airbus	Market total
Quantity (airplanes a week)	5	4	9
Price ($ million per airplane)	7	7	7
Total revenue ($ million)	35	28	63
Total cost ($ million)	5	4	9
Economic profit ($ million)	30	24	54

CHECKPOINT 14.3

Study Guide pp. 226–228

*e*Foundations 14.3

3 **Explain the dilemma faced by firms in oligopoly.**

Practice Problem 14.3

Isolated Island has two natural gas wells, one owned by Tom and the other owned by Jerry. Each well has a valve that controls the rate of flow of gas, and the marginal cost of producing gas is zero. Table 1 gives the demand schedule for gas on this island. What will the price of gas be on Isolated Island if Tom and Jerry:

a. Form a cartel and maximize their joint profit?
b. Are forced to sell at the perfectly competitive price?
c. Compete as duopolists?

TABLE 1

Price (dollars per unit)	Quantity demanded (units per day)
12	0
11	1
10	2
9	3
8	4
7	5
6	6
5	7
4	8
3	9
2	10
1	11
0	12

Exercises 14.3

1. A third gas well is discovered on Isolated Island, and Joey owns it. There is no change in the demand for gas, and Joey's cost of production is zero, like Tom's and Jerry's costs. Now what is the price of gas on Isolated Island if Tom, Jerry, and Joey:
   a. Form a cartel and maximize their joint profit?
   b. Are forced to sell at the perfectly competitive price?
2. Kodak and Fuji are the only major producers of high-speed photo film. Each company has developed a fast-speed film and aggressively advertises it. The two firms are locked in a duopolists' dilemma.
   a. Describe the dilemma facing Kodak and Fuji.
   b. Suppose that Fuji and Kodak were to secretly from a cartel. What do you predict would:
      i. Happen to the price of film?
      ii. Be the change in the two firms' advertising and research and development budgets?

TABLE 2

Quantity (units per day)	Total revenue (dollars per day)	Marginal revenue (dollars per unit)
0	0	
		11
1	11	
		9
2	20	
		7
3	27	
		5
4	32	
		3
5	35	
		1
6	36	
		–1
7	35	
		–3
8	32	
		–5
9	27	
		–7
10	20	
		–9
11	11	
		–11
12	0	

Solution to Practice Problem 14.3

a. If Tom and Jerry form a cartel and maximize their joint profit, they will charge the monopoly price. This price is the highest price that the market will bear when the quantity produced makes marginal revenue equal to marginal cost. Marginal cost is zero, so we need to find the quantity at which marginal revenue is zero. Marginal revenue is zero when total revenue is a maximum, which occurs when output is 6 units a day (see Table 2). The highest price at which 6 units a day can be sold is $6 a unit (see the demand schedule in Table 1).

b. The perfectly competitive price equals marginal cost, which is zero. In this case, output is 12 units a day.

c. If Tom and Jerry compete as duopolists, they will increase production above the monopoly level, but they will not drive the price down to zero.

14.4 GAME THEORY

Game theory is the main tool that economists use to analyze *strategic behavior*—behavior that recognizes mutual interdependence and takes account of the expected behavior of others. John von Neumann invented game theory in 1937, and today it is a major research field in economics.

Game theory
The tool that economists use to analyze *strategic behavior*—behavior that recognizes mutual interdependence and takes account of the expected behavior of others.

Game theory seeks to understand oligopoly and all other forms of economic, political, social, and even biological rivalries. Game theory uses a method of analysis specifically designed to understand games of all types, including the familiar games of everyday life. We will begin our study of game theory and its application to the behavior of firms by thinking about familiar games.

What Is a Game?

What is a game? At first thought, the question seems silly. After all, there are many different games. There are ball games and parlor games, games of chance and games of skill. But what is it about all these different activities that make them games? What do all these games have in common? All games share three features:

- Rules
- Strategies
- Payoffs

Let's see how these common features of games apply to a game called "the prisoners' dilemma." The **prisoners' dilemma** is a game between two prisoners that shows why it is hard to cooperate, even when it would be beneficial to both players to do so. This game captures the essential feature of the duopolists' dilemma that we've just been studying. The prisoners' dilemma also provides a good illustration of how game theory works and how it generates predictions.

Prisoners' dilemma
A game between two prisoners that shows why it is hard to cooperate, even when it would be beneficial to both players to do so.

The Prisoners' Dilemma

Art and Bob have been caught red-handed, stealing a car. Facing airtight cases, they will receive a sentence of 2 years for their crime. During his interviews with the two prisoners, the district attorney begins to suspect that he has stumbled on the two people who were responsible for a multimillion-dollar bank robbery some months earlier. But this is just a suspicion. The district attorney has no evidence on which he can convict them of the greater crime unless he can get them to confess. The district attorney decides to make the prisoners play a game with the following rules.

Rules

Each prisoner (player) is placed in a separate room and cannot communicate with the other player. Each is told that he is suspected of having carried out the bank robbery and that:

- If both of them confess to the larger crime, each will receive a sentence of 3 years for both crimes.
- If he alone confesses and his accomplice does not, he will receive an even shorter sentence of 1 year, while his accomplice will receive a 10-year sentence.

Strategies

Strategies
All the possible actions of each player in a game.

In game theory, **strategies** are all the possible actions of each player. Art and Bob each have two possible actions:

- Confess to the bank robbery.
- Deny having committed the bank robbery.

Payoffs

Payoff matrix
A table that shows the payoffs for every possible action by each player given every possible action by the other player.

Because there are two players, each with two strategies, there are four possible outcomes:

- Both confess.
- Both deny.
- Art confesses and Bob denies.
- Bob confesses and Art denies.

TABLE 14.5 PRISONERS' DILEMMA PAYOFF MATRIX

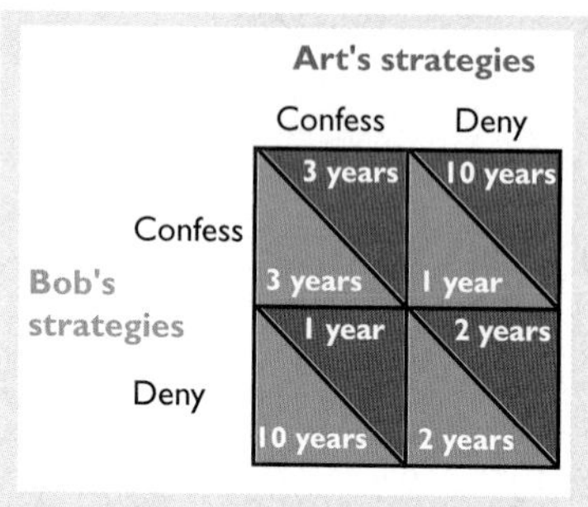

Each square shows the payoffs for the two players, Art and Bob, for each possible pair of actions. In each square, the red triangle shows Art's payoff and the blue triangle shows Bob's. For example, if both confess, the payoffs are in the top left square.

Each prisoner can work out exactly what happens to him—his *payoff*—in each of these four situations. We can tabulate the four possible payoffs for each of the prisoners in what is called a payoff matrix for the game. A **payoff matrix** is a table that shows the payoffs for every possible action by each player given every possible action by the other player.

Table 14.5 shows a payoff matrix for Art and Bob. The squares show the payoffs for each prisoner: The red triangle in each square shows Art's, and the blue triangle shows Bob's. If both prisoners confess (top left), each gets a prison term of 3 years. If Bob confesses but Art denies (top right), Art gets a 10-year sentence and Bob gets a 1-year sentence. If Art confesses and Bob denies (bottom left), Art gets a 1-year sentence and Bob gets a 10-year sentence. Finally, if both of them deny (bottom right), neither can be convicted of the bank robbery charge but both are sentenced for the car theft—a 2-year sentence.

Equilibrium

Nash equilibrium
An equilibrium in which each player takes the best possible action given the action of the other player.

The equilibrium of a game occurs when each player takes the best possible action given the action of the other player. This equilibrium concept is called **Nash equilibrium**. It is so named because John Nash of Princeton University, who received the Nobel Prize for Economic Science in 1994, proposed it.

In the case of the prisoners' dilemma, equilibrium occurs when Art makes his best choice given Bob's choice and when Bob makes his best choice given Art's choice. Let's find the equilibrium.

First, look at the situation from Art's point of view. If Bob confesses, it pays Art to confess because in that case, he is sentenced to 3 years rather than 10 years. If Bob denies, it still pays Art to confess because in that case he receives 1 year rather than 2 years. So no matter what Bob does, Art's best action is to confess.

Second, look at the situation from Bob's point of view. If Art confesses, it pays Bob to confess because in that case, he is sentenced to 3 years rather than 10 years. If Art denies, it still pays Bob to confess because in that case he receives 1 year rather than 2 years. So no matter what Art does, Bob's best action is to confess.

Because each player's best action is to confess, each does confess, each gets a 3-year prison term, and the district attorney has solved the bank robbery. This is the equilibrium of the game.

Not the Best Outcome

The equilibrium of the prisoners' dilemma game is not the best outcome. Isn't there some way in which the prisoners can cooperate and get the smaller sentence? There is not, because they cannot communicate with each other. Each player can put himself in the other player's place and can figure out what the other will do. The prisoners are indeed in a dilemma. Each knows that he can serve only 2 years if he can trust the other to deny. But each also knows that it is not in the best interest of the other to deny. So each prisoner knows that he must confess, thereby delivering a bad outcome for both.

Let's now see how we can use the ideas we've just developed to understand the behavior of firms in oligopoly. We'll start by returning to the duopolists' dilemma.

■ The Duopolists' Dilemma as a Game

The dilemma of Airbus and Boeing is similar to that of Art and Bob. Each firm has two strategies. It can produce airplanes at the rate of:

- 3 a week
- 4 a week

Because each firm has two strategies, there are four possible combinations of actions for the two firms:

- Both firms produce 3 a week (monopoly outcome).
- Both firms produce 4 a week.
- Airbus produces 3 a week and Boeing produces 4 a week.
- Boeing produces 3 a week and Airbus produces 4 a week.

The Payoff Matrix

Table 14.6 sets out the payoff matrix for this game. It is constructed in exactly the same way as the payoff matrix for the prisoners' dilemma in Table 14.5. The squares show the payoffs for Airbus and Boeing. In this case, the payoffs are economic profits. (In the case of the prisoners' dilemma, the payoffs were losses.) The table shows that if both firms produce 4 a week (top left), each makes an economic profit of $32 million. If both firms produce 3 a week (bottom right), they make the monopoly profit, and each firm earns an economic profit of $36 million. The top right and bottom left squares show what happens if one firm produces 4 a week while the other produces 3 a week. The firm that increases production makes an economic profit of $40 million, and the one that keeps production at the monopoly quantity makes an economic profit of $30 million.

Equilibrium of the Duopolists' Dilemma

What do the firms do? To answer this question, we must find the equilibrium of the duopoly game.

TABLE 14.6 DUOPOLISTS' DILEMMA PAYOFF MATRIX

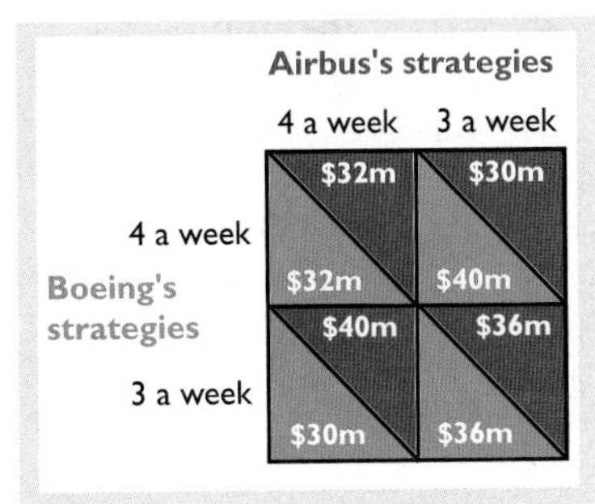

Each square shows the payoffs from a pair of actions. For example, if both firms produce 3 airplanes a week, the payoffs are recorded in the bottom right square. The red triangle shows Airbus's payoff, and the blue triangle shows Boeing's.

TABLE 14.7 DUOPOLISTS' DILEMMA'S EQUILIBRIUM

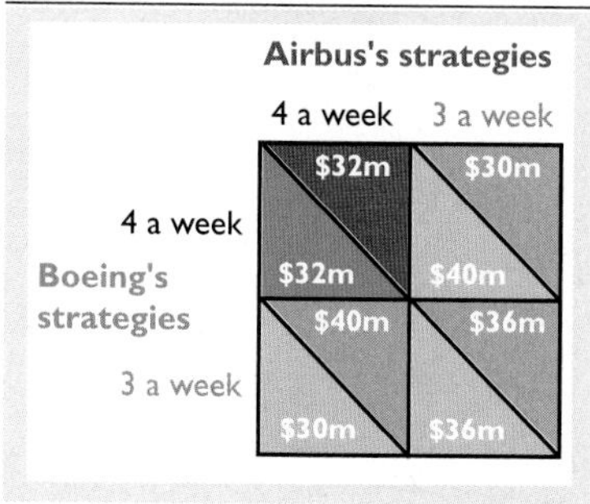

		Airbus's strategies	
		4 a week	3 a week
Boeing's strategies	4 a week	$32m / $32m	$30m / $40m
	3 a week	$40m / $30m	$36m / $36m

The equilibrium is a Nash equilibrium in which both firms produce 4 airplanes a week.

Using the information in Table 14.7, look at things from Airbus's point of view. Airbus reasons as follows: Suppose that Boeing produces 4 planes a week. If I produce 3 a week, I will make an economic profit of $30 million. If I also produce 4 a week, I will make an economic profit of $32 million. So I'm better off producing 4 a week. Airbus continues to reason: Now suppose Boeing produce 3 planes a week. If I produce 4 a week, I will make an economic profit of $40 million, and if I produce 3 a week, I will make an economic profit of $36 million. An economic profit of $40 million is better than an economic profit of $36 million, so I'm better off if I produce 4 a week. So regardless of whether Boeing produces 4 planes a week or 3 planes a week, it pays Airbus to produce 4 planes a week.

Because the two firms face identical situations, Boeing comes to the same conclusion as Airbus. So both firms produce 4 a week. The equilibrium of the duopoly game is that both firms produce 4 a week.

So, like the prisoners, the duopolists fail to cooperate and get a worse outcome than the one that cooperation would deliver.

Repeated Games

The games that we've studied are played just once. In contrast, most real-world games get played repeatedly. This fact suggests that real-world duopolists might find some way of learning to cooperate so that they can enjoy a monopoly profit.

If a game is played repeatedly, one player has the opportunity to penalize the other player for previous "bad" behavior. If Airbus produces 4 airplanes this week, perhaps Boeing will produce 4 next week. Before Airbus produces 4 this week, won't it take account of the possibility of Boeing producing 4 next week? What is the equilibrium of this more complicated dilemma game when it is repeated indefinitely?

The monopoly equilibrium may occur if each firm knows that the other will punish overproduction with overproduction—"tit for tat." Let's see why.

If both firms produce 3 airplanes in week 1, each makes an economic profit of $36 million. Suppose that Boeing contemplates producing 4 airplanes in week 2. This move will bring it an economic profit of $40 million and cut the economic profit of Airbus to $30 million. In week 3, Airbus punishes Boeing and produces 4 airplanes. But Boeing must go back to 3 airplanes to induce Airbus to cooperate again in week 4. Airbus now makes an economic profit of $40 million, and Boeing makes an economic profit of $30 million. Adding up the profits over three weeks of play, Boeing would have made $108 million by cooperating (3 × $36 million) compared with $106 million from producing 4 in week 2 and generating Airbus's tit-for-tat response.

What is true for Boeing is also true for Airbus. Because each firm makes a larger profit by sticking to the monopoly output, both firms do so, and the monopoly price, quantity, and profit prevail.

In reality, whether a duopoly (or more generally an oligopoly) works like a one-play game or a repeated game depends primarily on the number of players and the ease of detecting and punishing overproduction. The larger the number of players, the harder it is to maintain the monopoly outcome.

Duopoly in Computer CPUs

The CPU in your computer is the central brainpower of the machine. Until 1995, one firm produced all the CPU chips in PCs—Intel Corporation. Intel made a large economic profit by producing the quantity of chips at which marginal cost equaled marginal revenue and pricing the chips to ensure that the quantity demanded equaled the profit-maximizing quantity produced.

Then, in 1995, a small number of new firms entered the industry. One of them, Advanced Micro Devices, Inc. (AMD), quickly established itself as a serious challenger to Intel.

But in terms of market share and profit share, Intel dominates this market, as the pie chart shows. In 2000, both firms had a global market, with 55 percent of Intel's total revenue and 60 percent of AMD's total revenue coming from outside the United States.

If, as new firms entered this industry, they had maintained Intel's price and shared the market, together they could have made economic profits equal to Intel's profit. But AMD and Intel were (and remain) in a duopolists' dilemma. Intel has no interest in sharing its market with another producer. And to break into the market and take revenue and profit away from Intel, AMD must either offer a clearly superior product at the same price at Intel's or offer a similar product at a lower price.

AMD opted mainly for the second approach (although some chip experts say that AMD offers both a superior product and a lower price).

Setting aside the question of whether an AMD chip performs better than an Intel chip, it is clear that AMD has brought the price of CPU chips down. The bar chart shows the prices of some of the most popular CPU chips in March 2001. Notice that at comparable clock speeds, AMD chips are cheaper than Intel chips.

For example, all three Athlon chips that run faster than 1 GHz cost less than a 1 GHz Pentium III made by Intel.

At the low end of the product range, the AMD Duron chip is substantially cheaper than comparable-speed Intel Pentiums.

Notice, though, that to compete at this low end of the product range, Intel has introduced the Celeron processor at a lower price than the cheapest AMD chips.

Competition between Intel and AMD is like the duopolists' dilemma that you've studied in this chapter. The game is played on both price and product design and quality and across a range of differentiated products.

In 2000, Intel remained vastly bigger than AMD. But AMD's total revenue grew in that year by 63 percent. Intel's grew by 15 percent. If total revenue growth remains this unequal, AMD will become as large as Intel in less than 6 years.

This duopoly is going to be an interesting one to keep an eye on.

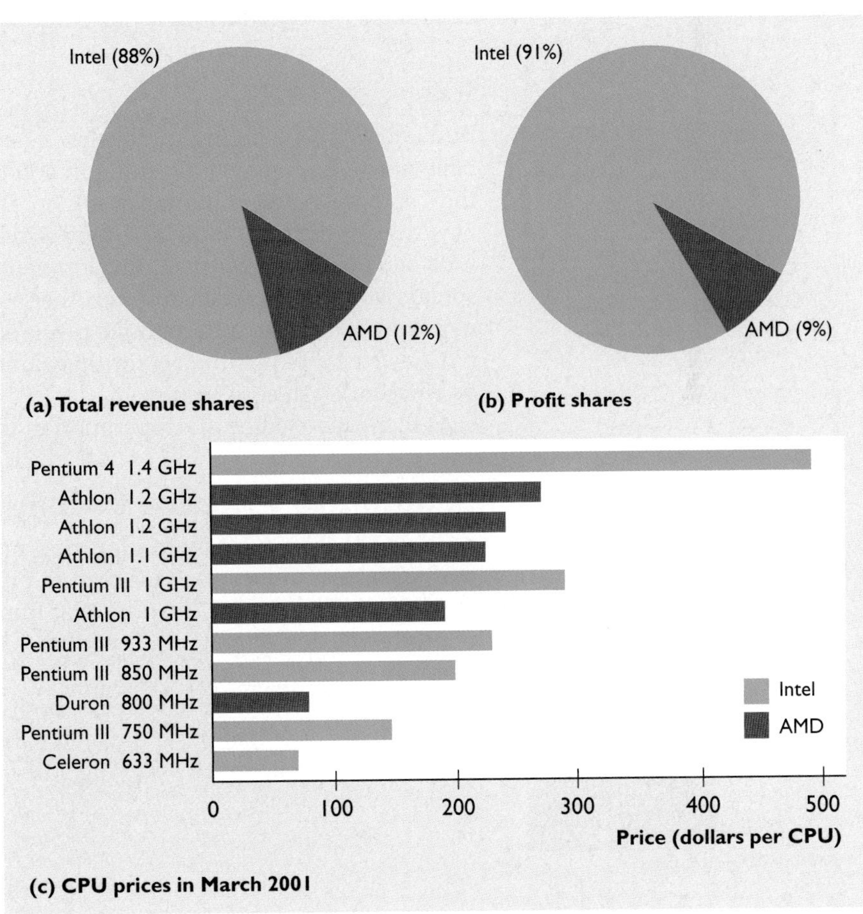

CHECKPOINT 14.4

Study Guide pp. 228–230

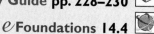

*e*Foundations 14.4

4 **Use game theory to explain how price and quantity are determined in oligopoly.**

Practice Problem 14.4

Bud and Wise are the only two makers of aniseed beer, a new-age product designed to displace root beer. Bud and Wise are trying to figure out how much of this new beer to produce. They each know that if they both limit production to 10,000 gallons a day, they will make the maximum attainable joint profit of $200,000 a day—$100,000 a day each. They also know that if either of them produces 20,000 gallons a day while the other produces 10,000 a day, economic profit will be $150,000 for the one that produces 20,000 gallons and an economic loss of $50,000 for the one that sticks with 10,000 gallons. And they also know that if they both increase production to 20,000 gallons a day, they will both earn zero economic profit.

a. Construct a payoff matrix for the game that Bud and Wise must play.
b. Find the Nash equilibrium.
c. What is the equilibrium if this game is played repeatedly?

Exercise 14.4

Bud and Wise are racing to develop a new brand of coconut milk that they both believe will be the next big thing in soft drinks. Bud and Wise each know that if they both spend $1 million a week on development, they will both develop the new milk at the same time and they will both earn zero economic profit from the milk and never recover their development cost. They also know that if one of them spends $1 million a week and the other spends nothing, the one that develops the new milk will make an economic profit of $2 million a week.

a. Construct a payoff matrix for this game.
b. Find the Nash equilibrium.
c. Is there any chance of cooperation in this research and development game?

Solution to Practice Problem 14.4

a. Table 1 is the payoff matrix for the game that Bud and Wise must play.
b. The Nash equilibrium is for both to produce 20,000 gallons. To see why, notice that regardless of the quantity that Bud produces, Wise makes more profit by producing 20,000 gallons. The same is true for Bud. So Bud and Wise each produce 20,000 gallons a day.
c. If this game is played repeatedly, both Bud and Wise produce the monopoly output of 10,000 gallons a day and earn maximum economic profit. They can achieve this outcome by playing a tit-for-tat strategy.

TABLE 1

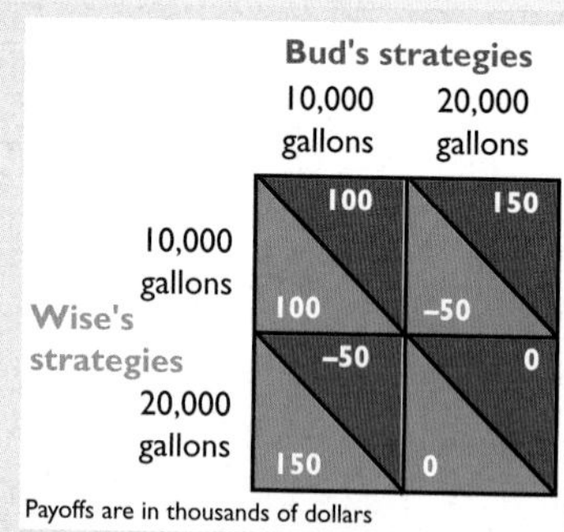

Wise's strategies \ Bud's strategies	10,000 gallons	20,000 gallons
10,000 gallons	Bud 100, Wise 100	Bud 150, Wise –50
20,000 gallons	Bud –50, Wise 150	Bud 0, Wise 0

Payoffs are in thousands of dollars

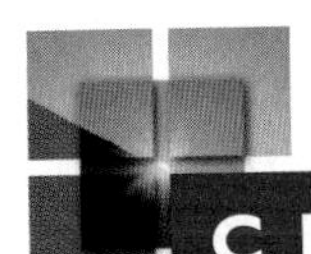

CHAPTER CHECKPOINT

Key Points

1 Explain how price and quantity are determined in monopolistic competition.

- Firms in monopolistic competition face downward-sloping demand curves and produce the quantity at which marginal revenue equals marginal cost.
- Entry and exit result in zero economic profit and excess capacity in long-run equilibrium.

2 Explain why selling costs are high in monopolistic competition.

- Firms in monopolistic competition innovate and develop new products to maintain economic profit.
- Advertising expenditures increase total cost, but they might lower average total cost if they increase the quantity sold by a large enough amount.
- Advertising expenditures might increase demand, but they might also decrease the demand facing a firm by increasing competition.
- Whether monopolistic competition is inefficient depends on the value people place on product variety.

3 Explain the dilemma faced by firms in oligopoly.

- Firms in oligopoly would make the same economic profit as a monopoly if they could act together to restrict output to the monopoly level.
- Each firm can make a larger profit by increasing production, but this action damages the economic profit of other firms.

4 Use game theory to explain how price and quantity are determined in oligopoly.

- Game theory is a method of analyzing strategic behavior.
- In a prisoners' dilemma, two prisoners acting in their own interest harm their joint interest.
- An oligopoly (duopoly) game is like the prisoners' dilemma.
- The firms might cooperate to produce the monopoly output or overproduce.
- In a one-play game, both firms overproduce, and the price and economic profit are less than they would be in monopoly.
- In a repeated game, a punishment strategy can produce a monopoly output, price, and economic profit.

Key Terms

FIGURE 1

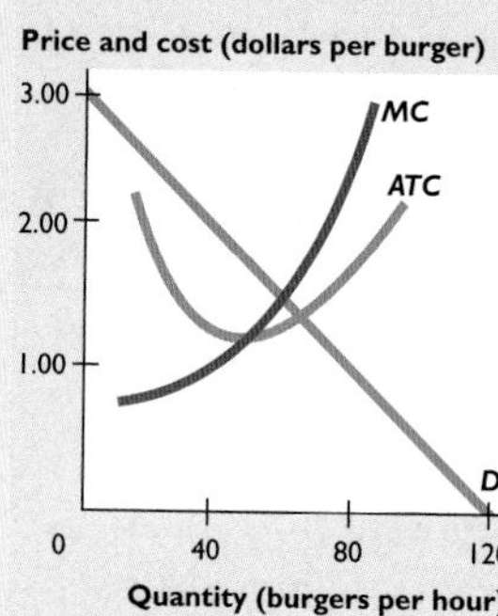

Exercises

1. Figure 1 shows the demand curve, marginal revenue curve, and cost curves of Bob's Best Burgers, a firm in monopolistic competition.
   a. What are Bob's profit-maximizing output, price, and economic profit?
   b. Do you expect other firms to enter the quality burger business and compete with Bob?
   c. Does Bob have excess capacity? If not, why not? Isn't excess capacity a feature of monopolistic competition?
   d. What happens to the demand for Bob's burgers in the long run?
   e. What happens to Bob's economic profit in the long run?
   f. Does Bob have excess capacity in the long run?

2. Use the link on your Foundations Web site to obtain information on Caribbean cruises.
   a. Is the cruise market an example of perfect competition, monopoly, monopolistic competition, or oligopoly? Explain your answer.
   b. Are these cruises differentiated products? Explain why and provide some information from the cruise lines' brochures.
   c. How do you think the prices of these cruises are determined?
   d. Do you think these cruises operate at capacity or less than capacity? Why?
   e. There has been a large increase in the number of boats serving the Caribbean cruise market in the last 10 years. Why do you think this entry occurred?

3. Isolated Island has two natural gas wells, one owned by Tom and the other owned by Jerry. Each well has a valve that controls the rate of flow of gas, and the marginal cost of producing gas is zero. The demand for gas on this island is zero at a price of $12 a unit, and for each $1 decrease in price, the quantity demanded increases by 1 unit.
   a. Create a payoff matrix for the game that Tom and Jerry play if their strategies are to produce the monopoly profit-maximizing quantity or to increase production to maximize their own profits given the production of the other firm.
   b. Find the Nash equilibrium for this game if it is played just once.
   c. Find the Nash equilibrium for this game if it is played repeatedly.

4. Jenny loves going to the movies (payoff of +100) and hates going to the ball game (payoff of –100). Joe loves going to the ball game (payoff of +100) and hates going to the movies (payoff of –100). But both Jenny and Joe prefer to go out together (payoff of +100 each) than to go out on their own (payoff of zero).
   a. Make a payoff matrix of the game that Jenny and Joe play.
   b. Is this game similar to the prisoners' dilemma or different in some way?
   c. What is the Nash equilibrium? What do Jenny and Joe do? Does it make a difference if the game is repeated many times?

Chapter 15

Regulation and Antitrust Law

CHAPTER CHECKLIST

When you have completed your study of this chapter, you will be able to:

1. **Distinguish between the public interest and capture theories of regulation, and explain how regulation affects prices, outputs, profits, and the distribution of surpluses between consumers and producers.**

2. **Describe U.S. antitrust law and explain how it has been applied in some landmark cases and how it is used today.**

When you consume water or use the local telephone service, you are buying from a regulated monopoly. Why are the industries that produce these items regulated? How are they regulated? Do the regulations work in the public interest—the interest of all consumers and producers—or do they serve special interests—the interests of particular groups of consumers or producers?

Microsoft has been charged by the U.S. Department of Justice with violating the antitrust laws. What are the antitrust laws? How have they evolved over the years? How are they used today?

This chapter studies government regulation of monopolies and U.S. antitrust law. The chapter draws on your earlier study of how markets work and on your knowledge of consumer surplus and producer surplus. It shows how consumers and producers can redistribute surpluses in the political marketplace, and it identifies who stands to win and who stands to lose from government regulation.

15.1 REGULATION

Regulation
Rules administered by a government agency to influence economic activity by determining prices, product standards and types, and the conditions under which new firms can enter an industry.

Regulation consists of rules administered by a government agency to influence economic activity by determining prices, product standards and types, and the conditions under which new firms can enter an industry. To implement its regulations, the government establishes agencies to oversee the regulations and ensure their enforcement. The first national regulatory agency to be set up in the United States was the Interstate Commerce Commission (ICC), established in 1887. Over the years until the late 1970s, regulation of the economy grew. At its peak, almost a quarter of the nation's output was produced by regulated industries. Regulation applied to banking and financial services, telecommunications, gas and electric utilities, railroads, trucking, airlines and buses, many agricultural products, and even haircutting and braiding. Since the late 1970s, there has been a tendency to deregulate the U.S. economy.

Deregulation is the process of removing restrictions on prices, product standards and types, and entry conditions. In recent years, deregulation has occurred in domestic air transportation, telephone service, interstate trucking, and banking and financial services. Cable TV was deregulated in 1984, reregulated in 1992, and deregulated again in 1996.

Economic Theory of Regulation

Two broad economic theories of regulation are:

- Public interest theory
- Capture theory

Public Interest Theory

Public interest theory
The theory that regulation seeks an efficient use of resources.

The **public interest theory** is that regulation seeks an efficient use of resources. Public interest theory assumes that the political process relentlessly seeks out deadweight loss and introduces regulations that eliminate it. For example, where monopoly exists, the political process will introduce price regulations or other measures to ensure that output increases and price falls to its competitive level.

Capture Theory

Capture theory
The theory that regulation helps producers to maximize economic profit.

Capture theory is that the regulations help producers to maximize economic profit. Capture theory assumes that the cost of regulation is high and only those regulations that increase the surplus of small, easily identified groups and that have low organization costs are supplied by the political process. Because of rational ignorance (see Chapter 9, p. 211), even though these regulations impose costs on others, they do not decrease votes if the costs are spread thinly.

The predictions of the capture theory are less clear-cut than those of the public interest theory. The capture theory predicts that regulations benefit cohesive interest groups, bring large and visible benefits to each member of the interest group, and impose a small cost on everyone else. The cost per person is so small that no one finds it worthwhile to incur the cost of organizing an interest group to avoid it.

Which theory of regulation best explains real-world regulations? Which regulations are in the public interest and which are in the interest of producers?

The Scope of Regulation

The past 20 years have seen big changes in the way the U.S. economy is regulated. We're going to examine some of these changes. First, we'll look at what is regulated and the scope of regulation. Next, we'll turn to the regulatory process and examine how regulators control prices, output, and economic profit. We'll see that firms might be regulated in several different ways, and we'll compare regulations that aim to serve the interest of consumers with regulations that arise when the producer captures the regulator.

The first federal regulatory agency, the Interstate Commerce Commission (ICC), was set up in 1887 to control prices, routes, and the quality of service of interstate railroads. Its scope later covered trucking lines, bus lines, water carriers, and oil pipelines. Following the establishment of the ICC, the federal regulatory environment remained static until the years of the Great Depression. Then, in the 1930s, more agencies were established: the Federal Power Commission, the Federal Communications Commission, the Securities and Exchange Commission, the Federal Maritime Commission, the Federal Deposit Insurance Corporation, and, in 1938, the Civil Aeronautical Agency, which was replaced in 1940 by the Civil Aeronautics Board. There was a further lull until the establishment during the 1970s of the Copyright Royalty Tribunal and the Federal Energy Regulatory Commission. In addition to these, there are many state and local regulatory commissions.

In the mid-1970s, almost one quarter of the economy was subject to some form of regulation. Heavily regulated industries—those that are subject to both price regulation and regulation of entry of new firms—were those that produced electricity and natural gas and telephone, air, highway freight, and rail services.

During the 1980s and 1990s, deregulation stimulated competition in broadcasting, telecommunications, banking and finance, and all forms of transportation (air, rail, and road, passengers and freight).

What exactly do regulatory agencies do? How do they regulate?

The Regulatory Process

Though regulatory agencies vary in size and scope and in the detailed aspects of economic life that they control, all agencies have features in common.

First, the president, Congress, and state and local governments appoint the people who run the regulatory agencies. In addition, all agencies have a permanent bureaucracy made up of experts in the industry being regulated and often recruited from regulated firms. Agencies have budgets, voted by Congress or state or local legislatures, to cover the costs of their operations.

Second, each agency adopts a set of practices or operating rules for controlling prices and other aspects of economic performance. These rules and practices are based on well-defined physical and financial accounting procedures, but they are extremely complicated and, in practice, hard to administer.

In a regulated industry, individual firms are usually free to determine their production technology. But they are not free to determine the prices to charge, the quantities to produce, or the markets to serve. The regulatory agency certifies a company to serve a particular market and produce a particular line of goods and services, and it determines the prices that may be charged. In some cases, the agency also determines the scale of output permitted.

To analyze the way in which regulation works, it is convenient to distinguish between the regulation of a natural monopoly and the regulation of a cartel. Let's begin with the regulation of a natural monopoly.

Natural Monopoly

We defined *natural monopoly* in Chapter 13 (pp. 310–311) as an industry in which one firm can supply the entire market at a lower price than can two or more firms. Examples of natural monopoly include local distribution of water, electricity and gas, and urban rail services. For these activities, most of the costs are fixed, so the larger the output, the lower is its average total cost. It is much more expensive to have two or more sets of pipes, wires, and train lines serving every neighborhood than it is to have a single set. The industries or markets that are natural monopolies change over time as technology changes. With the introduction of fiber-optic cables, both telephone companies and cable television companies can compete in urban areas that have a sufficiently dense population. So what were once natural monopolies are becoming more competitive industries. Direct satellite TV is a substitute for cable TV, but not a close substitute, and in many parts of the country, cable TV remains a natural monopoly.

Figure 15.1 shows the market for cable TV in the 20 states served by Cox Communications, based in Atlanta. The demand curve for cable TV is *D*. Cox's marginal cost curve is *MC*. That marginal cost curve is assumed to be horizontal at $10 per household per month—that is, the cost of providing each additional household with a month of cable programming is $10. Cox Communications has

FIGURE 15.1

Natural Monopoly: Marginal Cost Pricing

*e*Foundations 15.1 

A cable TV operator faces the demand curve *D*. Its marginal cost *MC* is a constant $10 per household per month. Its fixed cost is large, and the average total cost curve, which includes average fixed cost, is *ATC*. ❶ Price is set equal to marginal cost of $10 a month. At this price, ❷ the efficient quantity (8 million households) is served.

❸ Consumer surplus is maximized, shown by the green triangle. ❹ The firm incurs a loss on each household, shown by the red arrow.

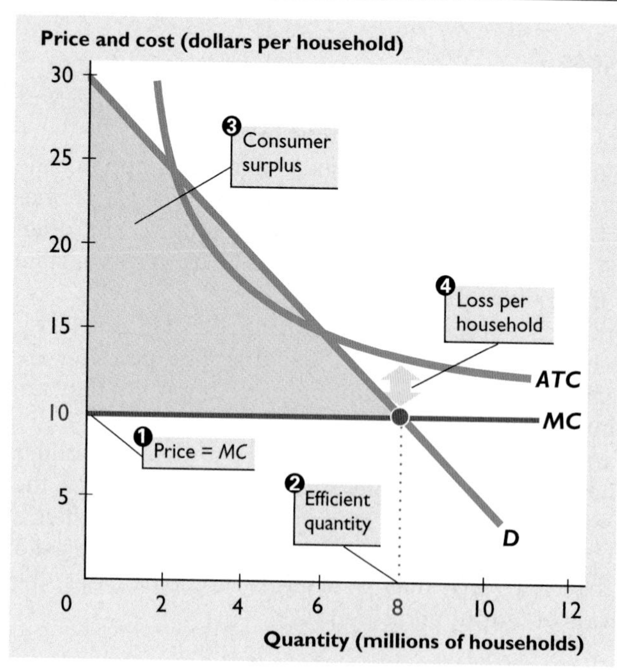

invested heavily in satellite receiving dishes, cables, and control equipment and so has large fixed costs. These fixed costs are part of the company's average total cost curve, shown as *ATC*. The average total cost curve slopes downward because as the number of households served increases, the fixed costs are spread over a larger number of households. (If you need to refresh your memory on how the average total cost curve is calculated, take a quick look back at Chapter 11, p. 271.)

Regulation in the Public Interest

How is cable TV regulated according to the public interest theory? According to public interest theory, regulation achieves an efficient use of resources, which occurs if marginal cost equals marginal benefit, which also equals price. As you can see in Figure 15.1, that outcome occurs if the price is regulated at $10 per household per month and if 8 million households are served. Such a regulation is called a marginal cost pricing rule. A *marginal cost pricing rule* sets price equal to marginal cost (see Chapter 13, p. 331). It achieves an efficient use of resources in a regulated industry.

A natural monopoly that is regulated to set price equal to marginal cost incurs an economic loss. Because the average total cost curve of a natural monopoly is downward sloping, marginal cost is less than average total cost. Because price equals marginal cost, price is less than average total cost. Average total cost minus price is the loss per unit produced. It's pretty obvious that a cable TV company that is required to use a marginal cost pricing rule will not stay in business for long. How can a company cover its costs and, at the same time, obey a marginal cost pricing rule?

One possibility is price discrimination (see Chapter 13, pp. 324–328). Another possibility is to use a two-part price (called a *two-part tariff*). For example, local telephone companies might charge consumers a monthly fee for being connected to the telephone system and then charge a price equal to marginal cost (zero) for each local call. A cable TV operator might charge a one-time connection fee that covers its fixed cost and then charge a monthly fee equal to marginal cost.

But a natural monopoly cannot always cover its costs in these ways. If a natural monopoly cannot cover its total cost from its customers and if the government wants it to follow a marginal cost pricing rule, the government must subsidize the firm and raise the revenue for the subsidy by taxing some other activity.

But as we saw in Chapters 7 and 9, taxes themselves generate deadweight loss. So the deadweight loss that results from additional taxes must be subtracted from the efficiency gained by forcing the natural monopoly to adopt a marginal cost pricing rule. As a result, it might be more efficient to permit the natural monopoly to charge a price that is higher than marginal cost. Doing so avoids taxing other parts of the economy to subsidize the natural monopoly and avoids creating a deadweight loss in those other parts of the economy.

For a natural monopoly to cover its total cost, its price must equal average total cost. The pricing rule that delivers this outcome is called the *average cost pricing rule,* a rule that sets price equal to average cost (see Chapter 13, p. 331). Because average total cost exceeds marginal cost for a natural monopoly, when price equals average total cost, the quantity is less than the efficient quantity, and a deadweight loss arises. Figure 15.2 illustrates the outcome for Cox Communications.

FIGURE 15.2
Natural Monopoly: Average Cost Pricing

*e*Foundations 15.1 

❶ Price is set equal to average total cost of $15 a month. At this price, ❷ less than the efficient quantity (6 million households) is served.

❸ Consumer surplus shrinks to the smaller green triangle. ❹ A producer surplus enables the firm to pay its fixed cost and break even. ❺ A deadweight loss, shown by the gray triangle, arises.

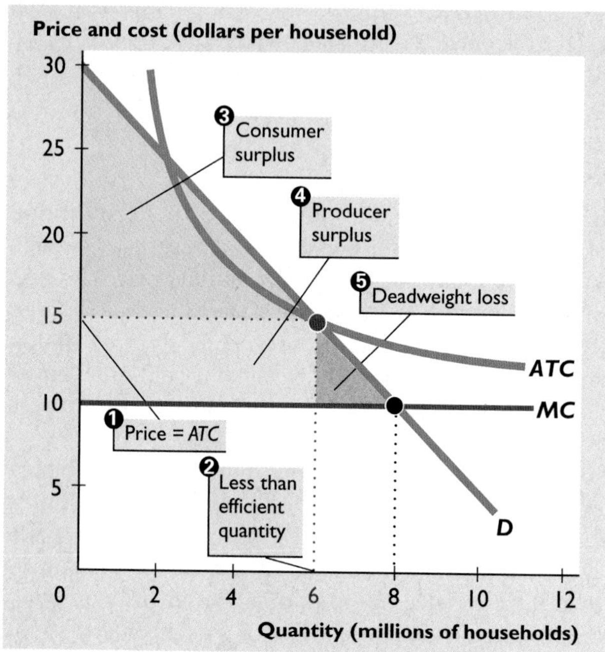

In Figure 15.2, to cover its costs, Cox charges $15 a month and serves 6 million households. Because fewer than the efficient number of households receives the service, a deadweight loss arises (shown by the gray triangle). This outcome is in the public interest—is efficient—if this deadweight loss is smaller than the loss from collecting the taxes to finance a subsidy under marginal cost pricing.

Capturing the Regulator

According to the capture theory, regulation serves the interests of the producer, which means maximizing the producer's profit. You learned in Chapter 13 (pp. 316–317) that a monopoly maximizes profit by producing the output at which marginal revenue equals marginal cost. The monopoly's marginal revenue curve in Figure 15.3 is the curve *MR*. Marginal revenue equals marginal cost when output is 4 million households. So a regulation that enables the producer to maximize profit will set the price at $20 a month.

But how can a producer go about obtaining regulation that results in this monopoly profit-maximizing outcome? To answer this question, we need to look at the way in which agencies determine a regulated price. A key method that is used is called rate of return regulation.

Rate of return regulation
A regulation that sets the price at a level that enables a regulated firm to earn a specified target percent return on its capital.

Rate of Return Regulation A regulation that sets the price at a level that enables the regulated firm to earn a specified target percent return on its capital is a **rate of return regulation**. The target rate of return is determined with reference to what is normal in competitive industries. This rate of return is part of the opportunity cost of the natural monopoly and is included in the firm's average total cost. By examining the firm's total cost, including the normal rate of return on cap-

FIGURE 15.3
Natural Monopoly: Maximizing Profit

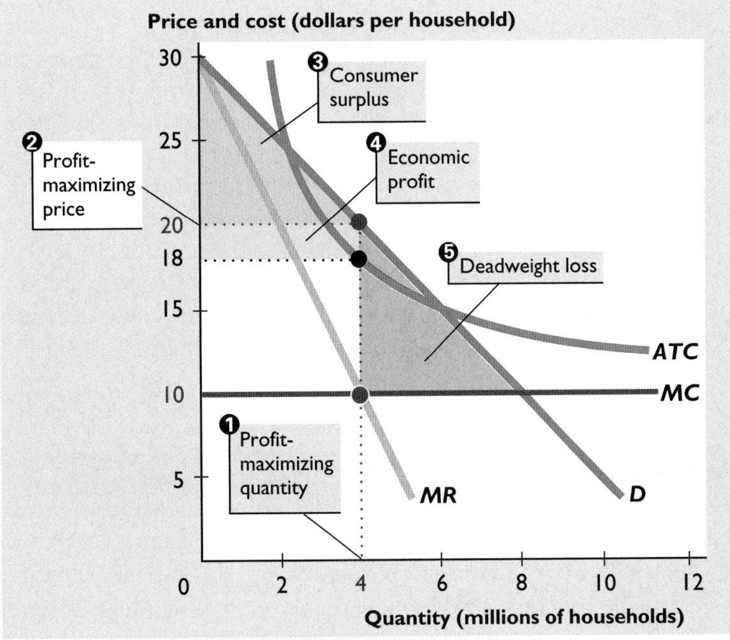

To maximize profit, the firm produces the ❶ quantity at which marginal revenue (*MR*) equals marginal cost (*MC*) and charges the ❷ profit-maximizing price. The firm earns an ❸ economic profit shown by the blue rectangle.

❹ Consumer surplus shrinks to the green triangle. ❺ The deadweight loss increases to the gray triangle. If the producer can capture the regulator, the outcome will be the situation shown here.

ital, the regulator attempts to determine the price that covers average total cost. So rate of return regulation is similar to average cost pricing.

In Figure 15.2, average cost pricing results in a regulated price of $15 a month with 6 million households being served. So rate of return regulation, based on a correct assessment of the producer's average total cost, results in a price that favors the consumer and does not enable the monopoly to maximize profit. In other words, the special interest group will have failed to capture the regulator, and the outcome will be closer to that predicted by the public interest theory of regulation.

But a feature of many real-world situations, which the above analysis does not take into account, is the ability of the monopoly to mislead the regulator about its true costs.

Exaggerating Costs The managers of a firm might be able to exaggerate the firm's costs. Or they might be able to disguise some of their profit as cost. By this device, the firm's apparent costs exceed the true costs. On-the-job luxury in the form of sumptuous office suites, limousines, free baseball tickets, golf competitions at expensive locations (disguised as public relations expenses), company jets, lavish international travel, and entertainment are all ways in which managers can make profits appear to be costs.

January 4, 2001

The California Power Quagmire

California's experiment with energy deregulation is not just a mess; it's a certifiable failure, according to everyone from the state's governor to the utilities that initially backed the scheme.

Questions

1. What are the problems with California's electricity supply industry?

2. Do you think the problems arise from deregulation or from regulation?

 eFoundations 15.1

Incentive Regulation and Deregulation

For some of the reasons we've just examined, rate of return regulation is increasingly being replaced by incentive regulation schemes. An **incentive regulation** is a regulation that motivates the firm to operate efficiently and keep its costs under

Incentive regulation
A regulation that motivates the firm to operate efficiently and keep its costs under control.

control. By 1990, 30 states had adopted incentive regulation schemes rather than traditional rate of return regulation for telecommunications. These new schemes take two main forms: earnings-sharing plans (adopted in Colorado, Connecticut, Florida, Georgia, Kentucky, Tennessee, and Texas) and price caps (adopted in California, New Jersey, Oregon, and Rhode Island).

Under earnings-sharing regulation, if profits rise above a certain level, they must be shared with the firm's customers. Some evidence suggests that under these types of regulations, local telephone companies are attempting to cut costs.

Under price-cap regulation, the regulators set the maximum price that can be charged and hold that cap (adjusted for inflation) for several years. By keeping costs under control, economic profits can be earned. But if costs increase and exceed the price cap, a shortage can arise, just as with a price ceiling, such as those that arise in the rent-controlled housing market that you studied in Chapter 7 (pp. 166–171). The crisis in the electricity supply industry in California has resulted from such a cost increase (alongside other problems).

Regulating Electricity in California

In 1996, California changed the way it regulates its electric power industry. The utilities own the lines that carry electricity to the final consumer, but face a ceiling price they can charge the consumer. The utilities buy power from the private producers and import any shortfall from neighboring states.

California electricity producers also face a price ceiling called the soft-cap price because it can be exceeded with permission from the regulator. The market price increased above the soft-cap price of $150 a megawatt and reached more than $500 a megawatt in April 2001 (see figure).

Regulations restrict California's utilities from entering into long-term supply contracts, so they must pay the current market price to meet demand.

In 2001, importing became difficult because the utilities incurred large losses and suppliers were reluctant to grant them credit. The result was electricity shortages and blackouts.

The reaction to the problems of California's electricity supply industry is that deregulation is a failure. This reaction is not supported by the facts. The industry is still regulated, and under rules that almost guarantee the problems it faced in 2001.

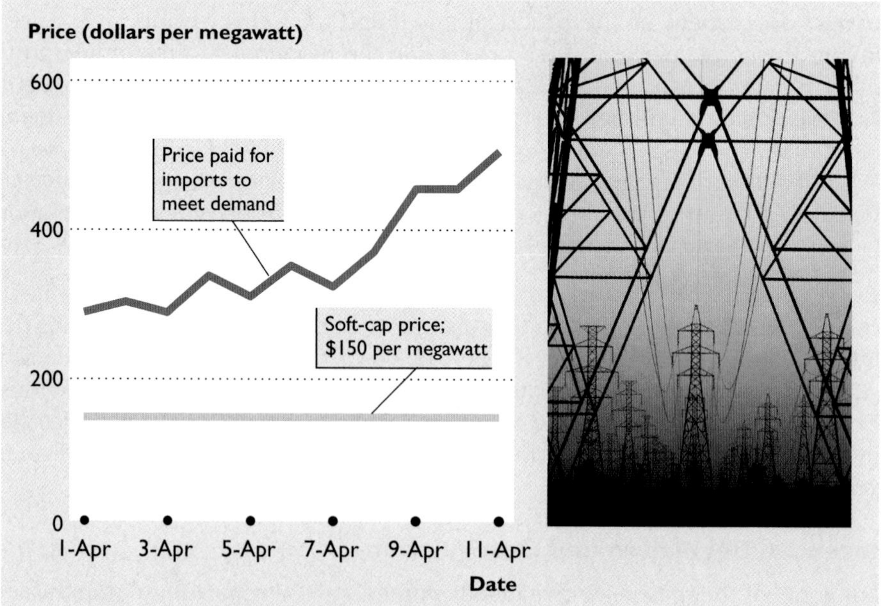

SOURCE: California Independent System Operator.

Oligopoly Regulation

An oligopoly is a market structure in which a small number of firms compete with each other. We studied oligopoly (and duopoly—two firms competing in a market) in Chapter 14 (pp. 348–357). There we saw that firms have an incentive to try to form a *cartel*—a collusive agreement among the firms in the industry that is designed to restrict output and achieve a higher profit. A profit-maximizing cartel behaves like a monopoly. It sets the same price and sells the same total quantity as a monopoly would.

Cartels are illegal in the United States and in most other countries. But international cartels, such as the cartel of oil producers known as OPEC (the Organization of Petroleum Exporting Countries), can sometimes operate legally. Illegal cartels can arise in oligopolistic industries. But as we also discovered in Chapter 14, each firm in a cartel has an incentive to cheat by increasing its own output and profit at the expense of the other firms. Such cheating unravels the monopoly situation and leads to a higher output rate, lower price, and smaller economic profit. Such an outcome benefits consumers at the expense of producers.

How is oligopoly regulated? Does regulation prevent cartels and monopoly practices or does it encourage those practices?

According to the public interest theory, oligopoly is regulated to ensure a competitive outcome. Consider, for example, the market for trucking tomatoes from the San Joaquin Valley to Los Angeles, illustrated in Figure 15.4. The market demand curve for trips is *D*. The industry marginal cost curve—and the competitive supply curve—is *MC*. Public interest regulation will regulate the price of a trip at $20, and there will be 300 trips a week.

Regulatory Roller Coaster

Cable television has been on a regulatory roller coaster. When cable first arrived, its prices were regulated. They were deregulated in 1984, but profits soared and prices were reregulated in 1992. Congress passed yet another deregulation law in 1996 and set March 31, 1999, as the date the Federal Communications Commission (FCC) would stop regulating most cable TV prices. On that date, federal price controls were removed from packages that included popular channels, such as CNN, Discovery, ESPN, and MTV.

Before the 1999 deregulation, consumers paid an average $31 a month for cable TV services.

Back in 1996, when Congress set the March 31, 1999, date, it expected to see effective competition among cable companies, but competition still has not developed.

When the 1992 regulated prices took effect in 1993, prices decreased at first and cut billions of dollars from cable bills. But in 1994, the FCC loosened the rules and prices began to rise. In mid-1996, cable rates increased sharply. Between 1996 and 1999, cable prices increased 24 percent, compared with a 6 percent rise in all prices on the average.

Until effective competition arrives, it is difficult to see an end to high cable prices.

FIGURE 15.4
Collusive Oligopoly

*e*Foundations 15.1 

Ten trucking firms transport tomatoes from the San Joaquin Valley to Los Angeles. The demand curve is *D*, and the industry marginal cost curve is *MC*. Under competition, the *MC* curve is the industry supply curve.

❶ Public interest regulation will achieve the efficient competitive outcome: a price of $20 a trip and 300 trips a week.

❷ Regulation in the producers' interest will limit output to 200 trips a week (where industry marginal revenue, *MR*, is equal to industry marginal cost, *MC*), and the price will be $30 a trip.

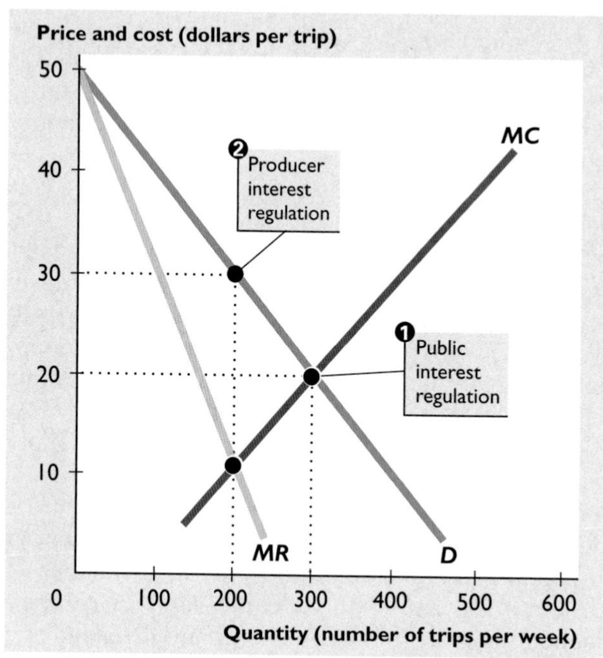

How would this industry be regulated, according to the capture theory? Regulation that is in the producers' interest will maximize profit. To find the outcome in this case, we need to determine the price and quantity when marginal cost equals marginal revenue. The marginal revenue curve is *MR*. So marginal cost equals marginal revenue at 200 trips a week. The price of a trip is $30.

One way of achieving this outcome is to place an output limit on each firm in the industry. If there are 10 trucking companies, an output limit of 20 trips per company ensures that the total number of trips in a week is 200. Penalties can be imposed to ensure that no single producer exceeds its output limit.

All the firms in the industry would support this type of regulation because it would help to prevent cheating and maintain a monopoly outcome. Each firm knows that without effectively enforced production quotas, every firm has an incentive to increase output. (For each firm, price exceeds marginal cost, so a greater output brings a larger profit.) So each firm wants a method of preventing output from increasing above the industry profit-maximizing output, and the quotas enforced by regulation achieve this end. With this type of cartel regulation, the regulator enables a cartel to operate legally and in its own best interest.

Cartel-like behavior occurs in many regulated activities in which the *purpose* of regulation is quality control but the *effect* of regulation is monopoly profit. One example is citrus fruit production in California and Florida, where the state citrus boards, whose purpose is to regulate the size and quality of fruit, also regulate the weekly sales of the producers. Another example is the provision of physicians' services. Regulation of the quality of doctors ends up regulating entry and achieving a monopoly price for their services.

CHECKPOINT 15.1

1 **Distinguish between the public interest and capture theories of regulation, and explain how regulation affects prices, outputs, profits, and the distribution of surpluses between consumers and producers.**

Study Guide pp. 236–240 

*e*Foundations 15.1 

Practice Problem 15.1

An unregulated natural monopoly bottles Elixir, a unique health product that has no substitutes. The monopoly's total fixed cost is $150,000, and its marginal cost is 10 cents a bottle. Figure 1 illustrates the demand for Elixir.

a. How many bottles of Elixir does the monopoly sell?
b. What is the price of a bottle of Elixir?
c. Is the monopoly's use of resources efficient?
d. How might the government regulate the monopoly in the public interest?
e. If the government introduces a marginal cost pricing rule, what will be the price of a bottle of Elixir, the quantity of Elixir sold, and the monopoly's profit?

FIGURE 1

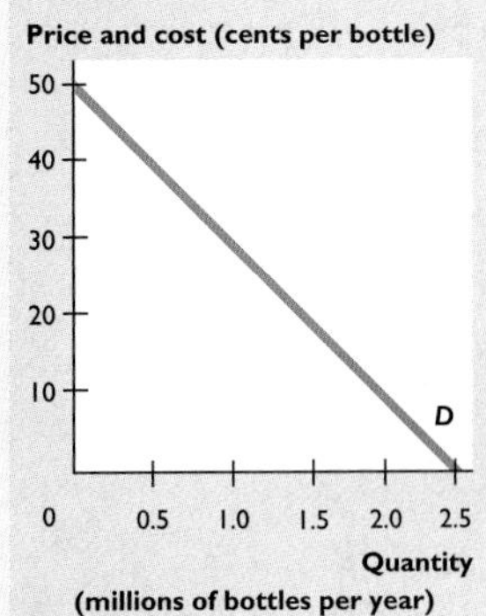

Exercise 15.1

An unregulated natural monopoly cans Mount McKinley air, unique clean air that has no substitutes. The monopoly's total fixed cost is $120,000, and its marginal cost is 20 cents a can. Figure 2 illustrates the demand for Mount McKinley air.

a. How many cans of Mount McKinley air does the monopoly sell?
b. What is the price of a can of Mount McKinley air?
c. If the monopoly captures the regulator, how might the monopoly be regulated?
d. If the monopoly can mislead the regulator about its costs, what is the maximum excess average total cost that it would claim?
e. Would the regulated monopoly use resources efficiently?

FIGURE 2

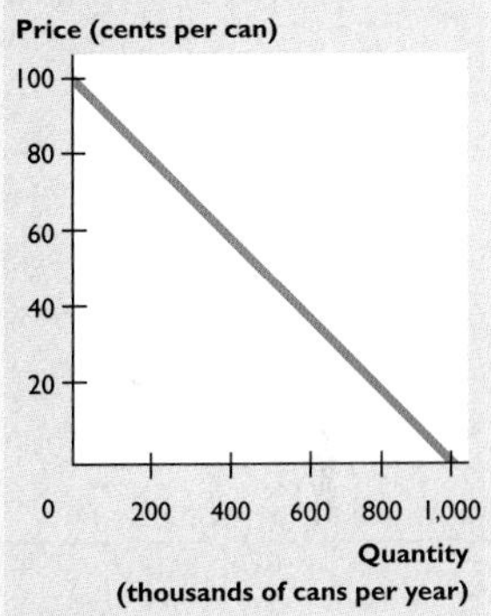

Solution to Practice Problem 15.1

a. The monopoly will produce 1 million bottles a year—the quantity at which marginal revenue equals marginal cost (Figure 3).
b. The price is 30 cents a bottle—the highest price at which it can sell the 1 million bottles (Figure 3).
c. The monopoly's use of resources is inefficient. If resource use were efficient, the monopoly would produce the quantity at which price equals marginal cost: 2 million bottles.
d. The government might use a marginal cost pricing rule or an average cost pricing rule to regulate the monopoly.
e. With a marginal cost pricing rule, the price will be 10 cents a bottle and the monopoly will produce 2 million bottles. The monopoly will make an economic loss of $150,000 a year. The monopoly will need a subsidy from the government to keep it in business.

FIGURE 3

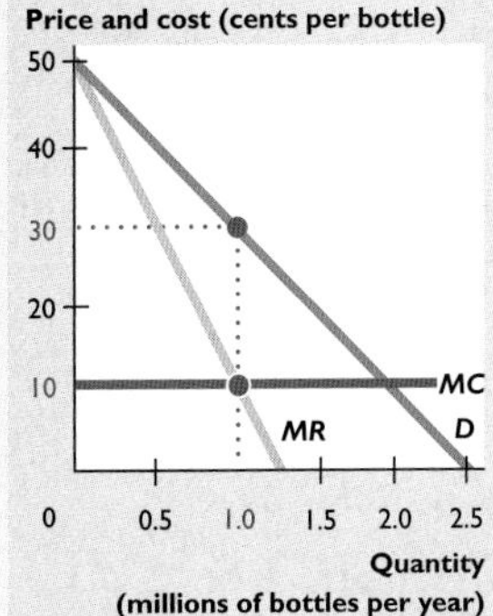

15.2 ANTITRUST LAW

Antitrust law
The body of law that regulates and prohibits certain kinds of market behavior, such as monopoly and monopolistic practices.

Antitrust law is the body of law that regulates and prohibits certain kinds of market behavior, such as monopoly and monopolistic practices. Antitrust law is enacted by Congress and enforced through the judicial system. Lawsuits under the antitrust laws may be initiated either by government agencies or by injured private parties. The main thrust of antitrust law is the prohibition of monopoly practices of restricting output to achieve higher prices and profits.

The Antitrust Laws

The U.S. antitrust laws are easily summarized. The first antitrust law, the Sherman Act, was passed in 1890 in an atmosphere of outrage and disgust at the actions and practices of J. P. Morgan, John D. Rockefeller, and W. H. Vanderbilt—the so-called robber barons. Ironically, the most lurid stories of the actions of these great American capitalists are not of their monopolization and exploitation of consumers but of their sharp practices against each other. Nevertheless, monopolies did emerge—for example, the spectacular control of the oil industry by John D. Rockefeller.

A wave of mergers at the turn of the twentieth century produced stronger antitrust laws. The Clayton Act of 1914 supplemented the Sherman Act, and the Federal Trade Commission, an agency charged with enforcing the antitrust laws, was created.

Table 15.1 summarizes the two main provisions of the Sherman Act. Section 1 of the act is precise. Conspiring with others to restrict competition is illegal. But Section 2 is general and imprecise. Just what is an "attempt to monopolize"? The Clayton Act and its two amendments, the Robinson-Patman Act of 1936 and the Celler-Kefauver Act of 1950, which outlaw specific practices, provided greater precision. Table 15.2 describes these practices and summarizes the main provisions of these three acts.

TABLE 15.1
The Sherman Act, 1890

e/**Foundations 15.2** 

Section 1:
Every contract, combination in the form of trust or otherwise, or conspiracy, in restraint of trade or commerce among the several States, or with foreign nations, is hereby declared to be illegal.

Section 2:
Every person who shall monopolize, or attempt to monopolize, or combine or conspire with any other person or persons, to monopolize any part of the trade or commerce among the several States, or with foreign nations, shall be deemed guilty of a felony.

TABLE 15.2
The Clayton Act and Its Amendments

*e*Foundations 15.2 

Clayton Act	**1914**
Robinson-Patman Act	**1936**
Celler-Kefauver Act	**1950**

These acts prohibit the following practices only if they substantially lessen competition or create monopoly:

1. Price discrimination.
2. Contracts that require other goods to be bought from the same firm (called tying arrangements).
3. Contracts that require a firm to buy all its requirements of a particular item from a single firm (called requirements contracts).
4. Contracts that prevent a firm from selling competing items (called exclusive dealing).
5. Contracts that prevent a buyer from reselling a product outside a specified area (called territorial confinement).
6. Acquiring a competitor's shares or assets.
7. Becoming a director of a competing firm.

Landmark Antitrust Cases

The real force of any law arises from its interpretation by the courts. The court rulings have been clear on price fixing (Section 1 of the Sherman Act) but less clear on attempts to monopolize (Section 2 of the Sherman Act and the Clayton Act). Rulings have fluctuated from favoring producers to favoring consumers. Table 15.3 summarizes some landmark cases.

Price Fixing

Court decisions have made any price-fixing deal a violation of Section 1 of the Sherman Act. Taking someone's life is a serious offense. But it is not always a violation of the murder law. Accidents and other involuntary causes of death are recognized as reasons not to convict someone of murder. In contrast, price fixing is *always* a violation of the antitrust law. If the Department of Justice can prove the existence of price fixing, a defendant can offer no acceptable excuse.

A 1927 case against Trenton Potteries Company and others first established this hard line, which is known as the *per se* interpretation of the law. The Latin term *per se* means "by or in itself." The court ruled that an agreement between Trenton Potteries and others to fix the prices of sanitary pottery violated the Sherman Act even if the prices themselves were reasonable. Price fixing *per se*—by and in itself—is a violation of the law.

In 1961, General Electric, Westinghouse, and other electrical component manufacturers were found guilty of a price-fixing conspiracy. This case was the first one in which the executives (rather than the company itself) were fined and jailed.

TABLE 15.3
Landmark Antitrust Cases

*e*Foundations **15.2** 

Case	Year	Verdict and Consequence
1. Price Fixing		
Trenton Potteries Company	1927	Guilty: Agreement to fix prices was *per se* a violation of the Sherman Act, regardless of whether the prices themselves are "reasonable."
General Electric, Westinghouse, and other electrical manufacturers	1961	Guilty: Price-fixing conspiracy; executives were fined and jailed.
Archer Daniels Midland	1996	Guilty: Price-fixing conspiracy; corporation was fined $100 million.
2. Attempts to Monopolize?		
American Tobacco Co. and Standard Oil Co.	1911	Guilty: Ordered to divest themselves of large holdings in other companies; rule of reason enunciated: only unreasonable combinations are prohibited under Sherman Act.
U.S. Steel Co.	1920	Not guilty: Although U.S. Steel had a very large market share (near monopoly), mere "size alone is not an offense"; application of the rule of reason.
Alcoa	1945	Guilty: Too big—had too large a share of the market.
Aspen Skiing	1985	Guilty: Owner of three of the four downhill ski facilities refused to offer an all-Aspen ticket and share revenues on a use basis with the owner of the other facility.
Spectrum Sports	1993	Not guilty: Although Spectrum Sports was the national distributor of sorbothane (used in athletic products), no evidence was present that the company had attempted to monopolize the market.

A recent costly example that also illustrates the application of the price-fixing law is that of Archer Daniels Midland. In 1996, this major producer of agricultural products was fined $100 million for conspiring with foreign producers to fix the prices of lysine and citric acid, two additives that are used in various food products.

Attempts to Monopolize

The most important early antitrust cases were those involving the American Tobacco Company and Standard Oil Company, which were decided in 1911. These two companies were found guilty of violations under the Sherman Act and ordered to divest themselves of large holdings in other companies. The breakup of John D. Rockefeller's Standard Oil Company resulted in the creation of the oil companies that today are household names, such as Amoco, Chevron, ExxonMobil, BP, and Sohio.

In finding American Tobacco Company and Standard Oil Company in violation of the provisions of the Sherman Act, the Supreme Court formulated the "rule of reason," which states that monopoly that arises from mergers and agreements among firms is not necessarily illegal. Only if there is an unreasonable restraint of trade does the arrangement violate the Sherman Act.

The rule of reason was widely regarded as removing the force of the Sherman Act itself. This view was reinforced in 1920 when U.S. Steel Company was acquitted of violations under the act, even though it had a very large (more than 50 percent) share of the U.S. steel market. Applying the rule of reason, the court declared, "size alone is not an offense."

Some people interpreted the Alcoa case, decided in 1945, as challenging the rule of reason. Alcoa was judged to be violating the antitrust law because it was too big. It had too large a share of the aluminum market. This relatively tough interpretation of the law continued through the late 1960s.

Of the many other cases concerning the attempt to monopolize, we look at two interesting and relatively recent ones. During the 1970s, the Aspen Skiing Company, which owned three of the four downhill ski facilities in Aspen, offered an all-Aspen ticket and shared the revenues with Aspen Highlands Skiing Corporation, which owned the fourth facility. Revenues were split on the basis of a survey of users. In 1977, Aspen Skiing refused to offer the all-Aspen ticket unless Aspen Highlands agreed to accept a low fixed share of the revenue. The all-Aspen ticket was not offered, and Aspen Highlands lost business. The court decided that the Aspen Skiing Company was attempting to monopolize.

When Spectrum Sports became the national distributor of sorbothane athletic products (sorbothane is a shock absorber), some injured companies alleged that Spectrum had attempted to monopolize. The court decided that Spectrum could not be considered to have attempted to monopolize the market without evidence that it had engaged in monopoly practices.

Today's Showcase: The United States Versus Microsoft

Encouraged by Microsoft's competitors, and not by the consumers of its products, the U.S. Department of Justice charged Microsoft with specific violations of the antitrust law. A trial on these charges began in 1998 and a final judgment was delivered in mid-2000. The judgment was still under appeal in mid-2001.

The Case Against Microsoft

The Department of Justice claimed that Microsoft:

- Possesses monopoly power in the market for PC operating systems.
- Uses below-cost pricing (called *predatory pricing*) and tying arrangements to achieve a monopoly in the market for Web browsers.
- Uses other anticompetitive practices to strengthen its monopoly in these two markets.

Microsoft, it was claimed, operates behind barriers to entry that arise from economies of scale. Microsoft's average total cost falls as production increases (economies of scale) because the fixed cost of developing an operating system such as Windows is large, while the marginal cost of producing one copy of Windows is small. An additional barrier arises because as the number of Windows users increases, the range of Windows applications expands, so a potential competitor would need to produce not only a competing operating system but also an entire range of supporting applications as well.

When Microsoft entered the Web browser market with its Internet Explorer (IE), it offered the browser for a zero price. This price was viewed as predatory pricing—an attempt to drive out the competition and monopolize a market. Microsoft integrated IE with Windows 98 so that anyone who uses this operating system does not need a separate browser such as Netscape Communicator. Microsoft's competitors claimed that this practice is illegal product tying.

Microsoft's Response

Microsoft challenged all these claims. It said that Windows competes with Macintosh and others and is vulnerable to competition from new operating systems. Windows dominates because it is the best product. It also claimed that integrating Internet Explorer with Windows 98 provides a product of greater consumer value. Instead of tying, Microsoft said the browser and operating system is one product. It is like a refrigerator with a chilled water dispenser.

In the final judgment delivered in June 2000, the court ordered that Microsoft be broken into two firms: one that produces operating systems and one that produces applications. Microsoft is appealing this ruling.

Breaking up a monopoly is a drastic action. Preventing one from emerging from a merger is much less radical and a goal that is routinely pursued by the Department of Justice. We end this chapter by examining the rules that guide these decisions.

Merger Rules

The Department of Justice uses guidelines to determine which mergers it will examine and possibly block on the basis of the Herfindahl-Hirschman index (HHI), which is explained in Chapter 14 (p. 338). A market in which the HHI is less than 1,000 is regarded as competitive. An index between 1,000 and 1,800 indicates a moderately concentrated market, and a merger in this market that would increase the index by 100 points is challenged by the Department of Justice. An index above 1,800 indicates a concentrated market, and a merger in this market that would increase the index by 50 points is challenged. Figure 15.5(a) summarizes these guidelines.

The Department of Justice used these guidelines to analyze two recently proposed mergers in the market for soft drinks. In 1986, PepsiCo announced its intention to buy 7-Up for $380 million. A month later, Coca-Cola said that it would buy Dr Pepper for $470 million. Whether this market is concentrated depends on how it is defined. The market for all soft drinks, which includes carbonated drinks marketed by these four companies plus fruit juices and bottled water, has an HHI of 120, so it is highly competitive. But the market for carbonated soft drinks is highly concentrated. Coca-Cola has a 39 percent share, PepsiCo has 28 percent, Dr Pepper is next with 7 percent, then comes 7-Up with 6 percent. One other producer, RJR, has a 5 percent market share. So the five largest firms in this market have an 85 percent market share. If we assume that the other 15 percent of the market consists of 15 firms, each with a 1 percent market share, the Herfindahl-Hirschman index is

$$\text{HHI} = 39^2 + 28^2 + 7^2 + 6^2 + 5^2 + 15 = 2{,}430.$$

With an HHI of this magnitude, a merger that increases the index by 50 points is examined by the Department of Justice. Figure 15.5(b) shows how the HHI would have changed with the mergers. The PepsiCo and 7-Up merger would have increased the index by more than 300 points, the Coca-Cola and Dr Pepper merger would have increased it by more than 500 points, and both mergers together would have increased the index by almost 800 points. The Department of Justice decided to define the market narrowly and, with increases of these magnitudes, blocked the mergers.

FIGURE 15.5
The HHI Merger Guidelines

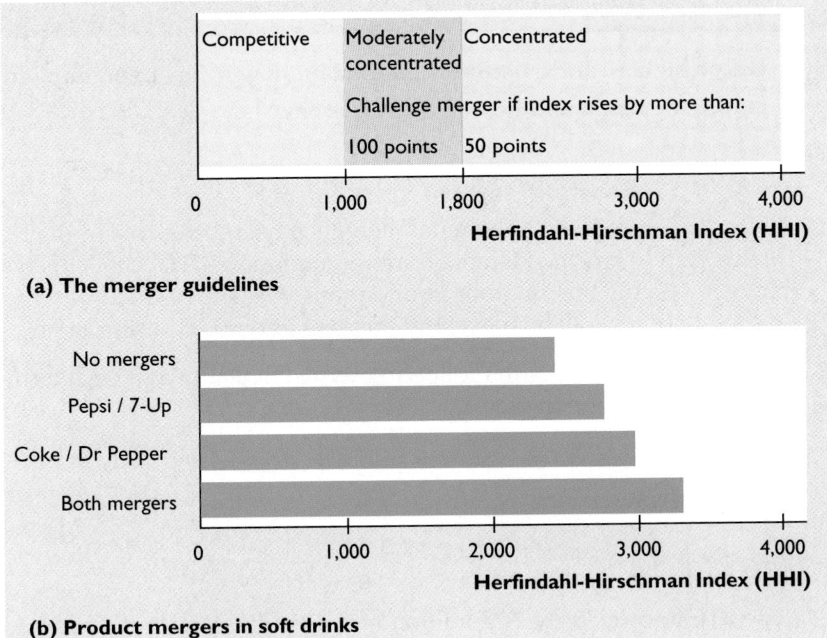

(a) The merger guidelines

(b) Product mergers in soft drinks

The Department of Justice scrutinizes proposed mergers if the HHI exceeds 1,000. Proposed mergers between producers of carbonated soft drinks were blocked in 1986 by application of these guidelines.

The AOL Time Warner Merger

There has been a wave of high-profile mergers during the past few years. One of them is the merger of AOL and Time Warner. The intention to merge was announced in January 2000 and the regulatory review was completed in January 2001.

AOL is the world's largest Internet service provider, with around 25 million customers. Time Warner is a leading media producer, which owns CNN, TNT, HBO, and the Cartoon Network; publishes *Time* and *People* magazines; and produces movies and music.

The idea of the merger was to create a large firm that produces both Internet content and access.

When the merger was approved, the Federal Communications Commission required the new firm to ensure that it would not prevent consumers from using an Internet service provider other than AOL to access its content.

With Internet service providers such as Microsoft MSN and Yahoo! and content providers such as Disney Corporation and News Corporation, the owner of Fox Broadcasting Company, and the other television networks, the AOL Time Warner merger clearly does not place any effective restriction on consumer choice.

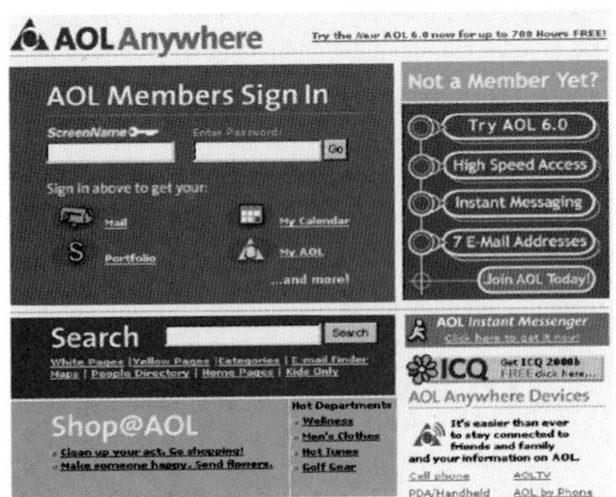

CHECKPOINT 15.2

Study Guide **pp. 240–244**

*e*Foundations **15.2**

2 Describe U.S. antitrust law and explain how it has been applied in some landmark cases and how it is used today.

Practice Problems 15.2

1. Since 1987, hundreds of hospital mergers have taken place in the United States. Rarely has the Federal Trade Commission (FTC) challenged a hospital merger. Use the link on your Foundations Web site to find out why the FTC decided not to challenge hospital mergers under U.S. antitrust law.
2. U.S. antitrust law uses the following terms. Explain what each term means.
   a. Attempt to monopolize
   b. Price fixing
   c. Rule of reason
   d. Tying arrangements

Exercises 15.2

1. The FTC approved the $27 million merger of BP Amoco PLC and ARCO only after they met the FTC's demands for substantial divestitures. Use the link on your Foundations Web site to see what some of the required divestitures were and why the FTC insisted on them.
2. In 1911, Standard Oil Company was found guilty under the Sherman Act and was ordered to divest. Today, some of the oil companies created as a result of the 1911 order have now merged to form large companies. Explain why Standard Oil Company was guilty under the Sherman Act, and explain why these recent oil mergers have been approved.

Solutions to Practice Problems 15.2

1. The FTC will not challenge a hospital merger if it will not substantially lessen competition in certain situations. Such situations include those in which (1) the merger would not increase the likelihood of market power either because strong competitors exist or because the merging hospitals were sufficiently differentiated, (2) the merger would allow the hospitals to reduce cost, or (3) the merger would eliminate a hospital that would probably have failed and exited the market.

2a. Attempt to monopolize is an attempt by a company to drive out its competitors so that it can operate as a monopoly.

2b. Price fixing is making an agreement with competitors to set a specified price and not to vary it.

2c. Rule of reason is a statement that monopoly that arises from mergers and agreements between firms is not necessarily illegal.

2d. Tying arrangements exist when a company does not offer a buyer the opportunity to buy one item without at the same time buying another item.

CHAPTER CHECKPOINT

Key Points

1 Distinguish between the public interest and capture theories of regulation, and explain how regulation affects prices, outputs, profits, and the distribution of surpluses between consumers and producers.

- The Interstate Commerce Commission, established in 1887, was the first national regulatory agency.
- Public interest theory predicts that regulation achieves an efficient use of resources. Capture theory predicts that regulation helps producers to maximize economic profit.
- At the peak of regulation, in the late 1970s, almost a quarter of U.S. output was produced by regulated industries.
- A natural monopoly is efficient if its price equals marginal cost.
- A natural monopoly maximizes its profit if its marginal revenue equals marginal cost and price exceeds marginal cost.
- Rate of return regulation makes price equal to average cost.
- Incentive regulation motivates a firm to earn an economic profit by keeping costs under control.
- Regulation has not lowered the profits of regulated firms, and the outcome of regulation is closer to the predictions of capture theory than to public interest theory.

2 Describe U.S. antitrust law and explain how it has been applied in some landmark cases and how it is used today.

- Antitrust law is used to control monopoly and monopolistic practices.
- The first U.S. antitrust law, the Sherman Act, was passed in 1890, and the law was strengthened in 1914 when the Clayton Act was passed and the Federal Trade Commission was created.
- All price-fixing agreements are in violation of the Sherman Act.
- The first landmark cases (against American Tobacco Company and Standard Oil Company) established the rule of reason, which holds that an attempt to monopolize a market is illegal; monopoly itself is not illegal.
- The Federal Trade Commission uses guidelines to determine which mergers to examine and possibly block based on the Herfindahl-Hirschman Index.

Key Terms

Antitrust law, 372
Capture theory, 362
Incentive regulation, 367
Public interest theory, 362
Rate of return regulation, 366
Regulation, 362

FIGURE 1

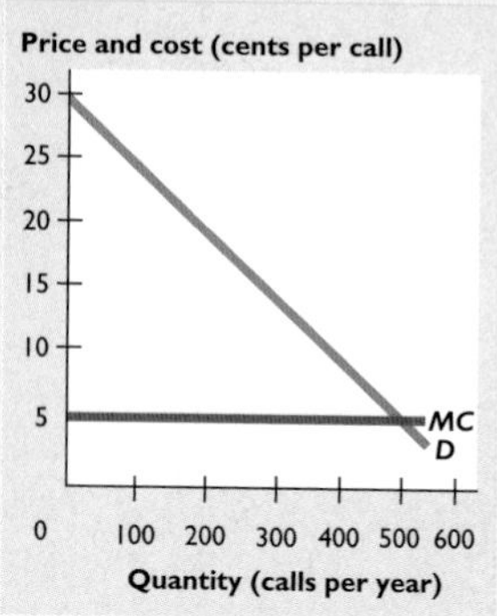

Price and cost (cents per call)

30, 25, 20, 15, 10, 5, 0

MC

D

100 200 300 400 500 600

Quantity (calls per year)

Exercises

1. Two phone companies offer local calls in an area. Figure 1 illustrates the market demand for calls and the marginal cost of a call for each firm.
   a. If these firms behave as a cartel, what price will the cartel charge for a call and what quantity of calls will be made?
   b. If the phone companies are regulated in the public interest, what will be the price of a call and what quantity of calls will be made?
   c. What will be the price of a call and the quantity of calls if the phone companies capture the regulator?
   d. In part (c), what is the deadweight loss?
   e. What regulation would lead to the resource use being efficient?

2. Use the link on your Foundations Web site to visit the Federal Trade Commission's site, where you can obtain information about Intel, the computer chip maker.
   a. What was the problem that the FTC had with Intel?
   b. What did Intel agree to do?
   c. Explain how Intel's agreement will influence the price, quantity, consumer surplus, and producer surplus in the market for computer chips.

3. Governments talk about regulating the Internet and taxing e-commerce. From what you know about how the Internet works and what e-commerce is:
   a. What difficulties do you think government will have in regulating the Internet?
   b. What difficulties do you think government will have in taxing e-commerce?
   c. What parts of current U.S. antitrust law do you think will be hard to enforce on companies that trade on the Internet?

4. Use the link on your Foundations Web site to visit the CNN Special on the California energy crisis.
   a. Describe the way in which electricity utilities were regulated in California before 1996.
   b. Describe the way in which the 1996 deregulation changed the regulations.
   c. Identify at least three areas in which the electricity industry of California remained regulated after "deregulation."
   d. Explain the probable effects of the price cap on electricity generated in California. (Hint: Use the model of price ceiling in Chapter 7.)
   e. How do you think the situation in California would be different if instead of price cap regulation, the state had introduced an earnings-sharing plan?

5. Use the link on your Foundations Web site to review the article "How the Government Plans to Tie Down the Microsoft Monster."
   a. What does the court want to happen to Microsoft?
   b. Who do you think would benefit from a breakup of Microsoft, the consumer of Microsoft's products or its competitors?
   c. Do you think that a breakup of Microsoft would be a move toward greater efficiency in the software industry, or would it create (or increase) the deadweight loss in that industry? Provide reasons.

Part 6

How Incomes Are Determined

Demand and Supply in Factor Markets

Chapter 16

CHAPTER CHECKLIST

When you have completed your study of this chapter, you will be able to:

1. **Describe the anatomy of the markets for labor, capital, and land.**
2. **Explain how the value of marginal product determines the demand for a factor of production.**
3. **Explain how wage rates and employment are determined.**
4. **Explain how interest rates, borrowing, and lending are determined.**
5. **Explain how rents and natural resource prices are determined.**

You've seen how markets for goods and services answer the first big question of economics: *What* goods and services get produced? The answer is the quantity that balances the buying plans of demanders and the selling plans of suppliers.

You are now going to learn how factor markets answer the other two big questions: *How* and *for whom* are goods and services produced?

First, we'll describe the anatomy of the labor, capital, and land markets. Then we'll learn what determines the demand for a factor of production. We'll go on to study demand, supply, and equilibrium in factor markets. These markets determine the quantities of factors of production that are used to produce goods and services, which answers the *how* question; and they determine the prices and incomes of the factors of production, which answers the *for whom* question.

16.1 THE ANATOMY OF FACTOR MARKETS

The four factors of production that produce goods and services are:

- Labor
- Capital
- Land
- Entrepreneurship

Factor price
The price of a factor of production. The wage rate is the price of labor, the interest rate is the price of capital, and rent is the price of land.

The first three factors—labor, capital, and land—are traded in markets that work like the markets for goods and services that you studied in Chapter 4. What a factor of production is paid—a **factor price**—is determined in a *factor market*. Entrepreneurship is different. Entrepreneurs create firms and hire labor, capital, and land in factor markets. The income of an entrepreneur is a profit (or a loss).

We'll begin by looking at the anatomy of the factor markets.

Labor Markets

Whether you're looking for a summer job or a permanent job after you graduate, you'll find it by searching in a labor market. Similarly, if you're running a business and want to hire some workers, you'll go to a labor market.

Labor market
A collection of people and firms who are trading labor services.

Job
A long-term contract between a firm and a household to provide labor services.

Labor consists of the work effort of people. And a **labor market** is a collection of people and firms who are trading labor services. Some labor is traded day by day, called casual labor. People who pick fruit and vegetables often just show up at a farm and take whatever work is available that day. But most labor is traded on a contract, called a **job**.

Labor is combined with *human capital*. Each person has a fixed (and equal) amount of time, but individual skills vary because individual ability and experience vary. More education and more experience bring more human capital. Also, individual productivity depends on how well the skills of a worker match the skills required by an employer. For these reasons, a large amount of search activity takes place in labor markets. People search for the best job they can find, and firms search for the best person to fill a particular job.

People find jobs by using a variety of search devices, such as leads from friends and family members, help wanted advertisements, job centers, and job-clearing Web sites such as monster.com.

The price of labor is a wage rate, which is expressed as dollars per unit of time—dollars per hour, day, week, month, or year.

Financial Markets

Capital consists of the tools, instruments, machines, buildings, and other constructions that have been produced in the past and that businesses now use to produce goods and services. These physical objects are themselves goods—*capital goods*—and are traded in markets, just as bottled water and toothpaste are. There are markets for earth-moving equipment, cranes, printing presses, Internet servers, and so on. The prices and quantities of capital goods are determined in markets just like those that you studied in Chapter 4.

Financial capital consists of the funds that firms use to buy and operate capital. The financial market is where firms get the funds that they use to buy capital. Firms are the demanders in the financial market. On the other side of a financial market are the people who have savings to lend.

Financial capital
The funds that firms use to buy and operate physical capital.

A **financial market** is the collection of people and firms who are lending and borrowing to finance the purchase of physical capital. The price of financial capital, which is determined in the financial markets, is expressed as an interest rate (percent per year).

Financial market
A collection of people and firms who are lending and borrowing to finance the purchase of physical capital.

The two main types of financial market are:

- Stock market
- Bond market

Stock Market

A **stock market** is a market in which shares in the stocks of companies are traded. A share in the stock of a company is an entitlement to a share in the profits of the company. Examples of stock markets are the New York Stock Exchange and NASDAQ (the National Association of Security Dealers Automated Quotation System). You can visit the Web sites of these stock markets and see the prices and the quantities of shares that are being traded minute by minute throughout the business day.

Stock market
A market in which shares in the stocks of companies are traded.

The growth of the Internet has created many new methods of participating in the stock market, and dozens of new firms offer services that enable anyone who is connected to the Internet to trade online.

Bond Market

A **bond market** is a market in which bonds issued by firms or governments are traded. A **bond** is a promise to pay specified sums of money on specified dates. To learn more about bond markets and how they are organized, you might visit the Bond Market Web site.

Bond market
A market in which bonds issued by firms or governments are traded.

Bond
A promise to pay specified sums of money on specified dates.

Land Markets

Land consists of all the gifts of nature. So there are many different objects in this category of the factors of production. What we call land in everyday speech is just one of these. Raw materials that we dig or pump from beneath the ground or ocean, such as metal ores, coal, oil, and natural gas, are also called land.

The market for land as a factor of production is the market for the services of land (of all types). These services are rented, and the price that is determined in a land market is a rent expressed as dollars per acre. The markets for raw materials are called **commodity markets**.

Commodity market
A market in which raw materials are traded.

Competitive Factor Markets

Factor markets vary in many ways. But most factor markets have one thing in common: many buyers and sellers. These markets are competitive markets. But some factor markets have elements of monopoly power—for example, those with labor unions. You can learn about this feature of the labor market in Chapter 17. In the current chapter, we study competitive factor markets.

CHECKPOINT 16.1

Study Guide **pp. 248–250** 

*e*Foundations **16.1**

1 Describe the anatomy of the markets for labor, capital, and land.

Practice Problem 16.1

To stage the Sydney 2000 Olympic Games, the Sydney Organizing Committee:

a. Borrowed money and sold sponsorships.
b. Built the Olympic Village and venues on a disused industrial site.
c. Hired and trained 46,000 volunteers and 20,000 security guards.
d. Built water- and waste-recycling plants in the Olympic Park.
e. Set up an Internet site, which averaged 1 million hits a day.
f. Staged some events in the streets of Sydney.

Divide this list into land, labor, physical capital, human capital, financial capital, and entrepreneurship.

Exercise 16.1

Visit the Web site of the Salt Lake City Winter Olympics of 2002. What are some of the factors of production that the Salt Lake City Committee is using to stage the Winter 2002 Olympics Games?

Solution to Practice Problem 16.1

Land: industrial site; Labor: volunteers and guards; Physical capital: Olympic Village, venues, recycling plants, Internet site, and Sydney streets; Human capital: the skill of the security guards and the trained volunteers; Financial capital: money borrowed and sponsorships sold; Entrepreneurship: the Sydney Organizing Committee.

16.2 THE DEMAND FOR A FACTOR OF PRODUCTION

The demand for a factor of production is a **derived demand**—it is derived from the demand for the goods and services that it is used to produce. You've seen, in Chapters 11 through 15, how a firm determines its profit-maximizing output. The quantities of factors of production demanded are a direct consequence of firms' output decisions. Firms hire the quantities of factors of production that maximize profit.

Derived demand
The demand for a factor of production, which is derived from the demand for the goods and services it is used to produce.

To decide the quantity of a factor of production to hire, a firm compares the cost of hiring an additional unit of the factor with its value to the firm. The cost of hiring an additional unit of a factor of production is the factor price. The value to the firm of hiring one more unit of a factor of production is called the factor's **value of marginal product**, which equals the price of a unit of output multiplied by the marginal product of the factor of production.

Value of marginal product
The value to a firm of hiring one more unit of a factor of production, which equals price of a unit of output multiplied by the marginal product of the factor of production.

Value of Marginal Product

Table 16.1 shows you how to calculate the value of the marginal product of labor at Max's Wash 'n' Wax car wash service. The first two columns show Max's *total product* schedule—the number of car washes per hour that each quantity of labor can produce. The third column shows the *marginal product* of labor—the change in total product that results from a one-unit increase in the quantity of labor employed. (See Chapter 11, pp. 263–267 for a refresher on product schedules.) Max can sell car washes at the going market price of $3 a wash. Given this information, we can calculate the value of the marginal product (fourth column). It equals price multiplied by marginal product. For example, the marginal product of hiring the second worker is 4 car washes an hour. Each wash brings in $3, so the value of the marginal product of the second worker is $12 (4 washes at $3 each).

TABLE 16.1
Calculating the Value of the Marginal Product

*e*Foundations 16.2 

	Quantity of labor (workers)	Total product (car washes per hour)	Marginal product (washes per worker)	Value of marginal product (dollars per worker)
A	0	0		
			5	15
B	1	5		
			4	12
C	2	9		
			3	9
D	3	12		
			2	6
E	4	14		
			1	3
F	5	15		

The price of a car wash is $3. The value of the marginal product of labor equals the price of the product multiplied by marginal product of labor (column 3). The marginal product of the second worker is 4 washes, so the value of the marginal product of the second worker (in column 4) is $3 a wash multiplied by 4 washes, which is $12.

The Value of Marginal Product Curve

Figure 16.1 graphs the value of the marginal product of labor at Max's Wash 'n' Wax as the number of workers that Max hires changes. The blue bars that show the value of the marginal product of labor as Max employs more workers correspond to the numbers in Table 16.1. The curve labeled *VMP* is Max's value of marginal product curve.

A Firm's Demand for Labor

The value of the marginal product of labor and the wage rate determine the quantity of labor demanded by a firm. The value of the marginal product of labor tells us the additional revenue the firm earns by hiring one more worker. The wage rate tells us the additional cost the firm incurs by hiring one more worker.

Because the value of marginal product decreases as the quantity of labor employed increases, there is a simple rule for maximizing profit: Hire labor up to the point at which the value of marginal product equals the wage rate. If the value of marginal product of labor exceeds the wage rate, a firm can increase its profit by employing one more worker. If the wage rate exceeds the value of marginal product of labor, a firm can increase its profit by employing one fewer worker. But if the wage rate equals the value of the marginal product of labor, the firm cannot increase its profit by changing the number of workers it employs. The firm is making the maximum possible profit.

So the quantity of labor demanded by a firm is the quantity at which the wage rate equals the value of the marginal product of labor.

FIGURE 16.1

The Value of the Marginal Product at Max's Wash 'n' Wax

*e*Foundations 16.2 

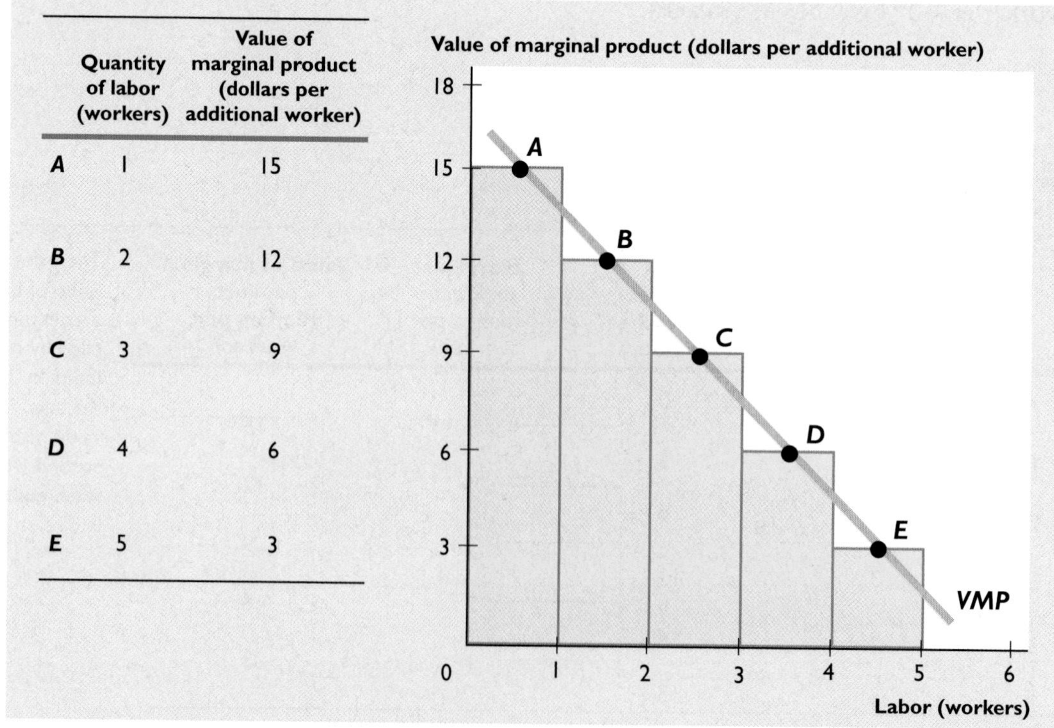

	Quantity of labor (workers)	Value of marginal product (dollars per additional worker)
A	1	15
B	2	12
C	3	9
D	4	6
E	5	3

The blue bars show the value of the marginal product of the labor that Max hires based on the numbers in Table 16.1. The orange line is the firm's value of the marginal product of labor curve.

A Firm's Demand for Labor Curve

A firm's demand for labor curve is also its value of marginal product curve. If the wage rate falls and other things remain the same, a firm hires more workers. Figure 16.2 shows Max's value of marginal product curve in part (a) and demand for labor curve in part (b). The *x*-axis measures the number of workers hired in both parts. The *y*-axis measures the value of marginal product in part (a) and the wage rate—dollars per hour—in part (b).

Suppose the wage rate is $10.50 an hour. You can see in part (a) that if Max hires 1 worker, the value of the marginal product of labor is $15 an hour. Because this 1 worker costs Max only $10.50 an hour, he makes a profit of $4.50 an hour. If Max hires 2 workers, the value of the marginal product of the second worker is $12 an hour. So on this second worker, Max makes a profit of $1.50 an hour. Max's total profit per hour on the first two workers is $6 an hour—$4.50 on the first worker plus $1.50 on the second worker.

If Max hired 3 workers, his profit would fall. The third worker generates a marginal product of only $9 an hour but costs $10.50 an hour, so Max does not hire 3

FIGURE 16.2
The Demand for Labor at Max's Wash 'n' Wax

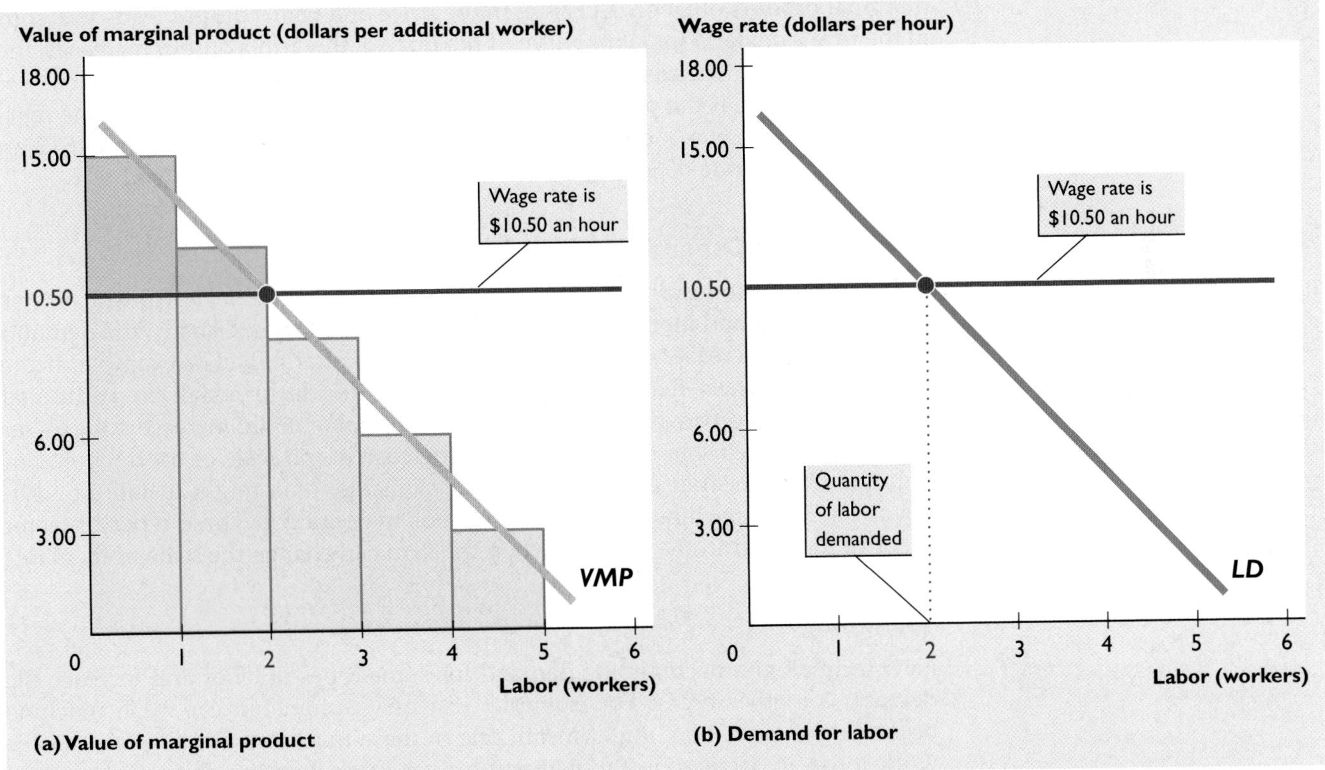

At a wage rate of $10.50 an hour, Max makes a profit on the first 2 workers but would incur a loss on the third worker (part a), so the quantity of labor demanded is 2 workers (part b). Max's demand for labor curve in part (b) is the same as the value of marginal product curve. The demand for labor curve slopes downward because the value of the marginal product of labor diminishes as the quantity of labor employed increases.

workers. The quantity of labor demanded by Max when the wage rate is $10.50 is 2 workers, which is a point on Max's demand for labor curve, *LD*, in Figure 16.2(b).

If the wage rate increased to $12.50 an hour, Max would decrease the quantity of labor demanded to 1 worker. If the wage rate decreased to $7.50 an hour, Max would increase the quantity of labor demanded to 3 workers.

A change in the wage rate brings a change in the quantity of labor demanded and a movement along the demand curve. A change in any other influence on a firm's labor-hiring plans changes the demand for labor and shifts the demand for labor curve.

Changes in the Demand for Labor

The demand for labor depends on:

- The price of the firm's output
- The prices of other factors of production
- Technology

The Price of the Firm's Output

The higher the price of a firm's output, the greater is its demand for labor. The price of output affects the demand for labor through its influence on the value of marginal product. A higher price for the firm's output increases the value of the marginal product of labor. A change in the price of a firm's output leads to a shift in the firm's demand for labor curve. If the price of the firm's output increases, the demand for labor increases and the demand for labor curve shifts rightward.

For example, if the price of a car wash increased to $4, the value of the marginal product of Max's third worker would increase from $9 an hour to $12 an hour. At a wage rate of $10.50, Max would now hire 3 workers instead of 2.

The Prices of Other Factors of Production

If the price of using capital decreases relative to the wage rate, a firm substitutes capital for labor and increases the quantity of capital it uses. Usually, the demand for labor will decrease when the price of using capital falls. For example, if the price of a car wash machine falls, Max might decide to install an additional machine and lay off a worker. But the demand for labor could increase if the lower price of capital led to a sufficiently large increase in the scale of production. For example, with cheaper capital equipment available, Max might install an additional car wash machine and hire more labor to operate it. These types of factor substitution occur in the *long run* when the firm can change the scale of its plant.

Technology

New technologies decrease the demand for some types of labor and increase the demand for other types. For example, if a new automated car wash machine becomes available, Max might install one of these machines and fire most of his work force—a decrease in the demand for car wash workers. But the firms that manufacture and service automatic car wash machines hire more labor—an increase in the demand for these types of labor. During the 1980s and 1990s, the electronic telephone exchange decreased the demand for telephone operators and increased the demand for computer programmers and electronic engineers.

CHECKPOINT 16.2

2 **Explain how the value of marginal product determines the demand for a factor of production.**

Study Guide pp. 250–252

eFoundations 16.2

Practice Problem 16.2

Kaiser's Ice Cream Parlor hires workers to produce smoothies. The market for smoothies is perfectly competitive, and smoothies sell for $4.00 each. The labor market is competitive, and the wage rate is $40 a day. Table 1 shows the workers' total product, *TP*:

a. Calculate the marginal product of hiring the fourth worker.
b. Calculate the value of the marginal product of the fourth worker.
c. How many workers will Kaiser's hire to maximize its profit?
d. How many smoothies a day will Kaiser's produce to maximize its profit?
e. If the price of a smoothie rises to $5, how many workers will Kaiser's now hire?
f. Kaiser's installs a new soda fountain that increases the productivity of workers by 50 percent. If the price remains at $4 a smoothie and the wage rises to $48 a day, how many workers does Kaiser's now hire?

TABLE 1

Workers	Smoothies per day
1	7
2	21
3	33
4	43
5	51
6	55

Exercise 16.2

Happy Joe's hires workers to produce wraps. The market for wraps is perfectly competitive, and wraps sell for $4 each. The labor market is competitive, and the wage rate is $40 a day. Table 2 shows the workers' total product:

a. Calculate the marginal product of hiring the third worker.
b. Calculate the value of the marginal product of the third worker.
c. How many workers will Happy Joe's hire to maximize its profit?
d. How many wraps a day will Happy Joe's produce to maximize its profit?
e. If the wage rate rises to $48 a day, how many workers will Happy Joe's now hire?
f. Happy Joe's now installs a new machine for making wraps and the productivity of workers doubles. At the same time, the price of a wrap falls to $3. How many workers will Happy Joe's now hire at $48 a day?

TABLE 2

Workers	Wraps per day
1	20
2	38
3	54
4	68
5	80
6	90
7	98
8	104

Solution to Practice Problem 16.2

a. The *MP* of hiring the fourth worker equals the *TP* of 4 workers (43 smoothies) minus the *TP* of 3 workers (33 smoothies), which is 10 smoothies.
b. The *VMP* of the fourth worker equals the *MP* of the fourth worker (10 smoothies) multiplied by the price of a smoothie ($4), which is $40.
c. Kaiser's maximizes profit by hiring the number of workers that makes $VMP = W$. Kaiser's hires 4 workers.
d. Kaiser's hires 4 workers, and they produce 43 smoothies. When Kaiser's hires the 4th worker, the *MP* of labor is 10 smoothies. The cost of the 4th worker is $40, so the *MC* of a smoothie is $40 ÷ 10 smoothies, which is $4 a smoothie. Kaiser's *MC* equals the price of a smoothie ($4 a smoothie). That is, $MC = P$, when Kaiser's produces 43 smoothies a day.
e. Kaiser's maximizes its profit by hiring 5 workers.
f. Kaiser's maximizes its profit by hiring 5 workers.

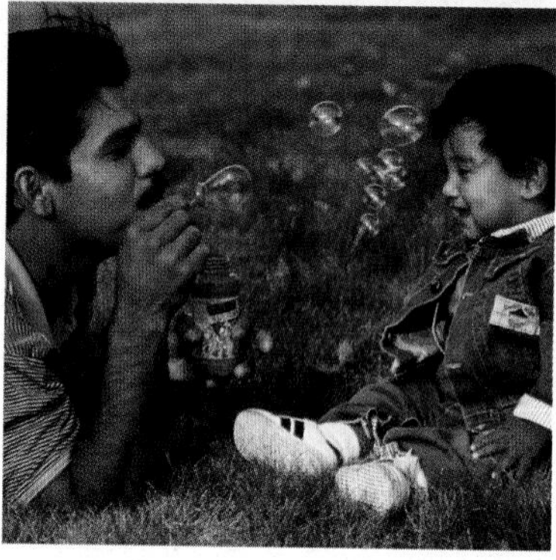

16.3 WAGES AND EMPLOYMENT

For most of us, the labor market is our only source of income. We work and earn a wage. What determines the amount of labor that we supply?

The Supply of Labor

People supply labor to earn an income. Many factors influence the quantity of labor that a person plans to provide, but a key factor is the wage rate.

To see how the wage rate influences the quantity of labor supplied, think about Larry's labor supply decision, which Figure 16.3 illustrates. Larry enjoys his leisure time, and he would be pleased if he didn't have to spend his evenings and weekends working at Max's Wash 'n' Wax. But Max pays him $10.50 an hour, and at that wage rate, Larry chooses to work 30 hours a week. The reason is that he is offered a wage rate that is high enough to make him regard this use of his time as the best available to him. If he were offered a lower wage rate, Larry would not be willing to give up so much leisure. If he were offered a higher wage rate, Larry would want to work even longer hours, but only up to a point. Offer Larry $25 an hour, and he would be willing to work a 40-hour week (and earn $1,000). With the goods and services that Larry can buy for $1,000, his priority would be a bit more leisure time if the wage rate increased further. If the wage rate increased above $25 an hour, Larry would cut back on his work hours and take more leisure. Larry's labor supply curve eventually bends backward.

FIGURE 16.3
An Individual's Labor Supply Curve

*e*Foundations 16.3 

❶ At a wage rate of $10.50 an hour, ❷ Larry is willing to supply 30 hours a week of labor. ❸ Larry's quantity of labor supplied ❹ increases as the wage rate increases up to ❺ a maximum, and then ❻ further increases in the wage rate bring a decrease in the quantity of labor supplied. Larry's labor supply curve eventually bends backward.

	Wage rate (dollars per hour)	Quantity of labor (hours per week)
A	40.00	30
B	35.00	35
C	30.00	38
D	25.00	40
E	20.00	38
F	15.00	35
G	10.50	30
H	5.00	0

Market Supply Curve

Larry's supply curve shows the quantity of labor supplied by one person as that person's wage rate changes. Most people behave like Larry. But different people have different wage rates at which they are willing to work and at which their labor supply curve bends backward. A market supply curve shows the quantity of labor supplied by all households in a particular job. It is found by adding together the quantities supplied by all households at each wage rate. Also, along a market supply curve, the wage rates available in other jobs remain the same. So, for example, along the supply curve of car wash workers, we hold constant the wage rates of car salespersons, mechanics, and all other types of labor.

Offer Larry more for car washing than for oil changing, and he will supply more of his labor to car washing. So the market supply curve in a given job slopes upward like the one in Figure 16.4, which shows the market supply curve for car wash workers in a large city.

Influences on the Supply of Labor

The supply of labor changes when influences other than the wage rate change. The key factors that change the supply of labor are:

- Adult population
- Preferences
- Time in school and training

FIGURE 16.4
The Supply of Car Wash Workers

*e*Foundations 16.3 

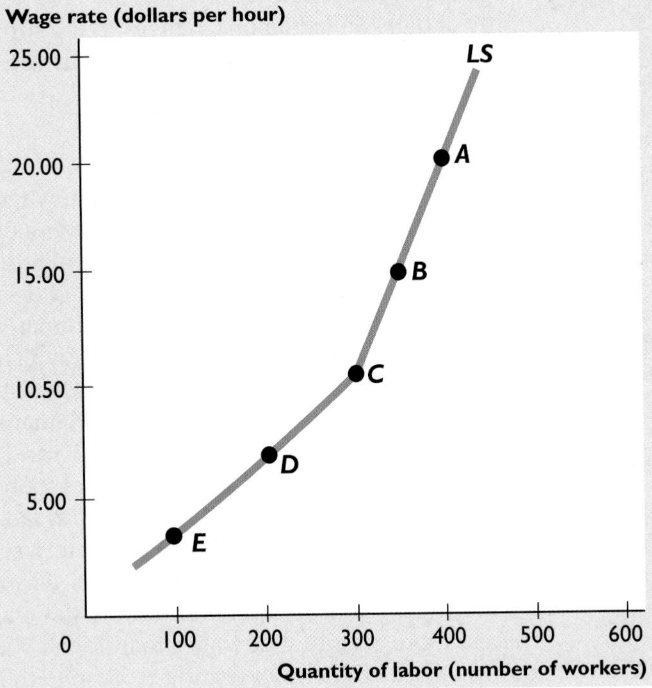

	Wage rate (dollars per hour)	Quantity of labor (workers)
A	20.00	400
B	15.00	350
C	10.50	300
D	7.00	200
E	3.50	100

The supply curve of car wash workers shows how the quantity supplied changes when the wage rate changes, other things remaining the same. In a market for a specific type of labor, the quantity supplied increases as the wage rate increases, other things remaining the same.

Adult Population

An increase in the adult population increases the supply of labor. Such an increase might occur because the birth rate exceeds the death rate. Or it might occur because of migration. Historically, the population of the United States has been strongly influenced by migration.

Preferences

In 1960, less than 40 percent of women had jobs. In 2000, 60 percent of women had jobs and the percentage was still rising. Many factors contributed to this change, which economists classify as a change in preferences. The result has been a large increase in the supply of female labor. At the same time, the percentage of men with jobs has shrunk slightly, from 83 percent in 1960 to 75 percent in 2000.

Time in School and Training

The more people who remain in school for full-time education and training, the smaller is the supply of low-skilled labor. Today in the United States, almost everyone completes high school and more than 50 percent of high-school graduates enroll in college or university (see Chapter 2, p. 41). Although many students work part time, the supply of labor by students is less than it would be if they were full-time workers. So when more people pursue higher education, other things remaining the same, the supply of low-skilled labor decreases. But time spent in school and training converts low-skilled labor into high-skilled labor. So the greater the proportion of people who receive a higher education, the greater is the supply of high-skilled labor.

When the amount of work that people want to do at a given wage rate changes, the supply of labor changes. So an increase in the adult population or an increase in the percentage of women with jobs increases the supply of labor. An increase in college enrollment decreases the supply of low-skilled labor. Later, it increases the supply of high-skilled labor. Changes in the supply of labor shift the supply curve, just like the shifts of the supply curves that you studied in Chapter 4 (p. 91).

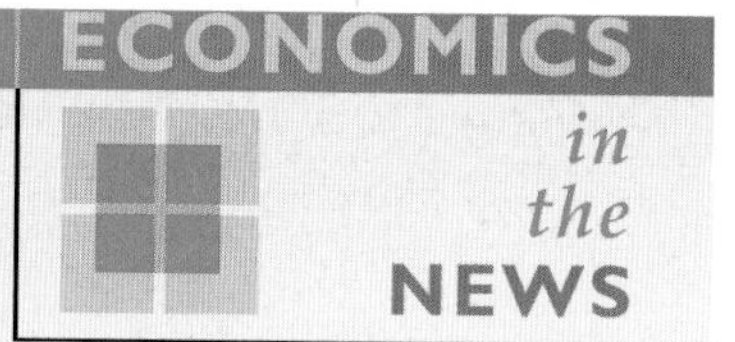

October 22, 1999

Expanding Nanny Industry

The nanny industry is expanding rapidly, and to help people comply with IRS rules on household employment, the provision of household payroll services is also expanding. Becky Kavanagh, president of the International Nanny Association, is reported to have said, "In the last five years, demand has been so great that there is actually a nanny shortage."

Questions

1. Why is the nanny industry expanding? Is the source of the expansion an increase in demand, an increase in supply, or an increase in both demand and supply?

2. Do you predict that the nanny's wage rate has increased, decreased, or not changed? Explain.

3. What do you think Becky Kavanagh means? Draw a demand-supply diagram to illustrate this statement. Do you think Becky is correct? Why or why not?

4. Why is the provision of household payroll services expanding?

5. What do you predict will happen in the nanny industry and the household payroll services over the next few years?

 *e*/**Foundations 16.3**

Labor Market Equilibrium

Labor market equilibrium determines the wage rate and employment. In Figure 16.5, the market demand curve for car wash workers, is *LD*. Here, if the wage rate is $10.50 an hour, the quantity of labor demanded is 300 workers. If the wage rate rises to $14 an hour, the quantity demanded decreases to 200. And if the wage rate falls to $9 an hour, the quantity demanded increases to 350. Figure 16.5 also shows the supply curve of car wash workers, *LS*, which is the same as that in Figure 16.4.

Figure 16.5 also shows equilibrium in the labor market. The equilibrium wage rate is $10.50 an hour, and the equilibrium quantity is 300 car wash workers. If the wage rate exceeded $10.50 an hour, there would be a surplus of car wash workers. More people would be looking for car wash jobs than firms were willing to hire.

In such a situation, the wage rate would fall as firms found it easy to hire people at a lower wage rate. If the wage rate were less than $10.50 an hour, there would be a shortage of car wash workers. Firms would not be able to fill all the jobs they had available. In this situation, the wage rate would rise as firms found it necessary to offer higher wages to attract labor. Only at a wage rate of $10.50 an hour are there no forces operating to change the wage rate.

Reallocating Labor

Technological change destroys some jobs and creates others. But it creates more jobs than it destroys, and *on the average,* the new jobs pay more than the old ones did. But to benefit from technological change, people must acquire new skills and change their jobs. During the 1990s, the number of jobs in coal mining, steel making, and many manufacturing industries declined. But the number of jobs in services industries, especially in computer and data services, expanded. Changes in demand and supply in these labor markets brought about these changes in employment along with associated changes in equilibrium wage rates.

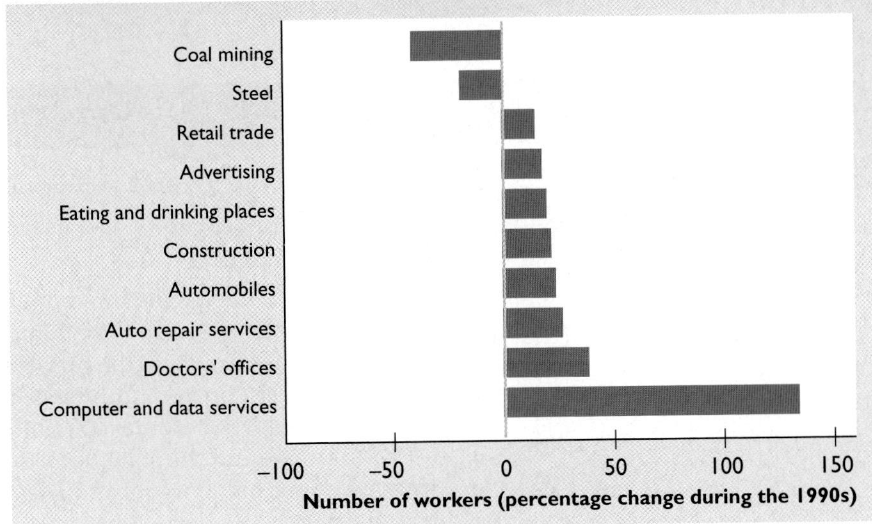

SOURCE: *Statistical Abstract of the United States,* 2000.

FIGURE 16.5
Labor Market Equilibrium

e/Foundations **16.3** 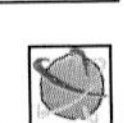

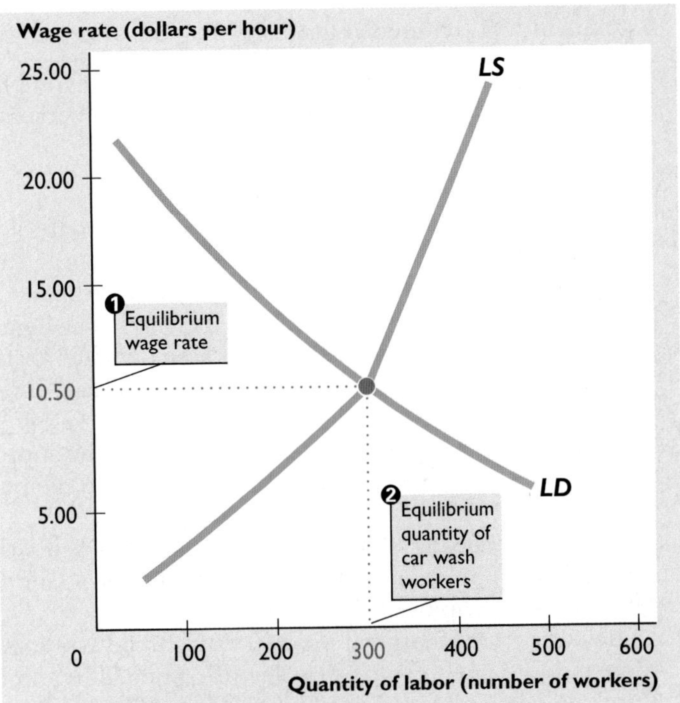

The labor market coordinates firms' demand for labor and households' supply of labor plans by changing the wage rate. The market is in equilibrium—the quantity of labor demanded equals the quantity supplied. ❶ The equilibrium wage rate is $10.50 an hour and ❷ the equilibrium quantity of labor is 300 workers.

If the wage rate exceeds $10.50 an hour, the quantity supplied exceeds the quantity demanded and the wage rate falls. If the wage rate is below $10.50 an hour, the quantity demanded exceeds the quantity supplied and the wage rate rises.

CHECKPOINT 16.3

Study Guide pp. 253–255 

e/Foundations 16.3

3 **Explain how wage rates and employment are determined.**

Practice Problem 16.3

Fast-food outlets in Greenville hire both teenagers and retirees. In Greenville, the following events occur one at a time and other things remain the same. Explain the influence of each event on the market for fast-food workers.

a. A new theme park opens and hires teenagers to sell tickets for its rides.
b. The new theme park becomes the hottest tourist attraction in the state.
c. Retirees from around the state flock to Greenville and make it their home.
d. The demand for hamburgers and fries decreases and as a result the price of a hamburger and fries decreases.
e. New technology in the fast-food industry decreases the marginal product of fast-food workers.

Exercises 16.3

1. Lifeguards are skilled workers who patrol beaches and swimming pools around the nation. Consider the market for lifeguards on the beaches of Southern California and explain how that market would change if:
   a. Beach holidays became less popular.
   b. New swimming equipment made it impossible for anyone to drown.
2. What effect do you think the predicted increase in Internet sales this year will have on the market for sales clerks?
3. More and more people use the Internet. What are three types of labor for which the demand will continue to increase and three types for which the demand will continue to decrease? Explain your answer.
4. As more people go to college, what changes do you predict will occur in the markets for college graduates and low-skilled workers?

FIGURE 1

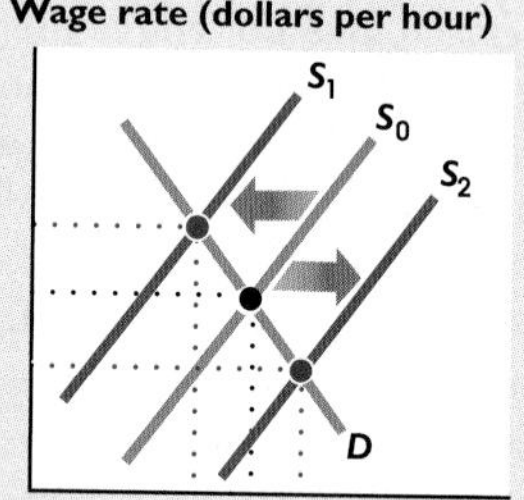

FIGURE 2

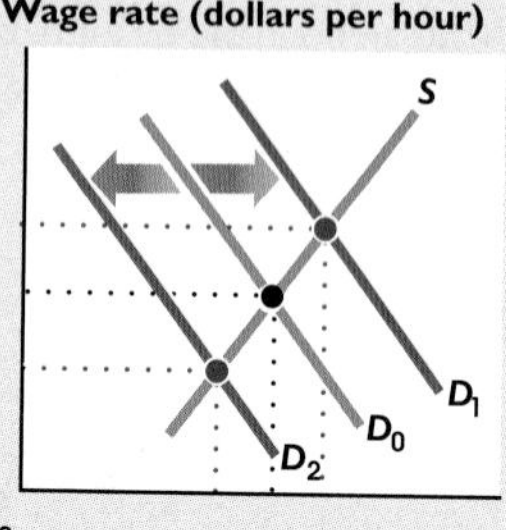

Solution to Practice Problem 16.3

a. Some teenagers prefer to work as ticket sellers, so the supply of labor in the fast-food market decreases from S_0 to S_1, in Figure 1. The wage rate rises, and the number of fast-food workers employed decreases.
b. The number of visitors to Greenville increases. The demand for fast food increases from D_0 to D_1 in Figure 2, so the demand for fast-food workers increases. The wage rate increases, and the number of fast-food workers employed increases.
c. An increase in the number of retirees increases the supply of fast-food labor from S_0 to S_2 in Figure 1. The wage rate falls, and the number of fast-food workers employed increases.
d. A decrease in the price of fast food decreases the demand for fast-food workers from D_0 to D_2 in Figure 2. The wage rate decreases, and the number of fast-food workers employed decreases.
e. A decrease in the marginal product of fast-food workers decreases the demand for fast-food workers. The wage rate falls, and the number of fast-food workers employed decreases (Figure 2).

16.4 FINANCIAL MARKETS

Financial markets are the channels through which firms borrow financial resources to buy capital. These financial resources come from saving. The price of financial capital, which adjusts to make the quantity of capital supplied equal to the quantity demanded, is the interest rate.

For most of us, financial markets are where we make our biggest-ticket transactions. We borrow in a financial market to buy a home. And we lend in financial markets to build up a fund on which to live when we retire.

Let's look at demand and supply in financial markets.

The Demand for Financial Capital

A firm's demand for *financial* capital stems from its demand for *physical* capital to produce goods and services. And the quantity of *physical* capital that a firm plans to use depends on the price of *financial* capital—the interest rate.

Other things remaining the same, the higher the interest rate, the smaller is the quantity of capital demanded. The quantity of capital demanded decreases if the interest rate rises, other things remaining the same, because the marginal product of capital diminishes as the quantity of capital employed by a firm increases.

For example, suppose that the interest rate is 4 percent a year and Amazon.com is planning to build a $100 million warehouse. The cost of this capital is 4 percent of $100 million, or $4 million a year. Amazon reckons that the value of the marginal product of this warehouse is enough to earn the $4 million a year that the capital will cost. Now suppose that the interest rate rises to 6 percent a year while all other prices remain constant. If Amazon goes ahead with its plan, it will now incur a cost of $6 million a year. In this situation, Amazon now scales back its warehouse plans and borrows less.

Two main factors that change the demand for capital are:

- Population growth
- Technological change

As the population grows, the demand for all goods and services increases, so the demand for the physical capital that produces them increases. Advances in technology increase the demand for some types of physical capital and decrease the demand for other types. For example, the development of desktop computers increased the demand for office computing equipment, decreased the demand for electric typewriters, and increased the overall demand for capital in the office. So the demand for financial capital increased.

The Supply of Financial Capital

The quantity of financial capital supplied results from people's saving decisions. Other things remaining the same, the higher the interest rate, the greater is the quantity of saving supplied.

A dollar saved today grows into a dollar plus interest tomorrow. The higher the interest rate, the greater is the amount that a dollar saved today becomes in the future. Other things remaining the same, if the interest rate rises, the opportunity cost of current consumption increases, so people cut their consumption and increase their saving.

The supply of saving changes if the amount that people want to save at a given interest rate changes. The main influences on the supply of saving are:

- Population
- Average income
- Expected future income

An increase in the population increases the supply of saving because it increases the number of potential savers.

Saving converts *current* income into *future* consumption potential. For example, saving can pay for a child's future college education or for consumption during retirement. The higher a household's income, the more it consumes both now and in the future. But to increase *future* consumption, the household must save. So other things remaining the same, the higher a household's income, the more it saves. Most households save a roughly constant proportion of their income. So as income increases, the supply of capital also increases.

Over their lives, most people try to achieve a level of consumption that fluctuates less than their income—that is, they try to smooth out the effects of income fluctuations on consumption. So the amount that a household saves depends not only on its current income but also on its *expected future income*. If a household's current income is high and its expected future income is low, it will have a high level of saving. But if its current income is low and its expected future income is high, it will have a low (perhaps even negative) level of saving.

Interest Rate Fluctuations

The figure shows the *real interest rate*—which is the interest rate that people *really* earn and pay after adjusting for the fact that inflation lowers the value of money—earned in the stock market and the bond market in the United States since 1960.

Interest rates fluctuate a lot because the demand for capital fluctuates much more than does the supply of capital. When rapid technological change brings an increase in the demand for capital, the real interest rate rises, as it did during the 1990s.

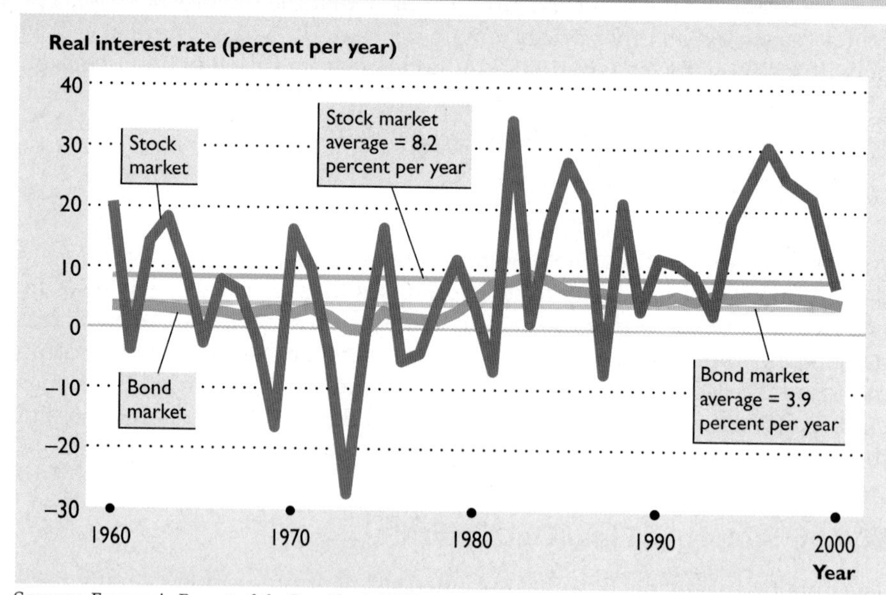

SOURCE: *Economic Report of the President*, 2000.

When the demand for capital grows slowly or decreases temporarily, the real interest rate falls, as it did in 1975.

The stock market is more volatile than the bond market, but it has a higher average real interest rate.

Young people (especially students) usually have low current incomes compared with their expected future income. They often consume more than they earn and go into debt. In middle age, most people's incomes reach a peak. At this stage in life, their current income is large and their expected future income is small because they anticipate stopping full-time work during their sixties. At this stage of life, saving is at a maximum. After retirement, people spend part of the wealth they have accumulated during their working lives, so saving falls again.

Financial Market Equilibrium and the Interest Rate

Figure 16.6 illustrates financial market equilibrium. The demand curve, *KD*, shows the relationship between the total quantity of financial capital demanded and the interest rate, other things remaining the same. And the supply curve, *KS*, shows the relationship between the quantity of financial capital supplied and the interest rate, other things remaining the same. Here, the equilibrium interest rate is 6 percent a year, and the quantity of capital is $200 billion.

Over time, the demand for capital and the supply of capital increase and the demand curve and the supply curve shift rightward. Population growth increases the demand for capital. And as the increased population earns a larger income, the supply of capital increases. Technological advances increase the demand for capital and bring higher incomes, which in turn increase the supply of capital. Because both the demand for capital and the supply of capital increase over time, the quantity of capital increases but the interest rate does not persistently increase or decrease (see the Eye On The U.S. Economy).

FIGURE 16.6
Financial Market Equilibrium

*e*Foundations 16.4

Interest rate (percent per year)

KS

KD

❶ Equilibrium interest rate

❷ Equilibrium quantity of financial capital

Financial capital (billions of dollars)

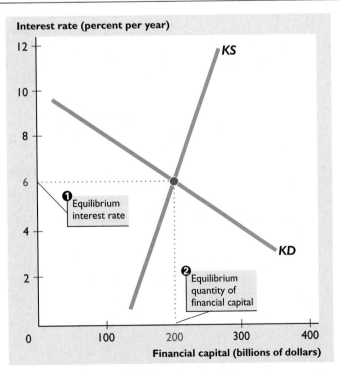

The demand for financial capital is *KD*, and the supply of financial capital is *KS*. Market equilibrium occurs at an interest rate of 6 percent a year with a quantity of financial capital of $200 billion.

CHECKPOINT 16.4

Study Guide pp. 255–257

eFoundations 16.4

4 **Explain how interest rates, borrowing, and lending are determined.**

Practice Problem 16.4

Wendy plans to open a Starbucks coffee shop. To do so, she will need \$50,000 to buy the franchise and \$20,000 to outfit the coffee shop. Wendy has \$15,000 in her bank account, and the current interest rate is 5 percent a year.

a. What is Wendy's opportunity cost of opening the coffee shop?

b. What is the quantity of financial capital that Wendy plans to get from the financial market?

c. What is the quantity of financial capital that Wendy plans to provide herself?

d. If demand for financial capital increases just when Wendy plans to go to the financial market, what will happen to her opportunity cost of the coffee shop? Explain your answer.

e. If the supply of financial capital increases just when Wendy plans to go to the financial market, what will happen to her opportunity cost of the coffee shop? Explain your answer.

Exercise 16.4

Lou plans to start a fish farm. To do so, he will need to buy capital goods that cost \$100,000. He will also need to hire some workers to help run the fish farm. The wage rate for fish farm workers is currently \$8 an hour, and he will need to hire 100 hours of labor per week. The interest rate is 3 percent a year. Lou has no savings.

a. What is the cost of the capital in Lou's fish farm?

b. Lou predicts that in the first 50 weeks, he will harvest no fish. How much financial capital is Lou planning to get from the financial market?

c. An exciting new technology now becomes available that allows Lou to replace the workers. The new technology costs \$10,000. How much financial capital will Lou now need to get from the financial market?

Solution to Practice Problem 16.4

a. Wendy's opportunity cost is 5 percent of the cost of the coffee shop, which is 5 percent of \$70,000 or \$3,500 a year.

b. Wendy needs \$70,000 but has \$15,000, so the quantity for financial capital that she requires is \$55,000 (\$70,000 minus \$15,000).

c. Wendy plans to provide \$15,000 herself.

d. An increase in the demand for capital will increase the interest rate. The interest rate that Wendy has to pay will exceed 5 percent a year and increase the opportunity cost of her coffee shop.

e. An increase in the supply of capital will decrease the interest rate. Wendy will pay less than 5 percent a year for her financial capital and decrease the opportunity cost of her coffee shop.

16.5 LAND AND NATURAL RESOURCE MARKETS

All natural resources are called *land*, and they fall into two categories:

- Renewable
- Nonrenewable

Renewable natural resources are natural resources that can be used repeatedly such as forestland—land in its everyday sense. **Nonrenewable natural resources** are resources that can be used only once and that cannot be replaced once they have been used. Examples are coal, natural gas, and oil—called hydrocarbon fuels.

Let's look first at the market for a renewable natural resource.

Renewable natural resources
Natural resources that can be used repeatedly.

Nonrenewable natural resources
Natural resources that can be used only once and that cannot be replaced once they have been used.

The Market for Land (Renewable Natural Resources)

The demand for land is based on the same factors as the demand for labor and the demand for capital. The lower the rent, other things remaining the same, the greater is the quantity of land demanded.

But the supply of land is special. The quantity of land is fixed, so the quantity supplied cannot be changed by people's decisions. People can vary the amount of land they own. But when one person buys some land, another person sells it. The aggregate quantity of land supplied of any particular type and in any particular location is fixed, regardless of the decisions of any individual. This fact means that the supply of each particular block of land is *perfectly inelastic*. Figure 16.7 illustrates the supply of a 10-acre block on Chicago's "Magnificent Mile." The quantity supplied is fixed at 10 acres regardless of the rent.

FIGURE 16.7
A Market for Land

Rent (dollars per acre per day)
2,000
S
1,000
Equilibrium rent
D
0
10
20
Land (acres)

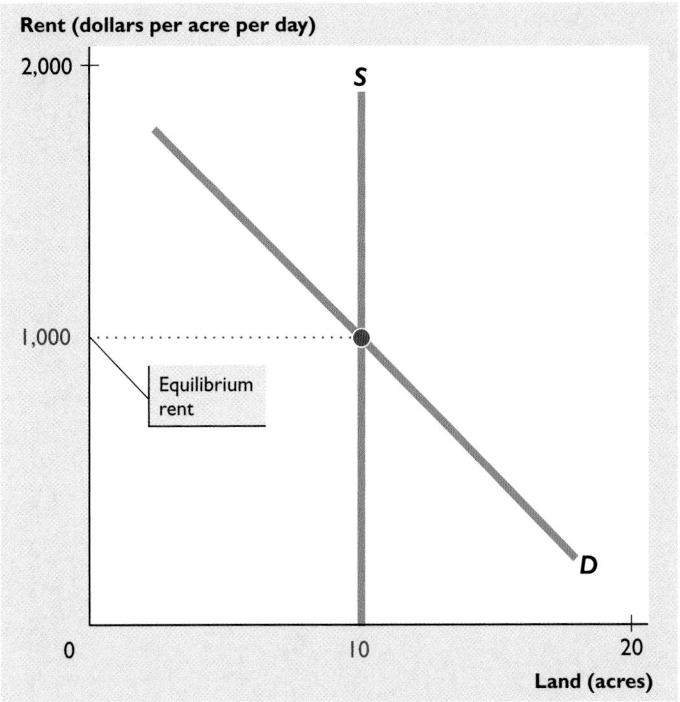

The demand curve for a 10-acre block of land is *D*, and the supply curve is *S*. Equilibrium occurs at a rent of $1,000 an acre per day.

Because the quantity of land supplied is fixed, the rent is determined by demand. In Figure 16.7, the demand curve is *D* and the equilibrium price (rent) is $1,000 per acre per day. The greater the demand, the higher is the rent.

Economic Rent and Opportunity Cost

Rent is a special kind of income because the resource that receives a rent would be available even if the rent were zero. Low demand would make the rent low, and high demand would make the rent high. But the quantity of land wouldn't change.

Land is not the only resource that is in fixed supply. Some human resources are too. There is only one Tiger Woods. This extraordinary golfer earns a large income because he has a high value of marginal product. A large part of Tiger Woods's income is called "economic rent." **Economic rent** is the income received by *any* factor of production over and above the amount required to induce a given quantity of the factor to be supplied. The income that is required to induce the supply of a given quantity of a factor of production is its *opportunity cost*—the value of the factor of production in its next best use.

Economic rent
The income received by *any* factor of production over and above the amount required to induce a given quantity of the factor to be supplied.

Figure 16.8 illustrates the economic rent and opportunity cost components of a factor's income. Suppose that the demand curve for Tiger's time were *D* and his supply curve were *S*. The wage rate would be $50,000 an hour, and Tiger would work 40 hours a week. His income is the sum of the red and green areas. The red area below the supply curve measures opportunity cost, and the green area above the supply curve but below the resource price measures economic rent.

FIGURE 16.8
Economic Rent and Opportunity Cost

*e*Foundations **16.5** 

Part of the income of a factor of production is ❶ opportunity cost (the red area), and part is ❷ economic rent (the green area). The figure shows the market for Tiger Woods's labor. At $50,000 an hour, Tiger is willing to work 40 hours a week. Tiger earns a large economic rent.

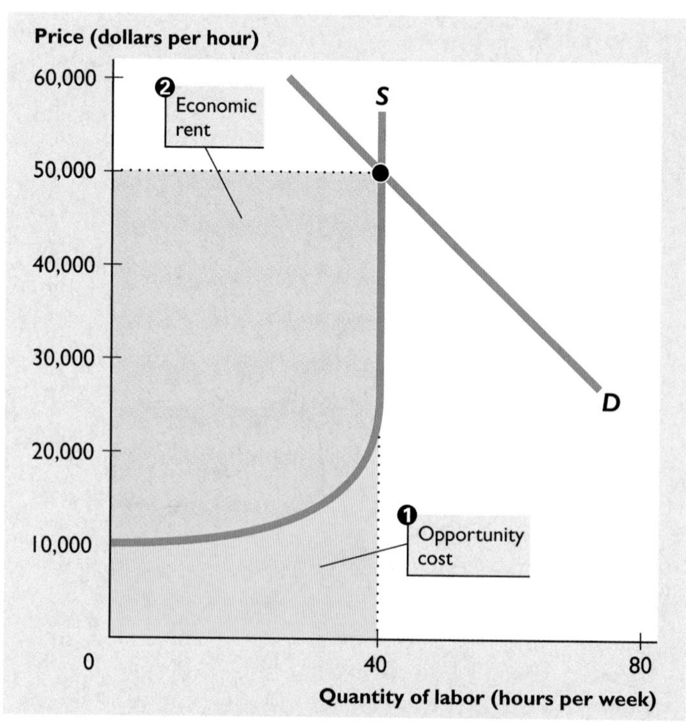

The Supply of a Nonrenewable Natural Resource

At a given time, the quantity of any natural resource is fixed and is independent of its price. Over time, the quantity of a nonrenewable natural resource decreases as it is used up. But the *known* quantity of a natural resource increases because advances in technology enable ever less accessible sources of the resource to be discovered.

Using a natural resource decreases its supply, which causes its price to rise. But new technologies that lead to the discovery of previously unknown reserves increase supply, which causes the price to fall. Also, new technologies that enable a more efficient use of a nonrenewable natural resource decrease demand, which causes the price to fall.

Over recent years, the forces that bring lower prices have outweighed those that bring higher prices and natural resource prices have fallen—see the Eye On The Global Economy.

You've now seen how competitive factor markets work. In the next chapter, we look more closely at the labor market and the reasons for earnings differences.

Natural Resources Prices

Thomas Robert Malthus (1766–1834), an English clergyman and economist, predicted in his best-selling *Essay on the Principle of Population*, published in 1798, that population growth would outstrip food production. Modern-day Malthusians such as ecologist Paul Ehrlich believe that Malthus is correct.

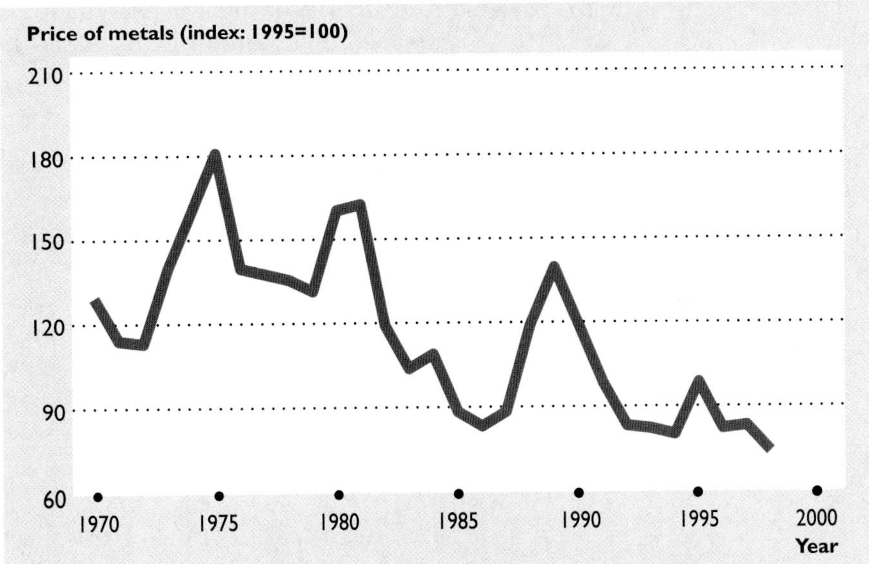

SOURCE: International Financial Statistics.

Julian Simon (who died in 1998) challenged the Malthusian gloom. He believed that a bigger population permits more people to work out better ways of using scarce resources, so the prices of exhaustible resources will fall. To demonstrate his point, in 1980, Simon bet Ehrlich that the prices of five metals—copper, chrome, nickel, tin, and tungsten—would fall during the 1980s. As the figure shows, Simon won the bet!

CHECKPOINT 16.5

Study Guide pp. 257–259

*e*Foundations 16.5

5 **Explain how rents and natural resource prices are determined.**

Practice Problem 16.5

Which of the following items are nonrenewable natural resources, which are renewable natural resources, and which are not natural resources? Explain your answers.

a. Beaches in Florida
b. Lake Powell
c. The Empire State Building
d. Silver mines in Arizona
e. The Great Lakes
f. National parks
g. Redwood forests
h. The Statue of Liberty

Exercises 16.5

1. New technology has allowed oil to be pumped from much deeper offshore oil fields than before. For example, the Hibernia project off Newfoundland in Canada has started production. What effect do you think the Hibernia project has had on the world oil price? Who will benefit from the Hibernia project? Explain your answer.
2. Water is a natural resource that is plentiful in Canada but not plentiful in Arizona and southern California. If Canadians start to export bulk water to Arizona and southern California, what do you predict will be the effect on the price of bulk water? Will Canada eventually run out of water?
3. In the 1970s, few people drank bottled spring water and the major producers of bottled spring water were in Europe. Today, lots of people drink bottled spring water. How has this increase in the demand for spring water been satisfied? Will this increase in demand lead to some springs running dry?
4. As cities grow, good farmland is gradually replaced with urban sprawl. Why do farmers sell their land to urban developers?

Solution to Practice Problem 16.5

Natural resources include all the gifts of nature. A nonrenewable natural resource is one that once used cannot be used again. A renewable natural resource is one that can be used repeatedly.

Nonrenewable natural resources include: silver mines in Arizona.

Renewable natural resources include: beaches in Florida, Lake Powell, the Great Lakes, national parks, and redwood forests.

The Empire State Building and the Statue of Liberty are national landmarks, but they are not natural resources. Labor and capital were used to build the Empire State Building. The Statue of Liberty was a gift from France and not a gift of nature.

CHAPTER CHECKPOINT

Key Points

1 Describe the anatomy of the markets for labor, capital, and land.

- Labor is traded on job contracts.
- Financial markets provide the funds that are used to buy physical capital.
- Natural resources are traded in land markets and commodity markets.

2 Explain how the value of marginal product determines the demand for a factor of production.

- The demand for a factor of production is a derived demand—it is derived from the demand for the goods and services that it is used to produce.
- The quantity of a factor of production that is demanded depends on its price and the value of its marginal product, which equals the price of the product multiplied by marginal product.

3 Explain how wage rates and employment are determined.

- Wage rates are determined by demand and supply in labor markets.
- Changes in technology bring changes in the allocation of labor.

4 Explain how interest rates, borrowing, and lending are determined.

- Interest rates are determined by demand and supply in financial markets.
- Real interest rates on stocks are higher on the average but fluctuate by more than those on bonds.

5 Explain how rents and natural resource prices are determined.

- Rents and natural resource prices are determined by demand and supply in land and commodity markets.
- Rents increase over time because the quantity of land is fixed.
- Nonrenewable natural resource prices have fallen because technological change has led to the discovery of new sources and made the use of natural resources more productive.

Key Terms

Bond, 385
Bond market, 385
Commodity market, 386
Derived demand, 387
Economic rent, 402
Factor price, 384
Financial capital, 385
Financial market, 385
Job, 384
Labor market, 384
Nonrenewable natural resources, 401
Renewable natural resources, 401
Stock market, 385
Value of marginal product, 387

Exercises

1. Through the 1990s, a larger percentage of high school students decided to go to college. What changes do you predict resulted from this increase in:
   a. The market for college graduates? Draw a demand-supply diagram to illustrate your answer.
   b. The market for college professors? Explain your answer.
   c. The market for high school graduates? Draw a demand-supply diagram to illustrate your answer.

2. If your college switched to online delivery of its courses, what changes do you predict would occur in the factor markets in the town where your college is located?

3. Suppose that Palm Island is the world's largest grower of coconuts and that the interest rate on Palm Island is 3 percent a year. The following events occur, one at a time. Explain the influence of each event on Palm Island's financial market and land market.
   a. Palm Island plans to build a $100 million airport on 100 acres—its first airport.
   b. Palm Island plans to double its population in 3 years by hiring well-educated people from the United States.
   c. The world price of coconuts is expected to increase by 200 percent next year and remain high for the next decade.
   d. Palm Island is short of entrepreneurs and plans to allow anyone with $1 million to immigrate to Palm Island.

4. Use the laws of demand and supply in factor markets to explain whether the following statements are true or false:
   a. New technology enables tomato growers to pick and pack tomatoes by machine. Tomato growers will now hire fewer workers and will be able to hire these workers at a lower wage rate than before.
   b. If soccer becomes more popular in the United States and basketball becomes less popular, basketball players will earn more than they do today.
   c. A recent new discovery of diamonds in the Yukon in Canada will lower the world price of diamonds and lower the wage rate paid to diamond workers in South Africa.
   d. As cars become more and more fuel efficient, the price of gasoline at the pump will fall.

5. Hong Kong is a much more densely populated country than the United States. How do you think the rent on land in Hong Kong compares with that in Chicago? Can you explain why the percentage of commercial buildings in downtown Chicago that is new is less than the percentage in Hong Kong?

6. "As more people buy Internet service, the price of Internet service will decrease. The decrease in the price of Internet service will lead to a decrease in the wage rate paid to designers of Web pages." Is this statement true or false? Explain your answer.

Chapter 17

Earnings Differences

CHAPTER CHECKLIST

When you have completed your study of this chapter, you will be able to:

1 **Explain why college graduates earn more, on the average, than high school graduates.**

2 **Explain why union workers earn higher wage rates than nonunion workers.**

3 **Discuss reasons why men earn more than women and whites earn more than minorities and predict the effects of a comparable-worth program.**

As you well know, college is not just a party. Those exams and problem sets require a lot of time and effort. Are they worth the sweat that goes into them? Is the payoff sufficient to make up for the years of tuition, room and board, and lost wages?

Many workers belong to labor unions and earn a higher wage than nonunion workers in comparable jobs do. How are unions able to get higher wages for their members than the wages that nonunion workers are paid?

Among the most visible and persistent differences in earnings are those between men and women and between whites and minorities. Certainly, a lot of individuals defy the averages. But why do minorities and women so consistently earn less than white men? Is it because of discrimination? Can comparable-worth programs help women and minorities?

In this chapter, we answer questions such as these by continuing our study of labor markets.

17.1 SKILL DIFFERENTIALS

Everyone is skilled, but the value the market places on different types of skills varies a great deal. So differences in skills lead to large differences in earnings. For example, a clerk in a law firm earns less than a tenth of the earnings of the attorney he assists. An operating room assistant earns less than a tenth of the earnings of the surgeon she works with. Differences in skills arise partly from differences in education and partly from differences in on-the-job training. Differences in earnings between workers with varying levels of education and training can be explained by using a model of competitive labor markets. In the real world, there are many different levels and varieties of education and training. To keep our analysis as clear as possible, we'll study a model economy with two different skill levels and two types of labor: high-skilled labor and low-skilled labor. We'll study the demand for and supply of these two types of labor to see why their wage rates differ and what determines that difference. Let's begin by looking at the demand for the two types of labor.

The Demand for High-Skilled and Low-Skilled Labor

High-skilled workers can perform a variety of tasks that low-skilled workers would perform badly or perhaps could not perform at all. Imagine an untrained, inexperienced person performing surgery or piloting an airplane. High-skilled workers have a higher value of marginal product than low-skilled workers. As we learned in Chapter 16, a firm's demand for labor curve is the same as the value of the marginal product of labor curve.

Figure 17.1(a) shows the demand curves for high-skilled and low-skilled labor. At any given level of employment, firms are willing to pay a higher wage rate to a high-skilled worker than to a low-skilled worker. The gap between the two wage rates measures the value of the marginal product of skill. For example, at an employment level of 2,000 hours, firms are willing to pay a high-skilled worker $25 an hour and a low-skilled worker only $10 an hour, a difference of $15 an hour. Thus the value of the marginal product of skill is $15 an hour.

The Supply of High-Skilled and Low-Skilled Labor

Skills are costly to acquire, and a worker usually pays the cost of acquiring a skill before benefiting from a higher wage. For example, attending college usually leads to a higher income, but the higher income is not earned until after graduation. These facts imply that the acquisition of a skill is an investment. To emphasize the investment nature of acquiring a skill, we call that activity an investment in human capital. *Human capital* is the accumulated skill and knowledge of human beings.

The opportunity cost of acquiring a skill includes actual expenditures on such things as tuition and costs in the form of lost or reduced earnings while the skill is being acquired. When a person goes to school full time, that cost is the total earnings forgone. However, some people acquire skills on the job. Such skill acquisition is called on-the-job training. Usually, a worker undergoing on-the-job training is paid a lower wage than one who is doing a comparable job but not undergoing training. In such a case, the cost of acquiring the skill is equal to the wage paid to a person not being trained minus the wage paid to a person being trained.

FIGURE 17.1
Skill Differentials

*e*Foundations 17.1 

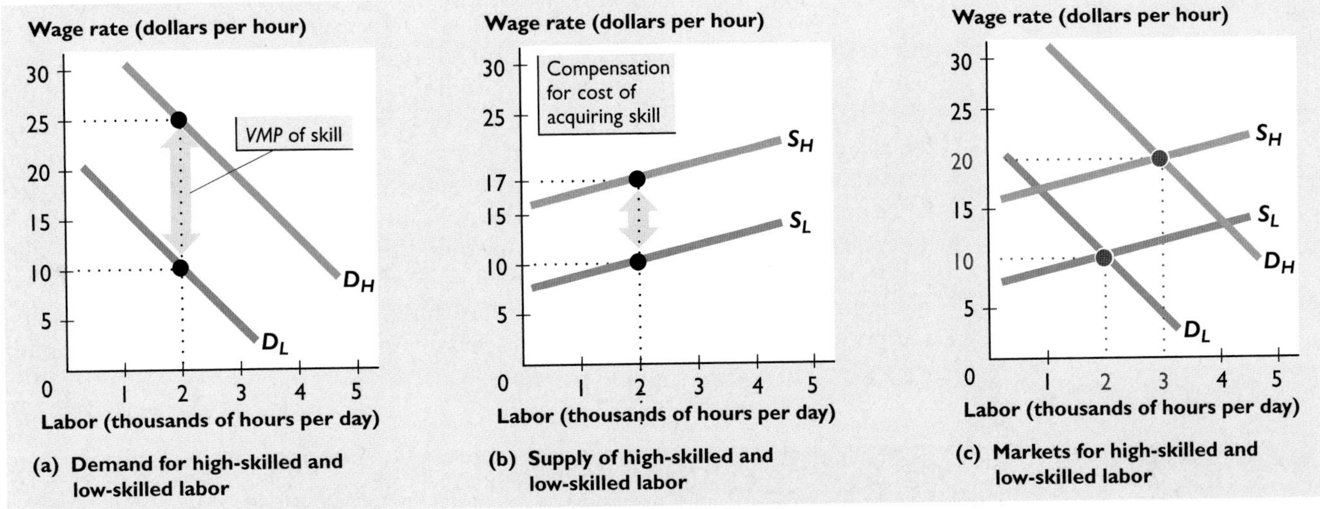

High-skilled labor has a higher *VMP* than low-skilled labor and a greater demand.

High-skilled labor bears the cost of acquiring skill.

The wage rate for high-skilled workers exceeds that for low-skilled workers.

The position of the supply curve of high-skilled workers reflects the cost of acquiring the skill. Figure 17.1(b) shows two supply curves: one for high-skilled workers and the other for low-skilled workers. The supply curve for high-skilled workers is S_H, and that for low-skilled workers is S_L.

The high-skilled worker's supply curve lies above the low-skilled worker's supply curve. The vertical distance between the two supply curves is the compensation that high-skilled workers require for the cost of acquiring the skill. For example, suppose that the quantity of low-skilled labor supplied is 2,000 hours at a wage rate of $10 an hour. This wage rate compensates the low-skilled workers mainly for their time on the job. Consider next the supply of high-skilled workers. To induce high-skilled labor to supply 2,000 hours, firms must pay a wage rate of $17 an hour. This wage rate for high-skilled labor is higher than that for low-skilled labor because high-skilled labor must be compensated not only for the time on the job but also for the time and other costs of acquiring the skill.

Wage Rates of High-Skilled and Low-Skilled Labor

To work out the wage rates of high-skilled and low-skilled labor, we have to bring together the effects of skill on the demand for and supply of labor.

Figure 17.1(c) shows the demand curves and the supply curves for high-skilled and low-skilled labor. These curves are exactly the same as those plotted in parts (a) and (b). Equilibrium occurs in the market for low-skilled labor where the supply and demand curves for low-skilled labor intersect. The equilibrium wage rate is $10 an hour, and the quantity of low-skilled labor employed is 2,000 hours. Equilibrium in the market for high-skilled workers occurs where the supply and demand curves for high-skilled workers intersect. The equilibrium wage rate is $20 an hour, and the quantity of high-skilled labor employed is 3,000 hours.

As you can see in part (c), the equilibrium wage rate of high-skilled labor is higher than that of low-skilled labor. There are two reasons why this occurs: First, high-skilled labor has a higher value of marginal product than low-skilled labor, so at a given wage rate, the quantity of high-skilled labor demanded exceeds that of low-skilled labor. Second, skills are costly to acquire, so at a given wage rate, the quantity of high-skilled labor supplied is less than that of low-skilled labor. The wage differential (in this case, $10 an hour) depends on both the value of the marginal product of the skill and the cost of acquiring it. The higher the value of the marginal product of the skill, the larger is the vertical distance between the demand curves. The more costly it is to acquire a skill, the larger is the vertical distance between the supply curves. The higher the value of the marginal product of the skill and the more costly it is to acquire, the larger is the wage differential between high-skilled and low-skilled workers.

Education is an important source of earnings differences. But there are others, and one of them is labor unions. Let's see how unions affect wages and why union wages tend to exceed nonunion wages.

Eye On The U.S. ECONOMY

Do Education and Training Pay?

The figure shows that there are large and persistent differences in earnings based on the degree of education and training. This figure also highlights the second main source of earnings differences: age. Age is strongly correlated with experience and the degree of on-the-job training a person has had. So as a person gets older, up to middle age, earnings increase.

Rates of return on high school and college education have been estimated to be in the range of 5 to 10 percent a year after allowing for inflation, which suggest that a college degree is a better investment than almost any other that a person can undertake.

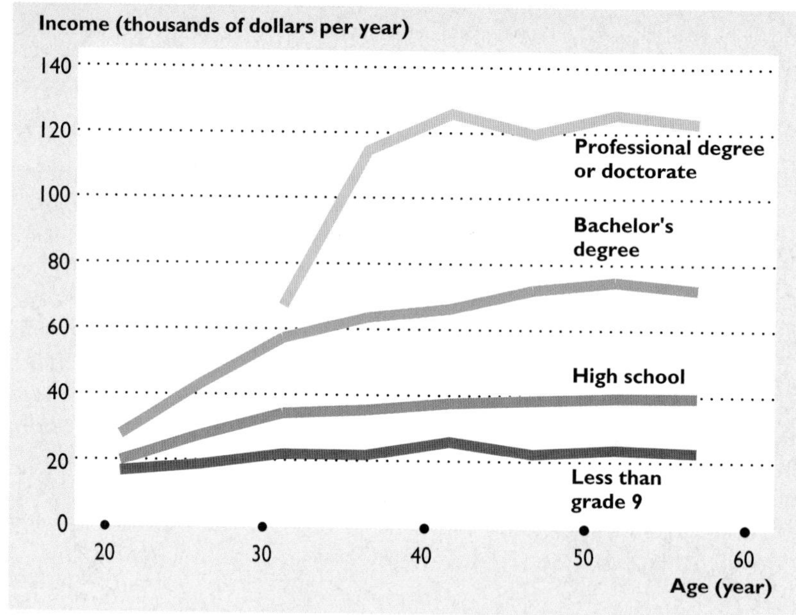

SOURCE: U.S. Bureau of the Census, *Money Income in the United States*, 1999.

Earnings of male employees at various ages and with varying school levels are shown. Earnings increase with length of education. For postgraduates, earnings peak in the mid-forties. For other groups, earnings peak in the mid-fifties. These differences show the importance of experience and education in influencing skill differentials.

CHECKPOINT 17.1

1 Explain why college graduates earn more, on the average, than high school graduates.

Study Guide pp. 264–267

eFoundations 17.1

Practice Problem 17.1

In the United States in 2000, 30 million people had full-time managerial and professional jobs that paid an average of $800 a week. At the same time, 10 million people had full-time sales positions that paid an average of $530 a week.

a. Explain why managers and professionals are paid more than salespeople.

b. Explain why, despite the higher weekly wage, more people are employed as managers and professionals than as salespeople.

c. If Internet shopping becomes very popular and the range of goods and services available on the Internet expands rapidly, what changes do you expect will occur in the market for salespeople?

Exercises 17.1

1. In the United States in 2000, 2 million people worked full-time in protective services and were paid an average of $600 a week. At the same time, 7 million people worked as full-time machine operators and were paid an average of $450 a week.
   a. Explain why people who are employed in protective services are paid more than machine operators.
   b. Explain why fewer people are employed in protective services than as machine operators.

2. In Canada and Australia, the manager of a manufacturing plant earns 20 times what the factory floor worker earns. In Hong Kong and Malaysia, such a manager earns 40 times what the factory floor worker earns. Can you explain this difference?

Solution to Practice Problem 17.1

The typical manager or professional has incurred a higher cost of education and on-the-job training than has the typical salesperson. The supply curve of managers and professionals, S_H, lies above that of salespeople, S_L (see Figure 1). The better education and more on-the-job training result in managers and professionals having more human capital and a higher value of marginal product than that of a salesperson, so the demand for managers and professional, D_H, is greater then the demand for salespeople, S_L.

a. and **b.** Demand for and supply of each type of workers determines the wage rate paid and the employment level. Figure 1 shows that the combination of demand and supply leads to a higher wage rate and to a greater employment level for managers and professional than for salespeople.

c. If people switch from shopping in person to shopping on the Internet, firms will requires fewer salespeople. The demand curve for salespeople will shift leftward, and fewer people will work in sales. What will happen to their weekly wage will depend on what happens to the supply of salespeople.

FIGURE 1

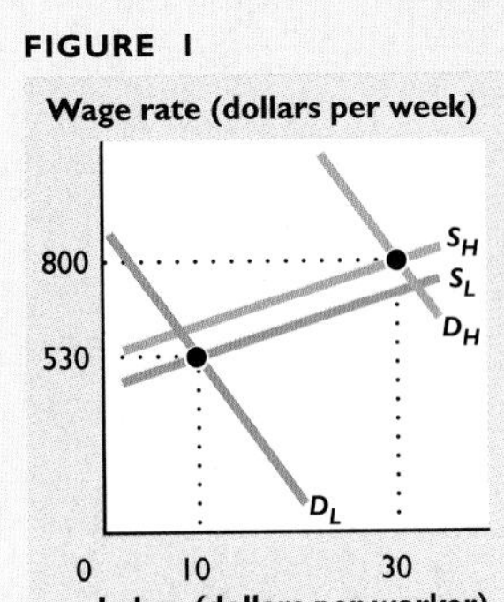

17.2 UNION-NONUNION WAGE DIFFERENTIALS

Labor union
An organized group of workers whose purpose is to increase wages and influence other job conditions for its members.

Craft union
A group of workers who have a similar range of skills but work for many different firms in many different industries and regions.

Industrial union
A group of workers who have a variety of skills and job types but work for the same firm or industry.

A **labor union** is an organized group of workers whose purpose is to increase the wage rate and influence other job conditions for its members. The union seeks to restrict competition and, as a result, increases the price at which labor is traded.

There are two main types of union: craft unions and industrial unions. A **craft union** is a group of workers who have a similar range of skills but who work for firms in many different industries and regions. Examples are the carpenters' union and the electrical workers union (IBEW). An **industrial union** is a group of workers who have a variety of skills and job types but who work for the same firm or industry. The United Auto Workers (UAW) and the United Steelworkers of America are examples of industrial unions.

Most unions are members of the AFL-CIO. The AFL-CIO was created in 1955 when two labor organizations combined: the American Federation of Labor (AFL), which was founded in 1886 to organize craft unions, and the Congress of Industrial Organizations (CIO), which was founded in 1938 to organize industrial unions. The AFL-CIO provides many services to member unions, such as training union organizers and acting as a national voice in the media and the political arena.

Union Membership

Unions vary enormously in size. Craft unions are the smallest, and industrial unions are the biggest. The figure shows the 12 largest unions in the United States, as measured by number of members. Union strength peaked in the 1950s, when 35 percent of the nonagricultural work force belonged to unions. That percentage has declined steadily since 1955 and is now only 12 percent. Changes in union membership, however, have been uneven. Some unions have declined dramatically, while others, especially those in the government sector, such as the State, County, and Municipal Employees union, have increased in strength.

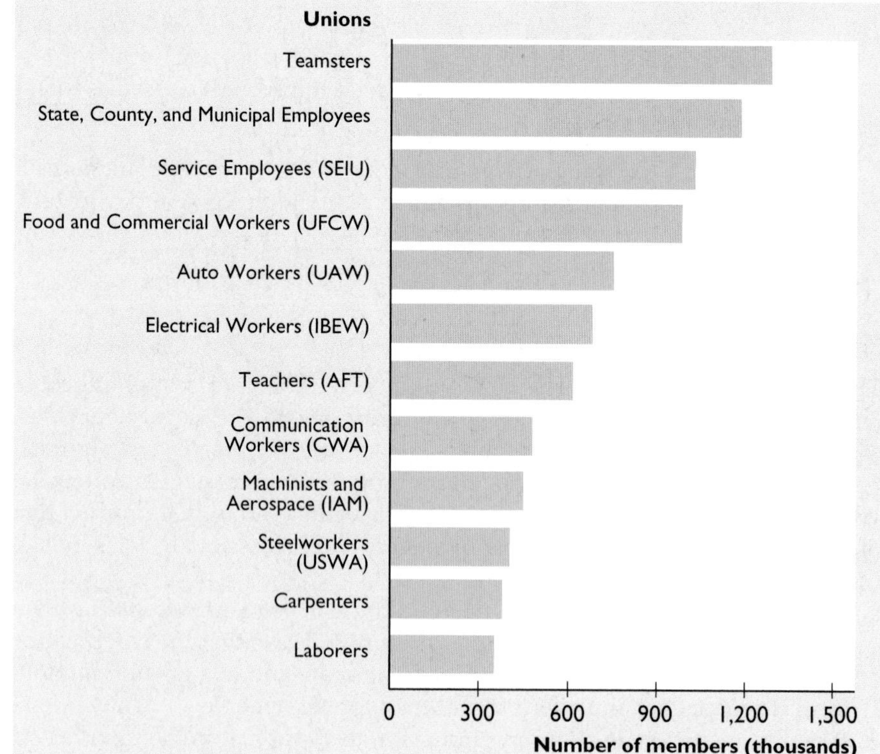

SOURCE: *Statistical Abstract of the United States.*

Union organization is based on a subdivision known as the local. The local is a subunit of a union that organizes individual workers. A local can take three possible forms of organization: an open shop, a closed shop, or a union shop. An open shop is an arrangement in which workers can be employed without joining the union—there is no union restriction on who can work in the "shop." A closed shop is an arrangement in which only union members can be employed by a firm. Closed shops have been illegal since the passage of the Taft-Hartley Act in 1947. A union shop is an arrangement in which a firm can hire nonunion workers but for such workers to remain employed, they must join the union within a brief period specified by the union. Union shops are illegal in the 20 states that have passed right-to-work laws. A right-to-work law allows an individual to work at any firm without joining a union.

Unions negotiate with employers or their representatives in a process called **collective bargaining**. The main weapons available to the union and the employer in collective bargaining are the strike and the lockout. A strike is a group decision to refuse to work under prevailing conditions. A lockout is a firm's refusal to operate its plant and employ its workers. Each party uses the threat of a strike or a lockout to try to get an agreement in its own favor. Sometimes, when the two parties in the collective bargaining process cannot agree on the wage rate or other conditions of employment, they agree to submit their disagreement to binding arbitration. Binding arbitration is a process in which a third party—an arbitrator—determines the wage rate and other employment conditions on behalf of the negotiating parties.

Collective bargaining
Union negotiations with employers or their representatives.

Although they are not labor unions in a legal sense, professional associations act in similar ways to labor unions. A professional association is an organized group of professional workers such as lawyers, dentists, or physicians (an example of which is the American Medical Association—AMA). Professional associations control entry into the professions and license practitioners, ensuring the adherence to minimum standards of competence. But they also influence the compensation and other labor market conditions of their members.

Union Objectives and Constraints

A union has three broad objectives that it strives to achieve for its members:

- To increase compensation
- To improve working conditions
- To expand job opportunities

Each of these objectives contains a series of more detailed goals. For example, in seeking to increase members' compensation, a union operates on a variety of fronts: wage rates, fringe benefits, retirement pay, and such things as vacation allowances. In seeking to improve working conditions, a union is concerned with occupational health and safety as well as the environmental quality of the workplace. In seeking to expand job opportunities, a union tries to get greater job security for existing union members and to find ways of creating additional jobs to increase its membership.

A union's ability to pursue its objectives is restricted by two sets of constraints—one on the supply side of the labor market and the other on the demand side. On the supply side, the union's activities are limited by how well it can restrict nonunion workers from supplying their labor in the same market as union labor. The larger the fraction of the work force controlled by the union, the more effective the union can be in this regard. It is difficult for unions to operate in markets where there is an abundant supply of willing nonunion labor. For example, the market for farm labor in southern California is very tough for a union to organize because of the ready flow of nonunion, often illegal, labor from Mexico. At the other extreme, unions in the construction industry can better pursue their goals because they can influence the number of people who can obtain skills as electricians, plasterers, and carpenters. The professional associations of dentists and physicians are best able to restrict the supply of dentists and physicians. These groups control the number of qualified workers by controlling either the examinations that new entrants must pass or entrance into professional degree programs.

On the demand side of the labor market, the union faces a tradeoff that arises from firms' profit-maximizing decisions. Because labor demand curves slope downward, anything a union does that increases the wage rate or other employment costs decreases the quantity of labor demanded.

Despite the difficulties they face, unions do operate in competitive labor markets. Let's see how they do so.

March 6, 2000

Wal-Mart Fights a Union

Wal-Mart Stores, Inc., is closing the meat department of a Texas store where meat workers recently held the chain's first successful vote to unionize.

Questions

1. How would you expect the wage rate of meat workers to change after they join a union?

2. Why might it be a rational decision on the part of Wal-Mart to close the meat preparation department in a store?

3. Would it have been a rational decision on the part of Wal-Mart to close the meat preparation department if the workers had not joined a union?

4. Is it efficient for the meat workers at Wal-Mart to join a union?

5. Should there be a law that prevents firms from doing what Wal-Mart has done?

 *e*Foundations **17.2**

Unions in a Competitive Labor Market

When a union operates in an otherwise competitive labor market, it seeks to increase wages and other compensation and to limit employment reductions by increasing the demand for the labor of its members. That is, the union tries to take actions that shift the demand curve for its members' labor rightward.

Figure 17.2 illustrates a competitive labor market that a union enters. The demand curve is D_C, and the supply curve is S_C. Before the union enters the market, the wage rate is \$10 an hour and 100 hours of labor a day are employed.

Now suppose that the workers in this market join to form a union. The union can attempt to increase the wage rate in this market in two ways. It can try to restrict the supply of labor, or it can try to stimulate the demand for labor.

Unions Change the Supply of Labor

Many unions control supply by organizing on-the-job training and limiting the number of workers who receive training. This action can restrict supply below its competitive level—to S_U. Employment decreases to 85 hours of labor, and the wage rate rises to \$12 an hour. The union picks its preferred position along the demand curve that defines the tradeoff it faces between employment and the wage rate.

If the union restricts the supply of labor, it raises the wage rate but decreases employment. But unions also try to increase the demand for labor. Let's see what they might do to achieve this outcome.

Unions Change the Demand for Labor

The union tries to operate on the demand for labor in two ways. First, it tries to make the demand for union labor less elastic. Second, it tries to increase the demand for union labor. Making the demand for labor less elastic does not eliminate the tradeoff between employment and the wage rate. But it does make the tradeoff less unfavorable. If a union can make the demand for labor less elastic, it can increase the wage rate at a lower cost in terms of lost employment.

FIGURE 17.2

A Union in a Competitive Labor Market

*e*Foundations 17.2 

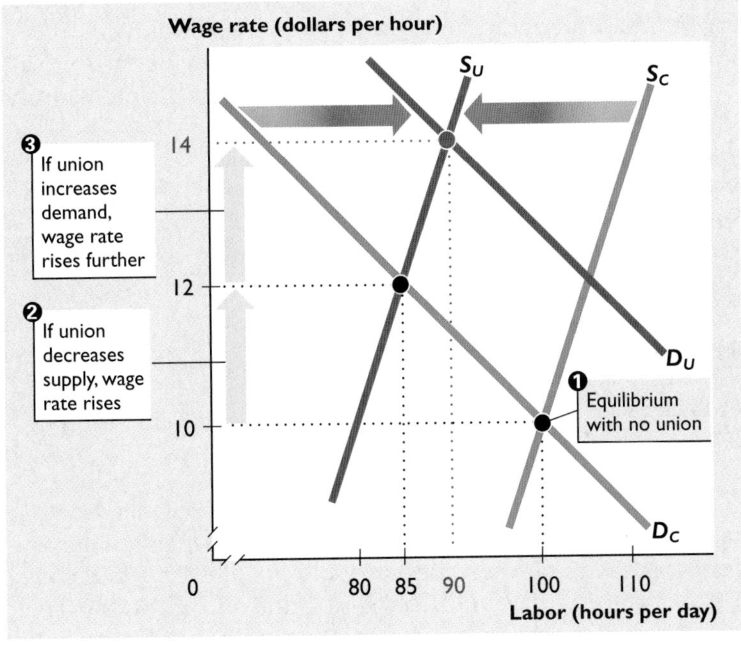

In a competitive labor market, the demand curve is D_C and the supply curve is S_C. ❶ Competitive equilibrium occurs at a wage rate of $10 an hour with 100 hours employed.

❷ By restricting employment below the competitive level, the union shifts the supply of labor to S_U. If the union can do no more than that, the wage rate will increase to $12 an hour but employment will fall to 85 hours.

❸ If the union can increase the demand for labor and shift the demand curve to D_U, then it can increase the wage rate still higher, to $14 an hour, and achieve employment of 90 hours.

But if the union can increase the demand for labor, it might even be able to increase both the wage rate and the employment of its members. Figure 17.2 illustrates the effects of an increase in the demand for the labor of a union's members. If the union can increase the demand for labor to D_U, it can achieve an even bigger increase in the wage rate with a smaller fall in employment. By maintaining the restricted labor supply at S_U, the union increases the wage rate to $14 an hour and achieves an employment level of 90 hours of labor.

Some of the methods used by the unions to change the demand for the labor of its members are to:

- Increase the marginal product of union members
- Encourage import restrictions
- Support minimum wage laws
- Support immigration restrictions
- Increase demand for the good produced

Unions try to increase the marginal product of their members, which in turn increases the demand for their labor, by organizing and sponsoring training schemes, by encouraging apprenticeship and other on-the-job training activities, and by professional certification.

One of the best examples of import restrictions is the support by the United Auto Workers union (UAW) for import restrictions on foreign cars.

Unions support minimum wage laws to increase the cost of employing low-skilled labor. An increase in the wage rate of low-skilled labor leads to a decrease in the quantity demanded of low-skilled labor and to an increase in the demand for high-skilled union labor, a substitute for low-skilled labor.

Restrictive immigration laws decrease the supply and increase the wage rate of low-skilled workers. As a result, the demand for high-skilled union labor increases.

Because the demand for labor is a derived demand, an increase in the demand for the good produced increases the demand for union labor. The best examples of attempts by unions in this activity are in the textile and auto industries. The garment workers' union urges us to buy union-made clothes, and the UAW asks us to buy only American cars made by union workers.

Because a union restricts the supply of labor in the market in which it operates, its actions increase the supply of labor in nonunion markets. Workers who can't get union jobs must look elsewhere for work. This increase in supply in nonunion markets lowers the wage rate in those markets and further widens the union-nonunion differential.

The Scale of Union-Nonunion Wage Differentials

We have seen that unions can influence the wage rate by restricting the supply of labor and increasing the demand for labor. How much of a difference to wage rates do unions make in practice?

Union wage rates are, on the average, 30 percent higher than nonunion wage rates. In mining and financial services, union and nonunion wages are similar. In services, manufacturing, and transportation, the differential is between 11 and 19 percent. In wholesale and retail trades, the differential is 28 percent; in construction, it is 65 percent.

But these union-nonunion wage differentials don't give a true measure of the effects of unions. In some industries, union wages are higher than nonunion wages because union members do jobs that involve greater skill. Even without a union, those workers would receive a higher wage. To calculate the effects of unions, we have to examine the wages of unionized and nonunionized workers who do nearly identical work. The evidence suggests that after allowing for skill differentials, the union-nonunion wage differential lies between 10 percent and 25 percent. For example, airline pilots who belong to the Air Line Pilots' Union earn about 25 percent more than nonunion pilots with the same level of skill.

We next look at a case in which an employer has a big influence on wages.

Monopsony

Monopsony
A market in which there is a single buyer.

A **monopsony** is a market in which there is a single buyer. This market type is unusual, but it does exist. With the growth of large-scale production over the last century, large manufacturing plants such as coal mines, steel and textile mills, and car manufacturers became the major employer in some regions, and in some places, a single firm employed almost all the labor. Today, in some parts of the country, managed health care organizations are the major employer of health care professionals. These firms have monopsony power in the labor market.

A monopsony employer decides how much labor to hire and pays the lowest wage at which it can attract the chosen quantity of labor. A monopsony makes a bigger profit than does a group of firms that compete with each other for their labor. Let's find out how they achieve this outcome.

A monopsony doesn't have a demand curve. But it has a downward-sloping value of marginal product curve. In Figure 17.3, we label this curve $VMP = D$ to remind us that it is also the demand curve in a competitive labor market. The

FIGURE 17.3
A Monopsony Labor Market

*e*Foundations 17.2 

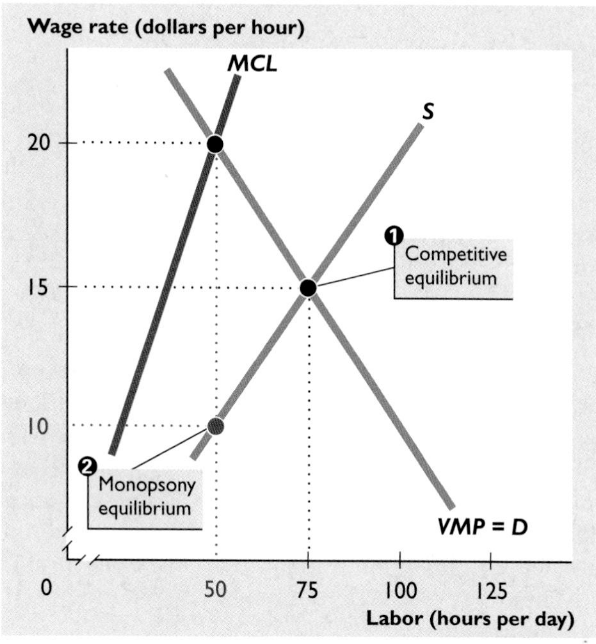

1. Competitive equilibrium occurs at a wage rate of $15 an hour with 75 hours employed.
2. A monopsony is a single buyer. In the labor market, its value of marginal product curve is *VMP* and it faces a labor supply curve *S*. The marginal cost of labor curve is *MCL*.
3. The monopsony maximizes profit by hiring the quantity of labor that makes the marginal cost of labor equal to the value of marginal product. The monopsony hires 50 hours of labor per day. It pays the lowest wage for which that labor will work, which is $10 an hour.

supply of labor curve, *S*, tells us the quantity of labor supplied at each wage rate and the lowest wage rate at which a given quantity of labor is willing to work.

A monopsony recognizes that by hiring less labor, it can pay a lower wage rate. For this reason, its marginal cost of labor exceeds the wage rate. The marginal cost of labor is shown by the curve *MCL*. The relationship between the marginal cost of labor curve and the supply curve is similar to the relationship between the marginal cost and average cost curves that you studied in Chapter 11. The supply curve is like the average cost of labor curve. Suppose a firm can hire 49 hours of labor for a wage rate of $9.80 an hour. The firm's total cost of labor is $480 an hour (49 hours × $9.80 an hour = $480.20, so we're rounding to the nearest dollar). Suppose that to hire 50 hours of labor, the firm must pay a wage rate of $10 an hour. The total cost of labor is now $500 an hour. So hiring the 50th hour of labor increases the total cost of labor from $480 to $500, which is a $20 increase. The marginal cost of labor is $20 an hour. The curve *MCL* shows the $20 marginal cost of hiring the 50th hour of labor.

To find the profit-maximizing quantity of labor, the firm sets the marginal cost of labor equal to the value of the marginal product of labor. In Figure 17.3, this outcome occurs when the monopsony employs 50 hours of labor. To hire 50 hours of labor, the firm pays $10 an hour, as shown by the supply of labor curve. But the value of the marginal product of labor is $20 an hour, which means that the firm makes an economic profit of $10 on the last hour of labor that it hires. Compare this outcome with that in a competitive labor market. If the labor market in Figure 17.3 were competitive, equilibrium would occur at the intersection of the demand curve and the supply curve. The wage rate would be $15 an hour, and 75 hours of labor a day would be employed. So compared with a competitive labor market, a monopsony decreases both the wage rate and the level of employment.

The ability of a monopsony to lower the wage rate and employment level and make an economic profit depends on the elasticity of labor supply. The more elastic the supply of labor, the less opportunity a monopsony has to cut the wage rate and employment and make an economic profit.

Monopsony Tendencies

Today, monopsony is rare. Workers can commute long distances to a job, so most people have more than one potential employer. But firms that are dominant employers in isolated communities do face an upward-sloping supply of labor curve and so have a marginal cost of labor that exceeds the wage rate. But in such situations, there is also, usually, a union. Let's see how unions and monopsonies interact.

Monopsony and Unions

When we studied monopoly in Chapter 13, we discovered that a single seller in a market is able to determine the price in that market. We have just studied monopsony—a market with a single buyer—and discovered that in such a market, the buyer is able to determine the price. Suppose that a union starts to operate in a monopsony labor market. A union is like a monopoly. It controls the supply of labor and acts like a single seller of labor. If the union (monopoly seller) faces a monopsony buyer, the situation is one of **bilateral monopoly**. In bilateral monopoly, the wage rate is determined by bargaining between the two sides. Let's study the bargaining process.

Bilateral monopoly
A market in which a monopoly seller faces a monopsony buyer.

In Figure 17.3, if the monopsony is free to determine the wage rate and the level of employment, the monopsony hires 50 hours of labor and pays a wage rate of $10 an hour. But suppose that a union represents the workers and can, if necessary, call a strike. Also suppose that the union agrees to maintain employment at 50 hours but seeks the highest wage rate that the employer can be forced to pay. That wage rate is $20 an hour. That is, the wage rate equals the value of the marginal product of labor. It is unlikely that the union will get the wage rate up to $20 an hour. But it is also unlikely that the firm will keep the wage rate down to $10 an hour. The monopsony firm and the union bargain over the wage rate, and the result is an outcome between $20 an hour (the maximum that the union can achieve) and $10 an hour (the minimum that the firm can achieve).

The actual outcome of the bargaining depends on the costs that each party can inflict on the other as a result of a failure to agree on the wage rate. The firm can shut down the plant and lock out its workers, and the workers can call a strike and shut down the plant. Each party knows the other's strength and knows what it will lose if it does not agree to the other's demands. If the two parties are equally strong and they realize it, they will split the difference and agree to a wage rate of $15 an hour. If one party is stronger than the other—and both parties know that—the agreed wage will favor the stronger party. Usually, an agreement is reached without a strike or a lockout. The threat—knowledge that such an event can occur—is usually enough to bring the bargaining parties to an agreement. But when a strike or lockout does occur, it is often because one party has misjudged the costs each party can inflict on the other.

Minimum wage laws have interesting effects in monopsony labor markets. Let's study these effects.

Monopsony and the Minimum Wage

In a competitive labor market, a minimum wage that exceeds the equilibrium wage decreases employment (see Chapter 7, pp. 173–175). In a monopsony labor market, a minimum wage can increase both the wage rate and employment. Let's see how.

Figure 17.4 shows a monopsony labor market in which the wage rate is $5 an hour and 50 hours of labor employed. A minimum wage law is passed that requires employers to pay at least $7.50 an hour. We've shaded the area below the minimum wage because a wage rate in this region is illegal. The monopsony in Figure 17.4 now faces a perfectly elastic supply of labor at $7.50 an hour up to 75 hours. Above 75 hours, a higher wage than $7.50 an hour must be paid to hire additional hours of labor. Because the wage rate is a fixed $7.50 an hour up to 75 hours, the marginal cost of labor is also constant at $7.50 up to 75 hours. Beyond 75 hours, the marginal cost of labor rises above $7.50 an hour.

To maximize profit, the monopsony hires the quantity of labor that makes the marginal cost of labor (*MCL*) equal to the value of its marginal product (*VMP*). That is, the monopsony hires 75 hours of labor. The monopsony pays the lowest wage rate at which it can attract this quantity of labor, which is the minimum wage of $7.50 an hour. The minimum wage law has succeeded in raising the wage rate by $2.50 an hour and increasing the amount of labor employed by 25 hours.

FIGURE 17.4
Minimum Wage in Monopsony

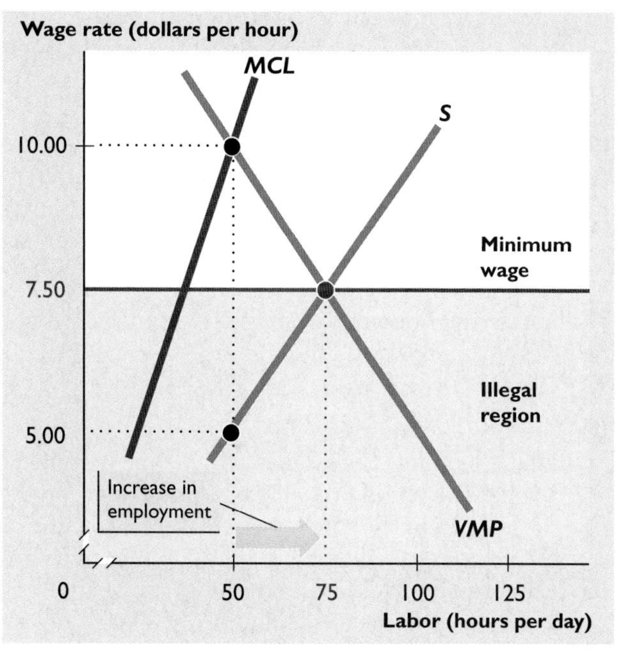

In a monopsony labor market, the wage rate is $5 an hour and 50 hours are hired. If a minimum wage law increases the wage rate to $7.50 an hour, employment increases to 75 hours per day.

CHECKPOINT 17.2

Study Guide pp. 267–271 

*e*Foundations 17.2

2 **Explain why union workers earn higher wage rates than nonunion workers.**

Practice Problems 17.2

1. In the United States in 1998, 98,000 people worked as flight attendants and earned an average of $17.00 an hour. Most flight attendants are members of a union, the Association of Flight Attendants. To be a flight attendant, a person must be a high school graduate, and formal training is provided by the airlines. The air transportation industry is competitive.
   a. If the flight attendants were not members of a union, how might the wage rate and number of flight attendants be different?
   b. Safety rules set by the Federal Aviation Administration (FAA) require one attendant for every 50 seats. If the union lobbies for a change in the safety rules and the FAA responds by requiring one attendant for every 25 seats, how might the wage rate and number of flight attendants change?
   c. If the union provided the formal training of flight attendants, how might the wage rate and number of flight attendants change?

2. Table 1 gives the demand and supply schedules of labor in a remote mining town. The mine is the only employer. What wage rate does the mine pay and how many workers does it employ?

TABLE 1

Wage rate (dollars per hour)	Quantity of labor supplied (workers)	Quantity of labor demanded (workers)
2	2	10
3	3	9
4	4	8
5	5	7
6	6	6
7	7	5
8	8	4

Exercises 17.2

1. In the United States in 1998, 30,000 elevator installers and repairers earned an average of $23 an hour. These workers must have a high school certificate, apply for their jobs through the union, and learn their trade through years of on-the-job training provided by the union. Most belong to the International Union of Elevator Constructors. The elevator sales and repair industry is competitive.
   a. If the high school graduates could apply to firms for jobs rather than the union, how might the wage rate and number of elevator workers change?
   b. If elevator companies rather than the union provided the on-the-job training, how might the wage rate and number of elevator workers change?

2. In Practice Problem 2, if the union lobbies for a minimum wage of $6 an hour, what now are the wage rate and the number of workers employed?

FIGURE 1

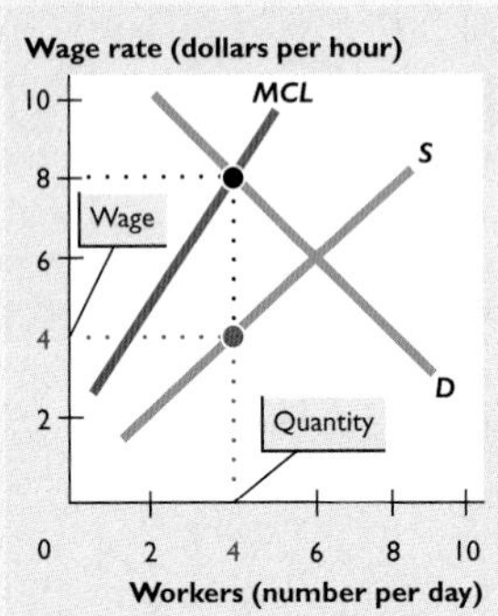

Solutions to Practice Problems 17.2

1a. The supply would not change because any high school graduate could be a flight attendant. The airlines provide the training, and so the demand would not change. The union probably has little impact on the flight attendant's wage.

1b. The change in the safety rules will increase the demand for flight attendants. The wage rate will rise, and the number of flight attendants will increase.

1c. If the union provides the training, it might restrict the number of people trained and so decrease the supply. The wage rate will rise, and the number of flight attendants will decrease.

2. The wage rate is $4 an hour, and the mine employs 4 workers (Figure 1). Table 2 shows the calculation of the mine's marginal cost of labor.

TABLE 2

Wage rate (dollars per hour)	Quantity of labor supplied (workers)	Total cost of labor (dollars per hour)	Marginal cost of labor (dollars per worker)
2	2	4	
			5
3	3	9	
			7
4	4	16	
			9
5	5	15	
			11
6	6	36	
			13
7	7	49	

17.3 SEX AND RACE WAGE DIFFERENTIALS

Why do women and minorities earn less per hour than white men? Is there discrimination against women and members of minority races, or is there some other explanation? We are going to examine four possible explanations for earnings differences:

- Job types
- Discrimination
- Differences in human capital
- Differences in the degree of specialization

Job Types

Some of the sex differences in wages arise because men and women do different jobs and the jobs that men do are better paid. But greater numbers of women today have jobs as bus drivers, police officers, and construction workers, all jobs that were traditionally done by men. Women enrolled in university courses in architecture, medicine, law, and accounting have increased from less than 20 percent of total students in 1970 to about 50 percent today.

But women and minorities earn less than white men even when they do the *same* job. So let's look at the other reasons why differences might exist, starting with discrimination.

Sex and Race Earnings Differences

The figure shows the earnings of different race and sex groups expressed as a percentage of the earnings of white men.

In 1999, white women earned, on the average, 76 percent of what white men earned. Black men earned 77 percent and black women earned 64 percent. The lowest-paid groups, men and women of Hispanic origin, earned only 60 percent and 55 percent respectively of white men's wages.

These earnings gaps have persisted over many years, and only that of white women has begun to narrow.

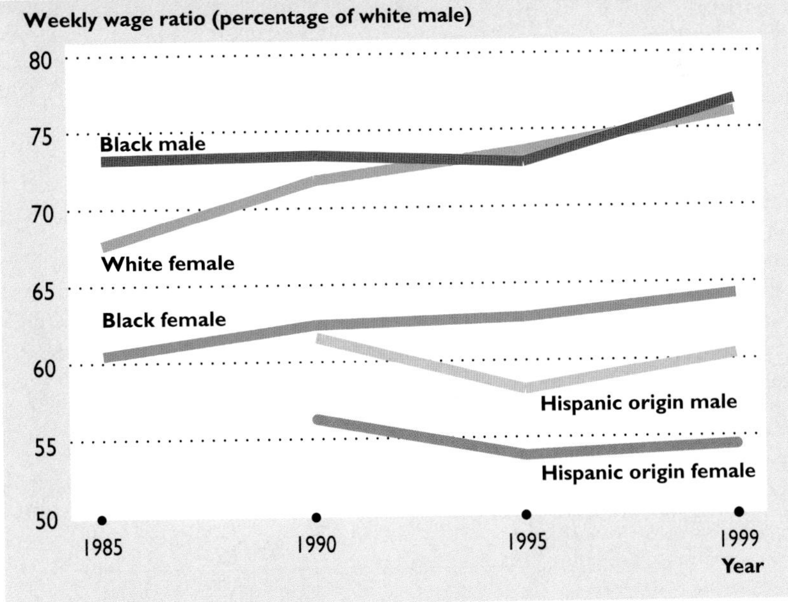

SOURCE: U.S. Bureau of the Census, *Statistical Abstract of the United States: 2000.*

Discrimination

Suppose that black females and white males have identical abilities as investment advisors. Figure 17.5 shows the supply curves of black females, S_{BF} (in part a), and of white males, S_{WM} (in part b). The value of the marginal product of investment advisors, as shown by the two curves labeled *VMP* in parts (a) and (b), is the same for both groups.

If everyone is free of prejudice about race and sex, the market determines a wage rate of $40,000 a year for all investment advisors. But if the customers of investment houses are prejudiced against women and minorities, this prejudice is reflected in wages and employment.

Suppose that the value of the marginal product of the black females, when discriminated against, is VMP_{DA}, where *DA* stands for "discriminated against." Suppose that the value of the marginal product for white males, the group discriminated in favor of, is VMP_{DF}, where *DF* stands for "discriminated in favor of." With these value of marginal product curves, black females earn $20,000 a year, and only 1,000 will work as investment advisors. White males earn $60,000 a year, and 3,000 of them will work as investment advisors.

Economists disagree about whether prejudice actually causes wage differentials, and one line of reasoning suggests that it does not. In the example that you've just studied, customers who buy from white men pay a higher service charge for investment advice than do the customers who buy from black women. This price difference acts as an incentive to encourage people who are prejudiced to buy from the people against whom they are prejudiced. This force could be so strong as to eliminate the effects of discrimination altogether.

FIGURE 17.5

Discrimination

*e*Foundations 17.3 

With no discrimination, the wage rate is $40,000 a year and 2,000 of each group are hired.

With discrimination against blacks and women, the value of marginal product curve in part (a) is VMP_{DA} and that in part (b) is VMP_{DF}. The wage rate for black women falls to $20,000 a year, and only 1,000 are employed. The wage rate for white men rises to $60,000 a year, and 3,000 are employed.

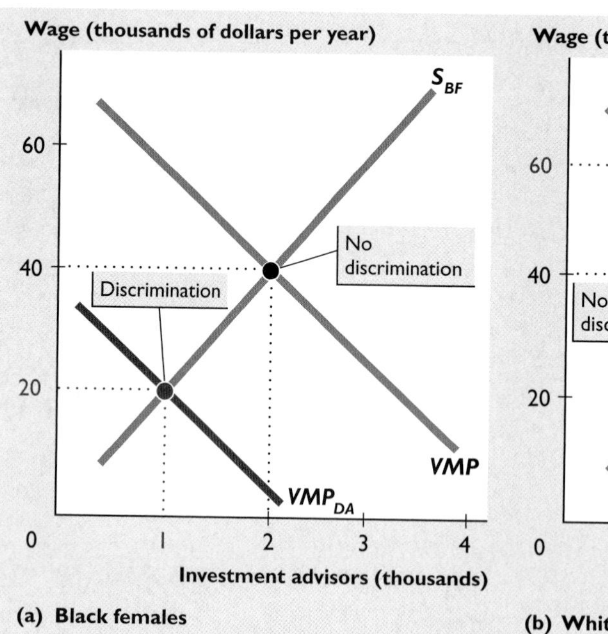

(a) Black females

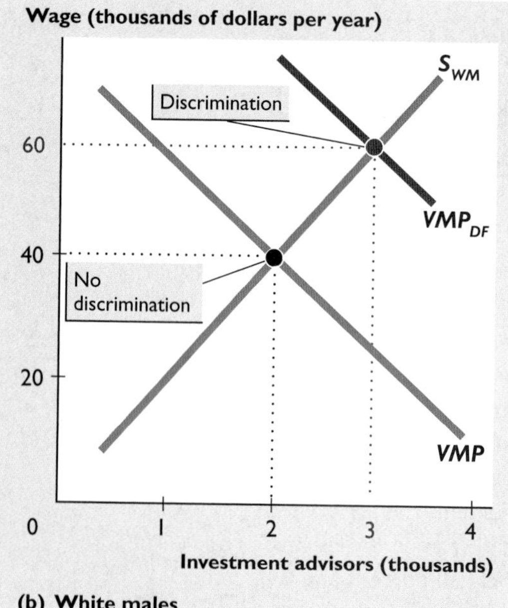

(b) White males

Suppose, as is true in manufacturing, that a firm's customers never meet its workers. If such a firm discriminates against women or minorities, it cannot compete with firms who hire these groups because its costs are higher than those of the nonprejudiced firms. So only those firms that do not discriminate survive in a competitive industry.

Let's now turn to the third possible source of wage differences: differences in human capital.

Differences in Human Capital

The more human capital a person possesses, the more that person earns, other things remaining the same. We use three indicators to measure human capital:

- Years of schooling
- Years of work experience
- Number of job interruptions

A larger proportion of men (25 percent) than women (20 percent) have completed 4 years of college. And a larger proportion of whites (24 percent) than blacks (13 percent) have completed a B.A. degree or higher. These differences in education levels among the sexes and the races are becoming smaller. But they have not yet been eliminated.

The more years of work and the fewer job interruptions a person has had, the higher is the person's wage, other things remaining the same. Interruptions to a career reduce the effectiveness of job experience and bring lower incomes. Historically, job interruptions are more serious for women than for men because women's careers have been interrupted for bearing and rearing children. This factor is a possible source of lower wages, on the average, for women. But maternity leave and day-care facilities are making career interruptions for women less common or at least shorter and less disruptive.

A final source of earnings differences, the relative degree of specialization of women and men, affects women's incomes adversely.

Differences in the Degree of Specialization

Couples must choose how to allocate their time between working for a wage and doing jobs in the home, such as cooking, cleaning, shopping, organizing vacations, and, most important, bearing and rearing children. Let's look at the choices of Bob and Sue.

Bob might specialize in earning an income and Sue in taking care of the home. Or Sue might specialize in earning an income and Bob in taking care of the home. Or both of them might earn an income and share home production jobs.

The allocation that they choose depends on their preferences and on the earning potential of each of them. The choice of an increasing number of households is for each person to diversify between earning an income and doing some home chores. But in most households, Bob will specialize in earning an income and Sue will both earn an income and take care of the home. It seems likely that with this allocation, Bob will earn more than Sue. If Sue devotes time and effort to ensuring Bob's mental and physical well-being, the quality of Bob's market labor will be higher than it would be if he were diversified. If the roles were reversed, Sue would be able to supply market labor that earns more than Bob.

To test whether the degree of specialization accounts for earnings differentials between the sexes, economists have studied two groups: never-married men and never-married women. The available evidence suggests that, on the average, when they have the same amount of human capital—measured by years of schooling, work experience, and career interruptions—the wages of these two groups are not significantly different.

Because labor markets bring unequal incomes, governments intervene in these markets to modify the wages and employment levels that they determine. One potentially far-reaching intervention is comparable-worth laws. Let's see how these laws work.

Comparable-Worth Laws

Congress passed the Equal Pay Act in 1963 and the Civil Rights Act in 1964. These acts require equal pay for equal work. They are attempts to remove the most blatant forms of discrimination between men and women and between whites and minorities. Minnesota and Wisconsin have passed laws that require that jobs with the same levels of training, skills, and responsibilities receive the same wages, regardless of whether the jobs are done by men or women or by blacks or whites. Paying the same wage for different jobs that are judged comparable is called **comparable worth**.

Comparable worth
Paying the same wage for different jobs that are judged comparable.

Figure 17.6 shows how comparable-worth laws work. Part (a) shows the market for oil rig operators, and part (b) shows the market for school teachers. The value of marginal product curves (VMP_R and VMP_T) and the supply curves (S_R and S_T) are shown for each type of labor. Competition generates a wage rate W_R for oil rig operators and W_T for teachers.

Suppose it is decided that these two jobs are of comparable worth and that the courts enforce a wage rate of W_C, for both groups. What happens? First, there is a shortage of oil rig operators. Oil rig companies are able to hire only S_R workers at the wage rate W_C. Oil rig companies cut back production or build more expensive labor-saving oil rigs. Also, the number of teachers employed decreases. But this decrease occurs because school boards demand fewer teachers. At the higher wage W_C, school boards demand only D_T teachers. The quantity of teachers supplied is S_T, and the difference between S_T and D_T is the number of unemployed teachers looking for jobs. These teachers eventually accept nonteaching jobs (which they don't like as much as teaching jobs), quite likely at a wage rate below that of teachers.

Although comparable-worth laws can eliminate wage differences, they can do so only by incurring costly unintended consequences. Comparable-worth laws limit job opportunities and create unemployment among workers whose wage rate they raise. And they make it hard for employers to hire workers whose wage rate is held down. Only in the rare case of a monopsonistic labor market does equalizing wage rates not create permanent surpluses and shortages of skills. In this situation, a comparable-worth law works in a similar way to a minimum wage law.

Effective Wage Policies

We have now surveyed the major sources of wage differentials. Of the various possible sources of differences in wage rates, one stands out: the level of education. On the average, people with postgraduate degrees earn much more than college graduates, who in turn earn much more than high school graduates, who in turn earn more than people who have not completed high school. This source of differences in earnings is the main one on which an effective policy can operate.

By pursuing the most effective education available in grade school, high school, and college and university, people can equip themselves with human capital that brings significantly higher earnings. But in today's rapidly changing world, education and human capital accumulation must be an ongoing enterprise. The most successful workers are those who are able to repeatedly retool and actively embrace each new technological advance. The least successful are those who get locked into a particular technology and are unable or unwilling to adapt when that technology becomes redundant. So an effective wage policy is one that emphasizes ongoing education and training.

FIGURE 17.6
The Problem with Comparable Worth

*e*Foundations 17.3 

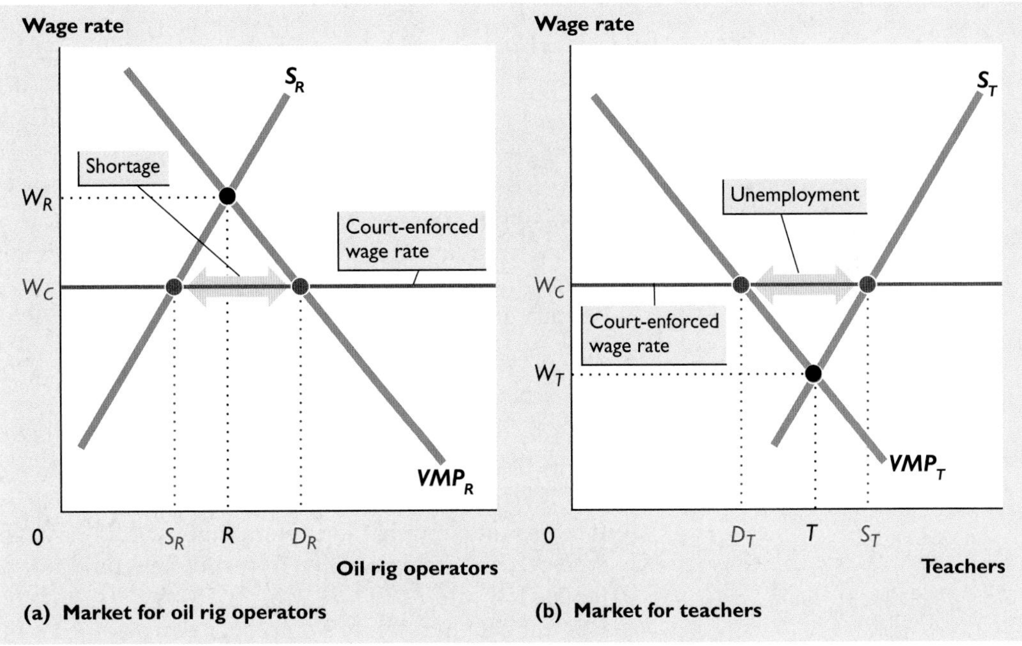

Part (a) shows the demand for and supply of oil rig operators, VMP_R and S_R, and part (b) shows the demand for and supply of school teachers, VMP_T and S_T. The competitive equilibrium wage rate for oil rig operators is W_R, and that for teachers is W_T. If an evaluation of the two jobs finds that they have comparable worth and rules that the wage rate W_C be paid to both types of workers, such a wage creates a shortage of oil rig operators and a surplus of teachers. Oil producers search for labor-saving ways of producing oil (that are more expensive), and teachers search for other jobs (that are less desirable to them and probably are less well paid).

CHECKPOINT 17.3

Study Guide pp. 271–274

*e*Foundations 17.3

3 **Discuss reasons why men earn more than women and whites earn more than minorities and predict the effects of a comparable-worth program.**

Practice Problem 17.3

Jenny is an attorney. Her husband, Pete, is an artist who works from home, takes care of the kids, and organizes the domestic help. Jodi, Jenny's classmate from Yale Law School, is also an attorney. Jenny and Jodi work the same number of hours a year, but Jenny earns $250,000 while Jodi earns only $175,000. Consider the following possible explanations for the income difference and explain why each might be correct or incorrect:

a. Jodi is less specialized than Jenny.

b. Jodi's employer is prejudiced against women lawyers and pays them less than he pays men.

c. Jenny's employer is prejudiced against men lawyers and makes a point of hiring women and paying them a high wage rate.

d. Jenny is a better lawyer than Jodi.

Exercise 17.3

The prize money for the U.S. Open tennis championship is the same for the men's and women's championships. But for the U.S. Open golf championships, the prize money is different. In 2000, the total purse for the men's competition was $4.5 million, with the winner getting $800,000, and for the women's competition the total purse was $2.75 million, with the winner getting $495,000.

a. Are women golfers discriminated against?

b. If the best women golfers are as good as the best men golfers, what might explain the difference in their prize money?

c. If the comparable-worth laws required the prize money of men and women golfers to be equal, how would the women's prize money and number of women golfers change?

Solution to Practice Problem 17.3

a. Jenny is specialized in market activity because of the flexible work arrangements of Pete, so it is possible that Jodi spreads herself across other activities that lower her market income.

b. It seems unlikely that Jodi's employer would pay women less than he pays men of comparable quality. If he did, he would not be able to hire some good female lawyers.

c. It is unlikely that Jenny's employer pays women a higher wage rate than the market rate. He would earn a larger profit by paying the market rate.

d. It is possible that Jenny is a better lawyer than Jodi in the sense that her value of marginal product is higher.

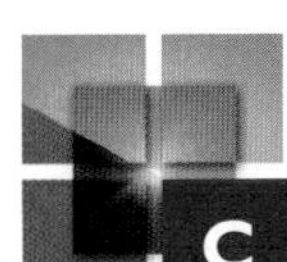

CHAPTER CHECKPOINT

Key Points

1 Explain why college graduates earn more, on the average, than high school graduates.

- Skill differentials arise from differences in value of marginal products and because skills are costly to acquire.
- Demand and supply in the markets for high-skilled and low-skilled labor determine wage rates.

2 Explain why union workers earn higher wage rates than nonunion workers.

- Labor unions influence wage rates by controlling the supply of labor.
- In competitive labor markets, unions obtain higher wage rates only at the expense of lower employment, but they try to influence the demand for labor.
- In a monopsony, a union can increase the wage rate without sacrificing employment.
- Bilateral monopoly occurs when a union confronts a single buyer of labor. The two parties bargain to determine the wage rate.
- Union workers earn 10 to 25 percent more than comparable nonunion workers.

3 Discuss reasons why men earn more than women and whites earn more than minorities and predict the effects of a comparable-worth program.

- Earnings differences between men and women and between whites and minorities arise from differences in types of jobs, discrimination, differences in human capital, and differences in degree of specialization.
- Well-paid jobs are more likely to be held by white men than by women and minorities. But discrimination is hard to measure objectively.
- Historically, white males have had more human capital than other groups, but human capital differences are falling.
- Women's careers have traditionally been interrupted more frequently than those of men.
- Men have been more specialized in market activity, on the average, than have women.
- Comparable-worth laws create unemployment in jobs on which the market places a low value and shortages of workers on which the market places a high value.

Key Terms

FIGURE 1

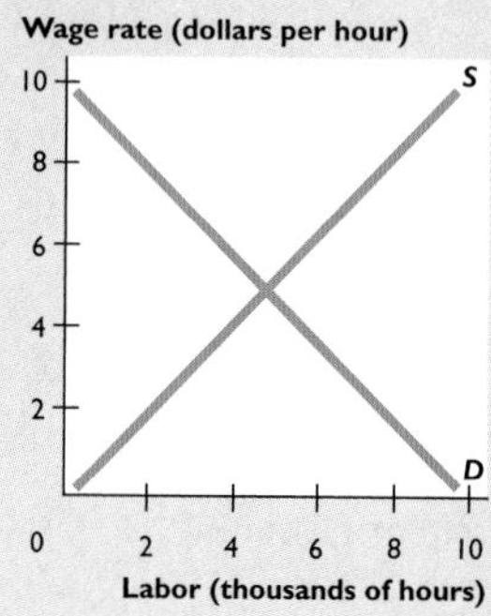

TABLE 1

Wage rate (dollars per day)	Number of workers	Quantity produced (bags of gold)
4.50	0	0
5.50	1	20
6.50	2	38
7.50	3	54
8.50	4	68
9.50	5	80
10.50	6	90
11.50	7	98

Exercises

1. Figure 1 shows the market for low-skilled workers. With training, low-skilled workers can become high-skilled workers. High-skilled workers have a marginal product at each employment level that is twice the marginal product of a low-skilled worker. But the cost of acquiring the skill adds $2 an hour to the wage rate that will attract high-skilled labor.
   a. What is the wage rate of low-skilled labor and how many low-skilled workers are employed?
   b. What is the wage rate of high-skilled labor and how many high-skilled workers are employed?
2. Suppose in Exercise 1 that high-skilled workers become unionized and the union restricts the number of high-skilled workers to 5,000.
   a. What is the wage rate of high-skilled workers?
   b. What is the wage differential between low-skilled and high-skilled workers?
3. A monopsony gold mine operates in an isolated part of the Amazon basin. The market for gold is competitive and the price of gold is $0.50 a bag. Table 1 shows the labor supply schedule (columns 1 and 2) and the mine's total product schedule (columns 2 and 3).
   a. What wage rate does the mine pay?
   b. How many workers does the mine employ?
   c. What is the miners' value of marginal product?
   d. If the miners form a union and lobby successfully for a minimum wage rate of $7.50 a day, how many workers does the mine employ?
4. In the United States in 1998, 133,000 aircraft mechanics and services technicians earned an average of $18.30 an hour, while 30,000 elevator installers and repairers earned an average of $23.00 an hour. The skill and training for these two jobs are very similar. If these jobs are judged to be of comparable worth and the government enforces the comparable-worth law, how will the markets for mechanics and elevator workers change?

5. Use the link on your Foundations Web site to visit the AFL-CIO and click on the "National Boycott List." Choose an item on this list that interests you and explain why the AFL-CIO is recommending a boycott of this item. Explain how not buying this item increases either the wage rate or employment level of union members.

6. Use the link on your Foundations Web site to visit the Bureau of Labor Statistics, BLS, and obtain data for the past three months on usual weekly earnings and the level of employment.
   a. What has happened to earnings and employment during the past three months?
   b. Try to explain the changes by using the tools of demand and supply.
7. Suppose that all nations agreed to permit the free movement of people. Which nations would be the biggest suppliers of immigrants? Which nations would attract most immigrants? Describe the world economy 10 years after the start of this process.

Chapter 18

Inequality, Poverty, and Redistribution

CHAPTER CHECKLIST

When you have completed your study of this chapter, you will be able to:

1 **Describe the inequality in income and wealth in the United States and explain why wealth inequality is greater than income inequality.**

2 **Explain how economic inequality arises.**

3 **Explain the effects of taxes, social security, and welfare programs on economic inequality.**

Fifty-three stories above Manhattan is a penthouse with unobstructed views of Central Park, the Hudson River, and the city skyline. Its price? $5 million. Not quite within view of this penthouse, but not far from it, is Fort Washington Armory in Upper Manhattan. What was opened as a temporary shelter in 1981 permanently houses close to 1,000 men, who sleep in one football-field-sized room. These men live on the edge of despair and in fear of AIDS and other life-threatening diseases.

Why are some people exceedingly rich while others are very poor? Are the rich getting richer and the poor getting poorer?

In this chapter, we conclude our study of income determination and the big *for whom* question by looking at economic inequality—its extent, its sources, and its potential remedies. We look at taxes and government programs that redistribute incomes and study their effects on economic inequality in the United States.

18.1 INEQUALITY IN THE UNITED STATES

We measure economic inequality by looking at the distributions of income and wealth. A household's income is the amount that it receives in a given period. A household's wealth is the value of the things it owns at a point in time.

Table 18.1(a) provides a look at the distribution of income in the United States in 1999 (the most recent year for which we have data). The median U.S. household income in 1999 was $40,816. The median is the middle, so 50 percent of households have incomes above the median and 50 percent have incomes below the median.

The table shows income inequality in three ways. First, it lists the percentages of total income received by each 20 percent group of households. The poorest 20 percent received 3.6 percent of total income, while the richest 20 percent received 49.4 percent of total income. Second, it lists the cumulative percentages of households and total income. For example, the poorest 60 percent of households received 27.4 percent of total income. Third, it lists the average income of each group. The average income for the poorest 20 percent was $9,940 a year.

Table 18.1(b) provides data on the distribution of wealth in the United States in 1998 (again, the most recent year for which we have data). In 1998, the median household wealth was $60,700. Wealth is distributed even more unequally than income. The poorest 90 percent of households owned only 29.1 percent of total wealth, and the wealthiest 1 percent owned 38.1 percent of total wealth. The average wealth of the poorest 40 percent of households was only $1,100, while that of the richest 1 percent was $10,204,000.

TABLE 18.1

Income Distribution and Wealth Distribution in 1999

(a) Income distribution: median household income $40,816

	Households		Income		
	Percentage	**Cumulative percentage**	**Percentage**	**Cumulative percentage**	**Average (dollars)**
A	Lowest 20	20	3.6	3.6	9,940
B	Second 20	40	8.9	12.5	24,436
C	Third 20	60	14.9	27.4	40,879
D	Fourth 20	80	23.2	50.6	63,555
E	Highest 20	100	49.4	100.0	135,401

(b) Wealth distribution: median household wealth $60,700

	Households		Wealth		
	Percentage	**Cumulative percentage**	**Percentage**	**Cumulative percentage**	**Average (dollars)**
A'	Lowest 40	40	0.2	0.2	1,100
B'	Next 20	60	4.5	4.7	61,000
C'	Next 20	80	11.9	16.6	161,300
D'	Next 10	90	12.5	29.1	344,900
E'	Next 5	95	11.5	40.6	623,500
F'	Next 4	99	21.3	61.9	1,441,000
G'	Top 1	100	38.1	100.0	10,204,000

Lorenz Curves

A **Lorenz curve** graphs the cumulative percentage of income (or wealth) on the *y*-axis against the cumulative percentage of households on the *x*-axis. Figure 18.1 shows the Lorenz curves for income and wealth in the United States based on the data in Table 18.1. Graphing the cumulative percentage of income against the cumulative percentage of households makes the Lorenz curve for income and the points on the graph correspond to the rows identified by the same letters in the table. For example, row *B* and point *B* show that the poorest 40 percent of households received 12.5 percent of total income (3.6 percent plus 8.9 percent).

Lorenz curve
A curve that graphs the cumulative percentage of income (or wealth) against the cumulative percentage of households. The farther the Lorenz curve is from a 45° line, the greater is the inequality.

Graphing the cumulative percentage of wealth against the cumulative percentage of households makes the Lorenz curve for wealth and the points on the graph correspond to the rows identified by the same letters in the table. For example, row *D*' and point *D*' show that the poorest 90 percent of households owned 29.1 percent of total wealth (0.2 percent plus 4.5 percent plus 11.9 percent plus 12.5 percent).

If income (or wealth) were distributed equally, each 1 percent of households would earn 1 percent of total income and own 1 percent of total wealth, and the cumulative percentage of income received by a given cumulative percentage of households would fall along the straight line labeled "Line of equality." The Lorenz curve is always below this line, and the closer the Lorenz curve is to the line of equality, the more equal is the distribution. You can see that the Lorenz curve for wealth is much farther away from the line of equality than is the Lorenz curve for income. The distribution of wealth is much more unequal than the distribution of income.

FIGURE 18.1
Lorenz Curves for Income and Wealth in 1999

*e*Foundations 18.1 

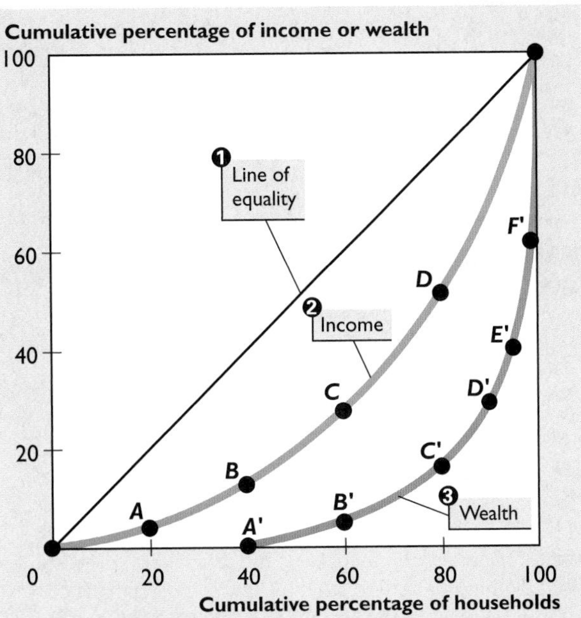

The cumulative percentages of income and wealth are graphed against the cumuative percentage of households. The poorest 20 percent of households received 3.6 percent of total income, and the richest 20 percent received 49.4 percent. The poorest 40 percent of households owned 0.2 percent of total wealth, and the richest 1 percent owned 38.1 percent.

SOURCES: U.S. Bureau of the Census, *Current Population Reports, P60-209, Money Income in the United States*, 2000; and Edward N. Wolff, "Recent Trends in Wealth Ownership, 1983–1998," Jerome Levy Economics Institute Working Paper No. 300, April 2000.

Inequality over Time

Income and wealth have become more unequal over the past few decades. And Figure 18.2 shows how the distributions of income and wealth have changed.

Change in Income Distribution

The share of income received by the richest 20 percent of households has increased from 43.7 percent in 1983 to 49.4 percent in 1999. The share of income received by all four other groups of households has decreased. But the decreased share is largest for the second and third poorest groups.

The higher-income groups have gained relatively more than the lower-income groups because rapid technological change has increased the return to education and skill. Everyone has benefited from the technological change, but the better-educated have benefited most. The result has been an increase in the spread between the hourly wage rates of the more highly educated and skilled and the less well educated and less skilled.

Change in Wealth Distribution

The share of wealth owned by the richest 1 percent of households has increased from 34 percent in 1983 to 38 percent in 1998. The share of wealth owned by all the other groups of households has decreased. And interestingly, the decreased share is largest for the next richest 4 percent. The remaining 95 percent of households have lost similar shares.

FIGURE 18.2
Trends in the Distributions of Income and Wealth

*e*Foundations **18.1** 

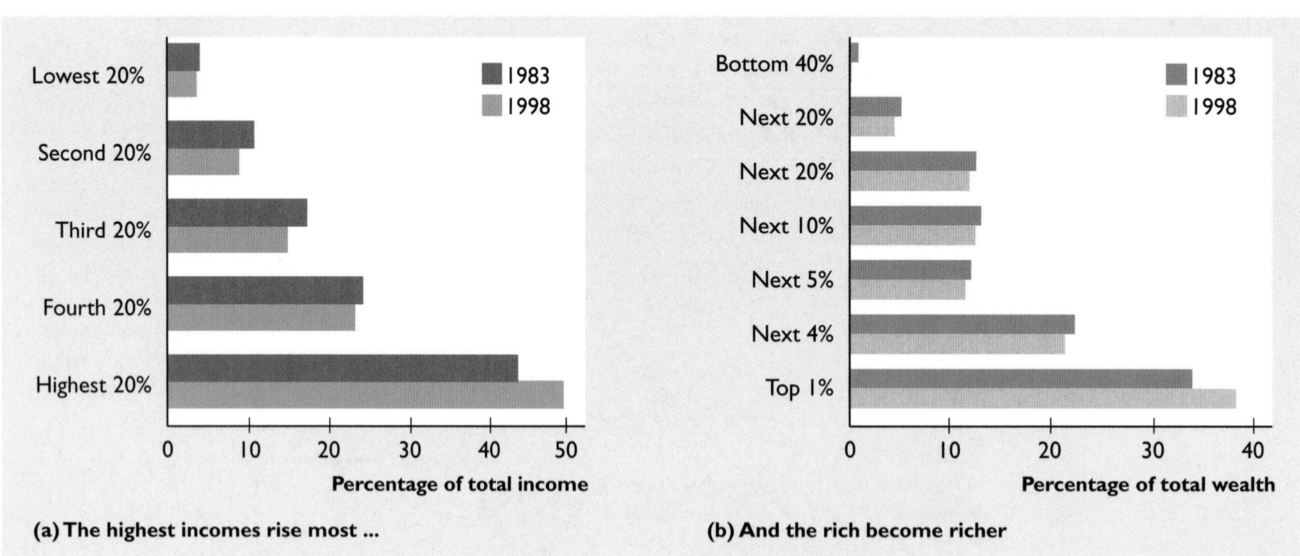

SOURCES: U.S. Bureau of the Census, *Current Population Reports*, P-60-209, *Money Income in the United States*, 2000; and Edward N. Wolff, "Recent Trends in Wealth Ownership, 1983–1998," Jerome Levy Economics Institute Working Paper No. 300, April 2000.

The distribution of income became more unequal between 1983 and 1999. The percentage of total income received by the top 20 percent increased, and the percentages earned by all other groups decreased.

The distribution of wealth became more unequal between 1983 and 1998. The percentage of total wealth owned by the top 1 percent increased, and the percentages earned by all other groups decreased.

The wealthiest households have a larger proportion of their wealth invested in stocks than do less wealthy households. So the wealthiest gained because of the extraordinary performance of the stock market during the 1990s. They gained most on the stocks of companies created by entrepreneurs in the information-age economy. But the fall in the stock market during 2001 generated larger losses for the wealthier households than for the poorer ones.

Who Are the Rich and the Poor?

The lowest-income household in the United States today is likely to be a black woman over 65 years of age who lives alone somewhere in the South and has fewer than nine years of elementary school education. The highest-income household in the United States today is likely to be a college-educated white married couple between 45 and 54 years of age living together with two children somewhere in the West.

These snapshot profiles are the extremes in Figure 18.3. That figure illustrates the importance of education, size of household, marital status, age of householder, race, and region of residence in influencing the size of a household's income. The range arising from education differences is the largest—from $17,300 a year for less than grade 9 to $70,000 a year for people with a bachelor's degree or higher. Household size, marital status, and age are also important. Race and region of residence have a much smaller effect than do the other four factors.

FIGURE 18.3

The Distribution of Income by Selected Household Characteristics in 1999

*e*Foundations 18.1 

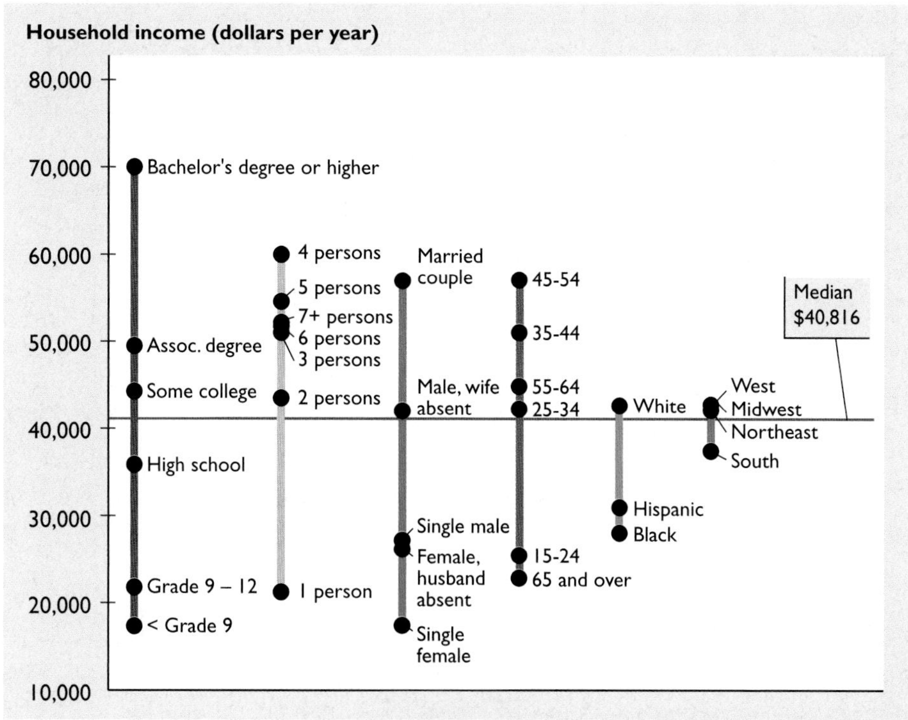

Education is the single biggest factor affecting household income distribution, but size of household, marital status, and age of householder are also important. Race and region of residence also play a role.

SOURCE: U.S. Bureau of the Census, *Current Population Reports*, P-60-209, *Money Income in the United States*, 2000.

Poverty

Poverty
A state in which a household's income is too low to be able to buy the quantities of food, shelter, and clothing that are deemed necessary.

Households at the low end of the income distribution are so poor that they are considered to be living in poverty. **Poverty** is a state in which a household's income is too low to be able to buy the quantities of food, shelter, and clothing that are deemed necessary.

Poverty is a *relative* concept. Millions of people living in Africa and Asia survive on incomes of less than $400 a year. Almost no one in the United States experiences this degree of poverty. But there are some very poor people in the United States compared with the average.

To measure the degree of poverty, the Social Security Administration considers a household to be living in poverty if its income is less than some defined level. The level varies with household size and is updated every year. In 1999, the poverty level for a four-person household was an income of $17,029. In that year, 32.3 million Americans lived in households that had incomes below the poverty level. Many of these households benefited from free health care and other government programs that raised the quality of their lives above the levels indicated by their low incomes.

Figure 18.4 shows that the distribution of poverty by race is unequal: 10 percent of white households, 24 percent of black households, and 23 percent of Hispanic-origin households live below the poverty level.

Poverty is also influenced by household status. More than 28 percent of households in which the householder is a female and no husband is present are below the poverty level, while 5 percent of other households are. Poverty rates in the United States are falling, especially for Hispanic and black families.

FIGURE 18.4
The Changing Poverty Rate in the United States

*e*Foundations **18.1** 

Poverty rates have fallen during the 1990s and more rapidly for black and Hispanic families. But poverty remains a bigger problem for black and Hispanic families than for white families.

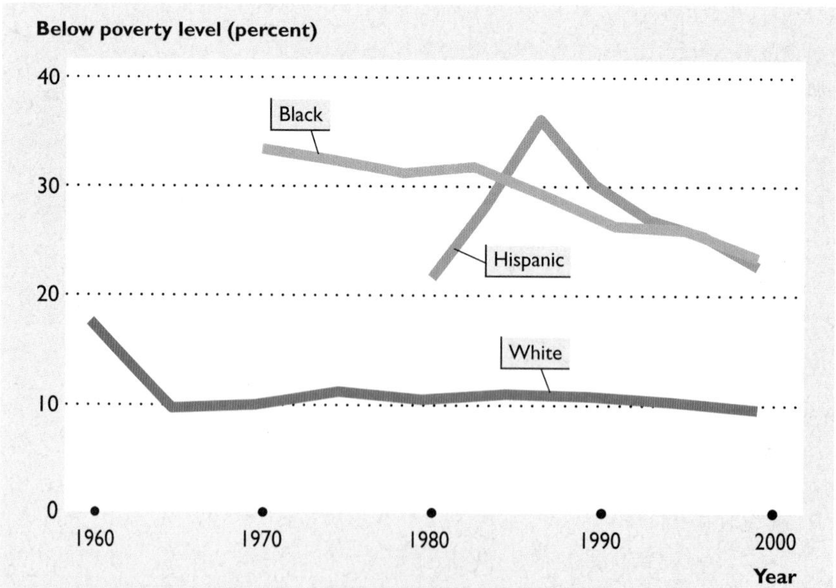

SOURCES: U.S. Bureau of the Census, *Current Population Reports*, P-60-209, *Poverty in the United States*, 2000.

Comparing Like with Like

To determine the degree of inequality, we compare one person's economic situation with another person's. But what is the correct measure of a person's economic situation? Is it income or is it wealth? If it is income, is it *annual* income, the measure we've used in this chapter, or income over a longer time period—for example, over a household's lifetime?

Wealth Versus Income

Wealth is a *stock*, and income is the *flow* of earnings that results from the stock of wealth. Wealth and income are two ways of looking at the same thing, and the interest rate determines the relation between them. Suppose that Lee's wealth is $1 million. If the interest rate is 5 percent a year, then Lee's income is $50,000 a year. We've converted Lee's wealth to an income. We can also convert his income to wealth. An income of $50,000 a year at an interest rate of 5 percent a year is worth $1 million—is a wealth of $1 million. So we can describe Lee's economic condition by using either his wealth or his income. At an interest rate of 5 percent a year, $1 million of wealth equals $50,000 a year of income.

But in Figure 18.1, the distribution of wealth is much more unequal than the distribution of income. Why? It is because the wealth data measure tangible assets only and exclude the value of human capital, while the income data measure income from both tangible assets and human capital.

Table 18.2 illustrates the consequence of omitting human capital from the wealth data. Lee's income is $50,000 a year, and Peter's is $25,000 a year. Lee's tangible assets are $800,000, and Peter's are $1,000. Is Lee twice or 800 times as well off as Peter? The answer is twice! The reason is that Peter's human capital is greater than Lee's. Peter's income from human capital is $24,950 a year, so using the 5 percent interest rate, Peter's human capital is worth $499,000. Lee's income from human capital is $10,000 a year, so his human capital is worth $200,000. Adding their human capital to their tangible assets shows that Peter's wealth is $500,000 and Lee's wealth is $1 million. Lee is twice as well off as Peter.

Because the wealth distribution data excludes human capital, the income distribution is a more accurate measure of economic inequality than the wealth distribution.

January 18, 2000

Income Gap of Richest and Poorest Widens

Two Washington think tanks report that the income gap between the poorest and richest U.S. families grew wider during the 1990s.

Questions

1. What are the facts reported by the Center on Budget and Policy Priorities and the Economic Policy Institute?
2. Why is this report controversial?
3. What are the main problems that arise in making income and wealth comparisons among individuals and families?
4. What are the main regional variations?
5. What are the data for your own state?
6. What are the policy implications of this report and the debate that surrounds it?

 *e*/**Foundations 18.1**

TABLE 18.2
Capital, Wealth, and Income

	Lee		Peter	
	Wealth	**Income**	**Wealth**	**Income**
Human capital	$200,000	$10,000	$499,000	$24,950
Tangible assets	$800,000	$40,000	$1,000	$50
Total	$1,000,000	$50,000	$500,000	$25,000

When wealth is measured to include the value of human capital as well as tangible assets, the distribution of income and the distribution of wealth display the same degree of inequality.

Annual or Lifetime Income and Wealth?

A typical household's income changes over time. It starts out low, grows to a peak when the household's workers reach retirement age, and then falls after retirement. Also, a typical household's wealth changes over time. Like income, it starts out low, grows to a peak at the point of retirement, and falls after retirement.

Suppose we look at three households that have identical lifetime incomes. One household is young, one is middle-aged, and one is retired. The middle-aged household has the highest income and wealth, the retired household has the lowest, and the young household falls in the middle. The distributions of annual income and wealth in a given year are unequal, but the distributions of lifetime income and wealth are equal. So because different households are at different stages in the life cycle, measured inequality overstates actual inequality. Inequality of annual incomes overstates the degree of lifetime inequality.

The Eye on the U.S. Economy reports one economist's attempt to measure lifetime inequality.

Consumption Inequality

Professor Daniel T. Slesnick of the University of Texas at Austin has provided a different view of inequality in the United States from the official view of the Bureau of the Census.

Instead of calculating the distribution of annual income, as the Census Bureau does, Professor Slesnick has calculated the distribution of consumption.

Consumption is superior to income for making comparisons of economic well-being for two reasons. First, consumption is the direct source of economic well-being. Second, consumption provides a good indicator of lifetime income.

Annual income is a poor indicator of lifetime income. A household has good years and bad years that average out. In a high-income year, the household saves more. In a low-income year, the household saves less (and might even eat into its assets by consuming more than its income).

The figure shows how a consumption-based measure of inequality changes the picture. While there is considerable inequality, there is much less inequality of consumption than there is of annual income. And in contrast to the picture presented by the annual income data, there is virtually no change in the degree of inequality between 1961 and 1995.

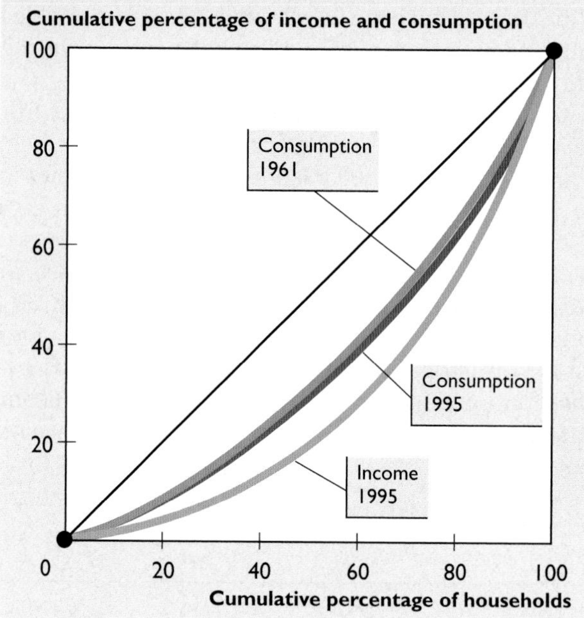

SOURCE: Daniel T. Slesnick, *Living Standards in the United States: A Consumption-Based Approach.* Washington, DC: The AEI Press, 2000.

CHECKPOINT 18.1

1 Describe the inequality in income and wealth in the United States and explain why wealth inequality is greater than income inequality.

Study Guide pp. 280–283

*e*Foundations 18.1

Practice Problem 18.1

Table 18.1 on page 430 shows the distribution of income in the United States, and Table 1 shows the distribution of income in Canada.

a. Draw the Lorenz curves for Canada and the United States.

b. Compare the distribution of income in Canada with that in the United States. Which distribution is more unequal?

TABLE 1

Households	Income (percentage)
Lowest 20 percent	7.4
Second 20 percent	13.2
Third 20 percent	18.1
Fourth 20 percent	24.9
Highest 20 percent	36.4

Exercise 18.1

Table 18.1 on page 430 shows the distribution of income in the United States, Table 1 shows the distribution of income in Canada, and Table 2 shows the distribution of income in the United Kingdom.

a. Draw the Lorenz curves for the United Kingdom, Canada, and the United States.

b. Compare the distribution of income in the United Kingdom with that in the United States. Which distribution is more unequal?

c. Compare the distribution of income in the United Kingdom with that in the Canada. Which distribution is more unequal?

TABLE 2

Households	Income (percentage)
Lowest 20 percent	3
Second 20 percent	5
Third 20 percent	14
Fourth 20 percent	25
Highest 20 percent	53

Solution to Practice Problem 18.1

a. The Lorenz curve plots the cumulative percentage of income against the cumulative percentage of households. Figure 1 shows the Lorenz curves in Canada and the United States.

b. The Canadian Lorenz curve lies closer to the line of equality than does the U.S. Lorenz curve. So the distribution of income in the United States is more unequal than that in Canada.

FIGURE 1

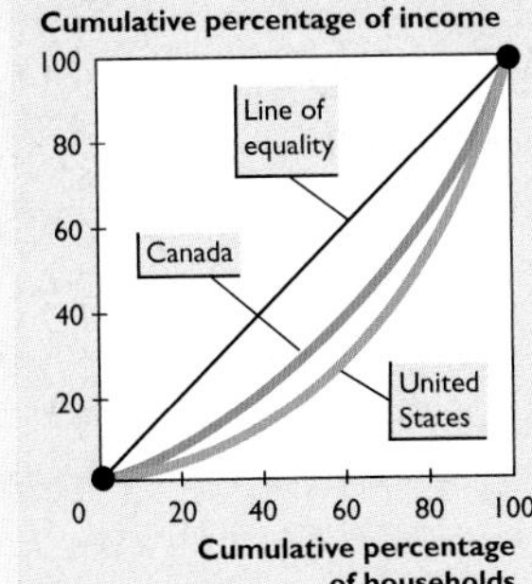

18.2 HOW INEQUALITY ARISES

A household's income depends on three things:

- Resource prices
- Resource endowments
- Choices

The distribution of income depends on the distribution of these three things across the population. The first two are outside our individual control and are determined by market forces and by history. From the viewpoint of each one of us, they appear to be determined by luck. The last item is under individual control. We make choices that influence our incomes. Let's look at the three factors that influence incomes.

Resource Prices

Everyone faces the same interest rates in capital markets, but people face differing wage rates in the labor market. And the labor market is the biggest single source of income for most people. To what extent do variations in wage rates account for the unequal distribution of income? The answer is to some extent, but wage differences cannot account for all the inequality.

A few extremely talented entrepreneurs who run successful businesses earn up to a billion dollars a year, and many more earn a few million dollars a year. Some unusually talented athletes, actors, and television performers, who earn millions of dollars a year, join these entrepreneurs at the top of the income ladder.

The highest-paid professionals, who earn a few hundred thousand dollars a year, stand a long way behind these rare people. But the highest-paid professionals earn around 3 times as much as high-skilled workers, who in turn earn around 4 times as much as low-skilled workers. So there is a big range in the incomes that people earn from their work.

Resource Endowments

There is a large variety in a household's endowments of capital and of human abilities. Differences in capital make a big contribution to differences in incomes. But differences in ability also contribute.

Physical and mental differences (some inherited, some learned) might have a normal, or bell-shaped, distribution—like the distribution of people's heights or weights. The distribution of individual ability across individuals is a major source of inequality in income and wealth. But it is not the only source. If it were, the distributions of income and wealth would look like the bell-shaped curve that describes the distribution of heights. In fact, these distributions are skewed toward high incomes and look like the curve in Figure 18.5. This figure shows income on the x-axis and the percentage of households receiving each income on the y-axis. In 1999, the median household income—the income that separates households into two groups of equal size—was $40,816. The most common income—called the mode income—is less than the median income. The mean income—also called the average income—is greater than the median income and in 1999 was $54,842. A skewed distribution like the one shown in Figure 18.5 is one in which many more people have incomes below the average than above it, a large number of people have low incomes, and a small number of people have high incomes. The distribution of (nonhuman) wealth has a similar shape to the distribution of income but is even more skewed.

The skewed shape of the distribution of income *cannot* be explained by the bell-shaped distribution of individual abilities. It results from the choices that people make.

Choices

Although many poor households feel trapped and do not have many options open to them, a household's income and wealth depend partly on the choices that its members make. You are going to discover that the choices people make exaggerate the differences among them and make the distribution of income more unequal than the distribution of abilities, as well as make the distribution of income skewed.

Wages and the Supply of Labor

At a high enough wage rate, an individual labor supply curve bends backward (see Chapter 16, p. 392). But over a large range of wage rates, the quantity of labor that a person supplies increases as that person's wage rate increases, other things remaining the same. Because the quantity of labor supplied increases as the wage rate increases, the distribution of income is more unequal than the distribution of hourly wages. It is also skewed, like the distribution shown in Figure 18.5.

FIGURE 18.5
The Distribution of Income

*e*Foundations 18.2 

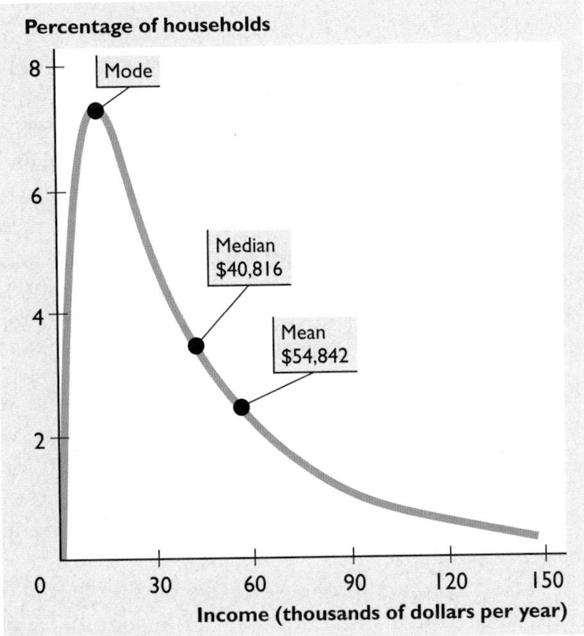

The distribution of income is unequal and is not symmetric around the mean income. There are many more people with incomes below the mean income than above it. Also, the distribution has a long, thin upper tail representing a small number of people who earn very large incomes.

To see why the distribution is skewed, think about three people: Jay, a high school graduate; Ken, an experienced electrician; and Lauren, a lawyer. Jay can earn $10 an hour, so he chooses to work 30 hours a week and earn $300. Ken has work and overtime opportunities at an average wage rate of $20 an hour, so he chooses to work for 45 hours a week and earn $900. Lauren can earn $100 an hour, so she works around the clock and puts in 54 hours a week to earn $5,400. The choices stretch out the incomes. The ratios of hourly wage rates are 1 for Jay, 2 for Ken, and 5 for Lauren. The ratios of the incomes are 1 for Jay, 3 for Ken, and 18 for Lauren. The median income of these three people is Ken's, $900, but the mean income is much higher. It is the average of $300, $900, and $5,400 and is $2,200.

Saving and Bequests

Another choice that results in unequal distributions in income and wealth is the decision to save and make bequests. A bequest is a gift from one generation to the next. The higher a household's income, the more that household tends to save and accumulate wealth across generations.

Saving and bequests are not inevitably a source of increased inequality. If a household saves to redistribute an uneven income over the life cycle and to enable consumption to be constant, the act of saving decreases the degree of inequality. If a lucky generation that has a high income saves a large amount and makes a bequest to a generation that is unlucky, this act of saving also decreases the degree of inequality. But two features of bequests make intergenerational transfers of wealth a source of increased inequality:

- Debts cannot be bequeathed.
- Mating is assortative.

Debts Cannot Be Bequeathed Although a person may die with debts that exceed assets—with negative wealth—debts cannot be forced onto other household members. Because a zero inheritance is the smallest inheritance that anyone can receive, bequests can only add to future generations' wealth and income potential.

Most people inherit nothing or a very small amount. A few people inherit enormous fortunes. As a result, bequests make the distribution of income persistently more unequal than the distribution of ability and job skills. A household that is poor in one generation is more likely to be poor in the next. A household that is wealthy in one generation is likely to be wealthy in the next. But there is a tendency for income and wealth to converge, across generations, to the average. Although there can be long runs of good luck or bad luck, or good judgment or bad judgment, such long runs are uncommon across the generations. But a feature of human behavior slows the convergence of wealth to the average and makes inequalities persist—assortative mating.

Assortative Mating Assortative mating is the tendency for people to marry within their own socioeconomic class. In the vernacular, "like attracts like." Although there is a good deal of folklore that "opposites attract," perhaps such Cinderella tales appeal to us because they are so rare in reality. Marriage partners tend to have similar socioeconomic characteristics. Wealthy individuals seek wealthy partners.

The consequence of assortative mating is that inherited wealth becomes more concentrated in a small number of households, and consequently, the distribution of wealth becomes more unequal.

CHECKPOINT 18.2

2 **Explain how economic inequality arises.**

Study Guide pp. 283–285

*e*Foundations 18.2

Practice Problem 18.2

An economy consists of 10 people, each of whom has the labor supply schedule shown in Table 1. The people differ in ability and earn different wage rates. Table 2 shows the distribution of wage rates that these people can earn. Calculate the:

a. Mean (average) wage rate.
b. Ratio of the highest to the lowest wage rate.
c. Mean (average) daily income.
d. Ratio of the highest to the lowest daily income.
e. Median income.
f. Mode income.
g. Compare the mean, median, and mode incomes.
h. Sketch the distribution of daily income for this economy and indicate the mean, median, and mode income on your graph.

TABLE 1

Wage rate (dollars per hour)	Hours per day
10	5
20	6
30	7
40	8
50	10

TABLE 2

Name	Wage rate (dollars per hour)
Alan	10
Bill	20
Carol	20
Denise	30
Ed	30
Frank	30
Gina	30
Hal	40
Ira	40
Jen	50

Exercise 18.2

In the Practice Problem, Alan decides that he needs to work harder and earn more. So he increases his work hours to 10 a week. Everyone else's labor supply schedule remains the same. Calculate the:

a. Mean (average) daily income.
b. Ratio of the highest to the lowest daily income.
c. Median income.
d. Mode income.
e. Compare the mean, median, and mode incomes.
f. Sketch the distribution of daily income for this economy, and indicate the mean, median, and mode income on your graph.
g. Sketch the Lorenz curves for this economy and the case in the Practice Problem.
h. Is the distribution of income more equal or less equal than in the Practice Problem?

TABLE 3

Name	Wage rate (dollars per hour)	Hours per day	Income (dollars per day)
Alan	10	5	50
Bill	20	6	120
Carol	20	6	120
Denise	30	7	210
Ed	30	7	210
Frank	30	7	210
Gina	30	7	210
Hal	40	8	320
Ira	40	8	320
Jen	50	10	500

Solution to Practice Problem 18.2

a. The mean wage rate is the average of the numbers in Table 2. Those numbers sum to \$300, and their average is \$30.
b. The highest wage rate is \$50 and the lowest is \$10, so the ratio of the highest to the lowest is 5 to 1.
c. The mean daily income is the average of the numbers in the last column of Table 3 and is \$227.
d. The highest daily income is \$500 and the lowest is \$50, so the ratio of the highest to the lowest is 10 to 1.
e. The median income is the one with 5 above and 5 below, which is \$210.
f. The mode income is the most common income and is also \$210.
g. The median equals the mode, and they are less than the mean.
h. Figure 1 shows the distribution of daily income in this economy.

FIGURE 1

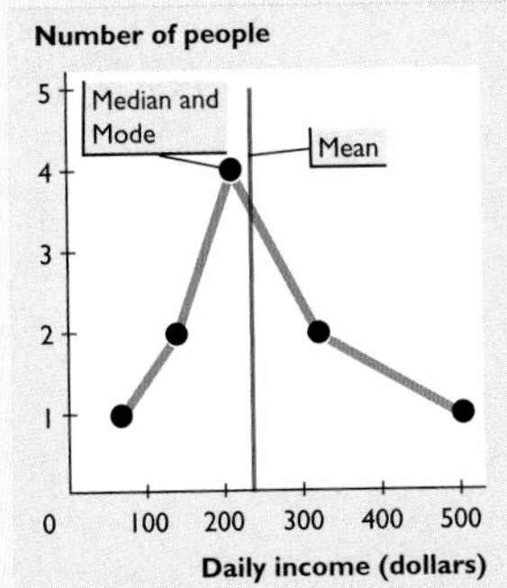

18.3 INCOME REDISTRIBUTION

The three main ways in which governments in the United States redistribute income are:

- Income taxes
- Income maintenance programs
- Subsidized services

Income Taxes

Income taxes may be progressive, regressive, or proportional (see Chapter 9, pp. 215–216). A *progressive income tax* is one that taxes income at an average rate that increases with the level of income. A *regressive income tax* is one that taxes income at an average rate that decreases with the level of income. A *proportional income* tax (also called a *flat-rate* income tax) is one that taxes income at a constant rate, regardless of the level of income.

The tax rates that apply in the United States are composed of two parts: federal and state taxes. Some cities, such as New York City, also have an income tax. There is variety in the detailed tax arrangements in the individual states, but the tax system, at both the federal and state levels, is progressive. The poorest working households receive money from the government through an earned income tax credit. The middle-income households pay 15 percent of each additional dollar they earn, and successively richer households pay 28 percent and 31 percent of each additional dollar earned.

Income Maintenance Programs

Three main types of programs redistribute income by making direct payments (in cash, services, or vouchers) to people in the lower part of the income distribution. They are:

- Social security programs
- Unemployment compensation
- Welfare programs

Social Security

Social Security is a public insurance system. The main component of Social Security is a program called OASDHI—Old Age, Survivors, Disability, and Health Insurance. Compulsory payroll taxes on both employers and employees pay for monthly cash payments to retired or disabled workers or their surviving spouses and children. In 1999, total social security expenditure was more than $500 billion, and 41 million people received an average monthly social security check of $721.

The other component of Social Security is Medicare, which provides hospital and health insurance for the elderly and disabled.

Unemployment Compensation

To provide an income to unemployed workers, every state has established an unemployment compensation program. Under these programs, a tax is paid based on the income of each covered worker, and such a worker receives a benefit when he or she becomes unemployed. The details of the benefits vary from state to state.

Welfare Programs

The purpose of welfare is to provide incomes for people who do not qualify for Social Security or unemployment compensation. They are:

1. Supplementary Security Income (SSI) program, designed to help the neediest elderly, disabled, and blind people
2. Temporary Assistance for Needy Families (TANF) program, designed to help households that have inadequate financial resources
3. Food Stamp program, designed to help the poorest households obtain a basic diet
4. Medicaid, designed to cover the costs of medical care for households receiving help under the SSI and TANF programs

Subsidized Services

A great deal of redistribution takes place in the United States through the provision of subsidized services—services provided by the government at prices far below the cost of production. The taxpayers who consume these goods and services receive a transfer in kind from the taxpayers who do not consume them. The two most important areas in which this form of redistribution takes place are education—both kindergarten through grade 12 and college and university—and health care. But neither necessarily redistributes from the rich to the poor.

In 2000–2001, students enrolled in the University of California system that were not residents of California paid annual tuition of $14,312. This amount was probably close to the cost of providing a year's education at UCLA or Berkeley. But California residents paid tuition of only $3,698. So California households with a member enrolled in the University of California received a benefit from the government of more than $10,000 a year. Many of these households have above-average incomes.

Government provision of health-care services has grown to equal the scale of private provision. Medicaid provides high-quality and high-cost health care to millions of people who earn too little to buy such services themselves and increases redistribution from the rich to the poor. Medicare, which is available to all over 65 years of age, is not targeted at the poor.

The Scale of Income Redistribution

A household's **market income** is the income it earns in factor markets before tax and excluding transfers from the government. We can measure the scale of income redistribution by calculating the percentage of market income paid in taxes minus the percentage received in benefits at each income level. The data available include redistribution through taxes and cash and noncash benefits to welfare recipients. They do not include the value of subsidized services such as college, which might decrease the total scale of redistribution from the rich to the poor.

Market income
The income a household earns in factor markets before tax and excluding transfers from the government.

Figure 18.6 shows how government actions change the distribution of income. The blue Lorenz curve in part (a) describes the market distribution of income. It is

Money income
Market income plus money benefits paid by the government.

not quite the same as that in Figure 18.1, which is based on money income. **Money income** is market income plus money benefits paid by the government. The green Lorenz curve shows the income distribution based on this measure. The orange Lorenz curve shows the distribution of income after all taxes and benefits, including Medicaid and Medicare benefits. The distribution after taxes and benefits is more equal than the market distribution. Figure 18.6(b) shows that redistribution increases the share of total income received by the lowest 60 percent of households and decreases the share received by the highest 40 percent.

Another measure of the scale of redistribution is provided by the sources of income at different points of the income distribution. The poorest 20 percent of households receive more than 70 percent of their income from the government. The second 20 percent receive around 40 percent and the richest 20 percent receive almost nothing from the government. They receive a third of their income from capital—interest and dividends from financial assets—but the other 80 percent of households receive only a constant 8 percent of income from capital.

FIGURE 18.6
Income Redistribution

*e*Foundations 18.3 

Taxes and income maintenance programs reduce the degree of inequality that the market generates. In part (a), the Lorenz curve moves closer to the line of equality. In part (b), the three lowest income groups gain and the top two income groups lose.

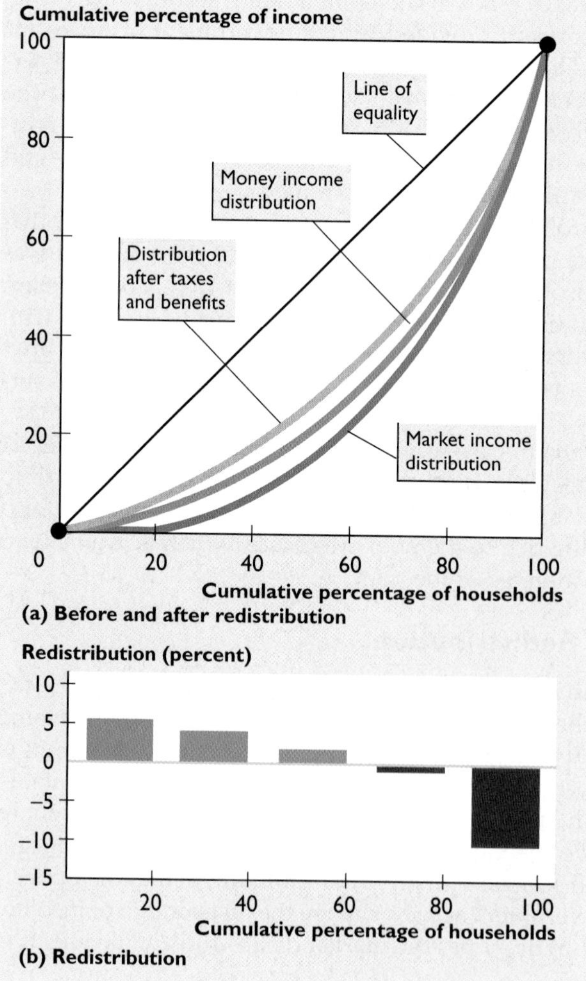

Source: U.S. Bureau of the Census, *Current Population Reports*, P-60-209, *Money Income in the United States*, 2000.

The Big Tradeoff

The redistribution of income creates the *big tradeoff* between equity and efficiency (defined in Chapter 6, pp. 148–149) that arises because redistribution decreases the total size of the economic pie to be shared. The redistribution bucket is leaky. The reason is that redistribution uses scarce resources and weakens incentives.

A dollar collected from a rich person does not translate into a dollar received by a poor person. Some of it gets used up in the process of redistribution. Tax-collecting agencies such as the Internal Revenue Service and welfare-administering agencies (as well as tax accountants and lawyers) use skilled labor, computers, and other scarce resources to do their work. The bigger the scale of redistribution, the greater is the opportunity cost of administering it.

But the cost of collecting taxes and making welfare payments is a small part of the total cost of redistribution. A bigger cost arises from the inefficiency—*deadweight loss*—of taxes and benefits (see Chapter 7, p. 164, and Chapter 9, pp. 216–218). Greater equality can be achieved only by taxing productive activities such as work and saving. Taxing people's income from their work and saving lowers the after-tax income they receive. This lower income makes them work and save less, which in turn result in smaller output and less consumption, not only for the rich who pay the taxes but also for the poor who receive the benefits.

Benefit recipients as well as taxpayers face weaker incentives. In fact, under the welfare arrangements that prevailed before the 1996 reforms, the weakest incentives to work were those faced by households that benefited from welfare. When a welfare recipient got a job, benefits were withdrawn and eligibility for programs like Medicaid ended, so the household in effect paid a tax of more than 100 percent on its earnings. This arrangement locked poor households in a welfare trap.

So the amount and methods of income redistribution must pay close attention to the incentive effects of taxes and benefits. Let's look at the way lawmakers are tackling the big tradeoff today.

A Major Welfare Challenge

Among the poorest people in the United States (see pp. 433–434) are young women who have not completed high school, have a child (or children), live without a partner, and are more likely black or of Hispanic origin than white. These young women and their children present a major welfare challenge.

There are about 10 million single mothers, and a quarter of them receive no support from their absent partners. The long-term solution to the problem of these women is education and job training—acquiring human capital. The short-term solution is welfare. But welfare must be designed to minimize the disincentive to pursue the long-term goal. This is what the current welfare programs in the United States try to do.

Passed in 1996, the *Personal Responsibility and Work Opportunities Reconciliation Act* created the Temporary Assistance for Needy Families (TANF) program. TANF is a block grant paid to the states, which administer payments to individuals. It is not an open-ended entitlement program. An adult member of a household receiving assistance must either work or perform community service. And there is a five-year limit for assistance.

These measures go a long way toward removing one of the most serious poverty problems while being sensitive to the potential inefficiency of welfare. But they don't go as far as some economists want to go. Let's look at a more radical reform of welfare, the negative income tax.

Negative Income Tax

Negative income tax is not on the political agenda. But it is popular among economists, and it is the subject of several real-world experiments.

Negative income tax
A tax and redistribution scheme that provides every household with a guaranteed minimum annual income and taxes all market income at a fixed marginal tax rate.

A **negative income tax** provides every household with a guaranteed minimum annual income and taxes all market income at a fixed marginal tax rate. Suppose the guaranteed minimum annual income is $10,000 and the tax rate is 25 percent. A household with no market income receives the $10,000 guaranteed minimum income from the government. This household "pays" income tax of *minus* $10,000, hence the name "negative income tax."

A household with a market income of $40,000 also receives the $10,000 guaranteed minimum income from the government. But it also pays $10,000—25 percent of its market income—to the government. So this household pays no income tax. It has the break-even income. Households with a market income of between zero and $40,000 receive more from the government than they pay to the government. They "pay" a negative income tax.

A household with a market income of $60,000 receives the $10,000 guaranteed minimum income from the government, but it pays $15,000—25 percent of its market income—to the government. So this household pays income tax of $5,000. All households with market incomes that exceed $40,000 pay to the government more than they receive from the government. They pay a positive amount of tax.

A negative income tax scheme can be set up to collect the same amount in taxes as it redistributes in guaranteed income and so break even for the government. To achieve this outcome, the guaranteed income is set at x percent of the average income and the tax rate is also set at the same x percent. In the above example, the negative income tax scheme breaks even if the average income in the economy is $40,000. In this case, the government pays out 25 percent of the average to everyone and collects 25 percent of actual income from everyone. But because actual income, on the average, is $40,000, the government collects $10,000 on the average. If the government plans to finance its purchases with the income tax, it will need to collect more in taxes than it pays out as guaranteed minimum incomes. So the tax rate will need to exceed the ratio of the guaranteed income to the average income.

Figure 18.7 illustrates a negative income tax and compares it with our pre-1996 arrangements. In both parts of the figure, the horizontal axis measures market income and the vertical axis measures income after taxes are paid and benefits are received. The 45° line shows the hypothetical case of "no redistribution."

Part (a) shows traditional redistribution arrangements—the blue curve. Benefits of G are paid to those with no income. As income increases from zero to A, benefits are withdrawn. This arrangement creates a welfare trap shown as the gray triangle. It does not pay a person to work if the income he or she can earn is less than A. Over the income range A to C, each additional dollar of market income increases income after redistribution by a dollar. At incomes greater than C, income taxes are paid and at successively higher rates, so income after redistribution is smaller than market income.

Part (b) shows the negative income tax. The guaranteed annual income is G, and the break-even income is B. Households with market incomes below B receive a net benefit (the blue area), and those with incomes above B pay taxes (the red

FIGURE 18.7
Comparing Traditional Programs and a Negative Income Tax

*e*Foundations 18.3 

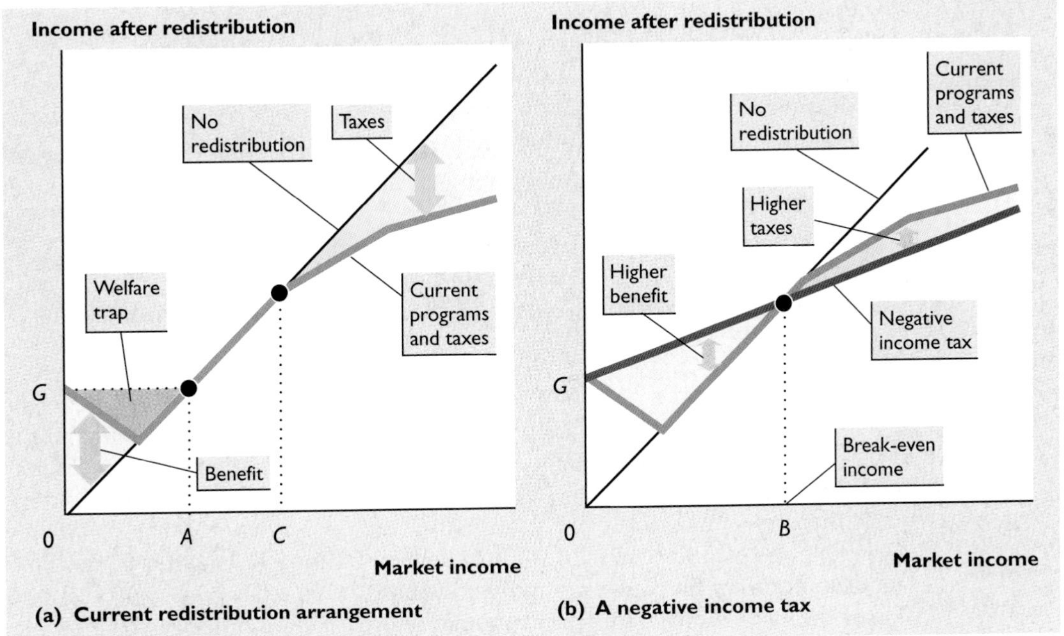

Part (a) shows traditional redistribution arrangements—the blue curve. Benefits of *G* are paid to those with no income. As incomes increase from zero to *A*, benefits are withdrawn, lowering income after redistribution below *G* and creating a welfare trap–the gray triangle. As incomes increase from *A* to *C*, there is no redistribution. As incomes increase above *C*, income taxes are paid at successively higher rates.

In part (b), a negative income tax gives a guaranteed annual income of *G* and decreases benefits at the same rate as the tax rate on incomes. The red line shows how market incomes translate into income after redistribution. Households with market incomes below *B*, the break-even income, receive net benefits. Those with market incomes above *B* pay net taxes.

area). A negative income tax removes the welfare trap and gives greater encouragement to low-income households to seek more employment, even at a low wage. It also overcomes many of the other problems arising from existing income maintenance programs.

A negative income tax does not eliminate the excess burden of taxation. Also, because it taxes all incomes, many low-income workers who pay no income tax under present arrangements would face a weakened incentive to work. It would also increase the marginal tax of the lowest-rate taxpayers. Only the highest-rate taxpayers would face lower rates and improved incentives.

Experiments conducted in Denver, Seattle, New Jersey, and other places in which a negative income tax has been compared with existing programs have yielded mixed results. The major objection to the idea is its cost. To provide an adequate basic income and cover other government expenditures, the tax rate would need to be high. Income redistribution will always be on the political agenda, and although off the front page today, the negative income tax might well return to the political stage, but probably not as a comprehensive scheme with a guaranteed income for everyone.

CHECKPOINT 18.3

Study Guide pp. 285–288 

e/Foundations 18.3

3 **Explain the effects of taxes, social security, and welfare programs on economic inequality.**

Practice Problem 18.3

Table 1 shows the distribution of market income in an economy. The government redistributes income by collecting income taxes and paying benefits shown in Table 2.

a. Calculate the income shares of each 20 percent of households after tax and redistribution.

b. Draw the Lorenz curve for this economy before and after taxes and benefits.

TABLE 1

Households	Income (millions of dollars per year)
Lowest 20 percent	5
Second 20 percent	10
Third 20 percent	18
Fourth 20 percent	28
Highest 20 percent	39

TABLE 2

Households	Income tax (percent)	Benefits (millions of dollars)
Lowest 20 percent	0	10
Second 20 percent	10	8
Third 20 percent	18	3
Fourth 20 percent	28	0
Highest 20 percent	39	0

Exercise 18.3

In the economy in the Practice Problem, the government replaces the current tax and benefit system with a negative income tax. Each household receives 20 percent of the average income, and each household pays a tax equal to 20 percent of its own income.

a. Calculate the income shares of each 20 percent of households after tax and redistribution under the new negative income tax scheme.

b. Draw the Lorenz curve for this economy before and after taxes and benefits.

c. Which economy do you predict has the higher average income and why: the one with the negative income tax or the one in the Practice Problem?

d. Which economy has the more equal distribution: the U.S. economy or the one with the negative income tax?

Solution to Practice Problem 18.3

a. To find the distribution of income, multiply the market incomes by the tax rates, subtract the taxes paid and add the benefits received to obtain the income after tax and benefits. Then calculate each group's income as a percentage of total income. Table 3 summarizes the calculations.

b. Find the cumulative shares from Table 3 to plot the Lorenz curve, shown in Figure 1.

FIGURE 1

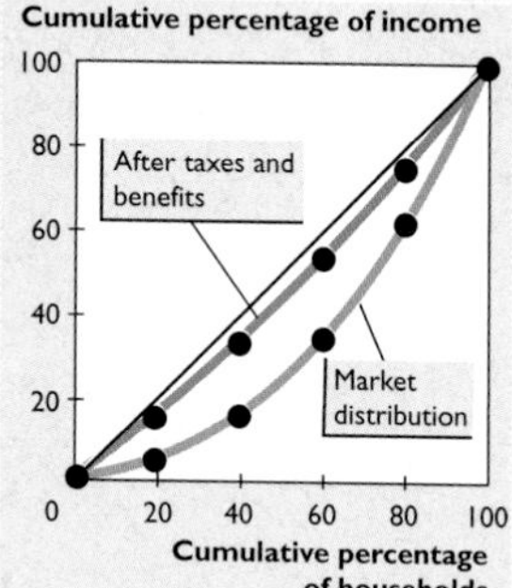

TABLE 3

Households	Market income (millions of dollars)	Tax paid (millions of dollars)	Benefits received (millions of dollars)	Income after tax and benefits (millions of dollars)	Income (percentage of total income)
Lowest 20 percent	5	0.0	10	15.0	16.0
Second 20 percent	10	1.0	8	17.0	18.1
Third 20 percent	18	3.2	3	17.8	19.0
Fourth 20 percent	28	7.8	0	20.2	21.5
Highest 20 percent	39	15.2	0	23.8	25.4

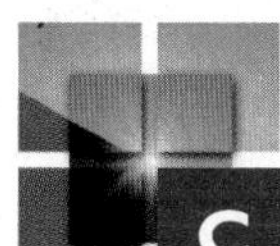

CHAPTER CHECKPOINT

Key Points

1 Describe the inequality in income and wealth in the United States and explain why wealth inequality is greater than income inequality.

- The richest 1 percent of Americans own almost one third of the total wealth in the country.
- Income is distributed less unevenly than wealth. Throughout the 1980s and 1990s, inequality increased.
- The poorest people in the United States are single black women with less than nine years of schooling who live in the South. The richest people live in the West and are college-educated, middle-aged, white households in which husband and wife live together.
- The distribution of wealth exaggerates the degree of inequality because it excludes human capital.
- The distribution of annual income exaggerates lifetime inequality.

2 Explain how economic inequality arises.

- Differences in income and wealth arise from differences in resource prices, endowments, and choices.
- People who face high wage rates generally work longer than those who face low wage rates, so the distribution of income becomes more unequal and more skewed than the distribution of wage rates.

3 Explain the effects of taxes, social security, and welfare programs on economic inequality.

- Governments redistribute income through income taxes, income maintenance programs, and provision of subsidized services.
- Income taxes are progressive.
- Redistribution creates a big tradeoff between equity and efficiency, which arises because the process of redistribution uses resources and weakens incentives to work and save.
- Traditional income maintenance programs create a welfare trap that discourages work, so poverty is persistent. Reforms seek to lessen the severity of the welfare trap. A more radical negative income tax reform would encourage those on welfare to find work but would increase the taxes on low-income workers.

Key Terms

Lorenz curve, 431
Market income, 443
Money income, 444
Negative income tax, 446
Poverty, 434

TABLE 1

Households	Income (percentage)
Lowest 20 percent	1
Second 20 percent	3
Third 20 percent	15
Fourth 20 percent	26
Highest 20 percent	55

Exercises

1. Table 1 shows the distribution of income in Australia.
   a. Draw the Lorenz curve for Australia.
   b. Compare the distribution of income in Australia with that in the United States. Which distribution is more unequal?

2. Imagine an economy with five people who are identical in all respects. Each lives for 70 years. For the first 14 of those years, they earn no income. For the next 35 years, they work and earn $30,000 a year from their work. For their remaining years, they are retired and have no income from labor. To make the arithmetic easy, let's suppose that the interest rate in this economy is zero; the individuals consume all their income during their lifetime and at a constant annual rate. What are the distributions of income and wealth in this economy if the individuals have the following ages:
   a. All are 45
   b. 25, 35, 45, 55, 65
   Does case (a) have greater inequality than case (b)?

3. Use the link on your Foundations Web site to visit the Economic Policy Institute's page on the Living Wage.
   a. What is the concept of the living wage?
   b. How does the concept of the living wage relate to the concept of poverty that you've studied in this chapter?
   c. How does the concept of the living wage relate to the concept of the minimum wage that you studied in Chapter 7?
   d. Do you think that the living wage is a solution to the problem of low income?

4. Use the link on your Foundations Web site to visit the Center on Budget and Policy Priorities and other sites and obtain information on President George W. Bush's tax cut proposals.
   a. What are the main elements in the President's tax plan?
   b. How do you think the President's proposals would change the Lorenz curve? Explain in detail.

5. Use the link on your Foundations Web site to obtain the article "Reengineering Social Security in the New Economy" by Thomas F. Siems, an economist at the Dallas Federal Reserve.
   a. What does Dr. Siems say is wrong with social security?
   b. How does he suggest the problems with social security be fixed?
   c. How would Dr. Siems's suggestions influence the distribution of income?

Part

7

Microeconomic Policy Issues

Chapter 19

International Trade

CHAPTER CHECKLIST

When you have completed your study of this chapter, you will be able to:

1. **Describe the patterns and trends in international trade.**
2. **Explain why nations engage in international trade and why trade benefits all nations.**
3. **Explain how trade barriers reduce international trade.**
4. **Explain the arguments used to justify trade barriers and show why they are incorrect but also why some barriers are hard to remove.**

Since ancient times, people have expanded their trading as far as technology allowed. Marco Polo opened up the silk route between Europe and China in the thirteenth century. Today, container ships laden with cars and machines and Boeing 747s stuffed with farm-fresh foods ply the sea and air routes. Why do people go to such great lengths to trade with those in other nations? Low-wage Mexico has a free trade agreement with high-wage United States. How can we compete with countries that pay their workers a fraction of U.S. wages?

In this chapter, you are going to learn about international trade. You will discover how all nations can gain by specializing in producing the goods and services in which they have a comparative advantage and trading with other countries. You will discover that all countries can compete, no matter how high their wages. And you'll learn why, even though international trade brings benefits to all countries, they nevertheless restrict trade.

19.1 TRADE PATTERNS AND TRENDS

The goods and services that we buy from people in other countries are called *imports*. The goods and services that we sell to people in other countries are called *exports*. What are the most important things that we import and export? Most people would probably guess that a rich nation such as the United States imports raw materials and exports manufactured goods. Although that is one feature of U.S. international trade, it is not its most important feature. The vast bulk of U.S. exports and imports are manufactured goods. We sell foreigners earth-moving equipment, airplanes, supercomputers, scientific equipment, movies, and magazines, and we buy televisions, VCRs, blue jeans, and T-shirts from them. Also, we are a major exporter of agricultural products and raw materials. We also import and export a huge volume of services.

Trade in Goods

Manufactured goods account for 50 percent of U.S. exports and for 60 percent of U.S. imports. Industrial materials (raw materials and semi-manufactured items) account for 17 percent of U.S. exports and for 20 percent of U.S. imports, and agricultural products account for only 7 percent of U.S. exports and 3 percent of U.S. imports. The largest individual U.S. trade items are capital goods and autos.

But goods account for only 74 percent of U.S. exports and 83 percent of U.S. imports. The rest of U.S. international trade is in services.

Trade in Services

You might be wondering how a country can export and import services. Here are some examples.

If you take a vacation in France and travel there on an Air France flight from New York, the United States imports transportation services from France. The money you spend in France on hotel bills and restaurant meals is also classified as a U.S. import of services. Similarly, the vacation taken by a French student in the United States counts as a U.S. export of services to France.

When we import TV sets from South Korea, the owner of the ship that transports them might be Greek and the company that insures them might be British. The payments that we make for the transportation and insurance are U.S. imports of services. Similarly, when a U.S. shipping company transports California wine to Tokyo, the transportation cost is a U.S. export of a service to Japan. U.S. international trade in these types of services is large and growing.

Trends in the Volume of Trade

In 1960, we exported around 5 percent of total output and imported around 5 percent of the goods and services that we bought. In 1998, we exported 11 percent of total output and imported 13 percent of the goods and services that we bought.

On the export side, capital goods, automobiles, food, and raw materials have remained large items and have held a roughly constant share of total exports. But the composition of imports has changed. Food and raw material imports have fallen steadily. Imports of fuel increased dramatically during the 1970s, fell during the 1980s, and increased again during the 1990s. Imports of machinery have grown and today approach 50 percent of total imports.

The Major Items That We Trade with Other Nations

The figure shows the U.S. volume of trade and balance of trade for the 25 largest items traded. If a bar has more red (imports) than blue (exports), the United States has a trade deficit in that item.

Transportation equipment, which is mainly automobiles but also includes airplanes and trucks, is the largest item traded. Electric and electronic machinery is also a large item. Services and travel are larger items than most goods.

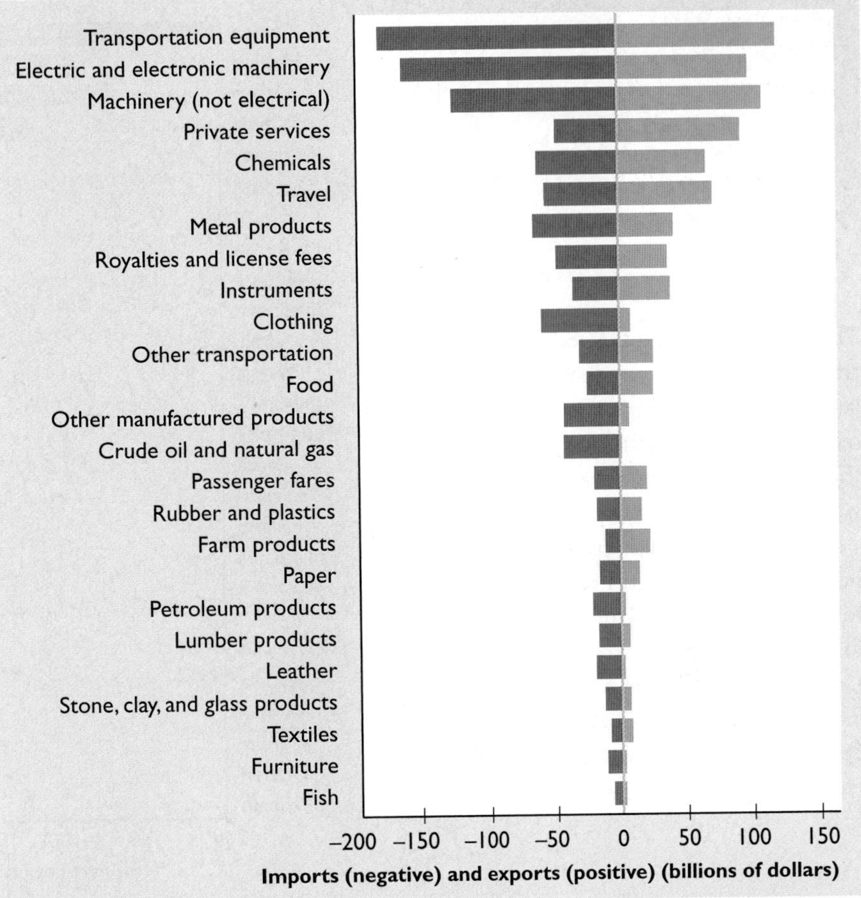

SOURCE: *Statistical Abstract of the United States*, 2001.

Trading Partners and Trading Blocs

The United States has trading links with every part of the world and is a member of several international organizations that seek to promote international trade and regional trade.

U.S. Trading Partners

Canada is the United States' biggest trading partner. Mexico and Japan are the second biggest and almost equal. Our other large trading partners are China, Germany, and the United Kingdom. But we also have significant volumes of trade with the other rapidly expanding Asian economies such as Hong Kong, South Korea, and Taiwan. Eye on the Global Economy on p. 456 shows the data for our 26 largest trading partners.

Trading Blocs

Trading blocs are groupings of nations in an international organization. The world today divides into three major geographical blocs, and the United States is a member of two of them. The two blocs of which the United States is a member are the North American Free Trade Agreement and Asia-Pacific Economic Cooperation. The other large bloc is the European Union. We'll provide a brief description of each of these groupings.

The Major U.S. Trading Partners and Volumes of Trade

The figure shows the U.S. volume of trade and balance of trade with its 26 largest trading partners. If a bar has more red (imports) than blue (exports), the United States has a trade deficit with that country.

Canada is the major trading partner of the United States by a big margin. Mexico and Japan come next, followed by China, Germany, and the United Kingdom. Trade with the newly industrialized countries of Asia (Taiwan, South Korea, Singapore, Malaysia, and Hong Kong) is also large.

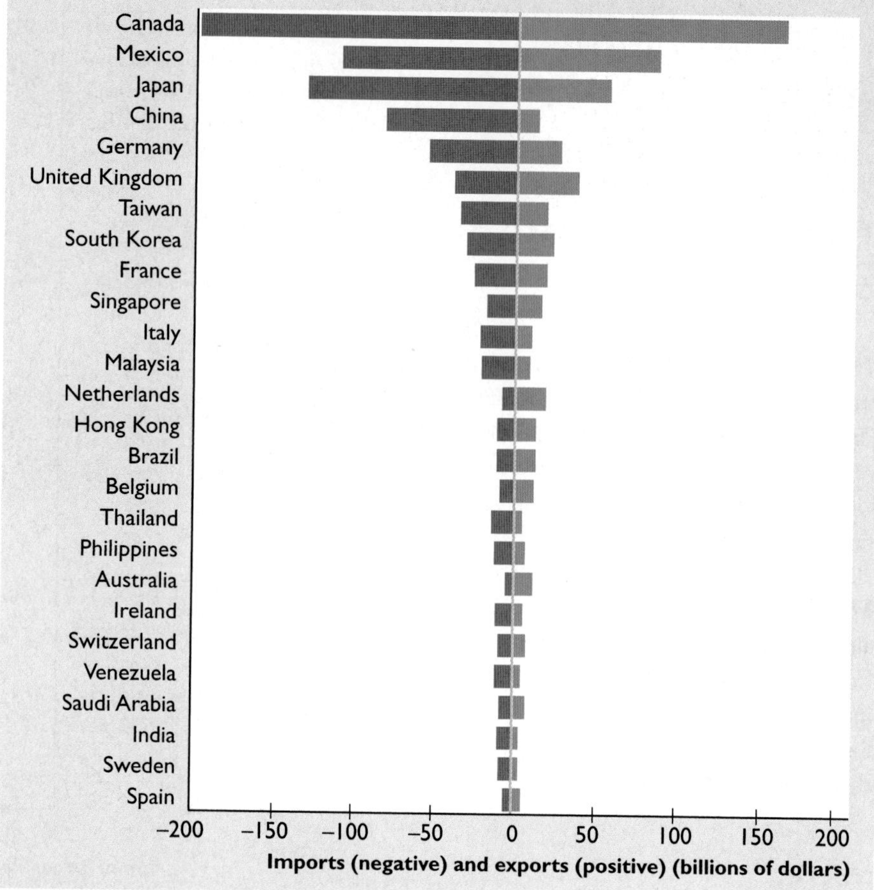

SOURCE: *Statistical Abstract of the United States*, 2001.

North American Free Trade Agreement The North American Free Trade Agreement, or NAFTA, is an agreement between the United States, Canada, and Mexico, to make trade among the three countries easier and freer. The Agreement came into effect in 1994. During the years since then, trade among the three nations has expanded rapidly.

The American continent consists of 35 nations and the governments of the 34 democracies (which excludes Cuba) have entered into a Free Trade of the Americas process. The objective of this process is to achieve free international trade among all the nations of the Americas by 2005.

Asia-Pacific Economic Cooperation Asia-Pacific Economic Cooperation, or APEC, is a group of 21 nations that border the Pacific Ocean. The largest of these are the United States, China, Japan, and Canada, but other significant members are Australia, Indonesia, and the dynamic new industrial Asian economies. In 1999, APEC nations conducted 44 percent of the world's international trade.

APEC was established in 1989 as an informal discussion group, but it has developed into an organization that promotes freer trade and cooperation among its member nations.

European Union The European Union, or EU, is a group of 15 nations of Western Europe. The EU began as the European Common Market when six countries (Belgium, Germany, France, Italy, Luxembourg, and the Netherlands) embarked on a process of economic integration in 1951. The EU is now developing its own money, the euro, and institutions of government that are more like those of a federal state than a group of independent states.

Balance of Trade and International Borrowing

The value of exports minus the value of imports is called the **balance of trade**. In 2000, the United States imported more than it exported. When a country imports more than it exports, it has a trade deficit and pays by borrowing from foreigners or selling some of its assets. When a country exports more than it imports, it has a trade surplus and lends to other countries or buys more foreign assets to enable the rest of the world to pay its deficit.

Balance of trade
The value of exports minus the value of imports.

CHECKPOINT 19.1

1 Describe the patterns and trends in international trade.

Study Guide pp. 294–296 

*e*Foundations 19.1

Practice Problem 19.1

Use the link on your Foundations Web site to answer the following questions:

a. In 1990, what percentage of Canadian production was exported to the United States and what percentage of total goods and services bought by Canadians was imported from the United States?

b. In 2000, what percentage of Canadian production was exported to the United States and what percentage of total goods and services bought by Canadians was imported from the United States?

Exercise 19.1

Use the link on your Foundations Web site to answer the following questions:

a. In 1990, what percentage of Mexican production was exported to the United States and what percentage of total goods and services bought by Mexicans was imported from the United States?

b. In 1998, what percentage of Mexican production was exported to the United States and what percentage of total goods and services bought by Mexicans was imported from the United States?

Solution to Practice Problem 19.1

a. In 1990, Canada exported 16.5 percent of total production to the United States and imported 14.4 percent of total goods and services purchased from the United States.

b. In 2000, Canada exported 34.6 percent of total production to the United States and imported 27 percent of goods and services purchased from the United States.

19.2 THE GAINS FROM INTERNATIONAL TRADE

Comparative advantage is the fundamental force that generates international trade. And comparative advantage arises from differences in opportunity costs. You met this idea in Chapter 3 (pp. 68–70), but we're now going to put some flesh on the bones of the basic idea. We'll begin by looking at an item that we export.

Why the United States Exports Airplanes

Boeing produces many more airplanes each year than airlines in the United States buy. Most of Boeing's production goes to airlines in other parts of the world. The United States is an exporter of airplanes. Why?

The answer is that the United States has a comparative advantage in the production of airplanes. The opportunity cost of producing an airplane is lower in the United States than in most other countries. So buyers can obtain airplanes from Boeing for a lower price than the price at which they could buy them from other potential suppliers. And Boeing can sell airplanes to foreigners for a higher price than it could obtain from an additional U.S. buyer.

So both countries gain. The foreign buyer gains from lower-priced airplanes. And Boeing's stockholders, managers, and workers gain from higher-priced airplanes. A win-win situation!

Figure 19.1 illustrates the effects of international trade in airplanes. The demand curve *D* shows the demand for airplanes in the United States. This curve tells us the quantity of airplanes that U.S. airlines are willing to buy at various prices. The demand curve also tells us the most that an additional airplane is worth to a U.S. airline at each quantity.

The supply curve *S* shows the supply of airplanes in the United States. This curve tells us the quantity of airplanes that U.S. aircraft makers are willing to sell at various prices. The supply curve also tells us the opportunity cost of producing an additional airplane at each quantity.

No Trade

First, let's see what happens in the market for airplanes if there is no international trade. Figure 19.1(a) shows the situation. The airplane market is in equilibrium when 400 airplanes are produced by U.S. aircraft makers and bought by U.S. airlines. The price is $80 million per airplane.

Trade

Second, let's see what happens in the market for airplanes if international trade takes place. Figure 19.1(b) shows the situation. The price of an airplane is determined in the world market, not the U.S. domestic market. Suppose that world demand and world supply determine a world equilibrium price of $100 million per airplane. In Figure 19.1(b), the world price line shows this price.

The U.S. demand curve, *D*, tells us that at $100 million per airplane, U.S. airlines buy 300 airplanes a year. The U.S. supply curve, *S*, tells us that at $100 million per airplane, U.S. aircraft makers produce 800 airplanes a year. So domestic production at 800 a year exceeds domestic purchases at 300 a year.

The quantity produced in the United States minus the quantity purchased by U.S. airlines is the quantity of U.S. exports, which are 500 airplanes a year.

FIGURE 19.1
An Export

*e*Foundations 19.2 

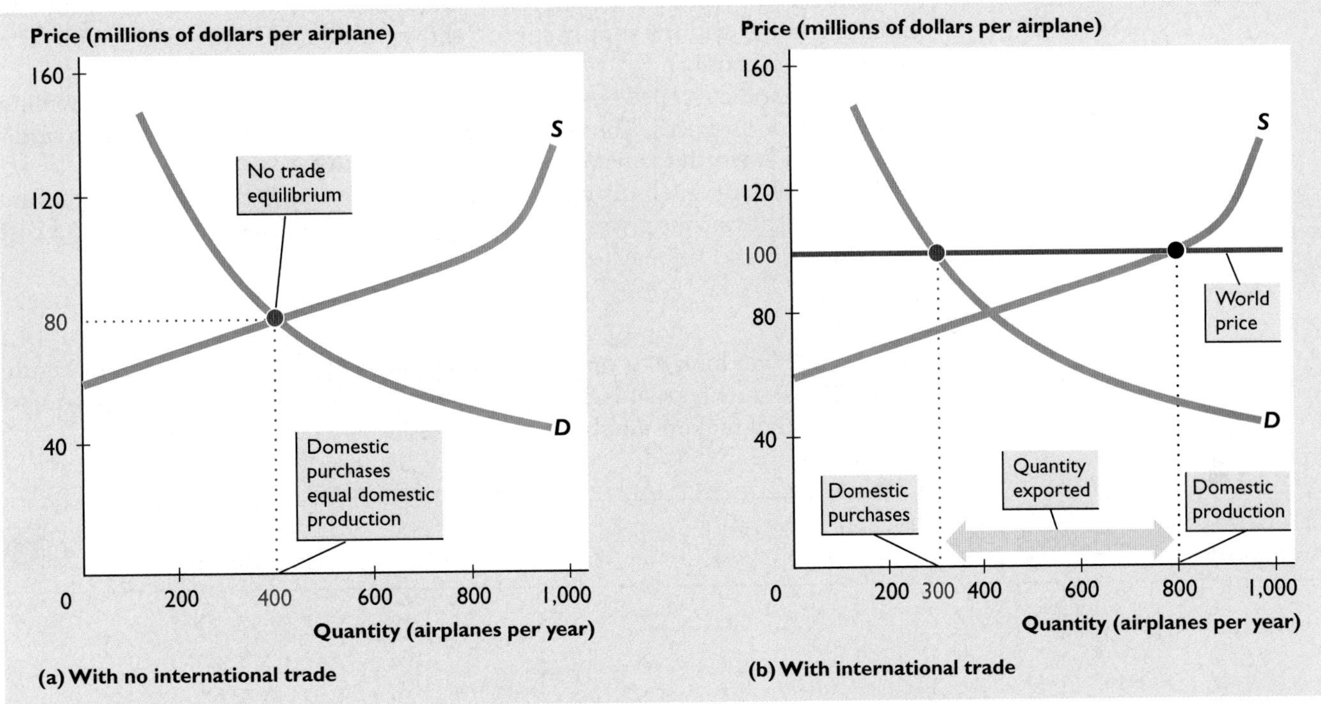

With no international trade in airplanes, the domestic demand and supply curves determine the price ($80 million per airplane) and the quantity produced and purchased (400 airplanes a year).

With international trade, world demand and supply determine the price, which is $100 million per airplane. Domestic purchases decrease to 300 a year, and domestic production increases to 800 a year; 500 airplanes a year are exported.

Comparative Advantage

You can see that U.S. aircraft makers have a comparative advantage in producing airplanes by comparing the U.S. supply curve and the world price line. At the equilibrium quantity of 800 airplanes a year, the world opportunity cost of producing an airplane is $100 million. But the U.S. supply curve tells us that only the 800th airplane has an opportunity cost of $100 million. Each of the other 799 airplanes has an opportunity cost of less than $100 million.

Why the United States Imports T-Shirts

Americans spend more than twice as much on clothing as the value of U.S. apparel production. That is, more than half of the clothing that we buy is manufactured in other countries and imported into the United States. Why?

The answer is that the rest of the world (mainly Asia) has a comparative advantage in the production of clothes. The opportunity cost of producing a T-shirt is lower in Asia than in the United States. So buyers can obtain T-shirts from Asia for a lower price than the price at which they could buy them from U.S. garment makers. And Asian garment makers can sell T-shirts to Americans for a higher price than they could obtain from an additional Asian buyer.

So again, both countries gain. The U.S. buyer gains from lower-priced T-shirts, and Asian garment makers gain from higher-priced T-shirts. Another win-win situation!

Figure 19.2 illustrates the effects of international trade in T-shirts. Again, the demand curve *D* and the supply curve *S* show the demand and supply in the U.S. domestic market only.

The demand curve tells us the quantity of T-shirts that Americans are willing to buy at various prices. The demand curve also tells us the most that an additional T-shirt is worth to an American at each quantity.

The supply curve tells us the quantity of T-shirts that U.S. garment makers are willing to sell at various prices. The supply curve also tells us the opportunity cost of producing an additional T-shirt in the United States at each quantity.

No Trade

Again, we'll first look at a market with no international trade, shown in Figure 19.2(a). The T-shirt market is in equilibrium when 20 million shirts are produced by U.S. garment makers and bought by Americans. The price is $8 a shirt.

FIGURE 19.2
An Import

*e*Foundations **19.2** 

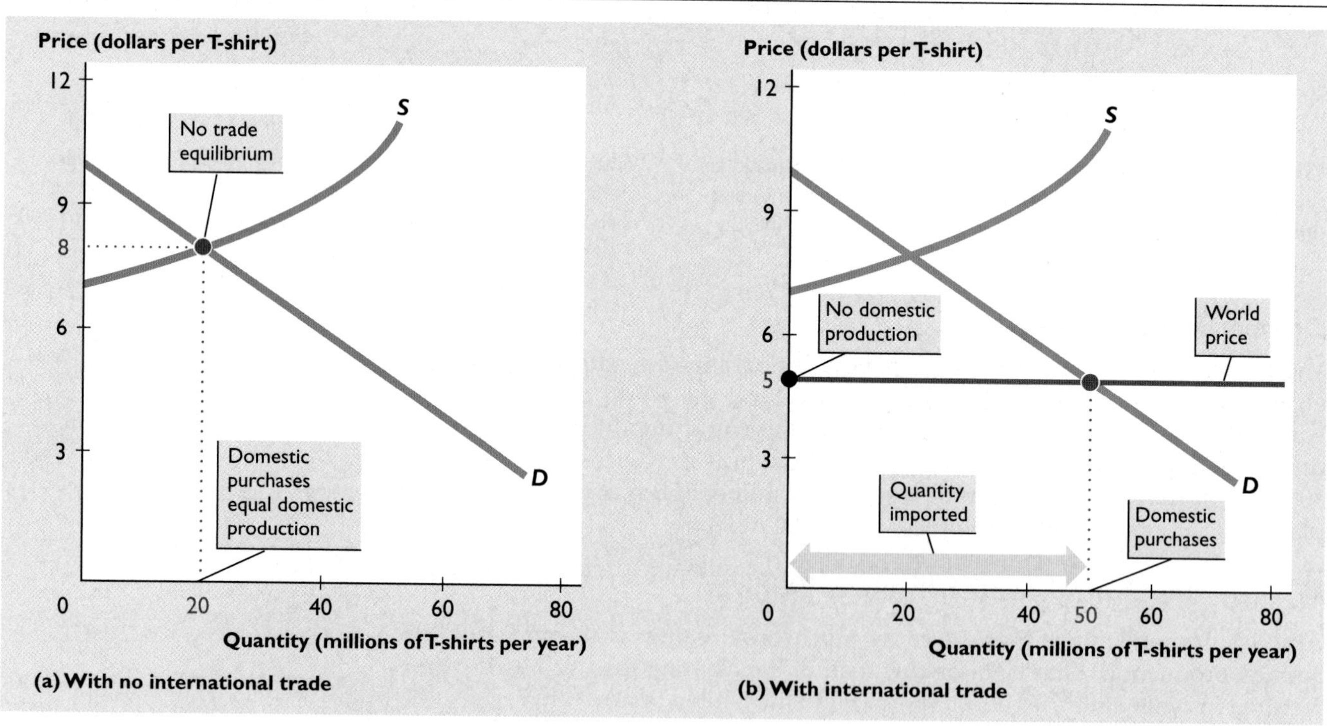

With no international trade in T-shirts, the domestic demand and supply curves determine the price ($8 per shirt) and quantity produced and purchased (20 million shirts a year).

With international trade, world demand and supply determine the price, which is $5 per shirt. Domestic purchases increase to 50 million a year, and domestic production decreases to zero. The entire 50 million shirts a year are imported.

Trade

Figure 19.2(b) shows what happens in the market for T-shirts if international trade takes place. Now the price of a T-shirt is determined in the world market, not the U.S. domestic market. Suppose that world demand and world supply determine a world equilibrium price of $5 per shirt. In Figure 19.2(b), the world price line shows this price.

The U.S demand curve, *D*, tells us that at $5 per shirt, Americans buy 50 million shirts a year. The U.S. supply curve, *S*, tells us that at $5 per shirt, U.S. garment makers produce no T-shirts. So there is no domestic production, and domestic purchases are 50 million T-shirts a year. The entire quantity of T-shirts purchased in the United States is the quantity imported.

Comparative Advantage

Now you can see that Asian garment makers have a comparative advantage in producing T-shirts by comparing the U.S. supply curve and the world price line. At the equilibrium quantity of 50 million T-shirts a year, the world opportunity cost of producing a T-shirt is $5. But the U.S. supply curve tells us that no U.S. garment maker has such a low opportunity cost, not even at smaller outputs. So Asian garment makers have a comparative advantage in producing T-shirts.

Gains from Trade and the *PPF*

The demand and supply model that you've just studied makes it clear why we export some goods and import others. But it doesn't show directly the gains from international trade. Another way of looking at comparative advantage uses the production possibilities frontier (*PPF*) that you learned about in Chapter 3. This approach shows the gains from trade in a powerful way, as you're about to discover.

Let's explore comparative advantage by looking at production possibilities in the United States and China.

Production Possibilities in the United States and China

To focus on the essential idea, suppose that the United States can produce only two goods: communications satellites and sports shoes. China can also produce only these same two goods. But production possibilities are different in the two countries.

If the United States uses all of its resources to produce satellites, its output is 10 satellites per year and no sports shoes. If it uses all of its resources to produce sports shoes, its output is 100 million pairs of shoes per year and no satellites. We'll assume that the U.S. opportunity cost of producing a satellite is constant. To produce 10 satellites, the United States must forgo 100 million pairs of shoes, which means that to produce 1 satellite, the United States must forgo 10 million pairs of shoes. That is:

The U.S. opportunity cost of producing 1 satellite is 10 million pairs of shoes.

In contrast, if China uses all of its resources to make satellites, it can produce 2 satellites per year and no sports shoes. And if it uses all of its resources to make sports shoes, it can produce 100 million pairs of shoes per year and no satellites. We'll assume that China's opportunity cost of producing a satellite is constant. To produce 2 satellites, China must forgo 100 million pairs of shoes, which means that to produce 1 satellite, China must forgo 50 million pairs of shoes. That is:

China's opportunity cost of producing 1 satellite is 50 million pairs of shoes.

The assumption that the opportunity costs of producing a satellite in the United States and in China are constant makes the point that we're illustrating in the simplest and cleanest way. We could assume increasing opportunity cost. We would reach the same conclusion that we'll reach here, but the story would be a bit more complicated and the point wouldn't jump out as clearly as it does by making the assumption of constant opportunity costs.

Figure 19.3(a) shows the production possibilities for the United States, and Figure 19.3(b) shows the production possibilities for China. The assumption that the opportunity costs are constant means that the two *PPF*s are linear. Along the U.S. *PPF*, 1 satellite costs 10 million pairs of shoes. And along China's *PPF*, 1 satellite costs 50 million pairs of shoes.

FIGURE 19.3
Production Possibilities in the United States and China

*e*Foundations **19.2** 

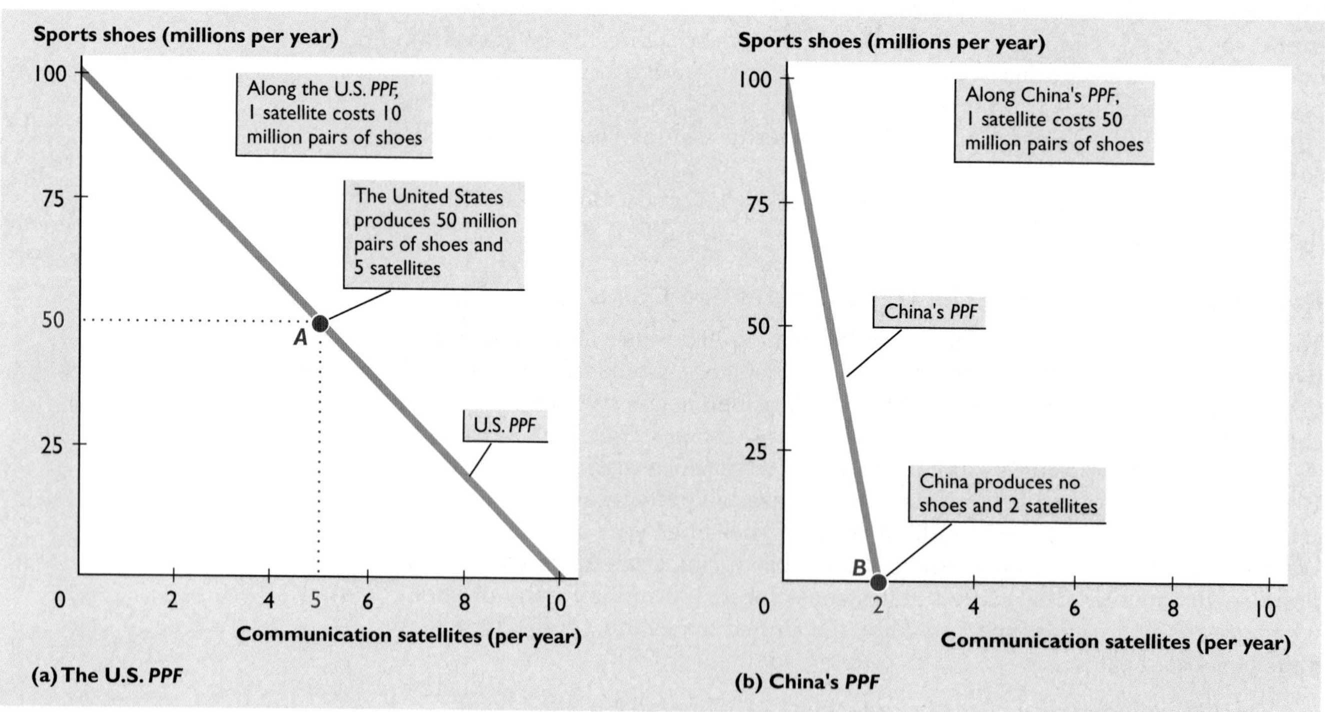

(a) The U.S. *PPF*

(b) China's *PPF*

The United States produces at point *A* on its *PPF* (part a), and China produces at point *B* on its *PPF* (part b). The opportunity cost of a satellite is lower in the United States than in China, so the United States has a comparative advantage in producing satellites. The opportunity cost of a pair of shoes is lower in China than in the United States, so China has a comparative advantage in producing shoes.

No Trade

With no international trade, we'll suppose that the United States produces 5 satellites and 50 million pairs of shoes at point *A* on its *PPF*. And we'll suppose that China produces 2 satellites and no shoes at point *B* on its *PPF*.

Comparative Advantage

In which of the two goods does China have a comparative advantage? Recall that comparative advantage is a situation in which one nation's opportunity cost of producing a good is lower than another nation's opportunity cost of producing that same good. China has a comparative advantage in producing shoes. China's opportunity cost of a pair of shoes is 1/50,000,000 of a satellite, whereas the U.S. opportunity cost of a pair of shoes is 1/10,000,000 of a satellite.

You can see China's comparative advantage by looking at the *PPF*s for China and the United States in Figure 19.3. China's *PPF* is steeper than the U.S. *PPF*. To produce an additional 1 million pairs of shoes, China must give up fewer satellites than does the United States. So China's opportunity cost of shoes is less than the U.S. opportunity cost of shoes. This means that China has a comparative advantage in producing shoes.

The United States has a comparative advantage in producing satellites. In Figure 19.3, the U.S. *PPF* is less steep than China's *PPF*. This means that the United States must give up fewer shoes to produce an additional satellite than does China. The U.S. opportunity cost of producing a satellite is 10 million pairs of shoes, which is less than China's 50 million pairs. So the United States has a comparative advantage in producing satellites.

Because China has a comparative advantage in producing shoes and the United States has a comparative advantage in producing satellites, both China and the United States can gain from specialization and trade. China specializes in shoes, and the United States specializes in satellites.

Achieving the Gains from Trade

If the United States, which has a comparative advantage in producing satellites, allocates all of its resources to that activity, it can produce 10 satellites a year. If China, which has a comparative advantage in producing shoes, allocates all of its resources to that activity, it can produce 100 million pairs a year. By specializing, the United States and China together can produce 100 million pairs of shoes and 10 satellites. With no trade, their total production had been 7 satellites (5 from the United States and 2 from China) and 50 million pairs of shoes (all produced by the United States).

So with specialization and trade, the United States and China can consume outside their production possibilities frontiers.

To achieve the gains from specialization, the United States and China must trade with each other. Suppose they agree to the following deal: China agrees to pay the United States 30 million pairs of shoes per satellite; the United States agrees to sell China 3 satellites a year at this price.

With this deal in place, the United States has 90 million pairs of shoes and 7 satellites—a gain of 40 million pairs of shoes and 2 satellites. China now has 10 million pairs of shoes and 3 satellites—a gain of 10 million pairs of shoes and one satellite.

Figure 19.4 shows these gains from trade. The United States originally produced and consumed at point *A*. It now produces at point *P* and consumes at point *A*'. China originally produced and consumed at point *B*. It now produces at point *Q* and consumes at point *B*'. As a result of specialization and trade, both countries can consume outside their production possibilities frontiers. Both countries gain from trade.

In this example, the United States can outproduce China and has an *absolute advantage* (see Chapter 3, p. 70), but it can get shoes at a lower cost by trading satellites for shoes with China. Gains from specialization and trade are always available when opportunity costs diverge.

Dynamic Comparative Advantage

Learning-by-doing
Repeatedly performing the same task and becoming more productive at producing a particular good or service.

Dynamic comparative advantage
A comparative advantage that a person (or country) obtains by specializing in an activity, resulting from learning-by-doing.

Resources and technology determine comparative advantage. But just by repeatedly producing a particular good or service, people become more productive in that activity, a phenomenon called **learning-by-doing**. **Dynamic comparative advantage**, a comparative advantage that a person (or country) obtains by specializing in an activity, results from learning-by-doing.

Hong Kong, South Korea, and Taiwan are examples of countries that have pursued dynamic comparative advantage vigorously. They have developed electronics and biotechnology industries in which initially they did not have a comparative advantage, but through learning-by-doing, they have become low opportunity cost producers in those industries.

FIGURE 19.4
The Gains from Trade

*e*Foundations 19.2 

If the United States specializes in satellites, it produces 10 a year at point *P*. If China specializes in shoes, it produces 100 million pairs a year at point *Q*.

If shoes and satellites are traded at 30 million pairs of shoes per satellite, both countries can increase their consumption of both goods and consume at points *A*' and *B*'. The gains from trade are the increases in consumption of the two countries.

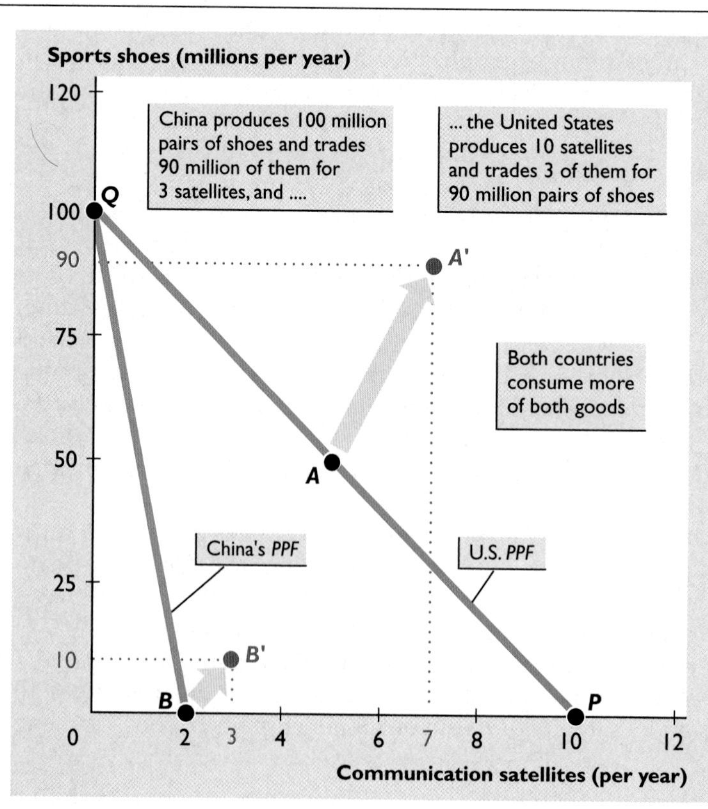

CHECKPOINT 19.2

2 **Explain why nations engage in international trade and why trade benefits *all* nations.**

Study Guide pp. 296–300 
e/**Foundations 19.2**

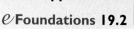

Practice Problem 19.2

During most of the Cold War, the United States and Russia did not trade with each other. The United States produced manufactured goods and farm produce. Russia produced manufactured goods and farm produce. Suppose that in the last year of the Cold War, the United States could produce 100 million units of manufactured goods or 50 million units of farm produce and Russia could produce 30 million units of manufactured goods or 10 million units of farm produce.

a. What was the opportunity cost of 1 unit of farm produce in the United States?
b. What was the opportunity cost of 1 unit of farm produce in Russia?
c. Which country had a comparative advantage in producing farm produce?
d. With the end of the Cold War and the opening up of trade between Russia and the United States, which good did the United States import from Russia?
e. Did the United States gain from this trade? Explain why or why not.
f. Did Russia gain from this trade? Explain why or why not.

Exercise 19.2

In 2001, the United States does not trade with Cuba. Suppose that the United States can produce 1,000 million units of manufactured goods or 500 million units of food. Suppose that Cuba can produce 2 million units of manufactured goods or 5 million units of food.

a. What was the opportunity cost of 1 unit of food in the United States?
b. What was the opportunity cost of 1 unit of food in Cuba?
c. Which country had a comparative advantage in producing food?
d. Suppose that the United States opens up trade with Cuba. Which good will the United States import from Cuba?
e. Will the United States gain from this trade? Explain why or why not.
f. Will Cuba gain from this trade? Explain why or why not.

Solution to Practice Problem 19.2

a. The U.S. opportunity cost of 1 unit of farm produce was 2 units of manufactured goods.
b. The Russian opportunity cost of 1 unit of farm produce was 3 units of manufactured goods.
c. The United States had a comparative advantage in producing farm produce because the U.S. opportunity cost of a unit of farm produce was less than the Russian opportunity cost of farm produce.
d. The United States imported from Russia the good in which Russia had a comparative advantage. The United States imported manufactured goods.
e and f. Both the United States and Russia gained because each country ended up with more of both goods. When countries specialize in producing the good in which they have a comparative advantage and then trade with each other, both countries gain.

19.3 INTERNATIONAL TRADE RESTRICTIONS

Governments restrict international trade to protect domestic industries from foreign competition by using two main tools:

- Tariffs
- Nontariff barriers

Tariff
A tax on a good that is imposed by the importing country when an imported good crosses its international boundary.

Nontariff barrier
Any action other than a tariff that restricts international trade.

A **tariff** is a tax on a good that is imposed by the importing country when an imported good crosses its international boundary. A **nontariff barrier** is any action other than a tariff that restricts international trade. Examples of nontariff barriers are quantitative restrictions and health and safety standards.

Tariffs

The temptation for governments to impose tariffs is a strong one. First, tariffs provide revenue to the government. Second, they enable the government to satisfy special interest groups in import-competing industries. But as we will see, free international trade brings enormous benefits that are reduced when tariffs are imposed. Let's see how.

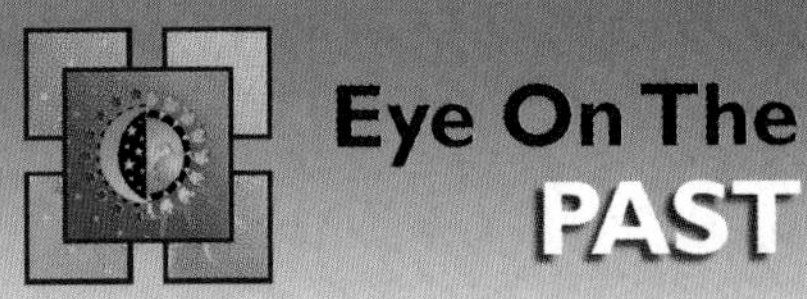

The History of the U.S. Tariff

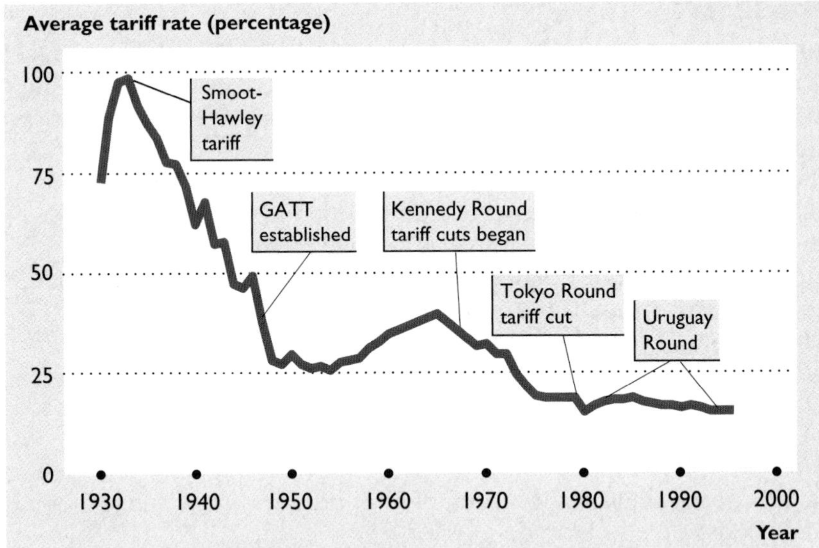

SOURCES: *U.S. Bureau of the Census, Historical Statistics of the United States, Colonial Times to 1970*, Bicentennial Edition, Part 1 (Washington, D.C., 1975); Series U-212: *Statistical Abstract of the United States: 1986*, 106th edition (Washington, D.C., 1985); and *Statistical Abstract of the United States: 1999*, 119th edition (Washington, D.C., 2000).

U.S. tariffs today are modest in comparison with their historical levels. The figure shows the average tariff rate—total tariffs as a percentage of total imports. Tariffs peaked during the 1930s when Congress passed a law known as the Smoot-Hawley Act. The General Agreement on Tariffs and Trade (GATT), an international agreement to eliminate trade restrictions that was signed in 1947, resulted in a series of rounds of negotiations that have brought widespread tariff cuts. Today, the World Trade Organization (WTO) continues the work of GATT.

The United States is a party to the North American Free Trade Agreement (NAFTA), which became effective on January 1, 1994, and under which barriers to international trade between the United States, Canada, and Mexico will be virtually eliminated after a 15-year phasing-in period.

To analyze how tariffs work, let's return to the example of U.S. T-shirt imports. Figure 19.5 shows the market for T-shirts in the United States. Part (a) is the same as Figure 19.2(b) and shows the situation with free international trade. The United States produces no T-shirts, and imports 50 million shirts a year at the world market price of $5 a shirt.

Now suppose that under pressure from U.S. garment makers, the U.S. government imposes a tariff on imported T-shirts. In particular, suppose that a tariff of 50 percent is imposed. What happens?

- The price of a T-shirt in the United States rises.
- The quantity of T-shirts bought in the United States decreases.
- The quantity of T-shirts produced in the United States increases.
- The quantity of T-shirts imported by the United States decreases.
- The U.S. government collects the tariff revenue.
- U.S. consumers lose.

FIGURE 19.5

The Effects of a Tariff

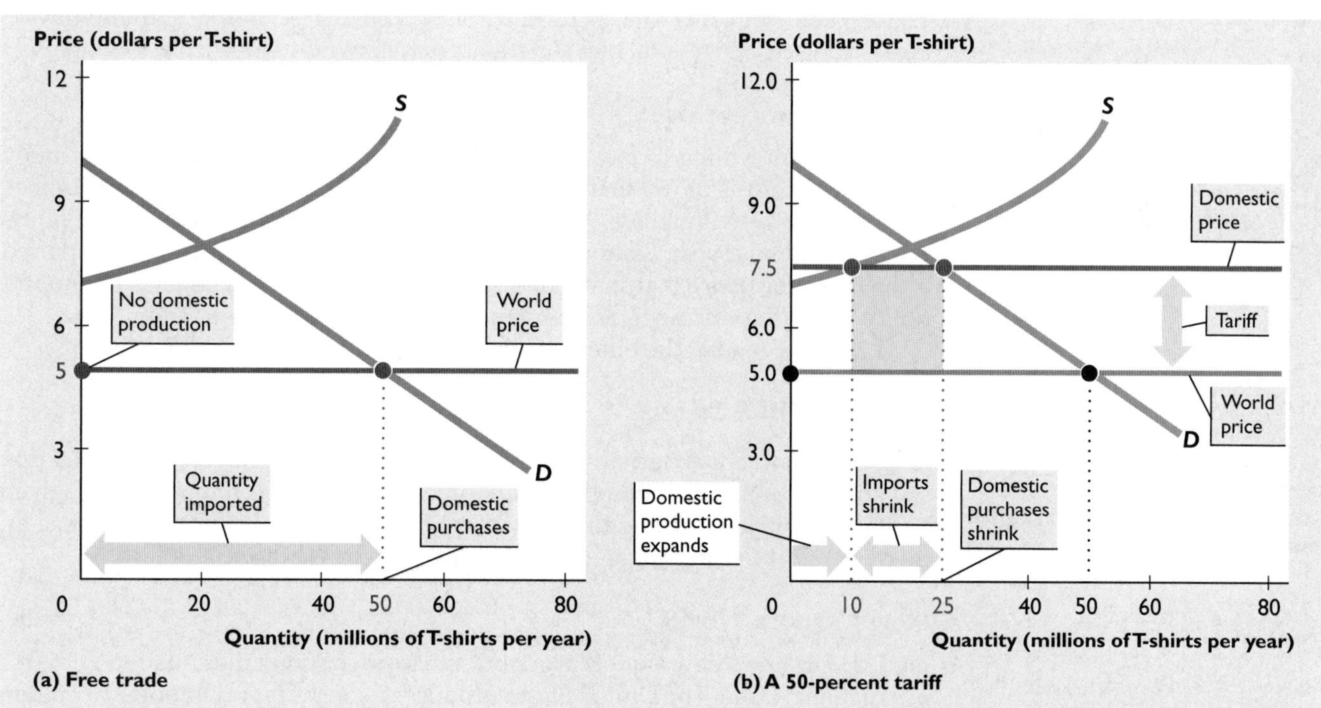

With free trade (part a), the United States produces no T-shirts and imports 50 million T-shirts a year.

In part (b), the United States imposes a tariff on imports of T-shirts. The domestic price equals the world price plus the tariff, so the tariff raises the price that Americans pay for a T-shirt.

The quantity of T-shirts demanded decreases, the quantity produced in the United States increases, and the quantity imported decreases. The U.S. government collects tariff revenue shown by the purple rectangle.

Rise in Price of a T-Shirt

To buy a T-shirt, Americans must pay the world market price plus the tariff. So the price of a T-shirt rises by 50 percent to $7.50. Figure 19.5(b) shows the domestic price line, which lies 50 percent (or $2.50) above the world price line.

Decrease in Purchases

The higher price of a T-shirt brings a decrease in the quantity demanded, which Figure 19.5(b) shows as a movement along the demand curve for T-shirts from 50 million a year at $5 a shirt to 25 million a year at $7.50 a shirt.

Increase in Domestic Production

The higher price of a T-shirt stimulates domestic production, which increases from zero to 10 million shirts a year—a movement along the supply curve in Figure 19.5(b).

Decrease in Imports

T-shirt imports decrease by 35 million from 50 million to 15 million a year. Both the decrease in purchases and the increase in domestic production contribute to this decrease in imports.

Tariff Revenue

The government collects tariff revenue of $2.50 per shirt on the 15 million shirts imported each year, a total of $37.5 million, as shown by the purple rectangle.

U.S. Consumers Lose

Americans are willing to pay $7.50 for the marginal T-shirt. But the opportunity cost of that shirt is $5. So there is a gain from importing an extra T-shirt. In fact, there are gains—willingness to pay exceeds opportunity cost—for all the T-shirts up to 50 million a year. Only when 50 million T-shirts a year are being imported is the maximum price that someone is willing to pay for a shirt equal to the opportunity cost of producing it. So restricting trade reduces the gains from trade.

Let's now look at the other tool for restricting trade: nontariff barriers.

Nontariff Barriers

Quota
A specified maximum amount of a good that may be imported in a given period of time.

A **quota**, which is a quantitative restriction on the import of a particular good that specifies the maximum amount of the good that may be imported in a given period, is a widely used nontariff barrier. The United States imposes quotas on many items, including sugar, tomatoes, bananas, and textiles.

How a Quota Works

Figure 19.6 shows how a quota works. Begin by identifying the situation with free international trade. The United States produces no T-shirts and imports 50 million shirts a year at the world market price of $5 a shirt.

Now suppose that the United States imposes a quota that restricts imports to 15 million T-shirts a year. The imports permitted under the quota plus the quantity produced in the United States is the market supply in the United States. This market supply curve is the one labeled $S + quota$ in Figure 19.6.

FIGURE 19.6
The Effects of a Quota

*e*Foundations 19.3 

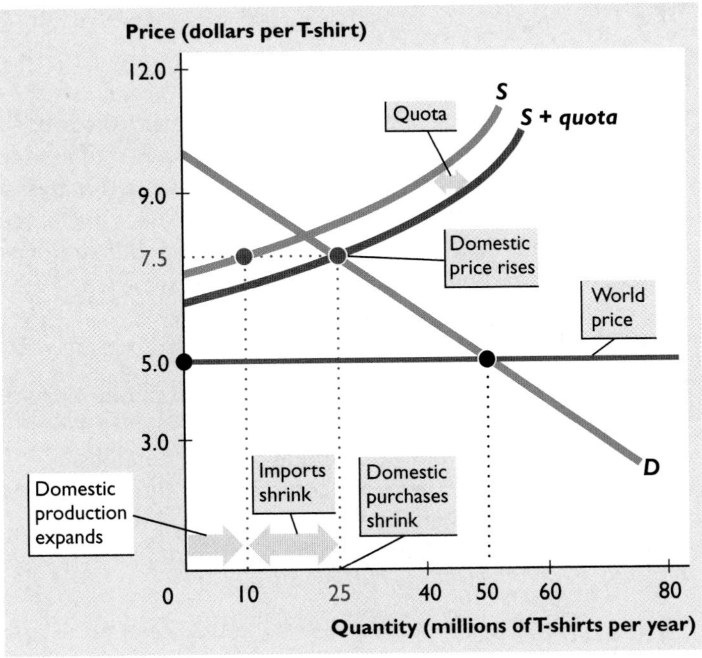

A quota of 15 million shirts a year restricts imports. This quota is added to the U.S. supply to give the market supply curve, *S + quota*. At the equilibrium price of $7.50 a shirt, the United States produces 10 million shirts a year and U.S. imports equal the quota of 15 million a year.

With this new supply curve, the U.S. price of a T-shirt is $7.50, the price that makes the quantity demanded by Americans equal the quantity supplied by U.S. producers plus imports. This quantity is 25 million shirts a year.

At a price of $7.50, U.S. garment makers produce 10 million shirts a year and U.S. imports equal the quota of 15 million a year.

We've made the outcome with a quota in Figure 19.6 the same as that with a tariff in Figure 19.5(b). But there is a difference between a tariff and a quota. In the case of a tariff, the U.S. government collects tariff revenue. In the case of a quota, there is no tariff revenue and the difference between the world price and the U.S. price goes to the person who has the right to import T-shirts under the import quota regulations.

Health, Safety, and Other Nontariff Barriers

Thousands of detailed health, safety, and other regulations restrict international trade. Here are just a few examples. All U.S. imports of food products are examined by the Food and Drug Administration to determine if the imported food is "pure, wholesome, safe to eat, and produced under sanitary conditions." In 2001, the scare of foot and mouth disease virtually closed down international trade in live cattle and beef. The European Union has banned imports of most genetically modified foods, such as U.S.-produced soybeans and Canadian granola. Australia has banned the import of U.S. grapes to protect its domestic grapes from a virus that is present in California. Restrictions also apply to many nonfood items. Although regulations of the type we've just described are not designed to limit international trade, they have that effect.

CHECKPOINT 19.3

Study Guide pp. 300–302

*e*Foundations 19.3

3 **Explain how trade barriers reduce international trade.**

Practice Problems 19.3

1. Before 1995, the United States imposed tariffs on goods imported from Mexico. In 1995, Mexico joined NAFTA. U.S. tariffs on imports from Mexico and Mexican tariffs on imports from the United States are gradually being removed. Explain how the removal of tariffs will change:
   - **a.** The price that U.S. consumers pay for goods imported from Mexico.
   - **b.** The quantity of U.S. imports from Mexico.
   - **c.** The quantity of U.S. exports to Mexico.
   - **d.** The U.S. government's tariff revenue from trade with Mexico.
2. The U.S. government has placed a ban on potato imports. Explain how this ban influences:
   - **a.** The price that U.S. consumers pay for potatoes.
   - **b.** The quantity of potatoes consumed in the United States.
   - **c.** The price received by Canadian potato growers.
   - **d.** The U.S. and Canadian gains from trade.

Exercises 19.3

1. In 2000, the U.S. Congress and Senate decided to extend an arrangement that limits the tariffs on imports from China. If the United States imposed higher tariffs on imports from China, explain how the higher tariffs would change:
   - **a.** The price that U.S. consumers pay for toys imported from China.
   - **b.** The quantity of U.S. imports of toys from China.
   - **c.** The quantity of toys produced in the Unitd States.
   - **d.** The U.S. government's tariff revenue from trade in toys with China.
   - **e.** The U.S. and Chinese gains from trade.
2. Australia has a comparative advantage in producing beef, but the United States sets a quota on beef imports from Australia. Explain how the quota influences:
   - **a.** The price that U.S. consumers pay for beef.
   - **b.** The quantity of beef produced in the United States.
   - **c.** The U.S. and Australian gains from trade.

Solutions to Practice Problems 19.3

1a. The price that U.S. consumers pay for goods imported from Mexico will fall.
1b. The quantity of U.S. imports from Mexico will increase.
1c. The quantity of U.S. exports to Mexico will increase.
1d. The U.S. government's tariff revenue from trade with Mexico will fall to zero.

2a. The price that U.S. consumers pay for potatoes will rise.
2b. The quantity of potatoes consumed in the United States will fall.
2c. The price received by Canadian potato growers will fall.
2d. Both the U.S. and Canadian gains from trade will decrease.

19.4 THE CASE AGAINST PROTECTION

For as long as nations and international trade have existed, people have debated whether a country is better off with free international trade or with protection from foreign competition. The debate continues, but for most economists, a verdict has been delivered and it is the one you have just seen. Free trade promotes prosperity for all countries: Protection reduces the potential gains from trade. We've seen the most powerful case for free trade: All countries benefit from their comparative advantage. But there is a broader range of issues in the free trade versus protection debate. Let's review these issues.

Three Arguments for Protection

The three main arguments for protection and restricting international trade are:

- The national security argument
- The infant-industry argument
- The dumping argument

Let's look at each in turn.

The National Security Argument

The national security argument for protection is that a country must protect industries that produce defense equipment and armaments and those on which the defense industries rely for their raw materials and other intermediate inputs. This argument for protection does not withstand close scrutiny.

First, it is an argument for international isolation, for in a time of war, there is no industry that does not contribute to national defense. Second, if the case is made for boosting the output of a strategic industry, it is more efficient to achieve this outcome with a subsidy to the firms in the industry, which is financed out of taxes, than with a tariff or quota. A subsidy would keep the industry operating at the scale judged appropriate, and free international trade would keep the prices faced by consumers at their world market levels.

The Infant-Industry Argument

The **infant-industry argument** for protection is that it is necessary to protect a new industry to enable it to grow into a mature industry that can compete in world markets. The argument is based on the idea of dynamic comparative advantage, which can arise from learning-by-doing.

Learning-by-doing is a powerful engine of productivity growth, and comparative advantage evolves and changes because of on-the-job experience. But these facts do not justify protection.

The infant-industry argument is valid only if the benefits of learning-by-doing not only accrue to the owners and workers of the firms in the infant industry, but also spill over to other industries and parts of the economy. For example, there are huge productivity gains from learning-by-doing in the manufacture of aircraft. But almost all of these gains benefit the stockholders and workers of aircraft producers such as Boeing. Because the people making the decisions, bearing the risk, and doing the work are the ones who benefit, they take the dynamic gains into account when they decide on the scale of their activities. In this case, almost no benefits spill over to other parts of the economy, so there is no need for government assistance to achieve an efficient outcome.

ECONOMICS *in the* NEWS

The Economist

March 22, 2001

At Loggerheads

For almost 20 years, Canada and the United States have been at war over softwood lumber. . . . The Americans claim Canadian producers are subsidized, and so have demanded countervailing duties on their exports, which are worth $7 billion a year. Canada retorts that . . . the Americans are indulging in plain old-fashioned protectionism.

Questions

1. Why might it benefit Canada and the United States to have free trade in softwood lumber?

2. Why might U.S. producers of softwood lumber want to limit Canadian imports?

3. Who benefits and who loses from limiting Canadian imports of softwood lumber?

 *e*Foundations 19.4

Infant-industry argument
The argument that it is necessary to protect a new industry to enable it to grow into a mature industry that can compete in world markets.

The Dumping Argument

Dumping
When a foreign firm sells its exports at a lower price than its cost of production.

Dumping occurs when a foreign firm sells its exports at a lower price than its cost of production. A firm that wants to gain a global monopoly might use dumping. In this case, the foreign firm sells its output at a price below its cost to drive domestic firms out of business. When the domestic firms have gone, the foreign firm takes advantage of its monopoly position and charges a higher price for its product. Dumping is usually regarded as a justification for temporary countervailing tariffs.

But there are powerful reasons to resist the dumping argument for protection. First, it is virtually impossible to detect dumping because it is hard to determine a firm's costs. As a result, the test for dumping is whether a firm's export price is below its domestic price. But this test is a weak one because it can be rational for a firm to charge a lower price in markets in which the quantity demanded is highly sensitive to price and a higher price in a market in which demand is less price-sensitive.

Second, it is hard to think of a good that is produced by a natural global monopoly. So even if all the domestic firms were driven out of business in some industry, it would always be possible to find several and usually many alternative foreign sources of supply and to buy at prices determined in competitive markets.

Third, if a good or service were a truly global natural monopoly, the best way to deal with it would be by regulation—just as in the case of domestic monopolies. Such regulation would require international cooperation.

The three arguments for protection that we've just examined have an element of credibility. The counterarguments are in general stronger, so these arguments do not make the case for protection. But they are not the only arguments that you might encounter. The many other arguments that are commonly heard are quite simply wrong. They are fatally flawed.

Fatally Flawed Arguments for Protection

Six commonly made but flawed arguments for restricting international trade are that protection:

- Saves jobs
- Allows us to compete with cheap foreign labor
- Brings diversity and stability
- Penalizes lax environmental standards
- Protects national culture
- Prevents rich countries from exploiting developing countries

Saves Jobs

The argument is: When we buy shoes from Brazil or shirts from Taiwan, U.S. workers lose their jobs. With no earnings and poor prospects, these workers become a drain on welfare and spend less, causing a ripple effect of further job losses. The proposed solution to this problem is to ban imports of cheap foreign goods and to protect U.S. jobs. The proposal is flawed for the following reasons.

First, free trade does cost some jobs, but it also creates other jobs. It brings about a global rationalization of labor and allocates labor resources to their highest-valued activities. Because of international trade in textiles, tens of thousands of workers in the United States have lost jobs because textile mills and other factories have closed. But tens of thousands of workers in other countries have gotten jobs because textile mills have opened there. And tens of thousands of U.S. workers have gotten better-paying jobs than textile workers because other export industries have expanded and created more jobs than have been destroyed.

Second, imports create jobs. They create jobs for retailers that sell imported goods and for firms that service those goods. They also create jobs by creating incomes in the rest of the world, some of which are spent on imports of U.S.-made goods and services.

Although protection does save some particular jobs, it does so at an inordinate cost. For example, textile jobs are protected in the United States by quotas imposed under an international agreement called the Multifiber Arrangement. The U.S. International Trade Commission (ITC) has estimated that because of quotas, 72,000 jobs exist in textiles that would otherwise disappear and annual clothing expenditure in the United States is $15.9 billion, or $160 per family, higher than it would be with free trade. In other words, the ITC estimates that each textile job saved costs consumers $221,000 a year.

Allows Us to Compete with Cheap Foreign Labor

With the removal of protective tariffs in U.S. trade with Mexico, prominent Texan Ross Perot said that jobs rushing to Mexico would make a "giant sucking sound" (see the cartoon). Let's see what's wrong with this view.

The labor cost of a unit of output equals the wage rate divided by labor productivity. For example, if a U.S. autoworker earns $30 an hour and produces 15 units of output an hour, the average labor cost of a unit of output is $2. If a Mexican auto assembly worker earns $3 an hour and produces 1 unit of output an hour, the average labor cost of a unit of output is $3. Other things remaining the same, the higher a worker's productivity, the higher is the worker's wage rate. High-wage workers have high productivity. Low-wage workers have low productivity.

"I don't know what the hell happened—one minute I'm at work in Flint, Michigan, then there's a giant sucking sound and suddenly here I am in Mexico."

SOURCE: © The New Yorker Collection 1993 Mick Stevens from cartoonbank.com. All rights reserved.

Although high-wage U.S. workers are more productive, on the average, than lower-wage Mexican workers, there are differences across industries. U.S. labor is relatively more productive in some activities than in others. For example, the productivity of U.S. workers in producing movies, financial services, and customized computer chips is relatively higher than their productivity in the production of metals and some standardized machine parts. The activities in which U.S. workers are relatively more productive than their Mexican counterparts are those in which the United States has a comparative advantage. By engaging in free trade, increasing our production and exports of the goods and services in which we have a comparative advantage and decreasing our production and increasing our imports of the goods and services in which our trading partners have a comparative advantage, we can make ourselves and the citizens of other countries better off.

Brings Diversity and Stability

A diversified investment portfolio is less risky than one that has all of its eggs in one basket. The same is true for an economy's production. A diversified economy fluctuates less than an economy that produces only one or two goods.

But big, rich, diversified economies like those of the United States, Japan, and Europe do not have this type of stability problem. Even a country such as Saudi Arabia that produces almost only one good (in this case, oil) can benefit from specializing in the activity at which it has a comparative advantage and then investing in a wide range of other countries to bring greater stability to its income and consumption.

Penalizes Lax Environmental Standards

A new argument for protection is that many poorer countries, such as Mexico, do not have the same environmental standards that we have, and because they are willing to pollute and we are not, we cannot compete with them without tariffs. So if they want free trade with the richer and "greener" countries, they must clean up their environments to our standards.

This argument for trade restrictions is weak. While everyone wants a clean environment, a poor country is less able than a rich one to devote resources to achieving this goal. The best hope for a better environment in the developing countries is rapid income growth through free trade. As their incomes grow, developing countries will have the means to match their desires to improve their environment. Also, because poor countries are willing to accept "dirty" activities (such as iron ore smelting and chemical production), it is easier for rich countries to achieve the high environmental standards that they seek.

Protects National Culture

The national culture argument for protection is not heard much in the United States, but it is a commonly heard argument in Canada and Europe.

The expressed fear is that free trade in books, magazines, movies, and television programs means U.S. domination and the end of local culture. So, the reasoning continues, it is necessary to protect domestic "culture" industries from free international trade to ensure the survival of a national cultural identity.

Protection of these industries is common and takes the form of nontariff barriers. For example, regulations often require local content on radio and television broadcasting and in magazines.

The cultural identity argument for protection has no merit, and it is one more example of rent seeking (see p. 476). Writers, publishers, and broadcasters want to limit foreign competition so that they can earn larger economic profits. There is no actual danger to national culture. In fact, many of the creators of so-called American cultural products are not Americans, but the talented citizens of other countries, ensuring the survival of their national cultural identities in Hollywood! Also, if national culture is in danger, there is no surer way of helping it on its way out than by impoverishing the nation whose culture it is. And protection is an effective way of doing just that.

Prevents Rich Countries from Exploiting Developing Countries

Another new argument for protection is that international trade must be restricted to prevent the people of the rich industrial world from exploiting the poorer people of the developing countries, forcing them to work for slave wages.

Wage rates in some developing countries are indeed very low. But by trading with developing countries, we increase the demand for the goods that these countries produce, and, more significantly, we increase the demand for their labor. When the demand for labor in developing countries increases, the wage rate also increases. So far from exploiting people in developing countries, trade improves their opportunities and increases their incomes.

We have reviewed the arguments that are commonly heard in favor of protection and the counterarguments against them. There is one counterargument to protection that is general and quite overwhelming. Protection invites retaliation and can trigger a trade war. The best example of a trade war occurred during the Great Depression of the 1930s when the Smoot-Hawley Tariff was introduced. Country after country retaliated with its own tariff, and in a short period, world trade had almost disappeared. The costs to all countries were large and led to a renewed international resolve to avoid such self-defeating moves in the future. They also led to the creation of GATT and are the impetus behind NAFTA, APEC, and the European Union.

Why Is International Trade Restricted?

Why, despite all the arguments against protection, is trade restricted? There are two key reasons:

- Tariff revenue
- Rent seeking

Tariff Revenue

Government revenue is costly to collect. In developed countries, such as the United States, well-organized tax collection systems exist that can generate billions of dollars of income tax and sales tax revenues. These tax collection systems are made possible by the fact that firms that must keep properly audited financial records do most economic transactions. Without such records, the revenue collection agencies (such as the Internal Revenue Service in the United States) would be severely hampered in their work. Even with audited financial accounts, some proportion of potential tax revenue is lost. Nonetheless, for industrialized countries, the income tax and sales taxes are the major sources of revenue and the tariff plays a very small role.

But governments in developing countries have a difficult time collecting taxes from their citizens. Much economic activity takes place in an informal economy with few financial records. So these countries collect only a small amount of revenue from income taxes and sales taxes. The one area in which economic transactions are well recorded and audited is international trade. So this activity is an attractive base for tax collection in these countries and is used much more extensively than in the developed countries.

Rent Seeking

The major reason why international trade is restricted is because of rent seeking. *Rent seeking* is lobbying and other political activity that seeks to capture the gains from trade. Free trade increases consumption possibilities on the average, but not everyone shares in the gain and some people even lose. Free trade brings benefits to some and imposes costs on others, with total benefits exceeding total costs. It is the uneven distribution of costs and benefits that is the principal source of impediment to achieving more liberal international trade.

Suppose that we had a tariff on T-shirts, as in the example that you studied earlier in this chapter. A few thousand (perhaps a few hundred) garment makers and their employees who must switch to some other activity would bear the cost of the United States moving to free trade. The millions of T-shirt buyers would reap the benefits of moving to free trade. The number of people who gain will, in general, be enormous in comparison with the number who lose. The gain per person will therefore be small. The loss per person to those who bear the loss will be large. Because the loss that falls on those who bear it is large, it will pay those people to incur considerable expense to lobby against free trade. On the other hand, it will not pay those who gain to organize to achieve free trade. The gain from trade for any one individual is too small for that individual to spend much time or money on a political organization to lobby for free trade. The loss from free trade will be seen as being so great by those bearing that loss that they will find it profitable to join a political organization to prevent free trade. Each group is weighing benefits against costs and choosing the best action for themselves. But the anti-free-trade group will undertake a larger quantity of political lobbying than the pro-free-trade group.

Compensating Losers

If, in total, the gains from free international trade exceed the losses, why don't those who gain compensate those who lose so that everyone is in favor of free trade? To some degree, such compensation does take place. When Congress approved the NAFTA deal with Canada and Mexico, it set up a $56 million fund to support and retrain workers who lost their jobs because of the new trade agreement. During the first six months of the operation of NAFTA, only 5,000 workers applied for benefits under this scheme.

The losers from freer international trade are also compensated indirectly through the normal unemployment compensation arrangements. But only limited attempts are made to compensate those who lose from free international trade. The main reason why full compensation is not attempted is that the costs of identifying all the losers and estimating the value of their losses would be enormous. Also, it would never be clear whether a person who has fallen on hard times is suffering because of free trade or for other reasons, perhaps reasons that are largely under the control of the individual. Furthermore, some people who look like losers at one point in time may, in fact, end up gaining. The young autoworker who loses his job in Michigan and becomes a computer assembly worker in Minneapolis resents the loss of work and the need to move. But a year or two later, looking back on events, he counts himself fortunate. He has made a move that has increased his income and given him greater job security.

It is because we do not, in general, compensate the losers from free international trade that protectionism is such a popular and permanent feature of our national economic and political life.

Competing with Low-Wage Nations

New Balance athletic shoes are made in two ways:

At a New Balance factory in Norridgewock, Maine, skilled workers who earn $14 an hour operate "see-and-sew" machines—$100,000 automated sewing machines guided by cameras. It costs $4 to make a pair of shoes in Maine.

At a subcontractor's factory in China, low-skilled women in their teens and early twenties who earn 40 cents an hour operate ordinary sewing machines. It costs $1.30 to make a pair of shoes in China.

New Balance is willing to pay the additional $2.70, which is about 4 percent of the retail price of a shoe, to produce shoes in the United States.

New Balance produces 25 percent of its output in the United States and the rest in Asia.

Nike, Reebok, and all the other makers of athletic shoes produce their entire output in Asia.

The Asian economies have a comparative advantage at making athletic shoes. Even when New Balance has invested heavily in equipment to make its U.S. work force much more productive than the Chinese work force, the labor cost alone of a pair of shoes is more than three times the cost in China. Add the capital cost to the equation, and New Balance pays much more for its shoes than do its competitors.

You would predict, and you'd be correct, that New Balance is not the most profitable shoemaker.

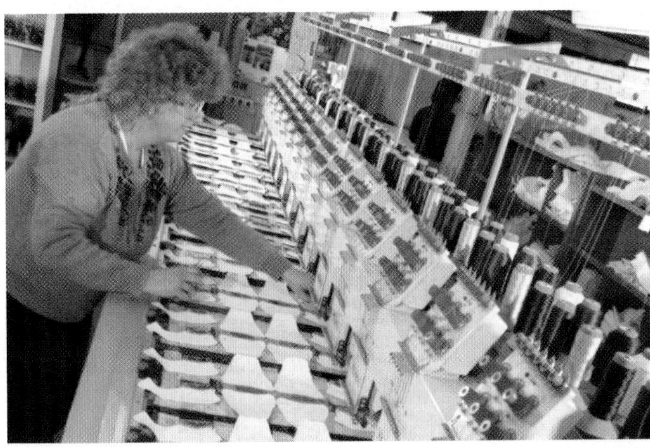

CHECKPOINT 19.4

Study Guide pp. 302–304 

*e*Foundations 19.4

4 **Explain the arguments used to justify trade barriers and show why they are incorrect but also why some barriers are hard to remove.**

Practice Problems 19.4

1. Japan sets quotas on imports of rice. California rice growers would like to export more rice to Japan. What are Japan's arguments for restricting imports of Californian rice? Are these arguments correct? Who loses from this restriction in trade?
2. The United States has, from time to time, limited imports of steel from Europe. What is the argument that the United States has used to justify this quota? Who wins from this restriction? Who loses?
3. The United States maintains a quota on imports of textiles. What is the argument for this quota? Is this argument flawed? If so, explain why.

Exercises 19.4

1. Texan Ross Perot has argued against NAFTA. What is his argument against a free trade zone in North America? What was wrong with Perot's argument? Whom did Perot see as the loser from NAFTA?
2. The Summit of the Americas in April 2001 decided to extend NAFTA to cover all of the Americas. What was President George W. Bush's argument for this extension? Who will be the winners? Who will be the losers?
3. Hong Kong has never restricted trade. What gains has Hong Kong reaped by unilaterally adopting free trade with all nations? Is there any argument for restricted trade that might have benefited Hong Kong?

Solutions to Practice Problems 19.4

1. Japan has used a number of arguments for low quotas on rice imports. Some of these are that Japanese consumers can get a better quality of rice from Japanese producers and that the quota limits competition faced by Japanese producers. The arguments are not correct. If Japanese consumers do not like the quality of Californian rice, they will not buy it. The quota does limit competition, but the Japanese quota allows Japanese farmers to use their land less efficiently. The big losers are the Japanese consumers because the price of rice in Japan is about three times the price paid by U.S. consumers.
2. The U.S. argument for a quota on imports of European steel is that European producers dump steel on the U.S. market. With a quota, U.S. producers will face less competition in the market for steel and U.S. jobs will be saved. Workers in the steel industry and owners of steel companies will win at the expense of U.S. buyers of steel.
3. The argument for a quota on U.S. imports of textiles is that textiles are produced in developing countries where labor is cheap. That is, the quota protects the jobs of U.S. workers. The argument is flawed because the United States does not have a comparative advantage in the manufacture of textiles and so a quota allows the U.S. textile industry to be inefficient. With free trade in textiles, the U.S. textile industry would exit but it would be smaller and more efficient.

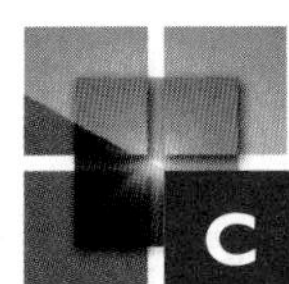

CHAPTER CHECKPOINT

Key Points

1 Describe the patterns and trends in international trade.

- Large flows of trade take place between countries, most of which is in manufactured goods exchanged among rich industrialized countries.
- Since 1960, the volume of U.S. trade has more than doubled.

2 Explain why nations engage in international trade and why trade benefits all nations.

- When opportunity costs between countries diverge, comparative advantage enables countries to gain from international trade.
- By increasing production of goods in which it has a comparative advantage and then trading some of the increased output, a country can consume at points outside its production possibility frontier.

3 Explain how trade barriers reduce international trade.

- Countries restrict international trade by imposing tariffs and quotas.
- Trade restrictions raise the domestic price of imported goods, lower the volume of imports, and reduce the total value of imports.
- Trade restrictions also reduce the total value of exports by the same amount as the reduction in the value of imports.

4 Explain the arguments used to justify trade barriers and show why they are incorrect but also why some barriers are hard to remove.

- The arguments that protection is necessary for national security, for infant industries, and to prevent dumping are weak.
- Arguments that protection saves jobs, allows us to compete with cheap foreign labor, makes the economy diversified and stable, protects national culture, and is needed to offset the costs of environmental policies are fatally flawed.
- Trade is restricted because tariffs raise government revenue and because protection brings a small loss to a large number of people and a large gain per person to a small number of people.

Key Terms

Balance of trade, 457
Dumping, 472
Dynamic comparative advantage, 464
Infant-industry argument, 471
Learning-by-doing, 464
Nontariff barrier, 466
Quota, 468
Tariff, 466

Exercises

FIGURE 1

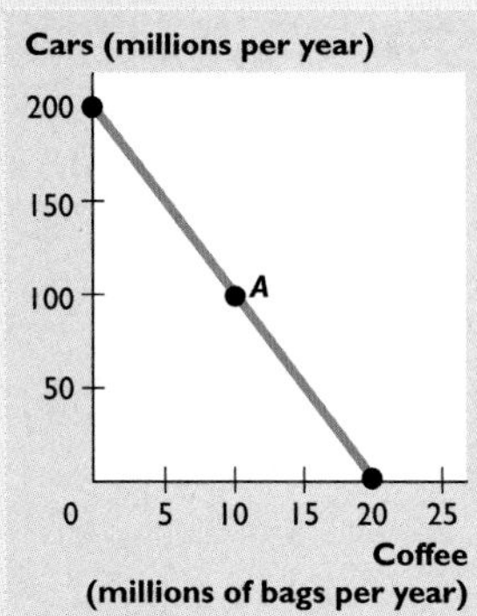

FIGURE 2

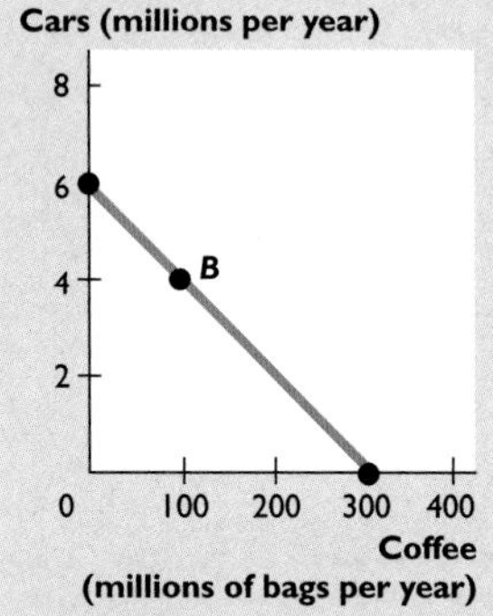

FIGURE 3

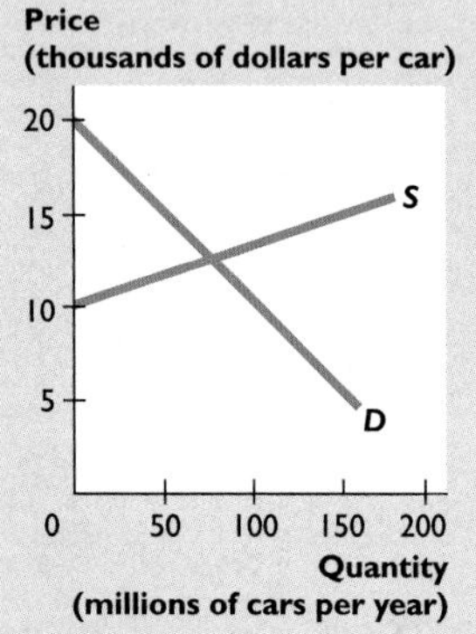

1. Suppose that with no international trade between the United States and Brazil, Figure 1 shows the U.S. production possibilities and the quantities of coffee and cars produced (point *A*). Figure 2 shows Brazil's production possibilities and the quantities of coffee and cars produced (point *B*).
   a. What is the opportunity cost of a bag of coffee in the United States?
   b. What is the opportunity cost of a bag of coffee in Brazil?
   c. Which country has a comparative advantage in producing coffee?
   d. Which country has a comparative advantage in producing cars?
   e. With free trade between Brazil and the United States, what does the United States import from Brazil and what does it export to Brazil? Explain your answer.
   f. Does Brazil gain from trade with the United States? Why or why not?

2. When free trade occurs in Exercise 1, the world price of a bag of coffee is 1/25th of a car. If Brazil completely specializes in coffee and exports half of it to the United States, show on two figures:
   a. The quantities of the two goods that Brazil consumes.
   b. The quantities of the two goods that the United States consumes.

3. Figure 3 shows the car market in Brazil when Brazil places no restriction on imports of cars. The world price of a car is $10,000. If the government of Brazil introduces a 20 percent tariff on car imports, what will be:
   a. The price of a car in Brazil?
   b. The quantity of cars imported into Brazil?
   c. The quantity of cars produced in Brazil?
   d. The government's tariff revenue?

4. Suppose that in Exercise 3, the Brazilian government introduces a quota of 50 million cars a year. Show on the figure:
   a. The price of a car in Brazil.
   b. The quantity of cars imported into Brazil.
   c. The quantity of cars produced in Brazil.

5. In the 1950s, Ford and General Motors established a small car-producing industry in Australia and argued for a high tariff on car imports. The tariff has remained through the years. In 2000, the tariff was cut from 22.5 percent to 15 percent. What was the argument for the high tariff? Is the tariff the best way to achieve the goals of the argument?

6. The Canadian government argues against free trade in magazines and movies. Why is the Canadian government concerned about the quantity of U.S. magazines and movies that Canadians see? What is wrong with the Canadian government's argument? Who in Canada gains from the government's argument?

7. The U.S. government imposes a quota on lamb imports from New Zealand and Australia. New Zealand and Australia have lobbied the U.S. government for an increase in the quota. What is the argument put forward by the New Zealand and Australian governments? What is the counterargument put forward by the U.S. government? Which argument is really an example of rent seeking?

Chapter 20

Farms and Cities

CHAPTER CHECKLIST

When you have completed your study of this chapter, you will be able to:

1. **Explain why farm incomes fluctuate and why the prices of farm products are on a downward trend.**
2. **Describe and evaluate the effects of government policies to stabilize farm incomes.**
3. **Explain why cities grow and evaluate tolls as a way of achieving an efficient use of roads.**

We spend 10 percent of our income on food. Ninety-seven percent of this food is produced on U.S. farms. We import only 3 percent of our food, and we export a similar amount of U.S.-produced food. Farms are an important component of the economy but they also present some special economic problems. In particular, farm incomes fluctuate more than other incomes. And the prices of farm products, the number of farm workers, and the number of farms are decreasing.

Although farms are vital to our lives, most of us have never seen one, at least not at close quarters. We live in cities. City life brings enormous economic benefits, but it also creates some special economic problems. Two of them are congestion on the roads and urban sprawl that eats into the surrounding rural land and increases our commuting time.

In this chapter, we study these economic issues in the United States today.

20.1 INCOMES AND PRICES OF FARM PRODUCTS

Heavy rain and flood, early frost, and drought all fill the lives of farmers with uncertainty. How do changes in farm output affect the prices of farm products and the total revenue of farmers? Let's answer this question by looking at the market for wheat.

Output Fluctuations in an Agricultural Market

Figure 20.1 shows the market for wheat. We're going to look at this market in three situations: in a normal year (part a), in a year in which conditions are unfavorable and the harvest is small (part b), and in a year in which conditions are unusually favorable and the harvest is large (part c).

In all of these years (and in all three parts of Figure 20.1), the demand curve for wheat is *D*. The demand for wheat is inelastic. Recall that demand is inelastic when the percentage decrease in the quantity demanded is less than the percentage rise in price (Chapter 5, p. 110). Once farmers have harvested their crop, they have no control over the quantity supplied, and supply is inelastic along a vertical supply curve. In normal climate conditions, the supply curve is S_0 (in all three parts of the figure). The price is determined at the point of intersection of the supply curve and the demand curve.

Normal Harvest

In normal conditions (Figure 20.1a), the demand curve *D* intersects the supply curve S_0 at an equilibrium price of $4 a bushel. The quantity of wheat produced is 20 billion bushels, and farm total revenue is $80 billion. We'll assume that the opportunity cost to farmers of producing wheat is also $4 a bushel. Then in normal conditions, farmers receive a total revenue that equals their opportunity cost of production and earn a normal profit. (Recall that economic profit is part of opportunity cost—Chapter 11, p. 259.)

Poor Harvest

Suppose there is an unfavorable growing season that results in a small harvest. What happens to the price of wheat and the total revenue of farmers? Figure 20.1(b) answers these questions. Supply decreases, and the supply curve shifts leftward to S_1. The quantity of wheat produced is 18 billion bushels. Demand is unchanged, so the demand curve is *D*. The equilibrium price rises to $6 a bushel.

What happens to farm total revenue? It *increases* to $108 billion. A *decrease* in supply has brought a rise in price and an *increase* in farm total revenue. Figure 20.1(b) shows the increase in total revenue from the higher price. Because the quantity decreases, there is a loss of total revenue of $8 billion (the red rectangle), but because the price rises, there is a gain in total revenue of $36 billion (the light blue rectangle). The gain in total revenue from the higher price exceeds the loss in total revenue from the smaller quantity sold by $28 billion, so farm total revenue increases from $80 billion in a normal year to $108 billion when the harvest is small.

Farm total revenue exceeds opportunity cost, so farmers are making an economic profit. But not all farmers share in this profit. Some farmers, whose entire crop is wiped out, suffer a decrease in total revenue and incur an economic loss. Others, whose crop is unaffected, make the gain and earn economic profits.

Bumper Harvest

Now suppose the opposite situation: There is an unusually favorable growing season that results in a large harvest—a bumper crop. What now happens to the price of wheat and the total revenue of farmers? Figure 20.1(c) provides the answers. Supply increases, and the supply curve shifts rightward to S_2. The quantity of wheat produced is 22 billion bushels. Demand is unchanged, so the demand curve is D. The equilibrium price falls to $2 a bushel.

At this price, farm total revenue *decreases* to $44 billion. An *increase* in supply has brought a fall in price and a *decrease* in farm total revenue. Figure 20.1(c) shows the decrease in total revenue. Because the price falls, there is a loss in total revenue of $40 billion (the red rectangle), but because the quantity increases, there is a gain of total revenue of $4 billion (the light blue rectangle). The loss in total revenue from the lower price exceeds the gain in total revenue from the larger quantity sold by $36 billion, so farm total revenue decreases from $80 billion in a normal year to $44 billion when the harvest is large. Farm total revenue is now less than opportunity cost, so farmers are incurring an economic loss.

Inelastic Demand

Farm total revenue increases with a small harvest and decreases with a large harvest because the demand for wheat is inelastic. This effect of the changes in the wheat harvest, price, and total revenue is an example of the *total revenue test* for elastic and inelastic demand (Chapter 5, p. 116.)

FIGURE 20.1

Harvests, Farm Prices, and Farm Total Revenue

*e*Foundations 20.1 

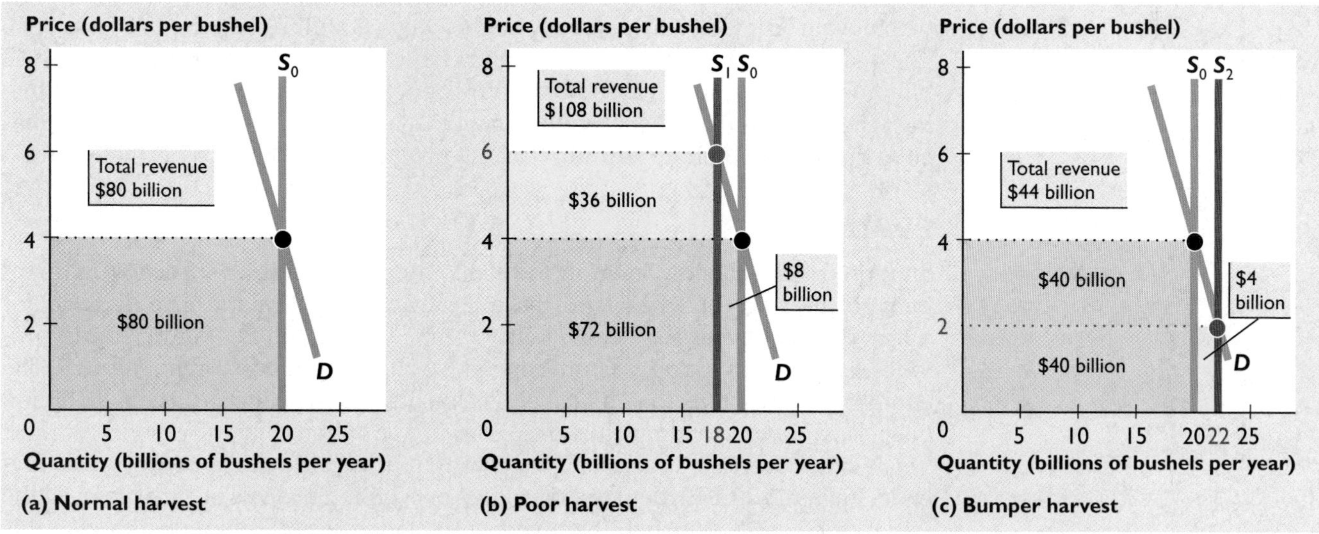

The demand curve for wheat is D. In normal times, the supply curve is S_0 and 20 billion bushels are sold for $4 a bushel. Total revenue is $80 billion.

A poor harvest decreases supply to S_1. The price rises to $6 a bushel, and total revenue increases to $108 billion—the $36 billion gain from the price rise exceeds the $8 billion loss from the smaller quantity.

A bumper harvest increases supply to S_2. The price falls to $2 a bushel, and total revenue decreases to $44 billion—the $40 billion loss from the price fall exceeds the $4 billion gain from the larger quantity.

Estimates of the elasticity of demand for farm products range from 0.2 to 0.4. At the low end of this range, a 10 percent change in price brings a 2 percent change in the quantity demanded and a 10 percent change in the quantity available brings a 50 percent change in price.

Why is the demand for food products inelastic? Recall that the main influence on the elasticity of demand is the ease with which a good can be replaced by a substitute. The demand for food products is inelastic because they do not have good substitutes. We must eat something every day, but there is a limit to what we want to eat. So the quantity of food demanded does not vary much when its price changes. It does change, though, because a change in price changes what people can afford to buy. So the demand for food products is not perfectly inelastic. But it is inelastic.

Demand Fluctuations in an Agricultural Market

Fluctuations in output are not the only source of volatile farm prices and incomes. Fluctuations in demand also have a big effect, as we'll now see.

We'll continue to study the market for wheat shown in Figure 20.2. And again, we'll look at this market in three situations. But this time, they are years in which the global economy: is normal (part a); experiences a slowdown, as it did during 2001, and demand decreases (part b); and experiences rapid expansion, as it did during the 1990s, and demand increases (part c).

In all of these years (and in all three parts of Figure 20.2), the supply of wheat is S. It is perfectly inelastic for the same reason as before. Once farmers have harvested their crop, they have no control over the quantity supplied.

Normal Year

In a normal or average year (Figure 20.2a), the demand for wheat is D_0. The demand curve intersects the supply curve S at an equilibrium price of $4 a bushel. The quantity of wheat produced is 20 billion bushels, and farm total revenue is $80 billion. We'll continue to assume that the opportunity cost to farmers of producing wheat is also $4 a bushel so that in a normal year, farmers receive a total revenue that equals their opportunity cost of production and earn a normal profit.

Low Demand

Suppose there is a slowdown in the economy and incomes decrease. What happens to the price of wheat and the total revenue of farmers? The demand for wheat decreases, and the demand curve shifts leftward to D_1. Figure 20.2(b) provides the answers. Supply is unchanged, so the supply curve remains at S. The equilibrium price falls to $2 a bushel. The quantity of wheat produced is 20 billion bushels, and farm total revenue decreases to $40 billion.

A small decrease in demand has brought a large decrease in farm total revenue. In Figure 20.1(b), demand decreases by 2 billion bushels at each price. At the initial price of $4 a bushel, the quantity demanded is 20 billion bushels, so this decrease in demand is a 10 percent decrease. But farm total revenue decreases from $80 billion to $40 billion, a 50 percent decrease.

Farm total revenue is less than opportunity cost, so farmers are incurring an economic loss.

High Demand

Now suppose that incomes grow more rapidly and demand increases. What now happens to the price of wheat and the total revenue of farmers? Figure 20.2(c) provides the answers. Demand increases, and the demand curve shifts rightward to D_2. Supply is unchanged, so the supply curve is *S*. The equilibrium price rises to \$6 a bushel. Farm total revenue increases to \$120 billion.

A small increase in demand has brought a large increase in farm total revenue. In Figure 20.1(c), demand increases by 2 billion bushels at each price, and at the initial price of \$4 a bushel, the increase in demand is a 10 percent increase. But farm total revenue increases from \$80 billion to \$120 billion, a 50 percent increase.

Farm total revenue now exceeds opportunity cost, so farmers are making an economic profit.

Inelastic Demand and Inelastic Supply

A change in demand brings a large change in price because demand is inelastic and, after the crop has been harvested, supply is perfectly inelastic. A small decrease in demand, with no change in the quantity available, needs a large change in price to restore market equilibrium. That is why when demand changes by a small amount, price and total revenue change by a large amount.

The Eye on the U.S. Economy looks at the actual price of wheat and confirms that its price does indeed fluctuate a great deal.

FIGURE 20.2

Demand Fluctuations, Farm Prices, and Farm Total Revenue

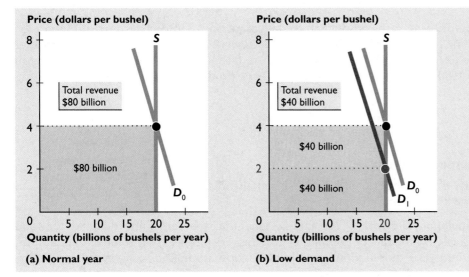

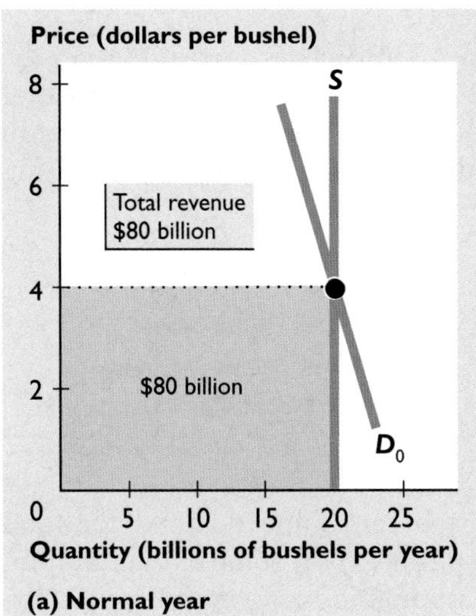

(a) Normal year

Price (dollars per bushel) · Total revenue \$40 billion · \$40 billion · \$40 billion · S · D_0 · D_1 · Quantity (billions of bushels per year)

(b) Low demand

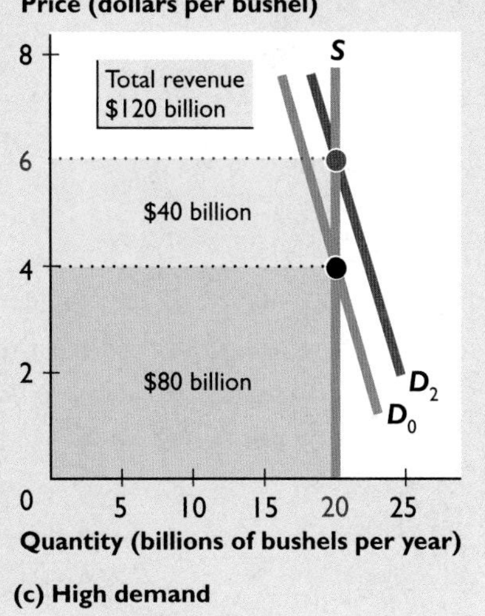

(c) High demand

The supply curve of wheat is *S*. The demand curve for wheat in normal times is D_0, and 20 billion bushels are sold for \$4 a bushel. Total revenue is \$80 billion.

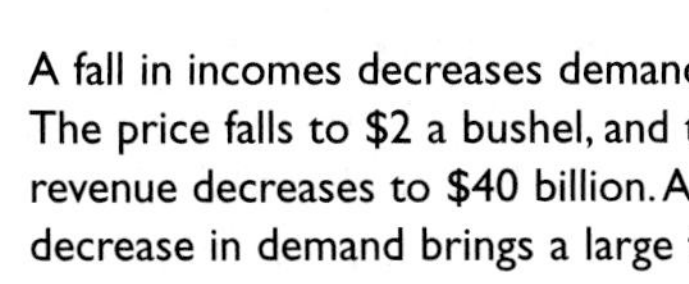

A fall in incomes decreases demand to D_1. The price falls to \$2 a bushel, and total revenue decreases to \$40 billion. A small decrease in demand brings a large fall in price and total revenue.

A rise in incomes increases demand to D_2. The price rises to \$6 a bushel, and total revenue increases to \$120 billion. A small increase in demand brings a large rise in price and total revenue.

The Fluctuating Price of Wheat

The figure shows the fluctuating price of wheat. The numbers are in 1996 dollars, which removes the effects of inflation on the price.

Notice two things about the price of wheat. First, it does indeed fluctuate. But second, it has a downward trend.

The fluctuating price is explained by the fluctuations in supply and demand combined with an inelastic demand.

The downward trend is the result of a tendency for supply to increase faster than demand. Technological advances in seeds and fertilizers have increased crop yields and brought a surge in supply that has outstripped the increase in demand that comes from population growth and rising incomes.

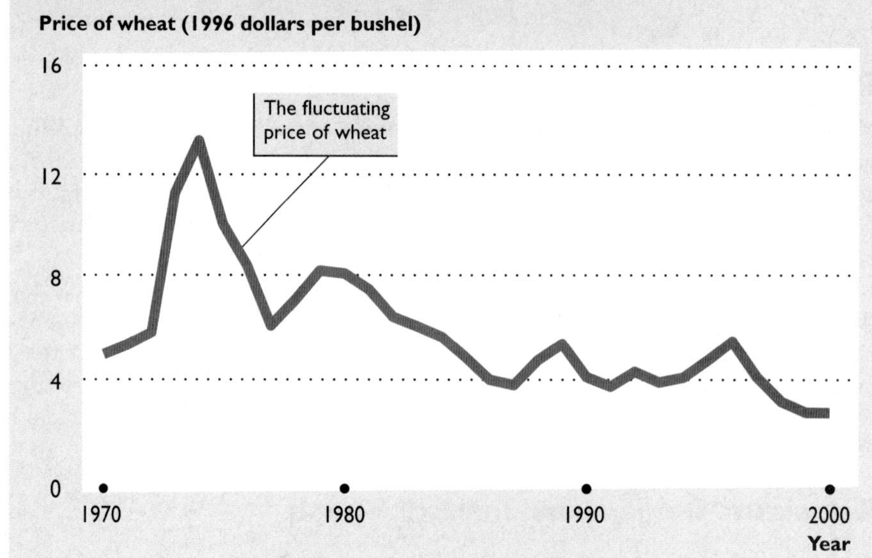

SOURCE: *International Financial Statistics*, International Monetary Fund, Washington, D.C.

Falling Prices of Farm Products

The prices of farm products have fallen and farm output has increased over the years. The prices of farm products in 2000 were 20 percent of their 1950 levels after the effects of inflation are removed. And farm output in 2000 was 280 percent of its 1950 level. Two interacting factors have produced falling prices and increasing output:

- An increase in demand
- An even greater increase in supply

Increase in Demand

Two main sources of the increasing demand for farm products are population growth and rising incomes.

Population Growth Other things remaining the same, the demand for food increases at the rate of population growth. U.S. farms export some of their output, so both U.S. population growth and world population growth influence the demand for U.S. farm output.

The population of the United States grows at a bit less than 1 percent a year. The world population grows at about 1.5 percent a year. So population growth increases the demand for U.S. farm products by about 1 percent a year.

Rising Incomes As incomes increase, the demand for food increases. The influence of income on demand is governed by the *income elasticity of demand*. The income elasticity of demand translates a given percentage increase in income into an increase in demand. Income per person in the United States and in the rest of the world grows at a rate of about 2.5 percent a year.

The income elasticity of demand for food is low because meeting that demand is a high priority. Even with a low income, people allocate their budgets to ensure that they get enough to eat. As incomes rise, people spend more on food by buying better food rather than more food. For example, a low-income family might buy chicken rather than beef. A high-income family might buy prime cuts of beef rather than lower grades of beef and chicken. But as a family's income rises, only a small percentage of the additional income is spent on food and a large percentage is spent on items that were previously out of reach, such as a larger home, a car, or a vacation.

As incomes rise, the income elasticity of demand for food falls. When a family has a high enough income to buy all the food it wants and of the quality it wants, then further increases in income lead to no change in the demand for food. The income elasticity of demand has fallen to zero. Many U.S. families have reached this position. But many have not, so the income elasticity of demand for food in the United States is about 0.14.

The presence of many more poor families in the developing countries means that the income elasticity of demand for food in those countries is higher than it is in the United States. In the poorest countries, the income elasticity of demand is about 0.8 (see Chapter 5, p. 127).

Demand Growth When we combine the effects of growth of income per person with the income elasticity of demand, income growth increases the demand for food by about 0.4 percent a year. Population growth adds another 1 percent to give a growth rate of demand of 1.4 percent a year, a growth rate that leads to a doubling of the level of demand in 50 years. And that is almost exactly what happened to the demand for U.S. farm products between 1950 and 2000: Demand doubled.

An Even Greater Increase in Supply

The supply of farm products has increased at a rapid rate because of an incredible pace of technological change and productivity growth. The farm sector has experienced productivity growth at approximately twice the rate of the rest of the economy. Despite the hype about the "new economy," it is the farm economy—the oldest economy—that has seen the fastest gains in productivity.

Productivity growth in agriculture occurs in seeds, fertilizers, and planting and harvesting equipment. Gains in all four areas were extraordinary during the twentieth century. These gains speeded up during the 1990s with the arrival of genetic technologies that led to the creation of controversial genetically modified foods. The result of all this technological change was an increase in supply that averaged around 2.6 percent a year.

Although the growth rate of supply of 2.6 percent a year doesn't look much larger than the growth rate of demand of 1.4 percent a year, maintained over 50 years, it makes an enormous difference to the *level* of supply. A growth rate of supply of 2.6 percent a year leads to a 90 percent increase in the level of supply in 25 years and a 260 percent increase over 50 years. That is exactly what happened to the supply of U.S. farm products between 1950 and 2000: Supply increased by 260 percent.

Supply, Demand, Price, and Quantity

Figure 20.3 summarizes the changes in demand and supply that occurred between 1950 and 2000. In the figure, both the price and quantity are index numbers, with the 1950 values defined to be 100. The demand for farm products in 1950 was D_{50}, and the supply was S_{50}. The demand curve and supply curve intersect at the equilibrium price and quantity of 100.

In the 50 years between 1950 and 2000, demand increased to D_{00}. The demand curve shifted rightward by 100 percent—a doubling of demand. You can see that doubling by noting that at the 1950 price of 100, the quantity demanded increased in 2000 to 200.

During the same 50 years, supply increased to S_{00}. The supply curve shifted rightward by much more than the demand curve. At the 1950 price, the quantity supplied in 2000 would have been 360 percent of the 1950 quantity.

The demand curve and supply curve in 2000 intersect at the 2000 equilibrium. The price is 20 percent of the 1950 price, and the quantity is 280 percent of the 1950 quantity.

This extraordinary increase in output and fall in price meant dramatic changes at the level of the individual farm. And despite the fact that supply increased, the number of farms decreased. In 1950, there were around 5,400,000 farms in the United States. By 2000, that number had fallen to barely 2,200,000—40 percent of the number in 1950. You can see that if the number of farms decreased and total output increased, output per farm must have increased even more. That is exactly what happened.

FIGURE 20.3

The Falling Price of Farm Products

*e*Foundations **20.1** 

Price and quantity are measured as index numbers with 1950 = 100. In 1950, demand was D_{50} and the supply was S_{50}, which intersect at the equilibrium price and quantity of 100.

By 2000, demand had increased to D_{00}—a 100 percent increase—and supply had increased to S_{00}—a 260 percent increase. The equilibrium price was 20 percent of the 1950 price, and the equilibrium quantity was 280 percent of the 1950 quantity.

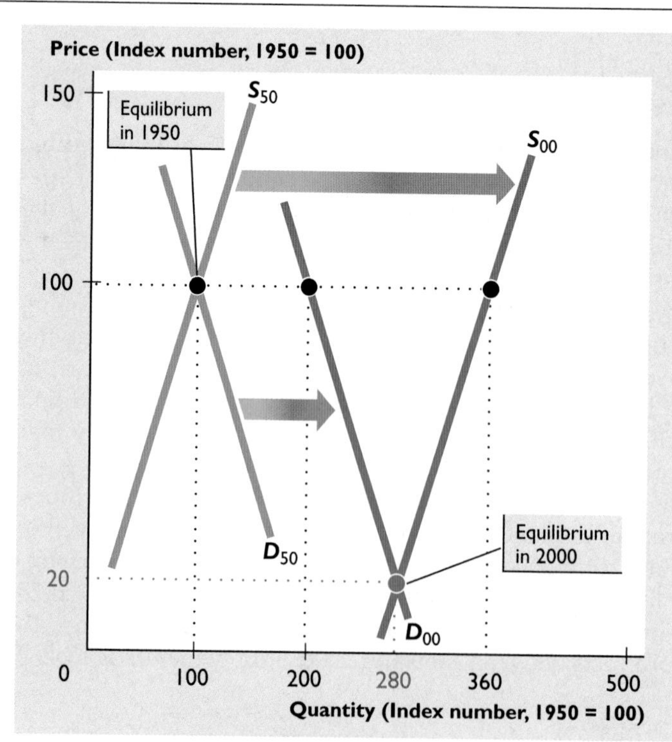

Down on the Farm

We can illustrate the effects of the technological change in farming by looking at a typical farm's average total cost curve (see Chapter 11, p. 271–272). Figure 20.4 shows the average total costs of a typical farm in 1950 and in 2000.

Farms operate in highly competitive markets, which we may assume are perfectly competitive. So they face a horizontal marginal revenue curve at the going market price. In 1950, that price was 100 (the index number for 1950 defined as 100) and the marginal curve was MR_{50}. If farms were earning normal profit in 1950, the average total cost curve was ATC_{50}. Minimum average total cost occurs at the 1950 output, which we define as 100.

Technological advances between 1950 and 2000 increased the output that can be produced by given inputs. Technological advances also increased the capital intensity of farming. So the fixed costs of farms increased relative to their variable costs. As a result, average total cost increased at low output levels (because average fixed cost increased) and decreased at high output levels.

We know (from Figure 20.3) that the price in 2000 was 20 percent of its 1950 level. So the marginal revenue curve in 2000 was MR_{00}. If farms earned normal profit in 2000, the average total cost curve was ATC_{00}. Minimum average total cost occurred at the 2000 output of 700—seven times the output of 1950.

Each farm, on the average, produced 700 percent of its 1950 output, but the number of farms in 2000 was 40 percent of the number in 1950. So total output in 2000 was 40 percent of 700 percent, or 280 percent, of its 1950 level. (Check that this percentage increase is the same as that shown in Figure 20.3.)

FIGURE 20.4
One Farm's Cost and Revenue Curves in 1950 and 2000

*e*Foundations **20.1** 

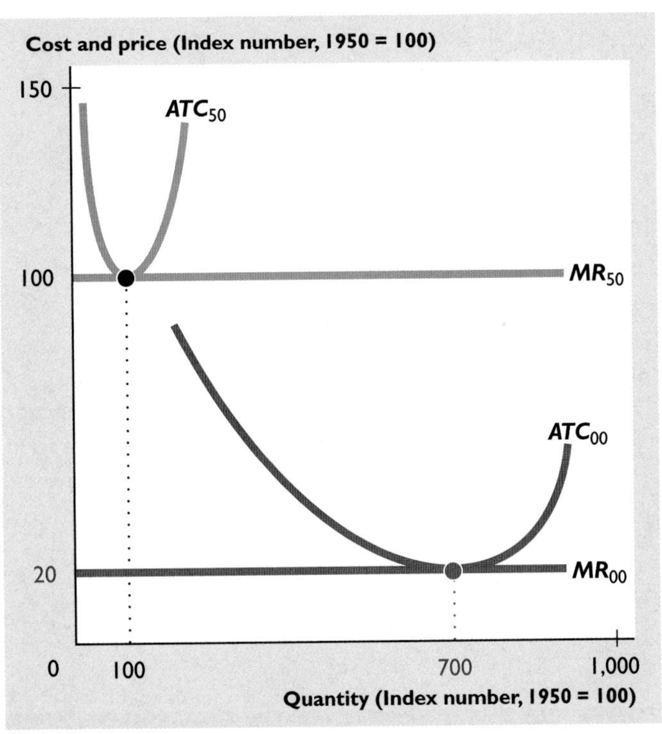

In 1950, a farm's average total cost curve was ATC_{50}. Between 1950 and 2000, technological advances increased the capital intensity of farming. In 2000, a farm's average total cost curve was ATC_{00}.

The Changing Farm Economy

You can see both the fluctuating and falling prices of farm products in Figure (a). The curve shows an index number of the average price of all farm products.

Figure (b) shows the dramatic increase in farm output. This output was produced by a decreasing number of farms. The table shows the number of farms at five-year intervals between 1950 and 2000.

Year	Number of farms (thousands)
1950	5,388
1955	4,654
1960	3,962
1965	3,356
1970	2,954
1975	2,521
1980	2,440
1985	2,293
1990	2,146
1995	2,196
2000	2,190

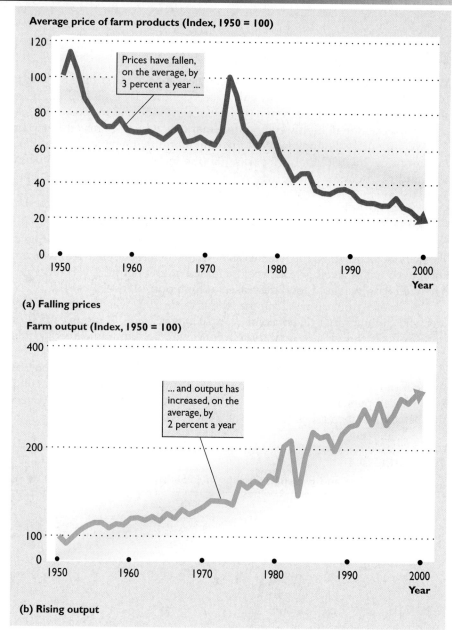

Average price of farm products (Index, 1950 = 100)

120
100
80
60
40
20
0

Prices have fallen, on the average, by 3 percent a year ...

1950 1960 1970 1980 1990 2000
Year

(a) Falling prices

Farm output (Index, 1950 = 100)

400
200
100
0

... and output has increased, on the average, by 2 percent a year

1950 1960 1970 1980 1990 2000
Year

(b) Rising output

SOURCE: Bureau of Economic Analysis.

The number of farms has shrunk because small, high-cost farms have found it ever harder to compete with large, low-cost farms. As technology has advanced, this competitive edge of the large farm has widened, so small farms have either left the industry or expanded to become large farms.

CHECKPOINT 20.1

1 **Explain why farm incomes fluctuate and why the prices of farm products are on a downward trend.**

Study Guide pp. 310–313 

eFoundations 20.1 

Practice Problem 20.1

Table 1 shows a demand schedule for oilseed in a normal year. The quantity of oilseed grown in a normal year is 50 million tons. In a boom year, the quantity demanded increases by 2 million tons at each price. In a slump year, the quantity demanded decreases by 2 million tons at each price. Calculate:

a. Farm total revenue in a normal year.
b. Price and farm total revenue in a normal demand year but with a bumper crop of 52 million tons.
c. Price and farm total revenue in a normal demand year but with a poor crop of 48 million tons.
d. Price and farm total revenue in a normal supply year but with a boom in demand.
e. Price and farm total revenue in a normal supply year but with a slump in demand.

TABLE 1

Price (dollars per ton)	Quantity demanded (millions of tons per year)
7	47
6	48
5	49
4	50
3	51
2	52
1	53

Exercise 20.1

Table 2 shows a demand schedule for maize in a normal year. The quantity of maize grown in a normal year is 100 million tons. In a boom year, the quantity demanded increases by 4 million tons at each price. In a slump year, the quantity demanded decreases by 4 million tons at each price. Calculate:

a. Farm total revenue in a normal year.
b. Price and farm total revenue in a normal demand year but with a bumper crop of 104 million tons.
c. Price and farm total revenue in a normal demand year but with a poor crop of 96 million tons.
d. Price and farm total revenue in a normal supply year but with a boom in demand.
e. Price and farm total revenue in a normal supply year but with a slump in demand.

TABLE 2

Price (dollars per ton)	Quantity demanded (millions of tons per year)
10	94
9	96
8	98
7	100
6	102
5	104
4	106

Solution to Practice Problem 20.1

a. The equilibrium price in a normal year is $4 a ton, so farm total revenue is $200 million.
b. With a bumper crop of 52 million tons, price falls to $2 a ton and farm total revenue falls to $104 million.
c. With a poor crop of 48 million tons, price rises to $6 a ton and farm total revenue rises to $288 million.
d. With a boom in demand and normal supply, price rises to $6 a ton and farm total revenue increases to $300 million.
e. With a slump in demand and normal supply, price falls to $2 a ton and farm total revenue decreases to $100 million.

20.2 GOVERNMENT POLICY IN AGRICULTURE

The U.S. government has been in the business of boosting farm incomes since the 1930s. The most recent redesign of the farm program occurred in 1996, when Congress passed the Federal Agriculture Improvement and Reform Act.

The 1996 act replaced arrangements that were introduced in the early 1970s. The old arrangements were based on a **price support system**, a system in which the government sets a price for a farm product and then buys any output that the farmer can't sell in the market at the support price.

Price support system
A system in which the government sets a price for a farm product and then buys any output that the farmer can't sell in the market at the support price.

For a range of crops called "contract crops" (wheat, corn, grain sorghum, barley, oats, rice, and upland cotton), the 1996 act replaced the price support system with a **production flexibility contract**. Such a contract provides a farmer with a support payment from the government over the 7 years through 2002 based on the number of acres covered by the contract and not based on production.

Production flexibility contract
A contract that provides a farmer with a support payment from the government based on the number of acres covered by the contract and not based on production.

The 1996 act retained but modified the details of the price support system for dairy products, sugar, and peanuts. The act also strengthened export promotion programs, especially for U.S. grain exports to emerging markets.

To understand the 1996 act and the reason it was passed, we need to see how farm incomes were supported under the earlier arrangements.

ECONOMICS *in the* NEWS

October 12, 2000

End Sugar Subsidies

The Global Alliance for Sugar Trade Reform and Liberalisation wants an end to U.S. and E.U. export subsidies and trade protection for sugar. The alliance says that such policies deny markets to developing countries and depress world prices by 40 percent.

Questions

1. How does the U.S. government support its U.S. sugar growers?

2. How does the European Union support European sugar growers?

3. What are the main problems that arise from U.S. and E.U. sugar subsidies for (a) the U.S. and European consumer, (b) sugar growers in other countries, and (c) consumers of sugar in other countries?

 *e*Foundations **20.2**

How Price Supports Work

Do price supports provide farmers with a larger income than they would otherwise have? What are the side effects of price supports? Let's address these two questions by examining how price supports work in the market for milk products.

Free Market Reference Point

Figure 20.5 shows the market for milk products. The demand curve is *D*, and the supply curve is *S*. With no government actions in this market, the equilibrium price would be $200 a ton and the equilibrium quantity would be 70 million tons a year. Farm total revenue would be $14 billion a year (70 million multiplied by $200 equals $14 billion). These price and output numbers are examples, not a description of our actual economy.

Effect on Output

Suppose that in the market for milk products, the government introduces a price support at $250 a ton. The government agrees that it will pay this price for any output that the farms can't sell in the market. With this offer in place, farms produce their profit-maximizing output, as shown by the market supply curve. Output increases to 78 million tons a year.

Because they can receive $250 a ton from the government, farmers are not willing to sell their output to consumers for less than this price. But at $250 a ton, the demand for farm products is only 66 million tons a year. The price support increases output and creates a surplus. In this case, the surplus is 12 million tons of milk products per year.

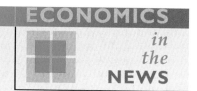

The surpluses that arise from price supports can be very large. And they lead to government holding stocks of unwanted farm output. For example, the U.S. and Canadian governments hold stocks of powdered milk. In the European Union,

FIGURE 20.5
The Effects of Price Supports

*e*Foundations 20.2 

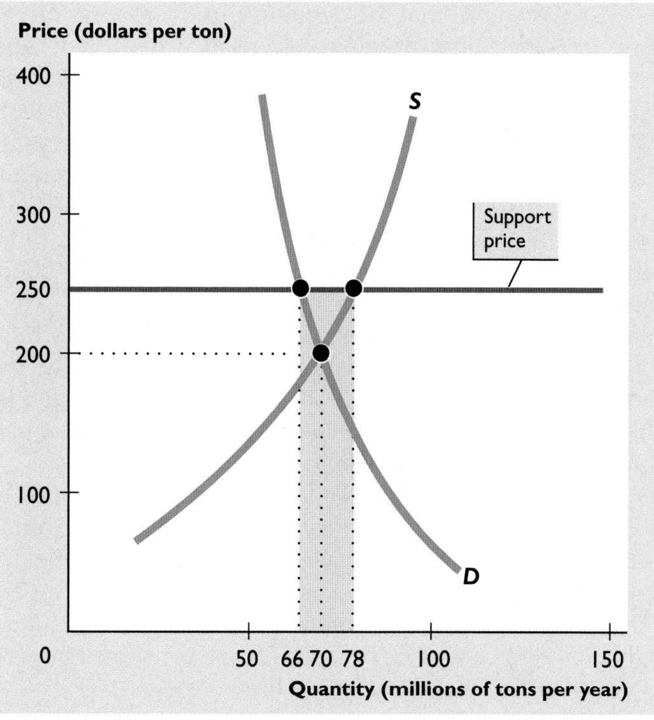

With no government actions, the equilibrium price is $200 a ton and the equilibrium quantity is 70 million tons a year.

With a price support at $250 a ton, output increases to 78 million tons a year, the quantity demanded decreases to 66 million tons a year, and the government buys the surplus of 12 million tons a year at the support price.

where price supports are high and government purchases of surpluses are enormous, huge inventories of powdered milk, butter, and even wine have accumulated.

Effects on Farm Incomes

Price supports do achieve their goal of increasing farm incomes. You can see how by comparing farm total revenue with price supports and without price supports. You've seen that without price supports, farms receive a total revenue of $14 billion. With price supports, farms sell 78 million tons for $250 a ton. Multiply these two numbers (on a pocket calculator), and we see that farm total revenue is now $19.5 billion, an increase of $5.5 billion. Farm incomes increase because farmers receive a higher price per unit sold and they produce and sell a larger quantity.

Effects on Consumers

Consumers lose from price supports. They pay a higher price for a smaller quantity. The loss to consumers in some cases is large. In Europe, consumers pay more than twice the price they would pay without price supports on a wide range of farm products. In the United States, the largest effects occur in the markets for sugar and milk. In these markets, the prices are about twice what they would be without price supports. Because farmers gain, it is not surprising that consumers lose. But it turns out that consumers lose more than farmers gain. Let's see why.

Inefficiency of Price Supports

Price supports are inefficient, and Figure 20.6 shows why. Recall that resources are allocated efficiently when marginal cost equals marginal benefit (Chapter 3, pp. 66–72). Also recall that the demand curve measures marginal benefit and the supply curve measures marginal cost, so at a competitive equilibrium, in the absence of externalities, resources are allocated efficiently (Chapter 6, pp. 134–141). The market for milk products in Figure 20.6 would be efficient if the price of milk were $200 per ton and the quantity were 70 million tons a year. At this price and quantity, marginal benefit and marginal cost would also equal $200.

Part (a) shows the farmers' gain. Farm total revenue increases by $5.5 billion, which is the sum of the blue and red areas in part (a). But to increase output, farmers must increase their costs. The supply curve tells about marginal cost, and the area under the supply curve shows us the increase in total cost (the red area). So only the blue area represents an increase in farm profit.

Part (b) shows the consumer-taxpayers' loss. The increase in farm total revenue equals the increase in consumer expenditures and taxes. In part (b), the sum of the green and purple areas shows this increased cost to consumers. The green area highlights the decrease in consumer surplus.

Part (c) isolates the social loss—the *deadweight loss*. The gain to farmers in part (a) is less than the loss to consumers in part (b) by an amount equal to the increase in farm total cost. This increase in farm total cost is the deadweight loss generated by price supports. Figure 20.6(c) highlights this deadweight loss as the gray area. The deadweight loss is larger than the loss that results from overproduction in Chapter 6 (pp. 144–145) because no one consumes the overproduction. It just gets stockpiled. So its entire cost is a loss.

FIGURE 20.6
The Inefficiency of Price Supports

e/Foundations 20.2 

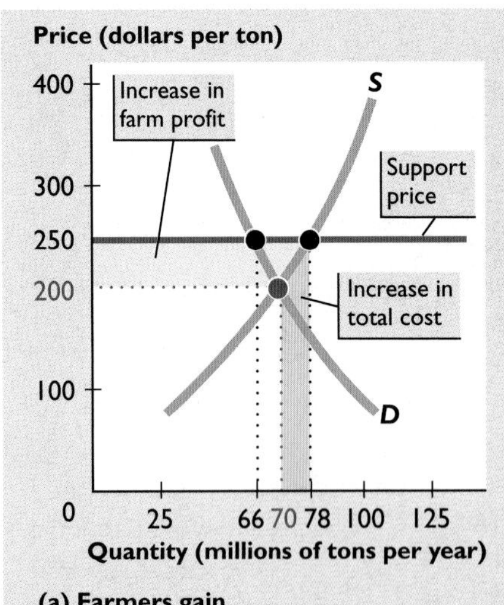

(a) Farmers gain

The support price increases farmers' profit, but farmers' total cost also increases.

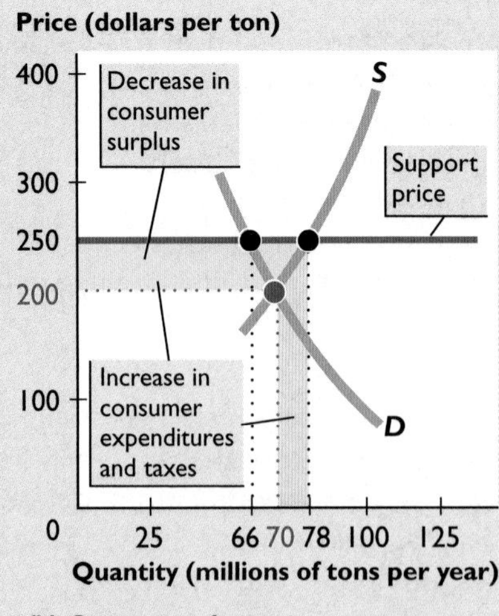

(b) Consumers lose

The consumer pays more for food and more in taxes and receives a smaller consumer surplus.

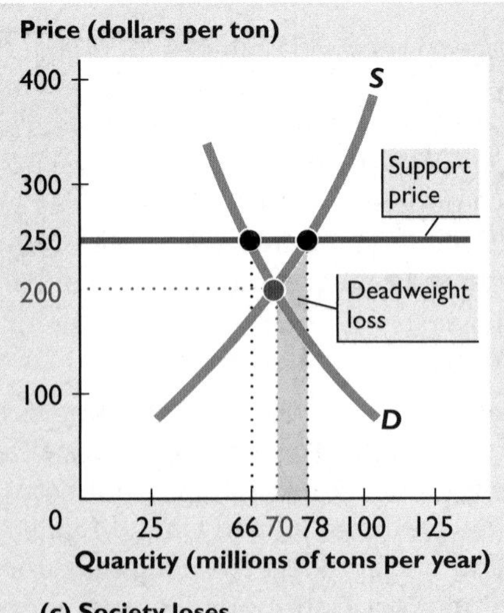

(c) Society loses

The total cost exceeds the total gain by a deadweight loss that equals the increase in total cost.

Production Flexibility Contracts

For many farm crops, the 1996 act replaced price supports with *production flexibility contracts*. Under these contracts, farmers receive a fixed payment per acre, not a payment per unit produced. The effect of these payments is to decrease a farm's fixed cost and leave its marginal cost unchanged.

A farm's supply curve depends on its marginal cost curve. And the quantity supplied is that at which marginal cost equals price. Because a production flexibility contract changes neither marginal cost nor market price, these new arrangements provide farmers with an increased income but leave the market price and quantity produced at their competitive equilibrium and efficient levels. So the new system avoids the social losses that arise from price supports.

But in sugar and dairy products, some element of price supports remains, so these products will continue to be a source of inefficiency. In the case of sugar, the inefficiency is extremely costly.

Farm Subsidies

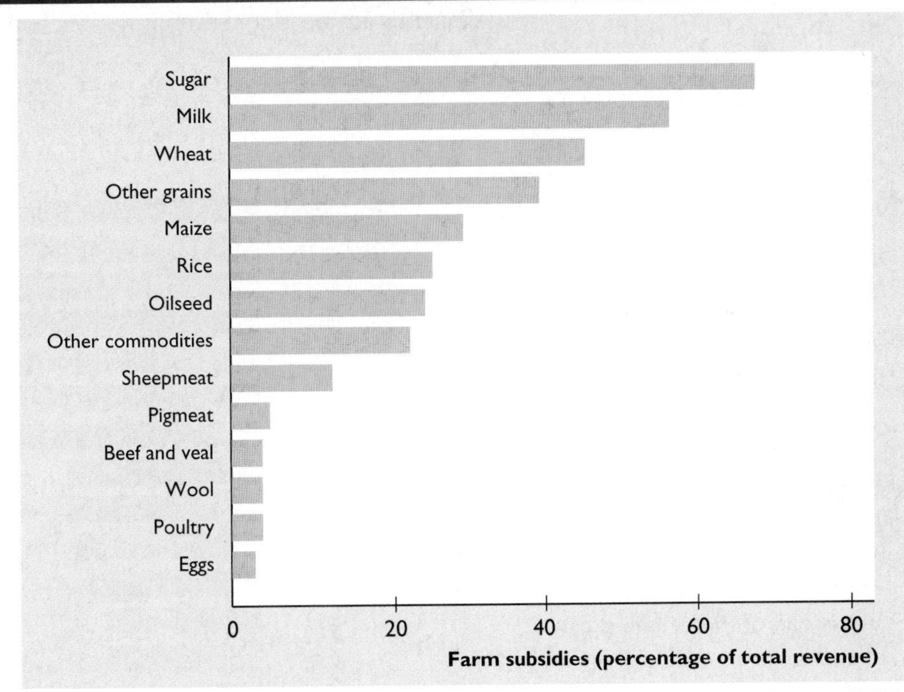

SOURCE: OECD.

The figure shows the percentage of U.S. farm total revenue that came from U.S. government subsidies in 1999.

In the case of sugar, almost 70 percent of total revenue is from subsidies. Sugar can be produced on the most efficient farms—most of them in Australia, the Caribbean, and other countries—for around half of what it costs to produce sugar on U.S. farms.

The government's support for the sugar industry is an example of the effects of *rent seeking*. The General Accounting Office, or GAO (a U.S. government agency), estimates that consumers pay $2 billion a year more for sugar and foods that contain it than they would if the program were scrapped and sugar were imported at the world market price.

The GAO also estimates that 42 percent of the sugar subsidies go to 1 percent of sugar farmers. Because the benefits are enormous, rent seeking is highly profitable.

The cost of the sugar subsidies, while large in total, is only around $5 per person per year. So there is little incentive for any one consumer of sugar to incur costs fighting the program.

Although the sugar subsidy is an extreme, milk subsidies are also large. Subsidies to grain producers represent a large part of total revenue.

Farm Subsidies and International Trade

Most countries subsidize their farms (see the Eye on the Global Economy below). And most use some form of price support system to boost farm incomes. You've seen how price supports increase output and create surpluses. They also diminish the amount of efficient international trade and depress the world price.

One of the ways in which support prices are achieved is to prevent imports by imposing quotas—quantitative restrictions on the quantities that may be imported. For example, the United States limits the import of low-cost sugar from Australia and the Caribbean, low-cost beef and lamb from Australia and New Zealand, and low-cost tomatoes from Mexico. These quotas lower the world demand for these products and their world prices fall.

Worse, because price supports increase domestic production, one of the ways in which governments try to dispose of their surpluses is to sell them abroad. So increased domestic production leads to an increase in supply in the rest of the world. The increase in supply further lowers the price in the rest of the world and lowers farm incomes in other countries.

Because most countries engage in these practices, the world market is oversupplied with food, world food prices are too low, and resources are allocated inefficiently in the global economy.

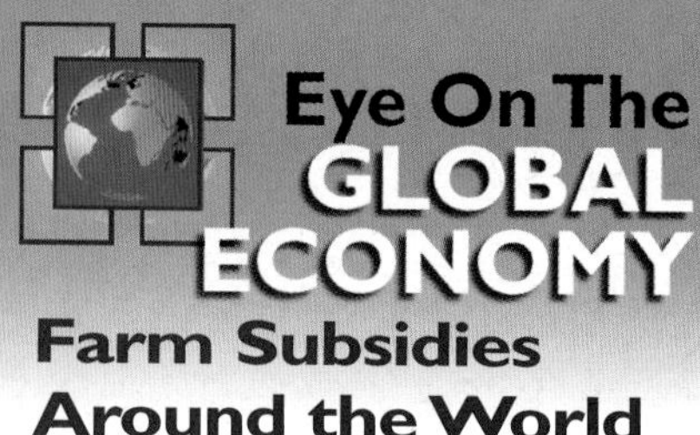

Farm Subsidies Around the World

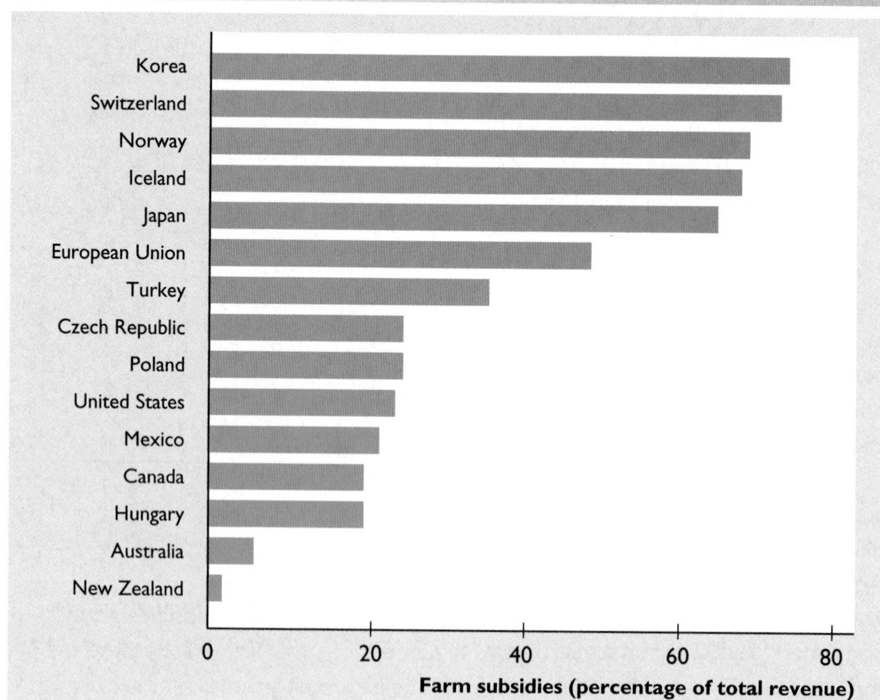

SOURCE: OECD.

Japan, the European Union, and a few small countries have high subsidies. Australia and New Zealand have the lowest subsidies.

Most countries, and the United States is one of these, have subsidies that average around 20 percent of farm total revenue.

Farm subsidies are an obstacle to free international trade and a major source of inefficiency in the global economy.

If the global food markets were efficient, the United States would have fewer farms and farm workers and would import more from developing countries. We would buy our food for a lower price, and farmers in poor countries would earn a larger income.

CHECKPOINT 20.2

2 **Describe and evaluate the effects of government policies to stabilize farm incomes.**

Study Guide pp. 313–316

*e*Foundations 20.2

Practice Problems 20.2

1. Table 1 shows the demand schedule and supply schedule for peanuts. The government decides to set a support price of $10 a ton.
   a. What are the quantities of peanuts produced and consumed?
   b. What is the quantity of peanuts bought by the government?
   c. What is the cost of the price support program to the consumer-taxpayer?
   d. Why is there a deadweight loss from the price support program for peanuts?
2. In the market described in Table 1, the government replaces the price support system with a flexible production contract that pays peanut farmers $100 million a year.
   a. What are the quantities of peanuts produced and consumed?
   b. What is the quantity of peanuts bought by the government?
   c. What is the cost of the price support program to the consumer-taxpayer?
   d. Who gains from this system compared with the price support in Practice Problem 1?

TABLE 1

Price (dollars per ton)	Quantity demanded (millions of tons per year)	Quantity supplied (millions of tons per year)
14	35	65
12	40	60
10	45	55
8	50	50
6	55	45
4	60	40
2	65	35

Exercises 20.2

1. Table 2 shows the demand schedule and supply schedule for rice. The government decides to set a support price of $5 a ton.
   a. What are the quantities of rice produced and consumed?
   b. What is the quantity of rice bought by the government?
   c. What is the cost of the price support program to the consumer-taxpayer?
   d. Is there a deadweight loss from the price support program for rice?
2. In the market described in Table 2, the government replaces the price support system with a flexible production contract that pays rice farmers $30 million a year. Do the farmers prefer this system to the price support in Exercise 1? Why or why not?

TABLE 2

Price (dollars per ton)	Quantity demanded (millions of tons per year)	Quantity supplied (millions of tons per year)
7	22	40
6	26	38
5	30	36
4	34	34
3	38	32
2	42	30
1	46	28

Solutions to Practice Problems 20.2

1a. The quantity produced is 55 million tons, and the quantity consumed is 45 million tons.

1b. The government buys 10 million tons.

1c. The consumer-taxpayer pays $550 million for 45 million tons compared with $500 million for 50 tons in a market without price support.

1d. A deadweight loss arises from the price support program because farmers use resources to produce peanuts that no one wants to buy at $10 a ton.

2a. The quantity produced is 50 million tons, and the quantity consumed is 50 million tons.

2b. The government buys no peanuts.

2c. Consumer-taxpayers pay $500 million for peanuts and $100 million in taxes.

2d. Consumer-taxpayers gain. With the price support, peanuts cost $550 for 45 million tons. With the flexible production contract, peanuts cost $500 for 50 million tons.

20.3 THE ECONOMICS OF CITIES

You saw in Chapter 2 (see pp. 38–39) that a quarter of the U.S. population lives in the six largest cities (or metropolitan areas) and more than one half of the population lives in cities that exceed 1 million people. Most metropolitan areas are growing in size and eating into the farmland that surrounds them. As cities get bigger, more and more people spend more time each day sitting in an automobile on a crowded and slow moving freeway or squeezed into crowded suburban trains and buses. Some people avoid the daily commute by living close to the center of the city. But to do so, they must pay a huge premium on the rent of a suburban home.

Why, with all the daily hassle that city life brings, do most people live in big cities? Why does anyone live in a city? The main answer is that city living brings large external benefits: external production benefits and external consumption benefits.

External Production Benefits

People living in densely populated communities are more productive (other things remaining the same) than people who are spread thinly over much greater distances. The daily interactions that easily occur in a big city are enormously productive. All the services that a firm needs are a few city blocks away, so transportation and communication costs are low. Also, living close to others permits synergies—output from a group that exceeds the outputs of each individual working alone—that would be difficult to generate by telephone, e-mail, or Internet chat technologies over larger distances.

External Consumption Benefits

Many services become feasible only in a large community. For example, a newspaper of the quality of the *New York Times* needs a very large local market to enable it to operate profitably. Restaurants and specialty services also need a large local market to be profitable. Also, choice is expanded in a large city. In a small community, there is usually one major event per day—a ball game on Monday, a concert on Tuesday, and so on. In cities, such as New York, Miami, or Los Angeles, there are several ball games, concerts, and other events every single day.

So cities arise because they increase productivity and expand consumption possibilities. But cities also create many interesting economic problems. Here, we're going to examine only two of them: the tendency for cities to expand, or urban sprawl, and the daily round of traffic congestion.

Urban Sprawl

The growth of a metropolitan area is limited by natural physical factors such as oceans, rivers, and mountains. For example, Los Angeles is bounded by the Pacific Ocean on the west and is encircled by mountains on the north, east, and south. The availability of an adequate supply of water also can limit the capacity of a city. But in some regions, natural barriers are not a dominant influence on the size of a city. The southeastern regions of the United States are particularly free from natural limits to growth. When natural barriers are absent, economic factors determine the size of an urban area. And we can summarize the economic factors as the unrelenting forces of demand and supply.

A Model of a City: The Basic Idea

Edwin S. Mills, a distinguished economist who has taught at MIT, Johns Hopkins University, Princeton University, and Northwestern University, suggested a clever way to use the demand and supply model to explain two features of a city: its geographical spread and its land prices (or rents). Figure 20.7 is a "map" of a Mills city.

Cities have a center and suburbs that surround the center and stretch out to the farmland that surrounds the urban area. Mills suggested that we idealize this description by thinking of a city as circular. No actual city is circular, but this assumption captures the idea of a center and suburbs.

In every city, land values (and rents) are highest at the center of the city and fall off as the distance from the center increases. In the model city, land values and rents depend *only* on the distance from the center. So there are circles that surround the center, and on each circle, the land values are equal. On circle *A*, all the land values are equal. On circle *B*, they are equal but less than those on circle *A*. And on circle *C*, they are equal but less than those on circle *B*. Circle *C* is the limit of the urban area, which is surrounded by farmland.

FIGURE 20.7
A Map of a Model City

e/**Foundations 20.3** 

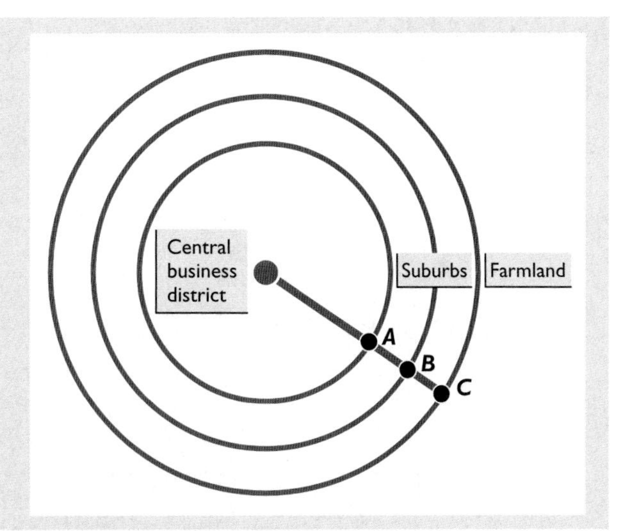

A model circular city has a central business district where the cost of land is highest. The value of land depends only on the distance from the center. On circle *A*, land values are equal. On circle *B*, they are equal but less than those on circle *A*. And on circle *C*, they are equal but less than those on circle *B*. Circle *C* is the limit of the urban area, which is surrounded by farmland.

The Demand for Urban Land

Because the model city is a circle, we can study the demand for and supply of urban land by taking a thin slice, like the slice along the line from the center through points *A*, *B*, and *C* in Figure 20.7.

Figure 20.8 illustrates this slice of the city. The *y*-axis measures the price of an acre of land, and the *x*-axis measures the distance from the city center.

The demand for urban land is the downward-sloping curve, *D*. This demand curve is a bit different from the standard one. At each point along the *x*-axis, there is only one acre of land available. The demand curve tells us the price that someone is willing to pay for that acre. At the city center (zero miles from the center), that price is $4,000 an acre in Figure 20.8. As we move farther away from the center, the price that someone is willing to pay decreases. The main reason why the willingness to pay decreases is the cost of transportation between the suburbs, where people live, and the city center, where people work. A longer commute makes people less willing to pay to live in a distant suburb.

The Supply of Urban Land

At the city center and at each distance from the center along a given slice, the quantity of land is fixed and its supply is perfectly inelastic. Its supply curve is vertical. So the demand curve determines the price of land. It actually costs $4,000 to buy an acre of land at the center of the city in Figure 20.8.

But there is an alternative use of land as farmland. The value of the land if used for farming depends on the income that an acre of land can produce for a farmer. The income that an acre of land generates in farming doesn't depend on

FIGURE 20.8

The Size of a City and Its Land Values

e/**Foundations 20.3** 

The demand curve for urban land, *D*, tells us the price that someone is willing to pay for an acre at each distance from the city center. The quantity of land is fixed and the supply of each acre is perfectly inelastic, so demand determines price. The value of land in farming is independent of location. The equilibrium limit of the city is 16 miles from the center.

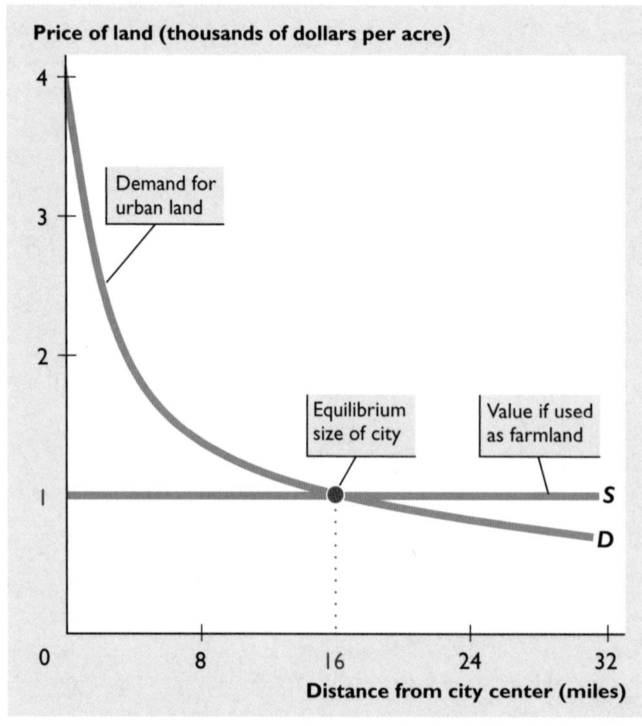

its location. Whether the land is close to the center or a long way from the center, its value in farming is the same.

Because the value of land used in farming doesn't depend on its location, the supply of land for urban use rather than for farm use is perfectly elastic and is shown by the supply curve *S* in Figure 20.8.

The Equilibrium Size of the City

Land is allocated to its highest-valued use. If land is worth more as farmland than as suburbs, it is used for farming. If land is worth more in suburban use than as farmland, it becomes suburbs. The equilibrium size of the city is the size at which the value of land in urban use equals its value in farm use. In Figure 20.8, the city limit is 16 miles from the center. At that distance, the value of land in urban use is $1,000, the same as that when it is used as farmland.

Why Cities Grow

There is one fundamental reason why cities grow: technological change. Advances in technology make land more valuable in urban use. Cheaper cars, improved freeways, and improved public transportation systems increase the amount that people are willing to pay for land in the suburbs. So the demand curve for urban land shifts rightward. Advances in agricultural technology increase farm yields per acre and enable farms to economize on land use. These advances lower the value of land in farm use. The combination of increases in demand and a falling value in farm use increases the equilibrium size of a city.

Qualifications and Modifications to the Basic Model

The basic model of a city that you've just studied provides insights into why cities grow and how land values are determined. But the model does not explain the precise details of any actual city. Some obvious modifications can be made to introduce additional realism. For example, highways and rail lines might be added. They increase the value of land close to the transportation artery and make the city shape more like a star than a circle. Natural objects also constrain the shape of the city.

The development of suburban centers and satellite cities also breaks the simple circular pattern. More complex models have been developed to describe the size and land values in these more realistic cities.

But these qualifications and modifications don't change the basic idea. Urban land is more valuable closer to the center, other things remaining the same. And farmland has the same value no matter where it is located. So the city limit is determined at the point of equality of the value of land in urban and farm use.

Environmental Externalities and City Size

The equilibrium size of a city might not be the efficient size. A city might grow too big if left to market forces. For this reason, land use is regulated and zoning laws are used to try to balance social marginal cost and social marginal benefit.

Rural land is valuable not only as farmland, but also as recreational land. And often, no one captures revenue from the recreational use of land, so the market undervalues this aspect of land use.

Also, a large urban area creates pollution of both air and land. So, again, limiting the size of a city or zoning within the city can improve an unregulated market-determined city size and land use.

Traffic Congestion

Every day, in every city, millions of people sit in cars and buses on congested highways. For several hours a day, freeways resemble expensive parking lots. Central city roads and streets are also congested for most of the business day. Why do freeways and city roads and streets get congested? Is congestion efficient? Is there a more efficient way of using our roads?

To answer these questions, let's think about a trip from *A* to *B*. Pick your own *A* and *B*. It might be from Ipswich to downtown Boston, Evanston to downtown Chicago, Riverside to central Los Angeles, West Palm Beach to Miami Beach, or any other urban trip. Figure 20.9 illustrates the economics of this trip.

Each traveler (and potential traveler) gets some value, or marginal benefit, from the trip. Arrange the travelers from the one who gets the greatest marginal benefit to the one who gets the lowest marginal benefit. Then make a graph of these marginal benefits, which will look like the marginal benefit curve, *MB*, in Figure 20.9. The person who values this trip the most receives a marginal benefit of $15. The traveler in the three thousandth vehicle receives a marginal benefit of $5.

The marginal cost of a trip depends on the number of vehicles using the road. The greater the number of vehicles, the longer the trip takes and the more it costs. The marginal private cost—the cost borne by one person—is the *MC* curve. When a person decides to take this trip, the cost is *MC*. But one more vehicle on the road slows the trip for everyone and adds to everyone else's cost. So the marginal *social* cost exceeds the marginal private cost. The curve *MSC* shows marginal social cost.

Each person decides whether to take this trip by comparing marginal benefit with marginal private cost. If *MB* exceeds *MC*, the person travels. If *MC* exceeds

FIGURE 20.9

The Cost of Congestion

*e*Foundations **20.3** 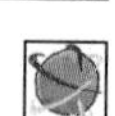

The marginal benefit of a trip is *MB*, and the marginal private cost is *MC*. Travelers balance marginal benefit and marginal private cost, so 3,000 vehicles per hour use the road. Marginal social cost, *MSC*, exceeds marginal private cost because of congestion. The road is overused, and a deadweight loss arises.

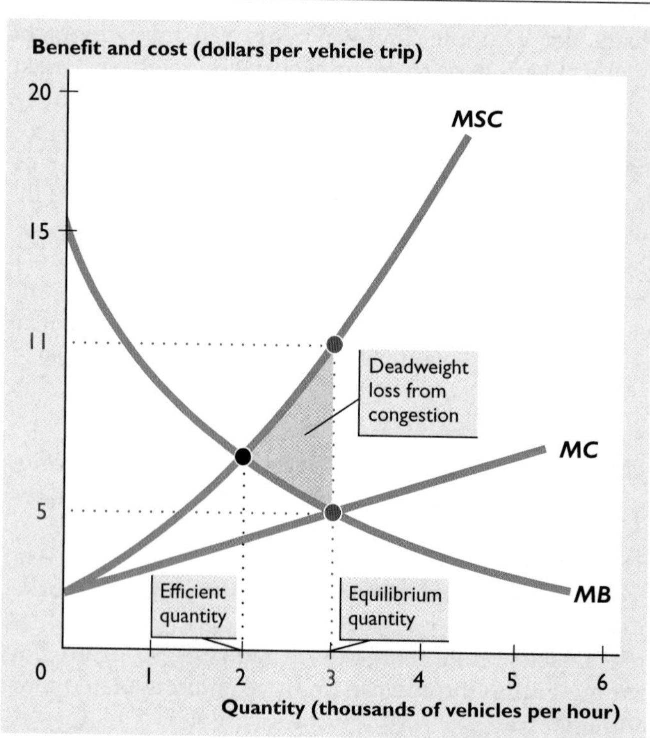

MB, the person stays home or travels at a different time. So the equilibrium number of vehicles is the quantity at which *MB* equals *MC*, which in Figure 20.9 is 3,000 vehicles an hour. Marginal benefit and marginal private cost are equal at $5.

This outcome is inefficient because marginal social cost exceeds marginal benefit. In Figure 20.9, *MSC* is $11 per trip and congestion generates a deadweight loss shown by the gray area.

Using Tolls to Achieve Efficient Road Use

Inefficient congestion arises because road users are not confronted with the social consequences of their choices. To achieve efficient road use, the cost to each user must reflect the marginal social cost. Introducing High-Occupancy Toll (HOT) lanes (or "Lexus lanes") is a way of achieving this outcome.

In Figure 20.10, a toll of $3.50 is introduced on the entire highway, not just on HOT lanes. The toll is added to the other components of marginal private cost to find the new marginal private cost curve, *MC*. The equilibrium number of vehicles now decreases to 2,000 an hour, and the use of this road is efficient.

Congestion decreases, but it might not be eliminated. With 2,000 vehicles an hour, traffic might still move slowly because of congestion. But it is the efficient quantity of congestion given the travelers' own assessments of the benefits and costs of a trip.

The marginal benefit curve shifts rightward at rush hour each day. So to achieve an efficient outcome, tolls would need to vary by time of day. At the morning and evening rush hours, the toll would increase, and during the rest of the day, it would decrease. The efficient toll might be zero at some parts of the day and night.

FIGURE 20.10
A Toll Reduces Congestion

*e*Foundations 20.3 

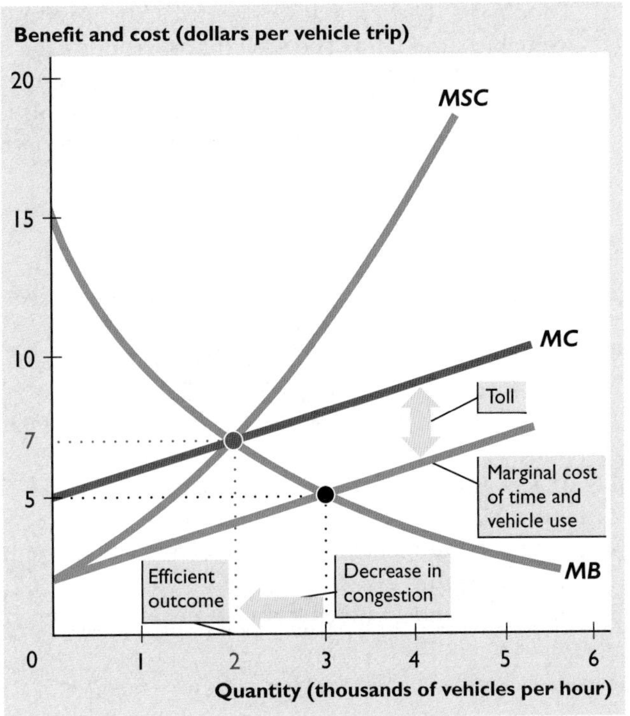

With a toll of $3.50, marginal private cost increases to *MC*. Travelers now decrease the quantity of trips to 2,000 vehicles per hour. Marginal social cost, *MSC*, now equals marginal benefit, *MB*, and the road is used efficiently.

CHECKPOINT 20.3

Study Guide pp. 316–319

*e*Foundations 20.3

3 **Explain why cities grow and evaluate tolls as a way of achieving an efficient use of roads.**

Practice Problem 20.3

In Figure 1, the demand for urban land in Concentric City in 2000 was D_0. In 2010, the demand had increased to D_1. Farmland around the city was selling for $4,000 an acre in 2000 and for $2,000 an acre in 2010.

a. What was the size of Concentric City in 2000?
b. What was the size of Concentric City in 2010?
c. What was the price of an acre of land at the center of Concentric City in 2000?
d. What was the price of an acre of land at the center of Concentric City in 2010?
e. What was the price of an acre of land 5 miles from the center of Concentric City in 2000?
f. What was the price of an acre of land 15 miles from the center of Concentric City in 2010?

FIGURE 1

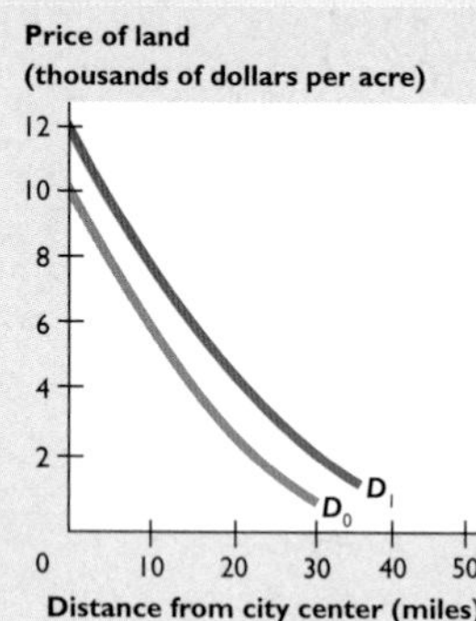

Exercises 20.3

1. In Concentric City in the Practice Problem and Figure 1, the value of each plot of urban land rises by a further $2,000 an acre by 2020. The value of land used in farming remains the same as it was in 2010.
   a. What is the size of Concentric City in 2020?
   b. What is the price of an acre of land at the center of Concentric City in 2020?
   c. What is the price of an acre of land 5 miles from the center of Concentric City in 2020?

2. People are worried that Concentric City is getting too big and is eating into valuable rural land. The area that surrounds the city is spectacularly beautiful and attracts many tourists, hikers, and campers.
   a. What is the economic problem that confronts Concentric City in 2020?
   b. What are some possible solutions to the economic problem that confronts Concentric City in 2020?

Solution to Practice Problem 20.3

a. The limits of Concentric City in 2000 were 15 miles from the center (at the intersection of D_0 and S_0 in Figure 2).
b. The limits of Concentric City in 2010 were 30 miles from the center (at the intersection of D_1 and S_1 in Figure 2).
c. An acre of land at the center of Concentric City in 2000 cost $10,000 (on D_0 in Figure 2).
d. An acre of land at the center of Concentric City in 2010 cost $12,000 (on D_1 in Figure 2).
e. An acre of land 5 miles from the center of Concentric City in 2000 cost $8,000 (on D_0 in Figure 2).
f. An acre of land 15 miles from the center of Concentric City in 2010 cost $6,000 (on D_1 in Figure 2).

FIGURE 2

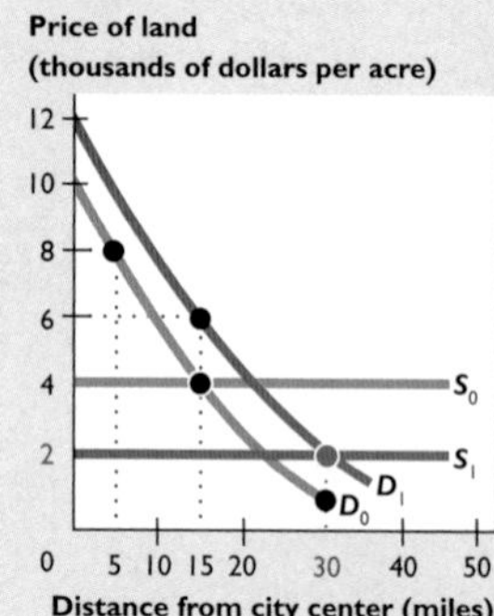

CHAPTER CHECKPOINT

Key Points

1 Explain why farm incomes fluctuate and why the prices of farm products are on a downward trend.

- Because the demand for farm products is inelastic, fluctuations in farm output bring large fluctuations in the prices of farm products and farm incomes decrease when output increases.
- Because the supply of and demand for farm products are inelastic, fluctuations in the demand for farm output bring large fluctuations in the prices of farm products and farm incomes.
- Population growth and rising incomes have brought an increase in the demand for farm products.
- Productivity growth in seeds, fertilizers, and planting and harvesting equipment has brought an increase in the supply of farm products.
- The increase in supply has exceeded the increase in demand, so the quantity produced has increased and the price has fallen.
- The output of the average farm has increased by a greater percentage than the increase in total output, and farm size has increased.

2 Describe and evaluate the effects of government policies to stabilize farm incomes.

- Price supports boost farm income, but they create a surplus of output, increase taxes, raise food prices, decrease the quantity of farm output consumed, and create a deadweight loss.
- Production flexibility contracts, introduced in the 1996 Farm Act, boost farm incomes and avoid the inefficiencies of price supports.

3 Explain why cities grow and evaluate tolls as a way of achieving an efficient use of roads.

- Cities grow because the value of land in urban use increases and the value of land in farm use decreases.
- Roads become congested because road use creates an external cost but road users take into account the private cost only.
- A toll can create the efficient use of roads, but an efficient toll would vary with the time of day.

Key Terms

Price support system, 492
Production flexibility contract, 492

Exercises

1. Explain why, in markets for farm products, a small change in (a) supply brings a large change in price and a change in the opposite direction in total revenue and (b) demand brings a large change in price and a change in the same direction in total revenue. Illustrate your explanations with appropriate diagrams. In your explanations, distinguish carefully between demand and quantity demanded and between supply and quantity supplied.
2. What are the main sources of falling prices of farm products? Do falling prices bring entry into farming or exit from farming? Do the reasons for falling prices make farms larger or smaller? Explain.
3. If farm incomes were boosted by a price support program that set the support price at the equilibrium price in a normal year, how would the program affect farm incomes, prices, production, consumer surplus, taxes, and deadweight loss:
   a. In a normal year?
   b. In a year with a bumper harvest?
   c. In a year with a poor harvest?

4. Use the link on your Foundations Web site to obtain information about U.S. tomato production and restrictions on international trade in tomatoes.
   a. Does the United States have free international trade in tomatoes? If not, what are the restrictions on international trade?
   b. Which countries produce tomatoes and export them to the United States?
   c. If U.S. tomato growers were assisted by a price support, what would happen in the tomato market?

5. Use the link on your Foundations Web site to obtain information about the U.S. sugar program.
   a. Evaluate the claim that U.S. sugar farmers are efficient.
   b. Evaluate the claim that the U.S. sugar program is wasteful.
   c. If sugar farmers were supported with flexible production contracts, how would the sugar market change?

6. Use the link on your Foundations Web site and read the document entitled "The Truth About Urban Sprawl."
   a. Summarize the general thrust of the argument in the document.
   b. Explain why you agree or disagree with the general thrust of the argument in the document. Pay special attention to the idea of the equilibrium size of a city and the efficient size of a city.
   c. If urban sprawl is a problem, how do you think it might be controlled? (Hint: Think about the remedies for externalities described in Chapter 8.)

7. Use the link on your Foundations Web site to learn how Singapore prices the use of its roads and uses other measures to control traffic volumes.
   a. What are the measures that Singapore uses to control road use?
   b. Do you think the Singapore solution is a good idea? Is it needed in the United States? Could it work in the United States?

8. Use the link on your Foundations Web site to learn about the HOT lane experiments that are being conducted around the nation. Use a diagram similar to Figure 20.10 to analyze the effects of introducing HOT lanes. [Hint: Think about what happens to the marginal cost of using the free lanes.]

Chapter 21

International Financial Markets

CHAPTER CHECKLIST

When you have completed your study of this chapter, you will be able to:

1 Describe a country's balance of payments accounts and explain what determines the amount of international borrowing and lending.

2 Explain how the exchange rate is determined and why it fluctuates.

Every single year since 1982, the United States has spent more on imports than it has earned on exports. During these years, imports exceeded exports by a total of $2.5 trillion! How can a nation spend more than it earns?

The world's three big currencies are the dollar, the yen, and the euro. The dollar (the currency of the United States) and the yen (the currency of Japan) have been around for a long time. The euro is new. It was launched on January 1, 1999, as the fledgling currency of 11 members of the European Union. Most of the world's international trade and finance is conducted using these three currencies. Currencies fluctuate in value. In 1971, one U.S. dollar bought 360 Japanese yen. In 1995, one dollar bought only 94 yen, and in 2000, it bought 108 yen. Why does our dollar fluctuate against other currencies? Is there anything we can do or should do to stabilize the value of the dollar?

In this chapter, you are going to learn about international finance. You will discover how nations keep their international accounts, what determines the balance of payments, and how the value of the dollar is determined in the foreign exchange market.

21.1 FINANCING INTERNATIONAL TRADE

When Sony Stores in the United States imports CD players from Japan, it does not pay for them with U.S. dollars—it uses Japanese yen. When a French construction company buys an earthmover from Caterpillar, Inc., it uses U.S. dollars. Whenever we buy things from another country, we use the currency of that country to make the transaction. It doesn't make any difference what the item being traded is; it might be a consumption good or a capital good, a building, or even a firm.

We're going to study the markets in which money—different types of currency—is bought and sold. But first we're going to look at the scale of international trading and borrowing and lending and at the way in which we keep our records of these transactions. Such records are called the balance of payments accounts.

Balance of Payments Accounts

Balance of payments accounts
The accounts in which a nation records its international trading, borrowing, and lending.

A country's **balance of payments accounts** record its international trading, borrowing, and lending. There are in fact three balance of payments accounts:

- Current account
- Capital account
- Official settlements account

Current account
Record of international receipts and payments—current account balance equals exports minus imports, plus net interest and transfers received from abroad.

Capital account
Record of foreign investment in the United States minus U.S. investment abroad.

Official settlements account
Record of the change in U.S. official reserves.

U.S. official reserves
The government's holdings of foreign currency.

The **current account** records receipts from the sale of goods and services to other countries (exports), minus payments for goods and services bought from other countries (imports), plus the net amount of interest and transfers (such as foreign aid payments) received from and paid to other countries. The **capital account** records foreign investment in the United States minus U.S. investment abroad. The **official settlements account** records the change in official U.S. reserves. **U.S. official reserves** are the government's holdings of foreign currency. If U.S. official reserves increase, the official settlements account balance is negative. The reason is that holding foreign money is like investing abroad. U.S. investment abroad is a minus item in the capital account and in the official settlements account. (By the same reasoning, if official reserves decrease, the official settlements account balance is positive.)

The sum of the balances on the three accounts always equals zero. That is, to pay for our current account deficit, we must either borrow more from abroad than we lend abroad or use our official reserves to cover the shortfall.

Table 21.1 shows the U.S. balance of payments accounts in 2000. Items in the current account and capital account that provide foreign currency to the United States have a plus sign; items that cost the United States foreign currency have a minus sign. The table shows that in 2000, U.S. imports exceeded U.S. exports and the current account deficit was $435 billion. We paid for imports that exceeded the value of our exports by borrowing from the rest of the world. The capital account tells us by how much. We borrowed $952 billion (foreign investment in the United States) but made loans of $553 billion (U.S. investment abroad). Our measured net foreign borrowing was $399 billion. Measurement error (recorded in the balance of payments accounts as a statistical discrepancy) was $36 billion. Our official reserves increased by $290 million, so rounding to the nearest billion dollars as we do in Table 21.1, they appear as a zero change.

You might better understand the balance of payments accounts and the way in which they are linked together if you think about the income and expenditure, borrowing and lending, and bank account of an individual.

The U.S. Balance of Payments

The numbers in Table 21.1 provide a snapshot of the U.S balance of payments in 2000. The figure puts this snapshot into perspective by showing how the balance of payments evolved from 1980 to 1998.

(Because the economy grows and the price level rises, changes in the dollar value of the balance of payments do not convey much information. To remove the influences of growth and inflation, the figure shows the balance of payments as a percentage of GDP.)

The capital account balance is almost a mirror image of the current account balance because the official settlements balance is very small in comparison with the balances on these other two accounts. A large current account deficit (and capital account surplus) emerged during the 1980s but declined from 1987 to 1991. Throughout the 1990s, the current account deficit increased.

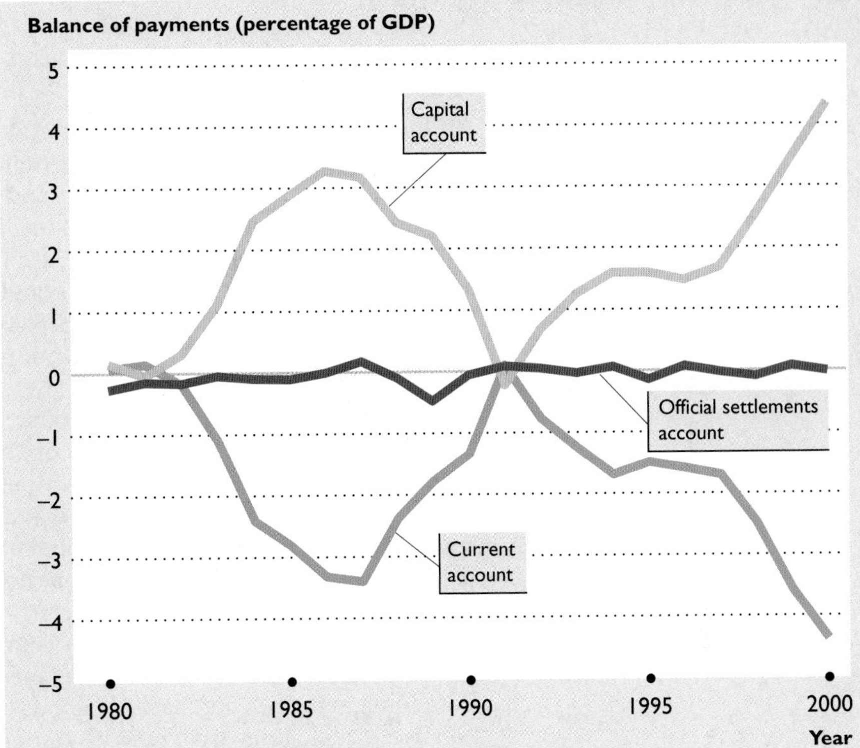

SOURCE: Bureau of Economic Analysis, U.S. Department of Commerce, Washington, D.C.

TABLE 21.1
The U.S. Balance of Payments Accounts in 2000

Current account	**(billions of dollars)**
Exports of goods and services	+1,070
Imports of goods and services	−1,438
Net interest	−14
Net transfers	−53
Current account balance	−435
Capital account	
Foreign investment in the United States	+952
U.S. investment abroad	−553
Statistical discrepancy	36
Capital account balance	435
Official settlements account	
Decrease in official U.S. reserves	0

SOURCE: Bureau of Economic Analysis, U.S. Department of Commerce, Washington, D.C.

Individual Analogy

An individual's current account records the income from supplying the services of factors of production and the expenditure on goods and services. Consider, for example, Joanne. She worked in 2000 and earned an income of $25,000. Joanne has $10,000 worth of investments that earned her an interest of $1,000. Joanne's current account shows an income of $26,000. Joanne spent $18,000 buying goods and services for consumption. She also bought a new house, which cost her $60,000. So Joanne's total expenditure was $78,000. The difference between her expenditure and income is $52,000 ($78,000 minus $26,000). This amount is Joanne's current account deficit.

To pay for expenditure of $52,000 in excess of her income, Joanne has to use the money that she has in the bank or she has to take out a loan. In fact, Joanne took a mortgage of $50,000 to help buy her house. This mortgage was the only borrowing that Joanne did, so her capital account surplus was $50,000. With a current account deficit of $52,000 and a capital account surplus of $50,000, Joanne is still $2,000 short. She got that $2,000 from her own bank account. Her cash holdings decreased by $2,000.

Joanne's income from her work is analogous to a country's income from its exports. Her income from her investments is analogous to a country's interest from foreigners. Her purchases of goods and services, including her purchase of a house, are analogous to a country's imports. Joanne's mortgage—borrowing from someone else—is analogous to a country's borrowing from the rest of the world. The change in her bank account is analogous to the change in the country's official reserves.

Borrowers and Lenders, Debtors and Creditors

Net borrower
A country that is borrowing more from the rest of the world than it is lending to the rest of the world.

Net lender
A country that is lending more to the rest of the world than it is borrowing from the rest of the world.

A country that is borrowing more from the rest of the world than it is lending to it is called a **net borrower**. Similarly, a **net lender** is a country that is lending more to the rest of the world than it is borrowing from it.

The United States is a net borrower, but it is a relative newcomer to the ranks of net borrower nations. Throughout the 1960s and most of the 1970s, the United States was a net lender to the rest of the world. It had a surplus on its current account and a deficit on its capital account. It was not until 1983 that the United States became a significant net borrower from the rest of the world. Between 1983 and 1987, U.S. borrowing increased each year. Then it decreased and was briefly zero in 1991. After 1991, it started to increase again. The average net foreign borrowing by the United States between 1983 and 2000 was $178 billion a year.

Most countries are net borrowers like the United States. But a small number of countries, including Japan and oil-rich Saudi Arabia, are net lenders.

Debtor nation
A country that during its entire history has borrowed more from the rest of the world than it has lent to it.

Creditor nation
A country that during its entire history has invested more in the rest of the world than other countries have invested in it.

A net borrower might be reducing its net assets held in the rest of the world, or it might be going deeper into debt. A nation's total stock of foreign investment determines whether the nation is a debtor or creditor. A **debtor nation** is a country that during its entire history has borrowed more from the rest of the world than it has lent to it. It has a stock of outstanding debt to the rest of the world that exceeds the stock of its own claims on the rest of the world. A **creditor nation** is a country that has invested more in the rest of the world than other countries have invested in it.

Flows and Stocks

At the heart of the distinction between a net borrower and a net lender on the one hand and between a debtor nation and a creditor nation on the other hand is the distinction between flows and stocks. Borrowing and lending are flows—amounts borrowed or lent per unit of time. Debts are stocks—amounts owed at a point in time. The flow of borrowing and lending changes the stock of debt.

The United States was a debtor nation through the nineteenth century as we borrowed from Europe to finance our westward expansion, railroads, and industrialization. We paid off our debt and became a creditor nation for most of the current century. But following a string of current account deficits, we became a debtor nation again in 1989.

Since 1989, total stock of U.S. borrowing from the rest of the world has exceeded U.S. lending to the rest of the world. The largest debtor nations are the capital-hungry developing countries (as the United States was during the nineteenth century). The international debt of these countries grew rapidly during the 1980s and created what was called the "Third World debt crisis."

Should we be concerned that the United States is a net borrower? The answer is probably not. Our international borrowing finances the purchase of new capital goods. In 2000, businesses spent $1,833 billion on new buildings, plant, and equipment. Government spent $336 billion on defense equipment and public structures such as highways, and dams. All these purchases added to the nation's capital and much of it increased productivity. Governments also spent on education and health care services, which increased human capital.

Current Account Balances Around the World

The U.S. current account deficit in 2000 is the major international payments deficit. No other country has a deficit remotely similar to that of the United States.

The next largest deficits are those of the developing countries in the Western Hemisphere—the nations of Latin America.

Japan and the newly industrialized Asian economies have current account surpluses, as do all other groups of countries.

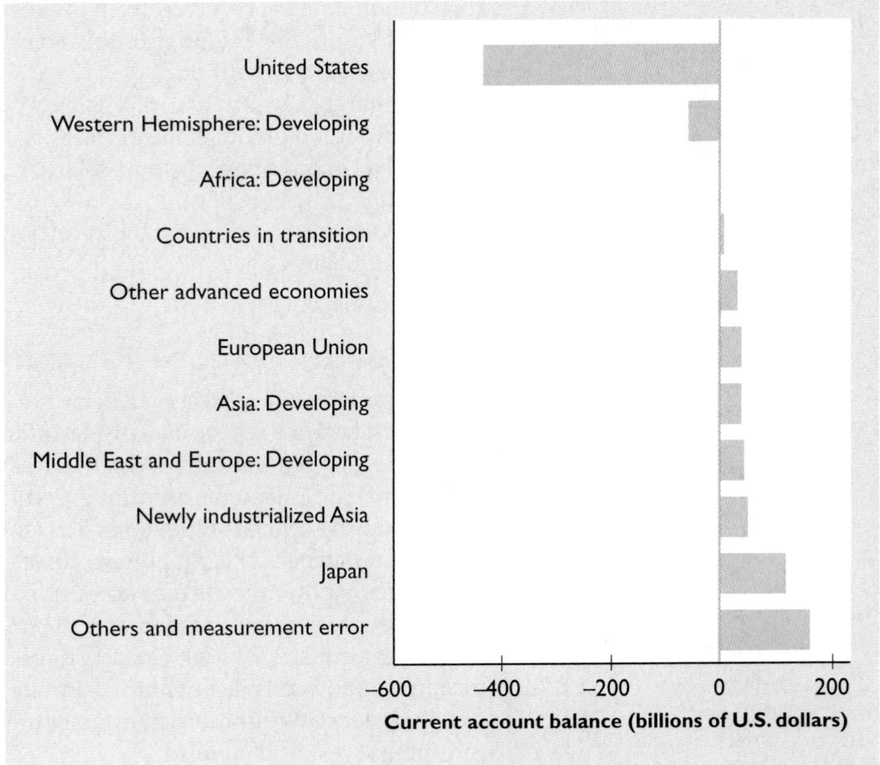

SOURCE: International Monetary Fund, *World Economic Outlook*, October 2000.

CHECKPOINT 21.1

Study Guide pp. 324–327 

*e*Foundations 21.1

1 **Describe a country's balance of payments accounts and explain what determines the amount of international borrowing and lending.**

Practice Problem 21.1

It is 2004 and the U.S. economy records the following transactions:

Imports of goods and services, $2,000 billion; interest paid to the rest of the world, $500 billion; interest received from the rest of the world, $400 billion; net transfers, zero; decrease in U.S. official reserves, $10 billion; capital account balance, $330 billion.

a. Calculate exports of goods and services, the official settlements account balance, and the current account balance.

b. Is the United States a debtor or a creditor nation in 2004?

c. If interest paid to the rest of the world increased by $100 billion, what would happen to the current account balance?

Exercise 21.1

It is 2005 and the U.S. economy records the following transactions:

Exports of goods and services, $1,800 billion; interest paid to the rest of the world, $550 billion; interest received from the rest of the world, $350 billion; net transfers to rest of world, $50 billion; capital account balance, $600 billion; decrease in U.S. official reserves, $10 billion.

a. Calculate the current account balance, the official settlements account balance, and imports of goods and services.

b. Has the United States become a larger or smaller debtor or creditor nation in 2005?

c. If imports increased by $100 billion, what would happen to the capital account balance?

Solution to Practice Problem 21.1

a. Because U.S. official reserves decrease by $10 billion, the official settlements account balance is a *surplus* of $10 billion. To find the current account balance, use the fact that the sum of the balance on the current account, capital account, and official settlements account is zero. The capital account balance is $330 billion and the official settlements account balance is $10 billion, so the current account balance is –$340 billion. To calculate exports of goods and services, use the fact that the current account balance (–$340 billion) equals exports (the number we seek), minus imports ($2,000 billion) plus net interest (–$100 billion) plus net transfers (zero). Exports of goods and services equal $1,760 billion.

b. The United States is a debtor nation in 2004. You can determine this fact because it pays out more in interest to the rest of the world than it receives from the rest of the world.

c. If interest paid to the rest of the world increased by $100 billion, the current account deficit would increase by $100 billion to $440 billion.

21.2 THE EXCHANGE RATE

When we buy foreign goods or invest in another country, we have to obtain some of that country's currency to make the transaction. When foreigners buy U.S.-made goods or invest in the United States, they have to obtain some U.S. dollars. We get foreign currency, and foreigners get U.S. dollars in the foreign exchange market. The **foreign exchange market** is the market in which the currency of one country is exchanged for the currency of another. The foreign exchange market is not a place like a downtown flea market or produce market. The market is made up of thousands of people: importers and exporters, banks, and specialists in the buying and selling of foreign exchange, called foreign exchange brokers. The foreign exchange market opens on Monday morning in Hong Kong, which is still Sunday evening in New York. As the day advances, markets open in Singapore, Tokyo, Bahrain, Frankfurt, London, New York, Chicago, and San Francisco. As the West Coast markets close, Hong Kong is only an hour away from opening for the next business day. Dealers around the world are in continual contact, and on a typical day in 2000, $1.5 trillion changed hands.

Foreign exchange market
The market in which the currency of one country is exchanged for the currency of another.

The price at which one currency exchanges for another is called a **foreign exchange rate**. For example, in August 2000, one U.S. dollar bought 108 Japanese yen. The exchange rate was 108 yen per dollar. We can also express the exchange rate in terms of dollars (or cents) per yen, which in August 2000 was a bit less than 1 cent per yen.

Foreign exchange rate
The price at which one currency exchanges for another.

Currency depreciation is the fall in the value of one currency in terms of another currency. For example, if the dollar falls from 100 yen to 80 yen, the dollar depreciates by 20 percent.

Currency depreciation
The fall in the value of one currency in terms of another currency.

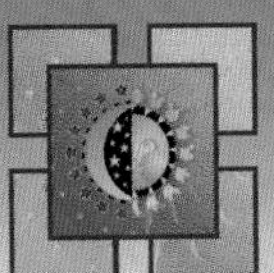

Eye On The PAST

The Dollar and the Yen Since 1980

The figure shows the exchange rate of the U.S. dollar in terms of the Japanese yen between 1980 and 2000.

From 1982 to 1995, and again in 2000, the value of the dollar fell against the yen—the dollar depreciated.

From 1978 to 1982 and again during 1996 to 1998, the dollar rose in value against the yen—the dollar appreciated.

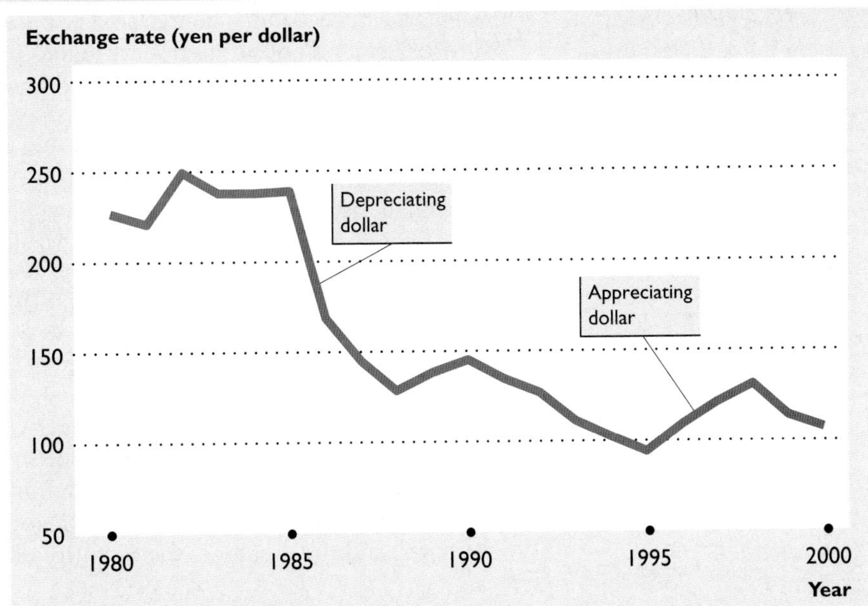

SOURCE: *Economic Report of the President*, 2001.

Currency appreciation
The rise in the value of one currency in terms of another currency.

Currency appreciation is the rise in the value of one currency in terms of another currency. For example, if the dollar rises from 100 yen to 120 yen, the dollar appreciates by 20 percent. When the U.S. dollar appreciates against the yen, the yen depreciates against the dollar.

Why does the U.S. dollar fluctuate in value? Why does it sometimes depreciate and sometimes appreciate? To answer these questions, we need to understand the forces that determine the exchange rate.

The exchange rate is a price—the price of one country's money in terms of another country's money. And like all prices, demand and supply determine the exchange rate. So to understand the forces that determine the exchange rate, we need to study demand and supply in the foreign exchange market. We'll begin by looking at the demand side of the market.

Demand in the Foreign Exchange Market

The quantity of U.S. dollars demanded in the foreign exchange market is the amount that traders plan to buy during a given time period at a given exchange rate. This quantity depends on many factors but the main ones are:

- The exchange rate
- Interest rates in the United States and other countries
- The expected future exchange rate

Let's look first at the relationship between the quantity of dollars demanded in the foreign exchange market and the exchange rate.

The Law of Demand for Foreign Exchange

People do not buy dollars because they enjoy them. The demand for dollars is a *derived demand*. People demand dollars so that they can buy U.S.-made goods and services (U.S. exports). They also demand dollars so that they can buy U.S. assets such as bank accounts, bonds, stocks, businesses, and real estate. Nevertheless, the law of demand applies to dollars just as it does to anything else that people value.

Other things remaining the same, the higher the exchange rate, the smaller is the quantity of dollars demanded. For example, if the price of the U.S. dollar rises from 100 yen to 120 yen but nothing else changes, the quantity of U.S. dollars that people plan to buy decreases. Why does the exchange rate influence the quantity of dollars demanded? There are two separate reasons, and they are related to the two sources of the derived demand for dollars:

- Exports effect
- Expected profit effect

Exports Effect

The larger the value of U.S. exports, the larger is the quantity of dollars demanded. But the value of U.S. exports depends on the exchange rate. The lower the exchange rate, other things remaining the same, the cheaper are U.S.-made goods and services to people in the rest of the world, the more the United States exports, and the greater is the quantity of U.S. dollars demanded to pay for them.

Expected Profit Effect

The larger the expected profit from holding dollars, the greater is the quantity of dollars demanded in the foreign exchange market. But expected profit depends on the exchange rate. The lower the exchange rate, other things remaining the same,

FIGURE 21.1
The Demand for Dollars

*e*Foundations 21.2 

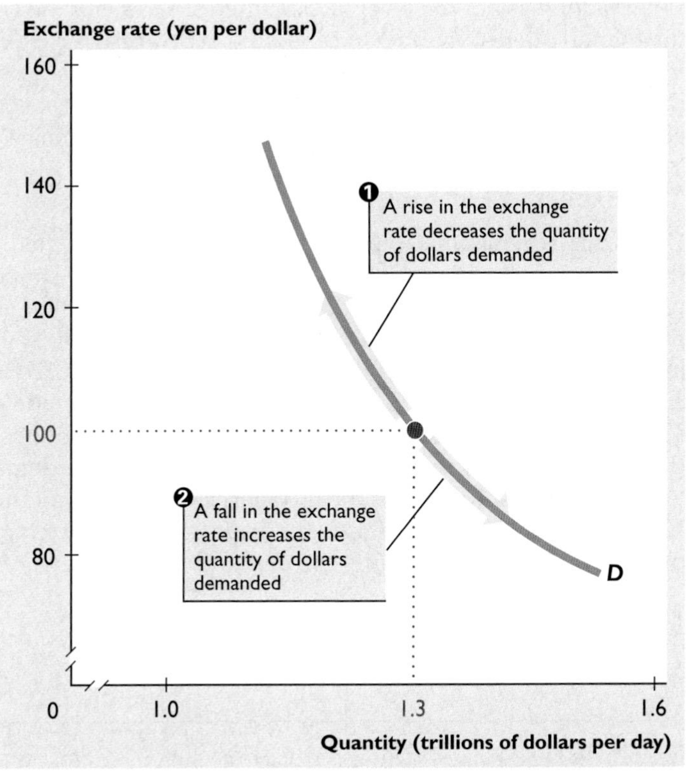

Other things remaining the same, the quantity of dollars that people plan to buy depends on the exchange rate.

1. If the exchange rate rises, the quantity of dollars demanded decreases and there is a movement up along the demand curve for dollars.
2. If the exchange rate falls, the quantity of dollars demanded increases and there is a movement down along the demand curve for dollars.

the larger is the expected profit from holding dollars and the greater is the quantity of dollars demanded on the foreign exchange market.

To understand this effect, suppose you think the dollar will be worth 120 yen by the end of the month. If a dollar costs 115 yen today, you buy dollars. But a person who thinks that the dollar will be worth 115 yen at the end of the month does not buy dollars. Now suppose the exchange rate falls to 110 yen per dollar. More people think that they can profit from buying dollars, so the quantity of dollars demanded increases.

Figure 21.1 shows the demand curve for U.S. dollars in the foreign exchange market. For the two reasons we've just reviewed, when the foreign exchange rate rises, other things remaining the same, the quantity of dollars demanded decreases and there is a movement up along the demand curve, as shown by the arrow. When the exchange rate falls, other things remaining the same, the quantity of dollars demanded increases and there is a movement down along the demand curve, as shown by the arrow.

Changes in the Demand for Dollars

A change in any other influence on the quantity of U.S. dollars that people plan to buy in the foreign exchange market brings a change in the demand for dollars and the demand curve for dollars shifts. These other influences are:

- Interest rates in the United States and other countries
- The expected future exchange rate

Interest Rates in the United States and Other Countries

U.S. interest rate differential
The U.S. interest rate minus the foreign interest rate.

People and businesses buy financial assets to make a return. The higher the interest rate on U.S. assets compared with foreign assets, the more U.S. assets they buy. What matters is not the level of U.S. interest rates, but the U.S. interest rate minus the foreign interest rate, a gap called the **U.S. interest rate differential**. If the U.S. interest rate rises and the foreign interest rate remains constant, the U.S. interest rate differential increases. The larger the U.S. interest rate differential, the greater is the demand for U.S. assets and the greater is the demand for dollars.

The Expected Future Exchange Rate

Other things remaining the same, the higher the expected future exchange rate, the greater is the demand for dollars. To see why, suppose you are Toyota's finance manager. The exchange rate is 100 yen per dollar, and you think that by the end of the month, it will be 120 yen per dollar. You spend 100,000 yen today and buy $1,000. At the end of the month, the dollar is 120 yen, as you predicted, and you sell the $1,000. You get 120,000 yen. You've made a profit of 20,000 yen. The higher the expected future exchange rate, other things remaining the same, the greater is the expected profit and the greater is the demand for dollars.

Figure 21.2 summarizes the influences on the demand for dollars. A rise in the U.S. interest rate differential or the expected future exchange rate increases the demand for dollars and shifts the demand curve rightward from D_0 to D_1. A fall

FIGURE 21.2
Changes in the Demand for Dollars

*e*Foundations 21.2 

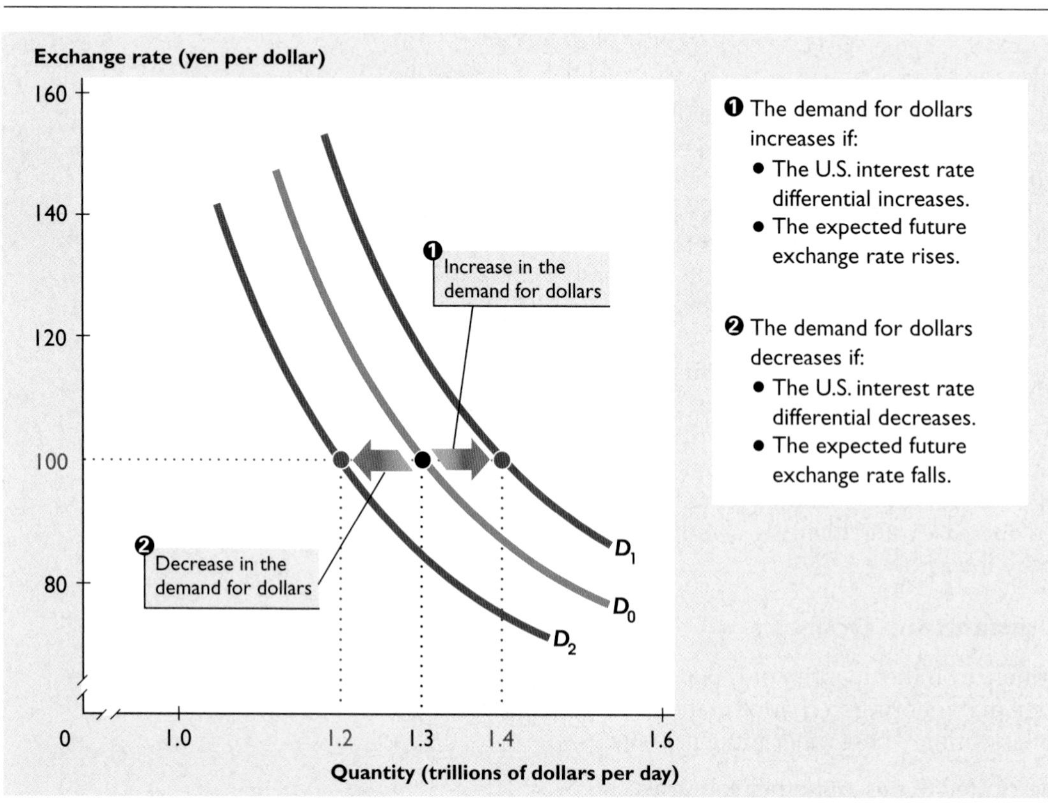
Exchange rate (yen per dollar)
160
140
120
100
80
0
1.0
1.2
1.3
1.4
1.6
Quantity (trillions of dollars per day)
1 Increase in the demand for dollars
2 Decrease in the demand for dollars
D1
D0
D2
1 The demand for dollars increases if:
• The U.S. interest rate differential increases.
• The expected future exchange rate rises.
2 The demand for dollars decreases if:
• The U.S. interest rate differential decreases.
• The expected future exchange rate falls.

in the U.S. interest rate differential or the expected future exchange rate decreases the demand for dollars and shifts the demand curve leftward from D_0 to D_2.

Supply in the Foreign Exchange Market

The quantity of U.S. dollars supplied in the foreign exchange market is the amount that traders plan to sell during a given time period at a given exchange rate. This quantity depends on many factors but the main ones are:

- The exchange rate
- Interest rates in the United States and other countries
- The expected future exchange rate

Let's look first at the relationship between the quantity of dollars supplied in the foreign exchange market and the exchange rate.

The Law of Supply for Foreign Exchange

Traders supply U.S. dollars in the foreign exchange market when people and businesses buy other currencies. And they buy other currencies so that they can buy foreign-made goods and services (U.S. imports). They also supply dollars and buy foreign currencies so that they can buy foreign assets such as bank accounts, bonds, stocks, businesses, and real estate. The law of supply applies to dollars just as it does to anything else that people plan to sell.

Other things remaining the same, the higher the exchange rate, the greater is the quantity of dollars supplied in the foreign exchange market. For example, if the price of the U.S. dollar rises from 100 yen to 120 yen but nothing else changes, the quantity of U.S. dollars that people plan to sell in the foreign exchange market increases. Why does the exchange rate influence the quantity of dollars supplied?

There are two reasons, and they parallel the two reasons on the demand side of the market:

- Imports effect
- Expected profit effect

Imports Effect

The larger the value of U.S. imports, the larger is the quantity of foreign currency demanded to pay for these imports. And when people buy foreign currency, they supply dollars. So the larger the value of U.S. imports, the greater is the quantity of dollars supplied on the foreign exchange market. But the value of U.S. imports depends on the exchange rate. The higher the exchange rate, with everything else the same, the cheaper are foreign-made goods and services to Americans. So the more the United States imports, and the greater is the quantity of U.S. dollars supplied on the foreign exchange market to pay for these imports.

Expected Profit Effect

The larger the expected profit from holding a foreign currency, the greater is the quantity of that currency demanded and the greater is the quantity of dollars supplied in the foreign exchange market. But the expected profit from holding a foreign currency depends on the exchange rate. The higher the exchange rate, other things remaining the same, the larger is the expected profit from selling dollars and the greater is the quantity of dollars supplied on the foreign exchange market.

For the two reasons we've just reviewed, other things remaining the same, when the foreign exchange rate rises, the quantity of dollars supplied increases and when the foreign exchange rate falls, the quantity of dollars supplied decreases. Figure 21.3 shows the supply curve for U.S. dollars in the foreign exchange market. In this figure, when the foreign exchange rate rises, other things remaining the same, there is an increase in the quantity of dollars supplied and a movement up along the supply curve, as shown by the arrow. When the exchange rate falls, other things remaining the same, there is a decrease in the quantity of dollars supplied and a movement down along the supply curve, as shown by the arrow.

Changes in the Supply of Dollars

A change in any other influence on the quantity of U.S. dollars that people plan to sell in the foreign exchange market brings a change in the supply of dollars and the supply curve for dollars shifts. Supply either increases or decreases. These other influences on supply parallel the other influences on demand but have exactly the opposite effects. These influences are:

- Interest rates in the United States and other countries
- The expected future exchange rate

FIGURE 21.3
The Supply of Dollars

*e*Foundations 21.2 

Other things remaining the same, the quantity of dollars that people plan to sell depends on the exchange rate.

1. If the exchange rate rises, the quantity of dollars supplied increases and there is a movement up along the supply curve for dollars.

2. If the exchange rate falls, the quantity of dollars supplied decreases and there is a movement down along the supply curve for dollars.

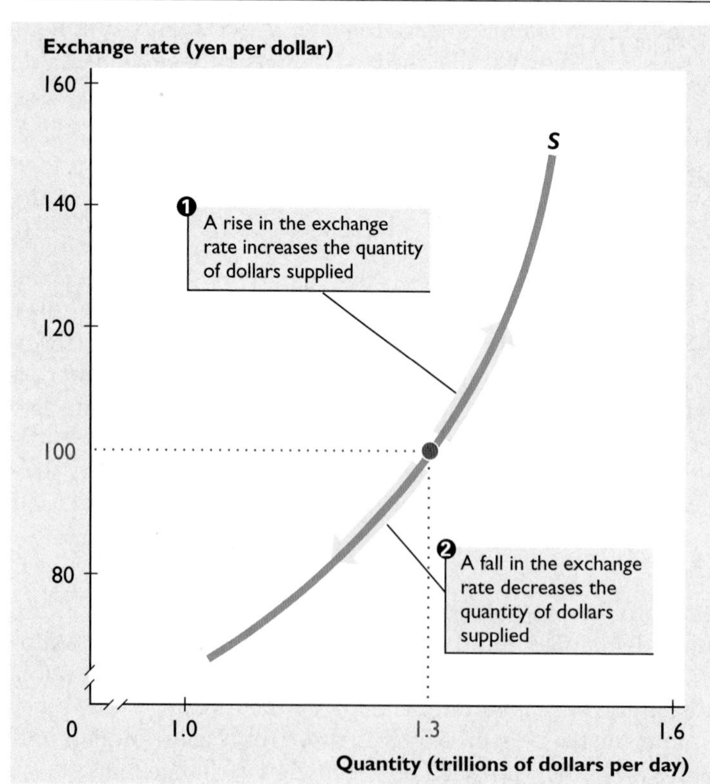
Exchange rate (yen per dollar)
160
140
120
100
80
0
S
1 A rise in the exchange rate increases the quantity of dollars supplied
2 A fall in the exchange rate decreases the quantity of dollars supplied
1.0
1.3
1.6
Quantity (trillions of dollars per day)

Interest Rates in the United States and Other Countries

The larger the U.S. interest rate differential, the smaller is the demand for foreign assets and the smaller is the supply of dollars on the foreign exchange market.

The Expected Future Exchange Rate

Other things remaining the same, the higher the expected future exchange rate, the smaller is the supply of dollars. To see why, suppose that the dollar is trading at 100 yen per dollar today and you think that by the end of the month, the dollar will trade at 120 yen per dollar. You were planning on selling dollars today, but you decide to hold off and wait until the end of the month. If you supply dollars today, you get only 100 yen per dollar. But at the end of the month, if the dollar is worth 120 yen as you predict, you'll get 120 yen for each dollar you supply. You'll make a profit of 20 percent. So the higher the expected future exchange rate, other things remaining the same, the smaller is the expected profit from selling U.S. dollars today and the smaller is the supply of dollars today.

Figure 21.4 summarizes the above discussion of the influences on the supply of dollars. A rise in the U.S. interest rate differential or a rise in the expected future exchange rate decreases the supply of dollars and shifts the demand curve leftward from S_0 to S_1. A fall in the U.S. interest rate differential or a fall in the expected future exchange rate increases the supply of dollars and shifts the supply curve rightward from S_0 to S_2.

FIGURE 21.4
Changes in the Supply of Dollars

*e*Foundations 21.2 

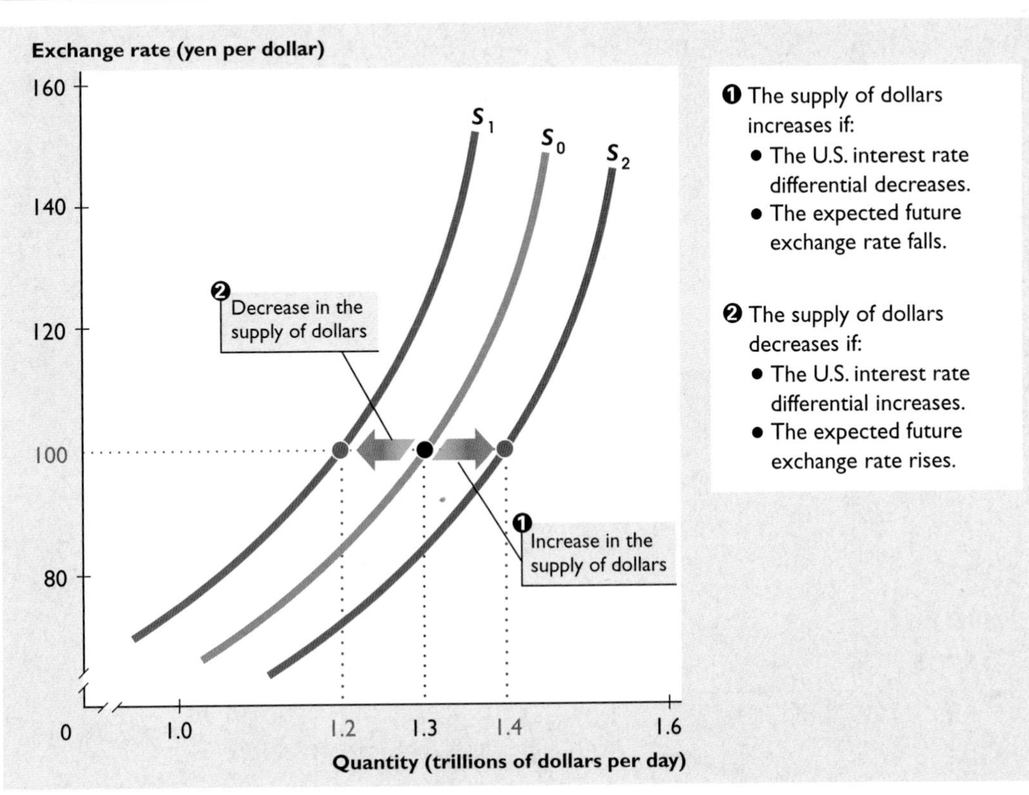
Exchange rate (yen per dollar)
160
140
120
100
80
0
1.0
1.2
1.3
1.4
1.6
Quantity (trillions of dollars per day)
S_1
S_0
S_2
❷ Decrease in the supply of dollars
❶ Increase in the supply of dollars
❶ The supply of dollars increases if:
• The U.S. interest rate differential decreases.
• The expected future exchange rate falls.
❷ The supply of dollars decreases if:
• The U.S. interest rate differential increases.
• The expected future exchange rate rises.

Market Equilibrium

Figure 21.5 shows how demand and supply in the foreign exchange market determine the exchange rate. The demand curve is *D*, and the supply curve is *S*. Just like all the other markets you've studied, the price (the exchange rate) acts as a regulator. If the exchange rate is too high, there is a surplus—the quantity supplied exceeds the quantity demanded. For example, in Figure 21.5, if the exchange rate is 120 yen, there is a surplus of dollars.

If the exchange rate is too low, there is a shortage—the quantity supplied is less than the quantity demanded. For example, in Figure 21.5, if the exchange rate is 80 yen, there is a shortage of dollars.

At the equilibrium exchange rate, there is neither a shortage nor a surplus. The quantity supplied equals the quantity demanded. In Figure 21.5, the equilibrium exchange rate is 100 yen. At this exchange rate, the quantity demanded equals the quantity supplied and is $1.3 trillion a day.

The foreign exchange market is constantly pulled to its equilibrium by the forces of supply and demand. Foreign exchange dealers are constantly looking for the best price they can get. If they are selling, they want the highest price available. If they are buying, they want the lowest price available. Information flows from dealer to dealer through the worldwide computer network, and the price adjusts second by second to keep buying plans and selling plans in balance. That is, price adjusts second by second to keep the market at its equilibrium.

FIGURE 21.5
Equilibrium Exchange Rate

*e*Foundations **21.2** 

The demand curve for dollars is *D*, and the supply curve is *S*.

❶ If the exchange rate is 120 yen per dollar, there is a surplus of dollars and the exchange rate falls.

❷ If the exchange rate is 80 yen per dollar, there is a shortage of dollars and the exchange rate rises.

❸ If the exchange rate is 100 yen per dollar, there is neither a shortage nor a surplus of dollars and the exchange rate remains constant. The market is in equilibrium.

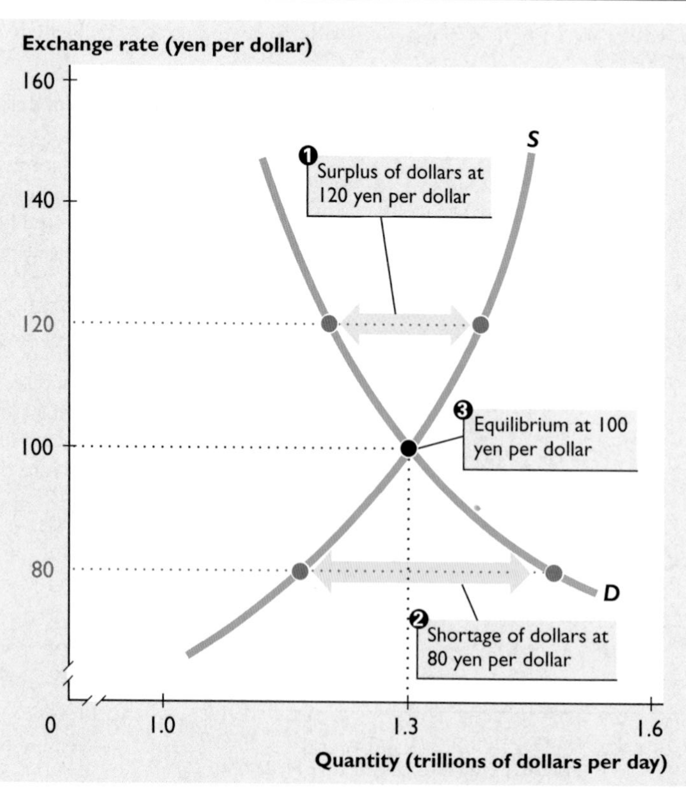

Changes in the Exchange Rate

If the demand for dollars increases and the supply of dollars does not change, the exchange rate rises. If the demand for dollars decreases and the supply of dollars does not change, the exchange rate falls. Similarly, if the supply of dollars decreases and the demand for dollars does not change, the exchange rate rises. If the supply of dollars increases and the demand for dollars does not change, the exchange rate falls.

These predictions about the effects of changes in demand and supply are exactly the same as for any other market.

Why the Exchange Rate Is Volatile

Sometimes the dollar depreciates and at other times it appreciates, but the quantity of dollars traded each day barely changes. Why? The main reason is that supply and demand are not independent of each other in the foreign exchange market.

When we studied the demand for dollars and the supply of dollars, we saw that unlike other markets, the demand side and the supply side of the market have some common influences. A change in the expected future exchange rate or a change in the U.S. interest rate differential changes both demand and supply, and they change in opposite directions. These common influences on both demand and supply explain why the exchange rate can be volatile at times, even though the quantity of dollars traded does not change.

Everyone in the market is potentially either a demander or a supplier. Each has a price above which he or she will sell and below which he or she will buy. Let's see how these common supply and demand effects work by looking at two episodes: one in which the dollar appreciated and one in which it depreciated.

A Depreciating Dollar: 1994–1995

Between 1994 and the summer of 1995, the exchange rate fell from 100 yen to a low of 84 yen per dollar. Figure 21.6(a) explains this fall. In 1994, the demand and supply curves were those labeled D_{94} and S_{94}. The exchange rate was 100 yen per dollar. During 1994, traders expected the U.S. dollar to depreciate. They expected a lower exchange rate. As a result, the demand for dollars decreased and the supply of dollars increased. The demand curve shifted leftward to D_{95}, and the supply curve shifted rightward to S_{95}. The exchange rate fell to 84 yen per dollar.

An Appreciating Dollar: 1995–1998

Between 1995 and 1998, the dollar appreciated against the yen. It rose from 84 yen to 130 yen per dollar. Figure 21.6(b) explains why this happened. In 1995, the demand and supply curves were those labeled D_{95} and S_{95}. The exchange rate was 84 yen—where the supply and demand curves intersect. During the next two years, Japan was in recession and the U.S. economy was expanding. Interest rates in Japan fell, and the yen was expected to depreciate. The demand for yen decreased, and the demand for dollars increased. The demand curve shifted from D_{95} to D_{98}. The supply of dollars decreased, and the supply curve shifted from S_{95} to S_{98}. These two shifts reinforced each other, and the exchange rate increased to 130 yen per dollar.

FIGURE 21.6
Exchange Rate Fluctuations

*e*Foundations 21.2 

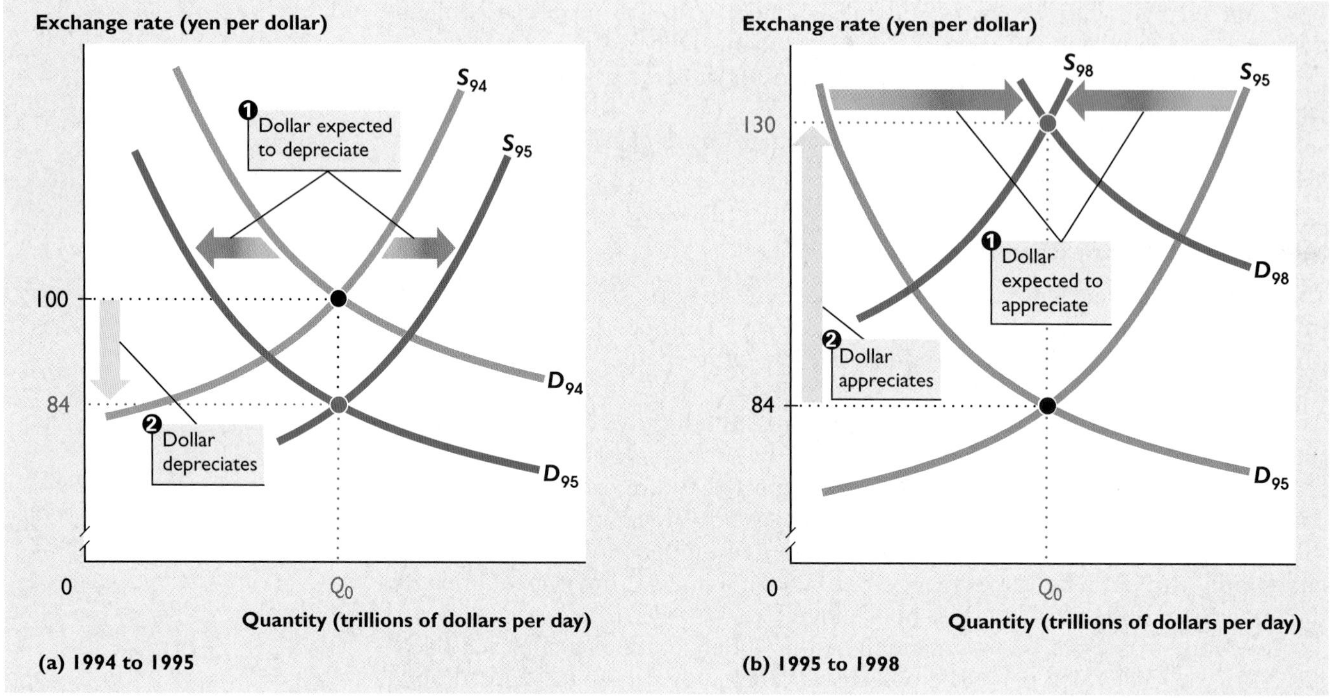

Exchange Rate Expectations

The changes in the exchange rate that we've just examined occurred in part because the exchange rate was expected to change. This explanation sounds a bit like a self-fulfilling forecast. But what makes expectations change? The answer is new information about the deeper forces that influence the value of money. There are two such forces:

- Purchasing power parity
- Interest rate parity

Purchasing Power Parity

Money is worth what it will buy. But two kinds of money, U.S. dollars and Canadian dollars, for example, might buy different amounts of goods and services. Suppose a Big Mac costs $4 (Canadian) in Toronto and $3 (U.S.) in New York. If the Canadian dollar exchange rate is $1.33 Canadian per U.S. dollar, the two monies have the same value. You can buy a Big Mac in either Toronto or New York for either $4 Canadian or $3 U.S.

Purchasing power parity
Equal value of money—a situation in which money buys the same amount of goods and services in different currencies.

The situation we've just described is called **purchasing power parity**, which means equal value of money. If purchasing power parity does not prevail, some powerful forces go to work. To understand these forces, let's suppose that the price of a Big Mac in New York rises to $4 U.S., but in Toronto it remains at $4 Canadian. Suppose the exchange rate remains at $1.33 Canadian per U.S. dollar. In this case, a Big Mac in Toronto still costs $4 Canadian or $3 U.S. But in New York, it costs $4 U.S. or $5.33 Canadian. Money buys more in Canada than in the United States. Money is not of equal value in both countries.

If all (or most) prices have increased in the United States and not increased in Canada, then people will generally expect that the value of the U.S. dollar on the foreign exchange market must fall. In this situation, the U.S. dollar exchange rate is expected to fall. The demand for U.S. dollars decreases, and the supply of U.S. dollars increases. The U.S. dollar exchange rate falls, as expected. If the U.S. dollar falls to $1.00 Canadian and there are no further price changes, purchasing power parity is restored. A Big Mac now costs $4 in either U.S. dollars or Canadian dollars in both New York and Toronto.

If prices increase in Canada and other countries but remain constant in the United States, then people will generally expect that the value of the U.S. dollar on the foreign exchange market is too low and that it is going to rise. In this situation, the U.S. dollar exchange rate is expected to rise. The demand for U.S. dollars increases, and the supply of U.S. dollars decreases. The U.S. dollar exchange rate rises, as expected.

Ultimately, the value of money is determined by prices. So the deeper forces that influence the exchange rate have tentacles that spread throughout the economy. If prices in the United States rise faster than those in other countries, the exchange rate falls. And if prices in the United States rise more slowly than in other countries, the exchange rate rises.

Purchasing Power Parity

Purchasing power parity (PPP) holds in the long run, but in the short run, large deviations from PPP can occur.

The figure shows the range of deviations from PPP in March 2001. The Japanese yen was overvalued by almost 30 percent. The Hungarian forint was the most undervalued currency.

According to PPP, an overvalued currency is one that will depreciate at some point in the future; an undervalued currency is one that will appreciate at some time in the future. But PPP does not predict *when* a currency will depreciate or appreciate.

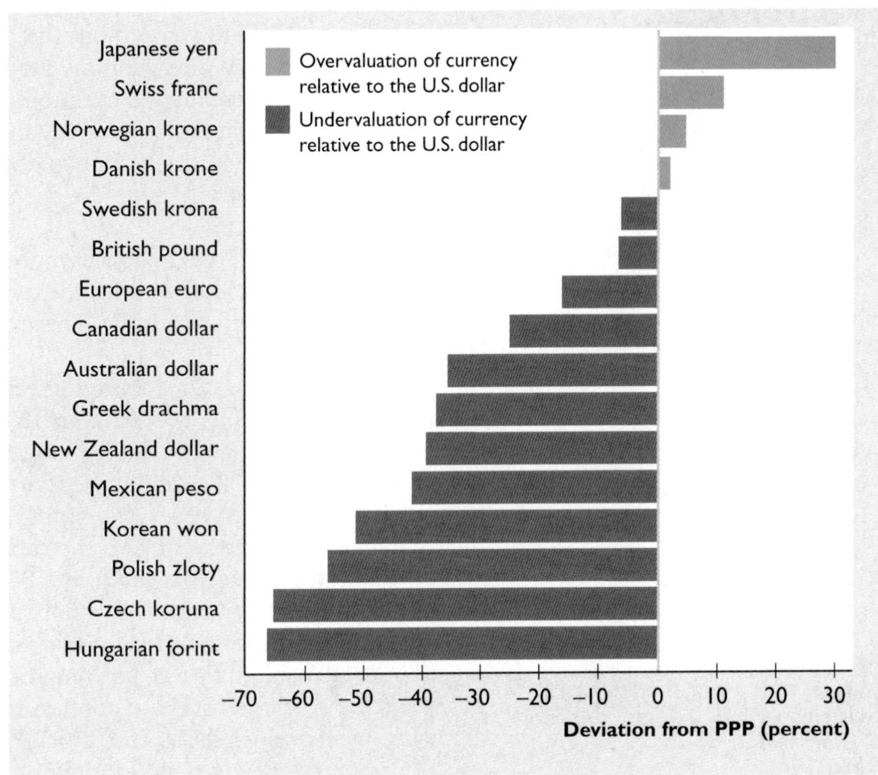

SOURCE: PACIFIC FX Service, University of British Columbia, March 23, 2001.

Interest Rate Parity

Suppose a Canadian dollar deposit in a Toronto bank earns 5 percent a year and a U.S. dollar deposit in a New York bank earns 3 percent a year. Why does anyone deposit money in New York? Why doesn't all the money flow to Toronto? The answer is: because of exchange rate expectations. Suppose people expect the Canadian dollar to depreciate by 2 percent a year. This 2 percent depreciation must be subtracted from the 5 percent interest to obtain the net return of 3 percent a year that an American can earn by depositing funds in a Toronto bank. The two returns are equal. This situation is one of **interest rate parity**—equal interest rates when exchange rate changes are taken into account.

Interest rate parity
Equal interest rates—a situation in which the interest rate in one currency equals the interest rate in another currency when exchange rate changes are taken into account.

Adjusted for risk, interest rate parity always prevails. Funds move to get the highest return available. If for a few seconds a higher return is available in New York than in Toronto, the demand for U.S. dollars rises and the exchange rate rises until expected rates of interest are equal.

The Fed in the Foreign Exchange Market

The Federal Reserve (the Fed) influences the U.S. interest rate, so its actions influence the exchange rate. When the U.S. interest rate rises relative to those in other countries, the demand for U.S. dollars increases, the supply decreases, and the U.S. dollar exchange rate rises. (Similarly, when the U.S. interest rate falls relative to those in other countries, the demand for U.S. dollars decreases, the supply increases, and the U.S. dollar exchange rate falls.)

But the Fed can intervene directly in the foreign exchange market. It can buy or sell dollars and try to smooth out fluctuations in the exchange rate. Let's look at the foreign exchange interventions the Fed can make.

Suppose the Fed wants the exchange rate to be steady at 100 yen per dollar. If the exchange rate rises above 100 yen, the Fed sells dollars. If the exchange rate falls below 100 yen, the Fed buys dollars. By these actions, the Fed changes the supply of dollars and keeps the exchange rate close to its target rate of 100 yen.

Figure 21.7 shows this Fed intervention in the foreign exchange market. The supply of dollars is S, and initially, the demand for dollars is D_0. The equilibrium exchange rate is 100 yen per dollar. This exchange rate is the Fed's target—the horizontal red line.

When the demand for dollars increases and the demand curve shifts rightward to D_1, the Fed sells \$0.1 trillion. This action increases the supply of dollars by \$0.1 trillion and prevents the exchange rate from rising. When the demand for dollars decreases and the demand curve shifts leftward to D_2, the Fed buys \$0.1 trillion. This action decreases the supply of dollars by \$0.1 trillion and prevents the exchange rate from falling. If the demand for dollars fluctuates between D_1 and D_2 and, on the average, is D_0, the Fed sometimes buys and sometimes sells but, on the average, it neither buys nor sells.

But suppose the demand for dollars increases permanently from D_0 to D_1. To maintain the exchange rate at 100 yen per dollar indefinitely, the Fed would have to sell dollars every day and buy foreign currency. The Fed would be piling up foreign currency and increasing U.S. official reserves.

Now suppose the demand for dollars decreases permanently from D_0 to D_2. To maintain the exchange rate at 100 yen per dollar indefinitely, the Fed would have to sell U.S. official reserves and buy dollars every day. Eventually, it would run out of foreign currency and have to abandon its attempt to fix the exchange rate.

March 29, 2000

The Euro Sags

The euro hit a new low against the yen this week as the new currency continued to weaken ahead of a key European interest rate decision due later this week.

Questions

1. What is the euro and when was it created?

2. What is the history of the euro-yen exchange rate?

3. Why do you think the euro fell against the yen in March 2000?

4. Use demand and supply analysis to explain the fall in the value of the euro. Pay special attention to the distinction between changes in demand (and supply) and changes in the quantity demanded (and supplied).

5. What can the ECB do to increase the value of the euro? Would it be wise to try to make the euro rise against the yen? Why or why not?

 *e*Foundations 21.2

FIGURE 21.7

Foreign Exchange Market Intervention

*e*Foundations 21.2 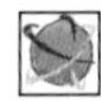

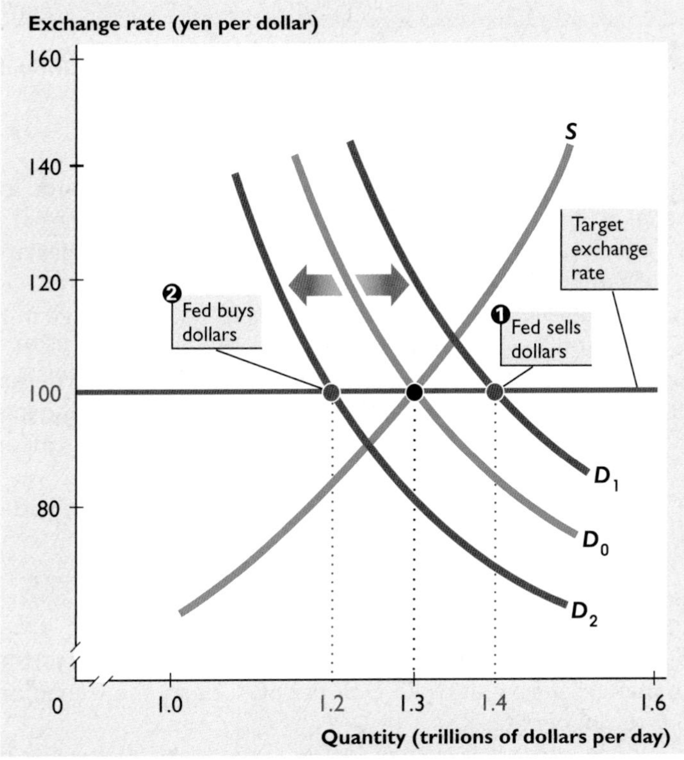

Initially, the demand for dollars is D_0, the supply of dollars is S, and the exchange rate is 100 yen per dollar. The Fed can intervene in the foreign exchange market to keep the exchange rate close to its target rate (100 yen in this example).

❶ If demand increases from D_0 to D_1, the Fed sells dollars to increase supply.

❷ If demand decreases from D_0 to D_2, the Fed buys dollars to decrease supply. Persistent intervention on one side of the market cannot be sustained.

Eye On The GLOBAL ECONOMY

The Sliding Euro

The Fed rarely intervenes in the foreign exchange market to support the value of the dollar. But the European Central Bank (ECB), based in Frankfurt, Germany, sometimes intervenes to support the value of its currency, the euro.

Launched in January 1999 at 1 euro = 1.16 U.S. dollars, the euro has been on a slide for most of its life. By October 2000, the value of the euro had fallen to 85 U.S. cents.

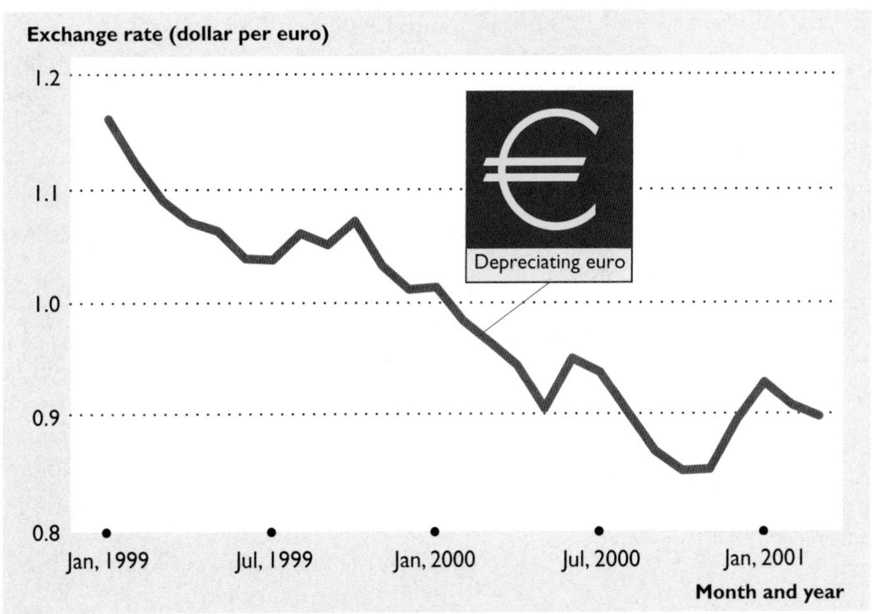

SOURCE: PACIFIC FX Service, University of British Columbia.

CHECKPOINT 21.2

Study Guide pp. 328–331
eFoundations 21.2

2 **Explain how the exchange rate is determined and why it fluctuates.**

Practice Problem 21.2

Suppose that yesterday, the U.S. dollar was trading on the foreign exchange market at 100 yen per dollar. Today, the U.S. dollar is trading at 105 yen per dollar.

a. Which of the two currencies (the dollar or the yen) has appreciated and which has depreciated today?
b. List the events that could have caused today's change in the value of the U.S. dollar on the foreign exchange market.
c. Did the events that you listed in part (b) change the demand for U.S. dollars, the supply of U.S. dollars, or both the demand for and supply of U.S. dollars?
d. If the Fed had tried to stabilize the value of the U.S. dollar at 100 yen per dollar, what action would it have taken?
e. In part (d), what effect would the Fed's actions have had on U.S. official reserves?

Exercise 21.2

Suppose that yesterday, the Canadian dollar ($C) was trading on the foreign exchange market at $0.75 U.S. per $C. Today, the Canadian dollar is trading at $0.70 U.S. per $C.

a. Which of the two currencies (the Canadian dollar or the U.S. dollar) has appreciated and which has depreciated today?
b. List the events that could have caused today's change in the value of the Canadian dollar on the foreign exchange market.
c. Did the events that you listed in part (b) increase or decrease the demand for Canadian dollars, the supply of Canadian dollars, or both the demand for and supply of Canadian dollars?
d. If the Bank of Canada had tried to stabilize the value of the Canadian dollar at $0.75 U.S., what action would it have taken?
e. In part (d), what effect would the Bank of Canada's actions have had on Canadian official reserves?

Solution to Practice Problem 21.2

a. Because the U.S. dollar costs a larger number of yen, the U.S. dollar has appreciated. The yen has depreciated because it buys fewer dollars.
b. The main events might be an increase in the U.S. interest rate, a decrease in the Japanese interest rate, or a rise in the expected future exchange rate.
c. The events that you listed in part (b) change both the demand for and supply of U.S. dollars. They increase demand and decrease supply.
d. To stabilize the value of the U.S. dollar at 100 yen per dollar, the Fed would have increased the supply of U.S. dollar in the foreign exchange market. The Fed would have sold U.S. dollars.
e. When the Fed sells U.S. dollars, it buys foreign currency. U.S. official reserves would have increased.

CHAPTER CHECKPOINT

Key Points

1 Describe a country's balance of payments accounts and explain what determines the amount of international borrowing and lending.

- Foreign currency is used to finance international trade.
- A country's balance of payments accounts record its international transactions.
- Historically, the United States has been a net lender to the rest of the world, but in 1989, that situation changed and the United States became a net borrower and a net debtor.

2 Explain how the exchange rate is determined and why it fluctuates.

- Foreign currency is obtained in exchange for domestic currency in the foreign exchange market.
- The exchange rate is determined by demand and supply in the foreign exchange market.
- The lower the exchange rate, the greater is the quantity of dollars demanded. A change in the exchange rate brings a movement along the demand curve for dollars.
- Changes in the expected future exchange rate and the U.S. interest rate differential change the demand for dollar assets and shift the demand curve.
- The lower the exchange rate, the smaller is the quantity of dollars supplied. A change in the exchange rate brings a movement along the supply curve for dollars.
- Fluctuations in the exchange rate occur because fluctuations in the demand for and supply of dollars are not independent.
- The Fed can intervene in the foreign exchange market to smooth fluctuations in the dollar.

Key Terms

Balance of payments accounts, 508
Capital account, 508
Creditor nation, 510
Currency appreciation, 514
Currency depreciation, 513
Current account, 508
Debtor nation, 510
Foreign exchange market, 513
Foreign exchange rate, 513
Interest rate parity, 524
Net borrower, 510
Net lender, 510
Official settlements account, 508
Purchasing power parity, 522
U.S. interest rate differential, 516
U.S. official reserves, 508

Exercises

1. The following data describe the economy of Antarctica in 2050:

Item	(billions of Antarctica dollars)
Imports of goods and services	150
Exports of goods and services	50
Net interest from abroad	−10
Net transfers from abroad	35
Foreign investment in Antarctica	125
Antarctica's investment abroad	55

   Calculate the following for Antarctica:
   a. Current account balance.
   b. Capital account balance.
   c. Decrease in Antarctica's official reserves.

2. Use the link on your Foundations Web site to visit FRED, the Federal Reserve Economic Database, and find data on the exchange rate and international trade.
   a. When did the United States last have a current account surplus?
   b. Does the United States have a surplus or a deficit in trade in goods?
   c. Does the United States have a surplus or a deficit in trade in services?
   d. What has happened to foreign investment in the United States during the past ten years?
   e. Do you think the U.S. balance of payments record is a matter for concern? Why or why not?

3. Use the link on your Foundations Web site to obtain data on the exchange rate of the U.S. dollar against two other currencies. Then:
   a. Use the demand and supply model to explain the changes (or absence of changes) in the exchange rates.
   b. What specific events might have changed exchange rate expectations?
   c. What forces might have prevented the exchange rate from changing?
   d. What information would you need to determine whether the central bank intervened in the foreign exchange market to limit the change in the exchange rate?

4. The U.S. dollar appreciates. State, with reasons, which of the following events could have caused these changes to occur:
   a. The Fed intervened in the foreign exchange market and sold dollars.
   b. People began to expect the dollar to appreciate.
   c. The U.S. interest rate differential narrowed.
   d. The U.S. current account went into deficit.

Ability-to-pay principle The proposition that people should pay taxes according to how easily they can bear the burden. (p. 222)

Absolute advantage When one person is more productive than another person in several or even all activities. (p. 75)

Allocative efficiency The most highly valued combination of goods and services on the *PPF*. (p. 67)

Antitrust law The body of law that regulates and prohibits certain kinds of market behavior, such as monopoly and monopolistic practices. (p. 372)

Average cost pricing rule A price rule for a natural monopoly that sets the price equal to average cost and enables the firm to cover its costs and earn a normal profit. (p. 331)

Average fixed cost Total fixed cost per unit of output. (p. 271)

Average product Total product divided by the quantity of an input. The average product of labor is total product divided by the quantity of labor employed. (p. 266)

Average tax rate The percentage of income that is paid in tax. (p. 215)

Average total cost Total cost per unit of output, which equals average fixed cost plus average variable cost. (p. 271)

Average variable cost Total variable cost per unit of output. (p. 271)

Balance of payments accounts The accounts in which a nation records its international trading, borrowing, and lending. (p. 508)

Balance of trade The value of exports minus the value of imports. (p. 457)

Barrier to entry A natural or legal constraint that protects a firm from competitors. (p. 310)

Benefit The benefit of something is the gain or pleasure that it brings. (p. 14)

Benefits principle The proposition that people should pay taxes equal to the benefits they receive from public services. (p. 222)

Big tradeoff A tradeoff between efficiency and fairness that recognizes the cost of making income transfers. (p. 148)

Bilateral monopoly A market in which a monopoly seller faces a monopsony buyer. (p. 418)

Black market An illegal market that operates alongside a government-regulated market. (p. 167)

Bond A promise to pay specified sums of money on specified dates. (p. 385)

Bond market A market in which bonds issued by firms or governments are traded. (p. 385)

Budget line A line that describes the limits to consumption choices and that depends on a consumer's budget and the prices of goods and services. (p. 230)

Capacity output The output at which average total cost is a minimum. (p. 341)

Capital The tools, instruments, machines, buildings, and other constructions that have been produced in the past and that businesses now use to produce goods and services. (p. 41)

Capital account Record of foreign investment in the United States minus U.S. investment abroad. (p. 508)

Capture theory The theory that regulation helps producers to maximize economic profit. (p. 362)

Cartel A group of firms acting together to limit output, raise price, and increase economic profit. (p. 348)

Ceteris paribus Other things remaining the same (often abbreviated as ***cet. par.***) (p. 10)

Change in demand A change in the quantity that people plan to buy when any influence on buying plans other than the price of the good changes. (p. 84)

Change in supply A change in the quantity that suppliers plan to sell when any influence on selling plans other than the price of the good changes. (p. 91)

Change in the quantity demanded A change in the quantity of a good that people plan to buy that results from a change in the price of the good. (p. 84)

Change in the quantity supplied A change in the quantity of a good that suppliers plan to sell that results from a change in the price of the good. (p. 91)

Circular flow model A model of the economy that shows the circular flow of expenditure and incomes that result from decision makers' choices and the way those choices interact to determine what, how, and for whom goods and services are produced. (p. 46)

Coase theorem The proposition that if property rights exist, only a small number of parties are involved, and transactions costs are low, then private transactions are efficient and the outcome is not affected by who is assigned the property right. (p. 188)

Collective bargaining Union negotiations with employers or their representatives. (p. 413)

Commodity market A market in which raw materials are traded. (p. 386)

Comparable worth Paying the same wage for different jobs that are judged comparable. (p. 424)

Comparative advantage The ability of a person to perform an activity or produce a good or service at a lower opportunity cost than someone else. (p. 73)

Complement A good that is consumed with another good. (p. 85)

Complement in production A good that is produced along with another good. (p. 92)

Constant returns to scale A condition in which, when a firm increases its plant size and labor employed by the same percentage, its output increases by the same percentage and its average total cost remains constant. (p. 278)

Consumer surplus The marginal benefit from a good or service minus the price paid for it. (p. 135)

Copyright A government-sanctioned exclusive right granted to the inventor of a good, service, or productive process to produce, use, and sell the invention for a given number of years. (p. 199)

Correlation The tendency for the values of two variables to move in a predictable and related way. (p. 11)

Craft union A group of workers who have a similar range of skills but work for many different firms in many different industries and regions. (p. 412)

Creditor nation A country that has invested more in the rest of the world than other countries have invested in it. (p. 510)

Cross elasticity of demand A measure of the extent to which the demand for a good changes when the price of a substitute or complement changes, other things remaining the same. (p. 125)

Cross-section graph A graph that shows the values of an economic variable for different groups in a population at a point in time. (p. 24)

Currency appreciation The rise in the value of one currency in terms of another currency. (p. 514)

Currency depreciation The fall in the value of one currency in terms of another currency. (p. 513)

Current account Record of international receipts and payments—current account balance equals exports minus imports, plus net interest and transfers received from abroad. (p. 508)

Deadweight loss The decrease in consumer surplus and producer surplus that results from an inefficient level of production. (p. 144)

Debtor nation A country that during its entire history has borrowed more from the rest of the world than it has lent to it; so it has a stock of outstanding debt to the rest of the world that exceeds the stock of its own claims on the rest of the world. (p. 510)

Decreasing marginal returns When the marginal product of an additional worker is less than the marginal product of the previous worker. (p. 264)

Demand The relationship between the quantity demanded and the price of a good when all other influences on buying plans remain the same. (p. 81)

Demand curve A graph of the relationship between the quantity demanded of a good and its price when all other influences on buying plans remain the same. (p. 82)

Demand schedule A list of the quantities demanded at each different price when all other influences on buying plans remain the same. (p. 82)

Derived demand The demand for a factor of production, which is derived from the demand for the goods and services it is used to produce. (p. 387)

Diminishing marginal rate of substitution The general tendency for the marginal rate of substitution to decrease as the consumer moves down along the indifference curve, increasing consumption of good x and decreasing consumption of good y. (p. 252)

Diminishing marginal utility The general tendency for marginal utility to decrease as the quantity of a good consumed increases. (p. 237)

Direct relationship A relationship between two variables that move in the same direction. (p. 26)

Diseconomies of scale A condition in which, when a firm increases its plant size and labor employed by the same percentage, its output increases by a smaller percentage and its average total cost increases. (p. 278)

Dumping When a foreign firm sells its exports at a lower price than its cost of production. (p. 472)

Duopoly A market in which there are only two producers. (p. 348)

Dynamic comparative advantage A comparative advantage that a person (or country) obtains by specializing in an activity, resulting from learning-by-doing. (p. 464)

Economic depreciation An opportunity cost of a firm using capital that it owns—measured as the change in the *market* value of capital over a given period. (p. 259)

Economic model A description of some aspect of the economic world that includes only those features of the world that are needed for the purpose at hand. (p. 9)

Economic profit A firm's total revenue minus total cost. (p. 259)

Economic rent The income received by *any* factor of production over and above the amount required to induce a given quantity of the factor to be supplied. (p. 402)

Economic theory A generalization that summarizes what we understand about the economic choices that people make and the economic performance of industries and nations based on models that have repeatedly passed the test of corresponding well with real-world data. (p. 9)

Economics The social science that studies the choices that individuals, businesses, governments, and entire societies make as they cope with scarcity. (p. 5)

Economies of scale A condition in which, when a firm increases its plant size and labor employed by the same percentage, its output increases by a larger percentage and its average total cost decreases. (p. 277)

Efficiency A situation in which the quantities of goods and services produced are those that people value most highly—in which we cannot produce more of a good or service without giving up some of another good or service that people value more highly. (p. 66)

Elastic demand When the percentage change in the quantity demanded exceeds the percentage change in price. (p. 110)

Elastic supply When the percentage change in the quantity supplied exceeds the percentage change in price. (p. 120)

Entrepreneurship The human resource that organizes labor, land, and capital. (p. 42)

Equilibrium price The price at which the quantity demanded equals the quantity supplied. (p. 95)

Equilibrium quantity The quantity bought and sold at the equilibrium price. (p. 95)

Excess burden The deadweight loss from a tax— the amount by which the burden of a tax exceeds the tax revenue received by the government. (p. 164)

Excess demand A situation in which the quantity demanded exceeds the quantity supplied. (p. 96)

Excess supply A situation in which the quantity supplied exceeds the quantity demanded. (p. 96)

Excludable If it is technologically possible to prevent a person from enjoying the benefits of a good or service. (p. 204)

Explicit cost A cost paid in money. (p. 259)

External diseconomies Factors outside the control of a firm that raise the firm's costs as *market* output increases. (p. 302)

External economies Factors beyond the control of an individual firm that lower its costs as the *market* output increases. (p. 302)

Externality A cost or a benefit that arises from production that falls on someone other than the producer; or a cost or benefit that arises from consumption that falls on someone other than the consumer. (p. 182)

Factor markets Markets in which factors of production are bought and sold. (p. 46)

Factor price The price of a factor of production. The wage rate is the price of labor, the interest rate is the price of capital, and rent is the price of land. (p. 384)

Factors of production The productive resources used to produce goods and services—land, labor, capital, and entrepreneurship. (p. 38)

Financial capital The funds that firms use to buy and operate physical capital. (p. 385)

Financial market A collection of people and firms who are lending and borrowing to finance the purchase of physical capital. (p. 385)

Firms The institutions that organize the production of goods and services. (p. 46)

Foreign exchange market The market that is made up of importers and exporters, banks, and specialist dealers who buy and sell currencies. (p. 513)

Foreign exchange rate The price at which one currency exchanges for another. (p. 513)

Four-firm concentration ratio The percentage of the value of sales accounted for by the four largest firms in an industry. (p. 338)

Free rider A person who enjoys the benefits of a good or service without paying for it. (p. 205)

Functional distribution of income The percentage distribution of income among the factors of production. (p. 44)

Game theory The tool that economists use to analyze *strategic behavior*—behavior that recognizes mutual interdependence and takes account of the expected behavior of others. (p. 353)

Goods and services The objects that people value and produce to satisfy human wants. Goods are physical objects, and services are work done for people. (p. 6)

Goods markets Markets in which goods and services are bought and sold. (p. 46)

Herfindahl-Hirschman Index The square of the percentage market share of each firm summed over the largest 50 firms (or summed over all the firms if there are fewer than 50) in a market. (p. 338)

Horizontal equity The requirement that taxpayers with the same ability to pay, pay the same taxes. (p. 222)

Households Individuals or groups of people living together as decision-making units. (p. 46)

Human capital The knowledge and skill that people obtain from education, on-the-job training, and work experience. (p. 40)

Implicit cost An opportunity cost incurred by a firm when it uses a factor of production for which it does not make a direct money payment. (p. 259)

Incentive An inducement to take a particular action. (p. 16)

Incentive regulation A regulation that motivates the firm to operate efficiently and keep its costs under control. (p. 367)

Income elasticity of demand A measure of the extent to which the demand for a good changes when income changes, other things remaining the same. (p. 126)

Increasing marginal returns When the marginal product of an additional worker exceeds the marginal product of the previous worker. (p. 264)

Indifference curve A line that shows combinations of goods among which a consumer is indifferent. (p. 251)

Industrial union A group of workers who have a variety of skills and job types but work for the same firm or industry. (p. 412)

Inelastic demand When the percentage change in the quantity demanded is less than the percentage change in price. (p. 110)

Inelastic supply When the percentage change in the quantity supplied is less than the percentage change in price. (p. 120)

Infant-industry argument The argument that it is necessary to protect a new industry to enable it to grow into a mature industry that can compete in world markets. (p. 471)

Inferior good A good for which the demand decreases when income increases. (p. 85)

Intellectual property rights The property rights of the creators of knowledge and other discoveries. (p. 199)

Interest Income paid for the use of capital. (p. 44)

Interest rate parity Equal interest rates—a situation in which the interest rate in one currency equals the interest rate in another currency when exchange rate changes are taken into account. (p. 524)

Inverse relationship A relationship between two variables that move in opposite directions. (p. 27)

Job A long-term contract between a firm and a household to provide labor services. (p. 384)

Labor The work time and work effort that people devote to producing goods and services. (p. 40)

Labor market A collection of people and firms who are trading labor services. (p. 384)

Labor union An organized group of workers whose purpose is to increase wages and influence other job conditions for its members. (p. 412)

Land The "gifts of nature," or *natural resources,* that we use to produce goods and services. (p. 38)

Learning-by-doing Repeatedly performing the same task and becoming more productive at producing a particular good or service. (p. 464)

Legal monopoly A market in which competition and entry are restricted by the concentration of ownership of a natural resource or by the granting of a public franchise, government license, patent, or copyright. (p. 311)

Linear relationship A relationship that graphs as a straight line. (p. 26)

Long run The time frame in which the quantities of all resources can be changed. (p. 262)

Long-run average cost curve A curve that shows the lowest average cost at which it is possible to produce each output when the firm has had sufficient time to change both its plant size and labor employed. (p. 278)

Long-run market supply curve A curve that shows how the quantity supplied by a market varies as the price varies and the number of firms in the market varies to achieve zero economic profit. (p. 303)

Lorenz curve A curve that graphs the cumulative percentage of income (or wealth) against the cumulative percentage of households. The farther the Lorenz curve is from a 45° line, the greater is the inequality. (p. 431)

Loss Income earned by an entrepreneur for running a business when that income is negative. (p. 44)

Macroeconomics The study of the aggregate (or total) effects on the national economy and the global economy of the choices that individuals, businesses, and governments make. (p. 5)

Margin A choice on the margin is a choice that is made by comparing *all* the relevant alternatives systematically and incrementally. (p. 15)

Marginal benefit The benefit that arises from a one-unit increase in an activity. The marginal benefit of something is *measured* by what you are *willing to* give up to get one more unit of it. (p. 15)

Marginal cost The cost that arises from a one-unit increase in an activity. The marginal cost of something is what you *must* give up to get one more unit of it. (p. 15); the marginal cost of producing a good is the change in total cost that results from a one-unit increase in output. (p. 270).

Marginal cost pricing rule A price rule for a natural monopoly that sets price equal to marginal cost. (p. 331)

Marginal external benefit The benefit from an additional unit of a good or service that people other than the consumer of the good or service enjoy. (p. 194)

Marginal external cost The cost of producing an additional unit of a good or service that falls on people other than the producer. (p. 184)

Marginal private benefit The benefit from an additional unit of a good or service that the consumer of that good or service receives. (p. 194)

Marginal private cost The cost of producing an additional unit of a good or service that is borne by the producer of that good or service. (p. 184)

Marginal product The change in total product that results from a one-unit increase in the quantity of labor employed. (p. 264)

Marginal rate of substitution The rate at which a person will give up good y (the good measured on the y-axis) to get more of good x (the good measured on the x-axis) and at the same time remain on the same indifference curve. (p. 252)

Marginal revenue The change in total revenue that results from a one-unit increase in the quantity sold. (p. 287)

Marginal social benefit The marginal benefit enjoyed by society—by the consumers of a good or service and by everyone else who benefits from it. It is the sum of marginal private benefit and marginal external benefit. (p. 194)

Marginal social cost The marginal cost incurred by the entire society—by the producer and by everyone else on whom the cost falls. It is the sum of marginal private cost and marginal external cost. (p. 184)

Marginal tax rate The percentage of an additional dollar of income that is paid in tax. (p. 215)

Marginal utility The change in total utility that results from a one-unit increase in the quantity of a good consumed. (p. 237)

Marginal utility per dollar spent The increase in total utility that comes from the last dollar spent on a good. (p. 241)

Market Any arrangement that brings buyers and sellers together and enables them to get information and do business with each other. (p. 46)

Market demand The sum of the demands of all the buyers in a market. (p. 83)

Market equilibrium When the quantity demanded equals the quantity supplied—when buyers' and sellers' plans are consistent. (p. 95)

Market income The income a household earns in factor markets before tax and excluding transfers from the government. (p. 443)

Market supply The sum of the supplies of all the sellers in a market. (p. 90)

Microeconomics The study of the choices of individuals and businesses, the interaction of these choices, and the influence that governments exert on these choices. (p. 5)

Minimum wage law A government regulation that makes hiring labor for less than a specified wage illegal. (p. 174)

Money income Market income plus money benefits paid by the government. (p. 444)

Monopolistic competition A market in which a large number of firms compete by making similar but slightly different products. (p. 286)

Monopoly A market for a good or service that has no close substitutes and in which there is one supplier that is protected from competition by a barrier preventing the entry of new firms. (p. 286)

Monopsony A market in which there is a single buyer. (p. 416)

Nash equilibrium An equilibrium in which each player takes the best possible action given the action of the other player. (p. 354)

National debt The total amount that the government has borrowed to make expenditures that exceed tax revenue—to run a government budget deficit (p. 50)

Natural monopoly A monopoly that arises because one firm can meet the entire market demand at a lower price than two or more firms could. (p. 310)

Negative externality A production or consumption activity that creates an external cost. (p. 182)

Negative income tax A tax and redistribution scheme that provides every household with a guaranteed minimum annual income and taxes all market income at a fixed marginal tax rate. (p. 446)

Negative relationship A relationship between two variables that move in opposite directions. (p. 27)

Net borrower A country that is borrowing more from the rest of the world than it is lending to the rest of the world. (p. 510)

Net lender A country that is lending more to the rest of the world than it is borrowing from the rest of the world. (p. 510)

Nonexcludable If it is technologically impossible, or extremely costly, to prevent a person from enjoying the benefits of a good or service. (p. 204)

Nonrenewable natural resources Natural resources that can be used only once and that cannot be replaced once they have been used. (p. 401)

Nonrival If the consumption of a good or service by one person does not decrease the quantity of the good available for someone else. (p. 204)

Nontariff barrier Any action other than a tariff that restricts international trade. (p. 466)

Normal good A good for which the demand increases when income increases. (p. 85)

Normal profit The return to entrepreneurship. Normal profit is part of a firm's opportunity cost because it is the cost of not running another firm. (p. 259)

Official settlements account Record of the change in U.S. official reserves. (p. 508)

Oligopoly A market in which a small number of firms compete. (p. 286)

Opportunity cost The opportunity cost of something is the best thing you must give up to get it. (p. 13)

Patent A government-sanctioned exclusive right granted to the inventor of a good, service, or productive process to produce, use, and sell the invention for a given number of years. (p. 199)

Payoff matrix A table that shows the payoffs for every possible action by each player given every possible action by the other player. (p. 354)

Payroll tax A tax on employers based on the wages they pay their workers. (p. 163)

Perfect competition A market in which there are many firms, each selling an identical product; many buyers; and no restrictions on the entry of new firms into the industry. (p. 286)

Perfect price discrimination Price discrimination that extracts the entire consumer surplus by charging the highest price that consumers are willing to pay for each unit. (p. 326)

Perfectly elastic demand When the quantity demanded changes by a very large percentage in response to an almost zero percentage change in price. (p. 110)

Perfectly elastic supply When the quantity supplied changes by a very large percentage in response to an almost zero percentage change in price. (p. 120)

Perfectly inelastic demand When the quantity demanded remains constant as the price changes. (p. 110)

Perfectly inelastic supply When the quantity supplied remains the same as the price changes. (p. 120)

Personal distribution of income The percentage distribution of income among individual persons. (p. 44)

Positive externality A production or consumption activity that creates an external benefit. (p. 182)

Positive relationship A relationship between two variables that move in the same direction. (p. 26)

***Post hoc* fallacy** The error of reasoning that a first event *causes* a second event because the first occurred *before* the second. (p. 11)

Poverty A state in which a household's income is too low to be able to buy the quantities of food, shelter, and clothing that are deemed necessary. (p. 434)

Price ceiling The highest price at which it is legal to trade a particular good, service, or factor of production. A rent ceiling is an example of a price ceiling. (p. 166)

Price-discriminating monopoly A monopoly that is able to sell different units of a good or service for different prices. (p. 312)

Price elasticity of demand A measure of the extent to which the quantity demanded of a good changes when the price of the good changes and all other influences on buyers' plans remain the same. (p. 108)

Price elasticity of supply A measure of the extent to which the quantity supplied of a good changes when the price of the good changes and all other influences on sellers' plans remain the same. (p. 120)

Price floor The lowest price at which it is legal to trade a particular good, service, or factor of production. The minimum wage is an example of a price floor. (p. 174)

Price support system A system in which the government sets a price for a farm product and then buys any output that the farmer can't sell in the market at the support price. (p. 492)

Price taker A firm that cannot influence the price of the good or service that it produces. (p. 287)

Principle of minimum differentiation The tendency for competitors to make themselves identical to appeal to the maximum number of clients or voters. (p. 210)

Prisoners' dilemma A game between two prisoners that shows why it is hard to cooperate, even when it would be beneficial to both players to do so. (p. 353)

Private good A good or service that can be consumed by only one person at a time and only by those people who have bought it or own it. (p. 204)

Producer surplus The price of a good minus the marginal cost of producing it. (p. 138)

Product differentiation Making a product that is slightly different from the products of competing firms. (p. 336)

Production efficiency A situation in which we cannot produce more of one good or service without producing less of some other good or service—production is at a point *on* the *PPF*. (p. 66)

Production flexibility contract A contract that provides a farmer with a support payment from the government based on the number of acres covered by the contract and not based on production. (p. 492)

Production possibilities frontier The boundary between the combinations of goods and services that can be produced and the combinations that cannot be produced, given the available factors of production and the state of technology. (p. 56)

Profit Income earned by an entrepreneur for running a business. (p. 44)

Progressive tax An increase in the average tax rate as income increases. (p. 215)

Property rights Legally established titles to the ownership, use, and disposal of factors of production and goods and services that are enforceable in the courts. (p. 187)

Proportional tax A constant average tax rate at all income levels. (p. 216)

Public good A good or service that can be consumed simultaneously by everyone and from which no one can be excluded. (p. 204)

Public interest theory The theory that regulation seeks an efficient use of resources. (p. 362)

Public provision The production of a good or service by a public authority that receives the bulk of its revenue from the government. (p. 196)

Purchasing power parity Equal value of money—a situation in which money buys the same amount of goods and services in different currencies. (p. 522)

Quantity demanded The amount of any good, service, or resource that people are willing and able to buy during a specified period at a specified price. (p. 81)

Quantity supplied The amount of any good, service, or resource that people are willing and able to sell during a specified period at a specified price. (p. 88)

Quota A specified maximum amount of a good that may be imported in a given period of time. (p. 468)

Rate of return regulation A regulation that sets the price at a level that enables a regulated firm to earn a specified target percent return on its capital. (p. 366)

Rational choice A choice that uses the available resources to most effectively satisfy the wants of the person making the choice. (p. 13)

Rational ignorance The decision not to acquire information because the marginal cost of doing so exceeds the expected marginal benefit. (p. 211)

Regressive tax A decrease in the average tax rate as income increases. (p. 216)

Regulation Rules administered by a government agency to influence economic activity by determining prices, product standards and types, and the conditions under which new firms can enter an industry. (p. 362)

Relative price The price of one good in terms of another good—divided by the price of another good.an opportunity cost. It equals the price of one good divided by the price of another good. (p. 233)

Renewable natural resources Natural resources that can be used repeatedly. (p. 401)

Rent Income paid for the use of land. (p. 44)

Rent ceiling A government regulation that makes it illegal to charge more than a specified rent for housing. (p. 166)

Rent seeking The act of obtaining special treatment by the government to create economic profit or to divert consumer surplus or producer surplus away from others. (p. 321)

Rival If the consumption of a good or service by one person decreases the quantity of the good that is available for others. (p. 204)

Scarcity The condition that arises because the available resources are insufficient to satisfy wants. (p. 4)

Scatter diagram A graph of the value of one variable against the value of another variable. (p. 24)

Search activity The time spent looking for someone with whom to do business. (p. 168)

Short run The time frame in which the quantities of some resources are fixed. In the short run, a firm can usually change the quantity of labor it uses but not the quantity of capital. (p. 262)

Shortage A situation in which the quantity demanded exceeds the quantity supplied. (p. 96)

Shutdown point The output and price at which price equals minimum average variable cost. (p. 291)

Single-price monopoly A monopoly that must sell each unit of its output for the same price to all its customers. (p. 312)

Slope The change in the value of the variable measured on the y-axis divided by the change the value of the variable measured on the x-axis. (p. 29)

Stock market A market in which shares in the stocks of companies are traded. (p. 385)

Strategies All the possible actions of each player in a game. (p. 354)

Subsidy A payment that the government makes to private producers that depends on the level of output. (p. 197)

Substitute A good that can be consumed in place of another good. (p. 84)

Substitute in production A good that can be produced in place of another good. (p. 91)

Sunk cost A previously incurred and irreversible cost. (p. 14)

Supply The relationship between the quantity supplied and the price of a good when all other influences on selling plans remain the same. (p. 88)

Supply curve A graph of the relationship between the quantity supplied of a good and its price when all other influences on selling plans remain the same. (p. 89)

Supply schedule A list of the quantities supplied at each different price when all other influences on selling plans remain the same. (p. 89)

Surplus A situation in which the quantity supplied exceeds the quantity demanded. (p. 96)

Symmetry principle The requirement that people in similar situations be treated similarly. (p. 147)

Tariff A tax on a good that is imposed by the importing country when an imported good crosses its international boundary. (p. 466)

Tax incidence The division of the burden of a tax between the buyer and the seller. (p. 158)

Taxable income Total income minus personal exemption and a standard deduction or other allowable deductions. (p. 215)

Time-series graph A graph that measures time on the x-axis and the variable or variables in which we are interested on the y-axis. (p. 24)

Total cost The cost of all the factors of production used by a firm. (p. 269)

Total fixed cost The cost of the fixed factors of production used by a firm—the cost of land, capital, and entrepreneurship. (p. 269)

Total product The total output produced in a given period. (p. 263)

Total revenue The total revenue from the sale of a good equals the price of the good multiplied by the quantity sold. (p. 116)

Total revenue test A method of estimating the price elasticity of demand by observing the change in total revenue that results from a price change (with all other influences on the quantity sold remaining unchanged). (p. 116)

Total utility The total benefit that a person gets from the consumption of a good or service. Total utility generally increases as the quantity consumed of a good increases. (p. 236)

Total variable cost The cost of the variable factor of production used by a firm—the cost of labor. (p. 269)

Tradeoff A constraint or limit to what is possible that forces an exchange or a substitution of one thing for something else. (p. 59)

Transactions costs The opportunity costs of conducting a transaction. (p. 188)

Trend A general tendency for the value of a variable to rise or fall. (p. 24)

U.S. interest rate differential The U.S. interest rate minus the foreign interest rate. (p. 516)

U.S. official reserves The government's holdings of foreign currency. (p. 508)

Unit elastic demand When the percentage change in the quantity demanded equals the percentage change in price. (p. 110)

Unit elastic supply When the percentage change in the quantity supplied equals the percentage change in price. (p. 120)

Utilitarianism A principle that states that we should strive to achieve "the greatest happiness for the greatest number. (p. 148)

Utility The benefit or satisfaction that a person gets from the consumption of a good or service. (p. 236)

Utility-maximizing rule The rule that leads to the greatest total utility from all the goods and services consumed. The rule is: 1. Allocate the entire available budget. 2. Make the marginal utility per dollar spent the same for all goods. (p. 240)

Value of marginal product The value to a firm of hiring one more unit of a factor of production, which equals price of a unit of output multiplied by the marginal product of the factor of production. (p. 387)

Vertical equity The requirement that taxpayers with a greater ability to pay bear a greater share of the taxes. (p. 223)

Voucher A token that the government provides to households that can be used to buy specified goods or services. (p. 198)

Wages Income paid for the services of labor. (p. 44)

INDEX

(continuation from page iv)

Chapter 1: p. 5 left and right: Scott Foresman/Addison Wesley Longman, Focus on Sports; p. 6 top: George Rose/Getty Images; 6 center: Owen Franken/Stone; 6 bottom: Digital Image © 2001/PhotoDisc, Inc.; p. 9: National Museum of Photography, Film, & Television/Science & Society Picture Library; p. 10: © Bettmann/CORBIS; p. 14 left: Digital Image © 2001/PhotoDisc, Inc.; p. 14 right: Copyright © David Young-Wolff/PhotoEdit; p. 16 left: Copyright © David Young-Wolff/PhotoEdit; p. 16 right: Copyright © Tony Freeman/PhotoEdit.

Chapter 2: p. 37 left: Digital Image © 2001/PhotoDisc, Inc.; p. 37 center: © CORBIS; p. 37 right: Digital Image © 2001/PhotoDisc, Inc.; p. 42 top and bottom: Digital Image © 2001/PhotoDisc, Inc.

Chapter 4: p. 80 left: Roderick Chen/Superstock; p. 80 center: AP/Wide World Photos; p. 80 right: © Steven Rubin/The Image Works; p. 99: Digital Image © 2001/PhotoDisc, Inc.

Chapter 5: p. 115 left: © Bennett Dean; Eye Ubiquitous/CORBIS; p. 115 right: Darama/Corbis Stock Market.

Chapter 7: p. 169: AP/Wide World Photos; p. 171: Digital Image © 2001/PhotoDisc, Inc.; p. 177: Digital Image © 2001/PhotoDisc, Inc.

Chapter 8: p. 182 left: © CORBIS; p. 182 right: © George Lepp/CORBIS; p. 183 left: © David & Peter Turnley/CORBIS; p. 183 right: © Neil Beer/CORBIS; p. 191 left: © Roy Corral/CORBIS; p. 191 right: © Doug Wilson/CORBIS.

Chapter 9: p. 205 left and right: © CORBIS; p. 223: Digital Image © 2001/PhotoDisc, Inc.

Chapter 10: p. 238 left: © CORBIS; p. 238 right: Hulton /Archive; p. 244: © John Henley/Corbis Stock Market.

Chapter 12: p. 287 top: Digital Image © 2001/PhotoDisc, Inc.; p. 287 bottom: © Jonathan Blair/CORBIS; p. 301 left: Jeff Zaruba/Corbis Stock Market; p. 301 right: ©2000 Richard Day/MIDWESTOCK; p. 305: © James Marshall/CORBIS.

Chapter 13: p. 310: Francisco Cruz/Superstock; p. 328: Courtesy of priceline.com.

Chapter 14: p. 336: ©Vincent Dewitt/Stock, Boston Inc./PictureQuest; p. 343: © Corbis Stock Market; p. 346: Courtesy of Nike, Inc.; p. 348: AP/Wide World Photos.

Chapter 15: p. 368: © CORBIS; p. 369: © Greg Pease/Stone; p. 377 top: AOL screenshot © 2001 America Online, Inc. Used with permission.; p. 377 bottom: © 2001 Time Inc. New Media. All rights reserved. Reproduction in whole or part without permission is prohibited. Pathfinder is a registered trademark of Time Inc. New Media.

Chapter 16: p. 384 left: © CORBIS; p. 384 center: AP/Wide World Photos; p. 384 right: Courtesy of Monster.com; p. 385: AFP/CORBIS; p. 392 top Serge Attal/Timepix; p. 392 bottom: © Kathi Lamm/Stone; p. 403: © Bettmann/CORBIS.

Chapter 19: p. 477 left: Jason Grow/SABA; p. 477 right: David G. McIntyre/BLACKSTAR.

Chapter 20: p. 490: AP/Wide World Photos; p. 498 left: Photo © Andy Manis; p. 498 right: © CORBIS.